PARTNERS IN SCIENCE

Howe Library
Shenandoah College
and
Conservatory of Music

Presented by

PARTNERS IN SCIENCE

Letters of James Watt and Joseph Black

Edited with Introductions and Notes by

ERIC ROBINSON and DOUGLAS McKIE

HARVARD UNIVERSITY PRESS
CAMBRIDGE·MASSACHUSETTS
1970

TO DAVID GIBSON-WATT

Contents

Acknowledgments   *page* viii

List of Letters, with dates   ix

Table of Chemical Symbols   xvi

Part 1 THE LETTERS

Introduction   3

The Letters   8

Part 2 THE NOTEBOOK

Introduction   425

The Notebook   431

Notes on Watt's Determinations   480

Index   491

Acknowledgments

A large number of the documents edited in this volume come from the family papers of Major David Gibson-Watt, M.C., M.P., and it is him first that we wish to thank for allowing us to publish them. In addition one of us is indebted to him for his generous hospitality on various occasions over several years, and for his unfailing helpfulness.

Our thanks are also due to Mr Arthur Westwood, the Assay Master, Birmingham; to the Librarian, the Birmingham Reference Library, and his Committee; and to the Librarian, Edinburgh University Library; for permission to publish manuscripts in their keeping. We wish also to thank the Royal Society for permission to publish James Watt's letter to Sir Joseph Banks.

Many points of annotation have required the generous help of other scholars and we have been greatly assisted by the careful researches, so willingly undertaken, of Miss E. Jack of Glasgow University Library, Mr D. Bryden of the Royal Scottish Museum, Miss D. M. Norris and Miss J. McCulla of Birmingham Reference Library, Mr M. F. Messinger of Shrewsbury Public Library and Mr G. L'E. Turner of the Oxford Science Museum. Mr J. A. V. Chapple of Manchester University has also been most helpful with bibliographical advice and Dr Geoffrey Talbot of Queen's University, Belfast, read some of the typescript at an early stage and offered helpful comments. If we have erred, it is no fault of theirs.

In work of this kind, the close attention of the careful typist is invaluable, and for this we wish to thank Miss P. Higgins of Manchester University and Miss L. Burrows and Miss M. D. Thomas of University College, London. In addition, for assistance with the transcription of some of the Robison letters we wish to thank Mrs G. Lea, and for extensive photographic work, Mr T. J. Collins of University College, London. The Chief Constable of Manchester, Mr W. J. Richards, also generously allowed the staff of the Police Forensic Laboratory to assist us with one difficult photographic problem, and we are most grateful to him and to them.

Eric Robinson
Douglas McKie

List of Letters

1768

Black to Watt	10 January 1768
Watt to Black	15 February 1768
Black to Watt	19 February 1768
Watt to Black	7 April 1768
Watt to Black	20 April 1768
Robison to Watt	8 July 1768
Black to Watt	31 October 1768

1769

Black to Watt	20 January 1769
Black to Watt	23 January 1769
Black to Watt	26 January 1769
Watt to Black	27 January 1769
Watt to Black	28 January 1769
Black to Watt	28 January 1769
Watt to Black	14 March 1769
Black to Watt	27 May 1769
Watt to Black	29 May 1769
Black to Watt	10 July 1769
Black to Watt	20 December 1769

1770

Black to Watt	28 February 1770

1771

Robison to Watt	22 April 1771
Keir to Watt	14 December 1771

1772

Keir to Watt	27 February 1772
Black to Watt	22 March 1772
Black to Watt	1 July 1772
James Russell to Watt	19 August 1772
Watt to Russell (Account)	
Black to Watt	1 October 1772
Watt to Black	15 December 1772
Black to Watt	23 December 1772
Black to Watt	26 December 1772
Black to Watt	31 December 1772

1773

Black to Watt	1 February 1773
Black to Watt	22 May 1773

1774

Black to Watt	23 February 1774

(No letters for 1775, 1776 and 1777)

1778

Black to Watt	27 November 1778
Watt to Black	12 December 1778

1779

Black to Watt	8 January 1779
Watt to Black (Two versions with draft)	13 January 1779
Black to Watt	20 January 1779
Black to Watt	8 February 1779
Alexander Black to Joseph Black	25 February 1779
Watt to Black (with copy)	3 March 1779
Black to Watt	6 March 1779
Watt to Black	11 March 1779
Black to Watt (with two drafts)	11 March 1779
Black to Watt	5 July 1779
Watt to Black	24 July 1779
Watt to Black	1 August 1779
Black to Watt	25 August 1779
Black to Watt	15 November 1779
Black to Watt	19 November 1779
Watt to Black	2 December 1779

1780

Black to Watt	7 January 1780
Watt to Magellan	1 March 1780
Watt to Black	1 March 1780
Watt to Magellan	9 March 1780
Watt to Black	9 March 1780
Black to Watt	15 March 1780
Watt to Magellan	20 March 1780
Watt to Magellan	29 March 1780
Watt to Black	17 May 1780
Watt to Black	30 May 1780
Black to Watt	3 June 1780
Watt to Black	9 June 1780
Black to Watt	1 September 1780

Watt to Black		15 October 1780
Black to Watt		18 October 1780
Watt to Black		25 October 1780
Black to Watt		27 October 1780
Watt to Black		9 November 1780
	1781	
Watt to Black		23 February 1781
Watt to Black		8 March 1781
Black to Watt		31 March 1781
Watt to Black		9 April 1781
Black to Watt		23 April 1781
Black to Watt		1 May 1781
Robison to Watt		22 October 1781
Watt to Robison		1 November 1781
	1782	
Black to Watt		7 September 1782
Watt to Black		13 December 1782
	1783	
Black to Watt		30 January 1783
Watt to Black		3 February 1783
Black to Watt		13 February 1783
Watt to Black		21 April 1783
Black to Watt		16 July 1783
Watt to Black		25 September 1783
Watt to Black		26 September 1783
Robison to Watt		22 October 1783
	1784	
Watt to Robison		20 January 1784
Robison to Watt		10 February 1784
Watt to Robison		9 April 1784
Robison to Watt		25 April 1784
Black to Watt		28 May 1784
Watt to Black		6 June 1784
Black to Watt		26 June 1784
Watt to Black		11 November 1784
	1785	
Black to Watt		10 June 1785
Robison to Watt		11 August 1785
Watt to Robison		18 August 1785

1786

Black to Watt	13 February 1786
Watt to Black	13 August 1786
Robison to Watt	15 August 1786
Black to Watt	? August 1786
Watt to Black	5 October 1786

1787

Black to Mrs Watt	28 December 1787

1788

Watt to Black	4 February 1788
Robison to Watt	5 February 1788
Robison to Watt	7 February 1788
Black to Watt	13 February 1788
Boulton (per Hodges) to Southern	15 February 1788
Watt to Black	7 April 1788
Watt to Black	8 June 1788
Robison to Watt	25 July 1788
Black to Watt	7 August 1788
Watt to Black	12 September 1788
Black to Watt	9 October 1788
Black to Watt	25 October 1788

1789

Robison to Watt	13 March 1789
Watt to Black	15 March 1789
Black to Watt	12 April 1789
Watt to Black	5 May 1789
Black to Watt	2 July 1789
Black to Watt	1 August 1789
Watt to Black	17 September 1789

1790

Black to Watt	30 November 1790
Watt to Black	5 December 1790

1791

Watt to Black	23 November 1791
Black to Watt	1 December 1791

1792

Mrs Watt to Black	6 November 1792

1793

Robison to Watt	7 March 1793
Robison to Boulton	7 March 1793

Robison to Watt		12 May 1793
Black to Watt		23 June 1793
Watt to Black		17 July 1793
	1794	
Black to Watt		16 January 1794
Black to Watt		10 May 1794
Watt to Black		15 May 1794
Black to Watt		6 June 1794
Watt to Black		9 June 1794
Watt to Black		25 June 1794
Black to Watt		30 June 1794
Watt to Black		3 July 1794
Watt to Black		31 August 1794
Black to Watt		9 September 1794
Black to Watt		28 October 1794
Watt to Black		8 December 1794
Black to Watt		13 December 1794
	1795	
Watt to Black		2 April 1795
Black to Watt		12 April 1795
Watt to Black		24 May 1795
Black to Watt		29 September 1795
	1796	
Black to Watt		4 January 1796
Watt to Black		7 January 1796
Watt to Black		1 June 1796
Black to Watt		28 July 1796
Watt to Black		9 October 1796
Watt to Robison		11 October 1796
Watt to Robison		24 October 1796
Robison to Watt		25 October 1796
Watt to Robison		14 November 1796
Robison to Black		? November 1796
Watt to Robison		19 November 1796
Robison to Watt		? December 1796
Robison to Watt Junior		27 December 1796
Enclosure—draft advertisement		
Robison to Watt		? December 1796
Black to Watt Memorial		1796
Robison to Watt Memorial		1796

1797

Robison to Watt jr.	1 January 1797
Robison to Ewart	3 January 1797
Watt to Black	15 January 1797
Robison to Watt	3 February 1797
Robison to Watt	7 April 1797
Mrs Robison to Watt	13 April 1797
Mrs Robison to Watt	29 April 1797
Robison to Watt	3 May 1797
Watt to Black	7 June 1797
Mrs Robison to Watt	8 June 1797
Black to Watt	13 June 1797
Watt to Black	16 October 1797
Black to Watt	11 November 1797
Keir to Watt and enclosure	24 November 1797

1798

Robison to Watt	14 January 1798
Watt to Black	7 February 1798
Black to Watt	8 [21] April 1798
Robison to Watt	4 May 1798
Black to Watt	12 May 1798
Watt to Black	21 May 1798
Robison to Watt	17 July 1798
Mrs Robison to Watt junior	4 September 1798
Robison to Miller	22 September 1798
Robison to Watt	[?] September 1798
Robison to Watt	15 December 1798

1799

Black to Watt	1 February 1799
Black to Mrs Watt	1 February 1799
Black to Watt	6 March 1799
Black to Watt	22 March 1799
Black to Watt	26 July 1799
Black to Watt	6 November 1799
Watt to Black	6 November 1799
Watt to Black	9 November 1799
Watt to Black	22 November 1799
Black to Watt	2 December 1799
Watt to Black	8 December 1799
Robison to Watt	11 December 1799

Watt to Robison	16 December 1799
Robison to Watt	18 December 1799
Robison to George Black junior	21 December 1799
P. Ewart to Watt	23 December 1799
Robison to George Black junior	28 December 1799

1800

George Black junior to Watt	4 January 1800
Robison to George Black junior	18 January 1800
Robison to George Black junior	20 January 1800
Watt to Robison	19 February 1800
Robison to Watt	25 February 1800
Watt to Robison	7 March 1800
Robison to Watt	23 July 1800
Robison to George Black junior	1 August 1800
Robison to Watt	9 September 1800
Robison to Watt	2 October 1800
Robison to Watt	[October 1800]
Robison to Watt	[October 1800]
Robison to George Black junior	18 October 1800
Robison to Watt	19 October 1800

1801

Robison to George Black junior	[January 1801]
Ferguson to Watt	2 February 1801
Robison to George Black junior	[9 October 1801]
George Black junior to Robison	[10 October 1801]
Robison to George Black junior	[?10 October 1801]

1802

Robison to Watt	18 January 1802

1803

Robison to Watt	19 April 1803
Watt to Robison	26 April 1803
Robison to Hamilton	14 August 1803
Mrs Robison to Watt	19 December 1803
Robison to Watt	20 December 1803

1804

Robison to Watt	30 July 1804

1805

Charles Robison to Watt	30 January 1805
Watt to Charles Robison	5 February 1805
Watt to R. Muirhead	7 February 1805

Mrs Robison to Watt	14 February 1805
Wilson to Watt	22 February 1805
Playfair to Watt	2 March 1805
Watt to P. Wilson	12 March 1805
De Luc to Watt	15 March 1805
Mrs Robison to Watt	17 March 1805
De Luc to Watt	23 March 1805
De Luc to Watt	31 March 1805
Jeffrey to Watt	26 March 1805
De Luc to Watt	6 April 1805
De Luc to Watt	16 April 1805
J. Watt's Recollections of his Friend Dr J. Robison	April 1805
Robison's letters in the possession of James Watt at his death	1805
Copy of Watt's Remarks on Robison's edition of Black's Lectures	4 January 1809
Watt to Banks	1 March 1815

Table of Chemical Symbols

▽ Water	⟁ Sulphur
▽ Earth	⩔ Spirit of Wine
△ Air	⊖⸱ or ⊖⸱ Fixed Alkali
F. △ Fixed Air	→ or > or + or < Acid
☉ Gold	> of ♇ Acid of Tartar
☽ Silver	⏀× Nitric Acid
♂ Iron	⏀ᐸ Nitric
☿ Mercury	⊕+ or ⊕→ Vitriol or Vitriolic Acid
Ψ Lime	⊕ᐸ Vitriolic
♇ or ♇ or ♇ Tartar	⊖+ or ⊖× Muriatic Acid

Part 1

The Letters

Introduction

At the University of Glasgow in the year 1757 or 1758, three men met
in the workshop of the university's scientific-instrument-maker—the
instrument-maker himself, James Watt, Professor Joseph Black, a
member of the teaching staff, and an undergraduate, John Robison.
The correspondence that follows tells the story of their friendship,
allowing for interruptions caused by Robison's long absences, until
first Dr Black died in 1799 and then Robison died in 1805, and the
survivor, James Watt, was left—Britain's greatest mechanical engineer
of his day and perhaps of all time. An association between the most
eminent chemist of Europe, which meant, at that time, the world, and
Europe's greatest engineer would be sufficiently interesting in itself but
when that association turns into a close friendship, nourished through
correspondence over many years, it takes on a still greater importance.
And the fact is that Black and Watt, neither of whom were demonstrative men, had a real affection for each other. Robison tells us how
Black rejoiced in Boulton and Watt's victory at law over the Hornblowers, saying amidst his tears: 'it is very foolish, but I can't help it,
when I hear of any thing good to Jamy Watt', while Watt himself
always did battle for Black's claim to be the discoverer of specific and
latent heats and was most jealous for his old friend's fame. As for
Robison who rose to be professor in the University of Edinburgh
after a distinguished career in St Petersburg, he was a lesser man
than the other two, continually plagued by illness, garrulous and
sometimes illtempered, but he did his duty by his old teacher,
Black, in editing his lectures, was a faithful friend to Watt, and
left behind him a devoted wife who could still write movingly in
defence of his character.

The correspondence of these three men and some of their friends pro-
vides a good deal of information about scientific and technical matters
in Britain during the 'take-off 'period of the Industrial Revolution.
Watt's letters demonstrate his range of interests—in the firing of delft
and stoneware, the manufacture of alkali from salt, the invention and
manufacture of scientific instruments, the invention and improvement
of his copying-press (a pioneer piece of office-machinery), the drawing
of plans for canals and harbour-improvement, the steam-engine and
the patent law—in these and many other matters, interesting side-lights

3

may be gleaned from the correspondence. In addition the letters also shed valuable light on many aspects of life in Britain in the later half of the eighteenth century. The economic historian will find material on the training and recruitment of skilled artisans, clerks and managers; the legal historian will be interested in the ways in which witnesses were assembled for the trial of Watt's steam-engine patent; the historian of technology and science will learn much about the channels by which information was disseminated at the beginning of the Industrial Revolution. For example, we can read in Robison's letters of the scientific and technical articles written by Robison for the *Encyclopaedia Britannica* on water-power, mills, and other matters of interest to the practising engineer; or of the simplicity with which Black lectured on chemistry so that it was, according to Robison, 'his great Aim to be completely understood by the most illiterate of his hearers', and so that 'any sensible dyer or Blacksmith or druggist' would understand everything that was said. Here is further proof of the practical application of science taught by at least two university teachers in this critical period of Britain's industrial development.

The letters also illuminate the difficulties of capital accumulation, the system of patronage and influence extending even to manufacturing and commercial employment, the range of contacts with foreign scientists, particularly French, the reception of Cort's newly-invented methods of iron-production by the race of existing iron-masters, and the experiments in pneumatic medicine, to mention only a few important subjects. There is surprisingly little triviality in the letters except perhaps in the discussion of their ill-health, but even this helps to remind us of what each of them managed to achieve despite their sufferings.

The letters help to round out our picture of James Watt, showing something of his early business as a maker of musical instruments and scientific apparatus, at a time when he wrote both of porcelain making and steam-engines in successive sentences. Black begs a pound of his shoe-varnish from him or tries to persuade him to go horse-riding; Robison tries to persuade him to become 'Master Founder of Iron Ordnance' to Catherine the Great of Russia; James Keir asks his advice on outlets for his glass production. His virtuosity is testified to in every letter. Watt is still, however, largely self-educated. He gives himself away by writing '*Detruitus*' instead of '*Detritus*' and Black has to point out his error, but he will still venture the odd sentence in French, and has undertaken by himself the study of German and Italian. Black faces problems of finding employment for his brothers and Watt, anxious to

4

help, seems to offer more than his partner, Matthew Boulton, is willing to fulfil. There is a note of impetuosity here, prompted by gratitude to Black, which one does not find often in his career. The correspondence continues with the exchange of information about mineralogy, lubricants for machinery, metallurgy, etc., intermixed with hints to each other for preserving their health or their ink.

Eventually, as Watt begins to prosper and his fame spreads, he turns to the defence of his patents at law, threatened particularly by the Cornish engineers, the Hornblowers, and he asks his old friends, particularly John Robison for evidence of his claim to have been the first to have invented the separate condenser, and for support of his assertion that his first patent was sufficient to enable a skilful mechanic to construct a steam-engine of his design. The letter that Robison writes to Watt in December 1796 describing himself discussing Watt's engine with fellow-scientists in St. Petersburg draws a picture of intellectual society in eighteenth-century Russia that helps to illuminate the history of that time. There are many similar shafts of light in this correspondence.

Much of the material in the book has not been published before, or, if published, published only in fragments. Thus some of the letters between Watt and Black and between Watt and Robison can be found in a very abbreviated form in J. P. Muirhead's *The Origin and Progress of the Mechanical Inventions of James Watt* (London 1854, 3 vols.), but by far the greater number of the letters in this correspondence are not mentioned there. It must be remembered, however, that in attempting to cover the whole of Watt's career, Muirhead was precluded by the great volume of Watt's surviving correspondence from quoting many important letters in full. It seemed valuable, therefore, to rectify this omission as far as concerns the correspondence of two of the greatest Scotsmen of the age. Muirhead also amended Watt's letters where he thought fit, silently inserting or changing marks of punctuation, altering spellings, and deleting Scotticisms. We have preferred to print the letters as they were written except that ampersands have been replaced by 'and' and that contractions have been expanded to help the reader in his study of the letters. Punctuation has been left unchanged but spaces have been left between sentences where no full-stop is given in the original. Square brackets [ ] are used for all editorial insertions and expansions, oblique strokes \ / for insertions written in the manuscripts themselves, and braces { } for authors' deletions. A table of chemical symbols is given on p. xvi. When the date of a letter has been written only at the foot of a letter, we have supplied the date at the head also.

5

Our footnotes have been kept short when the persons or places referred to are well-known but we have taken a little more space with the identification of lesser-known persons, places, books, etc. Addresses, endorsements and locations are also placed in numbered footnotes, but footnotes commenting upon the condition of the manuscript are indicated by daggers in order to distinguish them. For most of the letters we have been able to trace the original manuscript, but in some instances there only survives a mechanical copy made by a Watt copying-press. When there is only a mechanical copy in this way, this fact is indicated by an asterisk * after the number of the letter[1]: if there are in existence the original manuscript and a mechanical copy, the information is given by printing the number of the letter followed by the word 'and' and an asterisk.[2] In a very few instances we have been able to trace only a printed fragment as contained in Muirhead's *Mechanical Inventions*.

It is an exceedingly difficult problem to select the letters that deal with any one theme from the mass of surviving correspondence relating to James Watt. Our aim has been to print all letters between Watt and Black that we could find, together with all letters between Watt and Robison. To these we have added such letters as seemed to us most intimately related to the subjects dealt with in the correspondence between our three main characters and to be needed in order to clarify the part played by other persons closely involved. Naturally a certain arbitrariness has had to enter here and we must only hope that our readers approve of our choice and ask for their indulgence when they do not. If some readers feel that a wider selection of the Boulton and Watt papers should be published, that is a sentiment with which we heartily agree. The greatest number of letters come from Major David Gibson-Watt's family papers at Doldowlod and this location is abbreviated to Dol.; letters from the Boulton and Watt Collection at the Birmingham Reference Library are given the location B.R.L.; and the location of those from the Tew MSS. at the Assay Office Library, Birmingham, is given as A.O.L.B. Other locations are given in full.

In addition to the letters we have printed one or two memoranda relating to the friendship of the principal characters and, perhaps most important, a note-book recording Watt's experiments upon heat which is here printed in its entirety for the first time. To that note-book we have prefaced a separate introductory note, since its difficulties for the reader are quite different from those of the letters. We have also adopted different conventions for its publication, preferring to print it exactly as it stood, keeping ampersands, contractions, etc., but showing the corrections made by Watt to the experimental data at different dates. The note-book is so closely connected with several of the letters that we felt that it should not be published separately though it required special editorial treatment.

¹ Thus 196*.
² Thus 197 and*.

Letter 1

BLACK TO WATT

Enclosed in unaddressed cover, endorsed in Watt's hand: 'Dr.
Black January 20th 1768 enquiring when his Organ will be
ready' and numbered '20'. Dol.

[Enclosed in cover]   *10 January 1768*

Dear Watt

    You have never sent me the Copper Still and other things—nor will you write me a word—Pray when will the Organ[1] be ready—Unless I get it soon I shall be disappointed because I expect soon to have one of my neices in the house who can play upon it—I beg you would \immediatly/ send me the Still (i.e. the body not the head) the Manganese and Cobalt—and some Iron Potts which are lying in Dr. Wilsons[2] —to whom I beg my Comp[limen]ts and many thanks for the Therm[omete]r—Assure Mrs. Watt also of my best respects and beleive me ever Y[ou]rs

Joseph Black

Edinb[urgh] 10 Jan[uar]y 1768

  [1] Watt was asked by a Free-Masons' Lodge in Glasgow to build them an organ. He agreed but began by building a very small one for Dr Black which passed into the possession of John Robison. Watt also made guitars, flutes and violins.

  [2] Dr Alexander Wilson (1714–86) was Professor of Practical Astronomy in the University of Glasgow, 1760–84, and was succeeded by his second son, Dr Patrick Wilson, in 1786.

Letter 2

WATT TO BLACK

J. P. Muirhead MS. extract, B.R.L.

*James Watt to
Joseph Black,
15 February 1768*

'I have now a small share in the Delft work along with a new company.[1] We intend carrying on a stone [ware] manufactory likewise, and are

8

getting proper people for that purpose. You know Delft ware is at present burnt with wood in a square kiln having one mouth below to which the fuel is applied; it then goes into an arch and passes upward through cuts into the body of the furnace[2] from whence it issues in like manner into an arch above the furnace communicating with the chimney. This way of firing is not only expensive, but inconvenient; some parts of the kiln heating more than others, a great deal of ware being by that means spoilt.

Stone ware is burnt in a kiln like that of the common potters, having five mouths; the kiln is filled quite full of the cassettes excepting a small vacuity opposite each of the mouths; yet, though it is 12. ft. diameter, the ware in the middle is best burnt. A fat pit-coal is used for burning the stone-ware; the fire is continued for 48 hours; the colour of the ware depends greatly on the smoke of the coal.

In a little furnace I have, (the stove luted and the vent widened), I made a fire by filling half full of best soft coals, I gave them the full draught of a long chimney, but could never heat the part of the furnace above the fuel better than a bold red heat. I supplied it with fresh coals burnt them with a moderate draught of air till they ceased to smoke, then gave them the full draught; the upper part of the furnace was hotter than before, but could scarcely be called white hot. I put in cokes, and though I diminished the air and the draught of the chimney, in less than 15. minutes the furnace became of a bright white; the duration of the fire was double that of the coals. On opening the upper door and adding fresh cokes, it heated again in about 5. minutes to the white heat. I glazed Delft in an open muffle exposed to the vapours of the Coke; the colour was equal to any. yet I do not think that in large the heat of coke could be communicated to an equal distance from the fire as that of flaming fuel.

I intend, however, to try it for burning Delft thus:— I will make a small kiln like those used for stone-ware, lined within with fire-bricks; behind them an interstice filled with ashes, six or eight inches thick, then a wall of common bricks; the openings left for the flame in the stone furnace I will fill with cokes. I will make a door at the upper end of each opening for supplying fuel, at bottom a grate and dampers, and as the fuel will be as high as the perpendicular part of the wall, some holes may be made in that part for admitting air if occasion be. I intend to kindle the fire at the top, and give it very little air for the first twenty-four hours, after which it must be pushed with vigour for about six hours. In the furnace I mentioned I nutted fusible spar and flints, which

9

Pott could never do:— the glass transparent, colourless. I have, after some trouble, made a white glazing for stone-ware, like that of Delft, but whiter. I shall be glad to have your observations on the kiln before I begin it, which will be soon; and in return shall communicate a method of easily trying pottian[3] exp[erimen]ts much to your ease and satisfaction, with some observations on lutings, for which I have not room at present—J. Watt.'

[1] In 1763 Watt acquired an interest in the Delftfield Pottery Company. In 1766 white stone ware harder in the 'paste' than delft was introduced and this pottery was the pioneer of this ware in Scotland.

[2] Black's interest in furnaces is revealed in some of his early letters to his brother, Alexander. See D. McKie and D. Kennedy, 'On Some Letters of Joseph Black and Others', *Annals of Science*, September 1960, **16**, pp. 129–70.

[3] Johann Heinrich Pott (1692–1777), Professor of Theoretical Chemistry in the Academy at Berlin. His *Lithogeognosia* was published in 1746.

Letter 3

BLACK TO WATT

J. P. Muirhead MS. extract, B.R.L.

Joseph Black to
James Watt,
19 February 1768

'Some of Dr. Black's remarks in reply are worth giving:—* *
"I think your experiment upon coals and cokes promises a most useful improvement in the art of burning all sorts of earthenware, on account of the command it gives of the fire; for, supposing that the cokes will not give the due heat to so great a height as flaming fuel, they must still answer perfectly well if the kiln be only built so much the lower.* *
For my part I do not see what should hinder it to answer in the common proportions provided two things be well attended to, viz. a sufficient draught, and the confinement or preservation of the heat in the upper parts of the kiln; the only reason why the ware is best burnt in the middle of the stone-ware kiln is, that there the heat has no escape, and therefore accumulates. * * A kiln which is heated with flaming fuel may be said to be heated by means of a torrent of *liquid fire* which flows through it, but I am persuaded that cokes act mostly by a radiation like that of the sun. There is a pretty experiment in Nollets *Leçons de Physique*;[1]—he set two

mirrors, (made of pasteboard gilt), parallel to one another, and face to face, in the opposite sides of a room; in the focus of one, a bit of charcoal, and in that of the other, a little gunpowder;—he blew upon the charcoal to brighten it, and the gunpowder took fire. A candle, though a brighter object, would have done nothing in this situation. Is not this a pretty example of what charcoal can do in communicating heat to a distance? * * I believe I told you formerly that a Quaker chemist in Plymouth[2] sent me last year specimens of a Kaolin and Petunse which he has discovered, as he says, in immense quantities in Cornwall. The Kaolin is a beautiful white clay, full of minute scales of white talc, and of no extraordinary toughness. The Petunse is ground and made up for use, but he tells us that in its native state it is a granite. This day I burnt little cakes of each in covered crucibles, and along with them I also burnt a little of the purest sort of Fluor of which I have two or three varieties. The Kaolin burnt to a very pretty stone porcelain, of excessive hardness and strength; the Petunse melted like melted pitch down the side of the crucible, of a semi-transparent light gray colour. * *

[1] Abbé Jean Antoine Nollet (1700–70), experimentalist in electricity, published his *Leçons de Physique Expérimentale*, 6 vols, in Paris, 1754–64.

[2] William Cookworthy (1705–80), porcelain-maker. Started in a small drug business at Plymouth and travelled as a wholesale chemist. Discovered Cornish china clay between 1755 and 1758. Obtained a patent in 1768 which he afterwards sold to Richard Champion of Bristol.

Letter 4

WATT TO BLACK

J. P. Muirhead MS. extract, B.R.L.

*James Watt to
Joseph Black, Glasgow,
7 April 1768*

'I have tried the cokes for burning our Delft; they answer very well. The first time, I proceeded on the supposition of the Beaming of heat, and made my fires as you dress them. The kiln heated violently at the top, and the ware that stood at the bottom, within a few inches of the fuel, was scarcely at all baked, though the top of the same piles was very well fluxed.† I then placed a kind of grate brick-work before and over the fire thus, having a narrow slit before and wider ones at the sides, quite close

† At this point Muirhead has a note in margin: 'slight sketch'.

above except one small hole about 2. inches square; with this alteration, the kiln heats pretty equally, and makes very well-colored ware: the size of it is four feet diameter and four feet high, cylindrical, and closed at top by an arch having one foot of spring: the chimney is about 2. foot high and nine inches square. The only inconvenience is the ashes of the cokes getting into the cases, and sticking to the ware; this I intend to prevent by shutting the chimney where the fires are poked and by making the sagurs or cases closer. The ashes of the wood get into the cases in the other kiln, and, when not burnt off, produce those little black specks observable in the glazing of Delft.

I have contrived a glazing for stone-ware that will bear the ware to be burnt with it on it; for, if that was not the case, the trouble of putting the glazing on a hard-burnt close body would raise the price too high: but this can be sucked in upon a bisket, and, when burnt, is very little if any inferior in beauty to your china, which appears to me to be made of pipe-clay and petunse, and glazed with an opaque white glazing. What that glazing is, I have not discovered: my glazing is a glass of lead and tin without salts, which in great heats are apt to render the tin transparent, and at some time they prevent the glazing from running smooth on the ware without it be made very fusible, in which case it runs about. But I have by no means acquired all the knowledge I must have on this article, having just now little time to spare to it.'

Letter 5

WATT TO BLACK

J. P. Muirhead MS. extract, B.R.L.

James Watt to
Joseph Black, Glasgow,
20 April 1768

'I intended to have seen you in Edinburgh before now, but intended first to have my fire-engine finished, which has stood still too long. My health has been so languishing, that I have not got that completed, though considerably advanced. I shall be extremely happy to see you, and can communicate a great many particulars relating to earthern-ware. From an accidental experiment I found that p[ipe] clay may be burnt as white and hard as any porcelain. Nothing hitherto discovered can be wrought at the wheel with double the trouble that it can. If, therefore, this could be made to succeed in practice, nothing would be necessary for china but stone body. I have strange and incredible things to tell you about stone kilns, which if true, cokes will beat pit-coal even as to quantity or cheapness. Farewell—'

Letter 6

ROBISON TO WATT

Cover addressed: 'To/Mr. James Watt Merchant/Tronegate/ Glasgow' and endorsed in Watt's hand 'J. Robison July 1768.' B.R.L. Parcel 'A'.

Watford July 8 1768

dear Sir

I write this principally to thank you for the favour you have done me in introducing me to the acquaintance of Dr. darwin[1] and Dr. Small.[2] I can't tell how much I think myself obliged to you. I was quite charmed with the unaffected ease and Civility of darwin, and was particularly lucky in being introduced to him by one for whom he has so great a value. I met with no less kindness on the same account from Mrs. darwin You are happy in the Esteem of such worthy people. I was extremely sorry that my Situation hinderd me from taking all the advantage that I might have done of your recommendation. But I was obliged to hurry up to London, and Mr. Mcdowall did not seem so much interested in the subjects of our Conversation as to make me think of continuing them for any time. I spent one day (Tuesday) at Litchfield and was lucky enough to meet with Dr. Small at Mr. Darwin's, and along with him another most agreeable Man and your very warm friend, Mr. Boulton. Next day I went to Birmingham, and Mr. Boulton tho lame, was so kind as conduct me thro his vast works, and after Small carried me to Baskervilles varnishing Shop.[3] I was much struck with many appearances of ingenuity in Boulton's works. It is partly at his desire that I now write to you. In hopes that you had vigorously pursued the improvements of your fire Engine, and was getting your property secured, he has finished a building for one of your reciprocating Engines, and has waited delayd the erection of it on your account, because he says that he would be sorry to put the world in possession of an improvement of which you are the

Author. He is however in very great want of it, and [may] be obliged by necessity to finish it. He therefor earnestly begs that for his sake as well as your own you would lose no time. This he further says is the more necessary as one Edgeworth[4] has hit upon a thought pretty similar to yours, and has also conceived a circular Engine on your principles, and has even thought of employing ☿ as a preventative of friction in the same manner as in yours. Mr. Boulton has some reason for thinking that he has been a little indebted to you. Be this as it will Edgeworth is about to carry his Schemes into execution, there being at present great demand in this country for the improvement of the Engine. (The new navigation at Birmingham will require 3 Engines to supply it with Water). Along with this information he also told me that one Heatly,[5] I think he calls him, a person somehow employd by Dr. Roebuck[6] had got some ideas from you, and having extended them, is now about to publish upon the Subject\and claim the discovery/

You see my dear Sir how many reasons in a manner force you to bestir yourself in getting your porperty secured. I have fulfilled my promise to Mr. Boulton and Dr. Small by pressing the thing upon you in the strongest manner, and would fain hope that you will not neglect your interest.

I also thank you for your plan of a route thro' Keswick; this I found most delightful, beginning at Cockermouth, and going along the chain of lakes from thence to Winander mere. I was unlucky in my derbyshire route; I went across the Lead veins from North to South, by which means I saw only the Limestone stratum, nor was I much instructed at dovedale, nothing else showing itself there. I shall return that way if possible and have desired Dr. Darwin to mark out a route for me against that Time.

I beg my Compliments to Mrs. Watt and remain
Dear Sir
Your faithful Friend
John Robison

I lived at Dr. Mennishes
[Har]row near Watford Hartfordshire

---

[1] Erasmus Darwin (1731–1802), physician, inventor and poet. Member of the Lunar Society of Birmingham. See E. Robinson, *Catalogue of the Lunar Society Bicentenary Exhibition* (Birmingham, 1966) for short biographies of Lunar Society members.

[2] William Small (1734–75), physician and teacher. Member of the Lunar Society of Birmingham.

[3] John Baskerville (1706–75), writing-master and printer of Birmingham. Began in 1740 the manufacture of japanned ware, especially salvers, waiters, bread-baskets, tea-trays, etc. Famous for his type-founding; friend of Matthew Boulton.

[4] Richard Lovell Edgeworth (1744–1817), gentleman and inventor. Member of the Lunar Society of Birmingham.

[5] Joseph Hately was employed by the Carron Company as a millwright. He worked on Watt's experimental engine in 1770. In 1768 he obtained a patent for 'a new fire engine with a boiler, both of a particular sort'. He is next heard of in 1781 when he was seeking the patronage of John Wilkinson. His talents were despised by Boulton and Watt.

[6] John Roebuck, M.D. (1718–94), physician, manufacturing chemist and co-founder of the Carron Company.

[7] William Menish died on 6 April 1813 in his seventy-ninth year. As can be seen from Letter 62 he had been a pupil of Joseph Black in 1760–61. As he came to Glasgow in 1756 he must have been older than the average student. He later took up the manufacture of sal-ammoniac in Whitechapel Road, London (see the *Universal British Directory*, 1791) and the manufacture of hartshorn at the same address, 111 Whitechapel Road (see *Holden's Directory*, 1805). Either he or his younger brother, Henry, who graduated M.D. at Glasgow in 1763 may have been the 'Mr Menish' who was practising as a surgeon and apothecary in Chelmsford in 1780 (see *Medical Directory*).

Letter 7

BLACK TO WATT

Enclosed in unaddressed cover, endorsed in Watt's hand, 'Doctor Black 31st October 1768' and numbered '10'. Dol.

31 October 1768

Dear Watt

I desired Mr. Hill to send to you some things from the Laboratory which I must beg of you to pack up and send to me by the Carriers—among these are an absurd sort of still and a \tall/ head to it both of copper—the tall head you may sell as old Copper—the Still or Body, I wish to have opened above by taking off the top of it which is soldered on only with soft solder and that top is also to be sold as old Copper—the rest of the Body will serve me as a boiler and may be sent packed full of the other things—Mr. Hill may sell the oil of Vitriol Bottle and pay you the money—there are two or three Iron Potts in Dr. Wilsons which must also be sent—forgive me this trouble and beleive me ever

Yours Sincerely
Joseph Black

Edinb[urgh] 31 Octo[ber] 1768

[1] Ninian Hill (1728/9–90) was entered as a Fellow of the Faculty of Physicians and Surgeons of Glasgow in 1750. In Jones's *Directory of Glasgow* for 1787 appears the entry 'Hill and Montieth surgeons, Laboratory Shop, No. 54 Trongate'. See also *The Glasgow Chronicle*, 25 September 1777 which shows that Hill had a laboratory on King St. before removing to Trongate.

Letter 8

BLACK TO WATT

Endorsed in Watt's hand, 'Doctor Black January 20th 1769'
and numbered '11'. Dol.

20 January 1769

Dear Watt

I received yours today and expect some thing further when your leisure admits of it—I trouble you with this to beg you would send me a little of your Shoe vernish as my health does not allow me to prepare it at present—A pound will do or less if you cannot spare so much—and rather than scrimp me in the length of your letter {let me} make my compliments to Mrs. Watt and tell her I beg she will help you as Clerk that you may be saved part of the trouble of writing.

I am greived to the heart for my Freind N Hill———adieu———

J Black

Edinb[urgh] 20 Jan[uary] 1769

Letter 9

BLACK TO WATT

Endorsed in Watt's hand, ᴅᴏctor Black January 23 1769'
and numbered '12'. Dol.

Edinb[urgh] 23 Jan[uary] 1769

Dear Watt

I received yours this Day and am overjoyed to hear that Hill is something better   for Gods sake let me hear of him frequently—As to the Proposal of taking a Patent[1] I have no objection to it provided you are satisfyed that the thing will do and that You as well as Dr. Roebuck will join me in it—perhaps it would be best that I should apply for it in my own name alone giving you \two/ a private obligation to share the advantages of it with you and You going equal with me in the Expence —My reason for this is that I have no witnesses of my invention and of

16

. .

my right to the Patent but your selves two [*sic*] and you could not be admitted as witnesses if you were claimers of the Patent—or Parties—

I am sorry to hear of your bad health—It is the damp and wet weather I beleive destroys us both—

Y[ou]rs J. Black

---

[1] This refers to the proposed patent for alkali manufacture.
A full account of this undertaking will be in A. E. Musson and E. Robinson, *Science and Technology in the Industrial Revolution* (Manchester University Press).

Letter 10

BLACK TO WATT

Endorsed in Watt's hand, 'Dr. Black January 26 1769' and numbered '13'. Dol.

26 January 1769

Dear Watt

I imagine dispatch to be of great consequence in the Business which was the subject of my last and wonder you have delayed to answer me— with respect to Dr. Roebuck—I propose to offer him a Share upon the terms I mentioned but if he does not chuse it, I can easily find People here that will enter heartily into it—

Y[ou]rs
Joseph Black

Edinb[urgh] 26 Jan[uary] 1769

Letter 11

WATT TO BLACK

Cover addressed: 'Doctor/Joseph Black/Physician/Edinburgh', endorsed in Black's hand, 'From Mr. Watt 27 January 1769— about marine alkali', and numbered '5'. Dol.

Glasgow Jan[uary] 27th 1769

Dear Doctor

I rec[eive]d yours   Want of spirits prev[ente]d my writing you
sooner than yesterday   I have no doubt of Doctor Roebucks Chusing to

17

be concerned with you and of his being a valuable partner   my reason against the Experiments being made at Kinneil[1] is that it might be trusted to Improper people.   as he and I stand connected I cannot be concerned with you in that affair without him and Indeed if my health does not mend I cannot at all as I can be of no service to any body   In any case we would be much the better of an Industrious partner and the scheme if successfull will answer us all but would not wish you to take in any body till we have an Opportunity of meeting tho I \now/ think you should write the doctor directly   the sum of my experiments was that in a house of 18 feet wide 36 long and 15 high 9 tun of Alcali might be made in a year that is taking things at the Least   some processes gave much more   If I can I will write on Sunday with Acc[oun]t of Experiments etc.—I am yours sincerely

James Watt

[1] Kinneil was the residence of Dr John Roebuck. The house still stands near Borrowstoness, about three miles from Linlithgow, and was described as a 'very ancient and stately' mansion.

Letter 12

WATT TO BLACK

Cover addressed: 'To/Doctor Joseph Black/Physician/Edinburgh', endorsed in Black's hand, 'From Mr. Watt 28 January 1769—about marine Alkali', and numbered '4'. Dol.

Glasgow Jan[uar]y 28th
1769

Dear Sir,

   Calx exposed in a table plate 6 Inches diameter produced in a month 35gr. 140,000 square feet should then produce 112lb. per diem of dry salt free from Water—Cut into Cubes of $\frac{1}{2}$/In square and as many of them taken as filled about a Cubic foot, in 18 days it produced $1\frac{1}{4}$ Oz dry salt But when made into flatt plates with ridges to keep them asunder about a quarter of an Inch so that the air might pass between them it seemed to do more than in the other case, frost always facilitates the production but as far as I could observe it was only by hastening the Crystallization. It does not seem to be hastned by often watering With the solution but seemed to succeed best when the salt was allowed to run p[er] Deliqium. In every

18

case it operated only on the surface and breaking that produced a decomposition   nothing further can be known without more Experiment   this far however is certain that it never once failed producing
more or less. Now I must leave it to yourself whether it is worth while
to secure it for it is certainly one of the few things that can be compleatly
secured by a patent. Ninian Hill continues rather mending tho not out of
danger

Your's
James Watt

Letter 13

BLACK TO WATT

Endorsed in Watt's hand, 'Dr. Black January 28 1769 and
numbered '14'. Dol.

28 January 1769

Dear Watt

  I received both yours yesterday and today and have wrote to Roebuck
this night and promised to bring about a meeting of you and I at Kinneil
soon—I wish you could fix it for friday next and I am persuaded the ride
will do you good—that is if you can take care to keep your self warm a
horse back especially your feet which tho I beleive it difficult may be
effected by cloathing—I am getting a pair of boots of sufficient capacity
to contain two legs and six stockings—let me hear from you as to this
matter and God bless you—I am y[ou]rs

Joseph Black

I am impatient to discourse you about your health
Edinb[urgh] 28 Jan[uar]y 1769
In both your last letters you forget Poor Hill but I hope he is better

Letter 14

WATT TO BLACK

Cover addressed: 'Doctor Joseph Black/Physician/Edinburgh',
endorsed in Black's hand, 'From Mr. Watt 14 March 1769 and
1768 Marine Alkali and Pottery': also endorsed, apparently in
Watt's hand, below Black's, 'Trial of his Model of Fire Engine'
and numbered '2'. The 'and 1768' probably refers to Watt's
letter to Black of 15 February 1768. Dol.

Glasgow March 14th
1769

Dear Doctor

Receive inclosed the wire It would have been sent sooner but I was
confined to my bed most of last week with a sore throat attended with a
fever of which I am now quite well tho weak. I have got the slip pan I
mentioned to you just as I would have it by covering the bricks with a
sheet of Lead   it evaporates more than formerly and is not half so ready
to burn the Clay. the bricks wrought mostly by suction and dryed and
burnt the Clay next them if not constantly stirred   the Lead works
wholly by evaporation which is from the surface   the Clay is also
much tougher in the Lead pan   I made a tryal of my engine today the
full pressure of the Atmosphere on the piston is 750lb. the engine redily
lifted 625 and I believe will do still more   this was without any help
from the pressure of steam   let me know how you advance with the
Alcali when convenient

I am Dear Doctor
Your James Watt

Letter 15

BLACK TO WATT

Cover addressed: 'To Mr. James Watt/Merchant/in Glasgow'.
Dol.

Edinburgh 27 May 1769

Dear Watt.

I have been attempting to form the Lime into plates with the Instruments I shewed you but have not succeeded nor can I contrive any way

20

of doing it with moderate expedition or conveniency—I thought I could have wrought it so stiff and dry that the plates might have been cut off and set to dry without bending or loseing their form but find it impracticable—I wish you would make some trials of it and assist me in bringing the formation of these Plates (which is the first step) to be a practicable Art—I hope to be with you the begining of next month, when we shall converse more fully, but do what you can in the mean time—My Best Compliments to Mrs. Watt and all Freinds—and beleive me ever Y[ou]rs.

Joseph Black

Letter 16

WATT TO BLACK

Endorsed in Black's hand, 'Mr. Watt May 29th 68 or 69 Marine Alkali' and numbered '3'. Dol.

Glasgow May 29th [1769]

Dear Sir

I intend being at Kinneil on Thursday If you could be there at same time should be Glad as I long much to know If you have got any Alicalies made and their Success. Not long ago Dr. Small repeated his advice of dispatch. When I was last at Kinneil the Dr. wanted much to try the process there which for former reasons I am against unless I can find time when I am there with the engine to do something in it myself If you cannot come to Kinneil write to me there but say nothing but what is proper for the Drs. perusal My new Condenser[1] was tryed on Saturday and answers

Your's Sincerely James Watt

[1] This condenser is described in Watt's letter to William Small, 22 February 1769, A. O. L. B.

BLACK TO WATT

Cover addressed: 'To Mr. James Watt merchant/near the Cross/ Glasgow' and numbered '16'. Dol.

Monday 10 July 1769

Dear Watt

I received yours on Saturday and have also wrote to Handley[1] but forgot to mention whether I wanted the P[aten]t for England only or a more extensive one. If it be necessary to attend to this point of drawing the Petition I shall write again in a post or two which will be soon enough— When are you to be again at Kinneil and how long? let me have a line by the return of the Post—I wrote to my Brothers in London to call upon Handley and engage for payment etc but desired them to take no notice of the Business

Adieu
Joseph Black

[1] Thomas Handley, a solicitor. In 1771 his address was Thos. Handley and Co., Rolls Buildings, Fetter Lane, London. Correspondence from Handley to Watt, 1777–88, exists in the Birmingham Reference Library.

BLACK TO WATT

Endorsed in Watt's hand, 'Doctor Black December 20 1796' and numbered '17'. Dol.

Edinburgh 20 Dec[embe]r 1769†

Dear Watt

In the first place I desire you will charge the Postage of this heavy packet to my Account and forward the Inclosed and secondly I beg you will take the trouble to have a Pattern turned after the inclosed drawing and send it to Fairy[1] with orders to have 2 Casts of it in Iron as soon as possible—the two loops or Eyes on the lip may be Iron wire set in so as the melted metal may fasten upon it—When they are ready Pack them

† Letter torn down right-hand side.

up together with the Pattern and send them to me without delay and it will be still more obliging if you cram into the same box a good quantity of the richest of the Greenock Ore, I mean of the Gray [kind]   I shall be glad to hear what you have made of it—

Dr. Irvin[2] called upon me yesterday when I was abroad and left word that he was to set out for London early this morning—pray what carries him up at this time of year—I have lately examined the Therm[omete]rs which you blew for me and have found them most charmingly sized— I shall clean them and fill them some of these days and then I shall be upon you again to divide them, the coarse lump of a thing which you cut for me before I left Glasgow has been of great use—My best Comp- [limen]ts to Mrs. Watt and all freinds and beleive me ever

Y[ou]rs affect[iona]te[l]y
Joseph Black

[1] This is presumably the iron-founder father of John Farey, junior, engineer and historian of steam-engines.

[2] William Irvine (1743–87). Studied under Black at Glasgow, where he succeeded Robison as Lecturer on Chemistry in 1770.

Letter 19

BLACK TO WATT

Endorsed in Watt's hand, 'Dr. Black February 28 1770 and numbered '18'. Dol.

28 February 1770

Dear Watt

Send me Ten pounds More of the Manganese and send the light Tongs made for me by Wilson.

—I am convinced that the Manganese is the substance with which the Chinese Copper is Whitened[1]

Y[ou]rs
J. Black

28 Feb[ruary] 1770

[1] Black was wrong. Paktung is an alloy of copper, zinc and nickel.

23

ROBISON TO WATT

Endorsed, 'J. Robison April 1771'. B.R.L. Parcel 'A'.

St Petersburg Ap[ril] 22d 1771 OS.

——————I therefor obey with pleasure thy Order which I have just now received to write to You in order to see how you would relish the Scheme of coming here in quality of Master Founder of Iron Ordnance to Her Imperial Majesty. I made no hesitation in recommending my friend, because I was well acquainted with your knowledge in Metallurgy and Mechanics, and your intimate acquaintance with all the process as carry'd on at Carron; and because I was confident that if you yourself believed that you could undertake the Employm[en]t you would do honour to my recommendation; and my wishes to see you here, and my desire to serve Her Imperial Majesty and promote your Interest makes me readily submit to being eclipsed by you in my favorite Studies. I am not as yet able to tell you what may be your Encouragement, but I am sure that her Majesty's Generosity will make it very suitable to Her sense of the importance of the Employment. I write this only to know your Sentiments, and will take the first opportunity of informing you of what terms can be procured. You will no doubt consult with Dr. Roebuck upon this Subject. I also writ to him by order to know at what price the Carron Company can furnish Cannon. But it will be infinitely more agreeable to have a founder here—

To Mr. James Watt Engineer Glasgow

[In another hand]   London the 4 July 1771
If you choose to send to me your answer, proper Care shall be tacken of [it] you may only direct it as following

To
the Russian ambassador
in
Lower Grosvenor Street
London

Letter 21

KEIR[1] TO WATT

No cover. Dol.

Stourbridge
14 December 1771

Dear Sir,

Dr. Small informs me that you desire to know the result of my experiments on our method of procuring fossil alkali. My experiments are not sufficiently long continued, nor do I think that they were made with sufficiently large quantities of materials, to ascertain the quantity of alkali producible. I can only acquaint you that from a pound of dry salt I have obtained a quarter of a pound of dry, mild alkali, within a twelvemonth, and that the mass was not then exhausted, for it still continued to throw out more and more of the alkaline efflorescence. Some masses that had been kept 18 months were not exhausted. I make no doubt but the quantity of alkali producible is sufficient to make the Scheme profitable, if the excessive slowness of the process does not render the quantity of buildings, labor, etc., too great. When I was last in London I heard it mentioned by some persons curious in chemistry and who especially had made many attempts to discover the method of obtaining the alkali of common salt, that Dr. Black had actually discovered that method. I was afraid lest some persons might prevent our obtaining a patent, if we should think it necessary, by entering a caveat in general against all patents for obtaining alkali from sea-salt, especially as I found upon Inquiry that you and Dr. Black had not taken that precaution. I accordingly entered a caveat in my own name which caveat shall not prevent you or your friends connected in the Scheme from taking out a patent when you and they think proper. I was in hopes at that time to have offered my Service to you all to execute the Scheme if you chose to join me, as I had thoughts of renting a coal and salt work in Scotland. I am now fixed in an inland Country, and though I consume a great deal of alkali, yet I believe I must only wish success to those who chuse to undertake the scheme, I should nevertheless be glad to know when you are determined to take out a patent.—

Dr. Small acquaints me that he has written to You upon the Subject of the Glass trade in Scotland, and especially at Glasgow. You will oblige me much by informing me whether much (white or flint) glass is exported from Glasgow to America, *whence* the Glasgow merchants are supplied, at what *prices*, *discount*, *credit*, or other allowances, and whether You think I could come in for a share of that trade. To enable you to judge of this matter, I have sent you a list of prices of some goods with conditions of Trade, etc.—Dr. Small tells me you propose to be soon in England. I heartily [hop]e for the pleasure of seeing You here, and am [with] great regard,

Dear Sir,
Yours most Sincerely
James Keir

¹ James Keir (1735–1820), army officer, chemist and glass-maker. Member of the Lunar Society of Birmingham.

Letter 22

KEIR TO WATT

Cover addressed: 'Mr. Watt Ingeneer at /Glasgow/N. Britain'.
Dol.

Wordsley near Stourbridge 27th Feb[ruary] [1772]

Dear Sir

I return you many thanks for your information on the Glass trade at Glasgow, and would have acknowledged your favor sooner, but was a good deal puzzled about the intelligence you gave me, that the Merchants at Glasgow had glass delivered to them at prices a mere trifle higher than those I mentioned with 15 Months credit. I perceived that there must have been some mistake, and upon further inquiry I found that the prices are nearly the same, but no discount is allowed, whereas in my conditions, there is 20 per Cent. Disc[oun]t which is such an advantage as does much more than compensate for the difference of credit, and for the expence and risk of bringing Glass from Bristol or Liverpool to Glasgow. Our glass is preferred in London to the Newcastle, and I believe, justly. I doubt not but something may be done, and I suppose that the plan of keeping a warehouse might be the best, and of selling at the same prices as those of Newcastle, or only so much less as to obtain a preference. But at present I shall only think of{ selling }sending glass, as it is ordered, and I should imagine that the terms I mentioned might be sufficient inducement for a preference either to the Merchants who export, or to the Warehouse keepers of Glass (if there be any

such in Glasgow besides those belonging to the Newcastle company).—
I am much obliged to you for your offer of putting a few crates for a
trial into the hands of Mr. Hamilton.[1] When our canal is opened, (which
will be about the middle of May) I shall send some crates to Liverpool
to be forwarded to him.

The Surface from which I obtained the quantity mentioned of Alkali
was about a hundred Square inches. The mass was placed in a cellar, but
in other trials I found any part of the house from the uninhabited
Garrets to the cellars fit for the purpose; Nor can I say that I found any
circumstance to be necessary but a certain moisture, which must be
given either by a moist air as that of cellars, or by a frequent sprinkling
with water. If the mass be kept too moist, or too dry, the separation of
the alkali does not take place. I have more than once tryed the decomposition of vitriolated tartar and of nitre by the same method, but
without Success. I never tried the Salt of Sylvius. The alkali I{obtained}
\mentioned/ was mild, and as dry as could be without making it red hot.

Dr. Small has made a clock that shews hours, minutes and seconds,
strikes and repeats, with one wheel only, and without pinion or endless
Screw.[2]—I hope you have not laid aside thoughts of being in this
country some time this Spring or Summer.—I am

Dear Sir
Yours most Sincerely
Jame Keir

[Ink Note in James Watt's hand]
```
        100
   5 Square feet will yield 1 Lb per annum
   560 feet [will] produce one—Cwt
560 x 30 will produce one cwt. per day
   360
   ────
 33600
 16800
 ─────
```

9201600 22400

[Keir had previously written to Watt on the glass trade in Glasgow
14 December 1771 (Dol)]

[1] Gilbert Hamilton, merchant, was James Watt's cousin.
[2] See Patent No. 1048, A.D. 1773.

BLACK TO WATT

Cover addressed: 'To Mr. James Watt/Engineer/Glasgow'
and numbered '19'. Dol.

22 March 1772

Dear Watt

I got both your letters and have received the £100 for you this day   I called since upon Mr. Auld twice to leave the £50 with him but happened to miss him, shall call again tonight or tomorrow and shall send you his receipt by some other opportunity.

Am much obliged to you for this payment but beleive \me/ I did not receive it without some uneasiness lest you should lay yourself under Difficulties upon my account—Be assured that I dont desire any payments from you unless you can spare the money with Ease—I am happy to hear that affairs go on prosperously with You and have no doubt that your Health will mend as your Anxiety diminishes—Thanks for your kind Enquiries about me—I have no reason to complain, my Class is better this winter than ever before, and my health upon the whole no worse—but have been driven to one of the last shifts of a valetudinarian, a flannel shirt—which has however I think done me great service.

I have no chemical News, my attempts in Chemistry at present are cheifly directed to the exhibition of Processes and experiments for my Lectures, which require more time and trouble than one would imagine—Yet I could give you a more distinct process for the Purple precipitate of ⊙ than Montamye[1]—You offer me security for the rest of the money you owe me but you forget that I have already security for the greater part of it—The Bills I have upon you are First, One upon yourself and Jno. Craig[2] \conjunctly/ and severally for £150—the interest payed up to 7th June 1766—Secondly A Bill for £22:10. date 7th June 1766— —Thirdly A Bill for £50—date 14 Feb: 1766—upon the back of this last {dis I have} I have acknowledged receipt of the Principal but not of the Interest—since I got this present £50 from you —And I am indifferent about any further security for the rest than what I have already but if you have any reasons for chusing to change the security I have no objection—My Compliments to Mrs. Watt and all Friends and beleive me always

Yours with truth
Joseph Black

Edinburgh 22d March
1772
I have destroyed your Bill of the 16th upon Mr. Auld.

[Noted in Watt's hand on facing page].

$£222 . . 10$—
Interest $66 . . 12$—
_____
$£289 . . 2$
50—
_____
$£239 . . . 2$

[1] Didier François d'Arclay de Montamy (1702–1764), wrote a treatise on colours for painting enamels and porcelain, translated in J. H. Pott's *Lithogeognosia*.

[2] Jonathan Craig was Watt's partner in a mathematical-instrument-making business from 7 October 1759 until April 1765, when he died. He seems to have taken no part in the manufacturing side of the business but to have kept the books and advanced the greater part of the capital.

Letter 24

BLACK TO WATT

Endorsed in Watt's hand, 'Dr. Black July 1st 1772' and numbered '8'. Dol.

Edinburgh 1st July 1772

Dear Watt

I am much obliged to you for your attention to my Affairs. The risk which I run at present of losing the money you mention would have given me much more vexation had I not been habituated for a long time past to consider it as Money not to be counted upon—But as soon as I received Your letter however I wrote to A insisting upon an immediate Inspection of his Books and general View of his Affairs by Claud Marshall[1] to whom I also wrote upon the Same Subject and added that I should go west in a few days to receive Marshalls report. A. answered by the return of the Post promising to prepare the full state I desired, as soon as possible for Marshalls inspection, but begging 8 or 10 days to accomplish it which time he finds necessary on account of the Situation of his Family and the distressing news they have had from London—Upon the whole, he has lately expressed so strongly his sense of the Obligations he lyes under to me that I cannot suppose him capable of willfully deceiving or wronging me and am inclined to allow him full time for preparing his accounts—Upon the present occasion I happened to have some money in the hands of the Alexanders and a little also in the Douglass and Heron Bank[2] but have no anxiety about either of those Sums—I am afraid these confusions will delay the execution of the improvements of Air harbour[3]—pray are you pretty sure of the superintendancy of that Jobb—I had a conversation lately with Alexander and you may count upon him—

I hope soon to see you engaged in much greater and more profitable employments—

I am ever Yours
Joseph Black

[On separate slip enclosed, figures as follows:]

Debt to J. A. to J. B.

1771 January 2d a Bill	. . .	. £990..—..—	
May 27th paid	. . .	. 200..—..—	
1772 January 30th paid	. . .	. 60..—..—	
			786..19
		£730..—..—	127..11
			£914..10

1770 December 28th a bill	. .	. 119.. 7.. 6	
1772 May 13 Intrest on the last bill	.	. 8.. 4.. 4	
		£127..11..10	

1771 May 27th Intrest on £990. 4 mths 25 ds   19..16.. 5
1772 January 30th Intrest on £790. 8 mths 3 ds 26..13.. 3
    May 13th Intrest on £730. 2 mths 18 ds   10.. 9.. 6

£56..19.. 3 [sic]

---

[1] Claud Marshall, son of James Marshall, dyer of Glasgow, was a solicitor, admitted Notary Public in 1758 and Burgess and Guild Brother of Glasgow in the same year. He was appointed Commissary Clerk of Hamilton and Campsie in 1774 and was Dean of the Faculty of Procurators from 1804 until his death at the age of 74 in 1812.

² The Ayr Bank of Douglas, Heron and Co., stopped payment in June 1772. The 24th June was termed 'Black Wednesday', and long remembered for the misery entailed on all connected with the firms that failed. The cashier of the Canongate branch of Douglas, Heron and Co., was named Thomas Hogg and this may be the 'T.H.' referred to in Black's letter to Watt of 1 October 1772.

³ As will be seen from this correspondence, Watt did report on improvements to Ayr Harbour. He had previously prepared reports for new docks and a harbour at Port Glasgow.

Letter 25

RUSSELL TO WATT

Endorsed in Watt's hand, 'Proffessor Russel August 19 1772' and numbered '9'. Dol.

Edin[bu]r[gh] 19th Aug[us]t 1772

Dear Sir

I thank you for the perusal of the Reports and Plans of the Harbour of Air. I would have returned them much sooner, had not Com-[missione]r Clerk¹ desired to see them again. The other Reports you mention are not come to hand.

Have you forgot that I am in debt, or have you no distinct Acco[un]t of particulars? There is a large Eolus's Harp, a Monochord, and one, if not two drawing Machines. If there be two not accounted for, by Dr. Lind,² of those that lay sometime by me, that will be full evidence. Pray send an Acco[un]t to somebody with an order to discharge it.

I am

Dear Sir

Yours

James Russell³

As I am to be from home
for 3 or 4 days, I leave
this etc. to be sent
by the first Carrier

¹ Commissioner George Clerk, later Sir George Clerk. See p.123.

² James Lind, M.D. (1738–1812) went out as surgeon in an East Indiaman in 1766. He later settled in Windsor and became physician to the royal household.

³ James Russell (1754–1836), surgeon in Edinburgh and afterwards first professor of clinical surgery (1803–34) in the University of Edinburgh. He was a first cousin to Joseph Black, their mothers being sisters.

Letter 26

WATT TO RUSSELL

Cover addressed: 'Doctor Joseph Black/Physician/Edinburgh'
and endorsed, 'Settled Account with Proffessor Russell 1773'.
Also written on back, 'Alexander Smith/Pryse Walker'. Dol.

Proffessor Russel   *Glasgow Sep[tember] 2d 1765*

		Bought of James Watt			
1765 Sept[embe]r	A pair gogles 2/6 an Ivory folder 1/1		..	3..	7
	A monochord and box		..	9..	4
Nov[embe]r 13	An Eolus harp 21/ a key for ditto 1/6	1..	2..	6
	Pack box for Ditto 2/2		..	2..	2
June 22d	A pair bellows 12/		..12..	—
	A boiling water thermometer	1..	1..	—

£3..10.. 7

An Error in chargeing the price of the
   above Thermometer, of   1 : 1 : —

4 : 11 : 7

1765

July 19	3 drawing machines 63/ each	9 : 9 :
Sep[tembe]r 4	4 Ditto....Ditto.... 66/——	13 : 4 :
7[?]	1 Ditto .... 42/——	2 : 2 :
Oct[ober] 18	10 Ditto .... 63/——	31 : 10
31	3 Ditto from Mr. Clerk 66/——	9 : 18

70 : 14 : 7

Cash was paid him by Dr. Lind{ on my Account }[deleted in pencil] for
{ By Drawing Machines returnd }[deleted in pencil]
the following articles—

3 Machines at 45/——	6 : 15 : —
Cases to Ditto	: 4 : 6
2 Machines at 42/——	4 : 4 : —
5 Green Bags——	2 : 6
A Thermom[ete]r——	1 : 1 : —
6 Watch Alarms——	9 : —

32

[Enclosed on separate slip of paper:
    'Mr. James Watt D[ebto]r to Doctor Wilson
1769   £
    Jan[ua]ry 28   To an Elliptical Boiling Water Therm[ometer]— 2.2.0
    Received payment Alex[ande]r Wilson'.]

Letter 27

BLACK TO WATT

Numbered '7'. Dol.

Edinb[urgh] 1st October 1772

Dear Watt

I ought to ask your Pardon for giving you the trouble of this letter
and of an answer to it. for to tell the truth I have nothing to say that
should be intruded to disturb your meditations—Dr. Roebuck shewed
me part of a letter he had from you by which he concluded you were
in low spirits which I readily beleive as I hear that you have been
closely employed of late in deep Calculations—besides I have no
doubt that the faces of the People in Glasgow have been for some time
past screwed up with an unusual degree of Care and Anxiety and such
expressions of the Countenance are very infectious I wish I could
give you a dose now and then of my freind Huttons[1] Company, it
would do you a world of good

You express some concern on account of a freind of mine in distress,
lest I should be involved with him   I suppose you mean T.H.[2] With
regard to myself I am perfectly clear of him and was astonished this day
when I heard of his being arrested—I impute it to want of activity in
calling in his money and to the difficulty of getting accounts paid up
at present in Glasgow   I consider it as accidental and perhaps of little
consequence If I am wrong I beg you would write me a word upon it
—and you may at same time give me what you hear concerning
James Andersone[3]—I have not heard a word upon that Subject since
I was in Glasgow, except in general that all is gone, Lord knows where
—but I beg you will not write if you find it in the least troublesome
or are not at leisure—I have been at Lead Hills[4] lately and am at present

33

in pretty good health   for Gods sake take care of yours and beleive
me always

Yours most affectionately

Joseph Black

¹ James Hutton (1726–97), the geologist.
² See note above, p. 31.
³ This may be the James Anderson born in Hemiston in Mid-Lothian in 1739. He was a armer, writer, and a pioneer in the application of scientific knowledge to rural economy. He studied chemistry under Cullen at Edinburgh.
⁴ The principal lead-mines in Scotland were situated at Lead Hills and Wanlockhead on the border of Lanark and Dumfries-shire. The mines at Lead Hills were the property of the Earl of Hopetoun and those of Wanlockhead of the Duke of Queensberry.

Letter 28

WATT TO BLACK

No cover. Endorsed in Dr. Black's hand: '15 Dec[embe]r 1772'.
Edinburgh University Library.

Glasgow Dec[embe]r 15th 1772

Dear Doctor

I send you by this days coach, My plans of Tarbert and Crinan with sections of them both, the paralel lines in the sections were drawn by the help of the dividing Screw. You know I am no practised drawer and will therefore excuse deficiencys of neatness in the Plans particularly in the writing part, a great deal of which I was obliged to do by candle light and some of it while under the influence of a headach when my hand shakes considerably. It is at any rate more difficult to write neatly upon stiff paper with China Ink than you would imagine particularly when the paper has been much handled. There has likewise been some erasements in the Crinan plan, one occasioned by spilling some ink upon it when finished. I have brought a new skin on these places by a little paste which though it prevents their being so easily dirtyed does not render them less visible—As to the rest you may depend that not only the geometrical part is exact, but also that the face of the country is represented {as} very like   you will show them to our friends Mr Russel and Mr Clerk. The Report is wrote and mostly transcribed and I expect will be sent by Friday or saturdays coach. They have cost me much labour and I am afraid need as much excuse

34

as the Plans, but in essentials you will find them right—The expence of a 10 feet canal at Crinan is £49000—of a 7 feet De[pth] £36000 the 10 feet at Tarbert £24000—the 7 feet £18000

I hear of an acid somebody has discovered that turns water into Flint, do you know anything of it—My Compliments to all Friends particularly to the gentlemen mentioned and Dr Hutton

Your's sincerely
James Watt

P.S. Nothing has been done in your friend J.As affairs and I am told he is in great want

Letter 29

BLACK TO WATT

Endorsed in Watt's hand, 'Dr. Black December 23 1772' and numbered '5'. Dol.

23 December 1772

Dear Watt—

I received your Plans and Sections in perfect good order and your letter this day promising the report by tomorrows Coach. I should have advised you with the receipt of the Plans sooner but expected the report and proposed to write about both at same time

All who have seen the plans etc. are extreamly well pleased with them—Entre nous Mr. Clerk thinks it best that I should be employed to deliver them in to the board, as he supposes he will be appointed to examine and report his opinion of them to the board in that Case which would probably be otherwise were he to be the person who presented them from you. He read me that part of your letter to him which related to the money and desires you would write to me to give a rude estimate of the expence you have been at—he doubts if there be much ready Cash in the Receiver Generals hands but thinks it very reasonable that your expences should be refunded as soon as possible —I hope I shall have as much leisure during the Holidays as to read your Paper with attention and, I doubt not, with pleasure—

The Acid which converts water (in appearance) into Flinty earth is contained in the fluor phosphorescens, or flus spat not the gypseous

35

Spar but the fusible one—the account of it is in a pamphlet lately published by Foster—Titled—An easy method of Essaying and Classing mineral Subst[an]ces[1]—the Experiments on the fluor are an extract from A Memoir in the late Swedish Transactions—and the Translation excessively bad—Pray tell Dr. Wilson that Dr. Cullen[2] wants a Thermometer which he may send in by you or any other good opportunity the sooner the better—

My best Compliments to Mrs. Watt and beleive

Edinburgh 23 Dec[embe]r
1772

always Yours
Joseph Black

[1] Johann Reinhold Forster (1729–98), natural historian, published in London, 1772, *An Easy Method . . .* etc.
[2] William Cullen (1710–90), professor of chemistry in the University of Glasgow, and professor of medicine in the University of Edinburgh. Friend and colleague of Dr Black.

Letter 30

BLACK TO WATT

Endorsed in Watt's hand, 'Doctor Black December 26 1772' and numbered '6'. Dol.

26 December 1772

Dear Watt

I receivd Your report and propose to read it tomorrow along with Mr. Clerk and Dr. Hutton privately and you shall have our Criticisms if we have any to offer—in the mean time it is this day in the hands of Professor Ferguson[1] who having seen it yesterday in my Room was easily prevailed upon at my desire to look it over and mark any corrections of the language which he thought proper—he said he was very much pleased with the Stile and expression in general but found words here and there which he thought should be changed so I put it into his hands for that purpose—I perceive that the Sections cannot be conveniently applyed to the maps or compared with them so as to read both at same time—the east end being opposite the right hand in the one and the left hand in the other which might have been avoided and it is perhaps worth while to draw the Sections over again for that reason, but perhaps you may have other reasons for its being as at present—the Acid you enquire about is combined in the *fluor* with Calcarious Earth

36

alone—but adheres to it strongly—is separated by adding strong Vitriolic Acid to finely pulverized fluor and destilling the mixture, an Acid comes having the appearance and Odour of the muriatic, but the fumes of it corrode or roughen the Surface of the receiver—and form a crust of earthy concretion on the surface of Water placed in the receiver to condense them—the same earthy silicious matter was formed by these fumes when detached from the fluor in an Iron vessel upon their Strikeing a piece of wet charcoal suspended in their way etc.—more at meeting

for the present, remain
Yours
Joseph Black

Edinb[urgh] 26 Dec[embe]r 1772.

¹ Adam Ferguson (1723–1816), professor of philosophy in the University of Edinburgh, author of an *Essay on Civil Society*. He was Joseph Black's second cousin, his mother being an aunt of Margaret Gordon, Black's mother; in 1766 he married Black's niece, Katharine Burnett, daughter of Black's eldest sister, Isabel.

Letter 31

BLACK TO WATT

Endorsed in Watt's hand, 'Doctor Black December 23 1772' and numbered '4'. Dol.

Edinb[urgh] 31 Dec[embe]r
1772

Dear Watt

Your Freinds here have now read your Report and are extreamly well pleased with it—the Corrections of the language given by Mr. Ferguson and Mr. Russel are but very few and I shall add a few more when I return it to you—one Word occurs twice which I remember to have heard you use but mistakingly I mean *Detruitus*—the only Word of this kind is *Detritus* which is latin {but the french *detruire*} and means *worn or rubbed away*—but the french *detruire* has led you into a mistake both of the meaning in one place and orthography—I have corrected that word with my pen—and Mr. Ferguson had made a few corrections of single words before I told him that this Copy was to be presented to the Trustees—I shall deliver it to their Clerk with a Message or Card expressing your concern that it is but incorrectly transcribed and promising soon to exchange it for a fairer and more correct Copy

37

—I have not made any Exp[erimen]ts yet upon the Acid of Spar—but if you attend to the one I mentioned made with the ♂ vessel \(a bit of Gun barrel)/ and wet charcoal you will I imagine find an answer to the Question you put—Adieu and beleive me

Y[ou]rs
Joseph Black

I by no means think new Sections necessary

Letter 32

BLACK TO WATT

Endorsed in Watt's hand, 'Dr. Black February 1st 1773 favorable Report by Commissioner Clerk' and numbered '2'. Dol.

1 February 1773

Dear Watt

I received Yours and am sorry for your late indisposition—Yesterday Commissioner Clerk sent me the following line—"Edinb[urgh] 31st Janu[ary] 1773—D[ea]r Sir—I called yesterday to shew you a Scroll of a report I had made out very favourable for Mr. Watt, but no stronger than the merit of his performance deserves. I have also ordered our Secretary to reserve Money in his hands for payment and wish Mr. Watt would send in his Acc[oun]t without loss of time if he does not find it convenient to come in himself. The Report is now signed and delivered to our Clerk to be laid before the Board tomorrow—I am Y[our]s etc. G.C."

I shall endeavour to get your Report and return it to you with the slight remarks which were made on the Language—I suppose the Plans may remain where they are.

Yours ever
Joseph Black

Edinb[urgh] 1st Feb[ruary] 1773

[On other side a calculation:
'40/66/1   66/400/66
                    396
                    ———
                    400
          66'1

38

BLACK TO WATT

Endorsed in Watt's hand, 'Dr. Black May 22 1773' and
numbered '3'. Dol.

Edinb[urgh] 22d May 1773

Dear Watt

I cannot imagine you would pass thro this Town without calling
upon me and therefore suppose you are still in Glasgow—I must beg
the favour of you to bring when you come, the divided plate for
graduating Thermometers

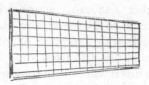

—Your machine with the Screw is admirable for its exactness but the plate will be exact enough for some
Operations I wish to have done—and it saves calculation

Compliments to Mrs. Watt and beleive me

ever Yours
Joseph Black

BLACK TO WATT

Endorsed in Watt's hand, 'Dr. Black February 23 1774' and
numbered '1'. Dol.

23 February 1774

Dear Watt

I am told that by the new law a Bill prescribes and becomes null in
6 years, I must therefore put you to the trouble of renewing those I
have from you which are already of too old a Date—One is for £150
accepted by yourself and John Craig date 7th June 1763 Interest paid to
7th June 1766—Another £22..10.. accepted by yourself only date
7th June 1766 no interest paid—I have also one for £50 but this is
discharged on the back with exception of Interest which was not
settled when I rec[eive]d the £50 from you—If you can pay me up
the Interest of the two first it will be very convenient at present as I shall
need a little money when I go into my new house—

Yours ever
Joseph Black

Edin[urgh] 23 Feb[ruary]   Accepted 2 bills for
1774   the £172..10 and interest
to this date

BLACK TO WATT

Cover addressed: 'Mr. James Watt/Engineer/at Redruth/
Cornwall' and numbered '65'. Dol.

Edinb[urgh] 27th Nov[embe]r
1778

Dear Watt

It is so very long since I have heard from you directly that some
account of your Prosperity from yourself would give me much more
than ordinary Pleasure I have heard from many hands that you have

succeeded in all your undertakings with your Engine to the Conviction and Surprize of all Unbeleivers and that even Smeiton[1] has been converted—In all this I also beleive, but for all that, some news of what you have done, comeing from yourself would be a great Cordial to Hutton and me—If you are to remain any longer in Cornwall you will have opportunitys to pick up great numbers of Specimens and I shall be obliged to you to lay out a few guineas for me—I would wish to have Specimens of the Rich Tin Ore and other minerals about 4 Inches square each—Small Specimens do not answer for my purpose—I was sorry to hear that Mrs. Watt complained a little of bad health so me time agoe and hope she is now grown stronger   make my kind Compliments to her and beleive me

yours affectionately
Joseph Black

[1] John Smeaton (1724–92), Engineer.

Letter 36

WATT TO BLACK

Cover addressed: 'To/Doctor Joseph Black/Professor of Chemistry/in the University of/Edinburgh', endorsed in Black's hand, 'Mr. Watt 12 December 1778' and numbered '59'. Dol.

Redruth Dec[embe]r 12th 1778

Dear Sir,

I received your kind letter of the 27 November and am very happy in the continuance of your and Dr. Huttons very kind wishes which shall study to deserve—I should long ago have wrote you of my proceedings but did not think that what I could impart merited much attention from you for though we have in general succeeded in our undertakings yett that success has from various unavoidable Circumstances produced small profits to us—The strug\g/les we have had with natural difficulties and with the ignorance prejudices and villanies of mankind have been very great but I hope are now nearly come to an end or vanquished

Mr Smeaton has behaved with the utmost Candour and friendship and has even reccommended a Customer to us more than once—Our

41

success here has equalled our most sanguine expectations   we have succeeded in saving 3/4 of the fuel over the engines here which are the best of the old kind in the Island—The large engine at Chacewater lately finished by us is 63 inches dia[mete]r, has a 9 feet stroke, makes when going out of hand under its full load 11 strokes per minute, works a pump of 17 inches dia[mete]r and 53 fathoms deep and moreover puts in motion a very strong Connection rod 25 fathoms long before it comes to the pump heads which rod and \the/ others which belong to 3 lifts of pumps weigh about 9 tuns the vis inertiæ of whi[ch] and its Counterpoize demands a very considerable power—This engine when going at the above rate burns 128 bushels of Welsh Coals per 24 hours —We have agreed to take £700 p[e]r ann[u]m for our part of the savings by this engine†

The water of this mine formerly baffled 2 Engines one a 66 and the other a 64 but though this is the rainiest season and the water the most plenty below ground we keep it very well under hitherto—but that you may know what a job it was, we were 3 months going at the above rate in forking or unwatering the mine. The whole country declared it impossible some on account of the known great qu[anti]ty of water and other from a belief that the engine could not work the pump to that depth

{The} \An/ universal confidence of the whole County in the abilities of the engine is now fully established and we have executed agreements for several others One of which will pay me better still and is also to do the work of two other engines larger than itself. Several mines formerly abandoned are likely to go to work again through virtue of our engines—we have 5 Engines of various sizes actually going here now \in this County/ and more in contemplation—So that our affairs wear a most smiling aspect to human eyes—*Le Roi de France dans son Conseil nous a Accorde un Privilege exclusif*[2] *pour faire et vendre ces machines en france* and we have now an engine actualy under hand for that kingdom —*but this entre nous*, Our affairs in other parts of england go on very well but no part can or will pay us so well as Cornwall and we have luckily come ammong them when they were almost at their witts end how to go deeper with their mines—In regard to [blank] the anxiety and vexation which I have undergone and still awaits me does not contribute to my health and the Climate here is not favourable to a valetudinarian as its Changes from heat to cold are frequent and sudden

† In margin, Watt wrote 'please not to mention particulars in public G.M.[1] is too fond of a good Bargain'.

and the storms of rain and wind excessive—yet in respect to Cold the air is mild the fields are still green and many plants in flower, we have had only one frosty morning yett—The weather is now so bad that I cannot pretend to get you many specimens of fossils this season but shall send you a few of the best mine tin stuff—I have seen no very Curious Copper ores—The yellow pyritous Ores are the great riches of the mines but some of them produce much grey ore which is generally friable—a list of such things as you want would be usefull as a guide—I shall soon return to Birm[ingham] for a few months—Mrs. Watt joins in best respect and sincere good wishes to you Mr. Clerk Dr. Hutton and all other friends Dear Sir

Yours most affectionately
James Watt

(near 5 o Clock a rainy day and no candle)

[1] Gilbert Meason, merchant, of Edinburgh. Meason was clearly concerned with the Wanlockhead lead-mine in Dumfriesshire. The Boulton and Watt Letter Books at the Birmingham Reference Library contain some fifty letters between Watt and Meason dated between 1776 and 1797.

[2] In 1778 Boulton and Watt were granted an exclusive privilege to make and sell their engines in France. The decree could not have the force of a patent until an engine had been tested by the Commissioners. This was the engine erected at the colliery of Monsieur Jary near Nantes.

Letter 37

BLACK TO WATT

Cover addressed: 'Mr. James Watt Engineer/Birmingham/by Ferrybridge' and numbered '64'. Dol.

Edinb[urgh] 8th Jan[uar]y 1779

My dear Watt

Your letter of the 12th Dec[embe]r gave us indeed very great and compleat Satisfaction—The performance of your Engine at Chace water is a wonderfull story and as you will immediatly begin to receive benefit from it and that it will facilitate and forward your Transactions with other People I am very hopefull it will have a good effect upon your health as there is certainly no greater cordial or promoter of health than Prosperity and Affluence when they happen to those who can enjoy them with temperance—I lately began to have some feeling of this, in consequence of my haveing got a nearer prospect than I ever had before of being able to live at my ease and independent of this rascally world which has cost me more vexation and anxiety than you will easily imagine—but by the last post I received News that have again sunk my Spirits not a little and made me pass a very Uneasy night—Two of my Brothers who have been a long time in Business in the mercantile way the one in France and the other in Spain first of all, went into Partnership at London about 16. Years agoe   after carrying on Business a while there, one of them took a farm near London for the sake of his young Children and soon after they both became so fond of Farming and so confident of success in that way that they very soon employed the whole of their Stock which was a very moderate one in this way   the Consequence has been what their Freinds dreaded—their Stock has been gradually diminishing untill it is totally gone and one of them has a Wife and a numerous Family—but I ask your Pardon for troubling you with this disagreable Story which you certainly have no connection with—I confess I was induced to mention it to you by a perhaps foolish Idea which took possession of my head last night during the agitation of my mind—It occurred to me that you might possibly find it convenient to employ the one or the other of them in some of your transactions abroad—What made me think of this was that they have both a mechanical genius and can draw very well—James (who is the married one) thought he would improve the art of Husbandry greatly by his improvements of the Plow and other farming machines— he published some time agoe a little treatise on this and other such subjects with the title of Observations on the Tillage of the Earth— which however is very ill written—But tho neither of them are quali- fyed to write a Book they are both of them perfectly honest and trusty —they have ingenuity and capacity for understanding machines—they have experience in business and they know the manners and language of the two Countrys where they were first settled—But I again ask your Pardon for using this freedom with you   you have no doubt taken your measures already and far be it from me to wish that you should put your self to any inconvenience upon my account—It however gives some releif to my mind that I have mentioned this to you while I am consulting with the rest of my Brothers what we shall do with them—With respect to the Ores & Minerals of Cornwall of which you propose that I should give you a list—I am too little acquainted with them and I beg you would give yourself very little

trouble about them except to send me some good peices of the Tin
Stuff and perhaps some also of the best and richest coloured Copper Ore

I am My Dear Sir

Yours affect[ionate]ly

Joseph Black

My best Complim[en]ts to
Mrs. Watt—

Letter 38

WATT TO BLACK

Cover addressed: 'Doctor Joseph Black/proffessor of Chemistry/
in the University of/Edinburgh/via Ferrybridge', endorsed in
Black's hand, 'Mr. Watt 13 January 1779', and numbered '58',
Dol.

Birmingham Jan[uar]y 13th
1779

Dear Doctor

Yours of the 8th came this day to hand   I had intended at any rate to
have sent you a few lines but am sorry for the cause which has accelerated that intention—I most sincerely wish that it was in my power to
have provided for for [*sic*] either or both of your Brothers according
to their deserts and my obligations to you; but that I cannot do—our
Business in france is only in its infancy yett—That is we have obtained
an arret of the king and Council for an exclusive privilege but that
cannot have the force of a patent untill we have erected an Engine and
after trial made thereof it has been reported by certain Commissarys
appointed by the *arret* that our engine is superior to the Common one
which we hope will easily be proved—We have agreed with a
M[on]s[ieu]r Jary[1] that the trial engine shall be {made} erected at a colliery he has near Nantes in Britany—And M[on]s[ieu]r Jary who is a
very ingenious man possest of the necessary \previous/ knowledge has
undertaken the care of the erection himself all to the finishing which
will require the attendance of some person practically acquainted with
the putting our Engines together, Untill this matter is finished our
property in the invention in that kingdom is dubious what may
happen in future we cannot determine but at present it would be
wrong in us to establish any agent in France—The only place which is

45

\now/ {at present} in our disposal which seems to be suited to the present State of your Brothers knowledge in Engine matters is that of Chief Clerk to our Engine Business here a person for which office is now wanted but the small matter we can afford to give would not be worthy his acceptance without it were considered as an interim occupation or a means of shewing his ability for better or more lucrative employment.

Mr. Boultons Book keeper at Soho seems to be inclined to leave him if that should happen and your Brother should be willing to take upon him the drudgery and Cons[tan]t attention such an Office requires for the money which is given to the present Clerk which is only (£80—) per year without any other perquisites—I think myself sure that Mr. Boulton will preferr your reccomendation and your Brother to any other person.† Mr. B. is lately gone to london and I have communicated to him the contents of your letter that he may see and converse with your Brothers and know in what line we can serve them and I hope some opportunity may present itself to him of reccommending them to some person who has some more beneficial office to bestow than we now have and on my part I shall inform you of any thing which appears likely—

The anxiety which I have suffered since I began this Business has been exceeding great as the difficulties have also been—It now begins to assume a more pleasing appearance but as it has unavoidably incurred a very Considerable debt we cannot with propriety call the profitts our own untill that debt be discharged which I hope will soon be the case, another Campaign in Cornwall will I expect do very great things—But to my sorrow I find that as Business encreases my Cares encrease in the same ratio which in a very considerable degree prevents the enjoyment of life—But lett us wave these cares for a moment— I sent you from Cornwall on the 29th of Dec[embe]r by the exeter waggon a small box directed to you to care of Mr. R[ichar]d Sinclairs at the Glasgow Wharf London containing such tin and copper ores as I could then obtain The tin stuff is as good as [I] have seen and pickit out of many tons and I believe you have there almost all the kinds commonly found excepting stream tin which I could not gett—The Copper ores are not so well sorted but are such as are commonly got and some of the richest grey kind with some poor yellow with the adhering matter of the lode which is called Caple I have sent also

† [in margin] excuse my mentioning such very poor offices, they are the best I can now offer and preferable to dependance

some few other stones such as I thought different from the stones of Scotland, but the varietys in Cornwall are not many the great excellency of the Country seems to be the quantities—what I have sent is not a curious collection but it is such as I could procure and will serve to shew the common and usefull produce of the mines This year I may possibly pick up some things which are rare or beautiful as my aquaintance and also interest with the Mine Captains will probably encrease—

It gives me real pain that you should think that I would {take}\make/ a trouble of the serving you or any person so closly connected with you as your Bro[the]rs I beg you will rest satisfied that nothing but the want of ability {would}\will/ hinder me from promoting their interest or that of any other person you interest yourself in. I can say no more about our employing them untill I have seen Mr. Boulton; but I shall be glad to hear from you in answer what is proposed for them—with Compliments to our friends I remain most sincerely your's—James Watt

Mr. Boulton at Mr. Will[ia]m Mathews[2] green Lettice Lane Cannon Street London will be there about a week

[1] He was 'Concessionaire des Mines du Nord en Bretagne'. His mines were coal-mines near Nantes, Loire Inférieure. He procured for Boulton and Watt a decree granting permission for a requisite trial to be made on his engine. He was furnished with drawings and instructions for the erection of an engine which was the first Watt engine on the Continent —1779.
[2] William Matthews [d. 1792] was Boulton's banker and agent in London.

Letter 39
WATT TO BLACK

Draft. Dol.

James Watt (Birmingham) to Dr Black. Jan[uar]y 13th 1779

Dear Doctor,

Yours of the 8th came this day to hand   I had intended at any rate to have sent you a few lines and am sorry for the cause which has accelerated that intention—I sincerely wish that it was in my power to have provided for either or both of your Brothers according to their deserts and my obligations to you but that I cannot do—our Business in france is only in its infancy yett—That is we have obtained an arret of the king and Council for an exclusive privilege but that cannot have

47

the force of a patent untill we have erected an Engine and after trial made thereof it has been reported by certain Commissarys appointed by the *arret* that our engine is superior to the Common one which we hope will easily be proved—We have agreed with a Mr. Jary that the trial engine shall be erected at a colliery he has near Nantes in Britany—And Mr. Jary who is a very ingenious man possest of the necessary knowledge has undertaken the care of the erection himself and all the finishing which will require the attendance of some person practically aquainted with the putting our Engines together. Untill this matter is finished our property in the invention in that kingdom is dubious What may happen in future we cannot determine but at present it would be wrong in us to establish an agent in France—The only place which is now in our disposal here is that of Chief Clerk to our engine business for which a person is wanted but the small matter we can aford to give would not be worthy his acceptance without it were considered as an interim occupation or a means of shewing his merit of a more lucrative employment—Mr. B's Bookeeper [*sic*] at Soho seems inclined to leave him if that should happen and your Brother should be willing to take upon him the drudgery and constant attention of such an Office for the money which is given to the present Clerk (£80 p[e]r ann[u]m) without any other perquisite I think myself sure Mr B. will preferr your reccomendation and your Brother to any other person   Mr. B is gone to London but I have communicated to him the Content of your letter that he may see and converse with your Brothers and know in what line we can serve them and I hope some opportunity may present itself to him of reccommending them to some more beneficial office that we now have to bestow and on my part I shall inform you of any thing which appears likely†

The Anxiety which I have suffered since I began this Business has been very great, as the difficulties have been   it now begins to assume a more pleasing appearance but as it has unavoidably incurred a very considerable debt we cannot with propriety call the profits our own untill that be discharged which I hope will be soon   another Campaign in Cornwall will I hope do great things

I sent you from Cornwall on the 29th of Dec[embe]r p[e]r exeter waggon to care of R[ichar]d Sinclair Glasgow Wharf London a small box containing some specimens of tin Stuffs and Copper ores—not the most curious but the most usefull products of the mines—I[t] gives me

---

†At the side of this paragraph, Watt has written 'excuse my mentioning such very poor offices   they are the best I can offer and preferable to dependance ——'

real pain that you should think I would construe into trouble the serving you or any person so closely connected with you as your Brothers; I beg you will rest satisfied that nothing but the want of abilitie will prevent my promoting their interest—I can say no more about employing them untill I have seen Mr. Boulton but shall be glad to hear from you in answer what is proposed for them

[Not signed]

Letter 40

WATT TO BLACK

Cover addressed: 'Doctor Black/Physician/Edinburgh/via Ferrybridge', endorsed in Black's hand, 'Mr. Watt 13 January 1779' and numbered '57'. Dol. The cover carries also the following:

'212
32
———
180
180°: 10: 40 Inches
10
————————
180)400(2¼
360
———   70
40   32
                       ——
                       38   ,

Birmingham Jan[uar]y 13th
1779

Dear Doctor

Yours of the 8th instant I received to day, and have also received a letter from your Brother some days ago—Mr. Boulton returned from London as proposed, staid 3 or 4 days here and returned thither on tuesday last, he brought with him a Mr. Perrier[1] \engineer/ from Paris who has bargained with us for engines to raise water to that City which we have found ourselves obliged to grant him on very moderate terms because our Arret not having yet the force of a patent we durst not risk any opposition—Mr. Perrier stuck so close to me to gett his

49

3—PIS * *

plans concerted that I had not an hours free conversation with Mr. B. during his stay, but took that opportunity to beg his exertions in your brothers behalf with which I doubt not he will comply—In relation to what I mentioned to you in my last—The Bookeeper at Soho does not leave his place as I then thought he might, he wanted an increase of Wages and was troublesome on that account but has chosen to remain at his former wages—Mr. Boulton thought from the short conversation he had with your brother that the plan I mentioned of Clerk to Engine business would not suit him and that it would rather have been an insult to offer it as we cannot offord more than £50 p[e]r annum in that place and, that circumstances otherwise might render it disagreable to him however much we might be disposed to treat him as our equal, and on these considerations did not offer it—The other place might have been more eligible as well as more profitable But the prospect of that is cut off, as mentioned, by the mans continuing who is acquainted with the business—when Mr. B. was last in London he heard a surmise that the Clerk at Shad[we]ll Waterworks² was likely to be displaced— I have begged him to enquire after that, (we have some interest there) and if any likely hood of that events having place to lett your B[rothe]r know, but not otherwise, as it would be wrong to give him false hopes —It is possible he might make interest to gett in there, and I have heard it is better than £100 p[e]r ann[u]m but he must submit to be domineered over by ignorant Londoners, the most unfeeling of all beings, I mean in what regards delicacy of sentiment—I have sent your letter and your Brothers to him by this nights diligence, with a renewal of sollicitations, to serve him in every way he can which I am sure he will do, being a man of a friendly disposition with a feeling heart— Some time ago it would have been easy to have provided your Brother with a place in this town but trade is now most exceedingly dull and many people turned out of Bread³   Mr. B has reduced his people at Soho from 600 or 700 to 150—however we shall try what can be done

When in Cornwall I had an Opportunity of seeing with mine own eyes Cast Iron which was grown soft by the vitriolic water in the mines, so soft that I cut it with my knife as easy as cheese—It retained its metallic colour and appearance—not unlike Black lead very soft and unctuous to the touch and full of very bright white \metalic/ particles —on drying it is said to become so hot as to burn paper but that I did not see and then becomes something harder than Chalk but friable—In the hurry of coming away I neglected to bring a specimen of it but shall next time I go It is only the inside of the pumps that become so the outside is rusty it happens in about 2 years time to half an inch deep into the mettal—The water seems to have a solution of grccn and bluc vitriol with much disengaged acid—

I have had a great deal to do lately, much vexation, many headaches from one of which I am just now recovered and feel myself not in a letter writing stile, otherwise should endeavour to render myself more amusing as I doubt not you have occasion for a cordial of that kind at present; but I can present you with nothing but my best wishes for happiness and prosperity—Make my best respests [to] Dr. Hutton Mr. Clerk and other friends and believe

ever most sincerely
Yours James Watt

[1] Jacques Constantin Perier (1742–1818), mechanical engineer, founded with his brother, Auguste Charles, a great manufactory at Chaillot. Interested in the application of steam-engines to coal-mines, water-works, etc.

[2] Between August 1778 and May 1779 three pumping-engines were set up for water-works in the London district at Richmond, Shadwell and Chelsea.

[3] This was a year of bad trade. T. S. Ashton in his *Economic Fluctuations in England, 1700–1800* (Oxford, 1959) reports that there were riots in Nottingham and Lancashire, including the burning of Arkwright's factory at Birkacre in October. There were also troubles in Staffordshire near Etruria.

Letter 41

BLACK TO WATT

Cover addressed: 'Mr. James Watt Engineer/at Soho/Birming-ham/by Ferrybridge' and numbered '63'. Dol.

Edinb[urgh] 20th Jan[ua]ry 1779

My dear Freind

I received your most kind letter of the 13th and am much obliged to you by the Concern you shew for my Brothers and your desire to assist them and if you have occasion soon to employ a Clerk for the Engine Business I for my part will certainly advise the Eldest Brother of the two who is not married to accept of the office whatever be the Salary which I by no means wish you to make a single penny more upon his account than what you would give to another—my reason is

51

that in the first place this would be doing something for himself whereas at present he is perfectly idle—and besides you and Mr. Boulton would have an opportunity of becomeing acquainted with his abilities and if you liked him might either give him the Clerkship of Soho in case of a Vacancy or some other such office—To tell you the Truth some such employment as these is the best suited to his present Circumstances for there are none of our Family opulent and we cannot furnish a Capital for him to begin Business again without distressing ourselves —which would be very imprudent on account of the uncertain Success of any Business in which he could at present engage himself as a Principal—I therefore write to him by this post to give him my opinion and advice with regard to this matter and shall desire him to call for Mr. Bolton if still in London but I cannot tell {what} how he will relish the proposal at first, it is not unlikely that it may cost him a few days to reconcile himself to it, he has been accustomed now for some time to a Country life and has expressed to me in former letters a strong partiality for it but I know that he wishes much to do for himself {and that his des} in some such way as the above and that his desires in point of emolument are extreamly moderate—

I am also much obliged to you for your attention with respect to the Ores and am my Dear Watt

Yours affect[ionate]ly
Joseph Black

Letter 42

BLACK TO WATT

Cover addressed: 'Mr. James Watt Engineer/at Soho/Birmingham/by Ferrybridge' and numbered '62'. Dol.

Edinb[urgh] 8th Feb[rua]ry 1779

My Dear Watt

I have a letter from my Brother Alexander who at my desire called upon Mr. Bolton at London, and upon the supposition that you may have an opportunity of deliberating whether you will employ him or not I send the letter inclosed as one means of knowing more about him than you can know at present—when you have read it and shewn it to Mr.

Bolton (if you think proper) send it back to me—It contains some strokes of his Character particularly in his answer to Mr. Bolton "that an honourable employment was more what he wished for at present than a lucrative one["] his only meaning in this was that he would rather have an employment in which he should be considered and treated as a Gentleman tho attended with small emoluments than one in which he should be treated as a Servant tho much more profitable—This is indeed a point upon which Alec is exceedingly Tender, he cannot bear to be roughly handled, he has that degree of pride or rather respect for his own person naturally—and it has not been diminished by his residence in Spain—but it is only such a degree of it as is a Subject of pleasantry among his freinds.   it is not in the least attended with selfishness or morosity—What he said of his Knowledge of Mechanics is so far true that he never studyed the {Subject} \Science/ in any regular manner and has not I beleive much knowledge of any of the general Principles—but I am sure that he has a natural genius for it and that he can draw with amasing accuracy and patience but in this work I beleive he is but slow—There is no doubt that the business he is the best qualifyed for at present is the keeping of accounts in which I sincerely beleive he would be extreamly exact and regular and this with a degree of honesty that is perfectly incapable of the smallest taint is not every where to be met with in this wicked World—But if you do not find it convenient or desireable to employ him tell me so frankly and without the smallest reserve—far be it from me to desire that you or Mr. Bolton should put yourselves to the smallest inconvenience upon his account or mine—I should reckon it unkind and unfreindly of you to treat me with any reserve or to put any constraint upon your self in this matter—It is certainly the Duty of his own Freinds to find a Provision for him and I only recommend him to you in Case you should find it your Interest to employ him—his Brother has been persuaded to give up all to his Creditors and become bankrupt that he may begin the World again in London as an Insurance Broker etc.—in which I hope he will succeed very well as he is chearfull and agreable and has many Freinds—I beg you will assure Mr. Bolton of my Gratitude for his kind and polite attention to Alec and beleive me ever

most affectionately
Yours
Joseph Black

ALEXANDER BLACK TO BLACK

Cover addressed: 'Doctor Joseph Black/In/Edenburgh'. Dol.

Morden 25 February 1779

My Dear Brother

I flattered my self from the interview I had with Mr. Bolton, that your freind Mr. Watt and him would have made me some proposal for an employment, particularly as I had hinted to them that a large salary was not what I was in search after—so much, as an honorable employment, with men of merit and character, with whom a rational man, may find comforts, far superior to those, an easy income may procure him, when depending on men of narrow minds and little education—but it seems that the only post they had to offer me was one, which is at present filled up, by a Scotch Gent[lema]n who had given them to understand that he would not not[*sic*] stay any longer with them, and I find that on Mr. Bolton['s] return to Birmingham he altered his mind and resolved to continue in their service during the time of his agreement—

Mr. Bolton made me many kind professions of the interest and pleasure he would take to serve me in all favourable occasions, and desired I should correspond with them when I thought their influence and recommendation might oblige me by obtaining any place I was in pursuit of—I had taken a resolution these two years past to get into some way of earning my livelyhood, as I saw no prospect of Jemmy's affairs and mine linked with his, terminating in any more favourable manner than what they have done—I therefore made many applications in different ways either to get into the line of Country occupation or that of merchandizeing but I cannot say I ever had any offer made me—I will continue my endeavours for I wish Jemmy and his dear family to reap entire every advantage that can accrew to them in a new settlement, from the kind protection and Influence of our family and freinds—the latter concerned with him in London have behaved with a generousity of which there are few examples, they loose every thing, and yet are indefatigable to extricate him from falling into the claws of some avaricious mean spirited individual   I imagine he will write to you in a few days to inform you what has been done—The family are in good health and salute you in the kindest manner   I remain ever

My Dear Brother

Yours most affect[ionate]ly

Alex[ande]r Black

Letter 44

WATT TO BLACK

Cover addressed: 'Doctor Joseph Black/Edinburgh/via Ferrybridge', and endorsed in Black's hand, 'Mr. Watt 3d March 1779' and numbered '56'.

Birmingham Mar[ch] 3d 1779

Dear Doctor

Since Mr. Boulton's return home about a week ago I have talked with him about your Brother who he has seen lately; he is of opinion that the most eligible place for your Brother would be in one of the public offices—Mr. Boulton has promised to use his interest with the people in power so soon as a place can be pointed out—His interest is considerable and would be much aided by the suppliants being *your* brother for {many} several of the people in power are amateurs of Science and pay you due respect as a philosopher—It remains with Mr. Black to lett us know of any vacancy that he thinks he may aspire to

The place I mentioned at Shadwell is not yett vacant though it is probable it soon may unless the person in office there can clear himself of a suspicion that he has taken bribes or at least suffered his masters to be cheated—

I return you his letter the sentiments of which do him honour and encrease the vexation I feel at not being able at present to serve him more effectualy

I am also sorry I should have misled you about our Clerkship I wrote from my feelings and did not consider every Circumstance which might thwart it

When I wrote you last I was in very poor health I am now a little better but crushed with Business which nobody can do for me and I cannot do half so much of as I ought

There is now in london a German who has made a self moving wheel which is said not to be actuated by fire, water nor air or any other known power It is said to be 12 feet dia[mete]r and raises a weight of 100 pounds 60 feet high in one minute

I do not put great faith in it and would be sorry it were true as it would demolish our Scheme He has sold the invention to some Gentlemen in London for £20.000—to be paid so soon as he proves the fact—

I ever remain
Most sincerely
Yours
James Watt

55

WATT TO BLACK

* Dol.

James Watt (B[irming]ham) to Dr Black   *Mar[ch] 3d 1779*

Dear Doctor

Since Mr. Boultons return home about a week ago I have had some discourse with him about your Brother—He has had another conversation with him from which he is of opinion that his most eligible line is a place in some of the public offices to obtain which Mr. B. has promised his interest which is considerable particularly when backt with your own and aided with the circumstances of the suppliant's being your Brother. It remains with your Brother to find out a vacancy and to advise us of it—†

Charles Greville[1] as I suppose you know is a man in power and an amateur of science and a letter from you to him might be of use provided any vacancy should occur within the limits of his jurisdiction   he is an acquaintance also of mine and my sollicitations shall not be wanting L[or]d Dartmouth[2] is also intimate with Mr. Boulton and has several times conferred small offices by his recommendation   There are also several others to whom we could apply if the place desired were a place of actual business and the salary not very high

The place I mentioned at Shadwell is not yet vacant but I think it probable it may soon be as the person in Office there has either been guilty of peculation or of gross neglect of duty which we shall be obliged by our own interest to expose so soon as we can produce sufficient evidence—we shall advise your brother to apply whenever we know of a vacancy there or in any other place which we think would suit him

I return you his letter   the sentiments contained in it do him great honour and add to the vexation I feel at not being able at present to do any thing for him

I am sorry I fed you with hopes about the place of our Clerkship   I was led by my feelings and did not immediately see the circumstances that might render it disagreable to him some of which were suggested by Mr Boulton and are unanswerable—When I wrote you last I was in very poor health   I am now a little better but crushed with Care and with business which nobody else can do for me and I cannot do the half of what I should do

† Then follow 9½ lines which have been crossed out by Watt.

There is now at london a German who has made a self moving wheel which is said not to be actuated by Fire water nor air or any other known power   it is said to be 12 feet diameter and raises a weight of 100 lbs 60 feet high in a minute   I do not put great faith in it and should be sorry it were true as it would demolish our scheme He has sold the invention to some Gentlemen in London for £20,000 to be paid when he proves the fact

[Then crossed out] [Our engine at Shadwell I have not seen but it is said to raise 600.000 Cubic feet of water one foot high with a bushel of Coals i.e. it raises 75,000 Cubic feet 80 feet high with that quantity—I scarcely believe this more than the other but I have better evidence as Mr Boulton says he saw it]

I ever remain
Most sincerely yours
James Watt

[1] The Hon. Charles Francis Greville (1749–1809), F.R.S.
[2] George Legge (1755–1810), third Earl of Dartmouth.

Letter 46

BLACK TO WATT

Cover addressed: 'Mr. James Watt Engineer/at Soho/Birmingham/by Ferrybridge' and numbered '61'. Dol.

Edinb[urgh] 6th March 1779

My Dear Watt
    I grudge the time I cost you and which you can very ill spare to read and answer my long letters, but it is long since I have given you any trouble before the present occasion of our correspondence and you must forgive me
    I rec[eive]d yours of the 13th Feb[rua]ry—in which you say Mr Bolton thought from the conversation he had with my Brother that the Clerkship of the Engine Business would not suit him partly on account of the small salary of £50 which you think is too small to be offered to him partly on that of other circumstances which \might/ render it otherwise disagreable to him
    With respect to the Salary I am sensible that it would be folly in you to give more than £50, as you can get a very good Clerk to answer your

purpose for that sum, but I could remove the difficulty upon that point by giving him a little addition to it while he should be in your Service

The other disagreable circumstances I am ignorant of but guess they might be little disputes with the men about their time of work and idleness in which they might sometimes behave in a bruteish and provokeing manner—What effect this might have I cannot tell but you will see from the enclosed which I take the liberty to send you that He has a strong desire to be connected with you Partly I must own on account of the difficulty he has hitherto found in endeavouring to get an employment to his mind—One Solid objection to your takeing him is that his Freinds will certainly endeavour to find a more profitable office for him and if they succeed you will be put to the inconvenience of changeing your Clerk and if this would in reality be very inconvenient to you I shall give you no further trouble but if you do not think this inconvenience of so much weight I wish you would still remain undecided untill I hear once more from you and from him, for I have wrote to sound him both with respect to the salary and to those disagreable circumstances above mentioned which occurred to my imagination—

The softened Iron which you describe put me in mind of a preparation of Iron similar in appearance (possibly the very same) which Dr. Knight was possessed of and which he valued on account of the fixed or permanent nature of its Magnetism—when once rendered magnetic he found it impossible to deprive it of that power or to change its poles   vide a Paper by Dr. Fothergill in Phil. Trans. Vol 66th—I hear that John Laurie[1] formerly employed as surveyor on the Canal—now a Landwaiter at Leith—has contrived a very ingenious machine for impelling air into Blast-Furnaces   it works by the pressure of water in Cylinders so that all Friction is avoided but this I only mention *entre nous* and wish you not to speak of it as I do not know what use he intends to make of it—My Compliments to Mrs. Watt and beleive me ever

Yours most affect[ionate]ly
Joseph Black

I attempted to pay the
postage here but they would
not receive it on account of
its going a cross road

---

[1] John Laurie, Landwaiter, appears in Edinburgh Directories from 1780 to 1794, until 1790 under 'Leith' and then in 1794 under 'Musselburgh'. He undertook work for the Edinburgh Council in 1765, 1769, 1783 and 1784. Laurie was a Mason. He described himself sometimes as 'Geographer'. No record seems to have survived of his blowing-engine.

WATT TO BLACK

Cover addressed: 'Doctor Joseph Black/Edinburgh/via Ferry-bridge', endorsed in Black's hand, 'Mr. Watt March 11th 1779' and numbered '55'. Dol. Also various calculations in crayon in Black's hand as follows:

No. 3   100 Tons   27   No. 1   100 Tons   19
                   95   95
                   ——   ——
                   135   95
                   243   171
                   ————   ————
                   2565   1805
        £25..12.. 2   £18.. 0.. 2
           3   3
        ——————————   ——————————
        22..12.. 2   15.. 0.. 2

                            No. 4   100 Tons   19½
                                              95
                                              ——
Also, in ink, '100 .. 20'   95
                                             171
                                              47
                                             ————
                                             1852
                            £18..10
                               3   deducted
                            ————————
                            15..10

                            No. 2   100 Tons   20½
                                              95
                                             ————
                                             147
                                             180
                                             ————
                                             1947
                            £16 per Ton.

On another part of cover (or fold of letter, in Black's hand: 'Mr. Berry Robert Ferguson Esq./Austin-Friars/London'. This is written in crayon.

Birm[ingha]m Mar[ch] 11th 1779

Dear Doctor
    I should be very ungratefull If I either grudged my labour or money

laid out in your service, therefore I beg no farther on that head—Mr Boulton is about 20 miles off settling the trial between a common engine and one we erected long ago which we have never been able to bring to a conclusion—He will be at home next week when we shall consider your last letter and advise, meanwhile thought it proper to lett you know the cause you could not have a speedy answer—

I invented a machine many years ago for blowing by the Compressing power of water without a water wheel which Model I gave to Mr John Anderson[1] for his Class but none of these water Machines answer well The air becomes damp and does not answer its end   its solvent power of water is encreased with its density   John Wilkinson[2] our founder has tryed many ways of using it but has given it up altogether in some engines he has lately erected—I say this that poor John may not put himself to any expence for unless he can get something from the Carron comp[an]y or others who are in infancy None of the old Standers will be drove out of the least Iota of their pres[en]t practice though an apostle came to teach them—I have been one of these foolish people who have undertaken to teach people how to do better and have found it a most difficult enterprize and have therefore given it up unless my interest be very much Concerned and even then the avarice the prejudices and the villany of mankind leave no stone unturned to cut of the profit and so, very often one finds it has not been ones interest

Lastly almost all the furnaces here are{ driven } \Blown/ by fire engines either mediately by water or immediately by an air Cylinder the friction of which is trifling and though this last way saves half the power very few practice it—I shall so soon as have opportunity try the magnetism of the soft Iron

I ever remain
Dear Doctor
Most sincerely yours
James Watt

remember me to all friends

[1] John Anderson (1726–96), Professor of Natural Philosophy of Glasgow, 1757–96, was interested in the improvement of scientific instruments. Under his care were the astronomical instruments bequeathed to the College in 1756 by Alexander MacFarlane. Watt was responsible for putting these instruments in order.

[2] John Wilkinson (1728–1808), the great ironmaster of Broseley.

BLACK TO WATT

Cover addressed: 'Mr. James Watt Engineer/at Soho/Birming-ham/by Ferry-Bridge'. Dol. Also Draft. Dol.

Edinb[urgh] 11th March 1779

My Dear Watt

I rec[eive]d yours of the 3d Inst[an]t yesterday but it unfortunately came too late to save you the trouble of receiveing another letter from me which I wrote a few days before. I am now perfectly satisfyed that the Clerkship to your Business would not suit my Brother. But you and Mr. Bolton have my most sincere and warmest gratitude for the Sympathy you have shewn for me on this occasion and I must beg you will return him my thanks in particular for his kindness and attention to him. I shall not fail to take the hint he has given and put both my Brother and other Freinds upon the look out and if any place can be found in the obtaining of which Mr. Bolton can assist us I shall not scruple to add the trouble we have given him already by begging the assistance which he has been so good as to offer—The last part of your letter relateing to the invention of a new moveing power made me uneasy on your account for a moment but I am persuaded it is some deception or mistake—Perhaps a heavy mass which bcing gradually brought into motion by a weak power may spend its accumulated force in lifting the weight—I can imagine something like this to be performed by Franklins Electrical Jack[1] —Is it possible to apply magnetism to such a purpose—had we a matter that could intercept the magnetic effluvia without being acted upon by them something might be done—did you ever try regulus of antimony It is said that this metal when mixed with Iron prevents the Iron from being attracted and if this be true in what manner can it act on this occasion but by intercepting the magnetic effluvia—for Iron is attracted tho mixed with all other metals—

Farewell and beleive me ever
Yours affect[ionate]ly
Joseph Black

[1] A device inventcd by Benjamin Franklin for turning a fowl for roasting.

Letter 49

BLACK TO WATT

Draft. Addressed: 'Mr. James Watt Engineer/at Soho/Birming-
ham/by Ferry-Bridge'. Dol. Unsigned and corrections in-
corporated in the other (signed) version.

Edinb[urgh] 11th March 1779

My Dear Watt

I received yours of the 3d Inst[an]t yesterday which unfortunately came
too late to save you the trouble of receiving another letter from me which
I wrote a few days before—I am now perfectly satisfyed that the Clerkship to your Business would not suit my Brother but you and Mr.
Bolton have my most sincere and warmest gratitude for the Sympathy
you have shewn for me on this occasion and I must beg you will return
him my thanks in particular for the kindness and attention he has shewn
him—I shall not fail to take the hint he has given and put Both my
Brother and other Freinds upon the Look out and if any place can be
{thought} found out in the obtaining of which Mr. Bolton can assist us I
shall not scruple to add to the trouble we have given him already by
begging the assistance which he has been so good as to offer

The last part of your letter relating to the new invention of a moveing
Power made me uneasy on your account for a moment but I am persuaded it is some deception or mistake—It may be a very heavy mass
which being gradually brought into motion by a weak power may
spend its accumulated force in lifting the weight—I can imagine something like this performed by Franklins Elec[trica]l Jack—but I cannot
imagine that it can lift the weight as high every minute. Is it possible to
apply magnetism to such a purpose—If we had a matter that could intercept the magnetic effluvia without being acted upon by them, I think it
would not be difficult to do great things—did you every [*sic*] try regulus
of antimony   it is said that this metal when mixed with Iron prevents
the Iron from being attracted by the Magnet and if this be true in what
manner can it act on this occasion but by intercepting the effluvia for Iron
is attracted tho mixed with all other metals

BLACK TO WATT

Further draft. Dol.

Edinb[urgh] 11th March 1779

My Dear Watt

I received Yours of the 3d Inst[an]t yesterday which unfortunately came too late to save you the trouble of receiving another letter from me which I wrote a few days before—I am now perfectly satisfyed that the Clerkship to your Business would not suit my Brother but you \and Mr. Bolton/ have my most sincere and warmest gratitude for the Sympathy you have shewn for me on this occasion and I{ also }\must/ beg you will return him my thanks in particular for the kindness and attention he has shewn him—I shall not fail to take the hint he has given and put Both my Brother and other Freinds upon the Lookout and if any { thing } place can be { thought } found out in the obtaining of which Mr. Bolton can assist us I shall not scruple to add to the trouble we have given him already by begging the assistance which he has been so good as to offer

The last part of your letter relating to the new invention of a moveing Power made me uneasy on your account for a moment but I am persuaded it is some deception or mistake—It may be a very heavy mass which being gradually brought into motion by a weak power may spend its accumulated force in lifting the weight—\I can imagine something like this to be performed by Franklins Elect[rical] Jack/ but I cannot imagine that it can lift that Weight as high every minute—Is it possible to apply magnetism to such a purpose—If we had a matter that could intercept the magnetic effluvia without being acted upon by them, I think it would not be difficult to do great things—did you every [*sic*] try regulus of antimony   it is said that this metal when mixed with Iron prevents the Iron from being attracted by the Magnet and if this be true in what manner can it act on this{ way }\occasion/ but by intercepting the effluvia for Iron is attracted tho mixed with all other metals

Letter 51

BLACK TO WATT

Cover addressed: 'Mr. James Watt Engineer/Birmingham'. Dol.

Edinburgh 5th July 1779

Dear Watt

I take the opportunity of one of our new Graduates Doctor Johnstone[1] who is going home your way to enquire after your health and
how matters go on with you, and he tells me besides that he beleives
his Father intends that he should settle in Birmingham some time hence—
He is a Very good and pleasant tempered lad and has exceeding good
Parts—I received the Ores from Cornwall and am greatly obliged to
you but hope that when you return to that Country you will continue
to pick up any remarkable good things for me when they come in your
Way—I must also beg some more of the Fluor, it is much more strongly
phosphorescent than the Derbyshire fluor and besides I want some of it
to make experiments upon the Acid—I met lately with a small specimen of Copper Ore said to come from Cornwall which I never saw
before and should be glad to have a larger Specimen of it or several
peices—At the first slight view it appears like a very rich grey Ore
mixed with some green or verdigrise Ore running thro it in small veins
and spots—but being examined more closely with a glass, the apparently grey parts are found to be not grey but of a deep transparent red
colour and give a \dirty/ red powder when bruised to dust—it is also
exceedingly rich and the little bit which I have contains some specks of
metallised copper—I know there is an artificial Substance made from
Copper which has a deep red Colour like Cinnabar in the lump but
I am perfectly sure that the above mentioned is an Ore and not
artificial   by the by however, if you know how the artificial red
matter is made I beg you will inform me—I have been told that it is
Copper mixed with Litharge and somewhat else—It appears to be
formed in some Process for separating ☽ or ☉ from the copper—
Mr. Meason shewed \us/ some time ago an article which was published in the Newcastle newspaper by Smeaton containing a Comparison of his Engine with yours in which he endeavoured to shew that his
engine is upon the whole equally advantageous to the proprietors of
Coal mines and insinuates that it will be more easily kept in order—
Supposing his reasoning to be perfectly just and fair which it has the

appearance of being, it is plainly however but an envious and malicious stroke at your Profits—as by diminishing these a little you turn the balance against him without dispute—

Pray what is become of the Foreigners Project for a perpetuum mobile—Hutton is well and greets you—My best Compliments to Mrs. Watt and beleive me ever

Dear Watt
Yours affectionately
Joseph Black

Do not write to me
untill you have leisure

<hr>

[1] Dr Edward Johnstone (1757–1851), a pupil of Joseph Black and friend of Erasmus Darwin, was physician to the Birmingham General Hospital.

Letter 52

WATT TO BLACK

Cover addressed: 'Doctor Joseph Black/Edinburgh/via Ferry-bridge', endorsed in Black's hand, '*Meditationes Physico Chemicae de origine Mundi*' and numbered '13'. Dol. Also ✶ omitting final paragraph. Dol.

Birmingham July 24th 1778
[*recte 1779*]

Dear Doctor

I received your letter of the 5th Curr[en]t by Dr. Johnson the other day—I was sorry that I could not send you some things more worthy of acceptance from Cornwall but imagined that their being the common workable ores would not render them the less acceptable—I woud have sent more of the fluor but did not conceive it to be worth sending And should not have sent it at all if I had not known it to be more luminous than any other I had seen—I have some notion that Calcarious earth is not its basis from the circumstance of there not being neither Calcarious earth nor gypsum in any part of Cornwall within 20 or 30 miles of the mines The Fluor is found both in the schistus and granite mines. I have seen the red Copper ore you mention but could not procure a specimen of it being scarce—The artificial substance you mention I have never seen unless you mean the rich red Copper slags

65

formed in seperating Copper from Litharge, which often occurrs in assaying, and resembles sealing wax—Mr. S[meaton]s publication[1] soon received a very able answer from a friend at newcastle and would have received a complete one if we had not judged it prudent to interpose; but all our endeavours could not prevent Mr. S: from a rejoinder to which we shall neither make nor authorize any printed answer— I detest paper war and S: has given us sufficient praises, let him keep the modest honour he aspires to of being the second best—between you and I we have it in our power to give a very sufficient and effectual answer to any of his publications but why should we labour to depreciate others when we have more work than we can properly do—All the publications in number 4. are to be seen in the newcastle Journals— I have not heard yet the event of the *perpetuum mobile*—It was to be tryed last week

I have little news in your way, I see you have great praises bestowed on your theory of fixt air by Maxquer[2] in the last edition of {your} his dictionary and am much pleased to observe that foreigners in general are disposed to award you the palm of priority of Invention which Priestly[3] has so invidiously huddled over—I have just rec[eive]d a new theory of the earth by Wallerius on Chymical principles in which {in} \after/ doing justice to your claim as inventor he attacks the facts themselves; but as he seems equally wrong in other Chymical matters. I conclude the old man doats—The title is *Meditationes Physico Chemicae de origine Mundi a Joh: Geo: Wallerio*. Stockholm 1779[4] I am most sadly teazed with the philosophers in this Country and their theorys of heat being only a vibration in bodies which seems to me highly improbable and not to be reconciled to many notorious facts—I see Macquer has defended it ably but has brought no conviction to me—I think that latent heat and difference of equilibrium will account for all its phenomena except the heat produced by friction   there I am at a loss

Our Engines answer now in every respect except the getting us money fast enough, they begin to do a little in that way and promise exceeding fair, but the rascality of mankind is almost beyond belief; however I perceive perseverance and dunning will conquer even that when one has a good cause—Mr. Garbett[5] lately did us the favour to settle be[twee]n a company here and us a bargain by which we get £217 per annum where they had the effrontery to offer us £30 p[e]r year not long ago—

I have lately had a short fever and sore throat which has weakened me a good deal   however I gett better fast; but am at all times most intolerably plagued with headachs† even to 3 days a week—My spirits are however tolerable—I remain, Dear Doctor

Most affectionately
Your's

Doctor Black James Watt

I have lately discovered a method of copying [writing] instantaneously, provided it has been written [the same day] or within 24 hours, I send you a specimen [and will] Impart the secret if it will be of any use to you [It enables] me to copy all my business letters—

¹ This refers to matter published by Smeaton in the *Newcastle Courant* 1779 about Boulton and Watt's Hawkesbury engine. See cutting in Birmingham Reference Library.
² Pierre-Joseph Macquer (1718–84), professor of chemistry in the Jardin du Roi, Paris, compiler of the famous *Dictionnaire de Chymie*, which went through many editions from its first (anonymous) appearance in 1766, and of other classic works on the theory and practice of chemistry. He was the greatest French eighteenth-century chemist before Lavoisier.
³ Joseph Priestley (1733–1804), Unitarian minister and scientist. Member of the Lunar Society of Birmingham.
⁴ Johan Gotschalk (not Geo.) Wallerius (1709–85), professor of chemistry in Uppsala (1750–67) and a very copious author. His *Meditationes* was published in 1779 as Watt says but this letter is dated 1778.
⁵ Samuel Garbett (1717–1803), merchant of Birmingham and John Roebuck's partner.
† [Tear in MS.]

Letter 53

WATT TO BLACK

Cover addressed: 'Doctor Joseph Black/Edinburgh/with a small parcel', and 'Mr. McGowan Called and left this packet Tuesday ½ past noon'. Endorsed by Black, 'Mr. Watt 1st August 1779' and numbered '54'. Dol. Also in Black's hand in crayon the following:

'Halkerston 2 winters—Dr. Steadman

Mr. Fox'
and in ink: 'Macartney
            Ogilvie'

Birmingham { July } August 1st
1779

Dear Doctor

I wrote to you the other day by post but having the opportunity of Mr. Garbetts going to Scotland—I send you a Specimen of an odd

67

substance found in Penelly lead mine in Shropshire about 9 miles easterly from the town of Montgomery—Some have supposed it zeolite (and I believe it is so) but it does not dissolve in acids nor melt by itself with the Blowpipe, but burns into a porcelane—There is no great quantity to be had and it lay all in a hole near the surface—shall be glad to have your opinion of it—I only tryed the opake kind, having got the other very lately

I ever remain Dear Doctor
very truely your's
James Watt

Please remember me to Mr. Clerk
and to Dr. Hutton—

Letter 54

BLACK TO WATT

Cover addressed: 'Mr. James Watt Engineer/Soho/Birming-
ham/per Ferry bridge' and numbered '59'. Dol.

Edinb[urgh] 25 Aug[u]st 1779

Dear Watt

I rec[eive]d both your letters, 24th July and the one by Mr. Garbett— and I much admire your Secret for copying writing—I shewed it last night to a Writer to the Signet who at first was much alarmed on account of the frauds which he thought it might give occasion to, he supposed that it needed only a little more address and ingenuity to enable you to copy writing of any age \and in any manner/—I thank you for your offer of the Secret but have no particular occasion for it as I very seldom need to Copy what I write—If it were peaceable times and money more plenty in the Kings pocket I think you might obtain some present or reward for communicating it to the Secretarys of State etc.—I also received the Samples of the fossil from Shropshire, it is the Spar called Cawk in Derbyshire, the Gypsum ponderosum as I now call it (formerly Gypseous Spar) you know the common appearance of it in mines, every where; that appearance however under which it is called Cawk by the English miners is so far as I know peculiar to England— The proofs of its being Gypseous are 1st its melting with a violent heat into an opake white mass which all Gypsum does when heated upon

68

an Earthen Support 2dly It being dissolved easily by Borax and when melted with it upon Charcoal forming a sort of hepar ⌬is You will ask why I call it Gypsum ponderosum; I answer because it differs from Common Gypsum by having for its basis a different Species of Calcarious Earth which being heavier than the Common Calcarious Earth is now called Terra Ponderosa and hence in part the great weight of the Gypsum Ponderosum—This terra ponderosa was discovered by some of the Swedish Chemists who first extracted it from the Spar and examined it—It burns to a sort of lime—forms a more insoluble Gypsum with Vitriolic Acid than the Common—and a very Crystallizable Compound with nitrous Acid—and it attracts Vitriolic Acid more strongly than Caustic fixed alkali does I have found it in the State of a Calcarious Spar or saturated only with fixed air at Lead Hills and shall send you a Specimen of it when I meet with an opportunity— I find by experiments made just now with my Blowpipe that common Gypsum will not make a hepar Sulphuris upon charcoal with *Borax* tho the Gypsum ponderosum will do it—but all Gypsums melt easily upon the earthen support with the blowpipe especially if they are ground to a fine powder and made into a paste with Water before the heat is applyed—and Common Gypsum as well as the other makes a hepar sulphuris very readily if melted upon the Charcoal with plenty of mild fossil alkali—

I have seen a fossil from the East Indies that is quite unknown in Europe—It is called Sparry Quartz \or rhombic Quartz/ and serves the same purposes in India that Emery does in Europe it even cuts all their Stones except the diamond. It is crystallized into rude but very distinct hexaedral Columns truncated at both ends length an Inch or $1\frac{1}{2}$ or 2, diameter not much less than the length—the surface is quite rough or rude no polish whatever—They appear to be formed in some sort of granite or whin Stone being attended with peices of felt spat—and some Schorl—They are easily broken down into peices and ground to a rough powder—the small peices are transparent with a slight tinge of a greenish yellowish colour and have much of the resinous appearance which is remarkable in the Diamond—They are in general rhomboidal like the fragments of Calcarious Spar the Stone being traversed \obliquely/ with innumerable flaws exactly in the same manner as Calcarious Spar—Tho this Stone is thus easily broken down the fragments and dust of it have an amasing hardness and sharpness cutting and tearing glass like the Devil—the Gentoos mix this Dust with melted Lac and of this mixture they form their wheels for cutting and

polishing—Mr. Clerk and Dr. Hutton desire me to send their Compliments and

I am ever
Dear Watt
Yours affectionately
Joseph Black

Letter 55

BLACK TO WATT

Cover addressed: 'Mr. James Watt, Engineer/at Mr. Thomas
Wilsons/Chace-Water/Cornwall', endorsed in Watt's hand,
'Doctor Black November 15th 1779' and numbered '58'. Dol.

Edinb[urgh] 15th Nov[embe]r 1779

Dear Watt

Since my last I had the pleasure of seeing Mrs. Watt in her way
westward with your two lovely Children and she flattered us with the
hope that we may see you here to fetch her home again—Mr. Henderson[1] was with her and among other things he told me a strange story of a
Menstruum they have at Birmingham which separates Silver from the
surface of Copper by dissolving the Silver only and leaving the Copper
untouched which I suspect is a mistake—I am desired by the Duke of
Buccleugh to apply to you for a communication of your Secret for
copying writing or taking a counter proof from it and if you chuse that
it should be communicated to him under the condition of Secrecy you
may perfectly depend upon his keeping it Secret—Your Machine at
Wanlock h[ea]d gives great Satisfaction—Hutton has seen it and he
says it goes and may be regulated like a pendulum Clock—it seems
Smeaton when there lately was very much struck with the regulating
Cocks which were then new to him—Hutton says that in your directions you dissapprove of *White Lead and Oil paint or Vernish* and
recommend *Whiteing or Chalk and Oil* as better for standing in the wet
or under water—pray let me know about this as I sometimes paint my
white Iron Vessels but observe that if water stands long in them it
softens the paint

I had something else to say but have forgot what it was and the post
hour is at hand—I pity your poor head in the Cursed Climate of Cornwall at this rainy Season—You are kindly remembered by your

Freinds here as Dr. Young and Lady—Com[missione]r Clerk etc. etc.—
and Mr. Davidson[2] the Crown Agent and his Lady desired me
particularly to make their acknowledgements to you for the goodness
and Civility you shewed their Son at Birmingham—I am ever

Dear Watt
most affectionately
Yours
Joseph Black

[1] Lieutenant Logan Henderson joined the firm of Boulton and Watt in 1776–77. He had
charge of the Torryburn and Byker engines in 1778 and in 1781 was in Cornwall with
Watt. He left the service of Boulton and Watt in 1782, after incurring Watt's suspicion
and dislike. He had some connections in 1785 with Jeremy Bentham presumably as a result
of his acquaintance with Samuel Bentham.
[2] John Davidson of Stewartfield and Haltrie, son of James Davidson, bookseller in
Edinburgh, became a Writer to the Signet in 1749. He was appointed Crown Agent and
was Deputy Keeper of the Signet from 1778 until his death in 1792.

Letter 56

BLACK TO WATT

Cover addressed: 'Mr. James Watt Engineer/at Mr. Thomas
Wilsons/Chace-Water/Cornwall'. Dol.

Edinb[urgh] 19th Nov[embe]r 1779

Dear Watt

I wrote you a few Posts agoe to enquire whether or not you inclined
to communicate your method of taking a counterproof from fresh
writing to the Duke of Buccleugh, I have been informed since that he
supported your Cause in the affair of the Patent and I know that he will
be inclined to befreind you in any other Business—and although you
should have formed a plan for deriving some benefit from it I think
you may very safely entrust him with the Secret in the mean time

But I have been applyed to since by two other Persons who wish
to be let into the Secret—One of them is Professor Ferguson of this
University whom you may also trust without the least scruple—The
other is Sir Will[ia]m Forbes the Banker a very worthy Man too who
requests it with great modesty and Submission and appears hardly to
expect it unless it be by paying for it in some shape or other, either by

71

purchasing the liquor from you with which it is done or paying a premium for a participation of the Secret and under the condition of Secrecy.—At the same time however that I could not avoid transmitting to you these applications I beg that you will act according to your own Plan without considering me as having any concern in the Matter—

I find the Perpetual moving Wheel is turning out a Bubble like all other such Projects—our Professor of Geometry here has a long and laboured letter from Cumin[1] which is plainly meant as an Apology to his Freinds and acquaintances here for his folly in having any concern with it

Farewell my Dear Freind and beleive me

Yours
Joseph Black

[1] Alexander Cummings, F.R.S., instrument-maker and friend of James Watt.

Letter 57

WATT TO BLACK

Cover addressed: 'Doctor Joseph Black/Edinburgh', endorsed in
Watt's hand, 'To Dr. Black December 2d 1779' and numbered
'12'. Dol.

Chacewater Dec[embe]r 2d 1779

Dear Doctor

Your letters of the 15th and 19th ultimo received. The post should have been answered sooner but have been exceedingly busy attending meetings and making calculations for an agreement with the proprietors of Wheal Virgin mine, which is at last stopt from the inability of the present Engines to draw the water, in fact they were wore out, as this is a matter of such moment as to be capable of affording \us/ above £2000 —a year if our Engines are adopted I hope you will excuse my silence—

Mr. Henderson ought not to have mentioned Mr. Keirs secret of disolving the silver from the Copper, which however is fact I having seen it done, though I know not by what means, The silver is disolved with rapidity and the Copper left bright and I think perfectly untouched —Mr. Boulton begs you would not mention the existence of it in your Class

I have found that Steam disolves white lead; and that White lead or

72

litharge renders lintseed oil more soluble in water than it is{commonly} other wise—English lintseed oil *not boiled with litharge or Lead*, and used with red ochre or with whiting is not so soluble in water but will also sooner or later be affected by it—If the oil be boiled with a small quantity of wax untill the wax be disolved, that is untill the mixture when cold is a semitransparent brown, it will be much less soluble in water, but must be used warm on account of its thickness—Steam also disolves Iron where it passes over it with velocity and the steams in this County also disolve Copper and brass particularly the latter—Mr. Keir has discovered a beautifull yellow Col[oure]d brass which forges hot like Iron and is as strong as Iron, say fully as strong and as stiff   he is making bolts of it for the navy

In relation to the copying scheme the state of it at present is as follows—I have given in a petition for a patent and it is now in train, but as my occupations and health cannot permitt me, to follow that business my self I have taken in 2 partners—Mr. B[oulto]n who is to be at the expence of the patent and Mr. Keir who is to manage the business—Our proposition is to open a subscription for 1000 persons who are to be put in possession of the secret; a quantity of proper paper and materials with a press for taking off the impressions at the rate of $5\frac{1}{2}$ guineas each; no one to be put in possession untill the whole is subscribed, as the thing is so simple and easy that after divulging it to a number we might lose the rest—We have reason to believe that such subscription will be immediately filled up, particularly as the price we have fixed is not much more if any more than the value of the press itself which will be made of Iron with *lignum vitae* Rollers—The Iron work jappanned Black—We cannot publish our proposals for the subscription untill the patent passes the seals the news of which I expect every day

In relation to the Duke of Buccleugh and the gentlemen for whom you pass your word they shall be accommodated with the first presses which are made, without waiting for the filling up the subscription or making any other terms with them than that of secrecy untill we have carried our point; and therefore would not have you mention price to them

I should without Hesitation communicate the whole to you but cannot do it without writing at least a sheet of paper and recalling my experiments and Ideas on the subject which at present would be a hardship on me when my head is filled with other business, the weather and my spirits both very bad.

73

In brief the first Idea was the forcing the ink through thin paper so as to appear on the other side, the second the improving the colour by wetting the paper with an astringent the third the depriving astringents of their colour, without depriving them of their effects as astringents— fourthly managing the operation so as to prevent the original being defaced or forced through to the other side—But the greatest part resides in the Mechanical Manoeuvre—all this to yourself *only*, at present

I hope the Duke will excuse a small delay in the communication which apart from any interested Consideration I should desire from my being unwilling to have my inventions come into the world imperfect —It gives me pain to be obliged to sell philos[ophi]cal discoveries but my circumstances render it necessary as to the world in general, as to my friends they shall welcome to it so soon as I am secured—

Cumming has certainly exposed himself by having any thing to do with Perpetual Motionists, every body has their failings and he though a first rate Mechanical philosopher believes in the {perpetual} possibility of a per[petua]l motion

I remain with the greatest sensibility of your friendship
Dear Doctor—Your's most sincerely
James Watt

Mr. B[oulto]n is here at present and joins in comp[liment]s to you— So far from taking it as a trouble to answer questions, you will perceive from what has been said, that the more names you send us the more will be obliged to you

Letter 58

BLACK TO WATT

Cover addressed: 'Mr. James Watt Engineer/at Mr. Thomas Wilsons/Chacewater/Cornwall' and numbered '57'. Dol.

Edinb[urgh] 7th Jan[ua]ry 1780

Dear Watt

I rec[eive]d yours of the 2d December and am happy to learn that you have such great Business on hand as the Wheal Virgin Engines for I cannot doubt that your Engines will be adopted—With respect to the Process for separating Silver from Copper Mr. Bolton may make himself perfectly easy I shall never make the least mention of it in any way whatever—Since my last I have found two Gent[leme]n besides the former who wish to be Possessed of your secret for copying writing —Mr. Smith who is now a Commiss[ione]r of the Customs here[1] and Doctor Cullen to whom it will be extreamly Usefull—but the way to get subscribers is to advertise   I have no doubt that great numbers would be found even in this poor Country and that upon the whole your Subscription will be immediatly filled up—Mr. Keirs invention of the strong and tough Brass promises to be an extreamly usefull one if it can be afforded at a moderate Price—last summer I examined the metal of some antient Weapons which are sometimes found in this Country and are made of a sort of Brass and found it to be Brass or Copper hardened with a small proportion of Tin—afterwards looking into Pliny I saw that the Antients made much use of Tin in the Composition of their Brassy Metals or Bronzes but that they were also well acquainted with the use of Calamine in makeing Brass—They considered all these Compositions as Copper variously coloured and modifyed and had the same name for them all (Æs)—and upon lookeing at their Copper Coins and Medals it is surprizeing to see what a variety of Colours there are among them and some of them very beautifull yellows—

Do you remember that I wanted some more of the Fluor from Cornwall—You may perhaps bring some for yourself too when I inform you of a Property of it which I lately discovered in making some experiments with the Blowpipe, it is that of being an excellent soldering flux when it is mixed with a certain proportion of Borax or fixed alcali—I know none equal to it for mildness with respect to Metals— Iron or Copper are dissolved and corroded very fast by Borax or by Common Glass but the above mixture tho it flows as thin as water and becomes as transparent when melted, does not corrode them at least not Copper in the smallest degree and even Iron is hardly touched by it —After trying its effect a while upon Copper I separated the bit of Copper from it and put a little bit of Iron to my Flux upon the Charcoal and then giving it a very strong heat with the blowpipe a minute globule of Copper which had remained took hold of the Iron and soon spread itself over the whole surface of it so as to copper it compleatly over—and I have no doubt that Iron may be silvered in the same manner—If the experiment were to be made in a furnace I suppose it would be necessary to use black-lead Crucibles as I suppose these would be more impenetrable to it than Earthen ones—

75

Farewell my dear Watt and may you long enjoy the Fruits of your long and hard Labours—beleive me

always yours affectionately
Joseph Black

Pray what is become of your
French business—

[1] Adam Smith, author of the *Wealth of Nations*, a close friend of Joseph Black, was appointed Commissioner of Customs for Scotland at the end of 1777.

Letter 59

WATT TO MAGELLAN[1]

* Dol.

Birmingham Mar[ch] 1st
1780

Dear Sir

Your favours of the 22 Feb[ruar]y I received on my return from Cornwall last week—Permit me *brevi modo* to say that You are a person we hold in great esteem, that our own experience will always weigh more with us than the reports or insinuations of others, and that the sole reason Mr. Boulton has not called upon you oftener is the hurry and vexation of business he has always been in in London which has prevented him from calling upon any of his numerous friends unless urged by business—I can give but short answers to your queries concerning Dr. Blacks ingenious doctrines of heat   it would require a volume to explain them fully—he has printed nothing himself—but there are two publications from which some part of his Theory may be gathered; though in my opinion too much blended with the Opinions and in one of them with the inconclusive experiments of the publishers. —The Books are written by a Doctor Duguid Lesly[2] and by Adair Crawford.[3]

I never saw nor heard of any Stockholm Accad[emi]e publication on the subject—but I know positively that Doctor Black was the inventor of these Experiments and Theorys and that prior to the year 1763, and that he has publickly taught them ever since, and I believe before that Æra.

I do not recollect exactly what quantity of heat is absorbed by ice when converted into water but I believe about 140°—ie, that it absorbs as much heat in the action of thawing as would have heated it 140°

above 32° if it could have continued in the form of ice—to understand this you ought to know that all bodies are sponges in respect of heat and some bodies can contain more of it and some others less, and that all liquids contain more heat than the solid substances by the melting of which these liquids are formed and that again when converted into vapour they can contain more heat than when in the state of Liquids—

The quantity of heat which is latent in Steam is 800° which added to its sensible heat {gives}\makes/1012° or in other words it will communicate to cold water as much heat as the water of which the steam is composed would do if it were heated to 1012° or as an equal *bulk* of Iron would do when heated to that degree I mean a piece of Iron equal in bulk to the bulk to the water which composed the steam

The vapour blown of from water by wind has the same share of Latent heat or perhaps more, on acc[oun]t of its being disolved in air—

The latent heat of Steam, I have said, will heat cold water as much as red hot Iron will, it is by that means it becomes sensible

Dr. Irvines theorys are nothing else but an explanation of Dr Blacks in other words, except that he has applyed these theories to account for the heating of the mixture of fluids such as ⊕+ and ∇ [form] and to show how much actual heat is contained in bodies or in other words what is the lowest degree of heat, in which he he [sic] has displayed very great Ingenuity and power of reasoning—I was the first that tryed experiments to find the quantities of heat absorbed by some metals by wood and by some other bodies in the year 1763 but invented no theories on the subject—it being done in consequence of Dr. Blacks discoveries—I have lately invented a method of copying writing expeditiously which I shall shortly publish by subscription

I hope you will be so good as to excuse Brevity and to believe me to remain

Dear Sir
Your Obliged Serv[ant]
James Watt

Mr. Magellan

[1] João Jacinto de Magalhaens (or Magelhaens), commonly called Magellan (1722–90) was of Portuguese origin. Came to England in 1764, F.R.S. 1774, and acted as a disseminator of scientific information, perhaps as a spy. He was a member of the Chapter Coffee House Society.

[2] Patrick Duguid or Patrick Duguid Leslie, M.D., *A Philosophical Enquiry into the Cause of Animal Heat*, etc. (1779).

[3] Adair Crawford (1748–95), a physician to St. Thomas's Hospital, London, and later Professor of Chemistry in the Royal Military Academy, Woolwich. Visited Scotland in 1776 and began his experiments on heat at Glasgow in 1777. His work, *Experiments and Observations on Animal Heat* (1779) had a second edition in 1788.

WATT TO BLACK

Cover addressed: 'Doctor Joseph Black/Edinburgh/via Ferry-bridge', endorsed in Black's hand, 'Mr. Watt 1st March 1780' and numbered '53'. Dol. Also incomplete * Dol.

Birmingham Mar[ch] 1st 1780

Dear Doctor

I should have answered your kind letter of the 7th January sooner, but the execrable weather bad health and the ordinary vexations attendant on business prevented me—before I received that letter Mr. B. had formed, Theoreticaly, notions of the use of fluor in soldering and plating silver upon Copper and had collected a ton of the spar—

I shewed him your letter and if you mean to make a property of it nothing will be done predjudicial to your interest; but I fear that it cannot be made a sufficient Object of Commerce: Its properties as a flux are well known to many of the Copper smelters but what you have suggested of its properties in soldering is I believe quite new—I have ordered a small cask to be filled with it and a few uncommon stones—to which I have added some Black tin in the situation it goes to the smelting house, on which you may experiment; one parcel is very pure from other ores—The Cask is sent to London \(by sea)/ to care of Mr. W[illia]m Mathews, our correspondent there to forward to you by sea The fluor is from Roskere mine—I had lately a letter from Mr. Magellan at London who was our agent in the french Business: Is I believe a Carthusian or Benedictine monk, by profession a dealer \in/ and retailer of philosophy, and perhaps a Spy—however that be he has acted honestly and honorably by us—he made many enquirys about your latent heat, which I answered in so far as was expedient—he wants to know when you invented it   I answered I could not tell but that you taught it before the year 1763—He says that Bergman[1] of Stockholm has published some memoir \lately/ in which he mentions that a professor Wiltke[2] of Stockholm did publish nearly the same fact long ago in the memoirs of Stockholm accad[em]y.

When in Cornwall I was shewn a Crystallization of the fluor in another form said to be artificial Quartz Christalls. It was done by steeping the fluor in ⊕+ and suffering it to remain there for some time. They were very small, seemed hexagonal Chissel pointed Christals—As

78

to their hardness I can say nothing as I was not suffered to touch them They were Chrystallized partly on the fluor itself and partly on the saucer in which it lay—I am very curious to know what is the basis of this Fluor—I suspect it is not lime as there are no Calcarious nor Gypseous substances in the neighbourhood There is however Chalcedony found in the same mine but this also seems to differ from Flints I believe I have sent you some specimens incrusted with it—The proposals for the Copying scheme will be soon published and some of the presses are making I shall send you some proposals as soon as ready—we have been obliged to raise the price to six guineas on acc[oun]t of more expence than we expected and the necessity of giving all the little implements along with it—Please make my respects to all friends and believe me to remain

Dear Doctor
Most sincerely
Your's
James Watt

Doctor Black

[1] Torbern Olaf Bergman(1735–84) succeeded Wallerius in the chair of chemistry in Uppsala in 1767, one of the great figures of eighteenth-century chemistry.

[2] Johan Carl Wilcke (1732–96), Professor of Experimental Physics at the Military Academy, Stockholm, and Secretary (1786–96) of the Swedish Academy, to which he contributed numerous memoirs on various branches of physics. See D. McKie and Niels H. de V. Heathcote, *The Discovery of Specific and Latent Heats* (1935).

Letter 61

WATT TO MAGELLAN

* Dol. Folder endorsed, 'Mr. to Watt's letters Mr. Magellan, dated Birmingham 1 March 1780 9 March 1780 20 Ditto— 1780', and numbered '5'.

Birmingham March 9th
1780

Dear Sir

I have just received your letter of the 8th inst[an]t my method of copying letters etc. extends only, at present, to the taking one copy from a letter in 24 hours after it is written (ie with certainty; for, some times, and by using proper methods it may be taken at a longer date) The two papers I sent you were an original and a copy of it.

Our proposals will be soon published and will be attended with specimens of the art—I shall do myself the pleasure of sending you one as soon [as] they are ready—The price of a licence to use the invention together with the Apparatus necessary (for a machine is requisite though not a cumbersome one) will be six guineas—The Machine alone would cost more money if we did not make a great number together; for we mean to make them very handsome and very good—

In relation to Dr. Blacks discoveries, you are wrong in thinking that they have not been published untill lately—There is if I reccollect right an account of them in a Quarto {Edition} Dictionary of Arts and Sciences published at Edinburgh in 1768 or thereabouts a second Edition of that dictionary is now publishing and the four first volumes which extend to F are come out and in these volumes you will find many of Dr. Blacks doctrines explained. They are printed by Balfour and Co[mpany] Edinburgh and I dare say may be had in London Consult among others the articles Evaporation, Fluidity Frost,—As to Professor Wilcke's discovery I know nothing of it except that it was given in to the accademy in 1772—and I must further inform you that very long prior to that date there were several Swedish and Danish students at Edinburgh who were perfectly acquainted with Dr. Blacks discoveries and capable of relating them

You seem to consider it as wrong in Dr. B not to have published his discoveries as he made them—in that I cannot agree with you. Every man who is obliged to live by his profession ought to keep the secrets of it to himself so far as is consistent with the use of them: It is

80

only People of Independ[en]t fortunes who have a right to give away their Inventions without attempting to turn them to their own advantage. According to your rule I should have published my fire engine or this Copying Scheme without securing them both by patent as I have done, but that way of proceeding will not make the pot boil. You might with equal propriety endeavour to persuade a man of fortune to divide his fortune with the public as a man of Ingenuity to publish his inventions as long as they afford him the means of subsisting—Indeed there is this difference that the man of Ingenuity from that weakness which is called the love of fame frequently publishes what he ought to conceal; for which the world is obliged to him; but the man of fortune seldom bestows his *money* with so liberal a hand—However I do not believe Dr. Black acted from the Motive of Covetousness but merely from the love of peace and quietness: and from the very laudable desire of perfecting his discoveries before he published them

If you do not publish Dr. B. as the first author of these discoveries you do him an injury and will be liable to have your own publication called in Question; but I promise myself that you will act impartialy and do justice among these great men

As to my own experiments in that way they are few and unconnected and I have at present no violent desire to shine forth in the page of Literary fame but I return you my most sincere thanks and remain

Dear Sir with esteem
Your obliged servant
James Watt†

†[At side of last page:
I never heard of the Spilsbury you mention to have had something like the copying scheme but as it is sometime invented he may have heard of it at second hand——]
[These last eight words are conjectural as they have been partially obliterated.]

WATT TO BLACK

Cover addressed: 'Doctor Black/Edinburgh/via Ferrybridge', endorsed in Watt's hand 'To Dr. Black March 9th 1780' and numbered '52'. Dol. Also on blank half-sheet, 'Dr. Crell of Brunswick November 69'. Also * Dol.

Birmingham March 9th 1780

Dear doctor

I wrote to you the other day and mentioned that Mr. Magellan had wrote to me for some acc[oun]t of your discoveries to which I had given such an answer as I thought was a prudent one that is I did not enter minutely into the subject and told him the time I knew you taught it publickly   To day I have another letter from him telling me he as been so much harrassed writing to his friends abroad concerning these new discoveries as published by Dr. Leslie and Dr. Crawford that he is printing in French a short account of them in which he means to atribute the discovery to Proffessor Wilkie and only to mention you in so far as your scholars have quoted you, which I think in all conscience is sufficiently little—They seem to have been too full of their own Theories to do justice to yours—I have wrote him in answer and insisted that he should do you justice as the first inventor—Magellan is I believe well meaning but no philosopher a mere gatherer of scraps and a bad writer but as he has an extensive correspondence he may circulate erroneous doctrines to the prejudice of your honour. I have therefore done my endeavour to stop him and if you chuse to furnish me with a few facts relative to the time etc. of your invention and an account of any publications in which it has been mentioned I will cause him publish them as from myself—I am really much vexed that you have lett so many plagiaries rob you of the honour of the greatest discovery this age has produced; but it is not yett\ too late/ to do well   I would write you the result of some experiments Dr. Withering[1] here has made on heating Iron red hot by hammering (at my instigation) but my head achs; lett it suffice that they confirmed your theory and were similar to what you once told me

I have seen Bergmans book, the date of Wilckes publication is 1772. Bergmans says very little on it, only that the heat thrown out by water in freezing is 72° of the swedish Thermometer—

I mentioned to Magellan that there have been several Swedish and

Danish students at Edinburgh who understood your theories, shall be obliged to you to confirm that by naming them—

I ever remain, Dear doctor
Your Affect[ionate] friend
James Watt

Dr. Black

[1] William Withering (1741–99), physician, botanist and chemist. Translated Bergman's *Sciagraphica*. Member of the Lunar Society of Birmingham. Published in 1785 his account of the use of digitalis in the treatment of heart-disease.

Letter 63

BLACK TO WATT

Cover addressed: 'Mr. James Watt Engineer/at Soho/ Birmingham/per Ferrybridge', endorsed in Watt's hand, 'Dr. Black March 15th 1780 dates of his discoverys' and numbered '55'. Dol.

Edinb[urgh] 15th March 1780

Dear Watt

I am in your Debt for two letters of a late Date   in the first you mention your haveing packed up a small Cask for me with Fluor etc— and you put a Question whether I wish to make a property of the discovery of the soldering Flux which it forms with Borax or alcaline Salts—to this I answer that I have no such intention and if you can apply it to any usefull purpose at Soho you are heartily welcome—The rest of that letter and the last are cheifly concerning the Subject of Lat[en]t Heat and Magellans Purpose of Publishing {upon} some history of it. Your anxiety with regard to this matter gives \me/ the greatest pleasure as it proceeds entirely from your Freindship for me and there is no person whose Freindship I value more highly—As Magellan has already got a Prejudice upon this Subject it may not be easy to set him right but I hope his Authority will not have very great weight in the mean time, and my present intention is to publish myself next Summer, if my health allows me which I confess easily suffers from working a little

As you must answer Magellans letter however I give you the following Facts—I began to give the Doctrine of lat[en]t Heat in My Lectures at Glasgow in the Winter 1757-58 which I beleive was the first winter of my Lecturing there \and I have/ or if I did not give it that winter I certainly gave it in the 1758-59 and I have delivered it every year since that time in my winter lectures—which I continued to give at Glasgow untill winter 1766-67 when I began to Lecture in Edinburgh The winter 1760-61 I had among my Scholars, the Hon[oura]ble Mr. Fitzmaurice Brother to the Earl of Shelburne and Dr. Menish now settled in England both of whom took notes I believe of many parts of my lectures—I was also attended the same year by Mr. George Farquhar[1] who is a Surgeon in London \and who went from Glasgow to Paris to finish his Education/—

The following winter I was attended by Dr. Irvin and Pat Wilson and about that time or soon after I read a Paper upon this Subject in the Philosophical or University Club at Glasgow—The winters 62-63 and 63-64 I was attended with numbers of Gentlemen at Glasgow many of whom will easily remember this Doctrine—and the winter 64-65 I had Simeon Desnitzky \and John Tretiakoff[2]/ the Russian Students then at Glasgow—Since I came here Dr. Crell[3] of Brunswic who is now engaged in some periodicall publications attended these Lectures in Nov[embe]r and Decemb[er] 1769—and in the {winter 177} same months of the year 1772 Dr. Henry Gahn[4] from Sweden attended my Course—I do not remember any other Foreigners than the above but could bring a multitude of other Evidences to prove the early date of my Doctrines on this Subject—And I should reckon the Testimony which you can give as equal to the greater part of them— you haveing been early acquainted with and directed by it in your pursuit of improvements upon the Steam Engine and incited to make Experiments with regard to it—In your last letter from Cornwall you mentioned your being very busy about the Wheal Virgin mine—Pray did you come to an agreement with the Company—

<table>
<tr><td></td><td>I am ever</td></tr>
<tr><td>Pray are \you/ to come this way</td><td>My dear Sir</td></tr>
<tr><td>to conduct Mrs. Watt home again</td><td>Yours affect[ionate]ly</td></tr>
<tr><td>or has she rejoined you already</td><td>Joseph Black</td></tr>
</table>

[1] Probably Mr Farquhar, formerly an army surgeon, Great Marlborough Street (*Medical Register* (1780)).

[2] S. E. Desnitskii and I. A. Tretiakov were sent by the government of Russia to the University of Glasgow to study science and mathematics, but their interests turned to law. Desnitskii translated Blackstone's *Commentaries* and became a principal advocate of the historical and comparative approach to the study of Russian law. Tretiakov's essay, *The Causes of the Fast and Slow Enrichment of Nations*, 1772, was the first Russian presentation of Adam Smith's ideas in political economy.

[3] Lorenz Friedrich von Crell (1744–1816), first professor of chemistry and mineralogy in Brunswick (1771–73), then professor of philosophy and medicine in the University of Helmstadt (1773–1810) and finally professor of chemistry in Göttingen. Famous also as the editor of *Annalen*.

[4] Johan Gottlieb (not Henry) Gahn (1745–1818), friend of Scheele and Bergman's assistant in Uppsala.

Letter 64

WATT TO MAGELLAN

★ Dol. Folder endorsed, 'Mr. Watt's letters to Mr. Magellan dated Birmingham 1 March 1780 9 March 1780 and 20 Ditto— 1780' and numbered '5'.

Birmingham Mar[ch] 20th
1780

Dear Sir

Since I did myself the pleasure to write to you last I have learnt the following particulars relative to the history of Dr. Blacks discovery which you may depend upon are facts—

Dr. Black gave the doctrine of latent heat in his lectures at Glasgow immediately on his being made proffessor there, which was in the year 1757-8 or in 1758-9 at latest; and taught it every winter at Glasgow untill 1766-7 when he began to lecture at Edinburgh—

In 1760-1 The hon[oura]ble Mr. Fitzmaurice, brother to Lord Shelburne, and a Dr. Menish, now settled near London attended his lectures, who both took notes. The same year, Mr. George Farquhar now a surgeon in London attended these lectures. The latter went to Paris the next winter to finish his education. In 1761-2 Dr. Irvine of Glasgow became his Scholar and Mr. Peter Wilson son to Dr. Wilson Proffessor of Astronomy at Glasgow

In 1764-5 Messrs. Desnitski and Tretiakoff both from Russia attended him—

Dr. Crell of Brunswick attended his Lectures at Edinburgh in 1769 and in Nov[embe]r 1772 Dr. Henry Gahn \from Sweden/ attended the lectures—There was also a Mr. Williamson a dane who attended him previous to that date I think about 1769—I myself became instructed in the doctrine about the year 1763, but I know for a certainty that it was taught much sooner, though I did not direct my studies that way before that time—Mr. Keir has reminded me that some account of it, he thinks a pretty full one, is contained in the Abbe Roziers Journal at the time it was published in Duodecimo—

I cannot pretend to give you lists of the numerous students Dr. Black has taught   I have mentioned a few, from the knowledge of \a/ friend, some of which you can satisfye yourself from as to the date of the discovery—The Abbe Roziers Journal is a sure proof that it was known in france at that time which I believe was before 1772 but as I have not the Book am not certain; but at any rate you see that it is possible that it was known in the farthest parts of Europe before 1772—but nevertheless Proffessor Wilcke may have invented the same thing independent {of Dr. Black} of any knowledge of Dr. Blacks doctrine—I have learnt further that Dr. Black means to publish on the subject himself this summer if his health which is very bad, permitts him

In the mean time I trust to your experienced candour to do the Doctor the Justice so ingenious a discovery merits and If you chuse you may give me as your authority for the foregoing facts; but I beg you may put them in a better dress if you publish them, as I am too much hurried to attend to stile—I always remain with esteem

Dear Sir
Your obliged serv[an]t

Mr. Magellan James Watt

Letter 65

WATT TO MAGELLAN

* Dol. Folder endorsed, 'Mr. Watt to Mr. Magellan. Birmingham 29 March 1780' and numbered '4'.

Birmingham March 29th
1780

Dear Sir

I have this moment received your favours of the 27th and at the same time the proofs of your work on latent heat, which I suppose have lain at the coach office for want of being directed to care of Messrs. Boulton and Fothergill Whenever you have anything to send to me send by the Diligence from the Castle and Falcon Aldersgate Street directed as above and it will be delivered immediately—I am sorry I had not longer time to peruse the proofs† (for I cannot prevail with myself to detain them any longer after having lain so long already). I must say that you have handled the subject *en maitre* and that your work makes it more intelligible than any publication I have seen on the subject, for Dr. Crawfords seems to be written only to adepts—I have made a very few remarks on the margin, which you may use as you please—If you please to publish any part of the letters I sent you, You may give me as your Authority for the whole of the dates of Dr. Blacks discoveries etc. contained in my last letter; for 800° being the quantity of latent heat in steam, or at least very nearly so, for it is more exceedingly difficult to ascertain the matter exactly, but please to observe that the experiment is originaly Dr. Blacks not mine, though I have repeated it often—I will also attest that Dr. Irvine of Glasgow about the year $177\frac{1}{2}$ [*sic*] invented a method of finding the quantity of Absolute heat in Bodies, from the heating of the mixture of ⊕+ and ▽ —he found that the specific heat or the capacity of the mixture to contain heat was less than the \sum of the/ specific heats contained in the two bodies before mixture and that consequently a quantity of heat was thrown out on mixing them and became sensible, from which he found out the quantity of Absolute heat contained in either of the two bodies, I cannot specify the quantity he found having no notes of it. However he found very nearly the same result from ice and water as from the other—Either Dr. Leslie or Dr. Crawford mention something of this discovery as made and taught by Dr. Irvine—you may also quote my own Authority for the bulk of steam being about 1800 times the bulk of water when the steam has 216° of Sensible heat This experiment is also exceeding difficult to make either in small or in Great, but that is the nearest I can give you

I find that we are not yet exactly agreed in our sentiments on the devoir of publication   however don't let that make us differ in other respects

If you had the happiness of being as well acquainted with Dr. Blacks Character as I am you would have taken his part perhaps more warmly —He is very far from concealing his discoveries he has always taught them publickly, and I fancy has had some thousands of scholars, He has not only taught them, but also all his acquaintance who would be at the pains of thinking on the subject. He is moreover a Gentleman of great modesty and of the utmost Candour towards other ingenious men

† [at side of page] I have sent off the proofs by this nights diligence.

87

As I observe this is only a part of a larger work, on philosophy I suppose, I shall be obliged to you to put me down as a Subscriber to the whole book which I shall be glad to have as soon as published

You [seem] to apprehend that the Copying Scheme may be made a bad use of, that I shall take care to prevent by publishing ink which cannot be copied and paper which being wrote upon by any ink is also incapable of yielding a copy—Mr. Boulton will be soon in London and will call upon you

I remain with great Esteem
Dear Sir Yours
James Watt

Mr Magellan

♂ ☉c ink

[At the side of page]
You may perhaps think I speak for the sake of my Country in favours [*sic*] of Dr. Black but it is only from personal friendship and desire of Justice to [Merit] for Dr. B is a native of France

Letter 66

WATT TO BLACK

Cover addressed: 'Doctor Joseph Black/Edinburgh' endorsed in Black's hand, 'Mr. Watt 17th May 1780' and numbered '51'. Dol. Also in Black's hand, 'Scotch Patent/Frauds'. Also ★ Dol.

Birmingham May 17th
1780

Dear Doctor

I take the opportunity of sending you by Capt[ain] Marr[1] a copy of Magellans book on heat—On which I shall make no other remarks, than that he has neither done justice to you nor to the remarks I furnished him with, most of which he has suppressed as being inconsistent with the Opinion he has taken up of Wilkes having a right to the honour of the discovery, merely because he printed first—I have found it in vain to argue with him, and have therefore given up the dispute as I found he thought himself right by his desireing me to do him the favour to send you the book; and I hope you will be philosopher enough to read him with patience, and if you publish any thing yourself I think the less notice you take of his wrongheadedness the better; at any rate save me harmless as I much dislike paper wars.—I took the liberty of sending you lately by J. Campbell 30 of our printed proposals for the Copying-Machines some of which I will be obliged to you to give to such friends as you think will take the trouble of showing them; and also to gett 2 or 3 of them stuck up in some Capital Booksellers Shops—We do not give any premium for taking in the subscriptions as the profits on selling the paper will prove a sufficient indemnification

We deliver the machines at London or at Hull free from any expence except that of packing boxes—We intend very soon to deliver out some machines to particular friends and to some of the first Subscribers and if you are to be at home shall send one of the first to you; but the greatest number \of those subscribed for/ cannot be got ready for some time yett. As his Grace the Duke of Buccleugh is to be served among the first I would be glad to be informed what size he will want his press whether only for Common post paper which requires 12 inch Rolls, or larger. Our present apparatus will make them as far as 16 inches long which will take a half Sheet of Imperial paper—The price is ½ a guinea an inch of the length of the Rolls

I ever remain
Dear Doctor
Yours sincerely
James Watt

Dr. Black

[1] Captain Marr was a naval officer; his wife was a cousin-german of James Watt.

WATT TO BLACK

Cover addressed: 'Doctor Joseph Black/Professor of Chemistry
in /the University of Edinburgh/via Ferrybridge', endorsed in
Black's hand, 'Mr. Watt 30th May 1780' and numbered '50'.
Dol. Also * Dol.

Birmingham May 30th
1780

Dear Doctor

I wrote to you lately by Capt[ain] Marr with Magellans Book on heat—To day I was informed by Mr. Keir that Alex[ande]r Fordyce[1] the late Banker had applied to parliament for an exemption from the duties on such quantities of Sea Salt as he should use for the purpose of preparing fossil alcali as [*sic*] his manufactury at North Shields near Newcastle As such a law if passed would confine the exemption to him no other person could afterwards attempt that process on an equal footing and as I have not totally laid aside all thoughts of the process we carried on for that purpose—and as Mr. Keir had invented a similar process about the same time we were at work upon it and is determined to go on with it upon his own account we have judged it proper, separately, to present petitions to the house of Commons praying to have the like exemption as Alex[ande]r Fordyce and as I by no means consider myself as the sole proprietor of that art and I had no time to Consult you I have petitioned the house on behalf of my self and you which I hope you will approve off and second with your interest and particularly write me a letter authorizing me to continue to use your name

I am my self at present in no capacity to engage in expensive projects, but at same time do not chuse to be cutt off at once from all prospect of reaping any benefit from a subject I bestowed much labour on—Mr. Keir I have mentioned means immediately to enter into the business but I am not in any shape to be concerned with him farther than this which he offers and I have accepted off as far as regards my self—He to take out a patent at his own expence and to grant to you and me licences to use the invention—He to be at the whole expence of this application to parlia[men]t for which we are never to repay him without we make use of the invention and in that case to pay him a proportional part—Or if you chuse to take out a patent in your own Name he will be silent and receive a licence from you instead of giving you one—on my own part I think his propositions fair and shall give him no opposition though I have found another way of doing the same thing I think easier—It is understood that in this convention all parties are to be on an independent footing in respect to one another only agreeing not to molest one another—I shall be happy to have your sentiments on this head as soon as possible as Mr. Keir will sett about his patent directly I have some reason to suspect a mistake either in your experiment on the quantity of latent heat in Steam or in my experiment on the bulk of Steam, I have in experiments not intended to be accurate and made since I came to England had different results in both Cases either the latent heat is 900° or the bulk of Steam ought to be only 1600 whereas your experiment makes the first 800° and my experiment makes the second 1800 If you mean to publish I wish you to try your exper[iment] again and with every attention I shall also try mine more effectually—If you do not publish this Summer, I will, as I will not longer run the risk of having the little pretension I have to literary fame run away with and I think I have completed the theory of the causes of the different heats at which ∇ boils under various pressures and have found the true series of the Curve

I remain most sincerely your's James Watt

[1] Alexander Fordyce, absconding partner, 1772, in the London banking house of Neale, ames, Fordyce and Down, brother of George Fordyce, M.D.

Letter 68

BLACK TO WATT

Cover addressed: 'Mr. James Watt Engineer/Soho/Birmingham/Via Ferrybridge' and numbered '56'. Dol.

Edinb[urgh] 3d June 1780

Dear Watt

I rec[eive]d yours of the 30th May and think your Proposal a very proper one that we should apply to Parliament to be put on equal footing with Mr. Fordyce in case he should succeed in obtaining an exemption from Duty for the Common Salt he shall use in his Manufactory of fossil alkali from Common Salt I saw in the newspapers mention of his Petition but I understood he meant to apply only for an exemption from the new additional Duty—I am perfectly willing to join you in this matter and therefore desire your instructions to direct me how I am to set about it— I also think Mr. Keirs Proposal a very fair one, to take out a Patent for himself immediatly at his own expence to carry on the said manufacture of which I beleive he was one of the first Inventors along with ourselves and afterwards when we shall chuse it to give us licences to manufacture also for ourselves, we in that case refunding to him our proportion of the expence of the Patent—I therefore heartily agree to this Proposal also— With respect to the latent heat of Steam—I have notes of an experiment of yours upon my principles made at Edinb[urgh] with a small Still J. Linds which makes the lat[en]t heat of ordinary Steam about 800°— this Exp[erimen]t was made in the year 1765—and soon after you made your Exp[erimen]t on the \latent/ heat of vapour in Vacuo which you estimated at 1000—I have also notes of an experiment made by Dr. Irvin in the 1764—with a common still—the data are a little inaccurate but it comes out at least 774° for the lat[en]t heat which came out of the Steam —and 750 and upwards for the heat which was employed in produceing it—I have no experim[en]ts of my own on this subject except some made at Kinneil Anno 1765 in a hasty kind of way upon a red hot Kitchin Table to measure that heat which enters Steam when it is formed—one of these experim[en]ts makes the lat[en]t heat 790°—Two others made in the same manner make it 807°—but I shall make some with more accuracy this Summer   my notes of your Experiment on the Dilatation of water when changed into Steam make it 1664 times the bulk of the water —I told Mr. Creech today of two more Subscribers for the Copying apparatus—viz. the Earl of Lauderdale and Will[ia]m Wilson writer here—There will be plenty of them if they once saw the thing put in practice

I am ever
Y[ou]rs
J. Black

[1] William Creech (1745-1815), the son of a Minister of Newbattle, was an eminent Edinburgh bookseller and publisher.

Letter 69

WATT TO BLACK

Cover addressed: 'Doctor Joseph Black/Physician/Edinburgh',
endorsed, 'Mr. Watt June 9th 1780' and numbered '49'. Dol.

London June 9th 1780

Dear Doctor

I am favoured with two letters from you   as to the first, I can only say
that if people will write with Ink that does not yield a copy, or take a
Copy themselves, no danger is to be apprehended   all \double/ trans-
ferred Copies on thick paper unless wrote on purpose are defective and
pale and very easy to be distinguished from originals—Mr. Keir has investigated the causes of inks not copying and we shall prepare and sell
ink of that species at a moderate price   it depends on the {want}
\absence/ of acid unsaturated—I subscribed for you and hope you will
accept of a Press which answers many purposes as well as the copying—
    Our pettition has not yett been read before the Committee but Mr.
Keir's has, and ours comes immediately on the meeting of Parliament
after this adjournment which is on Monday sennight   We are uncertain
whether Mr. F[ordyce] will condescend to carry us through with him,
but I am pretty confident that he must either do it or drop his Bill—For
besides us there are seven or eight more petitions to the same purpose.
But their processes are not formidable, part of them proceed on decomposing hepar sulphuris consequently must first make Glauber salt by ⊕+
and Fordyce is on the same plan only his process is more perfect, \than
the rest/   one man has a patent for doing it by F. ▽ Others only
exchange the vegetable for the Fossil ⊖- by elective attraction—I have
to prevent disputes come to a resolution to go half expence of the
patent with Mr. Keir and am getting a deed of convenant drawn
whereby he assigns to me half the property   you shall come in with me
for any share you desire; but Mr. Keir seems not willing to consider us
but as one person and I think it not worth while to object—I believe
Mr. Keir was as early in the process as ourselves or very nearly so—
We bind ourselves not to engage in any work for this purpose where we
have not {half} ¼ the property or profits and all licences to neutral
persons not be granted except by joint consent—I shall make the best
terms for you I can but at any rate you may depend on having half my
part if you chuse it   A patent cannot be assigned to more than 5 persons,
unless in the way of licence   I shall therefore try to gett your name as
one of these 5 {that is as} conjunct in the patent right but that is not to

93

say that you are not to have the $\frac{1}{2}$ share of the right granted me by Mr. Keir if you chuse it only that you shall have it as right not as licence—I shall write again about the latent heat   shall only mention that should be tryed by {sending some} condensing a quantity of steam in a given quantity of ∇ by weight and not to try too large quantities as cannot be weighed so exactly—We have had terrible doings here but I hope it is now over, I never saw or knew so many people overawed by a most despicable mob.[1]

I remain Dear Sir
Yours most sincerely
James Watt

[1]   The Gordon Riots of which Watt was an eye-witness.

Letter 70

BLACK TO WATT

Cover addressed: 'Mr. James Watt Engineer/Soho/Birming-ham/per Ferrybridge', endorsed in Watt's hand, 'Doctor Black September 1st 1780' and numbered '54'. Dol.

Edinb[urgh] 1st Sep[tembe]r 1780

My Dear Watt

I have expected a letter from you for some time but know well what a Struggle you have with Business and bad health so beg you will not put yourself to the least inconvenience or hurry to gratifye me but take your own leisure—to save you some trouble when you write I think it proper to let you know that I got a short History of Fordyces affair in the House of Commons Committee from my Brother from which it appears that Fordyce himself who applyed for a relaxation of the Duty on Salt was the author of its being refused because he could not get it to himself alone—but my Brother has not wrote me a word concerning our Patent or what was done in it and this I wish to hear of when it is convenient for you—I also beg leave to mention to you that I have never rec[eive]d the Box of Fossils which you wrote to me you had packed up for me the last time you were in Cornwall—If affairs had been more prosperous of late I should have saved you the trouble of writing and have made myself very happy by paying you a visit this Summer but the Situation of some of my Brothers and other Circumst[an]ces has made me excessively stingey of late—Adieu and beleive me ever

Y[ou]rs affect[ionate]ly
Joseph Black

Letter 71

WATT TO BLACK

Cover addressed: 'Doctor Joseph Black/Edinburgh/Via Ferrybridge', endorsed in Black's hand, 'Mr. Watt 15th October 1780'
and numbered '48'. Dol. Also * Dol.

Birmingham Oc[tober] 15th 1780

Dear Doctor

I duely received yours of the 1st Sep[tembe]r—I am exceeding sorry
to hear that any thing has happened which can distress your affairs, and
the more so that it has deprived me of the pleasure of seeing you here
which would have been a very great one I assure you—As Dr. R[oebuck]
continued in london and was constantly ferretting about in every public
office we thought it prudent to delay taking out the patent untill he
should take himself away which has only happened very lately and now
we are cool both Mr. K. and myself doubt whether it will be worth
while to take out a patent at all On my own part I have not had time to
try any exp[erimen]ts of consequence and in the state of my knowledge
on that subject I doubt much whether it would be sufficiently beneficial
though at same time I think improvements might be made on the process
which would render it so—Mr. Keir seems to me to place his principal
dependance on processes for decomposing hepar Sulphuris of which he
knows several—He does not however mean to use ⊕+ but some of the
cheap ☽ salts—He has now engaged with a Mr. Blair[1] in erecting a
works for that and other Chemical purposes about 8 miles from hence—
I wrote to London about your fossils but have not yett got any satisfactory intelligence about them—Shall cause further enquiries to be
made—Have you made any experiments yourself on the terra ponderosa
and what are they?—should be glad if you could send me a small parcel
of that earth \pure/ the same that you have tryed for I cannot find the
same properties in any which I have by me or have got from derbyshire—One Mr Fabroni[2] Librarian at Florence who was here last year
has discovered a cheap solvent of Caoutchouc—I have seen some Gauze
varnished with it but know nothing of the solvent. Its elasticity seems to
be preserved

Some years ago I sent p[e]r waggon via Manchester two Boxes containing a Copying Machine for you which I hope came safe to hand and
that you will accept and use it in remembrance of our friendship—That
business meets with Tolerable success though not so great as we had

reason to expect—Mr. Boulton is now in Cornwall concluding a bargain with the Wheal Virgin Adventurers, who are exceeding dilatory in their motions but I believe will come to—If they do it will be a great aquisition to us. All I pray for is peace and competence; Health I despair of. My Headachs have been worse than usual all this year and particularly so lately

I would have sent you a drawing of a Stand for the Machine but wait opportunity of a Frank

Mr. Garbett will bring any small parcel for me

I ever remain

Dear Doctor

Your Affectionate friend

James Watt

Shall be much obliged to you for your process for making the acid of ☿

Doctor Black

[1] Alexander Blair, like Keir a former army officer.

[2] Giovanni Valentino Mattia Fabbroni (1752–1822) deputy director under F. Fontana of the scientific museum in Florence. Translated the works of Cronstedt and Bergman into Italian.

Letter 72

BLACK TO WATT

Cover addressed: 'Mr. James Watt/Engineer/Soho/Birmingham/By Ferrybridge', endorsed in Watt's hand, 'Doctor Black October 18th 17 {79} 80 about Ink', and numbered '53'. Dol.

Edinb[urgh] 18th Oct[ober] 1780

My Dear Watt

I received your copying machine by the Waggon and as I learned by accident that one had arrived at same time for the D[uke] of Buccleugh I went after having studied my own a little, to Dalkeith, to set up theirs and shew them the managdement of it. These great Folk must have as much trouble and attention saved to them as possible—The Duke was not at home but I shewed it to the Duchess and I hear they have since tryed it with success and are very well pleased with it—For my part I was very much struck with the neatness and propriety of every thing belonging to it—but I am not satisfyed upon the Subject of your Inks tho of this

96

I have not uttered a syllable to any other person—nor shall I do it—You expressly prohibit the use of white wine in makeing Ink the reason for which I should be glad to know   It makes the very best Ink I have yet tryed—This letter is wrote with Ink made with strong white wine about 12 months past   it is perfectly free from the least symptom of mold-iness, flows remarkably black from the pen and becomes jet black by time. and it gives as perfect a Copy as yours or any Ink can do—It has another good property, that of takeing hold of the paper tho applyed with the lightest and most rapid strokes of the pen—I have met with Inks that were tormenting by their not taking hold of some kinds of Paper—John Robison complained to me lately of a bound Paper Book which would not take hold of his Ink   I sent him a little of mine and he was quite charmed with it—But another very great Excellence of white-wine Ink is the security of it from molding—both of your Inks have already molded with me even in the vials—I think I perceive in them the smell of Cloves which have some effect in preserving Ink but I know their power is not very great   I am at present of opinion that Spirit of wine is the best preservative, either added to water or as contained in strong whitewine—and I suppose it is this spirit which makes the Ink so fluent or so readily adherescent—I am sensible too that it encreases the disposition to sink but this is corrected easily with a little addition of Gum—so much for Ink—The First Student for my next Course who entered with me today is a Man from Birmingham called Bache   I asked about you, he said he was a little acquainted with you and that your Fire Engine was now bringing in between 5 and 6 Thousands regularly paid—I hope such good news will be confirmed when I hear from you—remember that you have 2 or 3 letters of mine to answer (and confounded long ones you'l say) but I dont mean to push you, take your own time, only look them over before you write to me   I have now received the Cornish Ores etc for \which/ I most heartily thank you—and shall give you no further trouble upon that subject—my Compliments to Mrs. Watt and beleive me ever

Yours most affectionatly
Joseph Black

After bragging so much of
my Ink I have spoiled my
letter by takeing a Copy with
too wet a paper

Letter 73

WATT TO BLACK

Cover addressed: 'Doctor Joseph Black/Edinburgh/via Ferry-bridge', endorsed in Watt's hand, 'to Dr. Black November [*recte* October] 25th 1780 on copying ink' and numbered '11'. Dol. In Black's hand in crayon, 'Laurence Inglis merch[an]t street'. Also * Dol. [In Williamson's *Edinburgh Directory* from 1773-90, there is an entry: 'Inglis Laurence, writer Merchant Street'].

Birmingham Oc[tobe]r 25th 1780

Dear Doctor

I received yours of the 18th to day—I am very much obliged to you for takeing the trouble to wait upon the Duke of Buccleugh to show the use of the Copying Machine, which I look upon as a great favour

I am sorry that the Ink you got with the machine did not prove good it was good when first made but from some cause not well understood yett by us, the Ink of which that was a part has deposited great part of its Colour and become very thin. That subject is attended with more difficulties than you can be aware of—The following qualities are required—1st that the Ink be capable of being made up in the form of a powder readily soluble in water 2dly that it be fitt for use in an hour of two after it is made—3dly that it be thin and flow readily from the pen 4thly that it do not grow thick or mould by keeping; nor yett deposite much sediment 5thly that it be capable of giving an impression without diffusion, soon after it is wrote with, 6thly that it shall be capable of yielding an impression at the end of 24 hours after it is wrote with and if would do it a longer date would be still more valuable, lastly that the Copy as well as the original keep its Colour

We have occasionaly made ink with all or most of these properties but I am sorry to say that we cannot always succeed which is the more mortifying as we do not know the causes

In order to make a soluble powder we have made an extract of the Galls by boiling in water, \evaporating to dryness/ but it seems that in spite of every precaution this process somehow renders part of the extracted matter unsoluble in $\triangledown$ and \I/ even think disposes part to precipitate afterwards Yett this form of a powder is what is most demanded. We propose to substitute in place of it a thick Robb[1] of Ink which with the addition of double its own quantity of $\triangledown$ shall make

98

ink. This method makes much better ink than the other but is much more bulky for carriage and I fear would not stand to go to the east indies—We have found that the Copying power resides in the Galls, that logwood has it not, that Ink made with vinegar or beer grows thick and loses the property of Copying, that acids communicate that property to ink which has lost it, that sugar also give it but thickens the ink and causes diffusion in the Copy besides that if much is added, the ink almost wholy leaves the original

I think that it also disposes the ink to precipitate very much—I will be much obliged to you for your hints upon this subject on which I should have enlarged further but happened not to take paper enough before my hand——L[or]d Dudley says that he spoke to Lord North about taking off the duty from Salts which he says he means to grant provided the revenue can be secured properly—

I am sorry that I cannot give you so good an account of our gains as you have heard Our income *if regularly paid* would be perhaps about £3000 p[e]r ann[u]m but it is not so, there are many deductions to be made and the expence of carrying on the business is great, as are our debts how ever our prospects are brilliant, our income increases yearly, will have a considerable increase soon in Cornwall, and a much greater one when Wheal Virgin setts to work about a year hence they are to pay £2500 per ann[u]m and Poldice which will go on at \the/ same time 1500 My situation hitherto has been of the most uneasy Sort, and I am so habituated to disappointment that even these splendid prospects cannot raise my spirits to par—Farewell [Signature missing]

Any of the gentlemen in Edin[bu]r[gh] who have subscribed for the machines may have them on writing to Mr. James Wood mason Stationer leadenhall street—who will direct to whom they are to pay them being answerable to us in that article

¹Robb = syrup. N.E.D.

BLACK TO WATT

Cover addressed: 'Mr. James Watt Engineer/Soho/Birming-
ham/By Ferrybridge', endorsed in Watt's hand, 'Dr. Black
October 27th 1780 > of ♀ and ▽ ponderosa' and also, 'Acid of
Tartar and Barite', and numbered '52'. Dol.

Edinb[urgh] 27th Oct[ober] 1780

My dear Watt

I rec[eive]d yours of the 15th the day after I wrote my last to you—I am
obliged to you for your kind concern about my affairs but I did not mean
that they were in the least embarassed, I am perfectly clear of my Brothers
and am resolved to keep myself free from all engagements but it is my
duty to give them assistance so far as I can without hurting myself—I
have put questions to you in former letters about your affairs \to/ which
you need not now give any answer haveing had a conversation with Mr.
Garbett which has satisfyed me—I beleive that better health is the only
thing you have reason to wish for now—do you avoid Butter? it is frequently the Cause of headachs, and most headachs like yours originate in
the Stomach either from rancidity or Acidity—Could not you try rideing to make yourself stronger? It is the only remedy I use for all my
complaints and there is none like it—It is probable that Cold is another
cause of your distresses and that it affects you cheifly in the feet and in
consequence of your sitting too much—The state of my mind with respect to the Patent is precisely the same with yours—I wish to make more
decisive Exper[imen]ts. I have made a few Exper[imen]ts upon the Terra
ponderosa and knew it to be a part[icula]r species of absorbent before I
heard of the Swedish experiments—It is the Basis of the heavy Gypseous
Spar and can be extracted from it by 1st Cementing the Powdered Spar
with Charcoal dust 2ndly applying pure aqua fortis \which/ will then
dissolve the Terra Pond[erosa]—filtre the Sol[ution] and evap[ora]te to
dryness and ignition to drive away the Nitr[ou]s Acid—when you will
have the Terr[a] pond[erosa] in form of Q[uick] Lime—or you may precipitate it from the Aqua fort[is]. I beleive with mild volatile alkali—It is
seldom found pure   its proper[ties] are to attr[act] Acids more strongly
than any caustic Alcali to form with the ⊕→ a Gyps. pond. perfectly insoluble—to form with the Nitr[ou]s Acid a Solution which crystallizes

—\Common/ Calcareous Earth when dissolved in Nitr[ous] Acid will not give Crystals and it was by this quality I discov[er]ed it to be a separate kind of Earth—Small quantities of the Terra ponderosa combined with fixed Air only have been got at lead hills among their Spars, in this State it forms masses composed of closely compacted and long slender crystals convergeing to a point—something like the Zeolite only the Crystals of the Terr[a] pond[erosa] are of a larger size and the mass is more transp[aren]t., greenish coloured and heavier than Zeolite—I beleive however that many fossilists may have it in England under the name of Scotch Zeolite, I shall send you a little of it but I have only a little to spare.

To extract the Acid from Tartar—take 5 ounces of perfectly good Quick lime beat it to small peices and throw it into an Earthern pot with 2 ounces of water at bottom, cover it up and let remain covered 12 or 24 hours, this is the best way of slakeing it—then boil it with 20 lbs. of water and one pound of Crem Tartar several hours—Cool—and decant the water which will contain the alkali of the Tartar   The white sediment is the Selenites Tartar[eu]s or Calx tartarisata—after washing it insipid put it into a large bowl and add ⊕→ *diluted with 3 waters* q.s. to form with the lime A common Gypsum or Calx Vitriolata, thus the > of ♀ is disengagd and dissolved in the liquor which is to be separated from the Gysp. afterwards by filtration—N.B. I perform this filtration by a similar process to that you will see described in the Edinb[urgh] Pharmacop[oeia] last Edition for filtrating Caustic Alcali from the lime—But how am I to know how much ⊕→ I should add? why thus take an equal quantity to the above of the same lime and haveing slaked it in the same manner—put it into a bowl with some water tinged with litmus or Cudbear and gradually add of the same diluted ⊕→ untill it be saturated which you will know by a permanent redness   that is the method I followed—but it is proper to use rather \less/ than the full proportion of the ⊕→ in decompounding the Selenit Tartareous   haveing filtrated the > of Tartar you may evap[ora]te it to dryness but with the most gentle warmth \like that of the Sun/ in the End—being redissolved again it will be quite pure—but it keeps ill in a fluid state being liable to moldiness

I shall be glad to see your \plan of a/ Table for the machine but I have go one already—it is three feet by 2—the machine is fixed at the right hand end of it, the rest of the \Table/ holds the two Books etc.—and it has a drawer the whole length of the Table which draws out of the left hand end—the pressing weight stands {upon} below the cross bar which connects the feet of the Table—and the drawer holds paper and every thing else

I am ever
Yours
Jos. Black

P.S. Send me the Plan of your Table for the sake of Mr. Ferguson Smith and others who have not yet got their machines

Letter 75

WATT TO BLACK

* B.R.L. Boulton and Watt Letter Books.

Birmingham Nov[embe]r 9th 1780

Dear Doctor

I am favoured with yours of the 27th and am much obliged to you for the two valuable processes it contains—I send you inclosed the Engraving of the stand for the machine, on which I have made 2 improvements since it was engraved. The one is making the Shelves draw out like those of a wardrobe and giving them sides and a back 2 inches deep, they run in guides which are fixed above the edges of the sides below their bottoms thus

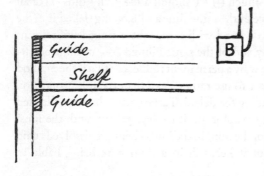

B, shows the manner the guides are fastened to the foot of the table. When the stand is made in this way the distance between the feet should be 25 inches and it ought to be 2 inches wider to admitt the books to be laid open into the Shelves—The second improvement is in the hinge which I have contrived so as to permitt the leaf either to fold up or down at pleasure—the use of folding up is to get at the drawer, and of folding down to prevent the leaf from warping while new and to prevent people from breaking the hinges by letting down the leaf without pulling out the drawer

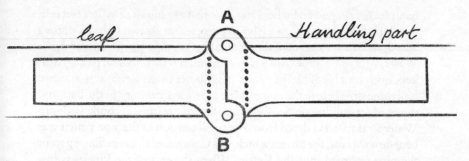

leaf

A

Handling part

B

The Joints A and B are connected by a piece of steel repre[sente]d by the prickt line
When the table folds up it folds at the {leaf A} Joint A When it folds down it folds at the Joint B.

We have made some discoveries in the nature of Ink since I last wrote to you on that subject and hope to do well with that article yett—You will please remark that the table is made as little bulk as it will admit of and being larger will in some cases be an advantage—

I ever remain, Dear Doctor,
Your's most sincerely
James Watt

Doctor Black

Letter 76

WATT TO BLACK

* Dol.

Experiments on Latent heat by James Watt

Birmingham 23d Feb[ruar]y 1781

A pipe of Copper was provided about 5 feet long, 3 inches of one of its ends bent downwards. The copper was about 1/50th. Inch thick, and the Diameter of the pipe was ⅝ of an Inch.

The Straight end of the pipe was fixed on the spout of a Tea Kettle from which the Pipe inclined upwards, so that the Bent end was about 2 feet higher than the spout of the Tea Kettle.

The Tea Kettle was filled with Water halfway up the entry of the Spout; the Lid was fixed Steam tight with some Oat Meal Dough. A Tin pan 4 Inches deep and 6 Inches Diameter had $2\frac{1}{2}$ pounds of Water put into it, which filled it nearly to $2\frac{3}{4}$ Inches deep. This pan was placed upon a Stand, and the very point of the Bent end of the pipe was Immersed in the Water, being first Shut with a Cork, through which a Small passage was kept open by a bit of Goose Quill. The Water in the Kettle was made to boil some time before the point of the pipe was Immersed in the Pan, and it was observed that no Sensible quantity of Steam was condensed into Water so as to fall in drops from the small portion of the pipe which was bent downwards, the Steam which was Condensed in the inclined part of the pipe returned into the Kettle. When the end of the Pipe was immersed in the Cold water, the Steam issuing from it was condensed with a Crackling noise, and began to heat the Water in Contact with it. The Water in the Pan being Constantly Stirred with a Circular Motion the heat was diffused through the whole, and the experiment was continued untill it was Judged that the Water in the Pan had acquired a proper degree of heat

Experiment first

The heat of the Water in the pan at beginning the Experiment was $43\frac{1}{2}°$. When the Exper[imen]t was ended the heat of the water was $89\frac{1}{2}°$ difference, or heat gained $46°$. The Weight of the Water at beginning the exper[imen]t was $2\frac{1}{2}$ pounds equal to 17280 Grains. After the experiment, by the Addition of Condensed Steam, the Weight of the water was 18032 Grains consequently the Steam Condensed into water was 752 Grains. Then 18032 Grains x by ($46°$ heat gained and by $\frac{1}{2}°$ allowed for the heat of the Pan $= 46\frac{1}{2}°$) $= 838488°$ which $\div$ by 752 Grains, the Weight of the Water, which when in the form of Steam contained that heat is $=$ $1115°$ But to this must be added the heat of the Water previous to the Experiment $43\frac{1}{2}°$ and gives $1158\frac{1}{2}°$ which is the sum of the sensible and Latent heat of the Steam reckoning from the o point of Fahrenheits Scale, from which if we deduct $213°$ the Sensible heat of the Steam remains $945\frac{1}{2}°$ its Latent heat The Water was weighed very Accurately, the Tin pan and a piece of oiled paper fitted to its inside being first Counter poised when they were quite dry. After the Water had received its heat from the Steam, it was thoroughly Mixed so as to be all of one heat.

Immediately after the Thermometer had shown what the heat was, which was in less than half a Minute, the water was covered with the Disc of oiled paper to prevent evaporation, which would otherwise have unavoidably lessened its weight during the Operation of Weighing. The

Thermometer with which the heats were measured became Stationary in less than 10 Seconds. The Duration of the exper[imen]t was generally from four to Six Minutes. The First and Second experiments were tried without the Cork in the Mouth of the Pipe, which was used in the *three* remaining ones. The Second experiment was supposed to have lost a little Weight as some few drops of Water were forced out by the Steam

The pan was set in a Cold place after the Experiment, where the Air was at 40° and Stood there for half an hour, when it was Considered that it was come to the heat of the Place 2 pounds of Water at 76° was then poured into it and after the Mixture the heat was found to be 75½° Then for every 35½° with 2 pounds of Water, there must be half a degree allowed for the heat of the pan, and half a degree for every 44° with 2½ Pounds of Water

5th March 1781 A Short Copper Pipe was procured, about 2 feet long and ¾ Inch dia[mete]r 6 Inches of one end of the Pipe was bent downwards and the Straight end was fixed in the nose of the Kettle the Cork was used as before. See Experiments No 6, 7 and 8

Number of Exper[imen]ts	Heat of Cold Water	Heat of Hot Water	Heat gained	Weight of Cold Water	Weight of Steam Cond[ense]d	Total Weight of the Water	Sum of heat above the o point	Latent heat
				Grains	Grs.	Grs.		
					Gr[ain]s	Gr[ain]s		
1	43½°	89½°	46°	17280	752	18032	1158½°	945½°
2	44½°	86½°	42°	17280	700	17980	1135½°	922½°
3	44½°	98°	53½°	17280	888	18168	1148½°	935½°
4	44½°	73½°	29°	17280	462	17742	1176½°	963½°
5	44½°	67¼°	22¾°	17280	365	17645	1155½°	942½°
6	47½°	87°	39½°	17280	636	17916	1173½°	960½°
7	49°	84½°	35½°	17280	582	17862	1153°	940°
8	47°	87½°	40½°	17280	667	17947	1150°	937°

N:B The 4th and 6th experiment are suspicious, in the 6th: it was thought that the Pan gained some heat from a hot board not withstanding that a thick woolen Cloth was always put under the pan—in the other experiments care was taken to put a board of the heat of the room under the cloth—nothing could be done with certainty untill the oiled paper dish was applied to the surface of [here the ms. ends]

WATT TO BLACK

* Dol.

James Watt (Birmingham) to Dr Black

Mar[ch] 8th 1781

Dear Doctor

Annexed I send you some experiments on the latent heat of steam made with all the accuracy I am master of The only point remaining is to ascertain the degree of accuracy of the thermometer used which I believe is tolerably good and I have examined the points of freezing and boiling ▽ on it and found them right—As soon as I am furnished with a Thermometer that can be thoroughly depended on I will make the Comp-[ariso]n and advise you—I made a great many more experiments but not having found out the loss of weight by evaporation during the weighing they were good for nothing—I shall be glad of your Criticisms on these experiments when convenient   I intend to try some others on similar subjects when leisure will permit but that is seldom and at this season I have such languid health that it is seldom I am fitt for them   I have according to your advice abstained from butter and fat and find no difference in my head aches tho I think my stomach is not quite so subject to be acid—excuse brevity and believe me ever to remain

Your's most sincerely
James Watt

Dr. Priestly is about publishing a new volume in which there are some curious facts particularly on nitrous air which maintain [sic] flame at a great rate but extinguishes animal life it is made by disolving Iron in solution of copper in nitrous Acid—He has also obtained great quantities of Dephlogisticated air from Allum and amazing quantities from Nitre by heat only—

My Business will not probably soon permit me to think or act in the Alkali business—I therefore told Mr. Keir to write to you about the patent he means to take out though I realy believe he means to follow some other process than the Ψ   some hepar one—As to myself I resign all thoughts of it, *sine die*

Yours again JW.

BLACK TO WATT

Cover addressed: 'Mr. James Watt Engineer/at Soho/Birmingham/by Ferrybridge', endorsed in Watt's hand, 'Dr. Black March 31st 1781' and numbered '51'. Dol.

Edinb[urgh] 31 March 1781

My dear Watt

I am much obliged to you for yours of the 8th and like your method of makeing the Experiments perfectly well—but in attempting to examine them I found an Error in the Calculation which immediatly stopped me —You say the weight of the condensing Water was at first 2½ *pounds* = *17280 gr[ains]* but 2½ pounds averd[upois] are equall to 17500 gr[ains]— as this affects all that follows I must beg your correction of it

In drawing out your Table I would like better the following method

Number of Experim[en]ts	Temp[era]ture of Cold ▽	Weight of Ditto including an allowance for the pan	Ditto after Condens[ation] of Steam	{ steam condensed }	Temp[era]ture after Ditto	additional heat × by the whole	the last sum ÷ by condensed Steam

No—I find yours is just as good, or any method by which the facts as they appear to the Senses are exactly recorded—Have you seen Scheeles Book on Fire[1]—I find it a most curious and ingenious Performance—how far it is Sound I cannot yet Judge

It is so very ill translated that you will find great difficulty in reading it and I wish I were at your lug to help you—My Compliments to Mrs. Watt and beleive me ever

Yours affect[ionate]ly
Joseph Black

Pray is the Money comeing in briskly

You still owe me £40 or some such matter but I do not desire to have it untill you are Rich

[1] Carl Wilhelm Scheele (1724 1786), chemist. His book *On Air and Fire* was published in 1777.

WATT TO BLACK

* Dol.

James Watt (Birmingham) to Dr. Black,   *Ap[ri]l 9th 1781*
£40.. 0.. 0
Forty Days after date please pay to the order of James Watt Forty
pounds sterling value received from ... Boulton and Watt
To Mr. William Matthews Merch[an]t—London No 6 Green lettice
lane
Pay to Dr. Joseph Black or order value in acc[oun]t—James Watt

Dear Doctor,

I was favoured with yours of the 31st 2 days ago   I am very much
ashamed of having been so long your Debtor, but I could not avoid it
without putting myself to some inconvenience as our Business never
defrayed its own current Charges untill last year and the product of that
was swallowed up in a very large pay[men]t: several P[aymen]ts we were
obliged to make at Christmas   I have therefore been always in debt to the
partnership but am now clear or nearly so. As to being rich that is out of
the question and to make you wait till then would be trespassing too
much on your patience which I have encroached upon too much already.
let it suffice that it is not now inconvenient to make the payment and that
I hope you will accept of my sincere thanks for the time you have indulged me—Whatever Ball[an]ce may be still due you I will either
settle with you at meeting or order you pay[men]t of immediately as is
most agreable
In relation to the experiments on latent heat I forgot in my last to
mention to you that upon examining the Grain weights that is the
Weights less than ½ an oz which I used in these experiments I found the
oz to be 432 of *these* grains and that upon a more exact scrutiny into
every thing concerned in the experiments I found that some of these
smaller weights were not exact subdivisions of others—I have therefore
since corrected all the weights so that 437½ of them are an oz avoir du
poise and have also compared the thermometer with 2 others and found
it to agree with them after which I have made 3 several experiments
which make the sum of the heats 1167°—1166°—1134°—In the first
exp[erimen]t a small quantity of the condensed ▽ was lost which might
make the Latent heat appear greater—The last exp[erimen]ts were not

objectible except that the last was continued untill the ∇ had attained
to 102°—In the exp[erimen]ts sent you as the ounce weight and the
half oz weight were exact subdivisions of the Pound the error could only
lie in the odd Grains and therefore whether we Calculate the oz as
containing 432 or 437½ grs it is still the same aliquot part of the pound
and by reckoning them so does not make above 1° in the result of most
of the experiments and in some none at all—
I was present the other day at Dr. Priestleys when he obtained excellent
dephlogisticated Air from Gypsum by a violent heat—It first produced
fixt Air and some phlogisticated air if I remember right—I have read
Scheeles Book on fire with Attention but as I looked on part of it as
borrowed from you without owning the obligation I was perhaps too
much out of humour to see its merit though I understood it very well—
I will however read it again on your reccommendation—Mr. Keir
asked me some time ago if I chose to continue to bear ½ expence in
extracting the $\ominus_r$ patent   I told him I did not chuse it as I could spare
no time from my present business to do anything in it—I reccommended to him to write to you about it   I was informed since by
another hand that he is taking out a pat[en]t for the 3 kingdoms and I
know that he is building very great works—If you think it worthy
any thing you should now make your terms—though I do not believe
he means to use that method yett I am not sure of it

[Then a large space]

                                    I ever remain with Affection your's JW

                                Letter 80

                            BLACK TO WATT

Cover addressed: 'Mr. James Watt Engineer/Birmingham/by
Ferrybridge', endorsed in Watt's hand, 'Dr. Black April 23d
1781 State of accounts' and numbered '50'. Dol.

                                Edinb[urgh] 23d April 1781

Dear Watt
    I rec[eive]d yours of the 9th Inst[an]t with your Dr[af]t for £40
indorsed to me of the same date payable in London 40 days after date

109

and addressed to Mr. William Matthews Merch[an]t in London which brings accounts between us very nearly to a balance   here follows a State of them

1st I have your Bill dated 14th Feb[ruary] 1766 for £50 payable to me one day after date on the back of which I have noted payment of the Principal Sum but not the Interest on the 19th March 1772—The Interest due at that time on this Bill was £15..5s.   this I have considered as balanced by the Organ which I got from you about that time and have noted this also the back of said Bill—

2dly I have my Bill on you accepted and dated 28th Feb[rua]ry 1774 for £141..10..—payable 100 days after date or on the 8th June 1774— on the Back of this Bill I have noted my haveing rec[eive]d from you a Bill on Mr. Rob[er]t Muirhead of Glasgow for £118..2..6 payable the 1st June 1776 which Bill was paid——turn [i.e. to next page]

	£	s.	d.
Interest of £141..10 from the 8th June 1774 when the Bill became due, to the 1st June 1776 when the payment noted on back of said Bill was made	13	19	11
Ballance which remained due of the Principal Sum—	23	7	6
Interest of this Ballance from 1st June 1776 to the 19th may 1781 when your £40 Indorsem[en]t to me becomes due.........................	5	16	1½
	£43	3	6½

Therefore when the above Indorsement for £40 is paid you will owe me only £3.. 3.. 6½ which may well remain untill we meet— and untill then you may keep this letter as a settlement of accounts between us—

I am sorry to find you expressing doubts of your becomeing rich— I assure you it will give me very great uneasiness if you do not—and I am anxious that you should wean yourself from your perpetual plodding and labour and accustom yourself to some amusement and relaxation by getting into pleasant Company in the Evenings and by makeing excursions to fly from business for a while—I have a notion that Buxton would do you good—Mrs. Roebuck and Miss will be there this Summer—and we have proposed it to Gilbert Meason who is not well—

I am perfectly satisfyed with your manner of makeing the Exper[i-men]ts on the latent heat of Steam and suppose you are equally right

in your Calculations but have not time at present to examine them—
Dr. Preistlys Exp[erimen]t upon Gypsum does not surprise me I
suppose the Vitriolic acid of the Gypsum became Phlogisticated and it
appears from Experience that in all Cases in which Bodies are Phlogisticated by application of heat alone to them a quantity of Empyreal
air is produced and according to Scheele it is produced by the Decomposition of a part of the heat—I wonder at your accusation of
Sch[eel]e for my part I am not sensible that he deserves [it] I wish we
had his Exper[imen]ts on Manganese and Arsen[ic] I have lately made
some on Manganeze and find the purest I can get contains some lead
and I suspect that the Metal you got from it was mostly Lead—The
Swedish Chemists also have got a Metal from it \they call it Magnesium/
which they say is hard and brittle and more difficult to melt than Iron—
but they found that this metal contained Iron and they never could
separate the whole Iron from it——Beware of—— He has no
Candour and I think he is not free from Hypocrisy and Malevolence
—I have had several letters lately from P. Wilson who has been
makeing some curious Experiments and tells me he has made an
improvement in the use of your \Copying/ Machine which you have
still further improved I shall be glad to know what this is—
Present my Compliments to Mrs. Watt and beleive me ever
Yours affect[ionate]ly Joseph Black

Letter 81

BLACK TO WATT

Cover addressed: 'Mr. James Watt Engineer/Birmingham/by
Ferrybridge', endorsed in Watt's hand, 'Dr. Black May 1st 1781'
and numbered '49'. Dol.

Edinb[urgh] 1st May 1781

My dear Watt
    I am much obliged to you for the notice you have given me in some
of your late letters of Mr. Keirs being about to take out a Patent for
the manufacture of fossil Alkali from Common Salt I am also advised of
it by my Brother James and have been considering these two days what
I should do—I have very little inclination to enage myself in a business

of that kind immediatly being in the present state of my health sufficiently occupied by my Lectures and other Dutys as a Professor but I am loth to relinquish the thing altogether and let it pass out of my reach

I should like best to retain a right to a participation of the Patent at any time hereafter when I chose it, I paying in that case a proportional share of the Expence of the Patent with Interest—If I remember right these were the Terms which Mr. Keir proposed to you or to us both formerly—I shall be much obliged to you if you will be so good as to converse with him upon my account which I give you authority to do, and let me know how he is inclined—make my compliments to him at the same time and return him my hearty thanks for an ingenious little apparatus which he sent me some years agoe—for trying the Effect of diff[eren]t Sub[stan]ces in diminishing Air—It gives me pain to give you this trouble knowing that you have enough of your own but I do not know what other method to take for opening a Correspondence with him upon this Subject and I am so ignorant about Patents that I shall be in danger of blundering—

Yours most affect[ionate]ly
Joseph Black

Letter 82

ROBISON TO WATT

Cover addressed: 'To Mr. James Watt/to the Care of Mr. Bolton/
Birmingham' endorsed in Watt's hand, 'Professor Robison
October 22d 1781' and numbered '1'. Dol.

Edin[bu]r[gh] Oct[obe]r 22 1781

Dear Sir

I have twice written† to you within these five Months, and as I have not received any answer, I am convinced that these Letters have not come to your Hands. My last related to an experiment on the gravitation of the Earth which I thought you would have an excellent opportunity of trying in Cornwall. Of this I shall write again very soon. I beg leave to trouble you on the Subject of my first. It was to sollicit your Employment for a young Lad, a near relation of mine,

---

†'not received' has been inserted above, presumably by Watt, who has underlined 'twice written'.

112

Peter Ewart[1] by name, who wishes to be educated as a Mill Wright, or in any good branch of the business of a Civil Engineer. I could not find so proper a Master as yourself, and I flatter myself that you would find him a very deserving Pupil. His father is a Clergyman near Dumfries, and has given the Boy a very good Education, but with other views. But the Boys inclinations are so much turned to mechanics, and his mind so much catched by any thing of this kind, that we all agree that this is the line of business in which he is most likely to succeed. His constitution is healthy and strong, so that he is perfectly fitted for the hard labour by which he is to get his living. If therefor you can find Employment for him, I shall look on him as setting out in the most favourable manner, and I will flatter myself that you will find some pleasure in being serviceable to the freind of an old acquaintance. What has made me write just now is that the Countess of Hoptoun [sic] has written in his behalf to Mr. Bolton, and has referred to my recommendation of him to you This will be unintelligible to you both if my Letter on this Subject has miscarried. I have directed this to Mr. Bolton's care in case of your absence, and beg the favour of your answer as soon as convenient, informing me whether you can do me this favour and on what terms. I ever am with great regard and best Wishes for your happiness

D[ea]r Sir
Your ob[edien]t h[um]ble Serv[an]t
John Robison

Be so kind as to offer my
Compliments to Mr. Bolton

[1] Peter Ewart (1767–1842), engineer. Apprenticed to Boulton and Watt as a millwright; later a cotton-spinner in partnership with George Lee; inspector of naval dockyards; vice-president of the Manchester Literary and Philosophical Society.

Letter 83

WATT TO ROBISON

* B.R.L. Boulton and Watt Letter Books.

Mr. John Robison

Cosgarne Truro Cornwall
Nov[embe]r 1st 1781

Dear Sir

Last post brought me your letter of 22d Oct[obe]r; but none of the other two you mention ever came to hand. I am exceedingly flattered

113

by your good opinion of me and if it can be made agreeable to Mr. Ewarts parents on the terms which we shall propose I shall be glad to have so usefull an Apprentice as your letter causes me to believe he will prove but as Mr. Boulton is not now with me I cannot fix the terms untill I see him or know his sentiments only this far, that the Apprenticeship must be for seven years, his parents to find him Clothes, and we paying him a reasonable allowance in place of board, which he cannot have at either of our houses—I should be very happy to try any experiment which you propose that is within my power; but I know not if you are apprized that this is not a mountainous County their being no hill higher than arthur's seat; but there is a \perfectly/ perpendicular shaft 150 fathoms deep under the surface and 110 fathoms below the level of the sea, but it must be remarked that shaft is very much encumbered with pumps and timber, so that I believe a line could scarcely be stretched from the top to the bottom without being bent— The drawing shafts are seldom perpendicular   otherwise they are Clear   I have no Barometer if any is required in the experiment and if you mean to weigh a body hanging by a wire to the bottom, by a weight at the top—I fear it cannot be done—nevertheless I shall be glad to know your experiment, and shall make it if I can and if it does not require long time for of that I am not master. The air and water in the mines here is frequently 70^d—caused by decomposition of minerals
With best respects to all my good friends with you
                                                                Dear Sir
                                        Your ob[edien]t humble serv[an]t
                                                              James Watt

excuse brevity I have som vexatious business to discuss this Post

Letter 84

BLACK TO WATT

Cover addressed: 'Mr. James Watt Engineer/Birmingham/per Ferrybridge', endorsed in Watt's hand, 'Doctor Black September 7th 1782 about the water of Wanlock head River', and numbered '48'. Dol.

Edinb[urgh] 7th Sep[tember] 1782
Dear Watt
    Mr. Meason applyed to me at your desire to examine the water with which his Engine is Supplyed, on account of its corroding the

piston rod—and I readily undertook it for your sake tho I should hardly have done as much for him his behaviour haveing put me out of humour with him—I rcccivcd from him first 1 bottle of water from the Cistern of the Engine and 1 bottle from the Boiler—but \afterwards/ applyed for more Samples and got 2 Bottles from the Cistern 2 from the Boiler 1 from an old Level which is the principal supply of the Cistern and 1 from a burn which is an assistant supply—here is the list of these as copied from his letter which came with them

1 bottle of Petersike water which is the Burn
1 bottle of Beltingrain old Level water
2 Bottles from the Cistern
2 Bottles from the boiler

I also received some crust about 1/12 of an Inch thick from the internal surface of the Boiler—

I made a number of Experiments with these waters of which I shall only give you the conclusive ones and the result—The result is that the Water of the Level contains a quantity of fixed air tho only a small quantity, it is perceptible in it as follows—1st it is perceptible by the taste of a person who has a delicate taste. 2dly When a Bottle of this water is opened and the water poured immediatly into a Glass the air begins to extricate itself and forms numerous and remarkable globules on the Surface of the Glass—or if poured from the bottle into a deep tube or Cylindrical Glass the air is seen to rise thro the water as in a fermenting liquor—3dly—When \I/ dropped 6 or 8 drops of Infusion of Litmus into a Glass of this water the Litmus was tingd quite red by it which redness afterwards gradually disappeared by letting the Glass stand the Litmus resuming its natural Colour—This is the nicest Exper[imen]t I know for the detection of fixed air in water and I think it is of Consequence to you since it appears that fixed Air in the water which supplyes fire Engines is an Enemy in more ways than one— and this Experiment will discover the smallest quantity of it—a quantity much smaller than what can be discovered by lime water— the above level water did not produce the least turbidness in lime Water in any proportion that I could mix them—

The Exper[imen]t is made thus—Pour into one Wine Glass about 3 inches deep of the water to be examined—Pour into another similar Glass as much pure Common water or destilled water—drop into each Glass 6 8 or 10 drops of Infusion of Litmus in destilled water but give the same number of drops to each glass and after stirring set the glasses together on a Sheet of white paper and look down into them—If there be fixed air in the water it will be manifestly red when compared with the other and this redness will afterwards gradually disappear—in a Glass of the above size and depth it will be about 48 hours before the redness is entirely \gone/

But if you use Cylindrical Glasses and fill them about 6 Inches deep the redness is more strickeing upon looking down into them and it may require 10 or 12 days to make it disappear—but waste of time is avoided in either case by boiling the \tinged/ water about a quarter of an hour which dissipates the redness at once—I also found that 20 grains weight of Limewater to each Ounce of the *Cistern Water* were sufficient to take off the red tinge—

From the other Exper[imen]ts I found, 1st That the Crusts of the boiler were merely calcareous with a small mixture of ochre—2d that the Level water did not contain Vitriolic acid in any form—3d That it contained a hardly perceptible quantity of muriatic acid and a small quantity of calcareous earth—4 The Burn Water turnd out much the same in the two last respects but was quite free from fixed air— The qualities of the water from the boiler you will easily imagine—

I must leave you to prescribe the Remedy—I suppose they cannot depend on the Burn water alone as it would freese in winter and the Remedy of lime water will subject the boiler to be more encrusted—

Your temporary expedient of mixing Soap with the lubricating grease may have some effect in preserving the Piston rod but it will not sensibly diminish the loss of power which the air occasions—

I am told there are found in Cornwall some Coarse Rubys Saphirs Hyacinths and Garnets in their native Crystallized State—If you can procure me two or three Specimens of each which would serve for shewing in my Lectures I would be content to give a little money for them You may perhaps know at what rate they can be had—When you see Mr. Keir present my best Compliments to him and many thanks for his Communications by Mr. Playfair[1] I shall always consider them as confidential and I wish I could give him any assistance but he has more knowledge of the matter than I

Dr. Hutton desires me to make his best Comp[limen]ts and I am ever

My Dear Watt
Yours affect[ionate]ly
Joseph Black

[1] John Playfair (1748–1819), mathematician and geologist. Joint-professor of mathematics in the University of Edinburgh, 1785–1805; became professor of natural philosophy, 1805.

Letter 85
WATT TO BLACK

Cover addressed: 'Doctor Joseph Black/Edinburgh', endorsed in Watt's hand 'December 13th 1782 about the Doctors discoveries and some that I claim', and numbered '47'. Dol. Further endorsed, 'Dr. Priestley's Experiments upon the conversion of Water into Air   The allusion in this letter to building my house on the Doctors ground relates only to the points herein mentioned and not to the inventions of the steam Engine'.

Birmingham, Dec[embe]r 13th 1782

Dear Doctor

I wrote you some time ago, and promised you some Growan Clay in its native state, but have not been able to fullfill my promise as though it has been sent off from Cornwall for some time it has not yett come to hand and I fear is lost—

Mr. De Luc[1] was here lately, and told me that he was now writing some thing on heat and on the nature of elastic fluids, and begged I would explain to him, some of my experiments and theories of that fluid which I complied with in part, but could not do it without first explaining your theories of Latent heat of which he wanted to know more than I could tell him or chose to do without your consent—He is a man of Great modesty and most engaging manners—Is a great Admirer of you from what he has heard of your discoveries; thinks you have been ill used by Dr. C[rawfor]d and other people who have endeavoured to Rob you of the merit of your discoveries and wishes to be made able to do you Justice. As he will take upon himself the trouble of being the Editor of whatever you please to communicate, either as received directly from yourself or through me. If therefore you should Chuse to communicate any thing, I think you may depend on his doing you Justice, in publishing as yours whatever you Claim

If it is not agreable to you to furnish any materials I shall only explain to him more fully your doctrine of the latent heat of steam; but in doing that I know not how to avoid mixing what may have been the suggestions of my own mind with what I have learnt from you which I would wish to {you} do as my suggestions may do your theory no honour—What I mean to tell him that I think my own, is the trying the experiment on the latent heat *in vacuo* and the finding it to be greater than under the pressure of the Atmosphere—The exp[erimen]ts to ascertain the different degrees of heat at which water boils under different pressures—the expansion which steam in its perfect state receives from heat and the experiments on the bulk of water when converted into steam together with a theory which I have devised which accounts for the boiling heats of the water not following a Geometrical progression, and showing that as {water} steam parts with its latent heat as it aquires sensible heat or is more compressed, that when it arrives at a certain point it will have no latent heat and may \under proper compression/ be an elastic fluid nearly as specifically heavy as water and at which point I conceive it will again change its state and become something else than steam or water   My Opinion has been that it would then become air, which many things had led me to conclude and which is confirmed by an experiment which Dr. Priestley made the other day in his usual way of Groping about, as he had succeeded in turning the acid into air by heat only, he wanted to try what water would become in like circumstances. He \under/ saturated some very caustic lime with an ounce of Water, and subjected it to a white heat in an earthen retort, He fixed a Balloon between the receiver and the retort, No water nor *moisture* came over but a quantity of Air $=$ in weight to water viz. 200 oz measures, a very small part of w[hi]ch was fixt air and the rest—of the nature of Atmospheric air but rather more Phlogisticated, he has repeated the experiment with the same results—Mr. Keir also presents his Compliments to you   he is going to publish a new edition of his dictionary and makes the same request that Mr. De Luc does—as he must now say some thing on the subject of heat which he formerly declined hoping you would have done it yourself; He wishes to have his information from the fountain head and to give to Caesar those things which are Caesars—In relation to these things which I look upon as my own If you think my title to any of them bad I will chearfully resign it if you claim it and shall at all events own that I have built my house on the foundation of your theory of Latent heat and that I owe a just way of thinking on these subjects to you—Mr. De Luc will be here again about the beginning of February, and I wish as soon as proves convenient that you would give me a few hints how you would have me act in the matter, as I have it much at heart to do what would prove most agreeable to you in it

It will also give me great pleasure to hear of your health and also that of all my good friends with you—to whom I beg to be remembered—My own health is as it usd to be none of the best, and I think my vexations encrease faster than my wealth—Mrs. Watt and my family are all well, she desires to be remembered to you. I remain Dear Doctor mostly [*sic*] Affect[ionate]ly Yours—J. Watt

I should have wrote more fully but you see I have exhausted the measure of paper which I had allowed myself—I should have told you that we have succeeded in making a tilting work perfectly regular by means of a steam engine and with one fourth part of the power which would have raised *the quantity of* ▽ *necessary to drive it* / hammer 120 lb— rises 8 inches—strikes about 300 blows pr minute / Cylinder 15 inches dia[mete]r / Cyl[inde]r 4 feet stroke

[1] J. A. de Luc (1729–1817). Born Geneva. Took up residence in London in 1770. Appointed reader to the Queen in 1773. Honorary Professor of Philosophy and Geology in Göttingen, 1798–1806. Returned to England and died at Windsor.

Letter 86

BLACK TO WATT

Cover addressed: 'Mr. James Watt Engineer/at Birmingham/ Via Ferrybridge', endorsed in Watt's hand, 'Dr. Black January 30th 1783 acknowledges my title to the discoveries mentioned in my letter of December 13th 1782' and numbered '47'. Dol.

30 January 1783

My dear Watt

There is nothing I meet with now that gives me so much pleasure as your letters, excepting those parts of them in which you mention your health and your vexations; when I come to these I exclaim "Good God why cannot I find the Philosophers Stone that I may be enabled to releive my Freinds from their Diseases and their Distresses."—But tho I feel a painfull Sympathy with you on such occasions I wish to hear every thing that relates to you and I would beg of you to write to me more particularly on this very Subject were I not Sensible that it would give you a great deal of trouble to explain such matters to me and in the busy restless state of your mind to add to your trouble would be unpardonable as I am persuaded that nothing would conduce so much to your releif and better health than relaxation and ease and amusement— You may however give me a few lines when you have any new Experiments or Discoveries such as you mention, to communicate. Early knowledge of these things being of some Consequence to me—I have thought upon your conversation with Monsieur de Luc and am very much flattered by his Opinion of me as I have a very high Esteem of his genius and abilities;—nor have I the smallest doubt of his Candor or any Suspicion that he would fail to do me ample Justice were he to be the Editor of what I have done on the Subject of heat—But I assure you that I have already prepared a part of that Subject for publication and that I am resolved next summer to prepare the rest and give it to the World such as it is—This is my fixed resolution and I am sorry that it is inconsistent with the freindly offer of Mons[ieu]r de Luc.

It gives me also particular concern that I cannot gratifye Mr. Keir[1] in this matter to whom I reckon myself under great obligations—but perhaps the inconvenience to both of these Gent[leme]n will not be great even if they should chuse to see what I have to say before they publish—it will delay their publications only some months or at most one year supposing that they were nearly ready at present†—as for what you have done on these Subjects you have certainly a right to communicate it to the Public in what manner you please but I think you ought to do it in such a manner as to derive from it some Profit as well as Reputation and if you chuse to make it a part of my Publication I shall certainly think myself bound to give you a share of what I make by it proportioned to the number of Pages which it fills and I shall willingly either receive it from you in your own composition or express it myself as well as I can—in which case it will be necessary that I pay you a Visit or that we have a meeting some how or other†— Having thus answered the principal part of your letter I can only for the present return you my thanks for the rest which contains very curious matter and some of it appearing to me very surprizing—but I have no time to spare just now—Adieu then and present my best Complim[en]ts to Mrs. Watt—I am

My Dear Freind—
Yours most affect[ionate]ly
Joseph Black

Edinb[urgh] 30 Jan[uar]y 1783

[1] This probably refers to James Keir's *Dictionary of Chemistry*, of which the first part was published in Birmingham 1789 and London 1790, but the second part never appeared.

† The section between the two daggers has been bracketed—presumably by Watt.

Letter 87

WATT TO BLACK

Cover addressed: 'Doctor Joseph Black/Edinburgh/via Ferrybridge', endorsed 'From J Watt 3d February 1783' and numbered '46'. Dol. Further endorsed as follows:

'Mr. Luc about to publish on heat
urges Dr. Black to publish his discoveries through him
Must otherwise himself publish his own claims
Annoyed by plagiarists of his improvements of the Steam
Engine
Mr de Luc is just returned from Paris and states Lavoisier
to be at work on the subject of heat
Dr. Priestleys Experiments on turning Water into Air
His own preconceived notions upon that subject'.

Birmingham Feb[ruar]y 3d 1783

Dear Doctor
    I wrote you some time ago informing you that Mr. De Luc was
intending to publish some thing upon elastic fluids and other subjects
connected with them and that he desired me to request from you the
communication of such of your theories and experiments on these subjects as you should judge proper which he would publish as your discoveries either as communicated by yourself or as communicated by
me as you should chuse, and at the same time he wished me to add
such experiments as I had made after you on the subject of steam—I
have yet received no answer to this letter which makes me fear that I
have been too presuming in my request, I hope however that you will
impute it to the desire I have to set your fame in the light it merits, and
which I think you have neglected too long. For my own part I have
little ambition or desire to publish any of the few experiments I have
made, but I find myself so sett upon by many of my friends to do it that
I cannot longer resist their importunities, though neither my health nor
leisure enable me to repeat the experiments with the necessary attention.
One thing promps me more than any other which is that we have been
so besett with plagiaries that If I had not a very good memory of my
doing it their impudent assertions would lead me to doubt whether I
was the author of any improvement on the steam engine, and the ill
will of those of those [*sic*] we have most essentially served, whether
such improvements have not been highly predjudicial to the common-
wealth. There is one fellow at Paris[1] who has the impudence to give

himself out as the author of the invention and is believed to be so there by many   I must mortify his pride, and assert my own rights which I cannot do more effectually than by showing His ignorance of the principles it is made upon. Mr. De Luc writes his Book in French and publishes it at Paris, and As he is an author which will be read by all men of philosophical learning there I look upon it as A good opportunity

I have a letter from him to day advising that he is just returned from paris and will be here in about a fortnight   I shall transcribe one paragraph of his letter

Les Chimistes de Paris s'occupent beaucoup Aujourdhui de la Chaleur et les Modifications des [sic] *ses transmissions de grand Mathematiciens se joignent a eux; car la Theorie de ces transmissions au Communications donnent lieux a de fort beaux problemes. Messrs. Lavoisier et De la Place² entrautres sont en grand travail et publieront. Enfin ill et* [sic] *certain qu'on commence a fouiller vivement dans les vraies bases de la Physique Ainsi je vous prie mon cher Monsieur a vous preter a y cooperer—*

Dr. Priestley has been going on with his experiments of turning water into air, and has discovered many facts which seem in some degree contradictory to each other. He finds the mixture of quick lime and ▽ heated in a glass vessel gives no air, only ▽, but that ▽ alone put into the stone ware retort gives air in great quantities ie. even the 8th part of its weight—That olive oil and or oil of turpentine in that earthen retort produce very pure inflamable air—That water being put into a gun barrel and distilled over slowly gives no air but on being confined by a cock and lett out by puffs it produces much air, which agrees with my theory and also coincides with what I have observed in Steam Engines—In some cases I have seen the 10th of the bulk of the water of Air extricated or made from it

Hopeing to hear from you soon—I am with a feeling remembrance of all my good friends with you my Dear Sir

Your's most Affectionately
James Watt

remember me particularly to
Mr. Clarke, Dr. Hutton and Mr. Robison—lett me hear how they do

---

¹ William Blakey, a hydraulic engineer, invented a steam-engine on Savery's principle used to operate pumps (see J. J. Bootsgezel, 'William Blakey, a rival to Newcomen', in *Trans. Newcomen Society*, 16 (1935–36), pp. 97–110). He petitioned through a friend against the extension of Watt's patent in 1775 but later withdrew.
² La Place, Pierre Simon, Marquis de (1749–1827), mathematician.

Letter 88
BLACK TO WATT

Cover addressed: 'Mr. James Watt Engineer/Birmingham/Via
Ferrybridge', endorsed in Watt's hand, 'Dr. Black 13th February
1783 ascribes to J[ames] W[att] the Sole honour of the invention
of the Steam Engine' and numbered '46'. Dol.

Edinb[urgh] 13 Feb[rua]ry 1783

My dear Watt

I rec[eive]d yours of the 3d Inst[ant] and by observeing the Dates I
see that you would receive my ans[wer] to your former, two or three
days after you wrote it—

In my last I acquainted you that it is my fixed Resolution to publish
next Summer—at present I am so much occupyed with the busyest part
of my Course and other matters that I cannot do any thing in that
Business—what you tell me in your last gives me a different notion of
Mr. De Luc's intention from that I had formed before   I had imagined
that he meant to publish in England and in the English Language—His
intention to publish in France and in the French Language makes a
consid[era]ble difference and if it was in my power to sit down just
now and give him an *Esquisse* of what I have done and mean soon to
publish on heat I should do it with pleasure† and I think it is very
proper for you to give him a short account of your Discoveries and
Speculations—and particularly to assert clearly and fully your Sole
right to the Honour of the { Discoveries } improvements of the Steam
Engine†—And there is one advantage which will attend this method of
Publication.—Mr. De Luc will naturally mention your Discoveries
with a proper degree of Esteem for their Value and Ingenuity, whereas
were you to be the first publisher of them yourself you would do it in
such a Cold and modest manner that Blockheads would conclude there
was nothing in it, and Rogues would afterwards by makeing trifleing
Variations vamp off the greater Part of it as their own and assume the
whole merit to themselves—I am greatly obliged to you for your
Philosophical News—and I assure you that the Freinds you mention
here remember you always with the greatest affection and Esteem

Mr. Clerks Elder Brother is lately dead and he is now Sir Geo[rge]
Clerk which will extricate him from many difficulties   his health however has been bad for some time but he is getting better—Dr. Hutton

† The section between the two daggers has been bracketed off—presumably by Watt.

has lost a few days agoe his Freind Doctor Young[1] who died suddenly apoplectic—The Doctor is much afflicted but being left one of the Tustees [sic] it keeps him busy and prevents him from resigning himself too much to his Greif—poor Mrs. Young I fear will not easily get the better of it—but the hour of the Post approaches—Farewell my dear Freind and beleive me most affectionately Yours

Joseph Black

[1] Thomas Young was Professor of Midwifery in the University of Edinburgh from 1756 to 1780, and is generally regarded as the founder of the obstetric school there, being the first to give systematic lectures on the subject. He was elected Dean of the Incorporation of Surgeons in 1756 and took his M.D. at Edinburgh in 1761.

Letter 89

WATT TO BLACK

Cover addressed: 'Doctor Joseph Black/Edinburgh/via Ferry-bridge', endorsed in Black's hand, 'From Mr. Watt 21 April 1783' and numbered '45'. Dol. Further endorsed in Watt's hand, 'Communicates his Theory of the Decomposition of Water'.

Birmingham April 21st 1783

Dr. Black

Dear Doctor,

Your two obliging letters I ought to have answered sooner, but according to Custom have delayed from Time to Time   I write this principally to urge you to publish your discoveries on heat as soon as possible, because many people are working and speculating on the subject, Among others Dr. Crawford is preparing a new Eddition of his work with Additions and retractations, and as he did no justice to your merit in his former work I expect no more in this. He has got the many to believe that he is the original inventor of the doctrines and has even caused it to be published that both You and Dr. Irvine had acknowledged under your hands that you have no pretensions to what he has published If you will do no more, lett me know what you have given up as his, and what you claim as your own.

Mr. De Luc came according to his promise and staid 10 days which time we principally employed in experiments of the latent heat in vacuo, but from the many causes of innacuracy could come to no other

124

conclusion than that at least the sum of the latent {heat} or sensible heat is always equal, that is that the latent heat encreases as the sensible decreases and in some experiments the sum of the heats appeared to be greater *in Vacuo* than in the Air. In all the experiments we build upon, the sensible heat of the steam was never more than 95° and in some not more than 75°—I have not begun yet to put my sentiments in writing—I shall consider it as a great honour to have the little I have been able to add to your Doctrines published along with them, as to any share of the profit it would be a shame for me to think of selling you doctrines which I learnt from you, and all I can do in that way will be but a small recompense for the many obligations you have laid me under. It would give me great pleasure to see you here, and I hope you will put your proposal in practice but lett me know the time you can come that I may be disengaged as much as possible from wor[l]dly concerns.

Dr. Priestley has made many more experiments on the Conversion of water into air, and I believe I have found out the cause of it Which I have put in the form of a Letter to him which will be read at the royal society with his paper on the subject, it is briefly this. By reducing metals in inflammable air, he finds they absorb it and that the residuum of 10 ounces out of 100 is still the same sort of inflammable air, therefore inflammable air is the thing called Phlogiston. 2dly when quite dry pure inflammable air and quite dry, pure Dephlogisticated Air are fired by the electric spark in a Close Glass vessel he finds after the vessel is cold a quantity of Water adhering to the vessel equal or very nearly equal to the weight of the whole Air, and when he opens the vessel under Water or Mercury it is filled within 1/200 part of it[s] whole contents, which remainder is phlogisticated air, probably contained as an impurity in the other airs

3d When he exposes to heat porous earthen retorts previously soaked in water or makes steam pass slowly through a red hot tobacco pipe The water or steam is converted into air either entirely or in great part according as the process is conducted—This conversion does not take place when the water is contained in mettalline or glass vessels and only in a small degree when the water is imbibed by Clay inclosed in a Glass vessel, and the conversion goes on much less rapidly when the earthen vessel is immersed in heated quicksilver

In the deflagration of inf[lamma]ble and dephl[ogisticate]d Air, the airs unite with violence, become red hot and on cooling totaly disappear, The only fixed matter which remains is *water*, and *water, light, and heat* are are [*sic*] all the products. Are we not then Authorized to conclude that water is composed of Dephlo[gisticate]d and inflam[ma]ble air or phlog[isto]n deprived of part of their latent heat, and that Dephlo[gisticate]d or pure air is composed of water deprived of its phlo[gisto]n: and united to heat and light and if light be only a modification of heat or a component part of Phlo[gisto]n then pure air consists of water deprived of its Phlo[gisto]n and of Latent heat?

The deflagration of pure and inflam[ma]ble air is owing to the dephlo[gisticate]d water having a more powerfull attraction for phlo[gisto]n than it has for latent heat when it is red hot, therefore one particle being made red hot heats the others, the attraction takes place and the whole is decomposed

In every case where dephlo[gisticate]d Air is produced substances are employed some of whose principles have a strong attraction for phlo[gisto]n and probably a stronger one than water has, and they are also such bodies as have water as one of their constituent parts and can retain it untill it becomes red hot, (nitre, allum, Gypsum, Nitre of Mercury etc.) or they are calces of Metals or earths which we know have powerfull attractions for Phlo[gisto]n and also for water, When these bodies are placed in proper circumstances they dephlo[gistica]te the water, it receives latent heat from the fire and becomes air, more or less pure

In the case of the porous earthen vessel The Clay attracts the w[ater] into its pores and robs it of some of its phlo[gisto]n   it thens becomes air   one particle of the Clay transmitts the phlogiston to another untill it reaches the outside of the vessel which gives it to the external air which can attract phlo[gisto]n from hot Clay, though the lat[t]er can attract it from water, therefore Clay moistened with water and placed in glass or metalline vessels can only produce limited quantities of Air because the Clay having no opportunity of parting with the phlo[gisto]n can take no [more] than what saturates it, and air by this process can never be obtained quite so pure as the external air. It being fact that the nearer the vessel is placed to the fire the more impure the air is

The above is a short and I am afraid not very clear Abstract of the letter, which will however serve to show you my drift

†{I hence now claim that Phlo[gisto]n consists of light and water calcinated . . .}

This idea is too new to be properly digested yet, and would not hold

† 4½ lines here scrawled over so as to render them illegible.

its ground therefore I have defaced it, and the other is not quite a week old yet

On distilling spirit of nitre in a glass retort and making the steam pass through a red hot tobacco pipe, you will produce dephlo[gisticate]d air in plenty, and the same with $\oplus$+, only in the latter case you have sulphureous acid to the bargain. Volatile Alkali is quite changed by the same process, and Spirit of wine and oils give inflammable air very pure.

It will give me pleasure to hear from you and I remain, Dear Doctor your's affectionately

James Watt

Letter 90

BLACK TO WATT

In Watt's hand: 'Dr. Black July 16th 1783 by the Marquis de Biancourt', and numbered '45'.

Edinb[urgh] 16th July 1783

Dear Watt

I am shamefully in your Debt but shall write to you tomorrow or next day—This is to introduce to you the Marquis de Biencourt[1] a French Gentleman who is makeing a Tour thro the Island and is a very amiable Character—

He takes pleasure in collecting Information of usefull manufactures and other improvements in the State of the Country but he neither understands nor speaks English—I know you can speak a little french to him but if there are other Persons in Birmingham who can speak it more fluently it will be doing him a favour to make him acquainted with them—He will not expect that you put yourself to any other trouble than that of giveing him a little of your Company and conversation

My best Compliments to Mrs Watt and beleive me

always
Y[ou]rs affectionately
Joseph Black

[1] Charles de Biencourt (1746/7-1824), soldier and politican.

127

WATT TO BLACK

Cover addressed: 'Doctor Black/Edinburgh' and marked, 'per favour *Mr Garbett*/with a parcel'. Endorsed in Black's hand, 'Mr. Watt 25 September 1783' and numbered '44'. Dol. Further endorsed in Watt's hand as follows:

> 'Mr. De Luc with him
> Sends Lavoisier and La Place's Memoir on Heat.
> Thinks they have not done Dr. Black Justice.
> Conceives that his Theory of Latent heat will be established.
> Dr. Witherings translation of Bergman's *Sciagraphia*
> Montgolfier's balloons
> Mr. Boulton about to visit Scotland.
> Mrs. Boulton dead.
> Visit from the Duc de Chaulnes.'

Dr. Black   *Birmingham Sep[tembe]r 25th 1783*

Dear Doctor,

I have long expected the pleasure of a letter from you, but have had none except a few lines by the Marquis de Biancourt. Mr. De Luc, who is here, desires his Compliments to you, and has sent along with this Messrs. Lavoisier and de la Place's *Memoire* upon heat which is a very well wrote paper though not free from Objections. It is a present to you from the authors, who I think might have done you the justice to have mentioned your name in it; but this and much more you bring on yourself by not publishing your discoveries. I think that as far as I can see into the matter that Dr. Irvines doctrines and Dr. Crawfords of capacity, will fall to the ground, and your original theory of Latent or essential heat be established—I send you also Dr. Witherings translation of Bergmans *Sciagraphia*, which if you approve of, it will Oblige me to mention in your Class—

The whole world is full of these flying balls at present I know very little more of them than you must have seen in the papers, except that Mongolfier[1] has found a method to make inflamable air by burning wet straw so cheap that he can fill a ball of 30 feet dia[mete]r for $\frac{1}{2}$ a Crown, but this method of doing this is a secret yet, at least if he has communicated it, it is only to the accademy, who were to send up a Ball of O this shape 70 long dia[mete]r, and 38 the small on last friday and 4 or 5 Criminals tyed to it. The Duke de Chaulnes[2] is here at present he does not seem to be deep as a man of Science, but is an Obliging affable man

My headaches have been rather less violent this summer but have been as frequent as usual and seem now to be returning to their former State

Please present my sincere Respects to Sir G[eorge] Clerk Dr. Hutton Mr. Robison and other friends, And believe me to remain Dear Doctor

Your Affectionate friend

James Watt

I forgot the principal purport of my letter which was to tell you that my friend Mr. Boulton will call upon you soon, and that your civilities to him will much oblige me, Mr. Garbett will introduce him, as his going via Ireland prevented me from writing by him. NB Mrs. Boulton is lately dead,

¹ Joseph Michel Montgolfier (1740–1810), balloonist and chemist. His brother, Jacques Etienne Montgolfier (1745–99) visited Birmingham.

² Marie Joseph Louis d'Albert d'Ailly, Duc de Chaulnes (1741–after 1789), chemist.

Letter 92

WATT TO BLACK

Endorsed in Black's hand, 'From Mr. Watt 26 September 1783' and numbered '43'. Dol. Further endorsed in Watt's hand, 'Introducing Mr., afterwards Dr. Pearson of Birmingham. Has sent him a Memoir on Heat by Lavoisier and La Place, and Dr. Witherings translation of Bergmans *Sciagraphia*'.

Birmingham Sep[tembe]r 26th 1783

Dear Doctor,

I beg leave to introduce to you Mr. Pearson of this place, who comes to Edinburgh to study Medicine, and proposes to attend your Class. I an not particularly aquainted with him but he bears the Character of an Ingenious and modest young Man, which character is confirmed by what I have seen of him.

I wrote you yesterday by Mr. Garbett, with Messrs. Lavoisier and De la Place's memoir on heat, and Dr. Witherings translation of Bergmans *Sciagraphia*, The perusal of both of which will I expect give you pleasure I shall be very glad to hear from you at your Convenience and [sic] remain

Dear Doctor

Your's Affectionately

James Watt

129

ROBISON TO WATT

Cover addressed: 'To Mr. James Watt/Birmingham', endorsed
in Watt's hand, 'Proffessor Robison October 22d 1783 about a
new Steam Engine Mr. Pearson System of Mechanics method
of computing power of a horse', and numbered '2'. Dol.

Edin[bu]r[gh] Oct[ober] 22. 1783

Dear Sir

I had the favour of Yours by Mr. Pearson, who seems to deserve the favourable things you say of him, and to whom I shall be glad to be of Service on your Acc[oun]t. I am glad of any thing which may happen to bring me to your remembrance, often regreting that our different pursuits have seperated me so far from a person whom I so much esteem and love. It would add greatly to the pleasure of my life could I be witness of the regard that is paid to your genius and the success which attends the exertion of your Talents. Beleive me there is noone who more sincerely rejoices in your prosperity {nor} or is more fully persuaded of your title to all the regard which is paid you. I am too far removed from you, to have any interest in flattering you, and you must therefore take this as the honest effusion of very affectionate regard.

I have advised Mr. Pearson to delay attending my Lectures (which he proposed to do this Winter) till he shall have acquired some mathematical Knowledge. It is the great misfortune of my Situation that few pupils come to me with such preparation as will enable them to acquire from my Lectures that only useful Knowledge which may be applied with confidence to the arts of Life. As I endeavour to conduct my Lessons in such a manner that *some* at least may do this, I render them less pleasing to the generality of my hearers, who aim at nothing but getting a superficial Knowledge, or, more properly speaking, whose only aim is a frivolous amusement. This renders me a very unpopular teacher, and as I cannot think of becoming a showman, I do not expect to grow rich in the profession. I have been at some pains in composing a system of practical Mechanics, which is now pretty far advanced, and I hope soon to have it fit for your inspection. I consider Machines as in motion, performing work. It is evident that this view must lead to or require very different maxims of construction from those which result from the equilibrium of machines, the only point of view in which they have been generally considered. Two capital questions occur here

1st the law by which the real resistance changes by a change in the velocity of the working part of the machine. 2d The law by which the real pressure of the power changes by a change in the velocity of the impelled part of the Machine. Both of these questions are very difficult, and our theory is too imperfect to give us general principles. I am promised the assistance of our Trustees for the Encouragement of Fisheries and Manufactures for determining these questions in some of the most important Cases, at least. You will judge of their importance from an example. I find by a numerous train of experiments that a horse tracking a boat performs the greatest quantity of work (estimated by the product of the force with which he stretches the track rope by the velocity of his motion) when he moves with 2/5 of that velocity with which he can move (without performing any work) during the ordinary working hours of the 24, and that in this Situation he is exerting a draught 9/23 of that which he can continue to exert on a still obstacle for the same time.

There has been lately with me a very ingenious young Man, named Ker, who imagines that he has made a great improvement on the first Steam Engine and proposes to apply for a patent. I advised him to correspond with you about it, as one in whose honour he could confide,

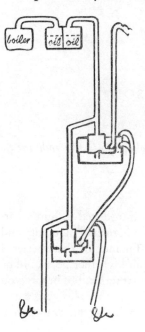

and who could inform him whether any person had been before him in the thought. He gave me leave to communicate it to you, requesting the favour of your opinion. You recollect the form given to this Engine by a Mr. Blakey. He adopts this form. But, in order to avoid the {necessity} inconveniences arising from the great expansive force of the Steam, employed for raising the water to a great hight, he divides the whole height into several short lifts, by making his Receiver communicate with different receivers, placed at different heights in the pit. He was not aware of the immense loss of Steam on such an extension of Surface. I advised him to make his Steam act on the Surface of a quantity of Oil containd in a great receiver, and to employ air alone for exerting the pressure on the other receivers. You will understand it by the annexed Sketch. His methods of emptying the vessels and of supplying the Air which may leak out, are extremely simple and ingenious, as is also his method of opening and shutting the Cocks in the first receiver. He has also proposed to remove the beam from the common Engine, making the piston fixed, and the Cylinder moveable, having the pump rods connected with it   He wishes for your information as to his originality also on this head, tho' I told him that I had published a scheme of this kind in the Universal Magazine above 26 years ago.[1] If you can find as much time I shall take it kind if you will drop me a line on these points, and that you will excuse this intrusion of

Dear Sir

Your most cordial Well wisher etc.

John Robison

P.S. It is 17 years since I filled balls of varnish with inflammable Air, and had them rise with great rapidity, but I never could get them to dry and remain firm. They burst like Sope bubbles.

[1] See *Universal Magazine*, November 1752, pp. 229-31, including diagram.

Letter 94

WATT TO ROBISON

*B.R.L. Boulton and Watt Letter Books.

Birm[ingha]m Jan[uar]y 20th 1784

Professor Robison

Dear Sir,

   When Mr. Boulton was in Scotland, you introduced to him a Mr. Renny a Millwright,[1] whom you mentioned as a man of ingenuity and application—We always have employment for men of that species I therefore give you the trouble of this to enquire whether he would be willing to agree with us for 5 years and on what terms; but before you ask him the question, I wish you to be satisfied in the following particulars, 1st whether he is perfectly sober, 2d whether his ambition is

132

moderate, and can for the term I have mentioned be contented with the station of a confidential servant: 3d Whether he is free from that \kind of/ self conceit that convinces a man that his own opinion is better founded than his masters or his senior's, and that will dictate improvements before he understands the subject. 4th Whether his ingenuity is in general well directed and not of that kind which leads a man from his business in search of Chimeras or novelties merely because they are such. As to his Ingenuity and abilities I take them for granted from the favourable report you made of him to Mr. Boulton, and I should also suppose his Integrity to be undoubted from your mentioning him at all

If you think he is perfectly or \tolerably/ free from the bad qualities I have mentioned, and otherwise disengaged, I will be obliged to you to ask him what he would come to us for—When he is sent on a journey about our business we allow his reasonable travelling charges, but when he is at any place where his stay is above a week he maintains himself

The employment we have for him is attending and directing the erection of Engines, once he is properly instructed for that purpose, and also working at the erection with his own hands (for we now keep no gentlemen engineers) and if he is not a man that likes to work and works neatly he cannot answer us. In consequence of our making Rotative Engines we shall also occasionally have employment for him in the Mill wright line, and have a considerable Job of that kind now before us, wherein he could be of use

It will not suit us to take a man for less than 5 years and instruct him in our business, because a great part of that time will elapse before he is so much master of it as to be essentially usefull to us, and if his time were shorter if he turned out well, we should be loth to part with him after having been at the expence and trouble of instructing him

I hope I may be excused saying that if he wishes to learn his business thoroughly he can have no better opportunity of gaining instruction and experience, and at the same time \of/ meeting with good treatment

I need say no more on this subject but that I will be obliged to you for an answer as soon as is convenient, as if it is not agreable to Mr. Renny to come to us we must turn our eyes to another quarter

Mr. Boulton joins in compliments to you and I remain

my dear Sir
Your sincere friend
James Watt

[1] John Rennie (1761–1821), civil engineer, first rose to fame as a result of his work for Boulton and Watt's Albion Mill, Blackfriars, London.

ROBISON TO WATT

A.O.L.B.

Edin[burg]h Feb[ruar]y 10 1784

Dear Sir

Your Letter of Jan[uar]y 20th should have been answered m[u]ch sooner, but Mr. Renney had been in the Country for ten days after I rec[eive]d it and my Letter to him has not come to his hands. Since I have seen him I have been so much harassed by Headaches that I could not converse with him. I must trust to your Goodness for an Excuse.

When I recommended Mr. Renny to the Notice of Mr. Boulton, it was in the full persuasion that if he had any use for him he would be found diligent faithful, and both intelligent and eager to learn. He has been at the greatest pains to educate himself, and is still prosecuting academical Education with great Assiduity, and has made considerable progress. What I considered as the most recommendable qualities of his Character was a modest opinion of himself, and a complete freedom from that troublesome ingenuity which you so justly think so useless to an employer. Indeed he has no title to such self conceit, for he is not at all what we usually call an ingenious Mechanic. His views are perfectly sober, and never lead him from his business in quest of novelties. So far I thought him a good Subject to put into the hands of a Friend, and I considered your Employment as a most valuable opportunity for him. But when I got your Letter I doubted whether your Views and his could be at all compatible. Renney has been for four years in business as a Master Millwright, and has executed some considerable Jobs with great success. He has lately built perhaps the best flour Mill in this Country, and having succeeded in this by reflecting on his former Experiences has a title to think that in Circumstances not very dissimilar, his Success may be still greater. In this Situation it cannot be ascribed to self conceit that it would be with some reluctance that he would sink from his present Station, even in this poor Country into that of a mere journeyman or, at best what we call a foresman I must therefore insist that you do not think the worse of him for this. But he is extremely desirous of serving you, and is by no means anxious about the immediate pecuniary advantages, being in a Situation which makes these of little Consequence to him. His object is to give himself the most

complete Mechanical Education that he could expect in your Employment, diversifyed as it now is by your rotative Engines. Nothing
he wishes for so much as to be introduced to business under your
Auspices, and therefor he would prize nothing so much as recommending himself to you by being useful to you in any way which is compatible
with his plans of self instruction. Your sole view being to obtain a trusty
Man to have some direction in erecting your Steam Engine he fears that
during a five year service, his task may have very little variety, and lend
little to his own improvement, as it will be allmost wholly devoted to
performances which are secured to you by patent. He begs however that
I will make an offer of his services to you upon Tryal, leaving the terms
to yourself. If at the End of a Year you find him a valuable acquisition,
and he sees that he will get that variety of information which he so much
wishes for, he doubts not but his Connection with you will be of longer
duration. He has not the least objection to working with his own hands,
and hopes that in that particular he will give you satisfaction. If you required it he could bring with him a good hand or two. I will make no
apology for this long detail. I could not do less for a person I think well of.
You will be directed by your own views, and I have no wish to press the
thing upon You.

Your question I have not yet completely resolved. It is not so simple as
it appears at first sight, and the solutions which have occurred to me are
limited to particular Cases. I am endeavouring to accommodate them
to the Circumstances which are the most likely to obtain in the application which you will make of it. I shall take the first spare hour which I
can obtain to finish what I have done.

I have the pleasure of informing you that You and Mr. Boulton were
unanimously elected Members of our infant Royal Society. As Secretary
I ought to have given you official Information a week ago, but I must
beg your Excuse, as I have had neither Leisure nor Spirits to do any
thing out of the Jog trot of my profess[io]n these many days. While this
severe weather continues I can hardly do any thing but sit before a warm
fire, with my face looking up to the Ceiling. In every other position I am
tormented with a Rheumatic pain in my head. I beg you will present my
respects to Mr. Boulton and request that he will accept of this Notification of his reception into the Royal Society of Edin[bu]r[gh]. I shall
procure a frank in a few days to enclose a Copy of our Statutes. When I
was lately in Glasgow, Dr. Wilson and Son spoke most affectionately of
you, and begged to be remembered of you by every opportunity. Peter
is now engaged on a most ingenious experiment for discovering whether

this planetary System is a set of Satellites to our Sun revolving round another Centre and in what quarter of the Universe that Center is placed. This he hopes to do by means of the aberration of light, as you will easily comprehend when I mention it. But I have no room to enlarge. Accept of my best wishes and believe me to be with great regard

D[ea]r Sir Your aff[ectiona]te friend
John Robison

Letter 96
WATT TO ROBISON

*B.R.L. Boulton and Watt Letter Books

Birmingham April 9th 1784

Proffessor Robison

Dear Sir

Your kind letter of the 10th Feb[ruar]y should have been answered sooner; but Mr. Boulton was absent, when I received it and for some time after, and when he returned we were both so beset with people who came here on business that we had no proper opportunity of talking over the { business } \matter/; and since that time I have been absent from home for more than a month and am very lately returned.

The truth is that to give a proper answer to the letter is attended with difficulty. On the one hand, such a person as you describe, would in all probability prove a desireable assistant in our business. And on the other hand, As he does not seem to be willing to agree with us for a term of years perhaps it would not be prudent in us to instruct him so far in our business as to be of signal utility to us Because a considerable portion of any short term must be spent in giving him instruction and experience, which he would in such case be under no obligation of exerting for our benefit, longer than the term of his agreement lasted, and consequently it would be more our interest to instruct some person whose views did not prevent him from engaging for a longer time; If any person were to be found with the same good qualities, and views more suitable to ours

As I had no intimation of his being in the Station of a Master Millwright, I hope that you and he will excuse the proposition I made, And at the same time I must add that a confidential Servant is not in this

136

country so degrading a situation as you seem to ap\p/rehend. Merit will always procure respect even in this degraded age.

As to the objection of his attention and instruction being directed solely to such businesses as are secured to us by patent, and therefore his experience of no use to him in future when free from Legal obligation to us. I answer that the use to which we wish to apply his talents is principaly Mill work, which must be the same whether wrought by water, wind or engines. He{ might}\may/ in the course of our business have an opportunity of seeing and making mills, for all sorts of purposes, besides various other mechanical instruments and operations which could not fail of being usefull to an intelligent man. and as to variety, the loss of our business is that we have too much of it to be able to get forward as fast as we wish

I shall only use one other argument on this head which is that if at twenty years of age I had engaged with any {body} \Respectable person/ as an upper servant for merely my board and clothing for seven years, I should in all probability have been both a richer and more respectable person that I now am and have past my life with more happiness —To come to the point, the greatest wages we give to any of our workmen (excepting one) is One Guinea a week and which we cannot go beyond without creating a mutiny; But if we think any mans services either on a particular occasion or at the end of the year merits more, we make him a present, more or less according to circumstances. and in some cases we have it in our power to throw other advantages in their way and always make them an allowance for travelling Charges when sent from home

If Mr. Renny does not think it for his interest to agree with us for five years I cannot desire it, but I do not think we should act wisely in agreeing for a shorter term. Nevertheless if he means to come to England and act for himself as a Master Mill wright, we shall reccomend \him/ to such business as may be in our power, provided that he engages to make no improper use of such matters as we may communicate to him in the course of our transactions together. We have it now in our power to get him employed in a considerable Job at London, which I expect will go forward this summer which though I cannot promise will be off immediate pecuniary advantage will at least serve to get him into Business. We should therefore wish to know what his determination is.

Mr. Boulton and myself return our sincere thanks to the Royal Society of Edinburgh for the honour they have done us in electing us members of it, and to you and our friends for your favourable opinion of us which we shall endeavour to merit. When you write to us as secretary we shall beg the favour of you to present our thanks to the society in a formal manner —I am extremely sorry to hear of your indisposition from which I hope you are now recovered and for which you have my best wishes, thanking you for the trouble you have taken in transacting the business with Mr. Renny thus far.

I remain
Dear Sir Yours Affectionately
James Watt

Letter 97

ROBISON TO WATT

Cover addressed: 'To Mr James Watt/Birmingham' and endorsed 'Proffessor Robison April 25th 1784'. A.O.L.B.

Edin[bu]r[gh] Apr[il] 25. 1784

Dear Sir

I deferred answering your Letter of the 9th instant for some days, because Mr. Renney had told me that having a little spare time he was determined to pass it in the North of England in viewing any thing which he could hear of in the line of his profession I imagining that I could easily persuade him to go as far as Birmingham, where he would have an opportunity of waiting on you This will accordingly be delivered to you by him, and I beg leave to recommend him to your Civilities and good Advices. If you can be useful to each other it will give me pleasure, and I am persuaded that your good Offices to him will be most thankfully received

I remain with great truth
D[ea]r Sir
Your aff[ectiona]te Friend and Serv[an]t
John Robison

Letter 98

BLACK TO WATT

Cover addressed: 'Mr. James Watt Engineer/Birmingham/by Ferrybridge', endorsed in Watt's hand as below, and numbered '44'. Dol.

'Dr. Black May 28th 1784
The State of his health and Engagements have prevented his writing and making any progress towards publishing.
___
Remarks on Lavoisier and La Places Theory of Heat
Receipt of Witherings *Sciagraphica*
___
Has given Dr. Freer a letter of introduction to Mr. Boulton upon Corts Process of makeing Iron
___
was pleased with Mr. Boulton's visit to him in the beginning of last Winter and delighted to form a friendship with [him]'

May 28th 1784

My dear Freind
 The great length of time during which I have been your debtor re-quires some apology from me   it has been occasioned by the following circumstances—I had made you a promise that I should in the Course of last Summer prepare some of my Lectures for the Press—When the Summer came I found my Self so much worn out with my Winters Labours and in such bad health with a Cough and defluxion from my breast that I was quite unfit to sit down to serious business—and during the rest of that Season I had other things in the way of College and other Business which broke my time and took up my attention in such a manner that I got nothing done—all this while I was ashamed to write to you after the promise I had made
 In the beginning of last winter when it became necessary to drop for some time all thoughts of such undertakeings I sat down to write to you but something prevented me from finishing my letter and it remains un-finished to this day—in short I feel that I am unfit to come under such engagements, I have not sufficient activity and spirits to be sure of ful-filling them and they are a load on my mind which encreases my disability
 I received Lavoisiers and la Place's memoir   their method for measur-ing quantitys of heat is ingenious but they have not used it with accuracy in some Cases, and there is reason to suspect from Mr. Wedgewoods

experiments in this way[1] that it cannot be practiced with exactness—I am told it was contrived by la Place—Be so good as to return my best Compliments to Mr. de Luc and many thanks for his trouble and attention to me—I rec[eive]d also Dr. Witherings Translation of Bergmanns [sic] *Sciagraphia* for which also be so good as to express my acknowledgements to him—I enclose those of the Medical Society to whom also he sent a Copy they delivered the inclosed to me in the beginning of winter to be forwarded to the Doctor whose address they were ignorant of and I let it lye by me untill I found leisure to write to you—I have taken the Liberty to give to Doctor Freer[2] from this Place a line of Introduction to Mr. Bolton I do not mean by this to recommend him in preference to Doctor Withering who has already and most deservedly gained your confidence Dr. Freer desired a letter of Introduction and his Merit and character are such that I could not refuse him—he was bred in our hospital as Physicians Clerk many Years during which he had ample opportunitys of attending all our Lectures and of acquiring practical skill—he was also very attentive diligent and prudent in his Conduct—and had much of the Confidence of the Physicians of the hospital—but his manner is so unpromiseing that he may find difficultys in getting forward on that account—We have lately had the pleasure to see Mr. Cort[3] From Gosport of whose important inventions in the manufacturing of Iron you have certainly heard, he is a plain Englishman without Science but by the dint of natural ingenuity and a turn for experiment has made such a Discovery in the Art of makeing tough Iron as will undoubtedly give to this Island the monopoly of that Business; he has shewn us an example of his Process here in the presence of a few Freinds and he wishes to have an opportunity of shewing it to Mr. Bolton and you; you will probably be astonished as I was at the simplicity and propriety of it and will wonder that it was not discovered sooner It is certainly both a far cheaper Process and an incomparably more perfect one than that hitherto practiced and it is much more likely to produce Iron without pores or Flaws—he has met with much illiberal treatment from many of the trade—The behaviour of the Manadger here was such as might be expected of him, illbred raillery and attempts at circumvention—It will be a deed well worthy of Mr. Boltons Humanity to settle matters if possible upon a general footing between Cort and the Trade; he is not greedy, and a very moderate allowance to him from the very great profits which his process will give them, will be a handsome reward for his Discovery

Few things have given me so much pleasure as the Opportunity I had in the beginning of winter to form an acquaintance with Mr. Bolton his

Connection with you had raised a strong desire in me to be acquainted with him and I found so much reason to \be/ satisfyed that the Connection is [a] fortunate and comfortable one that I was made happy on your account as well as in forming a Freindship with a Man of so much merit and worth—present my most respectful Compliments to him—and be assured that I ever am

My dear Freind
Yours most faithfully
Joseph Black

P.S. when I wrote the above I had seen Mr. Corts Process performed and had seen the Iron which it produced from the Common Cold-short carron Pigs subjected to a number of trials—It was remarkably soft and malleable while beat out into bars under the great hammer and formed Bars with Edges perfectly sound without a flaw in them—these Bars near $\frac{3}{4}$ Inch thick were very tough when Cold and when broken at last shewed a more fibrous fracture than any Iron I ever saw before—when the Ends of the fibres were turned to the Eye the fracture appeared remarkably dark coloured and the Smiths who saw it said it had the appearance of redshort—but upon trying to forge it they did not find reason to accuse it of that fault—Yet I am informed that when trial was made of it afterwards in the Plateing and in the Slitting mill it did shew some degree of a redshort quality—All the Same the Smiths however agreed that upon the whole it is good Iron, that it forges and files remarkably well and is very tough when Cold tho made from bad Carron Pigs

[1] Josiah Wedgwood (1730–95), the potter, began in 1780 a series of experiments on high temperature measurement resulting in the invention of his pyrometer.

[2] Robert Freer (1745–1827) came from Perth, took his M.A. at Aberdeen in 1765 and after studying medicine at Edinburgh, graduated M.D. at Aberdeen in 1779. He served as an ensign and surgeon in the American War. He began practising at Glasgow in 1779 and was Professor of Medicine in the University of Glasgow from 1796 to 1827, and physician to the Glasgow Royal Infirmary from 1797 to 1815.

[3] Henry Cort (1740–1800), born at Lancaster, was established as a Navy Agent in London at the age of twenty-five, 1765–75. About 1775 he moved to Fontley, near Fareham, where he erected a forge and slitting-mills. His new processes (patented 1783–84) revolutionized iron-making but he did not succeed in securing the rewards of his invention.

WATT TO BLACK

Cover addressed: 'Doctor Joseph Black/Physician/Edinburgh/
via Ferrybridge', endorsed in Black's hand, 'From J. Watt 6 June
1784 answered 26 Ditto', and numbered '42'. Dol.

Doctor Black   *Birmingham June 6th 1784*

Dear Doctor

The other day I received yours, without date   I am extremely concerned to hear of your bad health and spirits and sorry that I should have
plagued you about publication but I cannot bear to see so many people
adorning themselves with your feathers. And I still hope that if you cannot perform the task yourself you will find some man of ability and with
a greater quantity of animal spirits who will consent to be your Editor
and whom you will furnish with Ideas.

In the mean time every thing should give way to your health, you
should during the recess of College make a long excursion and leave care
behind you. It will give me the utmost pleasure to see you here, and to
contribute by every way in my power to your pleasure and comfort
when here   Our situation is healthy and clear of the Town, and the
country about affords many objects to interest and amuse you. I hope
therefore that you will take a sudden resolution and set out and if you can
bring Dr. Hutton with you so much the better. If you give me a little
warning I shall endeavour to get De Luc to meet you here; you will find
him one of the most amiable and entertaining of men. Previous to your
letter I have heard much of Mr. Cort's process for making barrs and
have seen a great deal of his Iron, though I cannot perfectly agree with
you as to its goodness yet there is much Ingenuity in the Idea of forming
the barrs in that manner, which is the only part of his process which has
any pretensions to novelty. The kind of Iron you describe is one of the
modifications of Cold short Iron and is known here by the emphatical
name of *rotten tough*. I have long known that almost any cold short Iron
may be brought to \that/ state, by rolling it very hot, or by drawing it
across the anvil so as to spin the Crystals into threads; and by certain
mechanical processes good Iron may be rendered Cold short. nevethe-
less in neither of the cases the quality of the Iron is {not} altered The
good Iron continues strong and the Cold short is very weak † I look on

† I speak only of the iron made from cold short by his process [written in margin]

142

Mr. Corts Iron as a Cold short whose crystalls are spun out by the rolling, and which is mixt with a large quantity of half metallized earth. It is tender to the file and soft to the hammer, rusts very readily, and ought never to be used where it is subjected to any strains, as it is very weak, therefore unfitt for Engine work Ship work etc. but good for nails, because easily wrought, but there the nailers complain that it wastes more than the com[mo]n cold short, I suppose because not so well freed from its cinder   Good Iron is hard under the hammer and stubborn to the chissel and file, breaks white, {sometimes} \generally/ granulated but the very best is fibrous and white like Silver—
I find I am getting into a dissertation on Iron which I must shorten

Mr. Cort has as you observe been most illiberally treated by his trade   they are ignorant brutes; but he exposed himself to it by exposing his process to them, before it was perfect, and they saw his Ignorance of the common operations of making Iron, laughed at and despised him; yet they will contrive by some dirty occasions to use his process or such parts as they like without acknowleging him in it. I shall be glad to be able to be of any use to him. He is now in this neighbourhood but as Mr B. is just setting out for Cornwall he could not see him before he went, being extremely hurried, and indeed I was glad to keep them asunder as Mr. B, occupies himself too much with other peoples business and too little with his own, and was lately much bit with the Ferromania

I send you inclosed my Draft on Gilbert Hamilton for £18.8sh.6d being the ballance due by me to you (for I reckon nothing on the organ which you placed to my credit)   It has grieved me much to have been obliged to have been so long owing you; but it is very lately that the sun began to shine on me, and I could not think of paying one friend by borrowing from another.

My health is as usual indifferent, and I feel I grow old and stupid. I have still however some desire for more knowledge which with the necessary attention to my family and business serves to keep me awake. With best respects to Doctor Hutton and all friends, I remain ever sincerely

Your's A[ffectionatel]y
James Watt

I again repeat that I most sincerely wish
you to come here as soon as you can
You have often told me that amusement was one of the best things
in life and I believed you and found it so—now do as ye bid
me do

Letter 100

BLACK TO WATT

Cover addressed: 'Mr. James Watt Engineer/Birmingham/By
favour of Mr. MacKenzie', endorsed in Watt's hand, 'Dr. Black
June 26th 1784' and numbered '43'. Dol.

Edinb[urgh] 26 June 1784

My dear Watt

I received Yours of the 6th Inst[an]t and am infinitely obliged to you
for your kind Anxiety about my health and invitation to come and see
you—with respect to the first I can make you easy by assureing you that I
have had better health upon the whole the last winter and Spring and
this Summer than formerly   in winter I had a Class of 220 effectives which
kept up my Spirits, and by walking regularly every day 3 or four miles
before dinner I preserved my Body in health and my mind fit for action
—Since I finished my Course which I did in good time the Business of
Graduations and a Set of Experiments for the Trustees on Ashes made in
differ[en]t parts of Scotland and a little practice have kept me employed
—The business of graduations breaks our time during the Summer and
requires not a little attention and along with a multitude of other things
which I wish to do in Summer and cannot attempt in Winter makes it
impossible for me at present to make the excursion you propose   It is one
of the pleasures however which I promise myself and keep in view but
the time for it is not yet come—You have formed a hasty and mistaken
notion of Corts Process, the mechanical improvements were those he
first contrived and got a Patent for which others attempted to elude and
cheat him out of—But he afterwards contrived an improvement in the
Chemical Part which I maintan still is Capital \and for which he has a
second Patent/—Two Companys at Newcastle and others in other
Parts of England have already made agreements with him to work under
his Patent—I see no reason why his Process should not produce Iron of
the very best Quality from good Pigs and beleive that it will—but if it
had no other merit but that of making from bad Pigs such Iron as we saw
made here which is of excellent quality for all ordinary uses it will still
prove an immense acquisition to Scotland.—I pray you be kind to him
when you see him, I assure you he is an honest worthy man—This will
be delivered to you by another honest and very ingenious Man Mr.
McKenzie,[1] he is an Engineer for Iron Furnaces or undertakes the
{building} planning and conducting of them and has uncommon know-

144

ledge in his Profession and a Philosophical liberality of mind—he has some proposal to make to you about erecting a fire Engine here and it is probable he may have occasion to apply to you again hereafter

I rec[eive]d the Bill you enclosed to me but I assure I do not intend to make use of it—I took the Organ from you with an intention to pay you for it when we settled acc[oun]ts and why do you talk now of haveing been in my Debt when the Sum in question is not equal to the 20 guineas which you set originally on that Instrument.—I am overjoyed to hear from you at last that the Sun begins to shine on you, that and Exercise if you will take it regularly will conduce more to your health than any thing—

I beg you will send me a slight Scetch of Dr. Witherings apparatus for makeing Aereal water—I have the description of it in Preistlys last Volume but there is no figure of it—   I am ever

Yours affect[ionate]ly

Joseph Black

<hr>

[1] Possibly Murdoch McKenzie, the elder (died 1797), surveyor and hydrographer.

Letter 101

WATT TO BLACK

Cover addressed: 'Doctor Joseph Black'Physician/Edinburgh/ via Ferrybridge', endorsed in Black's hand, 'From Mr. Watt 11 November 1784' and numbered '41'. Dol.

Birm[ingha]m Nov[embe]r 11th 1784

Dr Black

Dear Doctor

I sent you lately a copy of the paper on Dep[hlogisticate]d Air which I communicated to the Royal Society and \which/ will be printed in the next volume of their Transactions

It is far from being \well/ written, but I am every day more and more satisfied that the doctrines it contains are true however bold they appeared at first.—My bad health and my avocations, prevented me from sitting Close at it or thinking continuedly on the subject. It should therefore [be] considered as a parcel of detached scraps rather than any attempt at system, which made me put it into the form of a Letter—I inclosed in the same parcel a few copies for other friends which I beg the favour of

145

you to get delivered. The parcel went by a Mr. Walker of this place, who being going upon business may not perhaps be very expeditious

The following capital Experiments have been made lately by Dr. Priestly

Iron confined by dry mercury in dry Deph[logisticate]d air, on the focus of a lens beingthrown upon it, takes fire burns fiercely absorbs the dephlogisticatedvery rapidly and is perfectly calcined, no Inf[lamma]ble air is produced, but $\frac{1}{12}$ of the Deph[logisticate]d air is converted into fixt air, and there is scarce any appearance of moisture on the Glass

2. The Calx produced in the last experiment, being placed in the same circumstances in inf[lamma]ble air, is in the focu: of the lens reduced into Iron, the Inf[lamma]ble air is absorbed, no other air is produced, but the sides of the Glass stream with water. The Iron Loses weight and the water is = to it.

3. Iron gains $\frac{1}{3}$ of its, original, weight when thoroughly calcined

4. The Steams of water passed through a red hot copper tube produce no air

5. On putting some Iron turnings in the tube and passing steam through it. The Iron is calcined gains weight and yields $\frac{1}{2}$ more Inf[lamma]ble Air than would have done by vitriolic acid \no fixt air/

6. Inf[lamma]ble air absorbs water readily and becomes double specific gravity

7. Charcoal in the Copper tube, by steam yields a very large quantity of air which is \a/ mixture of Inf[lamma]ble and fixt air and is wholly reduced to ashes

8. 2 oz measures Spirit of wine (alcohol) passed in steams through the tube gave 1000 oz measures infl[amma]ble air, mixt with fixt air, in $\frac{1}{4}$ hour \3 drams water were deposited/. On sending through 2 oz measures more the tube was so much acted upon as to be pervious to the air, and on being broken was found to be calcined in the inside, the calx exactly ressembles Lamp black—The tube was no ways acted upon in any of the other exp[erimen]ts

9. The scales of copper, or calcined copper, placed in the focus of the lens in inf[lamma]ble air yields water the same as the Iron scales or calx does

The Iron calcined by water, does not differ from Iron calcined by air

There are more curious facts but they [do] not occur to me at present. but on the whole I think that poor Phlogiston will be perfectly saved from Mr. Lavoisiers sentence of annihilation, and I think myself bound in honour to help him up with his breeches, If I have Leisure

I am much Obliged to you for the friendly reception you gave Mr. Guyot[1] on my account and I trust you will find him exceedingly worthy of it—When you [see him] † please make my comp[limen]ts to him and tell him I received his very kind letter and shall write to him soon

Be also so good as to remember me kindly to all friends, and believe me to remain

Your's Most Affectionately
James Watt

† Tear in paper.
[1] A. Guyot of Passy was an intimate friend of De Lessert of De Lessert & Co., bankers in Paris. He may have been a partner in the firm.

Letter 102

BLACK TO WATT

Endorsed in Watt's hand, 'Dr. Black June 10th 1785' and numbered '42'. Dol.

10 June 1785

My dear Watt

This will be delivered by Doctor Sylvester[1] of Geneva who has passed two winters with us and whom I beg leave to recommend to your freindly notice He left Geneva in consequence of the late Disturbances in that City and change of Government which followed but he proposes to revisit it this Summer and will see your Son.—I have no news to give you but that Hutton has read two papers in our Philosophical Society which are much taken notice of—The Subject is the formation of fossils and the changes which our Globe has undergone—I beleive he will be persuaded to print them soon—Your Freind Guyot is very well and is to stay with us another twelvemonth

My best Compliments are presented to Mrs. Watt and I am ever

Yours most affect[ionate]ly
Joseph Black

Edinburgh 10 June
1785

[1] Dr P. Sylvestre was a Genevese, radical in politics, who in the 1790s resided at No. 1, Staple's Inn Buildings, Holborn. He studied in Montpelier for four years, then practised in Geneva for a year, followed by two years' study in Edinburgh. He was befriended by Dr Thomas Beddoes who recommended him to John Wilkinson.

ROBISON TO WATT

A.O.L.B.

No address

Edin[burgh] Aug[us]t 11 1785

Dear Sir

I trouble you with this at the request of Mr. Kier,[1] of whom I had formerly occasion to write you, desiring your opinion about his Improvement of Savary's Steam Engine.

He has invented a form for the Cylindric Wick'd Lamp so much superior to that of Mr. Argand[2] that there is little doubt of its supplanting

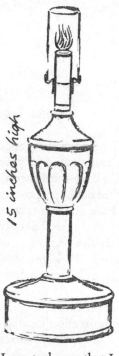

15 inches high

the other whenever it is seen. Mr. Kier wishes to sell his invention to the Trade, and it occurred to me that there was no person to whom it could be so properly offered as Mr. Boulton, as the patentees of the present Cylindrical Lamp will be most affected by the Sale of the new one. I have annexed a Sketch of the external form of the Lamp, by which you see that it has great advantage in point of Elegance. But its chief advantage consists in this that it can never overflow or have any dropping. It is filled without any separation of its parts, by merely taking off the Glass Cylinder \and Wick/ and pouring in Oil into the Top of the Tube. It will burn a wick of the Size of those of the patent Lamp about 10 hours, without any sensible diminution of brightness, and even for a much longer time, if of a less slender make. Nay, on the same principle, it can be made (at a greater Expence) to burn about 5 hours, the external form of it perfectly resembling a common Candlestick. I am not at liberty to be more particular, altho I can truly say that I made a Lamp on a principle nearly the same, in the year 1767, but with a common Wick. But as this is committed to me in confidence of Secrecy, I think myself tyed up for the same reason, altho the mere mentioning to an ingenious person the possibility of executing a Lamp of this form may suggest to him the principle on which it is done, I am confident that I have put it [in] safe Hands, and I think I may venture to promise that you will be pleased with the ingenuity and practical advantages of the construction when it is made known to You. May I therefore beg that you will mention it to Mr. Boulton. I believe that I should have addressed myself directly to him, but my long acquaintance with You gives me greater freedom of writing, and I hope that you will make this apology to Mr. Boulton, and that he will please accept of it, and will take the trouble of informing me whether he chooses to have any concern with the Invention. The Author puts a high Value in it, as you may naturally suppose, but if Mr. Boulton will enter into any transaction with him about it, there is no doubt of finishing it on equitable terms. The Man is poor, and ingenious. It has frequently occurred to me that Mr. Boulton could turn his ingenuity to account, and at the same time make it more profitable to the possessor than the narrow demand of Edin[bu]r[gh] can possibly do. He is a pretty good workman at the Lamp, and in Brass and hard wo[o]d turning he is exceedingly neat. He has lately made an Electrical Machine for me in the most accurate and complete Manner, and has a good notion of philosophical (not mathematical) instrum[en]ts in general. If Mr. Boulton would be so kind to him as to pay his Coach hire from this to Birmingham, he would wait on him with his Invention, and perhaps a more useful Connection to both might be the result.

I ought to apologize to You for this instrusion on your time and attention but I hope this is unnecessary, since the Ingenious are certainly the natural patrons of Ingenuity. I shall therefore say no more, but am, with most cordial wishes for your health and prosperity

Dear Sir,
Your ob[edien]t Serv[an]t
John Robison

¹ See Letter 93.
² Aimé Argand (1755–1803) was the inventor of the Argand oil-lamp. It was patented in 1784 and Boulton undertook its manufacture. The patent was later overthrown.

149

Letter 104

WATT TO ROBISON

Incomplete draft. A.O.L.B.

Birm[ingha]m Aug[us]t 18th 1785

Proffessor Robison

Dear Sir

It gave me pleasure to hear from you by the receipt of yours of the 11th [Blank] Mr. Boulton is now in Cornwall where he probably will remain for a month or two I shall transmit your letter to him this post While you wait his answer it may not be amiss for you to know the foll[owin]g particulars Mr. B. has only a small share in the lamp business I believe only ¼ The rest belongs to Mr. Parker[1] and to Mr. Argand the Inventor who is a most worthy and ingenious man

Mr. A. has made two sorts of his lamps which have the flame at top as you describe one of which is in sale the oil in it is raised by a pump about once in ½ an hour The other which I believe he has not yet published though it is about a year since he made it at which time he showed me a drawing of it, has the oil kept always at the same height by means of a shorter column of water which drains from an upper reservoir into a lower one, and is so contrived that while any of the oil remains it is kept exactly to the same level and this I apprehend is the principle of Mr. Keirs lamp—Mr. Argands patent is not for any form of a lamp but for the Cylindric wick and the Glass chimney, so that I apprehend any body using either of these improvements would lye within the patent. This matter will be soon tried, that is in the next term as Mr. Argand and comp[an]y have brought an action against certain people in London who have infringed on their pat[en]t

If his patentees should be defeated Mr. K's invention will be of no value, as not only the most valuable part of the contrivance will lie open to the tinmen at large who will run down one anothers prices, and if he \Mr. K/ were to have a patent for his particular method of supplying the lamp his enemies would unite again[s]t him as they have done against Argand and he would find his purse too shallow for Westminster hall from which Good Lord deliver us—If Mr. Ar[gan]d and Comp[an]y should gain the suit then Mr. K. cannot make nor sell his lamps in England without their leave and without his lamp has some thing in it preferable to theirs which Mr. A has contrived himself

I should hardly expect they would give him much for it, but as an Ingenious man and good work man they would probably employ him and give him proper wages, All that I have said you must consider as coming only from me and not from any of them, and as impartial, for I am no way concerned in it otherwise than \from/ my friendship for Mr. B. and Mr. A. The latter Gentleman is now in france and I apprehend that in no case any agreement could be made with Mr. K. untill his return

Mr. Renny

[1] William Parker, London glass-maker and instrument-maker, friend of Dr Priestley.

Letter 105

BLACK TO WATT

Endorsed in Watt's hand, 'Dr. Black February 13th 1786' and numbered '41'. Dol.

[Undated]
[*13 February 1786*]

My dear Watt

I have not time just now to indulge in the pleasure of writing you a long letter, of myself I need only to say that I am in good health and every thing going well—I apply to you on this occasion to beg that you would take the trouble to look out the letters I wrote you about Mr. Cort and his Process for refining Iron in an Air Furnace and that you would send Extracts of them or the letters themselves to my Brother—*Mr. James Black Bennet Street Blackfryars London*

Hutton is well and other of your Freinds here who always remember you with affection—Present my Compliments to Mrs. Watt and Your Worthy Freind Mr. Bolton and beleive always that I am

Yours faithfully,
Joseph Black

WATT TO BLACK

Cover addressed: 'Doctor Joseph Black/Edinburgh/via Ferry-bridge', endorsed in Black's hand, 'From Mr. Watt 13 August 1786 with answer' and numbered '40'. Dol. The answer appears to be missing.

Doctor Black   *Birm[ingha]m Aug[us]t 13th 1786*

Dear Doctor

I am happy in hearing by our friend Mr. Guyot, of your good health and prosperity which I hope will long continue—I should have thanked you long ago for your very kind enquiries after me during my illness in the Spring, but I have been so inert and have had so much more to do than was agreable to me, that I have been very remiss in all kinds of correspondence, and I had nothing very new wonderfull or agreable to impart.

I now write on the account of my friend Dr. Stokes[1] of Stourbridge, who I suppose you will recollect to have studied at Edinburgh. There being room for another Physician at Shrewsbury by the death of Doctor Owen,[2] he proposes to remove to that place and to be a Candidate for the office of one of the physicians to the \County/ Hospital there, and as in these cases, it is wished to have reccommendations from the universities where the Candidates have studied, as well as from other Physicians of eminence, he means to apply to you for such Character as you may think he merited while with you, and as my acquaintance with him has been of several years, I thought it a duty to inform you that his behaviour and Character among his friends here, will no ways disgrace any reccommendation you may be pleased to bestow upon him. His merit in his profession, I am not qualified to judge of, but I know him to be a man of industry {and} application and discernment with a nice sense of honour and propriety. Since he left Edin[bu]r[gh] he has been on the Continent and attended the Hospitals for some time at Paris and at Vienna. I need say no more, as your Character of him must be given from your own Observations, but I thought it might be proper for you to know that he had not changed for the worse since he left you

Doctor Priestley has lately made some new and interesting exp[eri-men]ts   he finds on disolving Charcoal by boiling in spirit of nitre that it produces a considerable quantity of air about half of which is nitrous air and the remainder a mixture of fixt and phlogisticated air, but most fixt air—The Charcoal had previously been kept for some time in a violent heat

He has also found some curious results by making the steams of the nitrous and vitriolic acids pass over metals kept redhot in an earthen tube impervious to air, but as my attention to philosophical subjects has much abated and I try no experiments of any kind myself, now, I cannot remember particulars, nor perhaps w[oul]d they be interesting to you

With Best wishes to you and Doctor Hutton and Comp[limen]ts to all friends, I remain, Dear Doctor

Your's Affectionately
James Watt

Mrs. Watt desires to be remembered to you kindly—

On looking over my letter I think I sh[oul]d have spoken of Dr. S in warmer terms, but I hate superlatives and always wish to say a little less than I think

---

[1] Jonathan Stokes (1755–1831), physician and botanist. Member of the Lunar Society of Birmingham.

[2] Dr Pryce Owen was physician at the Shrewsbury Infirmary from 22 November 1757 until his death in July 1786.

Letter 107

ROBISON TO WATT

Endorsed in Watt's hand, 'Proffesor Robison by Dr. Rogerson August 15th 1786' and numbered '3'. Dol.

Edin[bu]r[gh] Aug[ust] 15 1786

Dear Sir

This will be presented to you by my much esteemed freind Dr. Rogerson,[1] first physician to the Empress of Russia. Altho' his Merit and Reputation will give him a sufficient recommendation to your Civilities, I flatter myself that it will be an additional Satisfaction to you that you are at the same time conferring a favour on your old acquaintance. I shall indeed think myself much indebted to you for every attention which you show to Dr. Rogerson, whose Society and freindship were the chief comforts of my Life while I was in Russia. I am obliged to him, even at present, for giving me this opportunity of bringing to your remembrance one who is with great truth and esteem

D[ea]r Sir
Your faithful friend and Serv[an]t
John Robison

If there be any information concerning Russia which is interesting to you in the way of Business, I know no person who can give it you to better purpose, or who will do it more cordially

[1] John Rogerson was a nephew of James Mounsey, who had been chief royal physician to the Empress Elizabeth of Russia and to the Emperor Paul. Born in Dumfriesshire, he graduated M.D. at Edinburgh in 1765 and went to Russia in the following year, where he remained for fifty years and was one of the Empress Catherine II's most trusted advisers. He was admitted a Fellow of the Royal Society in 1779.

Letter 108

BLACK TO WATT

Endorsed in Watt's hand, 'Dr. Black August 1786—about Varnish wanted' and numbered '40'. Dol.

[n.d. August 1786]

My dear Watt

Any letter from you is a feast to me tho it do not contain philosophical news. I gave Mr. Campbell who is son to Lord Stonefeild[1] and nephew to Lord Bute a letter of introduction to you this Summer but contrary to his intention he went to London and returned without touching at Birmingham. Haveing been alarmed about your health not long before, I took the liberty in that letter to recommend what I have found the most beneficial in my own Case which is to take regularly a sufficient quantity of exercise. I make it a rule to walk above three miles every day before dinner if the weather is cool or ride two hours if it is warm; sometimes I walk four or five miles. this prevents the languor and weakness which oppresses me when I sit too much. I often feel a degree of this weakness when I begin my walk but it wears off by continueing. In the same letter I enquired of you whether the hard oil Vernish (Vernis Martin)[2] which is put on Snuff Boxes and Teatrays is sold at a reasonable price at London or Birmingham. I have a Mahogony Cistern or Tub 2 feet wide and a few inches deep which I want to vernish—In the end of April last I had the pleasure to see two of your men very good like lads who called on me at your desire. One of them talked a little of your haveing a Scheme among you for makeing waggons travel by means of your Engine Are you serious in such a design? Some of Gilb[er]t Measons men have been working at it and have made a small model but I have not such an opinion of their heads as to have much curiosity to see their model. it is reported they have taken a patent for it

What follows is for your Freind Dr. Stokes and I hope it will serve his purpose better than a formal attestation..—Be so good as to acquaint him immediatly with your haveing received it and that I beg he will accept of it as an answer to his letter which I received this day— my kindest Compliments to Mrs. Watt

[No signature]

[1] Lord Stonefield had seven sons, all of whom predeceased him. Archibald, the eldest, died in 1774, while John, the second, was the hero of the siege of Mangalore, where he died in 1783.
[2] Vernis Martin = Copal Varnish.

Letter 109

WATT TO BLACK

Cover addressed: 'Doctor Joseph Black/Edinburgh/via Ferry-bridge', endorsed in Black's hand, 'From Mr. Watt 5 October 1786' and numbered '39'. Dol.

Birm[ingha]m Oct[ob]er 5th 1786
Doctor Black

Dear Doctor,

I was much obliged to you for your letter and favours Dr. Stokes, who has however lost his election to the Hospital which is given to Doctor Berrington[1] a Gentleman of *Birth* and *Estate*. Doctor S. desired me to express his due sense of his obligation to you for your kind approbation of him

I have enquired after the varnish here. I believe there are several sorts, but apprehend you mean the Copal Oil varnish which is the best and dearest \White/ Oil varnish. The price is 10/ per Quart, but what quantity that will varnish I cannot inform you, nor easily learn from Nostrum mongers, there is also the Black amber varnish, which you know; it requires a heat of between 300 and 400^d to dry it thoroughly

The Copal varnish will not bear more than about 130^d and preserve its Colour, but will dry moderately hard in the summer air. If you will write to me how much you want I shall procure it and send it to you via London or by the Waggon

I am much obliged to you for your advice, in regard to my health, which I practise as much as I can. However the disease came on me by too much Exercise and not by too little I was in London, in very indifferent weather, and struggling to get my business done and to get home I exerted myself too much The animal spirits became exhausted and the vital powers sunk to a very Low ebb, When I walked or used any exercise I was seized with a quick breathing like a person in a fever, which at length became continual, I lived abstemiously by way of curing it, but I grew weaker. I made a shift to get home where Doctor Withering ordered me Decoction of Bark and Ether with volatile tincture of Guiacum, to eat nourishing and high seasoned food and to drink as much Madeira as I could; by following his advice I grew better {slowly} but have taken all summer to recover

I am now in tolerable good health and spirits, but I fear the first fit of vexation or anxiety will throw me back again, in spite of regimen or Medicine, but I must do the best I can, and it is lucky that {such} vexations do not dwell so long on my mind as they used to do, nor do so many things vex me

I am happy to hear by Mr. Guyot and some other of your pupils that your health is tolerable and I hope the summer has still improved it.

You know I have long had plans of moving Wheel Carriages by Steam and \I/ have even described them in one of my patents some years ago—I believe I shall make some experiments on them soon but have small hopes of their ever becoming usefull—

I beg to be remembered to Doctor Hutton and to all other friends— Mrs. Watt joins in best wishes to you and I remain

Dear Doctor
Yours Affect[ionat]ely
James Watt

<hr>

[1] Dr Thomas Berington was physician at the Shrewsbury Infirmary from 8 October 1766 to 6 April 1771 and again from 22 September 1786 to 7 October 1788.

Letter 110

BLACK TO MRS. WATT

Endorsed in Watt's hand, 'Dr. Black December 28th 1787 about
Mr. Geddes Engine' and numbered '39'. Dol.

Edinb[urgh] 28th Dec[embe]r 1787

Madam

You have made me happy with the prospect of Mr. Watts Visit and yours to my house   be assured that we can accomodate you all perfectly well and with the greatest pleasure. I shall expect to have notice from Mr. Hamilton a few days before

My freind Mr. Geddes[1] manager of the Glass works at Leith, begs that Mr. Watt will consider at his leisure of an answer to the following Questions. What might [be] the prime Cost of a Steam Engine to do the work of ten horses, in grinding Kelp and broken Pots and in turning the wheels for cutting and engraving Glasses? what might be the consumption of fewel, and what supply of water would it require— Mr. Watt may perhaps be better enabled to answer when he sees some part of the machinery which is \at/ present wrought with horses— present my best compliments to Mr. and Mrs. Hamilton and beleive me to be with best wishes for many happy \years/ to you all

Madam   Your most obedient humble
Servant
J. Black

[1] The Geddes family had many connections with the manufacture of glass: Archibald Geddes was the manager of the Leith glass-works. William Geddes owned the works at which his younger brother, John, gained the practical experience that he applied elsewhere (see A. Clow and N. L. Clow, *The Chemical Revolution* (1952), pp. 289 and 291).

Letter 111

WATT TO BLACK

Cover addressed: 'Doctor Joseph Black/Physician/Edinburgh',
endorsed in Black's hand, 'From Mr. Watt 4th February 1788'
and numbered '38'. Dol.

Birm[ingha]m Feb[ruar]y 4th 1788

Dear Doctor

I should have writen to you sooner after my arrival here, which was
on the Tuesday evening after I left you, but have had many letters to
write and not over much alive. We had a pleasant Journey considering
the season and it was of service to my health as it wrought off the
asthma   Mrs. Watt got a cold in the Newtown, which has not yet quite
left her, but she is much better. The children are well and James returns
you many thanks for the fossil wood. Mr. Boulton is in London, has
had no return of his nephritic comp[lain]t but is not well with a cold he
has got, he is much obliged to you for thinking on his case and would
be glad to hear from you at convenience if any thing farther occurs on
that subject. Doctor Priestly has made some new Experiments which
bear hard on the doctrine of the formation of water from Deph[log-
isticate]d and inf[lamma]ble airs   he seperated D[ephlogisticate]d air
from minium by heat in an earthen Glazed tube, and inf[lamma]ble
air from Iron \by heat only/, he dryed both the airs by means of fixt
ammoniac which absorbed about half of them   he then mixt them
and exploded them in a copper tube shut with a cock. (He was obliged
to have recourse to the Copper because he burst so many Glass
vessels)   after several explosions he obtained a small quantity of a blue
solution of copper which was examined by Dr Withering and Mr.
Keir and found to be a solution of copper in nitrous acid.

I have my doubts yet concerning these experiments but from them
it w[oul]d appear 1st that a very large proportion of *all airs* even
9/10 is water 2d that nitrous acid is a component part of D[ephlog-
isticate]d air as well as of phlo[gisticate]d air or at least that D[ephlog-
isticate]d and inf[lamma]ble together form it and that probably
phlo[gisticate]d air is some modification of the other two. He says that
both the D[ephlogisticate]d and inf[lamma]ble airs were the purest he
ever had and that the D[ephlogisticate]d had an exceeding small
proportion of phlo[gisticate]d if any. There it stands at present, but all

158

may be changed again in a few months, a fresh opening seems to be made for the phlogistonians and Mr. Lavoisier must mend his theories, or confute the experiments. Mr. Keir has printed some sheets of his dictionary, but goes on slowly, not quite through *acid* yet.

I beg to remind you of your promise to visit us this ensuing summer which I earnestly entreat you to keep, every body here who know [*sic*] you would be happy to see you and I hope you will bring Dr. Hutton with you, perhaps we may find some stones for him, and our Iron works will please you both At present I have nothing else new to inform you except one or two more formidable new invented fire Engines, but they give me little pain, they may vanish *in fumo* and leave only a stink behind them, or if they should suceed and be better than ours I can do something else or live in quiet on what I have got. at present we have a good many orders.

Mrs. Watt joins me in affectionate Compliments to you and Doctor Hutton with many thanks for your kind entertainment. She reproaches herself with having forgot to pay her hair dresser for our dressing and will be much obliged to you to do it for her and she [will]† take some opportunity of repaying you

I remain
Dear Doctor
ever Yours Affectionately
James Watt

† Tear in paper at seal.

Letter 112

ROBISON TO WATT

Cover addressed: 'To Mr. James Watt Engineer/Birmingham',
endorsed in Watt's hand, 'Proffessor Robison February 5th 1788
desireing me to purchase a Silver Cup for him, says he has been
very ill since he saw me', and numbered '5'. Dol.

Edin[burgh] Feb[ruar]y 5 1788

Dear Sir

You will perhaps be surprised at a letter from me chasing you home, but it comes in my usual Stile of Petition, a liberty for which nothing can plead my Excuse but my confidence in your friendly attention

In my few excursions into the Streets I have been rumaging the Shops for a handsome Silver Cup for a present to a person to whom I am much obliged, but every thing ornamental is done here so rudely that I am disgusted with the work. It occurred to me that at Birmingham, where such an immense quantity of plate is manufactured, and tools and molds for every kind of ornament are in profusion, a piece of work of this kind must be had in perfection, and I flattered myself that you would have no reluctance to exercising your Taste and your freindly attention to serve me. Permit me therefore, good Sir, to beg that you would take the trouble of procuring for me as handsome a thing as Twenty p[oun]ds or Guineas will purchase. I wish it to hold not less than three English pints, so as to serve for Porter, the use to which they are generally applied in this Country. I wish it also without a Cover, which is a considerable addition to the price, without adding to the appearance, because it is left by the Servant on the Side Board when the Cup itself is in Use. For the same reason (i:e: to make a good appearance at a moderate Cost) I have no objection to the Cup not being in the very fashion of the day, because a thing may be equally handsome of a year or two prior date, and the Silver Smith will be willing to part with it on more easy terms. To tell the truth I do not passionately admire Etruscan Simplicity when *outrée*, as is the mode just now. I saw one the other day four or five years old, which pleased me much. The handles were something in this Stile I dont mean to *order* one to be made with the ornaments in any particular Stile, because this brings an additional Expence but if you meet with such a thing, if

out of the ordinary jog trot fashion, so much the better: and I think that in this way I may have something handsome and honest like for the Sum I mentioned. This I do not wish to exceed, because it would look more like ostentation than the desire of a friendly remembrance by means of the Keepsake.

It is very possible that I am desiring of you a favour which will subject you to a trouble which woud be quite unreasonable. If so, I trust that you will frankly say that you have no ready opportunity of helping me to what I want, and I will immediately write to an acquaintance in London to look out for it. I should not have asked this favour if I had not thought that you could do it without difficulty on any of your morning walks among the Tradesmen, and I was certain that if this was the Case I would get my purpose better answered and at less expence, thro' your kindness than by applying to any other Person. After having said so much about this trifle I am almost ashamed to request that you would take the trouble of writing me a line or two informing me what I may expect thro' your good offices. I wish that I could give you any favourable acc[oun]t of myself but I have been exceedingly ill since I had the pleasure of seeing you, and see no prospect of amendment. But I allways am with the greatest Esteem

Dear Sir

Your ob[edien]t h[um]ble Serv[an]t

John Robison

NB I wish the engraving on the Cup to be of that kind most commonly put on plate, i:e, done with the chisel or scraper, which gives a brilliancy not to be had *au Burin*.

Letter 113

ROBISON TO WATT

Cover addressed: 'To Mr. James Watt/Birmingham/Via Ferrybridge', endorsed in Watt's hand, 'Proffessor Robison March [*recte*] February 7th 1788 orders Silver Cup Symingtons engine Dr. B[lack]s illness and amendment', and numbered '6'. Dol.

Edin[bu]r[gh] 7 Feb[rua]ry 88

Dear Sir

I was very sorry to learn by the 16th ult[im]o, and also by a Letter from Mr. Rennie that you have been so much indispos'd since your return home. I sincerely wish that this may find your health reestablish'd. I should have acknowledged the receipt of your obliging letter much sooner had I been able, but my disorder continues to torment me so much, that I am oblig'd even now to make use of another hand. I have formerly try'd the warm bath as you propos'd but without any relief and am now advis'd to try Sea bathing, upon the supposition that my disorder arisses from Rheumatism or Relaxation.

Accept of my best thanks for the pains you have been at about the Cup and be assur'd that it was without any ceremony and in confidence that you would execute the commission with chearfulness, that I wrote to you. Allow me then with the same frankness to request that you will order the Cup to be made at Mr. Bolton's Manufactory. I wish it to be of as Large a size as can be made out of forty ounces without being flimsy. It need not be stout, because in this Country it is not of very constant use. You desir'd me to send a sketch. but in my present condition I cannot easily do it   I can only say that I wish it not to have these extravagantly \simple/ Etruscan handles which are at present in vogue and which I sketch'd in my last. I should rather prefer a handle somthing like the other sketch, provided it does not require new patterns, which would increase expence. I should wish the handles to be rather odd than common. with respect to the ornaments on the Vase, I agree with you in rejecting all Imboss'd chasing and would have them done in Silversmith's Engraving. It should have on the sides an Oval for a Crest with Festoons of Flowers and Foliage hanging pretty deep. I think that the rim should have an neat bead struck on a fillet, and perhaps a narrow border in the stile of an antique frett or freize below it. I should like it rather Tall than broad with the handles rising a good deal above the brim. If it would not increase the Expence I should wish the Foot to terminate in a square plinth. I have only to add that as the Gentleman for whom I intend it will leave this Country in a Month, it will be necessary that it be set about immediately, and I must request that you will order it to be sent to me by the very first opportunity and draw upon me for the amount. be not offended at my repeating my wish of having it very neatly executed.

Our Friend doctor Black has been extreemely Ill for some time and the Physicians were much alarm'd about his case. I am happy to say that he is now thought out of all danger, and is again attending his Class. I hear that Symington's[1] Engine at Wanlockhead is working very well, giving ten strokes of eight feet per minute, with a Load of twelve pounds, but I am told that the steam supports a Column of water five feet high. Mrs. Robison begins to grumble at my causing her write such stuff. I must therefore conclude with her Compliments and our

[1] William Symington sought to evade Watt's patent by arranging the condenser and air-pump in the lower end of the cylinder itself. It is probably his father who is referred to here. He was responsible for the erection of engines at Torryburn and Wanlockhead, but his son also erected an engine at Wanlockhead. He built a number of engines until stopped by Boulton and Watt in 1796.

joint wishes for the health and happiness of you Mrs. Watt and your Family remaining D[ea]r Sir

Your's Most
cordially John Robison

Letter 114

BLACK TO WATT

Cover addressed: 'Mr. James Watt/Engineer/Birmingham/by Ferrybridge', endorsed in Watt's hand, 'Doctor Black February 13th 1788 aerated alkaline ∇ in praise of' and numbered '38'. Dol. Also endorsed by Watt, 'answered'.

13 February 1788

My dear Freind

I was happy to learn by yours of the 4th that you got well home, I had seen Gilbert Hamilton however before I received it, who had told me of your safe arrival notwithstanding of the vexatious adventure you had with the stupid driver

What I wished to say to Mr. Bolton was this, that a considerable number of Persons in this Country who had complaints proceeding from Stones in the Kidneys or Bladder have used the alcaline aerated water and that every one of them have been greatly releived and the greater number have been totally freed from the symptoms of their Disorder—they drink about half an english pint twice in the day, if they drink more, it generally purges but if any person can drink more without being purged by it I know not any reason why they should not —The Stomach agrees with this Remedy perfectly well, a freind of mine has taken it two years incessantly without ever finding it in the least disagrable and all this time it has kept him free from pain or uneasyness tho he was sorely afflicted before   We do not suppose that it has the power to dissolve the stone, but I am persuaded that it can prevent { new stones from } the formation of new stones and the encrease of those already formed—This opinion is founded on the nature of the Stone which has been the most successfully investigated by Scheele—he found it to be soluble in small quantity in hot destilled water and that the Solution gave a red tinge to the Infusion of Litmus —This Exper[imen]t which I have found true, and the readyness with

163

which the Stone is dissolved by the Caustic Alkali shows that it is of an Acid nature and that the proper antidotes for it are alkalines—and the Caustic alkali the most powerfull of any; but it cannot be taken for a continuance in such quantity as to act on the Stone, it fatigues the Stomach and Constitution and gives too much acrimony to \the/ fluids—whereas in the form of the Aerated alkaline water it is totally free from these inconveniences

I thank you for the communication of Dr. Preistlys Exper[imen]t—It is a sore cut on poor Mr. Kirwan[1] who founds his calculations on the Supposition that Inflammable Air is pure Phlogiston—You do not explain whether the half which was taken from the airs by the fixed Amm[onia] was the half of their bulk or the half of their weight

You are sure enough now of a visit from me in the course of this Summer if I am living—A cold blast of wind and rain to which I was exposed in the meadow on the 24th Jan[uar]y encreased my cold to such a degree that I was laid up by it and under the necessity of loseing blood 2 or 3 times   I am now recovering but a good deal weakened and when I am able to resume my Lectures I must make short work of it and then take a ramble for the greater part of the Summer—My Plan at present is first to go to Ireland and see some of my Brothers whom I have not seen for more than 20 years, and then to cross from Dublin to Hollyhead and come straight to you in my way to London—Hutton proposes some excursions for himself to the mountains of Scotland and I wished him after one of these to have joined me at Birmingham but his head at present is so full of the mountains that he has no relish for any thing else

Present my kind Compliments to Mrs. Watt and tell her that whenever you pass again together this way I shall be greatly dissapointed if you do not lodge with me, and I shall take care to give you more compleat Accomodation   in the meantime God bless you—I am Y[ou]rs. J. Black

I have paid Mrs. Watts Hairdresser whose whole demands amounted to 2 Shillings

[1] Richard Kirwan (1733–1812), F.R.S., a leading chemist of his time. Wrote on specific heats, mineralogy, geology etc. President of the Chapter Coffee House Society and later of the Royal Irish Academy.

Letter 115

HODGES TO SOUTHERN

Cover addressed: 'Mr. Southern/Mr. Watt's/Harpers' Hill',
endorsed in Watt's hand, 'Mr. Hodges estimate Silver Cup—
1788' and numbered '4'. A.O.L.B.

Soho 15th Feb[ruar]y 1788

Mr. Southern

Sir

Agreeable to your request the following is as near an estimate of a
Silver 3 pint *chaced* 2 handled Cup, as can be made—

Weight, from 34 to 40, ozs.
Fashion from £5: 15.—to £6. 10—
and Duty 6d. per oz—

NB. The fashions may be higher or lower than above mention'd
according to the *quantity* and stile of Chaced work—If tis' wish'd will
send you drawings—

I am
Sir Your obed[ien]t Servants
p[e]r M Boulton
Jno. Hodges

Letter 116

WATT TO BLACK

Cover addressed: 'Doctor Joseph Black/Edinburgh/Via Ferrybridge', endorsed in Black's hand, 'From Mr. Watt April 1788'
and numbered '37'. Dol.

Ap[ri]l 7th 1788

Dear Doctor

I am happy to find by your kind letter of the 2d that you continue to
mend, and I hope you will go on in that way, and not over do yourself
by too much exertion

As to myself I have continued to recover, though with some retro-
gradations ever since Mrs. W. wrote you   the fever continued lurking

165

for some time, though so as to be perceptable only by the state of my tongue {and} the cough and a great feebleness. By proper treatment it is now quite gone, and has taken the Asthma with it, (which was a very troublesome {circumstance} \symptom/) my ap\p/etite and digestion are good and I gain strength daily. I have still however a dry cough, and a disagreable expectoration, sometimes very salt, but these abate, as does a painful stitch in the fleshy part of my left breast, which has been mended by a blister. I should perhaps have sooner recovered my strength if my cons[t]itution would have permitted me to take bark, but it disagrees with me in every form and does me more harm than good, I am at present taking no medicine except a small dose of Rhubarb and tartar vitriol[a]t[e] twice a day, in which I have just begun   I have been out several times in a chaise but last week was such weather as has confined me, yet I have recovered much in that time, and hope soon to be in my usual health

Having thus fullfilled your request, I beg leave to conclude with best wishes for yourself and Doctor Hutton

My Dear Sir y[ou]r affect[iona]t[e]

James Watt

Mrs. Watt begs your acceptance of her thanks for your kind sollici-tude about my health.—We hope soon to have the pleasure of seeing you here   [Written at side of page]

Letter 117

WATT TO BLACK

Addressed: 'Doctor Joseph Black/physician/Edinburgh/X post' and endorsed in Dr. Black's hand: from 'Mr. Watt 8 June 1788'. University of Edinburgh Library.

Birm[ingha]m June 8th 1788

Doctor Black

Dear Doctor

I have been in some hopes of having the pleasure of hearing from you, I am glad to hear by Mr MacGowan and others that your health was pretty well reestablished and I hope it continues to mend and that we shall have the happiness of seeing you here this summer. I should be glad to know about what time we may expect you, as I mean to make some excursions and would regulate myself as much as I could by your motions.

Last week I sent by Swaine and Andertons waggon a box directed for you containing two Plated tea Urns one of which I beg your aceptance of and that you will send the other to Doctor Hutton with my best wishes   I write a short line to him by this post lest you should be out of Town, that he may open the Box and take out his urn. I hope they will please, all I can say in their favour is that the workmanship is good and the shape fashionable which now adays constitutes beauty

I have lately improved upon a hint I saw and made a new Instrument for measuring specific Gravities of liquids   it consists of { an } a syphon of two equal legs with a tube pined to the bend of it and a little valve in that pipe   One leg being immersed in water and the other in the

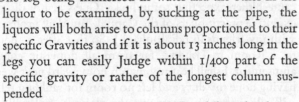

liquor to be examined, by sucking at the pipe, the liquors will both arise to columns proportioned to their specific Gravities and if it is about 13 inches long in the legs you can easily Judge within 1/400 part of the specific gravity or rather of the longest column suspended

I have nothing else now in the philosophical way except repetitions by Dr. P. of his experiments on the deflagration of D[ephlogisticate]d and inf[lamma]ble airs in which nitrous acid is always produced. as the deflagrations were performed in copper vessels the acid is saturated with Copper and is green but becomes blue on the addition of a small qu[anti]ty of common sprit of nitre. It appears however that more than 9/10 of the Liquor thus produced is water which probably in its own form constitutes the greatest part of the mass of All sorts of air. I think \it/ highly probable that the acid proceeds from the inf[lamma]ble air and that the D[ephlogisticate]d air acts the same part here that it does in the burning of sulphur and phosphorus

I have kept pretty well since I wrote last, but both the children have had the same sort of fever I had and are not fully recovered   yet— Mrs Watt Joins in best wishes to you

and I remain, Dear Doctor
Your's affectionatly
James Watt

ROBISON TO WATT

Endorsed in Watt's hand, 'Mr. John Robison by Mr. Ewart
July 25th 1788' and numbered '2' in bundle headed 'Miscellaneous Letters 1781-1790 No. 1 to 46'. Dol.

London, 25 July 1788.

Dear Sir

This will be presented to you by Mr. Peter Ewart, my Cousin, in the Employment of Mr. Rennie; I beg to recommend him to your kindness, not only for my Sake but on his own acc[oun]t, as a young man who will do credit to those who patronise him—Mr. Ewart will tell you my present Condition better than I have patience to write. I came hither expecting some lucky Guess at my disorder, among the extensive practitioners of the Capital. But they profess equal ignorance with my friends in Edin[bu]r[gh]. So that after a months confinment to a Room in London, far from all domestic comfort, society or amusement, I shall beat my march homeward next week, satisfyd with having done my duty and left no room for rankling reflection. But you will allow that my prospects are gloomy, and will therefore excuse the dulness of this Epistle. I could not think of missing such an opport-unity of being recalled to your remembrance, and of assuring you that I allways am with most affectionate Esteem and regard

D[ea]r Sir
Yours etc.
John Robison

Letter 119

BLACK TO WATT

Cover addressed: 'James Watt Esq./Buxton/to remain at the
Post Office till called for', endorsed in Watt's hand, 'Doctor
Black August 7th 1788' and numbered '37'. Dol.

London 7th Aug[u]st [1788]

My dear Sir

I had the pleasure to receive your letter of the 3d Curr[en]t and beg your pardon for haveing delayed so long to thank you for the kindness you shewed me at Birmingham. I shall never forget the goodness of my freinds there Mr. Garbetts letter procured me the most freindly reception from the Dean of Christchurch at Oxford,[1] who is one of the best and most agreable men I have ever known. he pressed me to lodge in his house which I did for one night and slept most comfortably —when I arrived at Woodstock I learned that the races were at Oxford and I found it difficult to get lodgeings even at Woodstock. but haveing Secured a bed I thought best to remain there 2 days or to the end of the races and I amused myself with Blenheim and my Book—had I forseen the obligeing reception which I met with at Oxford I should have staid but one day;—beside the Dean I had a young freind at Oxford, the professor of anatomy[2] who gave me the whole of his time—and I spent 2 compleat days there very agreably indeed at Windsor I spent a day and a half with our old freind Lind and visited Hirschel[3] and his Sister and had much pleasure in that Visit. Since I came here you may easily imagine I have not been idle—and I have reason to be thankfull that my health continues to improve. I cannot yet say when I shall leave London, but when I do leave it I shall wish to get home again as soon as possible and as I cannot travel very fast shall probably prefer the shortest way I cannot therefore promise to see you again on this occasion but beg to hear how buxton agrees with you

My Brother tells me that you have been desired to visit the Glass manufactory—I advised him to give you time to think on it and assured him you would do your best to serve the Co[mpany]—I found Mr. Rennie looking very thin and pale and complaining of his Stomach etc. —I am persuaded that he exhausts himself too much with running thro the endless streets of this monstrous City pray tell him it is my opinion he ought to avoid over fatigue of the Body as well as the mind —and frequently to employ the hackney Coaches—I learn from Edinb[urgh] that Dr. Hutton is gone to Isle o' man at the desire of the Duke of Athole and to meet his Grace there

My best wishes for you and Mrs. Watt and the bairns and I am

ever Most affectionatly

Yours

J. Black

[1] Cyril Jackson (1746–1819), dean of Christ Church, Oxford.
[2] William Thomson (1761–1803).
[3] Sir William Herschel (1738–1822), astronomer.

WATT TO BLACK

Cover addressed: 'Doctor Black/Mr. Byers/Charter house square/London', endorsed in Black's hand, 'From Mr. Watt 12 September 1788' and numbered '36'. Dol. The figures '30/246/8' and '6/240/40' are written above the address.

Birm[ingha]m Sep[tembe]r 12th 1788

Doctor Black

Dear Doctor

I received your kind letter at Buxton and should have wrote to you sooner after my return but thought you might have left London, until last night that I learnt from Mr. Boulton that you were still there. I found myself better of the Journey to Raven head[1] and from thence to Buxton, but did not perceive any benefit to arise from the use of the waters there. The drinking them caused an indigestion and costiveness, which obliged me to give up that use of them, at least to reduce it to one glass a day. The Bath seemed to agree well enough with me, yet I could feel that a longer use of it would have made me languid, this together with the rainy weather and incommodious lodgings made me come away after bathing 13 times. On the Journey home by way of Matlock and Derby I spent 3 days very agreably and was better than when at Buxton, since I came home, though I have had several fits of the Head ache more severe than have of late been usual, I have grown gradualy better and think myself better now than I was any time all last year, and very much better than when you were here, Mrs. Watt and the Children, especialy the latter, agreed very well with Buxton and got good appetites from the sharp air, though they made no use of the waters, and had the weather been better when I was there I think I should have received more benefit.

It will give me pleasure to learn how you are and if we may expect you to come this way—

I took the necessary memorandums at Raven head and think I can do some thing good for them, being now at work planning their motion. I have wrote to Herbert, our terms for a 14 horse Engine and only wait his orders to begin to it, which I wish to come soon as the winter approaches fast

I am sorry to learn that Mr. Rennie continues ill but hope that under your direction he will soon get better

Mrs. Watt joins in best wishes for you, and I beg you will present my Comp[limen]ts to your brothers, to Mr. Byers and to other friends remaining always

Dear Doctor
Yours most affectionately
James Watt

[1] Under an Act of 1771–3, monopoly of manufacture of plate glass was given to the Cast Plate Manufactory at Ravenhead, St. Helens.

Letter 121

BLACK TO WATT

Cover addressed: 'Mr. James Watt/Engineer/Birmingham/by Ferrybridge', endorsed in Watt's hand, 'Doctor Black October 9th about Calcarious cement and about Mr. Cappe', and numbered '36'. Dol.

Edinburgh, 9 October 1788

My dear Watt

Your kind letter of the 12th September found me still at London but longing for home and prepareing for my return to it. I left London about a week after and came by York and the weather being cooler than when I left home I felt more good from this journey than from the former ones especially now that I am rested. It gave me great pleasure to learn that your health too is improved   I beleive the journey and absence from business did more than the Water

On comeing home I opened the Box which you sent in June Dr. Hutton haveing left it untouched. We admired the elegance and good workmanship of the Tea Vases but were uneasy that you should have put your self to so much expence   We value them as a proof of your Freindship tho a superfluous one. I hope your Proposals have been accepted by the Plate Glass Company and that you have pleased yourself in the contrivance of their machinery   I am anxious that you should succeed uncommonly well in this undertakeing. At York I enquired for an old Glasgow College acquaintance and fellow student Dr. Cappe[1] a dissenting Clergyman there whose Son studied with us last winter and tho I did not find the Doctor at home I learned from Mrs. Cappe that one of his Sons has served an apprenticeship at

171

Birmingham and wishes now to be employed as a Clerk or Overseer in a manufactory   from what I heard he appears to have some mechanical genius   I was told that he has been contriveing a machine for cutting velvet at less expence than what is now required. I hope it will not be inconvenient for you to receive a visit from this young man and to give him your Opinion of his machine   I am not personally acquainted with him but know his Father and his brother and the rest of the family and have a high Esteem of them   I shall therefore send him a line of introduction to you. But he is at present at York to stay two or three weeks before he return to Birmingham. If you could be usefull to him by good Advice and assisting him to find an employment it would give me particular pleasure—I lately made a paste or cement which may be usefull to you on some occasions The materials are Quicklime rubbed to a fine powder (not slaked) and Melasses, beaten together to a tough adhesive paste—it adheres to every thing, metal, Glass etc., it neither swells nor contracts so far as I have perceived, and acquires gradually very great hardness and I beleive by time will resist the action of water to soften it—I suppose that an extract of Malt would be equally good with the Melasses, you may keep this to yourself. Present my best Compliments to Mrs. Watt and Mr. Bolton and the rest of the good freinds I found at Birmingham and beleive me always

Yours most affectionatly

Edinb[urgh] 9th Oct[obe]r   J. Black
1788

[1] Newcome Cappe (1733–1800) was the eldest son of the Rev Joseph Cappe of Leeds He matriculated at Glasgow in 1752. Minister of the Dissenting Chapel of St Saviour-Gate, York, 1755–1800.

Letter 122

BLACK TO WATT

Cover addressed: 'Mr. James Watt/Engineer/Birmingham/by favour of Mr. Cappe', endorsed in Watt's hand, 'Doctor Black October 25th 1788' and numbered '35'. Dol.

Edinb[urgh] 25 Oct[obe]r 1788

My dear Freind
    This will be delivered to you by Mr. Cappe who has been studying to contrive a machine for cutting velvet and who will probably ask

your opinion of it. he wishes to be employed as a Clerk or Overseer in some manufactory and will inform you of what he has done to qualifye himself and of the persons with whom he has hitherto served. It would give me much pleasure to hear that you found opportunitys of being usefull to him and I have no doubt of your inclination—

In my last I mentioned a Cement which I thought had some remarkable qualitys, but I have since found that my Judgement of it was premature, it shews a disposition to swell a little by time in consequence of which it has cracked {into} a plate of Glass, on which it was spread, into a great number of Peices. Dr. Hutton received your letter and is much obliged to you for your Map of Cornwall.—he joins me in best Compliments to Mrs. Watt Mr. Bolton and other Freinds

I am

Yours affectionately

J. Black

Letter 123

ROBISON TO WATT

Endorsed in Watt's hand, 'Mr. John Robison March 13th 1789 by Dr. Baader' and numbered '3' in bundle headed 'Miscellaneous Letters 1781–1790 No. 1 to 46'. Dol.

Edin[burgh] March 13 1789

Dear Sir

I take the liberty of introducing to your acquaintance Dr. Baader,[1] a young Gentleman who has been at this University for two or three Years. The confinement which my bad health has subjected me to has prevented me from being acquainted with him till very lately, and even then has given me very little opportunity of his conversation. This I regret exceedingly, because I find that he has given an attention to subjects connected with mechanical knowledge which is very uncommon, and I have met with very few who seem to have studied those things in the scientific manner he has done. Dr. Baader seems to have taken a strong predilection for this line of Study, and knowing that he has given more attention to it than would be proper as a mere amusement, has thoughts of making it a profession. For this purpose he will employ some time in seeing, both what information he may pick up by viewing the mechanical performances in England, and whether he may not find some opportunity of employment in the same way. I thought I could not do him a greater service than by recommending him to your Civilities, being confident that he may rely as much on your candor in advising him as in your abilitys to inform him—and I trust that you will not find him unworthy of your notice—I refer you to Dr Baader for any acc[oun]t of myself, and am with great esteem

D[ea]r Sir
Your aff[ectiona]te h[um]ble Serv[ant]
John Robison

[1] An engineer to the Court of Bavaria, Joseph von Baader later entered the service of the Earl of Balcarres who thought him to be the 'best and most ingenious mechanic in the world'. He was engaged to run the Haigh ironworks, since he claimed to have reorganized the ironworks at Coalbrookdale and those of John Wilkinson. The Haigh Ironworks did not, however, prosper under his control.

Letter 124

WATT TO BLACK

Cover addressed: 'DoctorBlack/Edinburgh/with a small parcel', endorsed in Black's hand, 'From Mr. Watt Birmingham November [recte March] 15 1789' and numbered '13'. Dol.

Birm[ingha]m Mar[ch] 15th 1789

Dear Doctor

I have not had the pleasure of hearing from you nor of you for a long time, and long much to hear how you have stood through this severe winter

I have long intended to have written to you, but having had my usual weak winters health, and for some time been tormented with business more than commonly vexatious I have delayed it from day to day—I have got some good stones of Tin from Cornwall for you which I shall send off by the waggon this week, one has some gold in it. The Mines there are perishing fast, they are in themselves poor and the prices of their produce still more so. Tin cannot be sold, at any price. Philosophical news I have none except what is contained in Dr. Priestleys paper which I send with this, begging the favour of you to deliver \to/ Dr. Webster[1] his copy, Lately Dr. P. has tried with all the accuracy he could whether any Phlo[gisticate]d air was decomposed in his process of Dephl[ogisticatio]n and finds that nitrous air well managed and Voltas eudiometer give exactly the same result of mixtures of Ph[logisticate]d and D[ephlogisticate]d airs consequently that in that process the inf[lamma]ble \nor D[ephlogisticate]d/ air has no action upon the phlo[gisticate]d With best wishes for you Dr. Hutton and other friends—I ever remain, Dear Doctor

Your's affectionately
James Watt

[1] Dr. Charles Webster was one of the physicians to the army and obtained the degree of M.D. from the University of Edinburgh in 1777. He practised in Edinburgh, officiated as one of the physicians to the Public Dispensary, read lectures on chemistry and published several works. He went to the West Indies as physician to the army and died there on 5 December 1795.

Letter 125

BLACK TO WATT

Endorsed in Watt's hand, 'Doctor Black April 12th 1789' and numbered '34'. Dol.

Edinb[urgh] 12th April 1789

My dear Freind

I received your letter of the 15th March which as I longed to hear from you was a most welcome one although the pleasure it gave me was allayed by some articles in it—your haveing been tormented with business more than commonly vexatious and the declining state of the Cornish mines cannot have a tendency to improve your health—In the end of last Summer it was certainly improved by the excursion you made to Buxton etc. I wish you would plan such another for this Summer and put it in practice as soon as possible After I came home in the beginning of October last I recruited health and flesh remarkably; still however I began my winters labours with some dread of the consequences but by liveing cautiously and fenceing out the Cold I have got on without one days interruption not however without some Colds and a good deal of Coughing but by taking early care of these colds they never became violent. Dr Hutton is perfectly well but John McGowan[1] had lately a Cold with inflammation in his breast for which

he was bled, he is still confined and is likely to cough and spit for a good while—
Return my gratefull thanks to Dr. Preistly and Mr. Keir for their freindly communications with which I have been much entertained and edifyed. As Mr. Keir is actually printing I hope we shall soon have the whole work published—your kind attention in procuring for me the large Tin Crystals is very obligeing. They are not yet arrived and I suppose have not been delivered to the Carrier so soon as you intended —It will require your Care and ingenuity to pack them so well that they may not break loose and go to logger heads during so long a Journey   I am
My dear Freind
Yours most affectionately
Joseph Black

[1] John McGowan was a member of the Oyster Club, founded in Edinburgh by Adam Smith, Joseph Black and James Hutton. He was a founder Fellow of the Royal Society of Edinburgh and had previously been a member of the Philosophical Society of Edinburgh.

Letter 126

WATT TO BLACK

Cover addressed: 'Doctor Joseph Black/Edinburgh', endorsed in Black's hand, 'From Mr. Watt May 5th 1789' and numbered '35'. Dol.

Birm[ingha]m May 5th 1789

Doctor Black

Dear Doctor
    Your letter of the 12th Ap[ri]l gave me much pleasure, as I had had at London some intimations of your having been ill, which however your Brother assured me had not been the case, I am glad nevertheless to have a confirmation from yourself. As you have found yourself so much stronger from last summers excursion I hope it will engage you to repeat it and that we shall have the happiness of seeing you here again.
    Soon after I wrote you last I was obliged suddenly to go to London, and did not send your stones off until my return about 2 days before I received your letter, they went in a small box by Swain and Andertons waggon and I hope are now safe with you. The stone with the grains of

176

Gold in it is from Garnan mine and the others from Polgooth near St. Austle. I hope Mr. McGowan is now recovered I am told inflammatory disorders are very rife here just now Dr. Withering is very ill with an inflammation in his Lungs which is the second time he has had it this season, he seems however to be upon the recovery. I got a cold at London that plagued me for some time and has left me the Asthma, very frequent and continued, it however does not do me much harm except making me very inactive, and unable to walk much, Mrs. Watt is just recovering from a severe fit of illness I believe of the nephritic kind, which confined her to her bed for some days, and the cold weather prevents her from going out, she desires her kind Compliments to you and wishes to consult you about our Little Daughters head aches which have been worse this season, but which I shall make the subject of another letter. When you may be at more leisure to answer it.

Dr. Priestley in trying to get pure dephlogisticated Air cheap has repeated one of his former processes with great success he fills an earthen [pipe] of about $\frac{3}{4}$ inch bore Glazed outside with bits of broken crucibles and sends the steam of oil of vitriol through it which produces a very great quantity of very pure D[ephlogisticate]d air free from any sulphureous smell, he has not yet examined the water through which it passed, but means to do it soon, he found no sulphur in the tube nor smell of it

The Antiphlogistians hold fast by their theory and Mr. Lavoisier has written a very able elementary book on Chemistry on that theory. The \1st Number/ of the Annales de Chymie by Lav[oisie]r Berth[olle]t Monge, and Fourcroy,[1] {are} is published and may be had soon from Mr. De Boffe Gerard street Soho London—I hear Dr. Crawford has discovered a remedy for Cancerous and scropholous diseases, it is the Terra ponderosa dissolved to saturation in ⊖÷ the dose from 2 to 12 drops in a glass of water twice a day he is to publish it soon

I recollect no other philosophical news—Mr. Boulton keeps pretty well by drinking the aerated alkali, he finds that mixing warm milk with it prevents its sitting heavy on the stomach

I remain Dear Doctor, very truly
Your Affect[iona]t[e] friend
James Watt

[1] Claude Louis Berthollet (1748–1822); Gaspard Monge (1746–1818); Antoine François de Fourcroy (1755–1809).

BLACK TO WATT

Cover addressed: 'Mr. James Watt/Engineer/Birmingham/by Ferrybridge', endorsed in Watt's hand, 'Doctor Black July 2d 1789' and numbered '33'. Dol.

[2 July 1789]

My dear Watt

I received your letter of the 5th May in which you made me expect another soon after on the Subject of your Daughters Headachs, I hope they have been less troublesome and that profitable Business has taken up your time, some person told me lately that an Engine of yours was to be set up in Portugal. I rec[eive]d the Tin ores which are rich and massy, but what I wishd most to have was a few of the regular crystals of as conspicuous a sise as those I saw in Mr. Boltons Collection but I have given you too much trouble already and can now apply to another hand viz. Raspe[1] who is at present employed in surveying the northeren and western part of Scotland to make usefull discoverys in the mineing way—We have got an ingenious young iron founder here one Cottrel who came from Birmingham and who has perfected a machine, which others had thought of and attempted, for threshing corn; it threshes 3 Scotch Bolls in the hour with one horse incomparably better and more perfectly than is commonly done by men and they are bespoke by the farmers faster than he can make them It can be set up in the end of a Barn or in a Space of ten feet square, it works in the scutching way

In your next give a word of news about what you have done for the Glass company—but the cheif reason for my writing at present is to beg your opinion of a Mr. Labrot or Lubrot[2] of Birmingham, whether he be an agreable man to live with and appears to understand his business and to be thriveing—whether it be advisable for a young man who wishes to enter into business at Birmingham to form a connection with him I shall take care to be discreet in the use I make of what you communicate—present my respectfull compliments to Mrs. Watt and love to the rest of your family—and beleive me

Yours most affectionately
Joseph Black

I have got a horse and
ride often which does me
much good—I wish you could try the same remedy
it is excellent against the asthma and tho you might
find it much too hard exercise at first, it is possible
you might bear it well afterwards, provided
always that you give your horse no corn, for that
makes them intolerably foolish and willfull

[1] Rudolf Erich Raspe (1736–94), German geologist and author, creator of 'Baron Munchausen'.
[2] The firm of Labrott and Hughes, merchants, appears in the Birmingham directories, first in 1787 at St Paul's Square and then in 1790 and 1800 at Fleet Street. Mr Frederick Labrott lived in Charlotte Street in 1790 and in Hagley Row in 1800.

Letter 128

BLACK TO WATT

Cover addressed: 'Mr. James Watt Engineer/Birmingham/turn
at Ferrybridge', endorsed in Watt's hand, 'Dr. Black August 1st
1789 about Jessy's health' and numbered '32'. Dol.

[1 August 1789]

My dear Watt
    I had the pleasure to receive your letter of the 11th Current and Mrs.
Watts addition   I thank you for what you have communicated and you
may depend on my discretion in the use of it. Mrs. Watts account of
Jessys[1] health appears to me sufficiently complete and I have no difficulty
in forming my opinion which is that medicines are only fit to palliate her
complaint and give a temporary releif but were they to be continued for
a long time without interruption they might do harm in place of good.
They may be used however with advantage when she happens to be
reduced to greater weakness than ordinary as she was in consequence of
her attending the day School. And the medicines most likely to be usefull are bitters, bark, and the rust of Iron. But the means from which I
would expect the most releif and amendment are proper exercise and
attention to Diet
    In the greater number of cases similar to Jessys these Headachs proceed
from disorder of the stomach in consequence of something haveing been

eaten which disagrees with it or is not digestible by it such as butter, cream, rich milk, fat meat, pye crust, acid or acescent substances, spices of different kinds and other things which tho easily digested by ordinary stomachs disagree however with particular constitutions. This disposition of the stomach to be disordered by such things proceeds therefore from a peculiarity of constitution and from weakness; by strengthning the whole system the powers of the stomach are strengthned and it becomes less liable to such disorders but we cannot hope to perform a compleat cure that will give security against a return. All that can be done is 1st To investigate by observation and afterwards avoid the foods etc. which disagree with the stomach and produce the headach and 2dly to strengthen the System; The most effectual and safe method of strengthning the system is to be often in the air and to take proper exercise. The best exercise for this purpose is rideing, especially when the weather is not very cold, in cold weather walking may be preferred. The Cold Bath is also a powerfull means for strengthning the System when there is enough of strength to bear it well. The journey or ramble which you propose cannot miss to produce good effects on the whole company. If you should turn your face northw[ar]ds and come this length I hope you will let me know and spend a few days with me—present my kind compliments to Mrs. Watt and the young folks and beleive me always

most affectionately yours
Joseph Black

Edinb[urgh] 1st August
1789
I have been much occupyed and sometimes absent from home since I rec[eive]d your letter and Mrs. Watts which has prevented me from answering sooner

[1] Janet(Jessy) Watt (1779–94), daughter of James Watt by his second wife, Ann McGrigor. Jessy's death and Gregory Watt's from consumption turned Watt's thoughts to the treatment of consumption by the inhalation of the newly discovered gases.

WATT TO BLACK

Cover addressed: 'Doctor Joseph Black/Edinburgh', endorsed
in Black's hand 'From Mr. Watt September 17th 1789' and
numbered '34'. Dol.

Doctor Black   *Birm[ingha]m Sep[tembe]r 17th 1789*

Dear Doctor

I received in due time your kind letter of Aug[us]t 1st and both Mrs
W[att] and myself hold ourselves much obliged to you for your advice
concerning Jessys health which we have pursued as far as we could, and
she is now much stronger and better of her head aches, the late violence of
which I think probably owing to her breeding teeth   Mrs W. is exceedingly much recovered from the complaint in her bowels by drinking
Cheltenham waters for a month and I hope is in the way of getting
perfectly well again, she can now walk 4 or 5 miles without Injury,
whereas before she set out on her journey she could not walk one mile
without being much disordered in her stomach and head   after leaving
chelt[enha]m we made a weeks tour into S. Wales which has done me
much good. The stay at Cheltenham was of little other service to me than
making me eat my breakfast more heartily, as I only drank a little of the
water a few times by way of experiment, and I found little to amuse me
there. At the same time I found myself unable to walk much and I cannot
now endure to ride on horse back; by perseverance in walking, tired or
not, and by the Jaunt I have pretty well recovered the use of my legs,
especialy since I came home; for health generally comes to me in consequence of a Journey not during the time of it, so that I have good hopes
of myself for the remainder of this year   I wish much to hear as good
an account of you and hope you will write soon

News I have little, Mr. Keir has published 200 pages of his dictionary
which as far as I can judge is an excellent and complete compilation, I
understand Elliot has bought the Copies. Dr. Priestley has also finished a
new edition of His philosophical works, arranged according to the subjects, but it is not yet gone to the press. Mr. Landriani[1] has written to me
that Mr. Klaproth[2] of Berlin has found Alcalis to consist of phosphoric
acid united to fixt air, but Mr. L. had not been informed of any particulars, and I do not understand how it can be. I have seen no curious
stones in my travels, except the calcarious stones in the Coteswold composed principaly of small eggs, not so distinct as the Ketton Stone. South

Wales is a tame Country, as far as Brecknock the limit of my travels, fine cultivated Valleys and gently sloping hills, the stones mostly a *very* hard grit, often laminated and hard lime stones like the Bristol lime and both these are attended with red marle

I beg to be remembered kindly to Doctor Hutton and to call other friends with you and remain, Dear Doctor

Your's sincerely and affectionately
James Watt

[1] Marsiglio Landriani (fl. 1780–1800), Italian natural philosopher, inventor of an early audiometer.
[2] Martin Heinrich Klaproth (1743–1817), German chemist, made many advances in chemical analysis.

Letter 130

BLACK TO WATT

Cover addressed: 'Mr. James Watt/Engineer/Birmingham/X Post', endorsed in Watt's hand 'Doctor Black November 30th 1790' and numbered '31'. Dol.

Edinb[urgh] 30th Nov[embe]r 1790

My dear Freind

I received your letter by Mr. Houlbrooke and shall not fail to pay all the attention in my power to him and the young Gentlemen under his Care. You had heard that my health had been better for a considerable time past than it was before   And it is true that I was better during the last Summer than I had been for a year or two past but I am liable to returns of the same disorder which had weakened me so much when I saw you at Birmingham—I had an attack of it in the month of March last—and another on the \night of the/ 27th of October {after} haveing delivered the first Lecture of my Course that Day—In 12 or 13 days however I was so far recovered as to proceed with my Course but I feel much weakness and a disposition in my lungs to be easily injured The Cold of this Season is also hard on me   I find it difficult to keep myself warm with any quantity of Cloathing and the exercise of walking which used to warm me fatigues me too much—I am also much less able for Study than formerly. In short I feel that I am wearing out and had circumstances permitted, I beleive the best thing I could have done this winter would have been to travel away to a warmer climate—As things stand however

182

I am engaged here—and that I may be able to go on the better I have commissioned a Sedan Chair from London—When I think of all this my Spirits are rather low and my Prospects discourageing—but this may be partly a consequence of the weakness induced by my late Illness—when I pick up more strength and courage I shall write you again—You have probably heard of the metallisation of some of the common Earths which has been effected in the Austrian Dominions

Assure Mrs. Watt Mr. Bolton and other Freinds of my best wishes and respects and beleive me allways

Yours most affectionately
Joseph Black

Letter 131

WATT TO BLACK

Cover addressed: 'Doctor Joseph Black/Edinburgh', endorsed in Black's hand, 'From Mr. Watt 5th December 1790' and numbered '32'. Dol.

Heathfield Birm[ingha]m Dec[embe]r 5th 1790

Doctor Black

My Dear Doctor

The receipt of yours would have given me much pleasure had it conveyed better accounts of your health, the present state of which makes me very uneasy. I wish I could give you any advice which could be of service to you. Have you tried the Comforts of the fleecy Hosiery, it is much recommended here. I approve much of the sedan which will tend to preserve you from some colds; but I must earnestly entreat you to \in/ practice the following Scheme, which you must approve as consonant to your own doctrines. Endeavour to get some one to read your lectures for you in the next winter, come to England in summer and in harvest proceed to the Continent and pass the winter at Nice, or else in the southern part of Italy, and turn your course northward as the heats grow troublesome, by which means you will enjoy 3 \Scotch/ summers running, besides the great benefit your health must receive from the Jolting and the view of strange men and things. I will not attempt to use my arguments with you, further than that a restoration of your health would give much pleasure to all your friends, and that in your complaints this seems the most likely way to attain it. My friend Dr. Withering has had many attacks of an inflammation in the Lungs, with Symptoms very similar to yours, he has hitherto been able to cure himself, and if you thought proper to state your case to him, I am sure that from his esteem for you he would give his opinion with pleasure

My recommendation of Mr. Holbrooke was not so warm as it might have been if some circumstances relative to his marriage with Miss Wilkinson had been otherwise; but he is a well informed sensible man and an agreable companion with whom I have formerly been in habits of some intimacy and I could not refuse him an introduction to you, though it is always against my conscience to trouble you with strangers.

I find the metalisation of the earths is contested, but surely the proof is easy, if they disolve the reguli in ☉✕ and precipitate with an alkali, they should again have the earths they set out with. I hear of nothing new here in the way of philosophy or chemistry and the french are so busy idolizing their liberty, that they are as idle

We are going on well enough in our business, but are attacked on many hands, and among the rest of our invaders are our *good friends* John Wilkinson and William Reynolds.[1] The former acts avowedly for his own interest, the latter from a purer motive, the good *of the public*, and the preventing our being paid for our merit more than we deserve. These and other things together with the failure of my own headpiece, make business exceedingly irksome to me; yet my health is much better than it has been, my headaches are less painful though more stupefying, so as frequently to render me unable to think.

W removed about 2 months ago to a new house about half a mile from Mr. Boultons, which is pleasant and commodious, but has cost me much more money than I think I had a right to lay out in that way.

Mrs. Watt has much recovered her health (principaly by the asistance of Cheltenham waters) the Children are well and I hear good accounts of my son James application to business at Manchester

I beg of you to keep up your spirits as well as you can, it will at least alleviate your Complaints   let me hear from you as frequently as is convenient and please also inform me how Doctor Hutton does   I was extremely sorry to hear of the loss of his sister which must have been a great shock to a man of his degree of affection and sensibility

Mrs. Watt joins me in best wishes for your health and happiness and

I remain

My dear friend

Your's most affectionately

James Watt

[1] John Wilkinson and William Reynolds, of Broseley and Ketley respectively, both ironmasters, pirated Watt's engine for their own use.

WATT TO BLACK

Cover addressed: 'Doctor Joseph Black/Edinburgh/X post',
endorsed in Black's hand, 'From Mr. Watt 23 November 1791'
and numbered '31'. Dol.

Heathfield
Birmingham
Nov[embe]r 23d 1791

Doctor Black

Dear Sir
It is very long since I had any letter from you and it gave me much pain
to hear some bad accounts of you lately, and also that Doctor Hutton
was indisposed. It will oblige me if you will write me a few lines upon
your own health and his, at your first convenience, or rather when you
find yourself inclined so to do, for I cannot wish to give you pain { with }
\by/ making it a duty.

The Hellish miscreants who committed so many outrages here,[1] by
banishing Dr. Priestley, have almost broke up our Lunar Society, at
least when we meet we have more politics than Philosophy so that I have
nothing new in the latter line, and the former is not worth troubling you
with, any farther than to tell you that this town is divided into 2 parties
who hate one another mortaly, that the professed Aristocrates are democrates in { principle } \practice/ that is encouragers of the mob; and that
the democrates, are those who have always contended for a police and
good goverment of the town, therefore are in fact aristocratic { in fact } at
least would have no objections to an aristocracy of which they themselves
were members—

I have heard that there is some body at Edinburgh makes artificial
marble. If you have heard of it I shall be obliged to you when you write
to mention whether it is a real stone, or an imitation by varnish or
enamel, if a stony composition resembling marble whether vitreous,
Gypseous or calcarious, all this only if you have seen or been informed of
the thing, for I do not wish you to have the trouble of enquiries

The reason of my enquiries is that I have been employed some time
upon an artificial Alabaster which I have brought nearly to the hardness
and semitransparency of marble—very much harder than any natural
alabaster, but I do not mean to make this publick and say little about it

until I see whether it can be made useful, to myself or family; for I have no great passion for fame now. I shall therefore be obliged to you not to mention it.

Mrs. Watt joins me in wishing you good health and good spirits, which are still more valuable, and we beg our best wishes may also be presented to Doctor Hutton, with comp[limen]ts to other friends

I remain

Dear Doctor

Yours affectionately

James Watt

[1] A reference to the Priestley Riots.

Letter 133

BLACK TO WATT

Cover addressed: 'Mr. James Watt Engineer/at Heathfield Birmingham/by Ferrybridge', endorsed in Watt's hand, 'Dr. Black December 1st 1791' and numbered '30'. Dol.

Edinb[urgh] 1st Decem[ber] 1791

My dear Freind

It is true that Dr. Hutton has been very ill and in great danger for some days, his Disorder was a suppression of urine which could not be re-leived by the Catheter or bougies, the bladder became much distended and very painfull and the urine began to be absorbed and to affect his head when we made a puncture and introduced a flexible pipe above the *os pubis* This gave him releif in the mean time—and a few weeks after the natural Passage began to open again and is now restored nearly to its natural State, very little of the urine being now voided by the artificial Passage—he was \first/ taken ill in the beginning of August or not long after it, and the danger he was in, together with the uncomfortable Prospect that was before him gave me such such [*sic*] a shock that I was much weakened by it. he is now however a great deal better and in good spirits, he begins to sit up out of bed and to do a little business—I exerted myself to get the better of the weakness which the above shock had brought on me by going often out in a chaise or on horseback when unfortunately in the beginning of September my horse fell and crushed my leg and foot

so ill that I was feverish and got no refreshing sleep for some time after—
This weakened me again and made me very anxious about the consequences—however by exerting myself and going out every day in a
chaise as soon as I was able for it I recovered so far as to be able for
lecturing when the time came—and have \been/ continued to lecture, I
find it necessary however to keep at home, or go abroad only in a chair or
carriage and am under the necessity of paying great attention to the
warmness of my cloathing—I mention this last that you may profit by it
—The horrible Disorders of Birmingham gave us much distress when
we heard of them   we were under strong apprehensions for our freinds
there and you in particular and it gives me pain to hear that the bad
humour has not yet subsided—you must surely take care hereafter to
have a strong Body of the military within a small distance of the town.
The artificial marble made here is made in the common way with
Gypsum Lime and other materials and the artist who is an Italian calls
himself a Scagliolist (Scagliola being their name for Gypsum or works in
Gypsum) he imitates some of the opake and coloured marbles very well
such as Siena and Brocatell and also the Porphyrys especially the deep red
or purple—but his white marble has no transparency whatever and is
absolutely ugly—one of the principal advantages of this art is the facility
of imitating inlaid work in marble in which flowers festoons and foliages
are represented, and which are extravagantly dear when executed in real
marble—Pray are you satisfyed that the Quartz which was found at the
root of the tree struck by lightning in Blenheim Park was really melted,
and melted by the lightning   If so it is a most extraordinary fact and
deserves to be compleatly ascertained—My best wishes attend Mrs.
Watt and the rest of your family and our freinds at Birmingham and I am
always

My dear Freind yours most affectionately
Joseph Black

MRS WATT TO BLACK

Cover addressed: 'Dr. Joseph Black/Edinburgh', endorsed in
Black's hand, 'From Mrs. Watt at Glasgow 6th November 1792'
and numbered '30'. Dol'

Glasgow Nov[embe]r 6th 1792

Dear Sir

I received a letter from Mr. Watt wherein he requested I would write
you wishing to have some account of your health and hoping that it may
not have suffered by the long tract of Bad weather which we have
had   he also desires me to inform you that Mr. Guyot a Gentleman which
you may remember spent two Winters about 6 or 7 years ago in Edinburgh
and had two french Gentlemen under his care and was recommended to
you by Mr. Watt   The family of De Lessert[1] with which he was connected and much esteemed by the destracted state of france are all dispersed
and Mr. Watt says—"Mr. Guyot wishes to resume his old employment
"and desires me to recommend \him/ to any one who has a young man or
"two to send abroad for their education (that are to study) not to cut a fig-
"ure and spend money, and has no objection to attending them in England
"or any of the Scotch Universities   He may be safely recommended as a
"man of firm character good temper Science and knowlege of the world
"with much application" I ought to have wrote you sooner but being
with my father in the country I delayed it till I came to town   I do not
know if Mr. Watt wrote you from Cornwall where Mr. Boulton \and
him/ were obliged to go as the Hornblowers[2] and others had erected
Engines which it is said was intirely B and W   I came to pay my father a
visit when Mr. Watt went to Cornwall   I am very sorry to hear that B
and W are obliged to com\m/ence a Law suit or lose Cornwall intirley
with the examples of former patent Trails   they have many fears the
suit will begin in a few days and they hope it will be ended before
Christmas What ever way it ends I hope Mr. Watt will find himself
better than the uneasy agitated state of mind he has been in for some
time would permit Him to be. I intend remaining here 12 or 14 days
longer   if you have any commands for Mr. Watt I will be happy to
carry them   I have entered Gregory[3] a student at the College

here Jessy and him beg to be remembered to you with best Compliments to you and Dr. Hutton I remain

Dear Sir
Yours
A Watt

[1] De Lessert and Co., Bankers in Paris.
[2] The famous family of Cornish engineers.
[3] Gregory Watt (1777–1804) was the much beloved son of James Watt by his second wife, Ann McGrigor. He had considerable talents and was interested in literature, chemistry and geology.

Letter 135

ROBISON TO WATT

Endorsed in Watt's hand, 'Jno. Robison March 7th 1793 by Mr. Booker' and numbered '7'. Dol.

Edin[bu]r[gh] March 7 1793

Dear Sir
I hereby recommend to your kind attention my young freind Mr. Booker, an amiable young Lad, and Son of one of the most excellent of human kind. His father is agent for the British factory at St. Petersburgh in Russia, and whether you consider his talents for business or the extraordinary worth of his heart, he is really a most uncommon Character. The Son is entitled to my best Services on his own account, and as he has been indulged with a Visit to Britain before setting down to laborious business I wish him to reap every advantage from the Journey, and therefor have taken the liberty of recommending him to your kind offices—It also gives me an opportunity of being brought to your remembrance, and has suggested a thought which I must take the liberty of troubling you with by post, Mr. Booker being just setting out, and I in too low a state just now to write. It concerns my Son whom I am going to breed up a Manufacturer. Adieu my good freind and give a kind reception to a longer Epistle in a few days from

Your affectionate and obliged humble
Serv[an]t
John Robison

Letter 136

ROBISON TO BOULTON

Cover addressed: 'Matthew Boulton Esq./Birmingham', and
endorsed, 'John Robison recommending Mr. Booker of St.
Petersburg'. A.O.L.B.

Edinb[urg]h March 7 1793

Sir

Permit me to introduce to your Civilities Mr. John Booker Jun[io]r
of St. petersburgh, now visiting this Country for Instruction and Entertainment. Mr. Booker Sen[io]r is Agent for the British factory at
Cronstadt, and a Gentleman of the most uncommon Worth and my
young friend is entitled to my best Services on his own account. I wish
him to see your magnificent Establishment with some advantage, and,
while I am sensible that I presume too far in taking this Liberty, I have so
much experience of your politeness and kind attention that I hope for
your Excuse

I am with respectful Esteem

Sir Your most obed[ien]t Serv[an]t
John Robison

Letter 137

ROBISON TO WATT

Cover addressed: 'To Mr. James Watt/Engineer/Birmingham',
endorsed in Watt's hand, 'J. Robison Edinburgh May 12th 1793
about putting his son to business', and numbered '8'. Dol.

Edin[bu]r[gh] May 12 1793

My dear Sir

Some weeks ago I took the liberty of recommending to your Civilities
a young friend from Russia, and hoped by this means to hear of you.
But he is gone home again, and his letter to me from London has by
some accident miscarried. In my letter to you I think I mentioned my
intentions of coming to England, and my hopes of seeing you. But my
Illness has been so distressing for these three months past that I have

hardly ever been able to sit up for a day together, and I fear that I have little chance of such an amendment as will make it prudent to venture the Journey. I must therefore have recourse to the feeble Substitute of letters to obtain from the kindness of others what I am no longer able to do for myself. And I flatter myself that you will forgive this application to your friendship, knowing that nothing could induce me to it but the persuasion that I have some share in your Esteem and your good wishes.

My eldest Son is just completing his 15th year, and I wish to fix him in the manufactoring line. His great relish for Chemistry, Mechanics, and other branches of natural Knowledge, makes him well inclined that way, and he has picked up a very considerable acquaintance with these things for his years. I should be happy to continue his academical Education much farther in this direction, but, unless he early begins to act, and to engage in the lower offices of the profession, his mind may get vain notions of Station, and may then feel some reluctance, if not disgust, in tasks which *must* be submitted to by a Youth who has nothing to trust to but his Education and his own hands. My Circumstances, with a family of five Children, and a precise income of £200, put an Apprenticeship, where a handsome premium is given, quite out of the question, and I must try to find some Master, who will take my Child, and breed him, *for his Services*. I have Relations in Glasgow, thriving people in that line, but I have so bad an opinion of the place, on account of its dissipation (and this of the coarsest kind) that I wish rather to send him to Manchester, where, by all accounts, the Ideas of folks in Business are much more sober, the habits of industry more prevalent, and where Scotch vanity will not thwart my views by making my Son consider his first employm[en]ts as degrading. I therefore intended going there with him this Summer, and try to find him a Master. But alas I am unacquainted with the way of getting a boy into business   in general I wished to find one who would take him and set him first of all to work with his hands, and during this time I must board him (if possible with his Master or some of his upper Servants). Then I hoped that he would be admitted into some department of trust, such as deliverer of yarn, or in short any thing above the mere work man—As he continues to make himself useful I hoped that he might get into employment where writing and Acc[oun]ts are required—and where, in time, he may get some small appointments, which will contribute to the expence of his Education. While this goes on he must recommend himself to his Employers by his Fidelity his talents and his Assiduity, and form to himself such connections and acquaintances as may help to his engaging in business on his own account—Such were my notions and expectations—but alas they are all without book, and I am quite ignorant whether any thing like this be practicable. Should I go to Manchester with him, I am little better off—for I cannot stir about, but am confined to my bed or a Couch for the far greatest part of the day. Before I can do any thing therefore, I must procure some acquaintance among the people of Business, such as are most likely to have use for a young lad to be so bred up for a confidential Servant, or who know such people. I know too well enough that a Boy totally unacquainted with the business is not a Servant but a burthen. You will now say to what End all this detail of difficulties— My good Freind I wish for your help—it strikes me that you must have connexions, acquaintances, and even influence, in Manchester. Perhaps you can recommend me to the Notice and Good Offices of some of your freinds who may inform me, advise me, and even assist me, and if you could venture to do this it would indeed be a great favour. I trust that you will sympathise with the anxiety of a Father, who for the first time, sends his Child from under his own Roof, and that you will not be inattentive to the pecularities of my Situation, rendered useless to my Family in the midst of my Life. Indeed my heart is very sore, to find myself a burthen where I shoud be a Support, and this at the precise time that my assistance is the most essential. My eldest Boy properly and successfully settled would be a prop and comfort to his Mother and a patron to his Brothers. I am sensible that I am asking a very serious favour and that a real friend alone will grant, and this not without hesitation. But I by no means wish you to do a thing inconvenient for yourself. I can only say that my Boy has been soberly brought up, unaccustomed to any luxurious or even refind habits. Indeed he is innocent like a Child, and I hope his dispositions accord w[it]h his Education— And I am not afraid that he will have any reluctance at any kind of work. I am apt myself to think him careless and lazy, but my acquaintances tell me I wrong him, and that he has done more than most boys of his years. I have endeavoured indeed to give him notions of cultivated manners. Perhaps this may be reckoned superfluous, and even inconvenient at the outset of *his* business. But I do not think him tainted with Scotch Vanity, the most hurtful of all casts of mind—If I could procure him admittance into the family of a Freind, where he could have a sober and creditable Society at an hour of Leisure, it would be to him a treasure, and a great protection against misconduct, which he knows would forfeit his admission. I flatter myself that his gratitude will correspond with the favours he receives, for I know him to be a warm hearted affectionate

Boy. But a parents partiality is always to be distrusted, and I am sensible that there will always be found about him failings which will require indulgence

Tedious as I have already been, I must still request your patience. I am distracted by variety of advice. I am told that there is little chance of finding a Master who can make any use of a Boy quite green, and that he must get some preparation here. Mechanical knowledge is represented as a great recommendation. One advises me to send him for two or three years to a MillWright—Another insists that he be bound for that time to a Clockmaker—these are precious years to be spent on a subordinate and an eventual part of Education, and I am loth to employ them in this Way. Another advice appears preferable—To get him employd here in some Cotton Mill, especially if I can get him particularly recommended to the Mechanical Overseer—In any Office here he must learn the necessity of Obedience Activity and Fidelity—and he will get m[u]c[h] opportunity of indulging his favourite Relish in this complicated Machine, and I am cheifly apprehensive of his being too much drawn aside by this attention Any notions I have yet got of these Matters make me prefer the weaving to the spinning branch—but my predilection is not great

Thus have I told you all my Tale—and have greatly fatigued your patience and entreat again your Excuse—My aim on the whole is to obtain from you both information Advice and Assistance—presupposing that you have numerous acquaintances among the Manufacturers, and can check me if you feel that I am going on improper grounds. I must go up myself—and want introduction—I cant have too many resources, and tho' Peter Ewart is there and will do much for me, I am perfectly confident that the influence of Mr. Watts Recommendation will be great—it would be most unreasonable to expect you to write such a letter as this, and yet even this does not convey a ten minutes conversation—but if you give me Encouragement I will come and see you before I do any thing decisive. Allow me then my dear Sir to hope for a few lines from you, and be contented with the grateful tho' barren and inefficient sentiments of my heart. I am with affectionate Regard

Yours
John Robison

Be so good as to give me your proper address—I have directed my Letter and dont like it—too late.

Letter 138

BLACK TO WATT

Cover addressed: 'Mr. James Watt Engineer/Birmingham', and endorsed in Watt's hand, 'Dr. Black June 23rd 1793/Congratulations on the marriage of his daughter and his sons taking to business   Upon Watt Juniors visit to the Continent Expresses a favourable Birmingham opinion of him'. Dol.

23 June 1793

My dear Freind

I should have wrote to you some time agoe to congratulate you on some late occurrences which must have encreased your comfort and happiness. The happy marriage of your daughter, the prospect of having your son settled in business and your own success which as I am informed has enabled you to secure a considerable Sum by an advantageous purchase of Land all this I assure You gave me the greatest pleasure, but most of all the last news I had from my brother that your health is at present good.—I was also most agreably undeceived lately with respect to your Sons visit to the continent concerning which reports were circulated which made me very uneasy on your account and at which I was the more astonished that when he was here I had formed a high opinion of his good sense. I hope that now your prosperity and ease will { will } continue to encrease and that your old age when it comes will be attended with all the happiness of which it is capable—I am desired by Mr. Geddes the manager of the glassworks at Leith to learn from you what will be the expence of setting up one of your Steam engines of a power equal to that of ten horses—Their work is much enlarged and the engine is wanted for grinding materials and for turning wheels etc. at which Cutters and engravers are at work—but what they wish to know is the Price of the { machine } \Engine/ itself independently of the machinery which it is to set in motion—and I suppose you can answer the question without any trouble—Be so good therefore as to give me the answer as soon as you conveniently can and beleive me always

Yours most affectionately

J. Black

Edinburgh 23 June 1793

WATT TO BLACK

Cover addressed: 'Doctor Joseph Black/Edinburgh', endorsed
in Black's hand, 'From Mr. Watt July 1793' and numbered '29'.
Dol.

Heathfield Birmingham July 17th
1793

Dr. Black

My Dear Sir

Your kind letter of the 23d of June came here in my absence, and I have
been so much agitated since that I could not write you, Mrs. W. advised
you of our having obtained a most complete verdict against one of our
many pirates, but the Judge unfortunately and in my opinion un-
necessarily reserved a law question for the opinion of the Court on which
we may split. In the mean time our enemies are as active as ever or more
so, and the Law is so very expensive that I fear in the end they will overcome by their numbers

I thank God however that my health and spirits are as good as I have a
right to expect and indeed better than they used to be, though I cannot
stand so much exertion—The information that I had purchased land was
premature, I have however secured some money on a Mortgage near
Glasgow and through Mr. Hamilton have lent some there on good
security and I hope have realized enough to enable me to support my
family, with œconomy, independent of future profits (If I can preserve
it in these perilous times) and that consideration is a great comfort to
me in the decline of life.

My Son James's[1] conduct has given me much uneasiness, though I have
nothing to accuse him of except being a violent Jacobin, that is bad
enough in my eyes, who abhor democracy, as much as I do Tyranny,
being in fact another sort of it. Young men will however presume to
think for themselves and of all their father's possessions set least value
upon their experience. I much dread the consequences of the opinions on
Government which have been propogated of late with so much industry.
The Rabble of this country are the mine of Gunpowder that will one
day blow it up and violent will be the explosion.

I am glad to hear from your brother that your health has been good this
last winter and I hope you will confirm it by rambling during the

summer, and that you will not forget that your friends here would have very great pleasure in receiving you, my house too is more convenient than it was and in a better situation

Mrs. Watt desires to join me in affectionate thanks for your kind directions in regard to Jessy's health which shall be attended to, I have the pleasure of informing you that she is much better, though she has had a return of fever yet it has been free from symptoms of inflammation, and I hope she will do well if the violent heat of the weather were a little moderated (we have had the therm[omete]r at 88° here in the Garden in the shade and it was at 90° at Hackney in the same circumstances) She goes out in the Chaise twice a day and begins to recover her appetite though not yet free from Cough

My absence and that of Mr. Southern[2] our agent has prevented us from answering Mr. Geddes queries but it shall be done to morrow in a letter to him

We have had no philosophical news since the affair of the frogs electricity except that Doctor Beddoes[3] is applying the antiphlogistic Chemistry to Medicine Azote and other poisonous airs to cure Consumptions and oxigene for spasmodic asthmas   he is at Bristol wells for the greater practice   Doctor Withering is returned very much the better for his passing the Winter at Lisbon, he was almost dead before he got away from England last october

With kind remembrance to Doctor Hutton and other friends

I remain always
My Dear Doctor
Your's affectionately
James Watt

[1] James Watt junior (1769–1848) followed his father in his interests in engineering and science, particularly chemistry and geology. After a short period of hectic Radicalism, he returned to England from France and settled into the family business.

[2] John Southern (1758–1815), one of the sons of Thomas Southern, of Wensley, near Wirksworth, Derbyshire, entered the service of Boulton and Watt in 1781 as an assistant to Watt. He was a very competent mathematician and a man of superior scientific knowledge. In 1810 he became a partner of the firm.

[3] Thomas Beddoes (1760–1808) M.D., physician and chemist. Patron of the young Humphry Davy, and father of Thomas Lovell Beddoes, the poet, Beddoes founded the Pneumatic Institute in Bristol for the treatment of disease by the administration of the newly discovered gases.

BLACK TO WATT

Cover addressed: 'Mr. James Watt Engineer/Birmingham/By Ferrybridge', endorsed in Watt's hand, 'Dr. Black 16 January 1794' and numbered '28'. Dol.

Edinb[urgh] 16 Jan[uar]y 1794

My dear Sir

I had the pleasure to receive your letter of the 24 Dec[embe]r with the present of the elastic Buckles for which Dr. Hutton and I are much obliged to you. We were also much gratifyed with the news you give us of your Son. And I am made happy by learning that Jessy is so much better

The good effects of the bloodings and cuppings do not surprise me but I should have hesitated to give the myrrh in such doses from the fear of its heating quality

I have however observed that medicines and even foods which stimulate the stomach give often a temporary releif to the lungs and breast of those in whom these last parts are liable to congestion from weakness. And they appear to me to do this by produceing a determination of the fluids towards the Stomach or exciting the nerves of that organ so much as to make those of other parts less sensible and irritable But that after such medicines have passed thro' the Stomach and entered the blood vessels they are apt to stimulate the heart and vascular system too much. In my case, who have weak lungs liable to inflammatory and other congestions I have found that a mild and moderate diet, a total abstinence from wine and other stimulants and great precautions against the bad effects of cold, are the best preservatives of health—I scarcely ever walk out in winter, but take a chair when I have occasion to go abroad and am never out in the evening—but it is true that if I were younger, I would not manage myself in the same manner. I should try to make myself a little more hardy—In Jessys case however colds are most carefully to be avoided and I have doubts of the propriety of airings in the carriage when the weather is cold. It must be judged of by their effects. If she likes the carriage, and is chearfull after it, not chilly and dull, it will do her good. If it have the contrary effects she will be the worse of it.   for every time that she is chilled or made dull by cold, the inflammatory diathesis will be more or less encreased. In makeing her take exercise be regulated by her own feelings of what she finds most agreable and pleasant and when the air or the Carriage appear too cold for her let her walk a while in a large room with a fire—I should think it dangerous to make her lay aside her flannel at this time of the year

The spring months are commonly very hard and trying for those who have weak health—on account of the cold mornings and evenings contrasted with the warm Sun in the middle of the day—Dr. Hutton is in excellent spirits, and I, after suffering a good deal, and almost loseing hopes in the beginning of winter, have now recovered my ordinary health—Dr. Hope[1] of Glasgow lately read a paper in our Phil[osophical] Society on the Strontian Spar (commonly supposed an Aerated Barytes) He proves satisfactorily that it is a particular species of alcaline earth different from Barytes and from Limestone but intermediate between them by the greater number of its properties—when combined with muriatic acid it forms a compound which being applyed \somewhat/ wet to the wick of a burning candle tinges the flame of a fine blood red, Calc[areou]s Earth{prod}has the same property but in an inferior degree —Dr. Hope gives to his new earth the name of Strontites—My affectionate Compliments to Mrs. Watt—Mr. Bolton and other Freinds— and beleive me always

Your most affectionately
Joseph Black

[1] Thomas Charles Hope (1766–1844), professor of medicine in Glasgow, succeeded Black as professor of chemistry in Edinburgh in 1799, discoverer of strontian.

Letter 141

BLACK TO WATT

Endorsed in Watt's hand, 'Dr. Black May 10 1794' and numbered '27'. Dol.

Edinburgh 10th May 1794

My dear Sir

I sit down to give you some account of the present state of your freind Guyot of whom I suppose you are anxious to have news   He wrote to you I beleive since he came here; I learned from him soon after his comeing that he had some disease or obstruction in his bowels and while he lodged with me for a short time I had an opportunity of enquiring about it and examining the state of it, but not satisfyed with this I persuaded him to take a consultation of Dr. Monro who also examined it very carefully— It is an irregular tumor under the left false ribs or under the Stomach, which produces difficult digestion and often vomiting of his food some time after it is taken, and which oppresses the surrounding parts and disturbs the action of the bowels in many respects—We gave him some medicines and directions without any hope of seeing his disease abate and after some time found it necessary to use palliatives only, he accordingly continued much in the same state untill the middle or towards the end of April—since which his disorder is evidently encreasing and his strength declineing and he is now reduced to great weakness. He is however perfectly resigned and composed and by the use of a little Laudanum and other palliatives enjoys frequently a good deal of ease, tho I do not think he can hold out long.—I understand that you lent him a little money and as he has ample funds for the repayment of it, he has taken care that it shall be done—Haveing given you this information about our worthy Freind I next must apply to you for news of your Daughter Jessy—I long much to learn what state she is in and what medicines she is now takeing, does she continue the use of the Gum Myrrh and has she acquired more strength than she had, has her pulse ever been quick or inclineing to the hectic—and what are the Symptoms of her Case at present—give me also some news of the State of your lawsuit—I do not know if you have heard that Dr. Hope of Glasgow has read a paper to our Society on the heavy Calcarious Earth \or Spar/ from Strontian which we at first supposed to be carbonate of Barytes He finds it to be a peculiar Earth of a middle nature between Calcarious Earth and Barytes. \and he gives it the name Strontites/—The most amuseing experiment with it is to saturate muriatic acid with it and get a muriate of it in long slender crystals. a little of these put on the wick of a burning candle tinges the flame of a beautifull red, the water of the crystals volatiliseing a little of the muriate, it produces this effect on the flame and the effect is renewed by applying a little of pure water afterwards to the same part of the wick. He has also discovered that both this Earth and the Barytes when the fixed air is driven out of them by a violent heat, will not only dissolve in water, but can be dissolved in greater quantity in hot water than in Cold and can be reduced to the form of Crystals composed of the pure Earths and water and containing a large proportion of water in their composition—an Abstract of his Exp[erimen]ts will appear in our next volume soon to be published, and the paper at length in the Volume that is to follow—

When you write to me be sure to let me know how Mr. Bolton is, and if he still uses the alkaline aerated water with the same advantage as formerly—

My own health is in its usual train, only that I am weaker in general and less able than ever to bear the least cold without suffering from it— With best wishes for Your good health and that of Mrs. Watt and the rest of your family

I am

My dear Sir

Yours affectionately

Dr. Hutton is remarkably
well and would enjoy
excellent Spirits if his
freinds were well around
him, but he feels much for
them and particularly for Guyot—

Joseph Black

Letter 142

WATT TO BLACK

Cover addressed: 'Doctor Joseph Black/Edinburgh', endorsed
in Black's hand, 'Mr. Watt May 15th 1794' and numbered '28'.
Dol.

Doctor Black   *Birmingham May 15 1794*

Dear Doctor

I am extremely sorry to hear such bad tidings of poor Mr. Guyot[s] health, who I was hopeful might have recovered under your care, as a Man of nice discernment {and} exemplary rectitude and a most sincere friend I shall lament his loss, with true concern. In respect to what he owes B and W we give ourselves no concern, and hope he will not in his present state waste thought upon it. I beg to be affectionately remembred to him. I shall write to him in a day or two, would have done so now, but am myself some what deranged from the effects of a yesterdays headach

Jessy is still in a very weak and relaxed state, and has been for sometime much molested by Hysterical fits which were at one time extremely violent, but have become less so either from the influence of the season, or from the use of the common palliatives, of which tincture of Castor and Laudanum mixed, and the *tinctura fuliginis* have been the most useful.

She still has a cough and expectoration, the latter of the common kind free from all symptoms of pus, and at sometimes when the expectoration is difficult she has pains in her chest and some tendency to inflamation, the remedy for which has been generally, an alkaline mixture I believe the volatile saline Julep with oyster shells Magnesia and some Sal tartari   this seems to operate by allaying the febrile symptoms and attenuating the Mucus. The Myrrh Medicine, was only given when most free from febrile Symptoms, to restrain the ever copious expectoration, which it has generally effected, but has seldom been continued so long as 10 days together and always laid asside on any appearance of pain in the side. It is the only tonic medicine which has agreed with her, all the others have speedily induced fever. At present she has feverish fits, especially after being exhausted by the Hysterics, they commonly go off of themselves, her great disease is weakness and want of appetite, which I think owing to a lurking fever, proceeding from or causing the affection of the lungs, We have very lately put an issue in her arm from it having had very good effects in some similar Cases, But we have the greatest hopes from air and exercise, and as soon as she can bear to travel one Stage a day, Mrs. W[att] sets out with her for the Coast of Hampshire, where Dr. Withering is to meet them and take the direction of her health. He has been at Lisbon during the winter, but has not found the same good effects from it that he did the preceding year, and a Hemoptoe warned him to fly from the approaching heats of that Climate. He will make some stay in Hampshire for the sake of the sea air and to avoid the fatigue of business here which he is no longer able to stand.

Our Lawsuit remains as it did, we expect an argument to take place on the special case next week, if the opinions of that Court are ag[ains]t us we shall proceed to take the opinion of the 12 Judges and ultimately to the House of Lords. In the mean time the Lord Chancellor has interdicted our antagonist from making more Engines and we expect will interdict the use of those that are made until the cause is finally decided.   all this is however enormously expensive and we are kept in suspence and anxiety.

Mr. Boultons health is tolerable, but would not be so without the use of the Alkaline water which he constantly uses and finds great relief from. It cannot however obviate all the effects of his own want of attention, of unceasing care and the approaches of old age—I lament you cannot give a better account of your own health, but hope you will employ the Summer in strengthening yourself ag[ains]t winter. If you could Join the party in Hampshire I am persuaded you would find benefit from it and I might have the pleasure of embracing you

As to myself my health is *tolerable* which is all I have now to expect, but I am grown intolerably stupid which is very unpleasant

Mrs. W. whose health keeps wonderfully good considering her unremitted attention to her daughter, desires to Join me in affectionate reme\m/brances to you and Dr. Hutton, who we are glad to hear suffers more for his friends than for himself   I return you thanks for your account of the Strontites which you had mentioned before, but your last account has been more full—I remain Dear Doctor

Your ever affectionate friend
James Watt

Letter 143

BLACK TO WATT

Endorsed in Watt's hand, 'Dr. Black June 6th 1794' and numbered '26'. Dol.

Edinb[urgh] 6th June 1794

My dear Sir

Soon after I received your last letter our worthy freind Guyot expired, he was excessively weakened and emaciated and died with the greatest tranquillity, and with expressions of being pleased with the attentions of his freinds to the last—he has left here in the hands of Sir William Forbes I. Hunter and Co[mpany][1] two or three hundred pounds after paying all his accounts, part of this money he got here and part was remitted to him from france since he came   You may therefore draw on the above Company for the Sum you lent him and desire them to place the bill to account with his heirs and if the bill is made payable to me I shall immediatly exchange it for one on London to your order, or for any other that you chuse—The plan of a journey which you were so kind as to propose for me would not at all suit me and most unfortunately I have an additional reason, since I wrote my last letter, for staying at home. My freind Hutton who was so hearty at that time was taken ill a few days after, with the same complaint that he had formerly so that an operation has been performed and he is at present confined to his bed—free however from pain, and in a condition to amuse himself with his books and writings but much the better of the attentions of his freinds—there is as yet no appearance of his recovering so well as he did before—

You need not hesitate to draw for the money You lent to Guyot, he left the most distinct account of the state of his affairs and had particularly noted down the Sum you had lent him—present my Compliments to Mrs. Watt Mr. Boulton and other freinds and beleive me always

Dear Sir
Yours affectionately
Joseph Black

[1] Sir William Forbes of Pitsligo (1739–1806) entered the firm of Coutts, bankers at Edinburgh in 1754 and soon became a partner changing the name to Forbes, Hunter and Co., in 1773.

Letter 144

WATT TO BLACK

Cover addressed: 'Doctor Joseph Black/Edinburgh', endorsed in Black's hand, 'From Mr. Watt 9th June 1794' and numbered '27' Dol.

Birm[ingha]m June 9th 1794

Dear Doctor

Your's of the 6th has found me in the hour of Grief   My Amiable and lovely daughter expired on Friday morning after a long suffering, the fever she had when I wrote you last proved a hectic of the most violent kind, which perhaps we might have seen sooner if we had not been misled by her violent hystericks. On perceiving a change in the expectorated matter I sent for Dr. Darwin, who gave little hopes but prescribed for the fever and other urgent symptoms, I then had Dr. Beddoes who attended her daily for a week, but also seemed to think the case desperate, She breathed fixt air from effervescing mixtures placed near her and some times inhaled it mixt with atmospheric, but without other apparent effect than its being grateful to her. The violence of her fever the hystericks and her great weakness prevented our trying the effect of other airs and of some active Medicines which were proposed. Yeast seemed to moderate very much the hot fit of the fever and I think she owed some{ease}\ease/ to the use of it. It has a tendency to purge which is easily counteracted by absorbents or ipecacuanha

The irritation to cough, sometimes convulsive, with the fever and a rapid pulse 120 to 130, brought on a hemorrage in the lungs of which she

203

expired in a few minutes   if that circumstance had not taken place, she might have suffered some days more of pain, but the disease was too far gone to admit of rational hopes of recovery. We have only the consolation to think that we did all to save her which was in our power, or the very able physicians we consulted could suggest as proper—Though Dr. Withering is not returned \home/ we had the benefit of his advice by \frequent/ letters by which his opinions corresponded with those on the spot as to the mode of treatment. Her mothers sorrow is very great, but she bears it well as or better than could well be expected, nor has her own health suffered so much as I feared it would from her unremitting attentions to her child. The loss to us both is great and irreparable but we must submit, and pay the more attention to those we have left. We propose a Journey to reinstate our health as soon after the last sad offices are performed, as may be possible

It adds much to our affliction to hear of Poor Guyots death and our friend Dr. Huttons severe illness from which we pray for his speedy recovery, and beg you will present our affectionate condolence

I hope you will pay that attention to your own health which your Judgement directs, and enjoy the benefit of the summer as much as possible—Mrs. W. joins in kind wishes to you and I remain

My dear Sir
Your affectionate friend
James Watt

I shall do the necessary in
regard to Mrs. Guyots money, as
soon as I can

Letter 145

WATT TO BLACK

Cover addressed: 'Doctor Joseph Black/Edinburgh', endorsed in Black's hand, 'From Mr. Watt 25 June 1794' and numbered' '26'. Dol. Also * B.R.L.

Birm[ingha]m June 25th 1794.

Doctor Black

Dear Sir

Inclosed is our draft at Sight, on Sir Will[ia]m Forbes, J. Hunter and Co[mpany] of which they have been advised at the date. The money advanced was £50—and the interest makes up the remainder

We shall be obliged to you after deducting postages and any other charges you may be at, to send us a draft on London for the remainder.

This Bill should have been sent you sooner but owing to the present state of my mind was entirely forgotten—

Mrs. Watt bears her loss, very well, and her health is tolerably good; but neither she nor myself can think on { our loss } \the subject/ without the utmost regret—We intend as soon as my affairs will permit to take a jaunt of a few weeks into Wales, but any letter you may be kind enough to write in our absence may be directed to James Watt Jun[io]r Soho.

I wish much to hear how Doctor Hutton recovers and how you are yourself, Mrs. W. joins me in sincerest and best wishes for both your welfares and I remain

My Dear Sir
Your's affectionately
James Watt

Letter 146

BLACK TO WATT

Endorsed in an unknown hand, 'Dr. Black June 30th 1794' and numbered '25'. Dol.

30 June 1794

Dear Sir

Inclosed I send a London Bill in return for your draught on the heirs of Mr. Guyot. Dr. Hutton is quite easy and in good spirits but confined to his house and without any appearance yet of complete recovery. I am better than I was lately and can walk about slowly but am very weak in the limbs—I hope you and Mrs. Watt will be the better of your Jaunt   it would have made your freinds here happy had it suited you to turn your face this way—Adieu and beleive me always

Yours most affectionately
Joseph Black

Edinb[urgh] 30th June 1794

WATT TO BLACK

Cover addressed: 'Doctor Joseph Black/Edinburgh', endorsed in
Black's hand, 'From Mr. Watt 3d July 1794' and numbered '25'.
Dol.

Doctor Black   *Birm[ingha]m July 3d 1794*

My Dear Sir

This day I received your's covering Bill value £50..8..3 to credit
of Mr. Guyots heirs

I am extremely concerned to find that your own health and Dr.
Huttons are so indifferent, I hope this fine weather will have effect on you
both, and hope you will not from aversion to exertion neglect any thing
which can conduce thereto

Mrs. W. continues to be much affected by our loss and suffers in her
health in consequence—my own health is wonderfully good, considering
the accumulation of Vexations and perplexities I am subjected to; but
like you my legs and feet fail me much, yet I crawl about tolerably—
Our Law affairs have delayed our Jaunt hitherto, but I hope that soon
there will be some decision, or at least term must end in a few days

Publick affairs wear a most Gloomy aspect and we are not without
fears of some bad doings at home—With kind remembrance to Dr.
Hutton—   I remain Most affect[ionat]ely
                                                    Your's etc.
                                                    James Watt

WATT TO BLACK

Cover addressed: 'Doctor Joseph Black/Physician/Edinburgh',
endorsed in Black's hand, 'From Mr. Watt 31 August 1794, and
numbered '24'. Dol.

Birm[ingha]m Aug[us]t 31st 1794

Dr. Black

My Dear Sir

Mrs. Watt and myself are anxious to hear of your health and Doctor Hutton's. We returned from a Jaunt into Wales about 3 weeks ago and I should have wrote to you sooner but had some hopes of hearing from you. Our Journey was rather agreable though the weather was far from being pleasant. We cannot say we gained much in point of health, but we were amused and our uneasy thoughts and regrets at times suspended.

To recite our infirmities or vexations cannot amuse you I shall therefore send you all the philosophical news I have—A person in Birm-[ingha]m produces Volatile alkali (as I am told) from the vitriolic salts with earthy bases, by mixing them with charcoal dust, heating them red hot and blowing air over them—Another person is said to have discovered a liquor which bleaches brown linen white in one minute and is prepared without either manganese or Sp.Sal.   this Man keeps his process secret as he means to take a patent for it.

At Doctor Beddoes sollicitation I have contrived an apparatus for easily preparing and collecting artificial airs for medicinal purposes which answers very well. It seemed to me that the inflammable air produced from charcoal and water was likely to be one of the most efficacious as being a solution of charcoal in infl[amma]ble air

I found however upon trial that it possessed virtues which my reasoning a priori could not infer.   One inspiration of it causes most violent vertigo, and when very pure the barely smelling it caused a person to fall down in the sleep of forgetfulness, from which he awakened without pain or uneasiness.† Dr. B. has given it in a case of incipient Phlisis [*sic*], which it cured

A young man in confirmed Consumption has had two doses of it from me, which he says have been of much service to him, the pain in his side and Dyspnea having left him

---

† [Note in margin] neither pure infl[amma]ble air nor pure fixt air produce these effects in any approach to this

The effects of the vertigo upon him, however, alarmed me so much that I have sent him to Dr. B.—The consequences or attendants on the vertigo are a quick weak pulse, which at last is almost suspended, great sense of cold and the person becomes cold to the touch. If continued too long apoplectic sleep would ensue, these symptoms soon go off and are suceeded by an agreable abatement of the Hectic heat. The safe [dose] is from 50 to 100 cubic Inches mixt with 12 times as much atmospheric air. The inspiration to be intermitted on the first appearance of vertigo—I produce fixt air of great purity, too pungent to be smelled to, from red hot chalk by dropping water upon it. 4 Cubic feet from 24 oz of chalk

Mrs. W. Joins me in requesting you will write soon and in sending our sincerest good wishes for your and Dr. Hutton's welfare and I remain

My Dear Sir
Your affectionate friend
James Watt

Letter 149

BLACK TO WATT

Cover addressed: 'Mr. James Watt Engineer/Heathfield/Bir-mingham', endorsed in Watt's hand, 'Dr. Black September 9th 1794' and numbered '24'. Dol.

Edinburgh 9th Sep[tember] 1794

My dear Freind

It gave me much pleasure to learn that you and Mrs. Watt were some-what releived by your jaunt and that you have been able to amuse your-self with philosophical contrivances and exper[imen]ts

Dr. Hutton still continues confined to his house and without any symptom as yet of his entire recovery, free from pain however and enjoying good spirits and amuseing himself with his own philosophical speculations and printing some of them—As for myself I am tolerably well, only feeling the effects of age encreasing upon me and reduced to the observance of a very strickt regimen, I have begun to prepare a legible copy of my Lectures, but by interruptions and defect of activity and strength I proceed very slowly—You have raised my curiosity by the mention of an apparatus of your contrivance; Is any description of it to be published soon?

I perceive you can throw water into it when the matter is red hot. The narcotic effects of the heavy inflammable air or carbonated hydrogen confirms me in the opinion I had of it in consequence of what happened to me at Glasgow when my Servant was thrown into a dangerous Stupor or apoplexy by it and I myself experienced, by being \less/ exposed to the breathing of it, very violent headachs—Dr. Goodwin[1] who made experiments on respiration here, would not be persuaded of it but alledged that all the bad airs not actually corrosive extinguished life not by any noxious quality but by filling the lungs to the exclusion of vital air. Is the production of volatile alkali, by the process you mention, a profitable manufacture—I have had Volatile alkali or rather Sal ammoniac produced by burning Coaks slowly with an addition of common Salt but I beleive this volatile \Alkali/ was contained in the Coaks as all the Substances which yield volatile alkali by destillation afford charcoals which retain a part of the Volatile alkali in them, and it is only such charcoals that are fit for making prussian Alkali—

The new bleaching liquor is perhaps some preparation of the Sulphureous or volatile vitriolic acid, which is the only thing I know beside the oxygenated muriatic that has the bleaching power—Does Mr. Keir still adhere to the doctrine of Phlogiston or has he abandoned it; Dr. Hutton still defends it in his own way and is printing about it. he desires me to return you his thanks and best wishes for your kind remembrance of him but was disappointed by haveing no news of the termination of your Lawsuit in your favour, it would be an high gratification to both of us—I am always My Dear Sir Yours and Mrs. Watts most affectionate well wisher and humble Servant

Joseph Black

[1] Dr Edmund Goodwyn, M.D. Edinburgh 1786, published in the same year in London, *The connexion of life with respiration*.

Letter 150

BLACK TO WATT

Dol.

Edinb[urgh] 28th October 1794

My dear Freind

I received in two franks from Bristol, Dr. Beddoes second pamphlet on the use which may be made of Gas's in medicine, with your description

209

of the apparatus you contrived for preparing them, but the plates referred to in this description were not sent or are not come to hand—The Doctor expressed by a former letter his wish that I should appear as a subscriber to his proposal for instituting a small hospital in which the usefullness of Gas's might be put to a fair trial, and I have no objection to the haveing my name set down for four or five guineas in such a Subscription, The Sum he wants cannot fail to be very quickly made up in *England* if his proposals are at all listened to, but in my opinion he does not do well to get into quarrels and disputes if they can possibly be avoided—I do not know how to address a letter to him and therefore trouble you with this that you may do the needfull in the Subscription, and I shall order the money to be payed to any person in London that you point out to me— Dr. Hutton continues in the same State without any appearance as yet of his being able to come abroad and I have had a little attack of my illness lately but it went off easily and I hope to be able to begin my Course as usual—present my kind respects to Mrs. Watt and beleive me always

Yours affectionately
Joseph Black

P.S. Looking again into the D[octo]r's Pamphlet I find he names Bankers in London who are to receive Subscriptions, I shall therefore write to Messrs. Coutts and Co[mpany] to set down my name and you need not take any trouble about it—

[1] Thomas Beddoes, M.D. *A Letter to Erasmus Darwin M.D. on a new Method of Treating Pulmonary Consumption*, 1793; or Thomas Beddoes, *Considerations on the Medicinal Use and on the Production of Facitious Airs*, 1794–96.

Letter 151

WATT TO BLACK

Cover addressed: 'Doctor Joseph Black/Physician/Edinburgh', endorsed in Black's hand, 'From Mr. Watt 8th December 1794 answered 13th Ditto' and numbered '23'. Dol.

Dr. Black   *Birm[ingha]m Dec[embe]r 8th 1794*

My dear Sir

Your last letter I immediately commun[icate]d to Dr. Beddoes, who thanks you for your observations to which he will pay respect—I would have wrote to you sooner but have been indisposed.

It gives me and your friends here much concern to find [you] so infirm, the beginning of the winter has been unkindly and Boisterous, but the weather is now fine, and we hope will prove more friendly to you. We sympathize most sincerely with Dr. Hutton and hope his sufferings are now alleviated.

It gave me pain that Beddoes had managed the sending his pamphlet so badly, when he sent it he had not got the plates, the engraver having disappointed him—I have last week sent a perfect copy for you and another for Dr. Hutton to Care of Gilb[er]t Hamilton which hope you have received

I shall soon send you to [sic] description of the apparatus better drawn up and Methodized, with considerable additions to the directions for obtaining the airs

The Medical people here have taken up the subject warmly and I hope will be able to produce some satisfactory results. It is said a Mr. Wathen[1] an Occulist has with the assistance of Dr. Thornton[2] cured two persons of *Gutta Serena* and one of perfect deafness, by means of Oxygene air— They have begun to try one here in *Gutta Serana*, but hitherto without success, A Consumptive patient in the last Stage has been much relieved from his hectic, dyspnea and pains in the Chest by Hydrocarbonate, which also enables him to Sleep without opium: Yet they do not hope for his recovery as he is too far gone—

Something above £100 has been subscribed in this town towards the Pneumatic institution and more is expected—The subscription will not be opened {till}† in London till the {spring}† meeting of parliament—

My complaints have been complicated, a disorder in my Stomach, Stitches in the breast, Asthma and extreme inactivity, it seems now on the mending hand

Mrs. Watt Joins me in best wishes to you and Dr. Hutton and I remain

Dear Doctor
Your affect[iona]te Friend
James Watt

I can send you some good manganese if you want any

---

† These words have a line through them—but this is not certain for 'spring'.
[1] Jonathan Wathen, a surgeon practising in London, was at one time a member of the governing body of the Corporation of Surgeons and a member of the Medical Society of London. He contributed articles to various journals including the *Philosophical Transactions*.
[2] Robert John Thornton (1768?–1837), physician and botanist.

BLACK TO WATT

Endorsed in Watt's hand, 'Dr. Black December 13th 1794' and
numbered '23'. Dol.

Edinb[urgh] 13 Dec[embe]r 1794

My dear Sir

I received your letter of the 8th Inst[an]t and hope your indisposition is now gone, for my part, my health has been mending ever since I last wrote to you and Dr. Hutton too enjoys good spirits tho confined to the house. The plates and description of the apparatus are not yet come to hand, but as they are committed to the care of Gilbert Hamilton I have no doubt of their comeing Safe—And I shall be much obliged to you for some good manganese, I have none of the best kind

I cannot form a judgment of the nature of your complaints at this distance but an inclined to advise nurseing and shunning the cold air—I find this regimen agree best with me, not to walk out in winter but to keep \to/ the house as much as possible and take exercise by walking an hour or half an hour in a large room that I have with a fire in it.   my bed too is warmed every night and my Cloaths every morning—This and a very antiphlogistic regimen when any \thing/ ails me are my Sovereign remedies but I am not in the least liable to stomach complaints or indigestion   my appetite and digestion are commonly rather too good—

Present my best wishes to Mrs. Watt and beleive me always

Yours affectionately

Joseph Black

WATT TO BLACK

Cover addressed: 'Doctor Joseph Black/Edinburgh', endorsed in
Black's hand, 'From Mr. Watt 2d April 1795' and numbered '21'.
Dol.

Birmingham Ap[ri]l 2d 1795

Dr. Black

Dear Sir

It is now a long time since I heard from you and I should have wrote to you sooner, but have been engaged in the disagreable business of our lawsuit and out of health and spirits. The improvement of the weather has tended to improve both the latter, but the former hangs like a Millstone about our necks, and I fear will be decided against us in the Court of Common pleas where we now are. If so we mean to remove it to the Kings bench where we hope there will be less quibbling upon *words*. Our late friend John Wilkinson has also taken this opportunity to turn against us, He has got into a lawsuit with his only Brother,[1] and accuses us of having combined with the latter against him, but we think this only a pretence, at least we have cleared up all he could alledge against us in that line, There is one comfort that he cannot do us much more injury as an enemy than he has done as a friend—

I have no philosophical news of my own, having not been well enough to attend to experiments lately; but the Pneumatick Medecine seems to have been of service in several cases which have come to my knowledge and there \are/ several intelligent practitioners at work upon it in different places, so that there is reason to hope that the Efficacy and general powers of these medicines will soon be known

Dr. Beddoes is publishing a new Edition of his Considerations with emendations new Experiments on Animals and Cases sent him from various practitioners—He has found that animals living some time in a mixture of carbonated Hydrogene and Common air, have the liver, venous blood, and Heart more florid than the comparative Animals living in common air This is contrary to his theory, but consistent with what has been observed here in Dr. Carmichaels[2] Pthisical patient who gained flesh and strength and became more florid in his complexion which was very pale—That patient has had a relapse from the late fall of snow and attendant cold but, is recruiting again, by the use of the same air

I believe I mentioned to you a patient with a very bad scrophulous ulcer treated by Mr. Barr[3] surgeon with oxygene air internaly, which immediately improved his general health and his sore put on a better appearance, but after some time an erysipelatous burning pain was felt in the sore which also became inflamed, Mr. Barr then mixed Hydrocarbonate air with the oxygene about 1 of the latter to 2 of the former, with 4 or 5 times as much common air. The pain soon abated the sore began to heal kindly and is now reduced to $\frac{1}{4}$ of the size it was, with every prospect of cure—Dr. C. has given the H.C. to a patient in the humid asthma whom it has cured, pro tempore at least—Mr. Henry[4] at Manchester has also succeeded in a similar case, and has also cured two cases of pertussis by the same air and though the patients were

seized by the late influenza \immediately/ afterwards, they did not relapse into the pertussis—Dr. Carmichael says that the oxygene air has
been of much service in a case of Chlorosis under his care The Hydro
carbonate seems to be a powerful antispasmodic and narcotic medicine
and procures sleep when all other means fail, Dr. C says he thinks it
most powerful when fresh made with all its charcoal suspended in it
and gives then only half the dose that he does of that which has subsided

I shall be very much obliged to you for a few lines to say how you
have stood through this very inclement winter, and how Dr. Hutton is
now, I wish I could devise some air which would be of use to him—
My friend Dr. Withering has kept tolerably well, by confining himself
to his house, where he is employed in preparing a new Edition of his
botany which is just going to the press he finds himself much the
worse of the motion of a Carriage or fatigue of any kind, which bring
on the Hemoptoe and an encrease of cough etc.—

Mrs. Watt joins me in best wishes to you and Dr. Hutton and I
remain

My Dear Sir
Your affectionate friend
James Watt

¹ William Wilkinson (1744/5–1808), also an ironmaster, and a close friend of Boulton
and Watt's sons.
² Dr John Carmichael graduated in medicine at Edinburgh in 1787.
³ Robert Barr, apothecary, Bristo Street, is recorded in the *Edinburgh Directory*, 1794.
⁴ Thomas Henry (1734–1816), apothecary of Manchester and member of the Manchester
Literary and Philosophical Society. He was an early industrial chemist and important in the
first experiments with chlorine bleaching. He translated Lavoisier's *Opuscules*.

Letter 154

BLACK TO WATT

Cover addressed: 'Mr. James Watt/Heath-feild/Birmingham',
endorsed in Watt's hand, 'Dr. Black April 12th 1795' and
numbered '22'. Dol.

Edinburgh 12th April 1795

My dear Watt

I had resolved to employ my first leisure to write to you before I received your letter of the 2d Curr[en]t I owed you thanks for your present

of Manganese which was a great present to me   I never had such good
Manganese before. It greives me think that this lawsuit should prove so
troublesome and expensive. The vexation of it is doubly hard upon
you whose Spirits are so often depressed by bad health. The pneumatick
medecine is neglected here. I have totally given up the practice of
Medicine being under the necessity of confining myself to the house in
Winter like Dr. Withering. I only go out to the Laboratory once a day
in my chair to deliver my Lecture. And our Physicians and Surgeons
are little inclined to give themselves trouble about any thing new,
especially the new pneumatic chemistry which very few of them
understand. I have heard only of one case of Cancer in the Hospital to
which they attempted to apply carbonic gas by means of a bladder but
they bungled and were not able to confine the Gas. Dr. Rutherfoord
who is a good Chemist is to give the clinical lectures this summer and
perhaps may attend to it.

I had the pleasure to reccive from Mr. G. Hamilton your last Edition
of the description of the apparatus. Have you made many of them, and
at what price?

Dr. Hutton has been close confined to the house for this twelve
months and is now without hope of releif from his confinement but
he enjoys good Spirits and is constantly employed in writing and
publishing. Mr. Kirwan has attacked his Theory of the Earth, and the
Doctor will not easily submitt to such an antagonist.

I caught a Cold, I beleive it was the influenza in the beginning of
February by venturing out to see Mrs. Ferguson whom we have lost
lately by a decay of her constitution and the severity of the winter

My Cold weakened me to a great degree and confined me close to
the house a complete month, Dr. Rotheram continuing the Lectures,
untill the beginning of March when I resumed them and have
continued them since and am gaining strength. I have taken a house in
the country near Leith where I propose to spend a few months of this
Summer to try the effect of such a change of air. Homoptoe is my
weakness, like Dr. Witherings, brought on cheifly by Colds and
changes of weather, my cure is always a mild abstemious diet and it is
fortunate that my Stomach bears such a diet perfectly well.

Has any person in Birmingham tryed to refine and manufacture
Platina? I am told that Dr. Ingenhouzs[2] at London has many things
made of it. What would a pair of small steel rollers cost such as are
used by the essay masters? A second \hand/ pair might perhaps be easily
got.

I have lately made an improvement on my penknife which might be taken up perhaps with advantage by some of your manufacturers My penknife was made by Capper and given me by Dr. Roebuck. It has a long narrow blade, not pointed at the extremity but a little rounded, that rounded part being blunt and smooth. I was accustomed to lengthen the slit of my pen by thrusting the extremity of the blade into the Slit from the inside of the pen and then {thrustin} pushing the edge forwards into the Slit to lengthen it. I think I have seen you do the same—But the obliquity of the edge produced by the ridge on one side of the knife which qualifyes it for giving the curved cuts necessary in makeing a pen always turned it to one side or made it difficult to lengthen the slit in a straight line along the pen. This difficulty I have removed by makeing a cutler grind down near half an inch of the ridge at the extremity of the blade and now it is as convenient a penknife as I can imagine

Present my best compliments and wishes to Mrs. Watt and to Mr. Bolton   I should be happy to hear that his health continues tolerably good

I am
My dear Sir
Your affectionate Freind
Joseph Black

[1] Daniel Rutherford (1749–1819), professor of botany in the University of Edinburgh, discoverer of nitrogen.

[2] Jan Ingen-Housz (1730–99), noted for his researches and discoveries on the action of light on growing plants.

Letter 155

WATT TO BLACK

Cover addressed: 'Doctor Joseph Black/Physician/Edinburgh', endorsed in Black's hand, 'From Mr. Watt dated London 24 May 1795' and numbered '22'. Dol.

London May 24th 1795

Dear Doctor

I should have answered your letter sooner but have been here attending the law, the result of which I wished to write you. The Court has sate in Judgement in our cause, The L[or]d Chief and Mr.

Justice Rooke made very able arguments in our favour. Justice Buller and Justice Heath against us, (Cornwall and Devonshire own these gentlemen) The votes being equal the court cannot decide we are therefore hung up until some Law lie or other expedient can be devised to loosen the knot. Mean while having *Justice*, the jury, and two Judges with us, we are trying whether the Chancellor will not confirm his Injunctions against the Aggressors. We are now in the same situation as before the trial, only that the piracy, being proved we can be aided by chancery

I have not your letter here but think the only article to be replied to was about a small rolling press. If you will mention the size I can get you one, the price of those about 4 inches long in the rolls, is about 3 or 4 guineas as far as I can remember—I have just enquired and find the prices here, for 3½ rolls is 4½ guineas and 4 inch rolls 5 guineas, but perhaps I may suceed better at Birm[ingha]m—These prices are independent of the stool which being a common 4 legged one can be better or at least *cheaper* had with you, for every thing in Joiner or carpenter work is abominably dear with us and the carriage will add to it

Dr. Beddoes has published a new Edition of his Considerations with some cases. The Birmingham ones I can attest, from my knowledge of the probity of the reporters. The Phthisical patient had a very bad relapse from the Snow Storm but has recovered it though from the effects of that there is doubts of a total Cure—B. writes me that he has accounts from Hull of a complete cure of Chlorosis by oxygene and of an incipient Phthisis by inf[lamma]ble air. If the success of these medicines vindicate the trouble, I think I can make a perfectly portable apparatus contained in a box about a foot square and 8 inches deep, and others even so small as to be carried in the pockets

I am very much concerned that our friend Dr. Huttons case is hopeless, but it is a great alleviation that his spirits support him under it. I hope the present fine weather will be use to both you and him and that you will make the best use of it by enjoying the country air

I had got pretty clear of my winters complaints but the late vile easterly winds gave me a cold which I find it difficult to get clear of, though it gets better Mrs. W. who is with me, has also had a dose of the same disease, but it has attacked her mostly with toothaches and Rheumatic pains, which are relieved at present

Political matters are out of my reach, at this conjuncture, the nation evidently suffers under the war, provisions of all kinds are enormously high *yet* the luxury and expence of this town suffers no restraint Our trade is less molested than it was under the late admiralty and the french trade suffers more but alas we have few countries to trade with and these have not money to spare

Mrs. Watt Joins in best wishes to you and Doctor Hutton and I remain

My Dear Sir
Yours affect[ionat]ely
James Watt

Letter 156

BLACK TO WATT

Endorsed in Watt's hand, 'Dr. Black September 29th 1795' and numbered '21'. Dol.

29 September 1795
Higher Hermitage near Leith
Links

My dear Sir

I had the pleasure to receive your letter of the 20th but unfortunately under an attack of one of my Colds which I had been free from ever since I came here in the beginning of June.   this day however I feel the return of health but as usual am considerably weakened but there is time enough to recover from that too before you pass thro' Edinburgh which I hope will not be prevented—You can have a bed with Mrs. Watt in my house and it shall be made in any manner that you desire— The weather promises to be fine but setting in for very cool nights, so take good care of yourself, never stirr out after dinner on any account— Dr. Hutton still enjoys a wonderfull degree of Courage and good spirits   I heard of him yesterday—Remember me kindly to Mrs. Watt and Mr. McGrigor[1] if you are still with him and beleive me always

My dear Sir
Yours most affectionately
Joseph Black

{Saturday}
Tuesday 29 Sep[tembe]r
1795

[1] James McGrigor, father of Ann McGrigor, Watt's second wife, was a bleacher in business near Glasgow. His son-in-law corresponded with him on the new chlorine bleaching process in 1787.

Letter 157

BLACK TO WATT

Cover addressed: 'Mr. James Watt Engineer/Heathfield/ Birmingham/by Ferrybridge', endorsed in Watt's hand, 'Dr. Black January 4th 1796 his treatment of his own case and directions for an issue', and numbered '20'. Dol.

Edinb[urgh] 4th January 1796

My dear Freind

May the year newly begun and many more be happy years to you. This is wishing you only better health for I think you have nothing else now to complain of. As for the injustice of the wicked and worthless it should not ruffle your mind now when you have had so much experience of it and know that it is to be expected from them, for my part such things make but little impression on me now tho' formerly they gave me excessive anguish. My health has continued to improve ever since you were here and I have hitherto gone on with my Lectures in my usual manner but I do not go abroad except in my chair

I impute my health to three causes 1. my Regimen, 2 An Issue at my breast and 3dly Currying my Self every morning—My Regimen is plenty of broth and vegetables at Dinner but scarcely one ounce of meat—The Issue is the easiest managed thing in the world and I am persuaded might help to keep off your asthma   One of Sandwells paper plasters with a little of the Unguentum e pulvere Cantharidum spread on the middle of it, first raises a blister, and two or three days after it must be \rubbed clean and/ dressed every day with a new paper plaster having the bulk of a pea of the Unguentum ex infuso Cantharidum spread \very thin and broad/ on the middle of it \but always rub it clean before this is applyed./ The application of the blister and the dressing of it afterw[ar]ds ought always to be performed in the morning, that the action of it may not interfere with sleep   managed in this way it gives no trouble whatever except now and then a degree of Itchyness which King James would have reckoned exquisite pleasure. The Currying is performed with a coarse woolen cloth in the morning when I am rising   I put it round my back and draw it tight with both hands which at the same time apply a part of it to my belly and by drawing alternately to one Side and the other I rub my Self all round at the same time —and afterwards rub my Shoulders and Arms in a very short time— After you left us I had some thoughts of trying the Hydro Carbonate and Dr. Hope prepared some for me before he left Glasgow, but as I grew better I never used it

Dr. Hutton continues in the same State, {only} but has rather more frequent fits of pain from the irritation of the Stone He is however very lively at times—I long to see your new improvements of the apparatus—the portable one will be a most acceptable present to me— Remember also that you promised to send me some of your Ink powders the most lately improved And do not forget to employ some person here to retail them, Or if you would direct your retailer of them in London to supply a retailer here {up} on the same terms as those on which he is supplyed with them it would do very well, as there \are/ Vessels running between London and Leith every week almost. Present Dr. Huttons and my kind Compliments to Mrs. Watt and your Son and beleive me always

yours faithfully.
Joseph Black

Letter 158

WATT TO BLACK

Cover addressed: 'Doctor Joseph Black/Physician/Edinburgh', endorsed in Black's hand, 'January 7th 1796 Mr. Watt' and numbered '20'. Dol.

Heathfield Birm[ingha]m Jan[uar]y 7th 1796

Doctor Black

My dear Friend
   Your letter of the 4th gives me great pleasure from the accounts it brings of your better health which I pray may long continue, and that you may enjoy many happy returns of the new year—When I was with you I was unwell, but gradualy grew better upon the road, not withstanding very indifferent weather, and since I got home have been much stouter and on the whole better than I have been these two last years, so that I have been able to work some in my laboratory, though I have not been quite free from complaints lately, such as pretty severe

headaches and a return of the spasms in my breast and stomach, which I now think proceed principaly from the latter as I have neither cough nor fever of any kind. The asthmatic complaint I have been very free from, at present quite so, except a very little upon lying down in bed

I have however been obliged to adopt a direct contrary regimen to yours viz. to eat no vegetables except bread but I have a good appetite and good digestion of animal food—As to the mental diseases I in great measure practise your counsel, and do not fall into the despondencies I used to do, and our affairs in general go on prosperously. Chancery seems disposed to do us justice on some of our pirates, but it is long winded. My son and Mr. Bs continue to apply to business, with the eagerness incident to well disposed young men—

I wish most sincerely you could have sent me better tidings of Dr. Hutton, his situation has given me much uneasiness. I wrote to him, I think, two Geological letters since I returned I hope he has received them and a small box of fossils I sent him, beg of him however not to answer them except when it can give him pleasure

I hoped before now to have sent you the portable apparatus, but it was long before I could get one finished and only one could be made until I was sure it was right (for I am now a terrible sceptic in new things) The trying it in various ways has taken me some time but it answers *completely* and more are making the first of which shall be yours—I have made some discoveries—I believe I now know the giddy making principle in Hydro Carbonate and believe it is not the charcoal

New fire tubes make stinking air, I imputed that to the Sulphur or plumbago of the Iron—to destroy that I filled a new fire tube with caustic Slackied [*sic*] lime and kept it 2 hours redhot, obtained some inf[lamma]ble air—filled the tube with charcoal and made H[ydro] C[arbonate] which smelt like phosphorus or red hot Steel—A quart mixt with 20 of C[ommon] A[ir] was inhaled by a healthy young man, without any sensible effect whatever, another quart was taken by another person with as little effect—The thing a wanting seemed to be the sulphur—Borings of cast Iron were mixed with the charcoal, the air smelt stronger but did not stink, In smelling to it I got a little \of it/, *a very little*, had slight and very transitory vertigo, which returned again rather more sensibly, on rising in the night, and was felt slightly next day I made some air from well burnt coals, smellt some what like soot and some what hepatick, vertiginous properties not tryed but not doubtful, was very inf[lamma]ble—The only doubt as to the sulphur-ated Hydrogene being the active part, arises from the charcoal, having

221

been frequently used before and thereby deprived of its bitumen or fixed oil, which I doubt not would produce similar effects to the sulphur, as all unburnt vegetable and animal substances I have tried produce very sickening and very stinking airs—New charcoal well burnd shall be tried when I can procure proper patients. In the mean time here is *certainly* a method to make H[ydro] C[arbonate] free from the vertiginous quality—What will be its virtues remains to be tried

To prepare it with certainty, in a prepared tube some lime may be mixed with the charcoal—Oxygene frequently or generaly has bad smells and much fixed air which I have long attributed to the cast Iron tube—a tube was prepared with lime, the manganese in coarse powder was mixed with lime (about ¼ in bulk) The air was free from smell or nearly so, and contained exceedingly little fixed air. The fine powder of the manganese and the lime were of a light brown, the inside of the larger grains was darker, I sifted them out and mixed them with more lime and subjected them to a second heat, the only produce was a little *inf[lammab]le* air—I thought there was more oxygene than usual from the manganese, but could not be certain as it varies considerably in different parcels

Now I mean to close my account by a *mechanical* Medicine for your complaint, At Dr. Beddoes instigation I have {made} contrived a machine which he has got made which he says he doubts not will cure hecticks and intermittents—I call it the rotative couch, a couch or *Cott* is suspended in a frame which turns round faster or slower as wanted upon a pivot placed under the centre of the patients body, but I think would be still better under the heart. Healthy persons placed \on it/ experience experience [*sic*] a glow (I suppose in the feet)† a phtisical [*sic*] patient sleeps better on it (when turned slowly) than in bed the hot fit of the Hectic has been prevented by it, and other favourable effects produced—Beddoes is also trying the inhalation of powders in pthisical cases (yellow bark, flor zin etc.) he thinks with good effect; they do not excite cough if used moderately—

I thank you for your prescription which I shall use when I become more indisposed, at present I wear a By[ssus] pitch plaister (ever since I left Glasgow) which I think has been of service

Mrs. W. Joins me in best respects and kindest wishes to you and Dr.

---

† [Marginal note] The intention of the machine was to drive the blood by the centrifugal force from the precordia to the extremities, to produce vertigo sleep and warm feet—I believe they turn it 20 times per minute

Hutton and with me desires to be remembred to Dr. Hope for whom we have both conceived much esteem, I remain

Your ever affectionate friend
James Watt

I mean to send you a few
precepts on the use of H.C. in
my next. The slight dose I mentioned
suspended my spasms for a day

Letter 159

WATT TO BLACK

Cover addressed: 'Doctor Joseph Black/Physician/Edinburgh'
and endorsed in Black's hand, 'From Mr. Watt, 1st June 1796'
and numbered '19'. Dol.

Doctor Black   *Heathfield June 1st 1796*

My dear friend

I have long been ashamed to write to you from my not having been able to fulfill my promise of sending the small pneumatick apparatus I promised you. I am grown old and not able to run after workmen as I used to be and our Young men have been very fully occupied with an unusual quantity of business, and latterly with a hot Contest with our pirates in Chancery, not yet decided. If you will join to these matters the abominable stupidity of workmen here when set about a new Job, you will excuse me, The apparatus is now however finished and packing up to be sent you per Waggon. I hope it will come safe and please. I think it all pretty well except some tin tubes, which are very vilely executed, but will answer the end and are easily replaced if they should not by some of your excellent tinmen.

I have been making no new experiments lately, but have had an opportunity of seeing the effects of Hydrocarbonate in Hemoptoe, in a man about 40, the disease was brought on by drunkenness, he spit blood to the ammount of a tea cup full in a night, in 3 days spit stinking pus, then I sent him to the dispensary, where he was blistered and got squill pills, two days after that I heard he was in bed with fever. I sent for him and gave him one pint H.C which caused vertigo   his pulse immediately fell 10 per minute and he had a good night free from

223

cough, the H C was increased to a quart per day and he continued to mend   his physician however directed a second blister   in a fews [*sic*] days after, by threshing (for he never ceased his labour) the Hemoptoe returned, and his pulse was 120 and strong, I gave him the H C a quart *twice* a day, the pulse soon abated and in 2 days he had an eruption all over his legs and arms extremely itchy, which with the continuance of the air seems to have completed his cure, his pulse is natural, the Cough is trifling and the expectoration has long ceased to be purulent, he has had no other medicine except a few opium pills. This account is I doubt not defective, but the effects of the H.C. upon the fever and cough seemed decided, at the two times I have stated, I doubt not the man might have been cured by other medicines but I apprehend could not have pursued out doors labour as he did with this

By the advice of Dr. Carmichael I gave oxygene air to a poor boy who has a caries in the os sacrum, of some standing, for the first month it seemed to do much good but his case now seems hopeless; unfortunately only small doses could be given, on account of his hectic, which large doses augmented—The H.C given in the hemoptoe was made by mixing cast Iron boreings with the charcoal and was potently vertiginifactive, I am going to try whether much *Iron* is not suspended or dissolved in the air. I have not heard of any other case wherein H.C. procured an eruption—I hear Dr. Priestley has by long and repeated mixture of nitrous air, absorbed $\frac{6}{10}$ of atmospheric air and Dr. Beddoes informs me that some person in England has absorbed nearly the whole by means of phosphorus and by means of Iron and Sulphur— You know that a mixture of Sulphur and Copper fileings on being heated takes fire and becomes intensely hot, Dr. B. says he has found that it previously emits a large quantity of azote or some air with all the negative qualities of azote! I had a visit of Count Rumford lately, with whom I am much pleased, both with his ingenuity and his communication thereof. We have tried his experiment of lining a copper pan with a silver one, *in contact* but *not soldered* together, Milk or other glutinous liquids may be boiled in it as long as you will without burning to the pan under the surface of the liquid, but the splashings up burn to the sides. I can not account for it, there is no water between the lining and the pan

We have been again obliged to attack two hordes of pirates, some have submitted and paid tribute and if tomorrows decision is favourable the rest must, these inroads upon our peace are however severely felt, and but for the good sense and indefatigable activity of Mr. Boulton

Jun[io]r and my son we must have succumbed, for want of animal life and Spirits—I have had no violent diseases this winter, yet I am neither strong nor active—My asthma seems to have entirely left me as well as the spasms in my breast, I believe the former was cured by some small doses of H.C. I got accidentaly in making experiments, the latter by small doses of camphor and a Dovers mixture, Mrs. Watt is well and my son Gregory has returned from Glasgow College, stout and in good health, loaded with a{c}cademical promise

I have had sometimes the pleasure of hearing accidentaly of your welfare, but I wish for a confirmation from your own hand and also for some account of Doctor Hutton, who I am sorry to hear has had no relief—Mrs. Watt joins me in best wishes for you both and I remain

<table>
<tr><td></td><td>My dear Sir</td></tr>
<tr><td>please be so kind as to</td><td>Your affectionate friend</td></tr>
<tr><td>remember me to Dr. Hope</td><td>James Watt</td></tr>
</table>

Dr. Withering has followed your example of putting an issue in his breast and I think has benefited thereby
The apparatus goes from here this day by Swaine and Andertons Waggons

Letter 160

BLACK TO WATT

Cover addressed: 'Mr. James Watt Engineer/Heathfield/ Birmingham', endorsed in Watt's hand, 'Dr. Black July 28th 1796   Receipt of portable Pneumatic Apparatus   Visit from Mr. Watt Junior' and numbered '19'. Dol.

Edinb[urgh] 28 July 1796

My dear Freind
I had the pleasure to receive your letter of the 1st June and more lately the apparatus perfectly safe. I am much pleased with it and especially with the simplification of the air receiver   When I shall use it I propose to employ stoppers of Glass or metal in place of the Corks, and along with the stoppers a small quantity of soft wax to make them airtight. Openings stopped up with Corks are not easily made airtight —The soft Wax I use is taken from Saussure[1] and is usefull on many Occasions—It is compounded of Olive oil 1, Resin 2, and Bees wax

225

4 parts well melted together and mixed—It is very adhesive and always ready for use

The Case you relate is a strikeing example of the efficacy of H.C. air but it was a favourable case, the man being in the vigourous time of life and having so much strength that he was able to labour. I am sorry to see that Beddoes is so absurd and wrongheaded as to set himself up as a Statesman and attack Mr. Pit[2] It must proceed either from a foolish conceit of his own abilities and Judgement or from a mean design to court a party. In packing up Apparatus's you should avoid the use of sawdust   it penetrated in this case more or less into every one of the bundles and other articles.

The visit I received from your Son gave me very great pleasure. It is a double comfort to me on his account and on yours to know that he is doing so well and that his manners are so pleasing. Dr. Hutton when free from pain is still in possession of his usual vivacity and activity in thinking and conversation and writing. But there are days now and then when he is distressed with painfull spasms of the bladder, occasioned by a Stone, and his sensibility is so acute that pain is to him uncommonly distressing. My own health has been but low for some time

I caught a Cold in the middle of April and it brought on me a degree of weakness and languor very distressing and of long continuance. I am now releived in a great measure from that symptom and from the Catarrh but I have another frailty, and that is weakness and stiffness of my loins and right leg proceeding from an old bruise and from Chronic Rheumatism which makes me very lame and awkward in walking—I hope to be releived when the weather becomes dryer and cooler as I was last year from the Same complaint. My best wishes attend Mrs. Watt and the rest of your Family and good Mr. Bolton and the rest of our mutual Freinds

I am always
My dear Sir
Yours most affectionately
Joseph Black

[1] Horace Bénedict de Saussure (1740–99), Professor of Philosophy at Geneva, particularly interested in meteorology, electricity and chemistry. Made several geological expeditions throughout Europe, 1758–1779.
[2] Dr Beddoes' attack on the younger William Pitt was entitled, *An Essay on the Public Merits of Mr Pitt*, London 1796.

WATT TO BLACK

Cover addressed: 'Doctor Joseph Black/Nicholson Street/ Edinburgh/per favour Mr. Withering', endorsed in unidentified hand, 'Mr. Watt to Dr. Black Heathfield 9 October 1796' and numbered '18'. Dol.

Heathfield Oct[obe]r 9th 1796

Doctor Black

My Dear Friend

I was duely favoured with your kind letter of July 28th but having nothing material to communicate, and having \been/ some time absent from home on an excursion to Bath, from which I received benefit, and since having had a good deal of vexatious business as usual, I delayed writing—I now take the opportunity of my friend Dr. Witherings son, William,[1] going to study at your university to write to you, and to introduce him to you, He is a modest Ingenious, uncorrupted young man, well informed for his age, especialy in Botany. He is also one who will not intrude upon you otherwise I should have waved the introduction

Soon after our return from Bath Mrs. Watt was called to Glasgow by the afflicting intelligence that her father had had an attack of apoplexy, from which he has never recovered, but remains in a State of Weakness and frequently of insensibility, little short of death. She consequently remains still there and Gregory is with her

In the month of June I lost my Daughter Mrs. Miller[2] who has left 4 children all very young, now under their fathers care, who is very much attached to them. These and some other losses of friends have affected me very much but I have borne up wonderfully under them, considering my natural habits; but these things *must* be borne they cannot be remedied.

My health for \some/ time after my Bath jaunt was better than its usual Standard, to which it seems now relapsing, the late east winds brought back my Rhematic [sic] affections in the arms sides breasts and shoulders and by the time I had got them a little subdued, the West Winds have brought on an attack of my dyspnea, so troublesome that yesterday I begun to try the effects of the Hydrocarbonate air upon it, seemingly with some success but I cannot be sure yet, as I have kept out of the wind all this day. It however has done no harm as I take \it/ in doses which cause the least possible vertigo, having experienced upon others that in general it is not necessary to produce that effect to any troublesome degree. It rather encreases the dyspnea immediately after taking it, which may be owing to the unnatural method of inhaling it, after an hour or two its sedative powers take effect, what the ultimate success is I shall inform you

Beddoes is publishing some select cases with observations in his manner, some of them are interesting In his politicks he is incorrigible, at least by me who have given him up in that line, and I am sorry to see that he is publishing another hit at the Doctors which I agree with you can do nothing but procure him enemies, who will be absurd enough to make war upon his doctrines in revenge

I thank you for your observations upon the apparatus Glass Stoppers were thought of, but they would much encrease the expence, and I find corks answer *sufficiently* well Oxygene Air has been found perfectly good after standing two months in the air holder. The soft wax is an old plaister of mine which I have often applied to diseased machines

I am very much concerned at your acc[oun]t of yourself and Doctor Hutton. I hope the summer has mended your complaints. I had an obstinate coldness in my left leg amounting frequently to pain and not easily removed by the heat of fire Dr. Withering directed a small blister to be applied to the nerve, just below the knee above its entry into the muscle, it has more than half cured the coldness which now is principaly below the ancle and probably another Blister above that end of the nerve might remove it but as it is now moderate I bear with it, query if some such treatment might not mend your Rheumatism?

We are deep in law again and have a trial coming on next December with a purse proud ignorant London Currier[3] who has turned maker of pirated Engines, and refuses to submit though now under the chancellers injunction, till trial. Please remember me affectionately to Doctor Hutton accept my best wishes, and believe me ever

truely your's
James Watt

My son James and Mr. Boulton
desire their best respects—

Oct[obe]r 13th. The Hydro carbonate was not efficacious. I was obliged to give it up after 4 doses, from its causing nausea like sea sickness which deranged my stomach, it however did no other hurt, and rather mended the spasmodic affections, for this complaint I fancy I should have taken it less diluted so as to cause vertigo—I have written to Mr. J. Robison requesting his advice or testimony concerning my invention and have sent him some abstracts of the accusations against me, and the Judges arguments after the last trial which I request you to look over and to add your remembrances to his, if your health and time permit

Adieu

I believe I must avoid the coming of the north or east wind for the cure of my asthma

[1] William Withering junior (1776–1832), physician, educated at Edinburgh, was his father's biographer. He is known to have attended a meeting of the Lunar Society.

[2] Mrs Miller was James Watt's daughter, Margaret, (1767–91), by his first wife, Margaret Miller.

[3] John Maberley, who was concerned with the Hornblower family, in pirating the Boulton and Watt engine. See B.R.L.: 'Considerations upon the measures to be adopted with Maberley, September 1796'.

Letter 162

WATT TO ROBISON

* B.R.L. Boulton and Watt Letter Books.

Heathfield Birm[ingha]m Oc[tobe]r 11th 1796

Proffessor Robinson
Edinburgh—

Dear Sir

It is with much reluctance that I trouble you in the business of this letter, but I flatter myself, that when you are informed of the motives, which urge me at present you will excuse me.—Ever since the Engine business was supposed to be profitable, Boulton and Watt have been molested with pirates of the invention. Unwilling to involve themselves in Law suits and sensible of the precarious tenor of all exclusive privileges in this country, they defended themselves by other means or winked at aggressions which were not of great magnitude until about 3 years ago, when the impudence of some aggressors and the powerful party which supported them, B and W found it necessary either to

229

bring an action against them or meanly to succumb under the combination, they preferred the former and brought their action in the Common pleas, where they obtained an unqualified verdict from the Jury, but the Judge thought proper to reserve some law questions for the opinion of the Court, which after long delay and two solemn arguments was divided, two Judges being in favour of B and W and two against them. The cause therefore remains undecided, There being in such case no appeal. However the Chancellor upon the strength of the verdict, granted injunctions to prevent, a considerable number of the pirated Engines from being used. These operations were however very expensive and served more to keep the enemy at bay than to produce profits to us. Other pirates in different parts emboldened by the indecision of the Court of C[ommon] P[leas] set us at defiance. We however obtained injunctions against them also   most of them submitted and paid our demands; but one Maberley a Currier in London who had set up a Manufactory of pirated Engines, held out and after several fruitless applications to Chancery at last obtained an order for a new trial which we *must* bring on next term and will probably be tried in the begginning of December next against which time we must collect all our forces. The proceedings in chancery have done this service that it has obliged our opponent to bring forward the greater part of his evidence, an abstract of which I shall send you, as well as the arguments of the Judges on the law points. You will see among other things that they alledge I was not the Inventor   some say that certain parts were in use before and others that the whole was invented by Dr. Roebuck, with whom I was acquainted till some time after the invention. In short the objections are multifarious and to every point; but the court held that it was sufficient if a skilful Mechanick acquainted with the Engines formerly in use could perform the invention from the specification it was good, though afterwards even that was called in question. Now my Dear sir I wish for your opinion on that general question, and also how far you know the method to be of my invention and not used or practised by others at that time. At the same time I hope you will favour us with your opinion of the answers to the particular philosophical or technical questions, say to the expedience or necessity of more particular description, which from the numerous modes in which the invention could be applied seemed to me at the time improper to be inserted as bounding the invention. I have put down my own thoughts upon the matter, copy of which I shall send you as soon as it can be made out

I believe the fact I there affirm to be true, that in a few hours after the idea struck me of condensing in a seperate vessel, I had arranged the whole in my mind and in a few days, had a model at work, which though defective enough in mechanism was in point of principle and in effect equal any made since

You know also I believe, the long wild goose chace I had in following various devises before I hit upon this simple idea, and also the pains I was at in endeavouring to condense the steam by external {condensation}\application/of cold water, to save the force necessary to draw the water out of the condenser, which at last I was obliged to give up, not from impracticability but expence

Knowing the state of your health and your avocations I am afraid to ask you to appear as a witness upon the trial if your opinions should be favourable, I shall only say that such appearance could not fail to be of great service to us, from your character, your Station, your Science and your knowledge of the invention, and that B and W would not withhold any expence which could make your Journey agreable. If your health or other circumstances render this request improper I cannot urge it. Feelings of the irksomeness of obligated reflection at our time of life have prevented me hitherto from troubling my friends in Scotland with this affair which has for years been a torment to me. At present had not Mr. Boulton and myself the assistance of our sons we must give it up, though the Stake is very great

I proposed to have come to Scotland this fall when I might have had the pleasure of a personal Conversation with you and other friends, but various matters of business have me delay till the weather has broke and deranged my feeble health so much that I am present confined to the house, by Asthma and other complaints, with a change of wind these may cure but my presence has become necessary here or in London to prepare for this highly disagreable business, in the best manner we can. So that even the cogent motive of fetching Mrs. W. from her attendance upon her father cannot operate as it would in other circumstances

Many things have of late years, and in this present year, have co-operated to depress my spirits and to lessen the enjoyment of life; but age and repetitions of affliction have lessened the acuteness of my sensations or at least the duration of acute sensations. Some of the diseases of youth have left \me/ but others at least equaly grievous have taken their place, and the activity of mind with the ardour of invention which served as stimuli to the corporeal powers have subsided. I might however still have some enjoyments if these pirates and law-suits would let my mind have rest

I must break off this disagreable subject   In my present state it would lead me too far and I should not forget that you are severely a fellow sufferer

my last Hobby horse has been experiments on the best means of producing factitious airs for Medicinal use and in some applications of them, which have been in many cases successful, in others they have failed, as all other medicines do. To myself they have been of no avail in any of my complaints

Our friend Mr. P. Ewart proves a very worthy and ingenious man, to whom we are under many obligations especially to his zeal for our interest. He has at present formed, as we hope a valuable connection at Manchester where he is at present but is expected back soon

With best wishes and respectful compliments to Mrs. Robison and all your family, I remain

Dear Sir
Yours affectionately
James Watt

I request the favour of an answer
as soon as convenient

please turn over

[Here follows Watt's letter to Robison of 24 October 1796]

Letter 163

WATT TO ROBISON

* B.R.L. Boulton and Watt Letter Books.

Heathfield Birm[ingha]m Oct[obe]r 24th 1796

Jno. Robison Esq
Edinburgh

My Dear Sir
Yesterday, only, I received your kind letter of the 15th. That I have not forgot you will appear from a letter I sent to you at Edinburgh, by Mr. William Withering which should be delivered at your house on Saturday last, to which I refer. I have been obliged to trouble many of my friends with these abominable law affairs but have hitherto, have only called those who lived near London, but now these scoundrels,—

the Hornblowers and others have leagued against us we must call all who are willing to help us. The state of your health and your disposition in too many bad points resembling my own prevented me troubling you while it could be avoided. I could and would descant with pleasure mixt with pain on the days of former years and on many points of your letter which come home to my feelings, but I also labour under low spirits, and might by what I should say tend to depress yours. I shall therefore on this subject only advise you to think better of yourself, do more think less and indulge the Bagatelle   In regard to your very cruel disorder, without I know more circumstances I can form no opinion. If it is an ulcer of any kind perhaps small doses of oxygene air and hydrocarbonate mixt might be of use as they have been in some bad cases of painful scrophula. Meanwhile be assured that you have never lost my good opinion, though from my pursuits and diseases I have not availed myself to your good will as I ought to have done. My path in life has been a Thorny one and even now though reasonably rich I am bowed down almost to the grave with cares of various kinds, to say nothing of half a dozen chronic diseases. In regard to happiness you have nothing to regret in not being linked with me, though I may have   Now let us to business, for as I set out for glasgow on Wednesday I have little time, my Journey and stay there must be hurried for I must be in London by the middle of November, if alive I propose if possible to see you in Edinburgh on my return

You will see from the papers sent you the objections and consequently the proper answers, I propose to send you my own general reply for your government, as soon as copy can be made—The point is to establish that I was the inventor that the invention was perfect as to the *saving steam and fuel* at the time of the patent 1769, and that the specification is sufficient to enable a Mechanick understanding Newcomens Engine to have constructed one with these properties

I did not invent this method piece meal but all at once in a few hours in 1765 I believe, The first step was the idea from the elastic nature of steam of condensing in a seperate vessel, 2d the getting out the water by a long pipe and the air by a pump, 3d that the pump would extract the water also 4th that grease might be used in place of water to keep the piston tight, 5th that Steam might be employed to press upon the piston in place of air 6 to keep the Cylinder warm.

The next day I set about it. The boiler was ready, I took a large syringe of Tom Hamiltons 2 inches dia[mete]r and a foot long that was the Cylinder. I made two tin ends to it with a pipe to convey steam to

233

both of them. I made a tin Condenser consisting of a pump about an inch dia[mete]r, and two small pipes about 10 inches long and ⅛ dia[mete]r immersed in a small round cistron, which I still have. I placed the Cyl[inde]r inverted tied a weight to the piston rod, blew out the \air and/ condensed water through the piston rod, which was hollow, and when I judged the Cyl[inde]r filled with steam, I drew up the piston of the pumps and the weight immediately followed, to my great Joy, all this was done in a day or two after I had contrived it, the other experiments you mention in the Encycl[opaedi]a were afterwards when I was bewildering myself with mechanism foreign to the invention and above all perplexing myself with trying to condense without injection. My patent is not for mechanism but for saving steam and fuel and perfectly applicable to the Engines which then existed. As you know my mechanical improvements the fruits of 20 years labour have nothing to do in this question, they are not protected by the patent, the steam wheel did actualy work with effect, but was superseded by the present modes which are superior.—You need not fear that it will be any breach of our blessed law to inform me of all you can bear evidence to, If I do not like any part of it I shall tell you and you may suppress it. Our law is not Justice nor the semblance of it, it is full of quirks which the witnesses must be aware of, otherwise they will injure the cause they mean to support, therefore they are so many advocates for their respective parties, only they must not tell falsehoods though they may conceal noxious facts, not trenching upon the Justice of the cause, Judges and Juries see the witnesses in this light and in cases such as mine it is the opinions of the most respectable witnesses, which determine them, for the Jury should give their { opinions } \verdict/ accordingly and the Judge his sentence unless there be some unfortunate law quibble beyond the reach of common sense which the judge reserves for the Court who have got over such prejudices, You will see that any evidence from Petersburgh must come too late, for this trial and besides the date you mention is after the patent and could avail nothing. I think Dr. Black may be able to assist your memory in some points, I have wrote to him—A principal question is supposing you to remember things nearly as I have stated them and are satisfied of the sufficience of the specification, could you come to London about the end of November, if your evidence should be deemed essential, when we know more fully what you would chuse to say. The favour is too great to ask, but if you think the journey might injure your health or affect your own affairs, refuse us flatly, but give us such other assistance as you can.

I would say much more but though the spirit is willing the flesh is weak. I would thank you for the very flattering things you say of me in the Ency[clopedi]a but I cannot find phrases In respect to the H[orn-blowe]rs they are mere thieves which you could not know. The steam collar was mine and in use before their patent, one of them saw it, also the expansive mode of using steam, their engine would not work till they also stole the air pump and lastly the condenser also. After all they were immensely under par when compared with ours, and by dint of fair trials and computations we have made them be laid aside. They have however the impudence and malice of devil. I shall endeavour to recollect about the strings at an [another time]

[Hiatus] At top of page letter concludes:
use it as you please. I like the Horners was in an error about the bulk of expanded steam, it loses head and loses bulk in what ratios I know not but so as to frustrate in great measure the expansive schemes, the good effect they have they owe to the moisture in the Cyl[inde]r—adieu god bless you with better health

Yours affectionate friend J. Watt

Letter 164

ROBISON TO WATT

Cover addressed: 'To Mr. James Watt/Engineer/Birmingham', endorsed in Watt's hand, 'Proffessor Robison October 25 1796 about his coming to England', and numbered '9'. Dol.

Edin[bu]r[gh] Oct[obe]r 25 1796

My dear Freind
    Your letter of the [blank] gave me infinite pleasure. I see you have not rec[eive]d my splenetic Epistle from the Country and that all my fears were bugbears of my own raising. Forgive me my good and old freind, and look only on the fair side of my conduct. Had my Esteem of you been less, you would not have been troubled with it. If any thing else can help me out, let it be my situation. I was sitting by an affection-ate Sister, whom I have left, never to see her again.
    You may depend on every service I can render you. But it fills me with regret that it is most likely that I can do you none   I have, perhaps rashly, engaged to teach my Class this winter, after an absence of five

years, and if my appearance be necessary during the Sessions of the Colleges it will be out of my power to give it My pain is so greivous that it would be impossible for me to come up except by very easy journeying: the smallest hurrying w[oul]d knock me up. If this did not put an end to my troubles, it w[oul]d destroy my Class and my Credit —for I am forced to tell you my worthy freind that I am shabbily used by our hon[our]able patrons (I believe I said something of this in my last) and they would not interpret in my favour my attempts to take a trip to London after being sick nine years. My Assistant was forced upon me with conditions so disgraceful to me that nothing but the security of the pension to my Wife would have made me accept But I will get my Assistant sounded at a distance to see if he will step in, and if he does, depend on my feeble aid. If this can't be done there is some chance that the snail pace of the Law may put off the necessity of my appearance till the beginning of May. Then I sh[oul]d gladly come up to you —If none of these ifs will do, is there not a way of the Chancery taking Evidence by Commission in Edin[bu]r[gh] But this must be enormously expensive, and it is giving you too high notions of any thing I can do. If any written declaration of my opinion can be of Use, I could then (not being limited by precise questions) say much more in detail what I recollect of the train of your thoughts and the sufficiency of the specifications I only want your instruction in what manner to proceed as an honest man—When I came to town Mrs. R was from home, the Room where my lumber drawers were was newly painted and locked to keep out my Boys—and when opened next day with some solemnity, the paper I expected was not to be found. This raised a laugh against me—but I am certain of having it—and will find it as soon as I have a moment to breathe. At present I am hurried amazingly all my apparatus in confusion and my first lecture to be tomorrow

I take it very kind that you tell me your own Situation, and sympathise with your afflictions. I had heard that you had derived great benefit from the use of Charcoal, but your letter destroys this satisfaction. My Case is most singular, the most perfect general health with *unceasing* torment. Yet I would rather bear this pure pain than any sickness—Racked by it as I am I sometimes trott my hobbys—one which you will laugh at I got accidentally the history of Free Masonry —which has I think led me into the French Revolution, or at least of the fixed plan by which the Cosmopolitical fanaticism has been propagated and is still spreading thro' Europe—Had I leisure I think I could give the public some useful information on this Subject.[1]—Farewell my

236

dear Sir—I write this in great confusion of mind—if any thing worth communicating occurs I will trouble you again Mean time accept of my best wishes, in which Mrs. Robison, who daily [hears]† your name and is well acquainted with you most cordially joins with
Dear Sir [signature cut out]
offer my best Compliments
to Mr. Boulton

† Paper torn here.
1 The following year John Robison published an extremely odd volume entitled: *Proofs of a Conspiracy against all the Religions and Governments of Europe, carried on in the Secret Meetings of Free-Masons, Illuminati and Reading Societies, etc.*, Edinburgh, 1797.

Letter 165

WATT TO ROBISON

★ B.R.L. Boulton and Watt Letter Books.

Heathfield Birm[ingha]m Nov[embe]r 14th 1796

Proff[esso]r Robison

Dear Sir

I wrote you a few hasty lines from Newcastle, to prepare you for the probable call we may be obliged to make upon your kindness.

Our sollicitor Mr. Weston is much pleased with your letter on our business, of which we sent him Extracts, and thinks your testimony will be of great importance to us, both as to the originality of my invention, and confuting the reports which as we apprehend have been circulated by Jo. Hately, and which if sworn to may have a very bad effect on our cause, and as to your opinions as a theoretical and practical Mechanick on the sufficience of the specification which will receive additional weight from your Proffession and from your appearance

These circumstances we hope will excuse our importuning you to do us the favour of personal attendance in London, as we can in no other way in the least avail ourselves of your testimony in a court of Law. Were it likely to injure your health, I could not ask the favour, but I hope it will not, but on the contrary, though it may cause you some temporary pain, will give more elasticity to your nerves and promote your future ease.

237

I hope also you will be able to procure leave of absence, and to prevail upon some proper substitute to teach for you, one argument which should have some weight in both these cases, is the enabling you to do an act of justice to your friends by declaring the truth and thereby assisting to rescue them from a conspiracy of pirates, (of {which} \whom/ we have discovered two fresh sets since I saw you.) I presume so far upon your good will as to say no more on the subject so far as regards yourself, and am persuaded if there should be any need Dr. Black will join his sollicitations to yours as to the leave of absence, please remember me kindly to him, with best thanks for the memorial he sent—It is supposed the trial will take place some day between the 5th and the 10th Dec-[embe]r ,but of this more fully when I can be better informed. We should wish you to be in London a few days before the trial, that you may be rested and prepared to answer the questions our counsel may put to you I hope you will now prepare for coming if you can possibly arrange your own affairs satisfactorily, as nothing can supersede the necessity of your evidence to us, except the trial being put off or deserted by the other party, an event not altogether improbable as they do not well know what they are about and we believe are not well prepared, but dupes to your friends H[ornblowe]r and H[atel]y and other such Hero's of their own tale

We had a pleasant Journey and recruited two material Evidences at Newcastle. I was pretty well on the road but have got an accession of Asthma since my return, owing to the cold damp westerly wind—Mrs. Watt and Gregory join me in best respects to Mrs. Robison and family and I remain

Dear Sir
Yours affectionately
James Watt

Your answer will find me here, as I send my son James to London in my place till near the time of trial, lest the air of that place should knock me up too soon

ROBISON TO BLACK

Probably sent by hand. Addressed 'To Dr. Black', endorsed in
Watt's hand, 'Professor Jno. Robison to Dr. Black Edinburg—
October 1796' and numbered '18'. Dol.

[? *November 1796*]
Sunday noon

Dear Sir

I had a letter yesterday from Watt, and find that I must needs go—
it will be with great satisfaction if I render him any essential service.
He bids me thank you for your excellent Memorial   I am sorry to feel
myself so much enfeebled in mind (by the Use of Opium) as well as in
Body that I cannot give much force to any thing that I have to say—
and as it is a trying situation, to be exposed to the round about tricks of
a parcel of Counsellors habituated to Villainy and skilled in puzzling
and entrapping, I am much afraid of being put out of temper. The
mere facts that I recollect scorn all attacks of this kind, but Watt says
that one Hately is ready to swear that Dr. Roebuck was the Inventor
and acknowledged to be so in the Neighbourhood—Now I recollect
Innuendos to this purpose, and have heard Gentlemen of Rank in the
Neighbourhood of Bo-Ness assert it with great Confidence. I recollect
some Facts, Cases of some of these, when they recanted, and of others
who persisted—I have even heard the doctor claim several subordinate
parts *of the Improvement,* and even say that Watt did not understand
what he was *gropeing* after, and could not go on without him. Should I
be sworn to declare the *whole* truth I must tell such things—and then
my *Conviction* of Watts Claim will be called mere matter of opinion.
This I am certain will provoke me—I must have a Conversation with
you, to learn the utmost extent of Roebucks Claims. They must be well
known to you—I think that he was not a complete convert to the
theory of latent heat at the time I was at Kinneil, or at least did not
understand it. For I remember his insisting that if the Condenser was
made of a great number of pipes, to encrease the Surface, it was of no
consequence how small the Cistern was, and that even hot water on
the outside would serve—and Watt complaind that he would not
acquiesce in the necessity of a very copious Injection (nor indeed of
any, which was watts first notion also) If this was the Case I should

239

speak boldly—If tomorrow about 2 oClock would not intrude too much on your time, or if you would admit me in the Evening to take a dish of tea with you, I think I should profit much by what I might learn from you—What you recollect might be connected with something which I knew and have forgotten

Mr. Watt writes me too that he has recruited two excellent Evidences at N[ew]castle—*per Contra* he has discovered two other Setts of pirates —and has suffered much from the damp weather on his journey—in so much that he is obliged to send his Son James to London in his place—I wish also to receive some instructions from you how to manage myself —how to avoid the Constipation which travelling generally produces, and which always gives me inexpressible torment. Be so good as to send me word whether I shall call about 2 oClock or about 5 or 6.

I am
D[ea]r Sir
Yours
J. Robison

[The blank space below the signature has been used to make the calculations shown below, possibly in Black's hand:

Valuation of the Property of Great Britain by Mr. Pitt anno 1796

Immoveable property . . .   1300,000,000,000

moveable Ditto supposed . .   2600,000,000,000

      National Debt 400,000,000   )3900,000,000,000(9750

                                             3600,000,000

                                             300 000 000

                                             28

                                             2 000 000 000

                                             2 000,000,000

                                               0

Next to the above note and extending to the opposite page is the following:

$$9750) \qquad \pounds$$

Suppose an Individual worth £20,000   (2.. 1.. 0⅓

$$19,500$$
$$500$$

There are also some figures in pencil   20

$$11\tfrac{3}{4} \qquad 8)313.\tfrac{7}{8} \qquad\qquad 10,000$$
$$4 \qquad\quad 24 \qquad\qquad\qquad 9750$$
$$3)47\ 15 \qquad 7 \qquad\qquad\quad 250$$
$$3 \qquad\qquad\qquad\qquad\qquad 12$$
$$17 \qquad\qquad\qquad\qquad\qquad 3,000$$
$$15$$
$$2$$
$$2$$
$$1$$

$$11$$
$$8$$
$$3)94 \quad 31$$

Letter 167

WATT TO ROBISON

* B.R.L. Boulton and Watt Letter Book

Heathfield Birm[ingha]m Nov[embe]r 19th 1796

Proffessor Robison
Edinburgh—

Dear Sir

I wrote to you from Newcastle and again since my return here, since which I am not favoured with any of your's

Our lawyers have now settled the trial to be at the Guildhall in the City of London for the sake of having a special Jury of Merchants, and desire us to have our witnesses in Town by the 5th but better they add if by the 3d Dec[embe]r

I intended with this to have sent you a remittance for your expences but have since thought it better that our agent Mr. Alex[ande]r Mackenzie should wait upon you, and tender them. You are best judge what you will require we have desired him to offer £100, and we hope to see you before more will be wanted—I hope you have been able to settle with your assistant and that no accession of bad health since I had the pleasure of seeing you will prevent your Journey—We shall be found in London at No. 13 London Street Fenchurch Street where we shall be happy to see you. I am sorry that the dilatoriness of decision among our council has not enabled me to write you positively sooner but hope that my last may have prepared you

I have found some letters of mine to Dr. Roebuck which serve to fix the date of the invention nearly and one to Dr. Small in 1767 which mentions distinctly the expansive Engine which Hornblower pretends to have invented much later, there are also abundance of letters from Old Hornblower in 1776 and later in which [there] is not the least mention of any invention of himself or any of his family but much which implies they had none then

John Roebuck is ready to declare that his Father always ascribed the invention to me   I have therefore requested his attendance, he can also give testimony to the invention from 1767 or thereabouts—

Mrs. Watt joins me in best respects and wishes to you Mrs. Robison and family and I remain, with comp[limen]ts to Dr. Black and other friends

Dear Sir
Yours sincerely
James Watt

Mr. Alex[ande]r Mackenzie
Writer to the Signet
Ramsay Garden is our agent
he is successor to Mr. W[illia]m Anderson.

Letter 168

ROBISON TO WATT

Cover addressed: 'Mr. Watt', and endorsed in Watt's hand, 'Jno. Robison, London December 1796 wishes to give his evidence in his own way and desires to know when he is to receive his instructions' and numbered '11'. Dol.

Dear Sir
The rambling materials for Evidence which occurred to me have turned out such a prolix Mass that I fear that neither yourself nor your Counsel will have patience to seperate the few Grains from the Chaff— I know that the things which I have to narrate, when taken alone are

frivolous in the extreme and it has often been matter of regret to me that I have put you and must yet put you to so much expence for a trifle that I now think you might have easily spared—But my fears made me think otherwise and put too high a value on what I had to say—Yet I still think that if the time can allow me to tie these trifling particulars together somewhat in the manner I have done here, they will have considerable Weight with a Jury of Men of liberal Minds, and that it will not hurt your Cause {if} should I in this manner give vent to that affection which is naturally excited by the recollection of our careless days and gay Scenes in a Mind not hackneyd in the bustle of Life, and softened by Suffering

You must excuse me to your Counsel for *appearing* to direct them in the Choice of their questions. This is not from Vanity, but from a Wish to have such interrogatories put to me, and in such an Order, as shall suggest and give room for my narration. I pray that I may be in such tolerable Condition on the day of Cause that I shall not be under the necessity of taking much opium, which always hurts my recollection

Let your Counsel garble this Farrago and throw away the rubbish— but I fear their Forensic Taste and that their habits have worn off from their minds the feelings of common life—I think that if I could get leave to tell my story in my own way it would have a better effect on persons of an ordinary way of thinking and feeling—But I shall obey their in- structions, having nothing at heart but your Service—

I could wish to know when I may expect to be instructed—this would leave me more master of my hours of idleness and I would then attend to some little things of my own—For I must run off the moment your Cause is desisted, as it would hurt me at Edin[bu]r[gh]to desert my Class longer than is necessary

I again request you to tell your Counsel before they cast their Eye on this paper that I do not presume to direct them in their questions, but I behoved to express such as should give me the opportunities of throwing out my mites of evidence

I regret exceedingly that I have not been able to enjoy your Company —but I wished to let Mrs. Robison see all that was possible—and *to be one of her Ciceroni*— days are sadly changed with me. I hoped to have shown her this place in a pleasanter way—This has fatigued me and when I come home I am in such pain that I am unable to come to you—I hope now to have more in my power, as the kindness of my friends have enabled us to do much of the Lyon business

Adieu good Sir and believe me
Monday ever yours J Robison

Letter 169

ROBISON TO JAMES WATT JUNIOR †

B.R.L. Misc. Box 35. Endorsed: 'Professor Robison London 27 December 96—With Advertisement for the newspapers respecting the trial with Maberley'.

[*27 December 1796*]

Dear Sir

I am sorry for having undertaken the proposed intimation of your Victory to the public—My door has never remained shut this forenoon and I have been unable to do more than scrawl out on scraps a paper a most imperfect Narration. I send it to your indulgence with all its sins upon its head—but your Attorneys will at once condemn it or pick out such hints as have not occurred to themselves

I wished to do something better, but am really too much fluttered by the unremitting bustle of this bustling City *Valeat quantum valere potest*

Your's in great truth

J Robison

† This is the covering note for the advertisement which follows. Edd.

Letter 170

ENCLOSURE: DRAFT ADVERTISEMENT

B.R.L. Misc. Box 35.

{ Yesterday} \On Friday last/ the {long depending} \important/ Cause Boulton and Watt against {several persons infringers of their patent rights}{ \Messrs/} \Hornblower and Maberley/ was heard in the Court of Common Pleas in Guild Hall before the Lord Chief Justice Eyre and a Special Jury, { who determined it in favour of the plaintiffs by a general Verdict}{ \and/}. The{ present} Action was \brought against the Defendants/ { brought against a Mr. Maberley and a Mr. Hornblower, for having erected Steam Engines with a seperate Condenser and other Apparatus}{ \of/}{ the sole Invention of Mr. James Watt of Glasgow,

244

and } for having { thus } infringed { a } \the Plaintiffs patent/ { granted him in 1769 } for a Method of lessening the Consumption of Steam and fuel in fire Engines.

{ The Case was opened for the plaintiffs by Mr. Sergeant Adair in the most able Manner } The defendants \in the prior proceedings/ had denied the { ir } Infringment { of the patent, and } \had/ offered to prove that Mr. Watt was not { intitled to its protection, because } the Invent { ion } \or/ was { not his }, and { \who/ } { that } { \to prove/ } in his Specification { enrolled in Chancery } { \was not sufficient/ } { he } had { insidiously } misled the public, { and concealed essential parts of the invention, for that it was of no use, and contained no information which would } { \could/ } { enable an Engineer to avail himself of the Invention. }

{ \After/ Mr. Sergeant Adair \had/ opend the Case for the plaintiffs { in the most able Manner } \which he did very fully/, { stating with philosophical precision } \explaining/ the original principles of Steam Engines, giving the history of their gradual Improvement from the Engine invented by the Marquis of Worcester to that of Newcomen, who totally changed its Nature and manner of action, and then stating, with philosophical accuracy the defects of { tha } Newcomens Engine, defects founded on the water and proportion of steam, and with equal precision \having/ described the Improvements mounted by Mr. Watt and his method of applying his principle to the Construction of a Steam Engine which should be free from all these defects and fully come up to the property assigned to it in the patent, namely the great saving of steam and fuel. } The Counsel for the defendants { seeing the Jury so fully instructed in the Nature of the Subject, } \in a very early stage of the Cause/ departed from their first averments admitted the Originality and Usefulness of Mr. Watts Invention, { and } \and/ { admitted } that { their Clients } /Defendants/ had { adopted the Invention of Mr. Watt } \infringed it/, and { boldly } rested { all on the insufficiency of the } \their Defence on the Objections raised against/ the Specification { and set the patent at defiance }.

The plaintiffs brought forward \Mr. De Luc Dr. Herschel [s]/ a Body of { the } most respectable { Evidence } \witnesses/ to prove the { super-abundancy of information } \sufficiency of/ { in } the Specification \and it appeared that they had a great many others in Court ready to be called if it had been necessary/ { This consisted of Gentlemen eminent for their physical knowledge, and the most reputable Engineers and even head Workmen, who all declared the Specification to be fully adequate to the communication of all the necessary instruction. This was opposed by a number of persons who called themselves Engineers, or persons well acquainted with the erection and management of Newcomen's Engine, who declared that they were not able from the most careful perusal of the Specification to erect an Engine which, like those of Boulton and Watt, should save Steam and fuel—It would appear no very difficult matter to find a very large body of Men who could emit such a declaration with a very safe Conscience—Yet, some of these, when conducted step by step by the examining Counsel, actually accomplished in succession all the things required for completing the Engine. And, so difficult was it to find a sufficient Number of persons who would acknowledge this inferiority of \apprehension/ that three Evidences called by the defendants viz Professor H——n——r and Mr. ——— gave evidence which was decidely for the plaintiffs.}

Mr. Sergeant le Blanc opened the Cause with no less dexterity for the defendants, and conducted his Argument with great Astuteness and perspicuity. Mr. Adair concluded his reply with congratulating this Country with possessing such a number of well instructed persons, able to carry into Effect the discoveries and invention of its Men of Genius that the defendants after having ransacked the Kingdom for Minds of an inferior Rank, seemed to have exhausted the Number, and \by mistake/ had furnished the plaintiffs with three of their most powerful Evidences

The Lord Chief Justice conducted the tryal with an impartiality and a complete knowledge of a very abstruse and difficult Subject, which does him infinite honour. His Charge to the Jury was equally conspicuous for perspicuity, instruction, and impartiality. The Jury without going out of Court, {brought in} \gave/ a general Verdict for the Plaintiffs with one shilling damages

And thus has the Patent Right of Boulton and Watt been defined and established by Law "a Method for saving Steam and fuel in Steam Engines", applicable to any form, and which may therefore be evicted from any form into which the ingenuity of pilfering pirates may introduce it

Whoever looks around him and observes the{numerous applications} \great number/ of these Engines which are employed in every quarter, not only for the purpose of draining Coal Mines where fuel is of little value, but for executing every Species of Manufacture, even when fuel is extremely dear, cannot but be pleased with seeing the ingenious Inventor fully protected by Law. And it must be a satisfaction to every reflecting mind to see the pretentions of ignorant and presuming tradesmen so effectually discouraged. Such persons by plausible exhibitions of Ingenuity, inveigle the unwary Employer, ruin him by expensive and fruitless projects, and thereby discourage them and others from all applications to Men possessed of Talents really able to serve them

We were happy in observing in the Evidence given in this tryal such proofs of \the/ skill and philosophical Information of our practical Engineers that we need not fear that any efforts of British Genius will ever be lost for want of hands fully able to execute its most difficult projects, by which the almost unparalleled Energy of this highly favourd Country{is incontestably demonstrated} may be still farther exhibited, to the admiration of the surrounding Nations And we think ourselves warranted to say that the Cotton Mills and the Engines of Boulton and Watt have been the most remarkable instances \and Means/ of this national Superiority†

The Defendants called {some} \several/ Witnesses to prove that the {Patent}\Specification/ was not sufficient, but of these two spoke nearly as forcibly in favour of its sufficiency as any of the Plaintiffs Witnesses— The testimony of the others produced no effect to alter the Impression made by the Plaintiffs Witnesses in their favour After a very able charge from the Cheif Justice the Jury instantly found a \general/ Verdict for the Plaintiffs with{Costs}nominal Damages \only/—the Plaintiffs \did/ not {insisting on}\press for/ more as \and/ in \such/{such}Cases \of Trespass/ Costs follow{such Damages}of course.

{The Defendants Counsel urged strongly for a special Verdict which was refused but they intimated an Inclination}

[The editors' conjectural reconstruction of the draft advertisement]

On Friday last the important Cause Boulton and Watt against Hornblower and Maberley was heard in the Court of Common Pleas in Guild Hall before the Lord Chief Justice Eyre and a Special Jury. The Action was brought against the Defendants for having infringed the Plaintiffs' patent for a Method of lessening the Consumption of Steam and fuel in fire Engines.

The defendants in the prior proceedings had denied the Infringment [and] had offered to prove that Mr. Watt was not the Inventor, and in his Specification had misled the public.

The Counsel for the defendants in a very early stage of the Cause departed from their first averments admitted the Originality and Usefulness of Mr. Watts Invention and that Defendants had infringed it and tested their Defence on the Objections raised against the Specification.

The plaintiffs brought forward Mr. De Luc Dr. Herschel [and] a Body

† At foot of page in reverse the following paragraph was added. Edd.

247

of most respectable witnesses to prove the sufficiency of the Specification and it appeared that they had a great many others in Court ready to be called it it had been necessary

The Defendants called several Witnesses to prove that the Specification was not sufficient, but of these 2 spoke nearly as forcibly in favour of its sufficiency as any of the Plaintiffs' Witnesses—The Testimony of the others produced no effect to alter the Impressions made by the Plaintiffs' Witnesses in their favour After a very able charge from the Cheif Justice the Jury instantly found a general Verdict for the Plaintiffs with nominal Damages only—the Plaintiffs did not press for more as in such Cases of Trespass Costs follow such Damages of course.

Letter 171

ROBISON TO WATT

Cover addressed: 'To Mr. Watt', endorsed in Watt's hand, 'Jno. Robison December 1796 London   correction of what he said in the tryal respecting conversation with Mr. Model and Epinus His plan of a Manual for Engineers and Mill wrights' and numbered '10'. Dol.

Dear Sir,

Some person told Mrs. Robison that you had thoughts of printing the Tryal. In this Case I wish it may not be too late for me to settle a doubt in my own mind about the Person to whom Mr. Model[1] was explaining the reason of his Ejaculation. Both Æpinus[2] and Dr. Kruse (a Gentleman eminent in that Country for Steel Works and great Knowledge in Chemistry, Magnetism etc.) were there that Evening, both singlely and together, and Kruse was very inquisitive about your discoveries, and was not unskilled (thro' my information) in Dr. Blacks Theory. I still think that it was Æpinus, and think that they were not both present at the time. For I have a sort of image in my mind of the Situation round the table, Model sitting by the Stove opposite to me and Æpinus at my left hand. I found him there. Kruse came in while we were chatting—and behoved to be sitting on my right (for it was a little Closet, in the rigour of winter) there being no more room. Æpinus went away, and therefore had it been Kruse to whom it was explained, he would have been on my right. But in

248

the recollection I have of the thing, I am certain that the person who looked at the papers along with me was on my left. If this be a circumstance of any Consequence, I could get it set to rights, for both are alive and I can easily write to them. If it be sufficient to say that Model, in order to explain the thing to a Gentleman present did so and so, there will be no occasion for further Enquiry

I find that I have overdone in the way of exertion. I naturally wished to have the pleasure of being the Cicerone to Mrs. Robison, and have raised the devil, not to be soon laid again. I regret this for nothing so much as the depriving me of the pleasure of chatting old stories with you. But I have always been so completely jaded before Night that I was fain to go into Dock. Excuse me then for taking this mode of writing some of my thoughts

I wished to take this opportunity of meeting with you to communicate my Intention (fleeting indeed) of printing a work on the employment of the Civil Engineer Millwright etc. such as might be useful to the *mere Workman*, might incite some to a further scientific, but elementary, knowledge of their profession, and furnish the means for this proficiency, and might also enable the person possessed of a proper degree of mathematical preparation to prosecute the difficult and interesting Articles as far as I can conduct him. This I thought might be accomplished by a Book in the following form. The running text should be intirely practical, containing no science, but only the results of scientific investigation, connected (when I am able) by some palpable reasoning. This should be accompanied by a set of Notes in which the Assertions in the Text are demonstrated in the plainest method that I can contrive so as to be really good Logic. This should be either accompanied by a second series of Notes, or have an appendix, containing the most complete discussion of every important and difficult Article. The Work should contain the principles of Mechanics, Hydrostatics, Hydraulics, and Pneumatics— Strength of Materials—Strains—proper disposition of both—Friction— Resistance of Mediums—of sand and of soft or ductile bodies Theory of Machines—including both the theory of their operation and of their best construction—The theory of their operation requires the minute discrimination of the modes of acting of the Natural Powers which may be imployd—Althis [sic] in a way totally different from the usual treatises of mechanics—these in my opinion treat only of equilibrium of Forces—but in a machine *doing work* this equilibrium is destroyed in one sense, while it remains perfect in another sense, viz the Equilibrium between the force *actually* impelling and the resistance *actually* exerted—

This will require the constant application of what I consider as the greatest discovery of Newton, viz his 39th proposition of Book I "That if AC be the line (straight or curve) along which a body is impelled or opposed by any force whatever, and if AD, BE, CF, etc are the forces at the points A, B, C, then ABED, ACFD etc are the augmentations or diminutions made on the Squares of the Velocities. 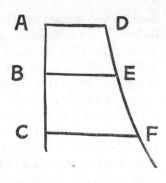 Then, let a ball, moving with any velocity whatever, pass thro a rampart whose thickness is AC, and which resists penetration in the points A, B, C, with forces as those ordinates, the whole diminution made in the square of the velocity will always be the same, viz ACFD—You will easily see that this gives the answer to every question in a working Machine, or a moving body, and is the leading proposition in dynamics— and you can form some Guess at the manner in which I should attempt to prosecute this Subject. Hydraulics must be traced from the same source, and will terminate (in as far as relates to the motion of the fluid itself) in a theorem similar to [?Briot's][3]. To form a further Judgement of my manner, you may look at the Articles *Philosophy*, *Physics*, Pumps, Resistance of Fluids, *Rivers*, *Roofs*, Rope making, Seamanship, Sound, Steam Engine, Strength of Materials, Stove, Steelyard, *Telescope*, Tides, Thunder, *Trumpet* (*Speaking*) Variation of the Cyclopedia Britannica. But in all this you must recollect that I came in at the Broadside of a Work already far advanced—I had to carry on two or three things Connected only by a Letter of the Alphabet, at once, and must del[i]ver them on a certain day. Nay I must accommodate myself to what was already printed, frequently against my own opinion—And in all without one exception, you see the very first draught, for I had not time to revise or remould—in general they are redundant, containing particular points pushed further than corresponds with the rest of the Article, because I always hoped to have time for a second writing where I might cull, and bring things to an even surface—this time never came, and they went to their home with all their Sins upon their heads.

Such is my intention, in those moments that I can refrain from crying with pain and almost cursing my Existence. I think then that I can execute the Jobb—but next day all changes to despair and a wish for my quietus— But the occupation will certainly do me good, by keeping me from brooding on my own Sufferings—and to bind myself by engagement, so as to have the whip hanging over my head \is also of use/—and, (to speak to you as to a trusty freind) it is all I can now do for an excellent Wife and four sweet Children. I fear that I cannot continue teaching— and thus I shall be reduced to my poor £200. Five years of this has, (notwithstanding the utmost economy, most chearfully and nobly exerted by Rachel,) run away with most of my savings. I need not tell you the situation of things. Suffice it that I have no expectations but from my own labours. I have never stepped beyond the sober station in which I was born, and my Wife, by her inflexible firmness, and her wise choice of plan, has made my finances show as well as double would do in other hands. But it cuts me to the Soul to think that I have for ten years secluded her, in the prime of life, from a Society which she would have orna- mented by her good Sense and cultivated manners, and if I could by this or any honest Employment add something to her Comforts, no labour would seem hard, but delightful

Now my good Freind you can greatly assist me here by your advice— You know the Market, and the Goods that suit it, and the demand for them. You also know something of the manufacture—particularly as to expence—this will be great, requiring many and some dear plates—I would not sell it—tho' I must join with me some Son of the Trade, that it may not be damned—A great Risk I dare not venture, because my little income is all appropriated—therefor to engage in such a plan rashly might be ruinous, and your sedate advice of great consequence to me— But further Many articles, you know well, are founded on vague enough principles and facts, collected from many quarters. It w[oul]d be an agreeable thing to myself, and would be some Credit to the work, to found the whole on a series of original and appropriated experiments made by myself. This leads to considerable expence of money and time. I have a good Situation for hydraulic Experim[en]ts at a Mill within 500 yards of my house at Boghall, with a small dam on the summit of a steep brow, and a fall of 50 feet. Other Exper[imen]ts on the strength of Matter on Friction etc, I shoud have great difficulty in, for want of great Apparatus and Workmen. For these I should apply to you—or perhaps come and place myself beside your Workmen—I should hope for such extracts from the myriads which you have made as you could with propriety communicate. In short, if you think the project feasable and worthy, I should hope for much friendly information and assistance— for which reasons I catch at this opportunity of laying my Scheme before you, begging that you would take it ad avisandum, when you have got home, and have a little quiet and leisure. I will remind you of it when I feel myself in the same situation. In the mean time I am under much obligation to you and those about you, for much instruction w[hi]c[h] I have gotten respecting both the state and the mechanism of your Engine. Allow me to beg that (if there be nothing inconvenient for You in it) {that} you would oblige me with a set of the drawings of the Engine in its different stages, from Newcomen's, with the most simple change into your form, the first change that you *really* adopt in pump Engin and your best single Engine (I have the double stroke Engine already). I wish to give them to my Son. He has a considerable relish for these things, and I wish to accomplish him as much as possible. But I hope you will make no ceremony of withholding them, if either you have none to spare, or if there appears the smallest inconvenience in granting them. From what you have already said, you may depend on it that, in my Class, I shall never go farther than an extempore hand sketch with Chalk in the presence of my Scholars—this I know is quite sufficient for giving them a scientific knowledge of the principles—I would fain ask another favor of this kind for my good friend Mr. Houston. He is fond of ingenious Constructions, and is much set on a built Beam for an Engine he will set up the ensuing Summer. Would you be so good as to cause any of your draftsmen to make a slight draft of one of your trussed Beams of this kind,

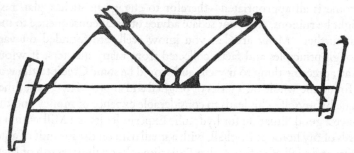

supposing it proper for small Engines. You know that Oak timber is rare and dear with us, and that this will be much stronger. When done, I would beg you to send it by post to George Houstoun Esquire[4] of Johnston by Paisley N Britain. I am under the greatest obligations to this Gentleman for his kindness to my Son, and I know he would think much of the favour

I have sufficiently tired your patience. When I look over what I have written I see that I have clavered too much, but I am not able to write another. Let it meet with indulgence and consign it to the fire, for it is *very unfit for any Eye but your own*, and I hope runs no risk of being seen by any other

[No signature.]

[1] J. G. Model (1711–1775), professor of pharmacy in the St Petersburg Academy.

[2] Franz Ulrich Theodosius Aepinus (1724–1802), mathematician, was Professor of Astronomy in the Academy at Berlin from 1755 to 1757 when he moved to St. Petersburg and taught in the Academy there. He published in 1759 his *Tentamen theoriae electricitatis et magnetismi*.

[3] Jean Bapiste Biot (b. 1774), Professor of Physics in the Collège de France, Paris. Astronomer and physicist.

[4] George Houston of Johnstone, cotton-spinner, is reputed to have erected the first steam-powered cotton mill in Scotland. He seems to have employed a Newcomen engine before installing Watt's engine.

Letter 172

BLACK TO WATT

Written in an unknown hand, the same as that of Robison's Memorial of the same date and numbered '60'. Dol.

[1] Memorial by Dr. Black respecting Mr. Watt's Invention of his Improvements on the Steam Engine etc. Written in 1796.

I became acquainted with Mr. James Watt in the year 1757, or 1758, at which time I was Professor of Medicine and Lecturer of Chemistry in the University of Glasgow. About that time, Mr. Watt came to settle in Glasgow, as a maker of Mathematical Instruments; but being molested by some of the corporations who considered him as an intruder on their privileges, the University protected him by giving him a shop within their precincts, and by conferring on him the title of Mathematical instrument maker to the University.

I soon had occasion to employ him to make some things which I needed for my Experiments, and found him to be a young man possessing most uncommon talents for mechanical knowledge and practice, with an originality, readiness and copiousness of invention, which often surprised and delighted me in our frequent conversations together. I also very soon had many opportunities to know that the goodness of his heart was equal to the acuteness of his judgment and understanding, and I therefore contracted with him an intimate friendship, which has continued and increased ever since that time. I mention these circumstances only to shew how it happened that I was thoroughly acquainted with the progress of his inventions, and with the different objects that engaged his attention while I remained at Glasgow and in a great measure ever since.

A few years after he was settled at Glasgow, he was employed by the Professor of Natural [2] Philosophy to examine and rectify a small workable model of a Steam Engine which was out of order. This turned a part of his thoughts and fertile invention, to the nature and improvement of Steam Engines, to the perfection of their Machinery, and to the different means by which their great consumption of fuel might be diminished. He soon acquired so much reputation for knowledge on this subject, that he was employed to plan and erect several Engines in different places, while at the same time he was frequently making new experiments to lessen the waste of heat from the external surface of the boiler and from that of the Cylinder. But after he had been thus employed a considerable time, he perceived that by far the greatest waste of heat proceeded from the waste of Steam in filling the cylinder with Steam. While the great cylinder is filled with steam for every stroke of the common engine, a great part of the steam thrown into it, is chilled and condensed by the coldness of the cylinder, before this last is heated enough to qualify it for being filled with elastic vapour, or perfect steam; he therefore perceived that by preventing this waste of steam, an incomparably greater saving of heat and fuel would be attained, than by any other contrivance. It was thus in the beginning of the year 1765, that the fortunate thought occurred to him of condensing the steam by cold in a separate vessel, or apparatus, between which and the cylinder, a communication was to be opened for that purpose, every time the steam was to be condensed, while the cylinder itself might be preserved perpetually hot, no cold water or air being ever admitted into its cavity.

[3] This capital improvement flashed on his mind at once, and filled him with rapture, and he immediately made an hasty trial of it which satisfied him of its value, employing for this purpose a large brass syringe which he borrowed from a friend.

His mind became \now/ very much employed in contriving the machinery by which this improvement might be reduced to practice, and he soon planned it to such a degree, that he thought he was ready to make an experiment on a large scale.

But here he was stopped by the want of funds, and he found it necessary to associate himself with some person who had money and spirit for such an undertaking, and to participate with him the advantages which might be derived from this invention. He addressed himself to the late

Doctor Roebuck, whose spirit for enterprise and improvement in arts, was very well known, and the Doctor accordingly received with Zeal the opportunity offered him. A small Engine was soon built in one of the offices of Kinneil house near Borrowstowness, where various trials were made and some difficulties surmounted, so as to give satisfaction

I must add that I was as much upon a footing of intimate friendship with Doctor Roebuck, as with Mr. Watt. The Doctor too had no small degree of mechanical knowledge and ingenuity, and was well qualified to perceive and value the talents of Mr. Watt. He had also much experience of the use of common Steam Engines in working his Colliery. He was withal ardent and sanguine in the pursuit of his undertakings, and was therefore a fortunate associate for Mr. Watt. [4] Mr. Watt was a valetudinarian more or less ever since I knew him, and his mind was liable to be too much depressed by little cross accidents or by the necessity of a greater expence than he had foreseen; whereas the Doctor was undaunted on such occasions, and roused Mr. Watt to disregard expence and to double his exertions until the difficulty was overcome. But Mr. Watt was the sole inventor of the capital improvement and contrivance above mentioned. I remember very well that it cost me some reasonings and conversations to inform the Doctor fully of the nature of Steam, of the great quantity of heat and fuel necessary to produce it, and of the importance therefore of preventing the waste of it.

While thus employed, Mr. Watts reputation for knowledge and skill in the engineering line, occasioned his having an offer made him to take the level and make the calculations for an intended Canal, which employment his circumstances induced him readily to accept. This, and other business of the same kind, filled up the greater part of his time for several years, and produced interruptions and delays of his experiments with his new Engine. But in the year 1769 being now completely satisfied of the practicability of his invention, he got the Patent for it, and in due time gave in his specification. There was much consultation between him and his friends about the terms most proper for this Specification. It ended in general opinion among them that he should not attempt to describe the machinery of the Engine, but take his Patent for the above [5] new and most important invention, or improvement, of making an additional vessel or apparatus distinct from the great cylinder or from that part of it in which the great piston moves, in which additional vessel or apparatus alone the steam was to be condensed by Cold, in consequence of its being made to pass from the Cylinder into this Vessel. The reasons for this opinion are sufficiently obvious. The above invention is the

Capital improvement; variations of the Machinery and Construction might be made in different ways, but which could have little effect in comparison with it, and had he given an exact description of the machinery and construction, which he had then planned, it might have limited him to that precise and particular construction and left others at liberty to evade his patent by varying the construction in points of little moment although they adopted his Capital improvement

This has in fact been the device of some of those who have attempted to encroach on his Patent, and rob him of his lawful right. They made variations of the construction and machinery but none of them were able to produce an Engine which approached to his in perfection and power, without adopting the above Capital and most important improvement. The number of ways however by which they have varied the machinery and the Construction, are sufficient to shew that Mr. Watt's specification was clear enough to enable an intelligent Engineer to take the advantage of his invention for the improvement of the Steam Engine and even to do it by different ways.—

Letter 173
ROBISON TO WATT

Written in an unknown hand, the same as that of the copy of Black's Memorial of the same date and numbered '57'. Dol.

Extract from a
Memorial by Dr. John Robison relative to his first acquaintance with Mr. Watt, and the improvements of the latter on the Steam Engine. Written in 1796.

My acquaintance with Mr. Watt began in 1758. I was then a Student in the University of Glasgow, and then studying the Science which I now profess to teach. Nat[ural] Phil[osoph]y. The University were then building an Astronomical Observatory. Mr. Watt came to settle in Glasgow as a Math[ematica]l and Phil[osophica]l Instrument maker, and was employed to repair and fit up a very noble collection of Instruments bequeathed to the University by Mr. McFarlane of Jamaica, a Gentleman well known to the scientific world. Mr. Watt had apartments, and a workshop within the College. I had, from my earliest youth, a great relish for the natural sciences, and particularly for Mathematical and

Mechanical Philosophy. I was eager to be acquainted with the practice of Astronomical observations, and my wishes were much encouraged by the celebrated Dr. Simpson Professor of Geometry, Dr. Dick professor of Nat[ura]l Phil[osoph]y, and Dr. Moor Professor of Greek, gentlemen eminent for their mathematical abilities. These Gentlemen brought me with them into Mr. Watt's shop, and when he saw me thus patronized and introduced, his natural complaisance made him readily indulge my curiosity. After first feasting my eyes with the view of fine instruments, and prying into every thing, I conversed with Mr. Watt. I saw a work-man, and expected no more, but was surprized to find a Philosopher as young as myself, and always ready to instruct me. I had the vanity to think myself a pretty good proficient in my favourite study, and was rather mortified at finding Mr. Watt so much my superior. But his own high relish for these things made him pleased with the chat of any person who had the same tastes with himself, or his innate complaisance made him indulge my curiosity and even encourage my endeavours to form a more intimate acquaintance with him. I loung'd much about him, and I doubt not was frequently teazing. Thus our acquaintance began.

It was interrupted in 1759. I left the College for the Navy, where I was a Midshipman four years, and was present in some of the most remarkable actions of that war. My health suffered so much by a seafaring life that I was obliged to give it up, much against my inclination, and return to my academical habits. I was happy to find Mr. Watt settled in Glasgow, as fond of Science as ever. Our acquaintance was renewed, I believe with Mutual Satisfaction. For I had now acquired some knowledge. I had lived in the closest intimacy with the late Admiral Sir Charles Knowles, and had been a good deal employed in Marrine surveys. I had been em-ployed by the Admiralty to make the observations for the trial of Mr. Harrison's famous Timepiece. In short my habits of life had been such that I reckoned myself more on a par with Mr. Watt, and hoped for a closer acquaintance. Nor was I disappointed, I found him as good and kind as ever, as keen after the acquisition of knowledge, and well dis-posed to listen to the information I could give him concerning things which had not fallen in his own way. But I found him continually striking into untrodden paths, when I was always obliged to be a follower. Our acquaintance at this time became very intimate, and I believe neither of us engaged far in any train of thought without the other sharing in it. I had had the advantage of a more regular education; This frequently enabled me to direct or confirm Mr. Watt's speculations, and put into a systematic form the random suggestions of his inquisitive

257

and inventive mind. This kind of friendly commerce knit us more to-gether, and each of us knew the whole extent of each others reading, and knowledge.

I was not singular in this attachment. All the young lads of our little place that were in any way remarkable for Scientific predilection were acquaintances of Mr. Watt, and his parlour was a rendezvous for all of this description. Whenever any puzzle came in the way of us we went to Mr. Watt. He needed only to be prompted, every thing became to him the beginning of a new and serious study, and we knew that he would not quit it till he had either discovered its insignificancy or had made some-thing of it. No matter in what line, Languages, Antiquity, Natural History, nay Poetry, Criticism and works of Taste. As to any thing in the line of Engineering, whether Civil or Military, he was at home, and a ready Instructor. Hardly any project, such as canals, deepening the River, Surveys or the like, were undertaken in the Neighbourhood, without consulting Mr. Watt; and he was even *importuned* to take the charge of some considerable works of this kind, though they were such as he had not the smallest experience in. When to this superiority of knowledge which every man confessed in his own line, is added the naive simplicity and candor of Mr. Watt's character, it is no wonder that the attachment of his acquaintances was strong. I have seen something of the world, and am obliged to say that I never saw such another instance of general and cordial attachment to a person whom all acknowledged to be their superior. But this superiority was concealed under the most amiable candour, and liberal allowance of merit to every man. Mr. Watt was the first to ascribe to the ingenuity of a friend things which were very often nothing but his own surmises followed out and embodied by another. I am well entitled to say this, and have often experienced it in my own case.

But the circumstance which made Mr. Watt's acquaintance so valu-able to me, was the trait of Character I have already mentioned. Every thing became to him a subject of new and serious study. Every thing be-came Science in his hands, and I took every opportunity of offering my feeble aid, by presenting systematically, and by the help of mathematical discussion, thoughts which he was contented with having suggested or directed. I thus shared the fruits of his invention, and with gratitude I here acknowledge my obligations to him for that strong relish which I thus acquired for rational mechanics, and which I have cultivated with great assiduity and pleasure all my life. I also shared with Mr. Mr. [*sic*] Watt a good deal of that subsidiary knowledge which he acquired as so many stepping Stones in his way to some favourite objects. He learnt the German language in order to peruse Leopold's *Theatrum Machinarum*. So did I, to know what he was about. Similar reasons made us both learn Italian. And so of other things. And I cannot now pass over another circumstance which endeared Mr. Watt to us all. He was without the smallest wish to appropriate knowledge to himself, and one of his greatest delights was to set others on the same road to knowledge with himself. No man could be more distant from the jealous concealment of a Tradesman, and I am convinced that Nothing but the Magnitude of the prospect which his improvement of the Steam Engine held out to him and his family, would have made Mr. Watt refuse himself the pleasure of communicating immediately all his discoveries to his acquaintances. Nay he could not conceal it. For besides the frankly imparting it to Dr. Black, and two or three more intimate friends, he disclosed so much of what he had been doing, that had it been in London or Birmingham, I am confident that two or three patents would have been taken out for bits of his method by bustling Tradesmen before he thought himself entitled to such a thing. And I have that confidence in the native honour and modesty of his character, that I do not believe that the contagion of plagiarism and Rivality, which he has lived in for thirty years past, has ever warped his mind so far as to make him assume to himself any thing that he thought the *serious* invention of another. I know indeed instances of his having made use of *Forms* of things which had been introduced by others *without thought*, and of which they did not perceive the proper situation or the advantage which knowledge like Mr. Watts could derive from them. As I see many of Mr. Watts' contrivances copied by ignorant Creatures who call themselves Engineers, merely because they are Wattses, and therefore must be good, though they are as often hurtful by being improperly employed.

Thus far Dr. Robison. The Memorial is long and enters into minute details of Mr. Watts invention (not now of moment as he has given the history of them himself) and gives answers to the Objections to his Specification. It concludes with an Anecdote so descriptive of the Powers of Mr. Watt's mind that it ought not to be omitted

"Every thing new that came into Mr. Watt's hands became a subject of
"serious and systematic study and terminated in some branch of science.
"Allow me to give an Instance. A Mason lodge in Glasgow wanted an
"Organ. The office bearers were acquaintances of Mr. Watt. We
"imagined that Mr. Watt could do any thing, and although aware *that*

259

"he did not know one musical note from another, he was asked if he could "build this Organ. He had repaired one and it had amused him. He said "Yes. But he began by building a very small one for his intimate friend "Dr. Black, which is now in my possession. In doing this, a thousand "things occurred to him which no Organ builder ever dreamed of. Nice "Indicators of the strength of the blast, Regulators of it etc. He then "began to study the philosophical theory of Music. Fortunately for me "no book was at hand, but the most refined of all, Smiths Harmonics. "Before Mr. Watt had half finished his organ, he and I were compleatly "masters of that most refined and beautiful theory of the Beats of im- "perfect consonances. He found that by the Beats, it would be possible "for him, totally ignorant of Music to tune this Organ according to any "system of temperament. And he did so, to the delight and astonishment "of our best performers. In prosecution of this, he invented a real mono- "chord of continued tone; and in playing with this, he made an obser- "vation, which had it been then known, would have terminated a dispute "between the first mathematicians in Europe, Euler and d'Alembert, and "which compleatly establishes the Theory of Daniel Bernouilli who "differed from these Gentlemen about the mechanism of the vibration "of musical chords, and as completely explains the harmonic notes "which accompany all full musical Notes, overturning the theories of "Rameau and Tartini. No wonder that the attachment to Mr. Watt was "strong, when persons of every taste and pursuit found in him an in- "exhaustible fund of instruction and entertainment."

See the Article "Temperament of Music" in the *Encyclopedia Britannica*, Edn. 1811, which is by Dr. Robison, where the Anecdote is related with some additional circumstances.

Letter 174

ROBISON TO JAMES WATT JUNIOR

Cover addressed: 'To James Watt Junior Esq/Birmingham' and endorsed in Watt's hand, 'Professor Robison Woodstock 2 January 1797   Intends to visit Soho'. B.R.L. M IV R.

Woodstock Jan[uar]y 1 1797

Dear Sir

Accept of our best wishes for many happy Returns of this day. We have got so far in our way home and my two Ladies are almost satiated with fine sights, tho to be sure, they have not been seen in their finest

Colours. Unsatisfactory as a hurried sight of Birmingham and Soho must be, I am unwilling that they should lose the only chance they may have, and mean to be there on Thursday Evening. I have used the freedom to write to you, that if your occupations should require your presence some where else at that Time, you may be so kind as to furnish us with a proper passport to Soho, and some introduction to Miss Boulton, to whom Mrs. Robison wishes to pay her respects. I saw at Oxford Mr. Jardine, Son of Prof[esso]r Jardine of Glasgow who begged to be kindly remembered to your family. Hopeing for your Excuse for this Liberty, I am

Dear Sir
Your most obed[ien]t h[um]bl[e] Ser[van]t
John Robison

Letter 175

ROBISON TO EWART

Cover addressed: 'To Mr. Peter Ewart/Soho/in Mr. Ewarts absence—enquire/for Mr. James Watt Junior', and endorsed in Watt's hand, 'Mr. Robison Birmingham 3 January 1797 Notice of his arrival at Birmingham'. B.R.L. M IV R.

3 January 1797

Dear Sir

Mrs. Robison and I got here to day ab[ou]t 4 o Clock, and as I am in a hurry to get home, and wishd to save all the time I could, I troubled Mr. James Watt Jun[io]r with a line from Woodstock on Sunday Night begging that he would put us on the way of seeing what is remarkable at Soho with dispatch. We had no great doubt of my Letter coming to hand, and, at any rate reckoned on finding Mr. Watt in Birmingham in a Moment. But, on enquiry we find that he neither lives here nor has a Compting house here. This puts me to some stand, and as it would be very strange for us to visit Soho as mere Strangers and go off without seeing either Mr. Watt or Mr. Boulton's family, I have troubled you to tell you that we mean to visit Soho tomorrow after breakfast and then proceed on our Journey, and we request of You that if Mr. James Watt is about the place, you would let him know this much and that we wish to present our respects to Miss Boulton en passant. Your taking this trouble would save us

a great deal of awkward Waiting and Enquiries, which my {anxiety} \hurry/ to get home makes very inconvenient
A word in answer would greatly oblige

D[ea]r Sir
Yours

Tuesday Evening 8 o Clock   John Robison

Letter 176

WATT TO BLACK

Cover addressed: 'Dr. Joseph Black/Physician/Edinburgh', endorsed in Watt's hand, 'To Dr. Black January 15th 1797' and numbered '17'. Dol.

Heathfield Jan[uar]y 15th 1797
Dr. Black

My Dear Friend
You have been informed by Mrs. W. of the fortunate issue of our trial at law and we received your kind congratulations upon the event. I did not write to you myself sooner, because I was much indisposed partly with a bad cold, but much more by the anxiety and attention such an affair required, which, though I neither gave way in the least to despair, nor had such acute feelings as I have been used to on {more} less serious occasions, took great effect upon me, so that even after the trial I remained nearly as much depressed as if we had lost it. The stimulus to action was gone and but for the attentions of my friends I ran some risk of falling into Stupidity. The getting away at last from the unwholesome air of London and the Journey home have greatly reinstated me, I have no particular complaints, except the cold sciatica in my leg and a general propensity to inaction, which however I strive against
In the whole affair nothing was so grateful to me as the zeal of our friends, and the activity of our young men which was unremitting. Our friend Mr. Robison exerted himself much and considering his situation did wonders, When we had got through a few of our witnesses, Our opponents thought it wise to give up their allegations against the priority of invention and also acknowleged their infringement, The Judge also complained of bad health and requested the trial might be shortned,

262

upon which we thought \it/ unnecessary to call Mr. Robison, and Mr. Roebuck, Our opponents however thought proper to call the former, but had reason to repent it and we were obliged to them for calling him as he gave a clear and decided Evidence against them and a Sketch he produced made by Mr. *Model* at petersburgh had considerable effect in convincing the Judge and the Jury, how few hints were necessary to enable a man of mechanical knowlege to execute the invention. I believe this was not strictly legal evidence but the court permitted it and the force of truth is great even when against law. Our opponents have not yet given us up, they mean to move in arrest of Judgement and if they cannot prevail in that to bring a writ of Error to take it to the Kings bench but it seems that writ is of slow progress and they probably cannot get it brought to an argument in less than a year and a half and in the mean time they are tied fast by injunctions from chancery, nor at any rate have we reason to fear the event after two decisive verdicts in our favour.

It gave us all much pleasure to hear that you have kept your health so much better than usual this winter and I hope it will continue through the remainder of it. I beg you will remember me kindly to Dr. Hutton. Beddoes in his last publication mentions some cases in which salt of soda was of singular service in complaints of the bladder. Whether it could afford our friend any relief you are the best judge.

Mrs. W. kept her health very well in London and escaped the colds which were so general there but since her return home has had an attack of her old Complaint of indigestion and vertigo, from which she is now recovering. She desires to be kindly remembred to you. Mr. Boulton has been remarkably well considering his age and disease and now he has shook off the terrors of the law seems quite renovated. Our new foundery is going on prosperously and I hope will in time prove productive of profit. I have some chemical facts to state to you, but I reserve them till I have verified them—With best wishes to you Dr. Hutton and other friends
                                         I remain my Dear friend
                                                Yours affectionately
                                                      James Watt

263

Letter 177

ROBISON TO WATT

Cover addressed: 'To James Watt Esq./Heathfield/by Birmingham', endorsed in Watt's hand, 'Jno. Robison Edinburgh February 3d 1797   embarassments on his return to Edinburgh on
account of the article Waterworks in the Encyclopaedia   Plan of
a work on practical Mechanics' and numbered '12'. Dol.

Edin[bu]r[gh] Feb[ruar]y 3 1797

My good Friend

You are no doubt surprised at my not having long e're now acknowledged Rec[eip]t of your Letter from Brimingham.† But I have not been
able to close my acc[oun]t of Expences. When I set out for London, I had
engaged to furnish the dictionary with the Article *Water* Works, and
had just begun it. It was to have completed what is containd in the
Articles Rivers and Resistance of Fluids, and form[e]d a pretty full
System of hydraulics, and acc[oun]t of the chief varieties of hydraulic
Engines. Altho Materials were ready, except the descriptions of the last
things, and I hoped to be able, in the Evening by the Road, and in Town,
to keep the press going, after having given them one Sheet. But, when I
attempted this, I found myself too much exhausted by the fatigue of the
day—and, in London, the eternal Crash and Bustle and jostle of Society
made it equally impossible. I wrote to the Editor, not to expect it, and to
make the best excuse he could, as there were several References from my
former Articles to this. And when I came away, I put all my papers into a
Box which I sent before me by the Waggon—on my Arrival (three
days after) I learned, to my great surprise and vexation, that he had made
a handsome apology, but made the purchasers expect it under the Word
Water *Works*, and he told me that, in consequence of a *demelée* with the
proprietors, he w[oul]d be in great distress, and lyable to a prosecution,
if I did not give the Article. There was no help for it, and tho' obliged to
to teach my Class (which, after five years Absence, required new Study) I
behoved to fag at this—and to crown my misfortune, my box is not yet
arrived, nor has yet left London. I had all to Spin out of my brain de novo,
and it is a sad piece of work, which I am ashamed and distressed about.
The worst was that I had most positively promised a Table for Briots

Formula of Uniform Motion; viz. $V = \dfrac{307\left(\sqrt{r} - 0,1\right)}{\sqrt{b}\,\sqrt{b + 1,6}} - 0,3\left(\sqrt{r} - 0,1\right),$

† 'Brimingham'—the old spelling.

and had actually computed it as 150 for r and 100000 for b, above a fort-nights hard work. I was unwilling to lose this (having bargained for a Guinea a day) and told the Editor that I would give an abstract, true to 4 decimals, which he accepted of. The Result of this Engagement has been that, since my return, I have sat up several times all Night and occupied every moment of the day that Pain would allow me to risk \in/ commit-ting my hasty thoughts to public Inspection. I am quite jaded, and almost spent, and have this day finished my Task, *et hic Castris armaque repono* I have two objects in plaguing you with all this. To apologise for what your habits of business must \cause to/ appear great remissness \in your Eyes/,—but chiefly to entreat you not only to look at the Article with the indulgent Eye of a kind Friend, but also to excuse its imperfections to others. I have spoken to some of the trade, and referred them to some of my articles for an opinion of my manner of treating these Subjects. This is the best information that a Tradesman can get, and unless he is informed of the hasty compilation of that Article, his opinion, or that of the friend in whom he confides, will be very unfavourable. Several of the young Men who are about you know of my concern with that work, and will naturally speak of it. And I know that the opinions of your Eleves are respected by those of the Profession. It is not therefore a trivial Matter to me what is thought of my performances. For as I formerly told you I have now no other way of doing a little for my little Family. I certainly see that I shall not be able to continue teaching, and am still afraid that I shall not make out this Course. I must therefore think seriously of the plan about which I consulted you in London and look to you for all the partial Encouragement that your candid opinion can afford me. Your Name and Mr. Boulton's, I am confident, will go far to recommend any thing that you can venture to patronise, and if I can contrive any method of making Use of it that will be decent either for myself or for you, I am confident of your friendly cooperation, and you may be equally so of my endeavours not to discredit your recommendation. Be assured that I duly prized the advices you gave me. Your sincere wish to serve me made you not scruple to say things not flattering to an authors notion of his own wisdom and importance. I look at the Repertory, which you told me had been a profitable Jobb, advising me to be a Contributor, on good terms. But this would be letting myself too much down, even if I could confide in your Information of its being a moneymaking project I am still of the opinion that a seperate Work will be best, at the same time that I accede to your notion of doing it in parts, by way of trying the Market. And I still expect advantages from a foundation of original

Experiments. Not that there have not been enough made—but they must be brought forward—and many of the most important, being complicated with Circumstances foreign to the Use I have to make of them, will require discussion which will tire the practical Reader. My present plan therefore is to go to my Farm as soon as my Class is over (if I am not able to read a Summer Course) and there prosecute a train of hydraulic and mechanical Experiments, convinced, by what you said, that I shall do it cheaper than in England as I first thought of doing—But there is an important Article on which I am very lame—the resistance opposed by the most general kinds of work done by Machinery—such as grinding—sawing—Tilthammering—Boreing—etc. This I must collect from Engineers—and here I expected much from your Experience—because your Engines afford the most accurate measures of the impelling power that can be found; so that if I wished to have a better measure of the power of Water acting by an Overshot Wheel than our poor theories afford, I could not do better than compare a good Mill with Mills which do the same kind of work when driven by one of your Engines   Questions of this kind, and questions concerning the absolute Strength of Materials, I expect to resolve by your help and that of professional Men about you. I expect that you would procure me the acquaintance of some such men —And I should derive much information from Conversation and from your Library—So that in completion of my plan, I should still plant my-self in your Neighbourhood before I publish, and *inform the public that I do so*, and that I have the Benefit of the Experience of Boulton and Watt. You see I am playing the tradesman, and putting the best foot foremost. But this should not alarm you for I too well know both your pressure of business and your state of health, not to be aware that much intrusion would be oppressive—Thus my dear Sir I open my mind to you, con-fident of your friendship, and duly sensible of its worth. And allow me to say, it will give me much satisfaction to spend some of my last days in society which so much delighted me in the early part of my Life

Before I enter on all this (which naturally figures much in my own Imagination) I will take the liberty of laying before you my plans of Experim[en]t for your Correction and advice—So much for business of this Sort

I was rec[eive]d by my Class with a plaudit. I gave my pupils a short account of what I had been about, and of the simple turn which the Cause took at last, which made it not more the Cause of Watt versus Horn-blower than of Science against Ignorance, When I finished, I got another plaudit that Mrs. Siddons would have relished. You must take your

Share of it—And now that the thing is over, give me leave to say that few things in my life have given me more sincere pleasure, and you oblige me greatly when you allow me the Satisfaction of thinking that my appearance was of essential Service   I have but few opportunities of feeling myself of any use, and it would have greatly mortified me had Brother LeBlanc not called upon me, and I had returned without opening my mouth, in return for so much expence to you and so long a Journey to myself. Had it not been this damned WaterWorks I Should have long ere now been as well as when I set out, and will now persist every day.

I cannot conclude this tedious Epistle without requesting you to remember me in the warmest manner to your Son and young Mr. Boulton. I cannot think on their behaviour to me without some pain. I was very ill that day at dinner, and two or three times declind going to the Foundery, saying that I was unwilling to give them the trouble of going there. It was not till a few minutes before I came out of the Works that I saw the extent of my obligation. Observing that the Engine was doing no work, I spoke of it with some surprise to a person standing beside me, and when he answered me "Surely no Sir, it was just to let you see it" The whole Compliment struck me at once, I saw the eager assiduity of the workmen to show me every thing, and immediately learned that it was holiday, and that every thing was done on my account. I shudder yet at the thoughts of it, for I was very near refusing altogether to go over, after so much trouble had been taken—it made me stupid, and I did not recover myself so far as to say how much I was obliged   I beg You to express my thanks to the young Gentlemen and assure them I shall never forget their kindness. And Mrs. Robison is equally sensible of her obligations to Miss Boultons kind hospitality, and begs you will present her best Compliments at Soho as well as at your own house— Apropos—will you take the trouble, some leisure hour, when otherwise disposed to write me, to give me a Scratch of the plan and dimensions of your house and offices. I am vastly taken with it, and have recommended it to a Freind (Mr. Ferguson Broth[e]r to Sir Adam of Kilkinan and Broth[e]r in Law to Mr. McDowall my quondam pupil) who is just going to build

Dr. Black is but poorly, and has been spitting more blood of late. I have set him and all here in the fidgets by your information of the dissimilarity of the oxygenous Airs from Metals and from Vegetables and they long to know the authority on which your Surmise is founded

What you say respecting the Illuminate shall be attended to as soon as I have breathed a little, but at present I am tired of pen and ink. This long

Epistle you will say is no proof of this. It shows how much I trust to your friendly patience—In two or three days I will send you the sum total of Charges, and in the mean time I remain with true regard

D[ea]r Sir
Your affect[iona]te Freind
etc
John Robison

My Compliments I pray to Mr. Boulton. I shall have the pleasure of writing to him in a very few days

Letter 178

ROBISON TO WATT

Cover addressed: 'To James Watt Esq./Heathfield/near Bir-mingham', endorsed in Watt's hand, 'Jno. Robison Edinburgh April 7th 1797   his sisters death,   receipt of B and W draft £31...1...6. His own bad health, Dr. Huttons death' and numbered '13'. Dol.

Edin[burgh] April 7 1797
My dear Sir
   I ask pardon for my awkward neglect to inform you of the Rec[eip]t of your draft on Mrs. Matthews for £31..1..6—I am so little habi-tuated to transactions of this kind that the propriety of immediately acknowledging receipt did not strike me and I partly waited the arrival of the present to Mrs. Robison. But this has not been the sole Cause. On Saturday the 25th ult[im]o I got acc[oun]ts of the death of my only sister at my House near Glasgow, and set off next morning for Boghall, and did not return till Sunday last. Altho' my loss was long expected, I feel the blank very much. I used to pass much of every Summer under her most affectionate Care, and this gave Mrs. Robison a little relaxation, as she was certain that I was as well looked to as if under her own Eye—But thus goes the world on—our Connexions gradually thin around us, and life becomes less worth caring for, and we shift the Scene in our turn with less regret. My own Situation is not very inviting, and I confess that it requires all my Sense of duty to my Wife and Children to make me wish to remain much longer with them, having no prospect but that of en-creasing Suffering or encreasing insensibility But I am not conscious of grumbling. Except my indisposition, I am conscious of my lot in life

being fully equal to my merits. I may have Capacity, but I want vigour of mind and activity, and have jogged on in a sort of easy and decent obscurity which I might have emerged from had I been more active. And I now confess that what I called virtuous Moderation in my own conduct was, in plain English, lazyness. I now repine at it, because the civil Station into which I have brought a family requires a better income to support it with decency, and without some painful Efforts, than I have been able to procure for them.

Your kind present has not yet come to hand. Mrs. Robison begs me to assure you of its being duly prized by her, and that she will always look with pleasure at any thing that brings to her recollection Persons with whom she enjoyed so many agreeable hours.

Dr. Black is greatly obliged to you for the trouble you have taken to state the Circumstances on which you found your opinion of the difference between the oxygenous Gases obtained by different processes, and will shortly write to you on the Subject. His health is better than when I formerly spoke of it. But he feels very strongly the loss of his amiable and worthy Freind and Companion Dr. Hutton. Dr. Black has not had Spirits enough to be able to see Dr. Hutton these several Months, till within a few days of his decease—He left, us without a struggle, in less than half a minute—after speaking with the utmost clearness—He was busy with another large volume and had engaged the Engraver to come and get his orders the day after that in which he died

I am Sorry that I cannot put more agreeable things on paper for you—but things will mend, and I hope still to have an opportunity of amusing You. Mean time I beg to be kindly remembered to all your good family, and to Messrs. Boulton and Miss Boulton, request in which my Wife and daughter most cordially join

Wishing you all good *Summer health* I remain with affectionate regard

My dear Sir
Your's
John Robison

MRS ROBISON TO WATT

Cover addressed: 'James Watt Esq./Heathfield/Birmingham',
endorsed in Watt's hand, 'Mrs. Robison Edinburgh April 13th
1797' and numbered '14'. Dol.

Edin[bu]r[gh] 13th April 1797

Your Box with its brilliant Contents arrived safe here last night for
which I beg you my D[ea]r Sir to present our best thanks to Mr. Bolton
and accept them also for yourself.

however superiour you Lords of the Creation are you are always encouraging us poor weak women in pride and Vanity—My pride indeed
was highly flatter'd in being so kindly remembered by those I so much
esteem, and my Vanity, but for a trifle I am with a heavy heart, going to
relate, would have been gratify'd to the utmost—but alas my Dear Sir you
know as well as I, every Joy must have its alloy in this World, how shall
I describe to you my feelings in perusing the Inventory of your Elegant
present to find it contain'd a duplicate of almost the whole of the Riches
I already possessed in the Silver way. I should not have told you this distressing circumstance my dear Sir but from a firm reliance that the
motive of your present will prevent your taking it amiss, as I am confident you wished it, not only, to be an Elegant, but a useful one, and as I
sincerely accept and wish to enjoy your kind intentions. I judged you
would more approve my frankly telling you so, than if I had with an
aching heart, penned you a Letter of thanks, and wrap'd up your
charming ware, to present, tarnish'd and perhaps unfashionable, to the
next generation.

I would need the pen of a Courtier to smoothe the rugged passage I
now come to, which is to beg your permission to return what I have and
honestly to inform you what I would wish to receive again, from you
and Mr. Bolton—besides having all you sent me I have a Large Goblet
or Cup, a Flagon, Tea pot, Milk pot and Cruets, but happily my Candle
sticks are of vulgar pinchbeck. I accept with pleasure the handsome pair
for the Tea table and shall be proud to be Illuminated by you also d[ea]r
Sir in the Dining room. and now that I am a Beggar, if you would not
think me too presuming, I would go on and ask a Tea Cady. These I
think will compleat my finery and my wishes.—Mr. Robison sends
many thanks for his pretty Standish

Euphemia also begs me to present her best Comp[limen]ts to Mr. Bolton and Mr. Watt with gratitude for their kind remembrance of her. She luckily had no shadow of the same before which allows her to feel the highest relish in the possession of her present, and if She had not been afraid to use it awkwardly, would have dip'd her Golden Pen to have said so herself.—I wish I could find any pen sufficient to make an adequate apology for this clumsy freedom, and trouble. I must entirely and solely trust to what first prompted me the hope I entertain'd you would be so good as excuse me in which pleasing expectation I remain my

D[ea]r Sir with Sincere regard
Yours Much Oblig'd
R. Robison

PS. I beg my best wishes to Mrs. Watt. I receivd her kind Letter and pray my dear Sir remember me kindly to Miss Bolton and Mr. R. Bolton and by no means forget my respect to Mr. James Watt whose Gallant entertainment I shall never cease to recollect and also to Mr. Gregory I saw Mr. Withering lately he speaks of being soon home—nothing you see Sir can stop me, but the end of my Paper Adieu again I beg my Comp[limen]ts to Miss Alston.

R.R.

Letter 180

MRS ROBISON TO WATT

Cover addressed: 'James Watt Esq./Heathfield/Birmingham', endorsed in Watt's hand, 'Mrs. Robison Edinburgh April 29th 1797' and numbered '15'. Dol.

Saturday 29th April Edin[bu]r[gh] 1797.

My Dear Sir

I am very sorry to give you all this trouble, but having receiv'd your favour of yesterday I must again scribble and plague you

I am perfectly satisfy'd with your first plan which includes the Branches   These will more than supply all my wants and wishes.

I was much disapointed you would not bestow upon me a few of these honied words (you speak of)   It is strange this commodity we never care for where plenty but as sincerity and these seldom go together I could

not expect it. I find I was just going on to teaze you with nonsense my
D[ea]r Sir so beging you again to remember me kindly to all my good
friends I will add no more than that I ever am with due Esteem and
regard

D[ea]r Sir,

Your much

Oblig'd and humbl[e] Serv[an]t

R. Robison

PS. I will most carefully pack up the Box and send it off, as directed on
Thursday next.

Letter 181

ROBISON TO WATT

Cover addressed: 'To James Watt Esq./Heathfield/Birming-
ham', endorsed in Watt's hand, 'Jno. Robison May 3d 1797—
requesting one of Sir Isaac Newton's letters from Mr.
B[oulton]. Sir Isaac's extraction' and numbered '16'. Dol.

Edin[bu]r[gh] May 3d 1797

My good Sir

I don't know whether Mrs. Robison has told you how much she
thinks of her own Judgement and Taste since she finds that her previous
Stock of Silver and plated Goods comprehended the very articles that
you thought most likely to be acceptable   I only know that your
Authority is now frequently made use of against my opinions. I was in
hopes of sending along with the returned Articles a specimen of Leith
Glass Manufacture which my Wife boasted of at Mr. Rennies, but it is
not yet ready—Your keepsake Standish is most welcome, but it will
require some time's Service to put it on a par with the homely apparatus
of my Study.

Mr. Boulton (to whom I request your kind remembrance of me) put
a wish into my brain that you will perhaps think very extravagant. He
told me that you had some Letters of Sir Isaac Newton's to Nicholas
Facio—I dare say you don't altogether refuse your Sympathy to my
superstitious veneration for every relick of that wonderful Man. I would
give any thing to have a Scrap, however insignificant of his writing, and
if your Collection could admit of any pruning, a twig or two would be
an inestimable present. I believe I told you that I had been on the hunt to
find documents of his Scotch Extraction, and that he himself firmly

believed that his Grandfather was a younger Son of Sir — Newton of that Ilk in East Lothian, and wrote to the last Man of the family requesting information whether some of the younger Sons did not attend James VI when he succeeded to the Crown of England—I am still in hopes of finding that Letter. Should I be able to render this descent probable, I will lodge an account of my Labours in the University Library—Would not that be a proper deposit for your Collection of Letters.

And this brings another thing in to my head—Would not a description and even a good Model of your Engine be a becoming present from You to the Museum of the University of Glasgow—I know that it would be received with great Affection and Respect.—Think of this at your Leisure, as also of a new doctorat that I am scheming with some hopes of Success, if we can find a proper Name for it—Doctor of Arts—a Collegium or Corporation of Scientific Engineers, with three degrees of Bachelor Master and Doctor—not merely academical honours, of no more value than the offices of a Mason Lodge, but to have Civil Consequences—As a Man must have a diploma to entitle him to a consulting fee, so should an Engineer etc. etc.—I had more to say—but the Wright has come to close the Box—so farewell—

Your faithful Freind and
Wellwisher
John Robison

Mrs. Robison begs to be remembred to Mrs. Watt, and would have written just now but has been much occupyd by some strangers who are with us

Letter 182

WATT TO BLACK

Cover addressed: 'Doctor Joseph Black/Physician/Edinburgh', endorsed in Black's hand, 'From Mr. Watt 7th June 1797 answered the 15th June' and numbered '16'. Dol.

Heathfield June 7th 1797

Dr. Black

My dear Friend

It is long since I had the pleasure of a letter from you. The afflicting intelligence of the loss of our worthy friend was communicated to me by

273

Mr. Robison. I sincerely sympathized with you but not being able to suggest any other consolations than must have occurred to you I forebore to write, especialy as from the then state of your health, I could not put you to the trouble of an answer. I have since had the satisfaction to hear that your health is better, and that you have hopes of being able to enjoy the summer, when it comes; I most ardently wish that you may.

I have no philosophical news to tell you and indeed the only thing material I have heard or seen lately is some account of Humbolds[1] experiments upon Galvanism, published in the Monthly magazine for May last, which are curious, and seem to confirm the idea of its being a different thing from electricity. In pneumatic medicine I have also heard of a case of the oozing of blood through the skin cured by oxygene air after every other means had failed, it was at Bath, I believe in the hospital.

Our law affairs continue in the same train as formerly   our adversaries are working to bring their writ of error and our counsel are opposing them step by step, we submit to the delay, because we have doubts about the opinion of the Judges in the K[ing's] bench, and in the mean time we are getting something by the patent. I am grown more callous than I was on these subjects, I believe principaly because I am less able to exert myself. It has however had the very bad effect of almost annihilating the little activity which I had remaining, so that I neither care to write nor yet to think long upon any subject, My friend Mr. Boulton is however as ardent after new schemes as he was 20 years ago   he is now at London about a new coinage of Copper penny pieces he has contracted with goverment for. The emergencies of the times I suppose prevent his getting the matter concluded with them. The nation seems at present in a dreadful situation   The M——rs seem to have lost our confidence and either cannot or will not make peace; while upon the other hand the opposition in order to get into place, are in the opinion of many saying and doing things which may urge on the desperate party to a civil war; already more than begun in the navy. There has been some violent work in Warwickshire   I have taken neither side, as I think both wrong and appeals to bludgeoned Mobs an inlet to such doings as they have had in France from which may heaven preserve us

Our Engine business is now carried on principaly by J[ames] W[att] Jun[io]r and Mr. Boulton Jun[io]r:, I however attend every day health and weather permits, My son Gregory has also taken to the Engine business and as well as the others gives great application, he has lately had an alarming attack of the influenza which has weakened him much but he is now pretty well recovered and taking tonicks under Dr. Witherings direction. The Dr. has also had lately a very violent fit of his usual disorder but is now recovering though slowly. He keeps up his spirits and activity in a most surprizing manner considering his great bodily weakness

Mrs. W. and myself are in our usual indifferent health   We have both had rather violent stomach complaints this Spring, but are now rather better and hope the Summer will reinstate us, we propose setting out on a Journey to Bath next week hopeing to derive benefit as we did last year. Mrs. W. and my sons Join in best wishes to you, and requesting the favour of a few lines from you at your convenience I remain

Dear Sir
Your affectionate friend
James Watt

Presumably Friedrich Heinrich Alexander von Humboldt (1773–1858), geographer.

Letter 183

MRS ROBISON TO WATT

Cover addressed: 'James Watt Esq./Heathfield/Birmingham',
endorsed in Watt's hand, 'Mrs. Robison June 8th 1797 receipt of
candlesticks' and numbered '17'. Dol.

8th June Edin[bu]r[gh] 1797

My Dear Sir
    I receiv'd in due course your last Letter of May 13th—and last night the Box in safety. I delay not a moment to inform you of its arrival as it is disagreeable to have our intentions frustrated by any cross accident   I admire your Taste again d[ea]r Sir on a larger scale, I have seen no candlesticks I think so handsome and would return again my best thanks but I know Mr. Watt needs not many words to inform him of my feeling of his kindness

    I was much mortifyd to hear your Health was still so poorly tho quit of a great deal of fatigue and the bad Air of London. I hoped you would be much relieved by geting home—the weather is more favourable now, at least the Season, tho' colder than it should be at present, but a few days more will surely bring us heat and then I am happy to think you will be

more easy and comfortable, what an incompleat shabby World this is   I
an often tempted to think, when I see good people suffer and often it is to
be seen, when the bad go free etc. but this is a bad subject—
we had some expectation of seeing you in Scotland lately, I hope Mrs.
Watt is well and recovering her spirits. I beg to be kindly remembred
to her. I would have written in answer to her kind Letter but am afraid
my pen has been rather troublesome in the Family as it is. I had a long
call from Dr. Black tother day which is a great rarity and favour, you
will be glad to hear he is in tolerable health and spirits just now. Mr. R
receivd your nice plan—but as he is abroad today I can say nothing from
him but suppose he will be writing soon.

I beg My Dear Sir you won't forget my best Comp[limen]ts to
Messrs. and Miss Bolton and your own young Gentlemen and without
further teazing you I remain Ever My Dear Sir with due Esteem

and regard Your
Much Oblig'd
Hum[b]le Serv[an]t
R. Robison

Letter 184

BLACK TO WATT

Cover addressed: 'Mr. James Watt Engineer/Heathfield/Bir-
mingham/by Ferrybridge', endorsed in Watt's hand, 'Dr. Black
13 June 1797 Dr. Huttons affairs' and numbered '17'. Dol.

Edinburgh 13th June 1797

My dear Freind
I have had the pleasure to receive your letter dated the 7th Inst[an]t.
It was my intention to write to you for some time past and especially on
occasion of the death of our freind, but being in bad spirits and learning
that John Robison had wrote to you I put it off—The Doctor left no
settlement and the winding up of his affairs will cost a little time and
trouble. His sister who succeeds to the whole of his fortune and who
never was accustomed to business and is quite unfit for it relys very much
upon me for advice and direction   I have therefore recommended to her
an Agent for the law part of the business, who will take good care of it
and manage it with judgment and decision, She has some relatives who

276

are very distant and who I am told would not succeed as heirs in law but we have become acquainted with a natural son of the Doctor whom he educated and has supplyed with money from time to time and to whom he intended some time past to leave a legacy—His name is James Hutton   he is about 50 Years old but has the appearance of being older   this is the consequence of long and close application to the business of the Post office at London where he was one of the Clerks   His health being much impaired he has, at present, leave of absence for the recovery of it and has retired to a country lodging near Workington. On hearing of the Doctors Death he came here and brought with him his leave of absence, in which there are strong expressions of the esteem and value they have for him in the post office. I have conceived a warm affection for this poor man, he is not unlike the Dr. in person and bald like him but not like him in the face, having more of the features of his mother, he is a most worthy modest man, of great assiduity and ability in business but has been so much confined as to be but little acquainted with the tricks of this world   He is married and has seven children, 4 sons and 3 daughters and one of his Sons, apprentice to a Surgeon at Workington is much spoken of for his genius and parts, He brought his eldest daughter with him to be his nurse and her manner and appearance shew that she has been well educated. His salary in the Post office afforded him a scanty and even insufficient subsistence for such a family but the Doctor allowed him to draw upon him when necessity required it, which Mr. H. did as seldom as possible.—As the Doctors property is considerable we hope to get a settlement made by Miss Hutton in which something handsome will be done for Mr. Hutton and his family. I am under great obligations to you for the present of your portable pneumatic apparatus   it has been very usefull to us in the chemical Course for some of the experiments. Doctor Hope is giving a short Summer Course at present the whole trouble of which he has taken to himself. he has a laudable ambition to attract notice and deserve esteem and I perceived when he first proposed this course that he wished to be the sole Lecturer in it. To this I readily consented and the truth is that I am not in a condition at present to take any share of the trouble. Since the Spring Season and beginning of Summer I have been afflicted with rheumatism and weakness of all my limbs which makes me totter and creep in walking like one under the infirmities of extreme old age. It does not distress me however in the night except by the difficulty of turning or moveing in bed and I get enough of sleep—In the day I can amuse my self with books and news and a little

277

work but am easily fatigued and I find that fatigue is very bad for me, it brings on a quick pulse and sometimes a little homoptoe which requires some time of rest and quiet to put it away—A chamber horse or spring Chair gives me the most convenient exercise at present, I cannot bear the jolting of a Carriage. You appear to me to have a more melancholy view of publick affairs than the occasion deserves. The mutiny of the sailors is not surprising, it is rather surprising that it has not happened oftener, they like a riot, are very ignorant and easily misled and I have no doubt that the industry and gold of the french and perhaps of opposition have been employed on this occasion. As for Ireland it has been in rebellion formerly and was always subdued by England, the Government there at present is very vigilant and I beleive judicious and it has so much power to reward informers, and deserters, that I have not much anxiety about the event—A good number of the troops employed there are scotch highlanders who are perfectly trusty, and exemplary by their sobriety and by their regularity and steadiness. They are esteemed by the Irish themselves even in the towns where there are the greatest number of disaffected Irish The conduct of opposition {of Opposition} is no doubt very bad but the nation in general has no confidence in them, and their furious unprincipled declamations have no effect but on the most ignorant and wrongheaded of the People and especially of London where they have conceit enough to think themselves Persons of very great consequence—Upon the whole I hope that better times are now not far off and that such institutions will be established for the defence of this country as shall secure us from foreign invasion. Present my kindest Compliments to Mrs. Watt and to your Sons and to Messrs. Boltons and beleive me always most affectionately Yours

Joseph Black

You tell me that your Son Gregory is taking Tonics. I hope he does not neglect gentle exercise on horseback which is the best of all Tonics for a young man like him

Letter 185

WATT TO BLACK

Cover addressed: 'Doctor Joseph Black/Edinburgh', endorsed
in Black's hand, 'From Mr. Watt 16th October 1797 by Mr.
Withering   answered 10th November Ditto' and numbered
'15'. Dol.

Heathfield Oct[obe]r 16th 1797

Dr. Black

My Dear Friend
   I should have wrote to you long ago if I had had any thing material to
inform you of; at present I embrace the opportunity of Mr. Witherings
Journey to enquire after your health, and to inform you of that of your
friends here. Philosophic news I have little, I saw lately a letter from Dr.
Odier[1] of Geneva who writes that the common Air in the valley of Gess
in piedmont has considerably more oxygene in it than the mixture of airs
given here as medicine being above 30 per cent oxygene which seems to
proceed from the water of the river which runs through it \and/ which
contains much air, 78 ox: ag[ains]t 22 azote. I have directed some queries
to be put to him respecting the health and diseases of the inhabitants of
that valley. He mentions also that he gives crude manganese powdered in
diseases of the stomach, dose 2 Scruples 4 times a day—He has also given
the magistery of bismuth with good effect in Gastrodynia and says that
both it and the Calx of Nickel which it frequently contains are very safe.
I should not however have courage to take either of them, but a medical
friend of mine here has sometime ago taken a dram of Manganese at
once without any effect whatever that he could perceive. You know the
giving the nitrous acid in the lues has been lately introduced, it has however had no effect in the cases in which it has been given in our hospital,
till lately Dr. Carmichael tells me two patients, who have taken it about
6 weeks begin to amend, no mercury has been given to them. I had
lately a { cough } \catarrh/ beginning with some fever, pains in my legs,
dry burning sore throat cough and spitting of very Salt mucus etc, in the
usual manner my serious colds \begin/{ do }   Dr. Withering desired me
to try the Hydro carbonate air. All airs breathed out of a bag cause
stitches in the muscles of my breast sides and shoulders, and disorder my
stomach, having however found the means of removing these com-

279

plaints, I took a pint of the H C in 20 pints of C[ommon] air   the sore throat got much better in a few hours, next morning the cough was better, and by taking 3 more doses of the H.C was cured. These doses caused no vertigo, but the last dose made me sickish and uncomfortable all the day after I took it, and I have observed in others I have given it to, that as the disease abated the air disordered them more so that the doses were obliged to be reduced

We made a long tour this summer, first to Clifton then to Bath from thence to Christ Church in Hampshire, Lymington Cowes and Southampton, and home by Winchester, stopping longer or shorter as we liked the place. We were out 2 months and by bathing at Bath and in the salt water, rideing and walking about, as much as the inconstant weather and our own Strength would permit, we all (Mrs. Watt Miss McGrigor Gregory and myself) received much benefit. The remains of Gregorys influenza left him at lymington   The rideing and walking and sea bathing being his only medicines, he got strong enough to take 14 mile walks on the loose flints of the sea beach. I found small doses of Rhubarb of great use in my stomach complaint, and should have enjoyed the jaunt more than I did had I not been tormented all the time with a severe lumbago and a gravelly complaint, the latter was removed by soda, but the former still remains though much mended. Our weather was in general unpleasant very windy and frequently exceedingly cold for the season. I was much disappointed in the appearance of that part of Hampshire and even of the isle of Wight. There are many parts of England much more pleasant. Trees grow very badly and there are few near the Coast from Christchurch to Lymington, those in the new forrest are stunted and weather beaten and seem as old as the forrest without being of large dimensions.

Mr. Boulton is busy with his coinage of pence (which you have no doubt seen) and they are sold as fast as they are made, though he makes 20 tons a week   in general he enjoys very good health and would be still better if he would attend a little more to himself and less to strangers, his son and daughter are also well—My Son James has been lately much plagued with headaches, caused partly by over attention to business, he is now on a jaunt for his health and I hear is better—Dr. Withering has upon the whole enjoyed better health this summer than usual, but has had several severe attacks of his complaint.

Mrs. Watt and the family here join me in best wishes to you and in requesting the favour of a letter from you, with some account how you

have passed the summer and how your health now is. With remembrances to such friends as you meet

I remain always
My Dear Sir
Your affec[tiona]te friend

The H.C. produced an effect
I little expected   it caused a
glow in my feet and skin and proved
considerably diaphoretic
I took no other medicine

James Watt

Tons
20
20 Ct wts
___
400 Ct wts
112
800
400
400
___
44800 libs
16
___
268800

20

12)716800(5973   3s..4d
60   £2986..13..4
__
11

716800 ounces 44800

[1] Dr Louis Odier the Elder, of Geneva, M.D., F.R.S. Edinburgh, author of *Epistola Physiologica*, Edinburgh, 1770.

Letter 186

BLACK TO WATT

Cover addressed: 'Mr. James Watt Engineer/Heathfield/Bir-mingham/by Ferrybridge', endorsed in Watt's hand, 'Dr. Black November 11th' and numbered '16'. Dol.

Edinb[urgh] 11th Nov[embe]r 1797

My dear Freind

I had the pleasure to receive your letter by Mr. Withering and the beautifull specimens of Mr. Boltons Copper Coinage which certainly surpasses every thing that ever was done before.—The proportion of oxygene gas in the air of the valley of Gess or Gex is not singular, Scheele found the atmosphere of Upsal containing the same proportion or one very near it if I rightly remember, and he made experiments on it every day for a whole twelvemonth in order to compare the state of that

281

atmosphere in the different months of the Year.—In the above mentioned Valley I suppose the water of the river throws out a part of its air in consequence of its becomeing less cold than it was in the higher grounds from which it descends. It was well thought of you to enquire about the health of the inhabitants of the Valley, and I shall be glad to hear his answer. In giving crude manganese for diseases of the Stomach Dr. Odier may have given an Oxyd of Iron, there is but little manganese to be found which does not contain Iron. As for Nickel, it is seldom or scarcely ever free from arsenic, his venturing on the use of it was therefore a bold measure and the powers of bismuth are (to me at least) so little known that it required boldness to venture on it also—The nitric acid has been tryed here for the cure of Syphilis, and at the first with great appearance of success but some of the patients relapsed and our practitioners are not disposed at present to trust to it. You have been very fortunate upon the whole in your trials of the H[ydro] C[arbonate] Air. I have not needed any such medicine lately, my great distress all this Summer having been rheumatism and weakness in my Sides and right shoulder but still more in my loins, A carriage tortured me and even a Sedan chair was scarcely endurable   I therefore was almost entirely confined to my house and continue so still, not being able to bear the cold of the external air. I however take some exercise, such as I am able for, in the house and I take enough of food, and I sleep abundantly—My wish in Summer was to try Bath or Buxton but I {never} \was/ not able to undertake such a journey, and your complaining now of Lumbago after having been at Bath has in great measure deprived me of my hopes from that quarter. My weakness in Summer was such that the smallest attempt to do any business fatigued me immoderately. I have now more *strength and ability for business* but am as stiff as an old horse and am under the necessity to use a Stick in walking, or creeping rather, through the house. I do not find myself in a condition or humour for Lecturing and have therefor left the whole of that business to Hope but I employ myself at home in planning improvements of the apparatus and getting them executed—Rhubarb is an usefull medicine to me as well as to you and I find that our home-made Rhubarb agrees with me better than what is named Indian Rhubarb; this last is stronger than ours, about double, but even half a dose it often gripes which the other never does with me— when I take our own as a laxative I take 15 grains which is just enough for me, and immediatly after swallowing it \mixed/ with a little tea well sweetened, I find it acceptable to my Stomach. A new method of cultivating it has been discovered which is a great improvement, It is done by earthing \it/ up every year after the Stem is dead and fallen, untill a{ little } mound or hillock is formed over it, Thus it gets a dry soil which is the best soil for it and the root forms new heads or strengthens and enlarges the old ones every year; I think I have heard that the gentleman who first tryed this method, found he could cut off some of the heads and leave the rest of the root to form new ones every year or every two years but in this I may be in a mistake.—I enquired at young Withering how his Father lived, and I suspect he uses too much animal food, I find Scot\c/h broth when well made an excellent nourishment, especially for old persons or for those inclined to plethora or inflammatory affections but the barley and vegetables must be well boiled, and the beef too to make them good, and if there be too much of the beef in them they are exceedingly Savoury but are heavy and heating and plethorific I am happy to hear that Mr. Bolton has now got employment for his coining machinery which gives him some satisfaction after the great expence it has cost him and I hope the specimen he is now giving will bring him as much business in the same way as he chuses to take—Assure him, and Dr. Withering and other freinds of my high esteem and best wishes, and your family in particular of my Sincere affection.

I always am
My dear freind
Yours most sincerely
Joseph Black

Letter 187

KEIR TO WATT

Cover addressed: 'James Watt Esq./Heathfield', endorsed in Watt's hand, 'J. Keir November 24th 1797 Mr. Robisons book' and numbered '9' in bundle headed, 'Miscellaneous 1797 and 1798 No. 1 to 26'. Dol.

24 November 1797

Dear Sir

I am very much obliged to you for you trouble in writing to Mr. Hamilton, who I hope will have it in his power to be of service to me   I have, as you recommended, written to him fully on the subject.—I return you Robison's book with many thanks for the curious and entertaining information it contains, though I confess I was surprized at the confusion and inaccuracy of a work written by one who I suppose is certainly, or has been, a man of ability. Some of his quotations I am certain are inaccurate. That from De la Place at page 232, I have found { so } upon comparison, to be so much so, as to be nonsense. I expect Dr. Priestley will not let him pass without a smart correction. I cannot believe that Priestley ever "boasted that he would blow up the religious establishment of his stupid and enslaved native country!' See p. 485; nor that the Doctor will accept the honour of the friendship of the bloody-minded Man mentioned in the same page. Nothing surely can be more contrary to Dr. Priestley's doctrines, than the accusation in page 430, that he denies a future state and "hopes to die like a dog".—I remember Metherie[1] has said foolish things on crystallization, but I can scarcely believe on Robison's authority, that he ever expected to discover what sort of crystallization, *God*{ was }\is/.—

All here join in best compl[imen]ts to Mrs. Watt and Miss Macgregor and I am   Dear Sir
                                    Yours most sincerely
                                          J Keir

[1] Jean Claude de la Métherie (1743–1817), Professor of Natural History in the Collège de France, Paris. Mineralogist and chemist.

Letter 188

Enclosed with previous letter.

[An enclosure most of which is in another hand. Keir's hand starts after X.] p. [232]

This quotation from De la Place is an *inaccurate* translation, and Robison's commentary has no connexion with the meaning of the text. The last sentence of De la Place is made nonsense by Robison. I have translated the last part below exactly.

"But the sublime results to which this discovery has led, are capable of consoling us for the small space assigned to us in the universe. Let us preserve and cherish these results, let us even extend them as the fruits of the sublime knowledge that we have acquired, and as the delight of thinking beings. They have renendered important services to Navigation and Geography: but their greatest benefit is that they have dissipated those fears with which we were struck by the extraordinary celestial phenomena, and destroyed the errors which arose from the ignorance of our true relations with nature; errors so much more fatal as the social order ought to rest solely in these relations. *Truth, Justice*; these are inimitable laws of this order. Far be from us the dangerous maxim that it is sometimes useful to depart from these, and to deceive or enslave men in order to insure their happiness. Cruel experience has shewn in all ages, that these sacred laws are never infringed with impunity. X (End of de la Place's book)

X Robison translates "that these laws are never totally extinct" which is nonsense and the passage in page 233 \and two last lines of page 232/ which, from their being marked with inverted commas, might be supposed to be quoted from De la Place, do not exist at all in the \French/ book.

Letter 189

ROBISON TO WATT

Cover addressed: 'To James Watt Esq./at Heathfield/near Birmingham', endorsed in Watt's hand, 'John Robison Edinburgh January 14th 1798 recommends Mr. Thomson to the Pneumatic institution price of copy right of proofs of a conspiracy' and numbered '18'. Dol.

Edin[bu]r[gh] Jan[uar]y 14 1798

My dear Freind

I had a Letter from a Freind a few days ago informing me that you was engaged in forming a useful and beneficent Establishment for the application of pneumatic Medicine, and you was looking about for a proper person for attending the dispensary. This Gentleman requested that I would recommend to your Notice Mr. Thomson,[1] as a Person well qualified to manage your apparatus and administer the Medicines. Mr. Thomson has studied in this University and means to take his degrees here. My friend says that his ardour for Chemical knowledge has long engaged his whole attention, and that he is well known to all the Anateurs of the Science to have made uncommon progress, and indeed to be one of the most accomplished Chemists in this Country—He speaks in the highest terms of Mr. Thomsons Integrity and indefatigable Industry. I know that my friend will not say so much in favour of any person without full persuasion of its truth, and I also know that he has had long acquaintance with him and therefore has had good opportunities of forming a just opinion of his worth—As Mr. Thomson says that

285

this occupation would of all others be most agreeable to him, and as I have great Confidence in the Judgment of the Person who recommends him to my good Offices with you, I have no hesitation to comply with his request, not doubting but that I am introducing to your Patronage a Person of Merit. I say all this however without any personal knowledge of Mr. Thomson's Abilities as a Man of Chemical Science, because altho' we have had some previous acquaintance, our Conversations never related to these Subjects. Besides, I acknowledge that my own acquaintance w[i]t[h] this branch of Chemistry is much too scanty to entitle me to engage Mr. Thomson in serious Conversation on the Subject. I am therefore in a situation somewhat awkward. Dr. Gleig[2] who recommends Mr. Thomson to me, without possessing much knowledge on this subject, is 'most intimately acquainted with what is going on here among the zealous Students, and knows their opinions of each other. I presume that it is on this authority that he speaks, and I presume you will think it very good authority, when a young man is considered as eminent amongst those who are pushing forward in the same line of pursuit—By this introduction there is a chance that I am serving a person of real Merit—this would give me real pleasure, and to you also.

I am glad to hear from Mr. Withering sometimes that you are holding pretty well out. Mrs. Robison and my daughter join with me in best wishes for your health and Comfort, and beg to be kindly remembered to Mrs. Watt and your Son. I had promised myself much pleasure from the acquaintance which my last winters visit had allowed me to make among your friends. But these were vain projects—I feel myself unable to make any use of the best opportunities, and must think of giving over the Struggle. I have been sadly deficient in my attention; for never was kinder attention paid to me than I met with from your Son and young Mr. Boulton. As you are my old friend I request you to plead my excuse w[i]t[h] both of them. I wished to write, particularly to Mr. James Watt, on some subjects of our Conversation—and I have more than once begun it—but my Spirits are quite depressed by continual Suffering, and really by fatigue, ever since I saw you. After teaching a winter and a summer Course, I went to the Country to recruit for the winters task   I was raised out of bed, and obliged to travel up and down more than 200 Miles before I stopped, sometimes in a Cart. This knocked me up so that I have never recoverd [from] it, and just now my struggle with my Class is all I am able for—Still however, excepting my continual pain, I am in perfect health, and could I get half a years rest, I should get back into my usual tolerable State—The abuse, and ridicule, and reproach which my

book has bro[ugh]t on me are inconceivable—the wretches here know how ill I am, and delight in tormenting me. They have even tried to alarm my family by threats of democratic vengeance—And my despotic Bookseller has contrived to deprive me of all advantage from the eagerness of the public to read the book. I am well assured that three thousand Copies are already sold, yet all that I can get for the Copy right from first to last is £150— I was so harassed by their modes of settling with me, which I was utterly unable to understand or to check, that I threw it up, and gave them the Copy right at their own price—so much for my talents as a bookmaker—*hic Castris Artemque repono*—I shall not trouble the press again—I sometimes think of your torments from your plea, and this makes me hope for your Sympathy with
Dear Sir
Your affectionate Freind
John Robison

Dr. Black is poorly—I see him very seldom, not being able to go out.

[1] Thomas Thomson (1773–1852), F.R.S., appointed Regius Professor of Chemistry in the University of Glasgow in 1818. His books exercised a great influence on the progress of chemistry in Britain.
[2] Possibly George Gleig (1753–1840), bishop of Brechin.

A

Letter 190

WATT TO BLACK

Cover addressed: 'Doctor Joseph Black/Edinburgh', endorsed in Black's hand, 'From Mr. Watt February 7th—1798 answered 21st April' and numbered '14'. Small diagram on cover. Dol.. Enclosed in this letter is the draft letter from Black to Watt dated 'Edinburgh 11th March 1779'.

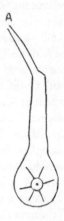

Heathfield Feb[ruar]y 7th 1798
Dr. Black

My dear Friend
    When I look at the date of your letter I am ashamed of being so long in answering it, but having nothing very material to impart I delayed from time to time

287

I have heard nothing more about the valley of Gex, at least nothing determinate and at present these abominable French have blocked up all access to it—The Manganese taken in doses of a scruple 3 times a day by Dr. Carmichael had no marked effect whatever, and much was not to be expected, as it is difficultly soluble even in vinegar—Nobody has had courage to try the bismuth—The nitric acid has been of no service here in Syphylis, but has been of great use in some liver cases and as a tonic being said to be more grateful to the Stomach than the vitriolic acid. In the hospital at Plymouth they continue to succeed with it and say they scarcely ever use Mercury There are accounts of its succeeding in several other places and As far as I learn it is every where a powerful remedy for the bad effects of Mercury.

It gave me great pain to hear of the state of your health, which however I hope has grown better since you wrote as at that time almost every body here had rheumatism or Sciatica. My returning from Bath with a lumbago ought not to discourage you. I went too late in the season and very hot weather coming on, I feared I might be weakned by over perspiration which made me leave it soon and retire to the sea coast, where we had cold enough weather. Buxton is more recommended for Rheumatisms than Bath, as not being weakening and if you think yourself able to bear the Journey I shall ask Dr. Witherings opinion upon it. I should think that something or other may be thought of which may relieve that disease. My lumbago has been much relieved by wearing an adhesive plaster so that it does not trouble me much except when I walk a good deal. Indeed I have enjoyed better health this Winter than I have done \in Winter/ for many years, my principal Complaint is in my Stomach which I ward off by avoiding all vegetables broths and slops, both Coffee and tea disagree with me, I drink cold water to breakfast and warm milk and water at tea time. This regimen with regularity in other respects keeps up a kind of negative health, but activity and industry are denied me. I am fortunate however in not having much use for them though their absence causes much regret and curtails my enjoyments—I have had another visit of the Catarrh lately but the H[ydro] C[arbonate] cured it again as before, at the expence of a headache or two. The Hydrogene is said to cure catarrhs and not to cause Headaches. I shall try it the next time I am unfortunate enough to catch cold—Dr. Withering says he has had better health this winter than he has had for 3 years past and hopes to make still further improvement in the course of the summer —Mrs. W. is pretty well though she has been much troubled with stomach diseases and Sciatica in the winter. Mr. Boulton and all your friends

288

at Soho are well and desire to be remembred to you, he is like to have further orders in the Coining way

Dr. Withering recommended to me to send Gregory to Cornwall for the winter to confirm his health he writes that he is well and has had nothing like a cold since he went, he is to stay till May. At the same time that he is securing his health he is acquiring knowlege in his business. The Winter there has been very rain but by the penzance register and that kept here we have had $1\frac{3}{4}$ inch more rain in Dec[embe]r than them, say$\{4\cdot1\}$Inches \3·04/ Cornwall 4·75 \Inches/ Soho,

Mrs. Watt joins me in wishing you much better health and such happiness as this world can give, and in begging the favour of you to remember us to such of our friends as may visit you and I remain

Your affectionate friend
James Watt

We are all here in some fear of a visit from the french and still more of our exhausting our national finnances, the late assessed Taxes are much cryed out against, but will be paid, there seems to be fewer disaffected than was, the french are hated in general

Letter 191

BLACK TO WATT

Cover addressed: 'Mr. James Watt Engineer/Heathfeild/Birmingham/by Ferrybridge', endorsed in Watt's hand, 'Dr Black April 21 1798' and numbered '15'. Dol.

Edinburgh 8th [21st] April 1798

My dear Freind

I duely received your kind letter of the 7th February You might have omitted any apology for its being so late, the experience I have of my own slowness and frequent inability to sit down and write disposes me at all times to make allowance for you. I thank you for the articles of medical news. I would not expect any effects from Manganese except perhaps when dissolved by some of the acids before it is taken but I have no doubt that Bismuth would act very powerfully one way or another. My health has been various since my last letter but on the whole very low, and since the beginning of this year I found necessity at two different times to lose some blood on account of oppression in my breast and an inflammatory disposition. I have also confined myself to a diet of milk

289

and vegetables the good effects of which I now experience my Cough being far less troublesome than it was. The warm weather also which we have now got contributes not a little to give me more ease. I have taken a house on the south side of the meadow where I shall have ample accomodation and hope the fresh air and grass milk will be of service to me.

As for Buxton or any other long journey I am quite unable for it at present nor have I any hopes that I ever shall be able to undertake it considering that I have now finished my 70th Year. What a difference there is between your stomach and mine. The insipid diet is necessary for me on account of my lungs and it is fortunate that my stomach can bear it. I do feel however sometimes the want of something more stimulating to my stomach than milk and sweets; a languor comes on which is very distressing, but lately I have found a remedy for this in the use of a little butter sprinkled with Salt and I digest the butter well which I formerly could not. Even this however I find must be used very sparingly and not without interruptions otherwise my breast begins to suffer again, and when my cough is encreased by that or by cold the \rheumatic/ soreness of the muscles of respiration makes it very distressing indeed. My best wishes attend Mrs. Watt and the rest of your family Present my Compliments also to Mr. Bolton Dr. Withering and others of your Freinds. Those you have here are in their ordinary. John Robison has carried on his Course this winter with very little interruption. As for myself, I have not once set my nose into the Laboratory nor do I beleive I shall ever again

But I am My dear Sir and ever shall be
Your affectionate Freind
I begun this letter the   Joseph Black
8th Inst[an]t but being fatigued
before I finished it I laid it
aside and such is my inactivity
that it lay still untill this day
        21 April 1798

ROBISON TO WATT

Endorsed in Watt's hand, 'Jno. Robison May 4th 1798 His sons
going to Manchester   Hydraulical Machine at Oulton in
Cheshire—Zurik spiral wheel for raising water' and numbered
'19'. Dol.

Edin[bu]r[gh] May 4 1798

My old and worthy friend,
  I cannot let Mr. Withering depart without taking the opportunity he
gives me of bringing myself into your kind remembrance, and expressing my earnest wishes for your Ease and Comfort. I need not trouble
you with any account of myself, because that would only give you pain.
Suffice it that unceasing pain has now got the better of me, and broken
my Spirits entirely, so that I am unfit for every thing. I have struggled
however, for the sake of my family, and finished my winters task, and
have even undertaken a Summer one—for we must live—and tho' it
encreases suffering, it is better than idly brooding over nearly the same
distress—I tryed your prescriptions, but the use of the Gasses destroyed
my appetite, which was indeed nearly gone before—finding that this
would immediately make me a sore burthen on those about me, I desisted
—Mrs. Robison and my daughter wish to be remembered by you, and
offer their Compliments to Mrs. Watt. My Son John is now at Manchester, with a Mr. Muirland, a Cotton Spinner. Sh[oul]d he ever come in
the Way of your Son Mr. James, may I request that he will show him
any little Civilities. Poor Lad, he is now launched into the World, to
shift *intirely* for himself, for I am useless to him. I have good hopes however, from his sobriety, and gentleness of temper. I gave him a Letter to
'Mr. Lee,[1] thinking that it will not be disagreeable to him to take some
notice of my Son, if he deserves it   God be with him
  I have been searching for your last kind Letter, but can't find it. You
spoke of a new hydraulic Machine—It occurs to me that one on the same
principle (announced near forty years ago by Dan Bernoulli[2] in his
Hydrodynamica) \was/ erected somewhere in Cheshire (I think at Oulton)
by a Clergyman, with Success. I think that the Zurick Machine, with a
Spiral pipe, taking in Air and Water alternately, when constructed with
attention to principle, is an excellent one. A Cylindric, instead of a flat
Spiral, gradually diminishing, so that the compressed Air may always

291

occupy an half of each Spire, will produce the greatest Effect, and, if the motion be slow, will raise more water than any thing I know. The construction is very delicate, and quite unfit for common hands. I made one just when I was growing ill, which gave me great Satisfaction   If any thing in your Situation, or of your Son's has occurred that would give me much pleasure, I hope that some leisure hour may allow you to make me happy with it—pray forget not to assure him of my best wishes. I dare not ask a line from him, tho' it would be highly prized. Please also to remember us to Mr. Boultons kind family. I wish to be remembered by You all, tho' I am not worthy of a thought and soon must be indifferent to it. Adieu my dear Sir, my good friend Adieu

Yours most cordially
John Robison

Dr. Black is now very feeble indeed   I have not been able to see him this long while, for I cannot go in upon him when my countenance betrays my own Suffering

---

[1] George Augustus Lee (1761–1826), partner in the well-known firm of Manchester cotton-spinners, Phillips and Lee.

[2] Daniel Bernoulli (1700–82), mathematician.

Letter 193

BLACK TO WATT

Endorsed in Watt's hand, 'Dr. Black/May 12th 1798/per Dr. A. Munro' and numbered '14'. Dol.

12 May 1798

My dear Sir

This line is to introduce to you Mr. Alexander Monro[1] He is the Son of my Worthy Collegue and is himself one of my young Freinds. On his way from London he proposes to pass through Birmingham and will no doubt have a desire to see the wonders of your industrious town. Be so good therefor as to make him acquainted with Your Son and with good Mr. Bolton who will put him into the proper train. Mr. Withering who has been here two winters is no doubt one of his acquaintances and may perhaps assist in making Birmingham the more agreable to him. You will therefore be so good as to take care that they be brought together if

it suits Mr. Monro. I hope you are recovered from the accident that be-
fell you, I mean the strain of your Tendo Achilles. The occasion of it
shewed that you had more boldness and enterprise than I could have
imagined—I am

My dear Sir

Yours most affectionately

Edinb[urgh] 12 May 1798   Joseph Black

Mr. James Watt Heathfeild

[1] Alexander Monro, Secundus (1773–1817), anatomist. Appointed Professor of anatomy
and surgery in the University of Edinburgh in 1755.

Letter 194

WATT TO BLACK

J. P. Muirhead, *Mechanical Inventions of James Watt*, 1854, vol. II,
pp. 257-58.

Heathfield, 21 May, 1798

*   *   In regard to the engine business, I now take little part in it, but
it goes on successfully. We are still engaged in law; but it gives us little
trouble, and we contrive to make it pay itself. The vexation it gave us for
a long time contributed much to impair my faculties of mind, and to
destroy that cheerfulness so necessary to happiness in this life. I have
learnt, however, to content myself with my present negative state, and
to thank Providence for having placed me in the situation I enjoy.   *   *

Letter 195

ROBISON TO WATT

Cover addressed: 'To Mr. Watt/Turf Coffee house' and endorsed in Watt's hand, 'John Robison Edinburg 17 July 1798',
B.R.L. M IV R.

Buccleugh place Tuesday Morn[in]g

Dear Sir

Mr. Geddes will be happy to see you at the Glass Works any time that
is convenient, and as you thought that half past 11 would suit you, I will

293

call on you at that hour, because I wish to accompany you, altho' my stay must be but for a few minutes. I regret exceedingly that my present condition almost incapacitates me for the enjoyment of my friends. It would otherwise have given me as much pleasure to have accepted Mr Geddises pressing invitation to dine with him, rather than come so early. But as I supposed that you was determined to be at Glasgow to night I thought it safest to keep to the hour you appointed. If however a later hour be more convenient for you, do not incommode yourself on my account. I am very insignificant, and only wish to get another hour of your Company. I was much mortified yesterday when my daughter told me that I could not ask you to take your bed with me as she had dismounted everything by her Mother's orders, to have the house furbished up against her return. Indeed it was but a selfish wish, for I should have been but a dull Companion. Long may you enjoy the pleasures of health and exertion. They have bid me farewell

Expect me at ½ past eleven and believe me with great Esteem

D[ea]r Sir
Yours
J Robison

Letter 196

MRS ROBISON TO JAMES WATT JUNIOR

Cover addressed: 'Mr. James Watt junior/Heathfield/Birmingham' and endorsed, 'Mrs. Robison Edinburgh 4 September 1798 Proposal for the education of Mrs. Millers children'. B.R.L. Muirhead Box 4 'A'.

Edin[bu]r[gh] 4th Sep[tembe]r 1798

My Dear Sir

I have now got home about a week ago, which time has been very busily employ'd owing to my long long absence or I would sooner have written to you—I saw you anxious and have been sorry my unavoidable occupations had delayd my telling you I have not been negligent of your commission.

I think I have found a place for your little folks that must yield you great satisfaction where their health manners and morals will be all compleatly attended to—It is the House of a Widow-Lady who has brought up a large Family of her own where I will often see them tho my Care will be quite superfluous, but before I say who the Lady is, I am desird to mention the Terms on which She would take the charge first that they are healthy children, and free of any disease—you made no difficulty of a board so I looked only for a place I thought particularly advantageous for the children where Tutorage would be thought of as well as maintainance   I proposed £40.—each, besides washing and schools etc.—perhaps their Father may not follow my Idea of the value of such a situation and think this high for children so very young, but as it is a thing quite new to the Lady and She Ignorant of the various charges by which small boards are made up, I mentiond that sum, indeed, She would not easily [have] been induced to the charge but on the temptation of dealing with me and I would beg you would allow me to stipulate for my part that I may have only yourself and no other person to correspond or transact the necessary business with— The Gentleman may be very worthy, and agreeable, but as I am entirely a Stranger to him, I would not like it, and I think it must be much easier for you to settle with him, and I should feel quite at ease in writing my mind to you—

If the child is found too difficult to manage in this situation I would then propose puting her into a Boarding School here kept by a very discreet woman where I think She would be as well off as is possible in a number, but I hope there will be no occasion for a change and that your interest in the child has misled your opinion.

be assured my d[ea]r Sir you may depend on my exertions in my power to assist you in the kind wishes of being of use to helpless Infants whose misfortune I feel great in losing their own proper guide

I hear your Father and Mrs. Watt are in Glasgow and that I missed seeing them in Moffat by being gone to Dumfries. Mr. Robison is just on the wing for Glasgow so I hope He won't fail meeting your Father I am afraid I won't be so lucky unless they come to Edin[bu]r[gh] perhaps your Father will be tempted, to see Dr. Black. The Doctor is remarkably well just now wonderfully stronger than in winter last.

I beg best comp[limen]ts to Miss Bolton and the two Gentleman I hear Mr. Mathew Bolton means to trust himself in this country but I can scarce believe it.—tell him if it is so I shall be very happy to see him.

Mr R and Euphemia beg to be remembred

Adieu D[ea]r Sir and believe me
Ever yours Sincerely
R. Robison

ROBISON TO MILLER

Cover addressed: 'To Mr. Miller/by favour of Mr. Watt',
endorsed in Watt's hand, 'proffessor Robison to Mr. Miller
September 22d 1798 about placing his daughters with Mrs.
Wright' and numbered '20'. Dol.

Tontine Inn Sep[tembe]r 22 1798

Dear Sir

I am sorry that I have not had the good fortune to meet with you during the short stay that I am able to make in Town just now. I found a letter lying for me from Mrs. Robison, relating to the Subject you spoke of when I had the pleasure of seeing you. She then told me that she was disappointed in her expectation of getting your daughters placed with a very worthy and accomplished person, who had been in the habit of bringing up young Ladies, but had declined continuing the business, her situation in life having considerably changed My Wife had hoped that, by the help of some friends, she might prevail—but it would not do.

I had mentioned to Mrs. Robison my wish that she would desire her Mother to take Charge of Mr. Watts Grandchildren Indeed, when your Brother in Law first spoke to me of the thing, that wish was in my thoughts. I cannot give you a better reason for it than by saying that the Manner in which Mrs. Wright brought up her own Children directed my choice in the most important transaction of my Life, and I have had the experience of more than twenty years to convince me that I had acted wisely.—But, when I hinted this wish to my Wife, I had no great hopes of success. My Mother in Law is a most sensible worthy person, and has the same notions of female accomplishments that I have myself, and therefore I must think them right—but she has the reluctance that I suppose every Gentlewoman has, to appear in any other character than the Instructor of *her own* Children. I was therefore afraid to offend her by the proposal. But I am happy that Mrs. Robison has done it and has prevailed; for I am certain that under Mrs. Wrights Care, your daughters will be as if they were under the Eye of an affectionate and a wise Mother, who will pay minute attention to their health their Education, and their principles. I am sorry to say that every thing we see around us at present makes me particularly anxious about this last Circumstance, a Circumstance which, twenty years ago, no body had any fears about.

It would be ridiculous affectation for me, who am an entire Stranger to you Sir, to pretend any particular attachment to your Children. But Mr. Watt is one of my oldest Freinds, and I was also happy in the acquaintance of your Mother in Law; and on these accounts should feel much satisfaction in contributing to the welfare of their dependants. I don't know how it is, but my good freind has the Art of winning the hearts of all the Ladies that get a sight of him, and I have sometimes been mortified by seeing my helpmate more anxious to please him than to please myself. I see that she has taken up this matter with all the warmth of affection. I am selfishly glad of this. For as your Father in Law and I have been long freinds, I am happy in every thing that helps to continue the Connection, and that gives me the hopes that our children will also be freinds. Mrs. Wright lives within two hundred yards of me, so that Mrs. R. and I will see your daughters almost every day

I'm afraid that I have trespassed on your patience by this long tattle; but I had no other way of conversing with you on the Subject, as I am obliged to return immediately to my little concerns in the country. I shall be in Glasgow in a few days again, and will make it my business to meet with you. Mean time accept of my best wishes, and believe me to be with great Regard

Dear Sir
Your faithful
humble Serv[an]t
John Robison

Letter 198

ROBISON TO WATT

Cover addressed: 'To Mr. Watt', endorsed in Watt's hand, 'Jno. Robison September 1798' and numbered '21'. Dol.

Dear Sir

I came to town last night, but was too much jaded by jolting along a very bad Road to be able to call on you. Pray let me know at what time this forenoon I may call on you. I can come out by eleven oClock, and have nothing to do but to see you and make another call in your Neighbourhood. I wish also to meet with Mr. Miller In consequence of a letter I found lying for me from Mrs. Robison. I should be glad to fall in your way without obstructing your visits among your Friends here—but I am altogether unfit for company, not being able to sit in one posture for any time, nor suffer any constraint. I therefore shun all large companies. But if I could be admitted to a breakfast, or a forenoon or evening chat, it would be a great feast to me.

I ever am, D[ea]r Sir
Your's most truly
J. Robison

Tontine Inn Friday Morn[in]g

Letter 199

ROBISON TO WATT

Cover addressed: 'To James Watt Esq./at Heathfield/near Birmingham', endorsed in Watt's hand, 'Proffessor Robison December 15th 1798   Iceland Crystal—His sons visit to me' and numbered '22'. Dol.

Edin[bu]r[gh] Dec[embe]r 15 1798

My dear Sir

Agreeably to the kind invitation by you and Mrs. Watt, I have written to my Son John at Manchester to ask leave of absence that he may wait on you during the Christmas Holidays, and have his glad answer that his Master approves of his Visit—It is with some anxiety that I think of his being introduced to your acquaintance, but I have had such accounts of his proper conduct since he has been so far from my own Eye that I flatter myself you will see nothing to check the partial attention which your goodness would lead you to pay to the Son of an old freind. And I even hope that he may reap some solid advantage from the visit—For I will hope that if you observe any thing about him that may be amended, you will, in great kindness to me, let him perceive your sentiments.—He is so much habituated to think of Mr. Watt not only as eminent in his profession, but as wise any [and]†worthy, that I am perfectly certain that your words and your opinions, as to life and behaviour, will make more impression on him than those of his father or any other Mortal—Be not offended at my speaking in

† 'any' written in error for 'and'.

298

this way, but let a father's anxiety meet with your sympathy—the prosperity and the good conduct of my Children seem now the only enjoyment that is left me. *Never ceasing* torture has now incapacitated me from all mental occupation, as it has long disabled me for any bodily recreation or exercise—Yet my constitution holds out most wonderfully, and I never have either sickness or headache, so that I am able, by a little more suffering, to teach my Class, and not be a useless burthen to my family

I was happy to learn from Mr. Lawson and others that you continue in the same comfortable plight that I saw you in. My best wishes for its continuance ever attend you—Mrs. Robison joins with her's, and begs to be held in kind remembrance, recommending her son at the same time to Mrs. Watts kindness—I will also request you to speak in his behalf to your Son. It is likely that I may write him myself, under cover to John, but I cannot count on this, because I am really much dispirited at present, having been unusually ill for these ten days past. Mr. James is not one who will pay much regard to Etiquette, and will not, I am persuaded withhold his kindness. Nor will he, I hope, expect much from a raw youth, who cannot recommend himself either by Genius or Accomplishments—But I am speaking too much on the subject

Dr. Black has continued pretty much in the same trim you saw him in—I have seen him but seldom, but have always found him chearful and pleasant, tho' very feeble indeed, but free from any thing that alarms him. The last time I was there, Dr. Hope told us that a Mr. Kennedy had discovered a very great quantity of Soda in our Whinn Stone, and still more in the basaltic Columns of Arthur's Seat. I think he said that the last held about 1/9 of its weight of dry Soda. Could you fall on an easy process for \its/ emancipation, I think poor Caledonia might bleach and glaze all Europe for a while

Something always made me forget to tell you that I have, several years ago, observed some most curious optical properties of Iceland Crystall, that are more puzzling than even its double refractions. I had proceeded a good length in classing them, and have nearly reduced them to general Laws—but my observations were but rough, so that I was not in a condition to subject them to public View. I got an apparatus made for repeating them with the precision that was necessary for insuring me that my laws were exact—but this cruel disorder totally prevents me. I have begun them several times, and the stirring of body that was necessary always brought on such paroxysms of pain as not only stopped my proceeding, but made me ill for a day or two—I am uneasy at the thoughts that they should be lost, for some of the facts are extremely curious and amusing—I inform you of this, in hopes that you may know some person of optical Curiosity and mathematical taste, who would take up the Affair where I have left it, and prosecute the experiments with Zeal.—I would send him a variety of fine Specimens possessing that singular property, and an abstract of my leading Observations—I am no longer anxious to be the Author, and only wish the thing to be prosecuted—If I am not mistaken I once shewed you one of the most remarkable facts,—I first observed it in Canada, among a parcel of Specimens found in a Parson's drawer plundered by our Sailors. When I came to London, I went to Ben Martins[1] Lectures and, to curry favour with him, I gave him my Specimens—he added some observations to what I shewed him, and made a pamph[l]et of it—I found the same property, or at least, one connected with it, in chrystals found in the Freestone at Castlesemple, and I think I shewed it to you—But it was not till 1788 that I was able to see their connexion, by getting some beautiful Specimens from Mr. Stanley, just returned from Iceland—I will send you some, with a note of a general Observation, which comprehends most of the facts—Now my good Freind, if you can find any person who will engage in this research with interest and ability, you will greatly oblige me

Farewell my dear Sir and beleive me with affectionate regard Your's

John Robison

[1] Benjamin Martin (1704–82), mathematician, instrument-maker and itinerant lecturer in science.

Letter 200

BLACK TO WATT

Cover addressed: 'James Watt Esq./Heathfeild/Birmingham/by Ferrybridge', endorsed in Watt's hand, 'Dr. Black February 1st 1799 J. Roebuck' and numbered '13'. Dol.

Edinburgh 1st Feb[rua]ry 1799

My dear Freind

The good news you sent to John Robison has given much pleasure to all your freinds here, And Mrs. Watt was so good as to communicate to me the same from Birmingham by a letter which I received from her this day. We hope that when you shall have secured the fruits of this Victory you will not engage yourself again in Patents and Lawsuits which have cost you so much anxiety and so much expence. You should study now to enjoy relaxation from business and the amusements which are the most suited to your taste, but above all relaxation and Ease and gentle exercise and change of air. You need not be anxious now about your fortune. It is already abundant, and it will encrease constantly even while you are sleeping—It is however one of the follies of old age to be too intent on the accumulation of Riches and I feel in myself a degree of that inclination Those of us especially who have made a little fortune by \our/ own {own} industry set a high value on Riches on account of the labour which they have cost us and when time has put an end to other enjoyments one of our greatest pleasures is to encrease the hoard. We do not consider that it is already sufficient for every reasonable purpose. We have acquired a taste and a habit which we indulge. If you can be amused with the works of Horace you will find in them many pleasant allusions to this folly and ingenious expositions of the absurdity of it. I was proposing to write to you before I saw your letter to John Robison. I wished to know whether any thing had occurred to you with respect to my Brother or the younger Hutton. I have some of his drawings which are copies of landscapes in water colours and very good. From what I have heard of him I have reason to beleive that he would be uncommonly attentive and assiduous in business. His father I know by personal acquaintance to be one of the best of men. He has a sound head for business and a goodness of heart, a strictness of integrity, a degree of modesty with respect to his own merits and an overflow of gratitude to those who befreind him which are rarely to be met with. His eldest son who is here studying surgery is also an excellent young man and I am persuaded that the fathers Character and the effects of his care in educating his children have pervaded them all. But there is another Person whose present Situation gives me rather more concern. I mean poor John Roebuck. You have probably heard of the injustice done him by the Company who set up the Iron Furnaces near Alloa. His dispute with them was referred to Arbitrators who have taken more than 12 months to consider of it. and no prospect yet of a speedy decision. In the mean time he is perfectly miserable, depending on his Wifes freinds for the Subsistence of his Family and receiving their aid in the most humiliating way. He is anxious to get any employment whatever by which he might do something for himself. He has been acting the Engineer lately in improveing Lime works for the Earl and Countess Dowager of Morton and has been very successfull, but having volunteered it he gains nothing by it but their good will—I think he is better qualifyed for Engineering than any other business. but I beleive he would Accept at present any employment. I know that you will feel abundantly for him and will be equally anxious to serve him so that I need not add any more to excite You but may leave You to think on what may be done for him And give me your thoughts when you have Leisure—Mrs. Watt does not say any thing particular about your health—Mine has hitherto been incomparably better than it was last winter and I still persist in my milk diet

Farewell my dear freind and beleive me always

Yours affectionately

Joseph Black

Letter 201

BLACK TO MRS WATT

Cover addressed : 'Mrs.Watt/Heathfeild/Birmingham/by Ferry-bridge', endorsed in Watt's hand, 'Dr. Black February 1799' and numbered '13'. Dol.

Edinburgh 1 Feb[rua]ry 1799

Dear Madam,

I return You a thousand thanks for the good news you have given me by your letter of the 27 Jan[uar]y. Professor Robison also received one from Mr. Watt himself inclosing a newspaper in which there is an imperfect account of the trial and decision. I hope this will put an end to all trouble and anxiety about this business. In answer to your kind enquiries about my health I have the pleasure to inform you that I am incomparably better this winter than the last. I am not able (it is true) to withstand the Cold air, and never go out except in my chair and that but Seldom But I take exercise in the house and am free from distress of any kind, my Rheumatic pains being all gone, a weakness only of my limbs being left which I cannot expect now to recover but I can easily go up and down stairs, which I was scarcely able for last winter—I write by this post to Mr. Watt and if he is still in London and to remain a little longer You may forward my letter— I am truely Madam

Your much obliged and obedient humble Servant

Joseph Black

BLACK TO WATT

Cover addressed: 'James Watt Esq./Heathfeild/Birmingham',
endorsed in Watt's hand, 'Dr. Black/March 6th 1799/
J. Roebuck' and numbered '11'. Dol.

Edinburgh 6th March 99

My dear Freind

You cannot imagine how gratefull John Roebuck was when he received the assistance you sent him lately. He shewed me your letter, his Eyes brimfull. and when he attempted to express his sense of your kindness his voice failed him. But I have the pleasure further to inform you that the arbitration of his dispute with the Alloa Company has at last taken a favourable turn for him both the Arbiters being now satisfyed that he has been treated with gross injustice. The only difficulty is about the quantum of damages but that question too is in a good train. It is not probable however that these will be much more than what will enable him to pay his debts. This Cause has made him known to some of our Lawyers and they have conceived much esteem for him. They approve his proposal to become an Engineer and say that some of those they are under the necessity of employing write reports so badly composed and expressed that they cannot understand them. From what I can learn however engineering is but an uncertain and poor business in Scotland. But it is the only plan he can form at present, and one way by which you may assist him in it, is to put a paragraph into your next letter to me of the following import if you approve of it, Viz. "That you are glad to hear that Mr. Roebuck proposes to take up the business of a professional Engineer He being uncommonly well qualifyed for it, by his liberal education which will give clearness to his Reports and that authourity and Credit to which his natural Character of Uprightness and Integrity shall well entitle them and as the bent of his genius \and the lines of business in which he has been hitherto engaged/ have led him more to the study of engineering and of the Sciences connected with the mechanical and chemical Arts than to any other You highly approve his setting out in that line and hope he will meet with due Encouragement". If you think it proper to write to me to this effect, I shall give him an extract from your letter to shew to his Freinds

Your last letter gave me much uneasiness as I see no end to your anxiety and troubles. If it \were/ possible to end the dispute by arbitration or compromise I have no doubt you would think of it but that is probably impossible or might be followed by bad consequences

I can only pray that your health and strength may be preserved under such a pressure of greivances.

I am always
Yours affectionately
Joseph Black

Letter 203

BLACK TO WATT

Cover addressed: 'James Watt Esq./Heathfield/Birmingham' and endorsed, 'Dr. Black Edinburgh March 99—Young Hutton'. B.R.L. Box 1 (MISC).

Edinb[urgh] 22d March 1799

My dear Freind

I received your letter of the 17th and write this line only to let you know that young Mr. Hutton is to join you very soon at Birmingham. He has been for some time and is at present in the counting House of a West India Merch[an]t or factor at London where he was taken in to give him some knowledge and experience in Book keeping etc. but not bound, and without any Salary. To that situation he has no likeing and would quit it immediatly, but is requested by the Merch[an]t to stay a fortnight longer only that his place may be Supplyed—

Yours always
Joseph Black

Letter 204

BLACK TO WATT

Endorsed in Watt's hand, 'Doctor Black July 26th 1799' and numbered '10'. Dol.

Edinburgh 26th July 1799

My dear Freind

I had the pleasure to receive Yours of the 21st and am happy to learn that you are at length escaping from the cursed torment of Lawsuits. It was a fellow-feeling with poor John Roebuck, I suppose, which made you advise him to be moderate or even low in his demands rather than to persist in claims which would require a long time to discuss them and the issue of which would probably fall far short of what he ex-

304

pected. His arbitration is now in the hands of the Ultimate and decisive arbiter, the Sollicitor General, who is a sound headed worthy and resolute man and I beleive will do him all reasonable justice and I hope soon too

I am glad that young Hutton is likely to please you. I have never Seen him but he has been described to me as an amiable Lad and I have endeavoured by a letter which his father has communicated to him to give him proper impressions of his duty to you and Mr. Bolton. Your anxiety about my health is very kind and pleasing to me and I have the happiness to be able to reward your kindness with very good accounts of it. You perhaps may not have heard of an attack on my lungs which I had near \the beginning or/ middle of May. It was preceded with chronic Coughs and Catarrhs and Rheumatisms for a considerable time and ended at last in an Haemoptoe which after a few days became suddenly very violent and peripneumonic, the sensation of it was that of very quick Suffocation if I had not been bled freely. It confined me to bed for some days and lowered my Strength very much and my Spirits and my hopes of health; but by Silence and Quiet and caution and nursing I recovered much faster than I expected and was able to remove to my house at the Meadow on the 2d or 3 of June, and since that time my recovery has made an happier progress than ever before. No Rheumatisms now and I am grown much stronger than I was last summer, being better able to walk and to bear the motion of a Carriage and the impression of the fresh air. All this I impute to more Caution in my Diet. Milk is the most nourishing and stimulateing part of \it/ excepting a little Salt which I take with my Vegetables, and I find by experience that I formerly took too much of it, Viz an english pint of it or near to that quantity commonly to my dinner Now I take less than half a pint to that meal and I find that this is abundance to do me good. I have now no Cough and my Sleep is excellent and I enjoy every comfort that I can desire and expect. I fondly hope that now when your mind will be more at its ease being relieved from the anxiety of lawsuits you will enjoy amusements and Relaxation and Quiet These are the principal Comforts of an old man and they will tend greatly to improve your health—My affectionate good wishes attend You and Mrs. Watt and the rest of your Family and good Mr. Bolton and I am

Always
My Dear Sir
Sincerely Yours
Joseph Black

305

BLACK TO WATT

Endorsed in Watt's hand, 'Dr. Black November 6th 1799 about
nitrate of ammonia' and numbered '9'. Dol.

Edinburgh 6th Nov[embe]r 1799

My dear Freind
  I have received Dr. Beddoes's Notice which contains some most
extraordinary Facts. There is mention in it of your having made a little
tryal of the Gazeous Oxyd of Azote (Dr. Preistly[s] deph[l]ogisticated
Nitrous Air) I beg to be informed particularly how you prepared it
and in what dose you took it etc. etc. My reason for putting you to this
trouble is that Beddoes hints that all depends on its being well prepared and promises instructions to be given hereafter But I am impatient to try it on a Freind of mine who is in a deplorable state of
Hypochondriacism with symptoms that threaten derangement and
the shocking consequences that might follow therefrom. I write to
Beddoes himself by this post and hope to get some of his instructions
but wish to learn also what you know and think of it. I heard some
good news relating to you from Mr. Playfair our Professor of Geometry who Was lately in Cornwall and other parts of England   He told
me that your Son and Mr. Boultons had been there this Summer and
had collected a very handsome Sum of the arrears which were due to
the Company—estimated by the mine-masters at about 40.000—Long
may you live and enjoy health with your present well earned good
fortune—I have continued this whole summer past {to have} in better
health than I had the former one and I still enjoy it. I find reason to
impute it all to the regulation of my Diet in point of Quantity as well
as Quality—and I always take exercise, in the house or out of it. I saw
mention in the Newspaper of the death of Dr. Withering at Birmingham on which I condole with you but am yet uncertain whether it was
the Father or Son—My best wishes attend You and Mrs. Watt and all
the rest of your Family and I am always

Yours affectionately
Joseph Black

Mr. James Watt Sen[io]r

WATT TO BLACK

Cover addressed: 'Doctor Joseph Black/Edinburgh', endorsed
in Watt's hand 'To Dr. Black November 6th 1799 on return
from a Jaunt to the West' and numbered '10'. Dol.

Dr. Black   *Heathfield Nov[embe]r 6th 1799*

My dear Friend

It gave me much pleasure to learn from your letter of 26th July that your health was then so much better than usual, which from a letter of Miss Alston to Mrs. W. I am happy to hear still continues, but I wish for a confirmation from yourself—I have lately made a 2 months Tour in the South western Counties and for the whole time excepting about 10 days we had most uncomfortable weather, which made me fear for you. It has been very cold, windy and rainy even on the south coast. Yet all the watering places were full of company. The prospect of the Harvest was very dismal upon the higher grounds much wheat spoiled and the barley and oats looking miserably. But in return the crop of apples was superabundant and ripened better than any other fruit this season—Among other places I was at Clifton where I found Dr. Beddoes much taken up trying a new Air, what Dr. Priestley called dephlo[gisticate]d nitrous air, which when properly prepared, Mr. Davy his assistant had found to be respirable—He prepared it from the Nitrate of Ammonia by distillation in a heat of about 300°. In greater heats it is decomposed and nitrous acid and azote produced

This Gas seems to have great power on the nervous System, in some patients it gives great hilarity and disposition to motion, without leaving lassitude—But in those disposed to be Hysterical it excites the fit. Some paralyticks have been cured by it and others relieved; but powerful as it is upon the nerves it seems to have little action upon the arterial system, as it does not affect the pulse. It is not {acid and} irritating and does not seem to hurt the lungs of those who have breathed it, though it is breathed pure

I tryed the hot bathing and pumping at Bath for my Sciatica and cold leg, for a fortnight. The Rheumatick feelings were mended but the cold in the leg remains. I have however greatly recovered the lameness owing to my broken tendon, merely by time and the force of nature so that I can now walk 3 or 4 miles in a day, and though my General health has not suffered any material amendment from the

Journey; yet I am less languid than when I set out, and I am persuaded have been saved from worse health which I should probably have had at home during such weather, Mrs.W. who{were}\and her sister were/ with me have also been well

News here there is none—We have not yet got all our cornish recusants brought to obedience and must still call some of them before the Courts at Westminster but we hope that will be {simp} straight forward work; with others who have paid, we have compounded for a part of our demands for peace sake. Our situation is therefore{mor} very much more pleasant than it was last year. Our Manufactory goes on well under our sons management and we have more orders for Engines than ever, though the patent is nearly expiring

Mr. Boulton is now coining halfpence for government and will have authority to issue them in a few days. He keeps his health very well for a man of his age, though occasionally troubled with the Gravel, for which he drinks alcaline water

Mrs. Watt my Sons and other friends here desire to be kindly remembred to you and Join me in best Compliments to Professor and Mrs. Robison and other freinds with you—I have heard nothing of Mr. Roebuck since you wrote me. I suspose [sic] the vacation has prevented the decision of his cause. I shall be glad to hear of him

Wishing you a continuance of good health and happiness I remain

My Dear Sir
Your affectionate friend
James Watt

WATT TO BLACK

Cover addressed: 'Doctor Joseph Black/Edinburgh', endorsed in Watt's hand, 'To Dr. Black November 9th 1799 on Nitrous Oxide' and numbered '9'. Dol. There is also on the cover a calculation as follows:

'   3/213 at 1/4
          71
      ─────────────
      52/0/28/4/14   '

Heathfield Nov[embe]r 9th 1799

Dr. Black

My Dear Friend

I wrote to you a few days ago mentioning Some general facts about the Gaseous oxide and today received your kind letter which I immediately answer—I have never prepared any of that gas, but took a trial of it at the pneumatick institution at Clifton.[1]

It is prepared from the nitrate of Ammonia, they saturate vol[atile] Alkali with nitric acid, to neutrality by the test paper and evaporate slowly in Glass vessels to dryness. Ammonia must be added from time to time during the evaporation as it grows acid—This salt is put into a Glass retort and exposed to a heat of about 300°, ie untill it just emits air. If the heat is greater the Gas is partly decomposed and nitrous acid and azote are formed. The nose of the retort enters into a \Conical/ Glass

tube about 3 feet long   the other end of

which enters into the lower opening of one of my Air holders filled with water, which is gradualy displaced by the air, some of which is absorbed by it for which reason the same water is employed over and over again —The air should stand 24 hours before it is used that any nitrous acid which it contains may be absorbed. This is the substance of what I have been told concerning the preparation of it. The dose is from 3 to 7 quarts which is put into a bag without any admixture of common air. The patient breathes {into} out of and into the bag, holding his nose, until 1st rapid convulsive breathing and 2dly vertigo and feeling of suffocation ensue, then the nose being released, he inspires from the bag and expires through the nose until the air is exhausted—The time is from 1 to 1½ minute. I took first 2 quarts diluted with 4 of Common air without much effect, then 3 quarts with an equal quantity of Common air, the rapid breathing and commencement of vertigo took place and I felt a glow in my *Cold* (not *numbed*) leg. Soon after I took 4 quarts pure, and felt the same effects in a greater degree, my leg did not resume its coldness all that day, and I thought I felt *rather* more lightsome than usual but not very remarkably so, the day being hot and otherwise exhausting I had not headache or depression after it, but felt for an hour or two some uneasiness in the trachea such as I have felt from oxygene air, which gradualy went off. Mrs. Watt took some but said it would have made her hysterical if continued and complained much of the said uneasiness in the chest, as did a gentleman who took several doses of it in my presence It appears that like the other gasses it has very different effects on different people, but seems to hurt nobody's lungs as Mrs. Beddoes who has taken it often has been very lately recovered from a pulmonary complaint which threatned her life. As far as I have been able to learn from several of the parties who inspired it the accounts published of their sensations are perfectly Just, being in general taken {with} from their own written accounts—The first paralytic patient could walk about very well when I saw him \two months ago/ and confirmed the account the Dr. has published, the second was just admitted but was some what relieved. The taste of the air is slightly acid sweet and astringent, like a very weak solution of Sugar of lead—I am so much convinced of its efficacy that I am preparing to make some of it in hopes that it will cure my leg which is a very great grievance independant of the fear of its becoming paralytick—I have got some of the Salt which is prepared for Dr. Beddoes by a Chemist here, priced 8/6 per lb. At first it seems to disagree more or less with most patients but they seem soon to remark only its good effects and I believe that even the nervous and hysterical could soon to [sic] brought to use it beneficialy if given dilute and in small doses at first. I shall be happy if what I have said can be of any use to you or your friend—

It gives your friends here much pleasure to hear that the amend-[men]t of your health still continues, which I hope will carry you well through the Winter—My Worthy friend Dr. Withering had several very severe attacks of his disorder during the Spring and Summer which weakened him so much that he gradualy sunk under them during my abscence. His loss is very much felt by me both as a Physician and disinterested adviser in all my concerns, and he is generally lamented

We have received from the Cornish people between 30 and 40 M

310

which is much below what was due to us from the payers, but of which from various deductions I shall not be much the richer; but I can now sleep in peace Some of them as I mentioned still hold out, but I believe must Pay as we have brought actions ag[ains]t them in which they cannot now dispute the validity of the patent

I beg leave to recommend to you Mr. East a Student in medicine now at Edinburgh, who will call upon you, he is a modest young Man eager after knowlege and will not be troublesome

I am pinched for time so cannot Copy my letter, and may therefore make repetitions. Mrs. Watt Joins in best wishes and I remain

My Dear Sir
Your affect[iona]te friend
James Watt

[1] The inhalation of nitrous oxide at 'laughing gas' parties is often associated with Humphry Davy who was Beddoes's assistant at this time.

Letter 208

WATT TO BLACK

Cover addressed: 'Doctor Joseph Black/Edinburgh', endorsed in Watt's hand, 'To Dr. Black November 22d on nitrous oxide' and numbered '8'. Dol.

Dr. Black   *Heathfield Nov[embe]r 22d 1799*

My Dear Friend

Yesterday I was present at the preparation and trial, of some of this new air, at Dr. Carmichael's in Birm[ingha]m and as I expect that the particulars may be useful to you I have sent them below

The Nitrate was prepared by Cope and Biddle[1] chemists Birmingham, price 8/6 per lb I am informed they proceed as follows. To strong spirit of nitre Christallized Volatile] Alkali is added to saturation, some part immediately Christallizes and the remainder does so by evaporation, which is pushed to dryness

13 oz of this salt was put into a 3 pint Glass retort in a sand heat, and the neck of the retort connected with the Hydraulic bellows, of my pnematic appar[a]tus to the other side of which was adapted an air holder filled with water

The heat was raised untill the salt melted and begun to boil when it

311

begun to produce air, the production soon became rapid and filled the bellows, which was emptied into the air holder by discharging the water from the latter. Another air holder was applied, but though the furnace was dampt the salt boiled furiously and the production of air was proportioned so that we could not change the air holder without losing much air, that which escaped filled the place with nitrous fumes. The heat however abating the production grew less rapid towards the end. and finally the salt totaly evaporated and left the retort clean—In all about 3 cubic feet were obtained, besides what escaped—

After standing 4 hours about 6 quarts were taken out of the 1st Air holder, which was breathed by a Gentleman present for about 2 minutes, He was affected with vertigo and felt a thrilling and prickling in his hands and legs, which went off in about 10 minutes

Another person by a similar dose, or rather larger was affected in the same manner though in a greater degree   he could not stand and his eyes stared, he said he felt as if he had drunk too much wine, both these Gentlemen repeated the dose with the same effects. The air when they left off breathing still greatly increased the light of a candle—More \persons/ were willing to try but the air holder was exhausted. This air smelt of nitrous acid but was not acrid and neither of the Gent[leme]n complained of their throat or breast or any other permanent effect, nor had any of them any disposition to dance etc—The second air holder of air tasted so strong of aquafortis that nobody chose to take any of it. The third was considerably better, but not thought quite safe—All of them will probably become so when they have deposited the acid by a day or two standing—The error in the preparation was the using a sand heat, Dr. Beddoes uses a chaffing dish which he removes or covers when the salt boils much. He suspends his retort in an Iron wire cage.

I learn that the 1st patient at Clifton remains cured and is gone to work at his trade as a Taylor, that the second is in a fair way, and that they are making great progress with some very deplorable cases taken in since, to one of whom they have given 72 Quarts per day. There are also several consumptive patients who receive great benefit from living in Cowhouses and it appears that it is the effluvia of the Dung which produce the good effects.

Mrs. Watt Joins me in best wishes to you and friends and hopeing to hear from you soon I remain

My dear Sir
Your affect[ionat]e freind
James Watt

A Mr. Tuffen of London a very worthy friend of mine requested me to recommend his nephew Mr. Braune to you—I did not consent as I know your situation does not permit you, to be troubled with too many young men. He is an acquaintance of Mr. Este whom I mentioned to you before, but I believe not so well informed. If you should chuse to see him E. will bring him. I know not the Young man but his Uncle is one of the most benevolent and friendly men I know

¹ Cope and Biddle, chemists, Bradford Street, appear in the Birmingham directories from 1790 to 1818. The firm actually existed over a longer period. In 1788 it was John Cope, 40 High Street, and by 1823, John Cope, again, 43 High Street. This was probably John Cope junior. Mrs B. Biddle (ob. 1797) was a daughter of Sampson Lloyd.

Letter 209

BLACK TO WATT

Cover addressed: 'James Watt Esq./Heathfield/Birmingham/ by Ferrybridge', endorsed in Watt's hand, 'Dr. Black December 2d {1800} 1799   His last letter—' and numbered '8'. Dol.

Edinb[urgh] 2d Dec[embe]r 1799

My dear Freind

I am very much obliged to you for your three letters the last of which was of the 22d Nov[embe]r. They have given me much usefull and satisfactory information I have only 2 or 3 questions more to propose—1st Is your Air holder proof against acid Vapours and secure from being injured by them—2. How many Quarts are there in a cubic foot? I might learn this by looking into my books but I suppose you have the answer quite ready. 3dly. You say this Gas does not quicken the pulse nor hurt the Lungs and that Mrs. Beddoes who has been taking it has lately recovered from a pulmonary Complaint which threatned her Life—Pray what was this pulmonary Complaint—was it Homoptoe or Inflammation—and is her recovery imputed to her taking the Gas.

You Enquire for John Roebuck. I have not seen him these 4 or 5 months past. The two arbitrators on his affairs did not agree and therefore the Business passed (by original Contract) into the Hands of the Kings Sollicitor(Bob Blair) for a final decision   Roebuck from over anxiety to have it soon settled prevailed with me to write the Sollicitor a letter representing the extreme distress of his situation and begging a

313

Speedy Decision.† I fear this letter has given Offence, or that the Sollicitor dislikes the business or thinks John Roebucks demands a great deal too much At least I have not heard of any decision {yet}, although the Sol[icito]r was consulted in May. and I suppose J[ohn] R[oebuck] is ashamed to call on me, as he owes me a little money which he promised to pay when his dispute was decided. I did not expect however that he would be able to pay me even then. We have had for some weeks a state of the atmosphere almost stagnant attended at the same time with a humid Coldness—This and little indiscretions by visiting some of the Cold rooms of my house made me contract a Cold with stuffing of the Head and Stupidity but no material distress and now by my being more Cautious {it is} the Symptoms of it are almost gone, not quite however as you may perceive by this letter

I pray for all happyness to You and Yours, and our Freinds with you I have seen one of Mr. Boultons halfpence in the hands of Mr. Este. they are beautifull indeed; Have not yet seen Mr. Braune but shall remember him

Yours faithfully and affectionately
Joseph Black

† The words 'Speedy Decision' are written in larger letters, evidently for emphasis

Letter 210

WATT TO BLACK

Cover addressed: 'Doctor Joseph Black/Physician/Edinburgh',
endorsed in Watt's hand, 'To Dr. Black December 8th 1799 on
nitrous oxide' and numbered '7'. Dol.

Heathfield Dec[embe]r 8th 1799
Dr. Black

My Dear Friend

In answer to your question of the 2d inst[an]t I cannot say whether the air holders are *perfectly* proof against the acid vapours of the nitrate of amm[oni]a But Dr. Beddoes uses these air holders and I heard no complaint. I have used one twice and have yet seen no bad effects upon it. When well Jappanned I know they can resist aqua fortis itself for a long time. The vessel is out of all sight the most convenient for the purpose—2d a cubic foot contains $6\frac{1}{10}$ ale gallons, nearly, and each

314

gallon contains 4 quarts, consequently there are about 24½ quarts in a cubic foot, and the ale quart is that we measure air by—3d I have not heard of any persons lungs being injured by the Gas, except when it was manifestly acid and even then the injury was not permanent, in its proper state it is not any ways irritating has inded a subacid taste, but not so much as 1/20 of fixed air would give to common air—I do not know the nature of Mrs. Beddoes complaint, but that she was Hectic with cough and thought to have an incipient consumption, of which she was cured by Digitalis. This gazeous oxide was not given her as a remedy, but on the contrary she was by her husband forbid to take it. She however chose to have a will of her own and took it at the institution unknown to him, and afterwards continued it for the same reason other Ladies take brandy viz. the pleasure it gave her. I know Dr. B. considers [it] as dangerous in pulmonick complaints, on account of the quantity of oxygene it contains and its stimulating effects. It has hitherto only been prescribed as far as I know in cases of diminished sensibility such as palsy; but seems not proper in Hysteria and Epilepsy—

The nitrate seems to be difficultly prepared to be always of the same quality, Mr. Biddle who prepares it has made some parcels very deficient in powers while other parcels proved very good and the cause is not known—Mr. Davy told me that it cristallizes with very different proportions of ammonia and that much of the latter flies off during the evaporation. I am disposed to think that the very reverse process should be employed in makeing it that is followed namely, that instead of adding the dry cristallized amm[oni]a to the acid, the latter should be added gradualy to a strong solution of the amm[oni]a till it approached to neutrality. When there is too much ammonia it does not mix with the air, but sublimes in substance. Since I wrote you Mr. Biddle and some other gentlemen were preparing some of this gas and having no proper apparatus and a barometer tube of about 3/16 inch diameter to conduct the air from the retort to an inverted aqua fortis bottle in which they were to receive it. The retort was one of 3 pints contents and they had about 4 oz of the Salt. The heat was applied by a chaffing dish and a fire shovel interposed when the ebullition was too great; but as the salt takes violent fits of ebullition which do not soon subside by removing the heat, some of the salt boiled over and choaked their small tube, soon after which the retort burst with a loud report and threw the boiling salt and bits of the retort upon the faces and cloathes of the assistants—To avoid such accidents, the tube should be wide enough to embrace the neck of the retort at one end

315

and small enough to go easily into the lower orifice of the air holder at the other end and not less than 2 feet long.

I have prepared two small quantities of the gas operating only upon 2 oz of the salt. The first time I obtained only 2/3 of a 12 quart air holder, say 8 quarts, and all the salt was evaporated   I observed that I had dryed the salt before the fire until all the water of cristallization was gone or nearly so, and that the water of the air holder might have absorbed much of the air. Therefore in the second operation upon the same quantity I added some water, and used the former water in the air holder, I obtained 12 quarts of air and had between 2 and 3 drams of the salt remaining in the retort. The air in both cases was of an indifferent quality and did not produce the effects upon me that the air I had breathed at Clifton did, but brought on some acute Rheumatisms as the oxygene used to do, upon me—It however made a candle burn with an enlarged flame fully as much as oxigene would have done. I therefore suspect that it may be the ammonia which gives the peculiar virtue of this gas, especialy as in some cases Hydro carbonate produces similar warming effects

I am sorry to find you are indisposed, but hope that by a continuance of your usual precautions, you will soon get over it   The weather has been abominably damp, but is now drier and mild for the season, which I hope will prove beneficial to you—Your account of J.R. \John Roebuck/† tallies with my conjectures   he rates himself too highly and is too greedy of money. Every man must if he is prudent be content to move in the sphere which the world assigns him, and it is only superlative abilities which can set their opinions at defiance. I hope however that he is applying to some business to maintain him in the mean time. I remain always, Yours affectionately—James Watt

[Added in margin] We are all well here and all join in best wishes to you

† J. R. underlined in pencil and John Roebuck written above in pencil in another hand.

316

ROBISON TO WATT

Cover addressed: 'To James Watt Esq./Heathfield/Birmingham', endorsed in Watt's hand, 'Professor Robison December 11th 1799   Dr. Blacks death—on the Friday preceding' and numbered '23'. Dol.

Edin[bu]r[gh] Dec[embe]r 11 1799

My dear Sir

Colonel Burnet has devolved on me the mournful Task of informing You of the Loss of your dear freind Dr. Black, who died last Friday. Knowing how severely you must feel this long expected stroke, I should hardly have accepted of the unpleasant office, were it not in my power to tell you that his End was such as his most affectionate freind would wish; without a groan, and without warning. The Servant had set down his little dinner before him while he was busy with a Tinman about a pan for warming his Mess—Some time after, a Gentleman called—the Servant opened the door, and announced him the doctor sitting as usual, on the End of the Sopha, with his back to the door, and his legs lying along the Sopha. He made no answer, and John told the Gentleman that his Master was asleep, and desired him to call again —and then went down Stairs—but, recollecting that the doctor had scarcely had time to prepare and eat his little Mess, and that he never had observed him fall asleep at dinner before, he went up again, opened the door, and stepped forward till he could see his Masters face. He saw him with his Eyes shut, and having his Bason of Milk standing between his thighs, supported by his right hand—Thinking him asleep, and the Milk in no danger of spilling, he went back again, and shut the door—but as he was going down Stairs, his heart misgave him, and he returned, and came forward and called him by name pretty loud— got no answer—he then took hold of his hand, and felt all cold—in short, found, as he said, that his poor Master had given over living— the bason was not fully supported by its position, and was really kept up by Dr. Blacks hand

What an enviable close of Life—to every Man—and to our dear freind, it was inestimable—You know that his mind was elegance itself—He sometimes hinted his uneasyness at the thought of becoming silly, or slovenly, or squalid—and even of the last Struggle of life—and

317

could not bear the thought of any undecency of conduct or appearance —his wish was completely gratified—for life must have ceased without a pang—the Servant told me that for an hour there was not any change observable on his countenance—had skilful people been about him, that sweet countenance might have been preserved—when I saw him next morning the lips had been allowed to contract.

Dr. Black had been in remarkably good spirits ever since the beginning of Autumn, and was as busy as a Man hanging by his slender thread could be—He was scheming a new Laboratory, to be built by subscription, of which he was to be the Contriver and the Architect— and never was without some gentle occupation.—Elegance and propriety modelled every thought, and his every Sketch has a beauty which would be highly prized, if found at Herculaneum. *Quando ullum inveniemus parem?*

I think that You, my dear freind, and Mr Geddes of Leith, had the greatest share of Dr. Blacks esteem and affection. I am now proud of having had some of his attentions. You know well that he was both a sagacious and a delicate judge of character, and that Dr. Blacks favourable opinion[s] are an honour to any Man. I owe to him my first introduction to the notice and acquaintance of Men of Science and Worth, and his Countenance gave me more confidence in myself.— When I returned from London,\at/ the account which I gave him of your triumph over Hornblower and Co[mpany] he was delighted, even to tears. He said "it is very foolish, but I can't help it, when I hear of any thing good to Jamy Watt"

I think our excellent friend well away from a World that is no longer worth living in, and I envy his Situation, not tied to it by those whom he has brought into it, and must leave in it. We are posting as hard as we can to brutality and barbarism, and must, I think, soon shake hands w[i]t[h] confusion and calamity, I am decidedly of opinion that when Man ceases to respect himself as the subject of a moral government of the World, he will soon cease to think it beneath him to live like a brute, depending only on himself, and minding nothing but himself.—but enough of this

pray remember me to your Son James, and tell him that I received his Letter by Mr Este, but have been so ill, during the beginning of my annual labours, that I have had no Spirits to write to any person. Had I been in any tolerable health, I should have had much pleasure in the acquaintance of a person so well informed. But at present, I am unfit for every thing—besides, there is something about that Gentleman

318

which hinders me from trusting him with confidence. I am persuaded that we think very differently on some very interesting subjects. And now my dear Sir farewell—may the winter pass smoothly and all at your Fireside be hearty. So prays,

Your affectionate
Friend and Serv[an]t
John Robison

Please offer my best Compliments to
Mr. Boulton's Family

Letter 212

WATT TO ROBISON

J. P. Muirhead, *Mechanical Inventions of James Watt*, 1854, vol. II, pp. 263-64.

Heathfield, Dec[ember] 16th, 1799.

MY DEAR SIR,—Your letter of the 11th, containing the afflicting intelligence of Dr. Black's death, I received yesterday. I had written to him on the 8th in answer to one of his of the 2nd; but little did I think that it was our last correspondence, or that my friend no longer existed amongst the living! In that letter he had mentioned his having had a cold, from which, he said, he was considerably recovered, and hoped by his usual prudent management to be soon well!

His death was certainly often expected by us all, but of late we had been flattered by the accounts he gave of his improved health; so that when it happened, it was totally unexpected. In respect to himself, life has not for many years been very desirable; yet he had his enjoyments in his own schemes, and in the welfare of his friends, which no man enjoyed more, and with all his infirmities he was still an useful member of society, whose loss will be much felt.

Like you, I may say, to him I owe in great measure my being what I am; he taught me to reason and experiment in natural philosophy, and was always a true friend and adviser, whose loss will always be lamented while I live. We may all pray that our latter end may be like his; he has, truly, gone to sleep in the arms of his Creator, and been spared all the regrets attendant on a more lingering exit.

319

I could dwell longer on this subject, but regrets are unavailing, and only tend to enfeeble our own minds and make them less able to bear those ills we cannot avoid. Let us cherish the friends we have left, and do as much good as we can in our day! * *

Letter 213

ROBISON TO WATT

Cover addressed: 'To James Watt Esq./Heathfield/by Birmingham', endorsed in Watt's hand, 'Proffessor Robison December 18th 1799 about his undertaking to Edit Dr. B[lack]s Lectures   account of his first axquaintance with the Doctor with dates' and numbered '24'. Dol

Edin[bu]rg[h] Dec[embe]r 18 1799

My good Freind
    Let me begin by thanking you for your kind remembrance of my Son—and let me entreat you to add to the favour your good Advice It will be received from You with reverence, and will have great influence on his Conduct—He is out of Employm[en]t, and I am uneasy about his situation so far from me, and unoccupied—but to bring him away from Manchester would be burying him alive. An opportunity of speaking for him may chance to occur to You. Be assured that you will recommend a sober, sweet tempered, and good principled Youth, who has never offended me, or given me an hours serious disquiet. In talents, he is as I was at his Age—possesses scraps of many things, but without that vigour of mind that makes one well founded in any thing—and, like me, he has neglected his opportunities of scientific improvement, particularly in Mathematics. But, being fond of Natural knowledge and Mechanics, like me, he may yet bring up some of his Leeway. Mr. Houstoun assures me of his freedom from all bad habits or inclinations, sober and modest, tho' sometimes apt to speak as if better informed than he really is—but this is the usual foible of youth To your kindness I commend him.
    None of the faculty can say any thing distinctly on the immediate Cause of our dear friends death. I was mistaken in saying that he was

sitting with Legs up, on the Sopha—he was in his Chair, with his bason of Milk on his knees, supported by one hand, the other leaning on the Arm of the Chair, and his Chin resting on his breast, as he usually slept after dinner. Any extravasation in the Lungs must have provoked a Cough, or a wry face, or caused some movement. Mr Geo Bell, who saw him within five minutes after his death. (for the Servant had seen him alive about that time before) tells me that there was not the smallest appearance of his having had an uneasy sensation. He thinks that it was a paralytic affection of the diaphragm, of which the Dr. twice before complained to his father, saying that "he had {catched} caught himself forgetting to breathe"—The heart, beating but feebly, ceased at the first omission of a stimulus from the pulmonic Vein (I think it is called). I have heard that Col Townshend died in one of his exhibitions of stopping his heart, and that it was without the least struggle—So departed our friend

My first acquaintance with Dr. Black began in your Rooms, where you was rubbing up McFarlanes Instruments. Dr. Black used to come in, and, standing with his back to us, amuse himself with Birds Quadrant, whistling softly to himself, in a manner that thrilled me to the heart—I tryed to imitate him, and he came in one day while I was doing it, and was close up to me before I perceived him. I blushed, and he smiled, I thought good humouredly—Next evening I came in upon you by candle light—and you immediately said to me, rather coldly, that the professors had forbidden you to admit the Students—I was mortified, and imagined that I had offended Dr. Black by my whistling—But a few days afterwards I was drinking Tea with Mrs. Leishman was telling her some curious things that I had seen in a Coalpit of my father's. Dr. Black came in, and she repeated it to him. He turned to me very kindly and desired me to try whether a frog would live in the place (it was filled with choke damp) and said that he would like to know—You may be certain that I hasted to make the tryal—and took the first opportunity of meeting the doctor in the Area, to tell him that the frog lived well enough, tho' both Mice and Sparrows died instantly—In the End of 1758, when I went to Sea, and had a favour to ask of the professors, Dr. Black spoke very handsomely of me—this I learned at my return—but we had no further acquaintance till then, or rather till 1764, and his marked attention to me (as he told me not long ago) was owing to my saying distinctly, and giving reason for it, that Dr. Dick, my professor, had infinitely more knowledge than his Successor, who was much more popular. Indeed Dr.

321

Black has often said to me that dick was one of \the most/ sensible and manly fellows he ever knew. Thus did my acquaintance begin—and I have found him uniformly kind and friendly, without his giving me particular encouragement to cultivate closer intimacy My Wife happened to please him, in her taste both of dress and of \furniture/ and he soon saw that she was proud of his Approbation—this led him frequently into conversation on matters of ornament, of which he was a most delicate Judge—Of late he has frequently made my house a breathing place in his Walk, and chatted with Mrs. R. with great good humour and confidence. I believe none of his female freinds more tenderly regret his death.

But I am forgetting a principal purpose of my Letter. The doctors friends, confiding in my Regard, *have done me the honour* of proposing that I shall prepare his Chemical Writings for the press, and \have resolved\ to publish them without delay, to prevent imperfect publications from other hands. It would delight me to pay this last mark of my Respect—but my state of health is such that I am disposed to shrink from the task. My general health is without fault; but the pain I suffer never quits me one minute of my waking hours, and I am frequently, for a day together, so much tortured, that I cannot command my thoughts, or keep steady sight of an object Dr. Ferguson will be in town tomorrow, and we shall then look over the papers. If they seem to require much alteration, or study, my regard for the Reputation of our Freind obliges me to decline the Charge—But if not, and if you will promise me your assistance I will venture. during my College duty (till May) I will just transcribe without alteration—leaving a blank page on every leaf—I will come and take lodgings near You, and consult with you on doubtful occasions, and submit the whole to your correction— I think that it will not be an unacceptable occupation for some of your spare hours. You was much with the Dr. during his most important researches, and know \dates and/ anecdotes, which will support his Claims to originality and priority; and you can recollect some of the vehicles, by whom some of his thoughts became known to others. I may avail myself of this knowledge without committing You in the least—I trust that you will thus unite with me in this last Office of freindship, and will hope for your answer as soon as convenient. Mrs R and my Girl beg to be kindly remembered to Mrs. Watt—Adieu my dear Sir believe me

Your aff[ectiona]te Fr[ien]d
John Robison

322

Dec[embe]r 29. The foregoing was written ten days ago—and in that interval Col Burnett and Mr. Black have not ceased pressing me to undertake the agreeable task. I agreed to it on condition of having Dr. Fergusons assistance—He came to town the day before yesterday, and sent for me. From his discourse I imagined that he was going to undertake it, and I recommended strongly the solicitation of your help, of which he fully saw the importance. I was much surprised yesterday by Mr. Black coming to me, as if nothing had passed, and requiring my positive Answer whether I would be the Editor of his Uncles Writings —I said that as Dr. F certainly meant to take that Office on himself, I could not interfere, and that I thought that Dr. Blacks Reputation could not be in better hands, and that his Edition would come with singular propriety from so near a Relation, and one so eminent as a Writer—Mr B still insisted that it was a mistake, and that all with whom he had consulted named me as the fittest person—I would not however put myself in so awkward a situation with a Gentleman whom I greatly respected—This occasioned some Conversation at home with Dr. Ferguson   He came to me this Morning and told me that all that he thought of doing was to have a fair transcript made of the doctors Lectures; and that he imagined that this would be the most acceptable form in which they could appear—and that if it was thought proper by Dr. Blacks freinds, he should put his Name to that fact that the Edition was an authentic Copy of the Manuscript—but that he would never think of adding or abstracting a Word. Dr. Hope (who had the free use of every paper) having said that many Scraps were only memorandums, and that the Lectures on the elastic fluids have never been written anew, and only notes of accommodation to new opinions occasionally inserted—Therefore it appeared to others whom Mr. Black had consulted that the form of publication recommended by Dr. fferguson could not be rigidly adhered to, and Mr B was determined not to ahdere to it, but to allow more liberty to the Editor, w[hic]h w[oul]d necessarily require study, and a competent familiar acquaintance w[i]t[h] the subject—This being the Case, and Dr. Ferguson having said that such a task would be too serious for him to engage in— even if he thought it the proper way of proceeding, which he was not yet clear about—When he was so precise in his declaration, I then thought myself at liberty to accept of the Charge which so highly honoured me. For surely, to be in the public opinion a person well thought of by a Judge so sensible, so candid, and so severe, or at least so cautious as Dr. Black, is a great honour to any Man. But I wish that I

323

may not have allowed myself to {here} go out of my bounds, by this flattering proposal, and by the agreeable thought of paying this last respect to a highly valued person. I am perhaps, not enough aware of the difficulty of the task—especially in that part of it in which our freind's reputation is most critically concerned, the theory of latent heat, of the Equilibrium of heat, and the constitution of the permanently elastic fluids—This will demand a most minute attention, that I may be able to state with accuracy what were Dr. Blacks sentiments. I am in some hopes of finding among the papers of our dear Friend the plan, at least, of a complete Exposition of his Sentiments— For Mr Black shewed me yesterday a paper written by the doctor with his pencil, intended as a preface to a dissertation on these subjects, in which he speaks of himself always in the third person—This will be most valuable—But, my dear Sir, in the whole of my proceeding in this Matter, I have presumed to rely on your friendly Aid—You were much about him in that interesting time of his life, and knew his thoughts on these subjects at all times—You knew many dates, which are important, and even the train of his thoughts—You knew many experiments on which he rested—I know that, cautious as he was, he was so clear in his conception of the efficient Circumstances of an experiment, that when he had obtained one, sufficiently simple, he rested on it like a geometrical Axiom, and used to despise the multiplicity of experiments with which the Germans generally stuffed their writings—therefore he made but few—but they were simple, perspicuous, and conclusive; and I shall take Care to make him appear as he was—*simplex munditiis*—I think that it will not be a disagreeable occupation for you to help me in my Endeavour to shew our Freind to the World as he was for his inspiring elegance of thought, and his talent of exhibiting that thought in luminous plainness and simplicity   Alas alas I fear much that when I have done my best, and perhaps pleased the general public, those who enjoyed Dr. Blacks intimacy will say that I have made a grim or a clumsy picture—But I must not allow myself to despond, and you must help to keep up my flagging Wing

My plan is, in the first place to make a fair transcript of the doctors Lectures, with an intervening blank *Leaf* between every *page* This shall be either with my own hand, or \done/ in my sight—I shall thus be master of the whole, and for the Gaps which require to be filled up, and perhaps some things which may be omitted with *propriety*—Thus prepared, I will come to you—You will look over the MS, and point out what things require particular attention, and where a Note may be of Use, either to illustrate or confirm—You will also help me to judge what abridgment may be proper (if at all) in the description of apparatus and operations, which {are} were listened \with pleasure/ to by uninformed hearers, to whom every thing is new and mysterious, but which may seem rather inferior to a Man so eminent as Dr. Black— In short I wish, and I hope, to print nothing without *your* imprimatur

Mr Black tells me that he has found a large bundle of your Letters, all neatly rolled up in a Case, and dated on the Ends. He has not looked into any, being extremely delicate, I think, in every thing, and unwilling to look into affairs which do not concern him. You frequently wrote to Dr. Black on scientific Subjects, and communicated to him your exper-[imen]ts and I have been told that his sentiments were much influenced by what he had on your authority respecting the new doctrines. As you had the start of every person in the decomposition of Water. I imagine therefore that some valuable information may be had from this Corres-pondence—but Mr. Black thinks that your consent is necessary, before he opens a letter—because, said he, Mr. Watt may have communicated to my Uncle, in confidence, information of which he avails himself in his business, and has no intention to make it public. If you desire it, I make no doubt but that Mr. Black will send you the whole bundle unopened; for he seems a very gentlemanly young Man. The doctor indeed always spoke of him in terms of particular regard, and has made him the greatest sharer of his Fortune. This, in Feb[ruar]y last amounted to £18,700, and must now considerably exceed £20,000. It is divided into 10,000 Shares, and is parcelled out among a great Number of Nephews and Nieces. Several annuities revert to Mr Geo Black, besides the largest share in the present partition.† I am somewhat surprised at his having left nothing to Dr. ffergusons eldest son Adam, who seemed to have much of his Confidence, was much about him and was employed to transact little matters for him. The daughters get £400 apiece (200 shares). I do not hear any exceptions made to the distribution that Dr. Black has made. Mr. Geddes of Leith knows the situation of all his Rela-tions, and thinks the partition made with great judgment; with particular attention to the need which each individual has for his assistance, and even to the chance of his making a good use of it. He \the d[octo]r/ grounds the preference given to Mr Geo Black on the good opinion he entertains of him on account of the attention which he had paid to his Father, who had been unfortunate in business, and his Son made a handsome settle-ment of an annuity out of his own Salary. Again my dear sir Adieu—

† [Heavily deleted] If you recollect any little thing which the Dr made habitual use of

Let me hope to hear soon from you and that you will grant me the help I solicit. I shall make my Visit at any time that will least disturb you, and therefore beg to know when will be the most convenient. Keep, I pray, in kind remembrance

Your aff[ectiona]te Freind

J R

Letter 214

ROBISON TO GEORGE BLACK JUNIOR

No cover. Endorsed in an unidentified hand: 'Doctor Robison/ Edinburgh/December 1799'. Edinburgh University Library.

Buccleugh place dec[embe]r 21 1799

Dear Sir

When, through the partial suggestion of Mr Geddes, you turned your thoughts toward me as a person fit for conducting the publication of dr Blacks chemical Writings, and \when/ he hinted it to me, it surely was not surprising that I should be pleased with a thing that both did me so much honour, and would engage me in an occupation so agreeable as paying this public mark of my respect to your Uncles Name. Nor will you blame me for listening too willingly to the proposal, and perhaps thinking it more serious than You intended. It was too flattering not to be cherished by me.

But I have had time to cool a little, and to reflect on the weight of the Task which I was about to take upon me My Spirit is indeed most willing, but my ability to do any thing of this Nature is so cruelly hurt by the distraction of unceasing, and generally acute pain, that I dare scarcely venture to write for the public Eye, even in my own line. I fear therefore that I may make a worse figure on any other Subject—But what makes me most fearful is the precariousness of my Health. If the severity of this Winter should be unusually hard on me, it may unfit me for doing any thing, and thus, after depending on me, you may be disappointed Perhaps I ought not to trouble You with these anxieties of my own Mind, and should say at once that I dare not engage in the Employment. But I trust that your Goodness will make you pardon this fluctuation between my fears and my wishes to do a thing so much to my liking, and so honourable to me, if properly done

Allow me just to say that if any other person is proposed to You for this Office, that shall appear to dr Ferguson and others concerned, to be

326

qualified for the task, then I beg that you will not allow yourself to be swayed by any delicacy in regard to me, on account of what has already been said to me on the subject, or any expectations which that may have raised in me. I am so conscious of the risk you run by my bad health, that I shall acquiesce without repining, and be ready to give any assistance in my power—I repeat what I formerly said, that if Mr. Watt would undertake it, there is not a Man living who can do it so well, or do it with more delight. He is my superior in chemical knowledge and Experience, and was continually with Your Uncle during his most original Researches. I was in Russia during part of this time   If Mr Watt has not yet withdrawn himself so much from Business as to have Leisure for this Occupation, and if I shall undertake it, my resolution is to go to Birmingham as soon as my College duty is over (viz at the End of April) and \I/ will pass the Summer beside him, and submit every sheet to his Inspection. By thus availing myself of Mr. Watts knowledge, and his Zeal for dr Blacks fame, it may be hoped that our performances will not be unworthy of the public Notice

I naturally wish for dr Ferguson's coming to Town, that we may see distinctly in what condition the Chemical papers are. I shall then be able to judge with more precision whether I am able to fit them for impression

I trouble you with this, chiefly to set you free from every thought of indelicacy with respect to myself, if any other person has been pointed out as well qualified for conducting the Business, and I hope you will excuse my not doing it in person, because the trouble of dressing for going abroad is so fatiguing to me, and so apt to raise a fit of greater pain, that I go very little out.   I remain with great regard Dear Sir

Your most obed[ien]t
and faithful Serv[an]t
John Robison

Letter 215

EWART TO WATT

Endorsed in James Watt's hand, 'P. Ewart December 23d By Mr. Robison Junior' and numbered '37' in bundle labelled 'Miscellaneous 1799 and 1800'. Dol.

[December 23d 1799 Manchester]

Dear Sir

I am very sorry that I cannot have the pleasure of writing you this Christmas although I did hope at one time that I should have been able to avail myself of your kind invitation but particular circumstances prevent me from leaving home for more than a day or two at present—Mr. Robison feels himself much obliged to you for your kind attention—He is much liked here but it is very difficult for a young man to get into good employment in a Manufactory at present—I have applied in various quarters for him without success—We must wait for better times when people will probably have more occasion for young men—I beg to be kindly presented to Mrs. Watt and remembered to all friends and I remain with the greatest respect

Dear Sir
Your most obed[ien]t Serv[an]t
Peter Ewart

Letter 216

ROBISON TO GEORGE BLACK JUNIOR

Addressed: 'To George Black Esqr./Nicholson Street' and endorsed in an unidentified hand: 'Professor Robison/December 1799'. Edinburgh University Library.

Buccleugh place dec[embe]r 28 1799

Dear Sir,

Not being able to wait on you I am under the necessity of writing you a tedious letter, which I must entreat you to excuse

You cannot doubt but that I thought myself much honoured and gratifyd by the proposal made me by You and Col Burnett to be the Editor of your excellent Friends Chemical Writings. You know that I hesitated accepting of so flattering a proposal, because I feared that my precarious state of health might occasion a disappointment, after you had depended on me. I was less diffident (perhaps than I ought) of my abilities, because Mr Watts attachment to dr Black, and his regard for myself, insured me in every assistance from him, who knows more of the Science, and also of every thought of the doctor's concerning it than any man in Europe; and who would be the fittest Editor of all, if his Occupations and his health would allow him to undertake it

I declined looking at dr Blacks Papers till dr Ferguson should come to town, and was resolved to be greatly directed by him as to the form of the publication, whether it should profess to be an Edition of dr Blacks chemical Lectures, or a System of Chemistry extracted from them, in conformity to his views, and insisting particularly on his discoveries—I also relied on dr Fergusons judgment as to the Season most proper for the publication. I was therefore much pleased when I got a message yesterday from Mr Ferguson telling me that he waited for me at your house—and when I found that he was of the same opinion with myself as to the time of the publication, that it should not be thought of before next winter—this relieved me from my greatest fears—because when I have such time allowed me, I have little doubts of being able to execute the task—I can now, for the first time, say that I embrace your proposal of being the Editor, and that I shall not disappoint You

But I was somewhat surprised at first by dr Ferguson's speaking of looking out for some Student to copy the lectures fairly under his inspection. This looked as if he was thinking of taking charge of the Work —I could not but highly approve of it, as a thing becoming so near a Relative, and because the publication, under his Name, would derive great advantages from his Eminence as a philosopher and as a good writer. I therefore heartily acceded to every thing he said as to the propriety of having the Copyist in the house with him, and never quitting sight of a single paper. And when I heard dr Ferguson express himself sensible of the importance of Mr Watts informations and determined to obtain his help, I considered Your Uncles Writings and his Fame as in the best possible hands—I took my leave, and came home, perfectly satisfied, and thought no more of the Matter, presuming that every thing had been settled among dr Blacks Friends

But when You came to me this morning, and seemed to adhere to your first proposal, and still to consider me as the person engaged to execute this task, I was a good deal distressed. The proposal does me much honour, and I should have accepted of it with the greatest Satisfaction. But I cannot think of interfering in an Office, which dr Ferguson will discharge with so much propriety, and execute with credit to himself, and greatly to the satisfaction of the public. This would put me in a very unpleasant Situation with a Gentleman whom I greatly respect—perhaps I am mistaken in thinking that Dr Ferguson in[c]lines to be the Editor of his Friends Writings—But, even if I am mistaken, what you said this morning, "that it would be some time before He can have the Copyist in his house" would rob me of half of the time that I had allotted, and prevent me from getting Mr Watts Assistance—I had resolved to begin immediately to have the Lectures fairly copied, by my own hand, or in my sight—and then; being master of the subject, I would have gone to Birmingham.—Now if dr Ferguson keeps the papers, this plan is stopped completely

As things now stand, You must be sensible that any thing further on my part would be indelicate and improper, till dr Fergusons intentions are distinctly known.—I am ready to undertake the task, if it be entirely in my Offer, and if I get the papers in a few days—but I cannot interfere, nor take it upon me, unless it be my own Work and Study—I must be the responsible person—and there are articles which will require study. Those, in which dr Blacks Claims to discovery are most concerned, namely the doctrine of Heat, and all the new doctrines in Chemistry, will require it—for I am pretty certain that these Lectures are not written anew, but accommodated to the Creed of the day, rather containing an exposition of the opinions of others than dr Blacks decisions. I have heard him say that he would not be surprised at seeing all those doctrines overturned again—this does not look like complete acquiescence in those doctrines, and I expect to find such Articles in an imperfect State.— About such points I would converse at large with Mr Watt, but I could not ask him to write me long dissertations on them—Mr Watt is completely informed on those points, and I know that his Letters were the first grounds of dr Black's change of opinion—for Watt was the discoverer of the Composition of Water (which discovery is the Basis of all the new doctrines) and corresponded with the doctor about it—Such reasons make me anxious to have as much time as can be allowed. I should certainly publish nothing without dr Fergusons approbation, and should think myself much obliged to him for his assistance and Correction I have no experience as a Writer, and should therefore have great deference for his opinions in this respect—But I must act according to my best judgment in everything relating to the science, being responsible for a fair and accurate exposition of dr Blacks opinions. The Study must be my own.

I entreat your Excuse for this tiresome Letter—but You must be sensible that an Ecclaircissement is necessary on this point—whether dr Ferguson means to be the Editor, or whether that duty is to be entrusted to me—which-ever be your Resolution, you may depend on any help that is in my power—As I presume that my own Lectures on Chemistry, when I succeeded dr Black, may be considered as the fullest Copy of his Lectures (for I had no chemical knowledge but through him) they are at dr Ferguson's Service whenever he sh[ould] require them.

It will be obliging if you will take the trouble of informing me what is

330

the real state of the Matter, and whether th[ere] will be any occasion for
my thinking any more about it—I remain, with great Regard

Dear Sir
Your most obed[ien]t
and humble Serv[an]t
John Robison

To Geo. Black Esqr.

Letter 217

GEORGE BLACK TO WATT

Cover addressed: 'James Watt Esq./Birmingham' and endorsed
in Watt's hand, 'Geo Black Junior Edinburgh January 4th 1800
on Dr. Black's Death Professor Robison has undertaken to
publish his lectures. Has delivered to him all Mr. Watt's letters
in a sealed packet' and numbered '7'. Dol.

Edinburgh, 4 Jan[uary] 1800

Sir
     From the very strict friendship and Intimacy which subsisted between
You and My late Revered Uncle Doctor Black, I shoud immediately
have Written you upon my Coming to Edinburgh on the Melancholy
occasion of his death but found that Professor Robison had already done
so—That Gentleman has kindly undertaken to transmitt to posterity the
Lectures and Chemical Writings of our late Friend, in which He hopes to
derive much advantage from your Assistance, You being, as Mr.
Robison frequently expresses, the fittest Person in Europe to perform
the Task which He has undertaken, if your Health and other Avocations
woud permit it—From your being so zealous a Friend of My Uncles,
Might I presume to request, that you woud have the goodness to assist
Mr. Robison with any information which woud contribute to support
the high Character, which the Doctor has already established for Originality and Priority in Discovery—this is one Motive for publishing His
Writings and your kind Assistance will be considered a very particular
Obligation
     I have Collected all your Letters and given them Sealed up, in charge
to Mr. Robison, from them He Mr. Robison coud no doubt collect

331

much usefull Information, but woud not take the liberty of granting it, without your Permission—

Edinburgh 4th January 1800

I remain Sir Your Most
Obed[ien]t Servant
Geo. Black Jun[io]r

Letter 218

ROBISON TO GEORGE BLACK

Addressed: 'To Geo Black Esqr./S. Bridge Street' and endorsed in an unidentified hand: 'Doctor Robison/January 1800'. Edinburgh University Library.

Buccleugh place Jan[uar]y 18 1800

Dear Sir

I have attempted to make a scroll of an Agreement, but find it a task for which I am wholly unfit. I never have had occasion to do such a thing before, and know not how to set about it—I dont mean as to the Law forms, but even as to the Circumstances which both You and I must have in view. This ignorance or awkwardness has made me prolix, fearing that I should omit some necessary Circumstance—I have no anxiety in transacting a piece of Business [as] a Gentleman, when it is to be ended by ourselves—but when others may be concerned than either You or I, it is necessary to make it equally easy, and equally secure, for them also. Although I have my fears on this hand, on account of my frail Courage, yet I am not without hope that You and I shall bring it to a Close without any other.

You will please to put the scroll into the hands of your Attorney that he may immediately make a proper Scroll—I must show that to my assistant in such Matters, and shall then return it to you to be engrossed for signature etc

If you are not otherwise engaged I would beg that you would do me the favour of taking a bit of dinner with us tomorrow—Not being a College day I am less fatigued and more able to enjoy the pleasure of a friends Company. If you are otherwise engaged, I shall still hope to have the pleasure of seeing You before you leave this Country.

I am with great Esteem and Regard
Dear Sir
Your faithful
h[um]ble serv[an]t
J Robison

332

ROBISON TO GEORGE BLACK JUNIOR

No cover. Endorsed in an unidentified hand: 'Professor Robison January 1800'. Edinburgh University Library.

Buccleugh place Jan[uar]y 20 1800

Dear Sir

I have received the Chest You sent me, containing a number of paper Slips or Cases, each of which is titled in the hand writing of the late dr Black, purporting them to be the Manuscript Notes of his Chemical lectures, as he was accustomed to deliver them. They are numbered, by another hand, from No 1 to No 128, inclusive and appear to comprehend the whole Course of Lectures. The chest also contains a Copy of Notes taken by some Student in 1773, bound in four Volumes, and several parcels of old notes and extracts from different Authors; of which I cannot give a list.

As You have done me the honour to put these papers into my hand, that I may fit and prepare them for publication, I have looked thro' them with due attention. I find them to be, in many places, nothing more than Memorandums to speak from. In other places, the train of the subject is interrupted by repetitions from yesterdays lecture, or references to processes going forward in the Laboratory—Many of them are on scraps of paper, much altered and interleaved—and the whole are filled with chemical symbols and contractions

This being the state of the Manuscript, the arrangment proposed by dr Ferguson is impossible; and even the writing a fair Copy becomes a more intricate Business than I expected. To put the Manuscript in a form which will exhibit dr Blacks Sentiments with Fidelity, and after a manner not unworthy of him, will be a Work of much Study, and considerable delicacy.

I must presume that You entrust this to my Judgment, and to my regard for the Memory and Reputation of your late excellent friend; and that You authorise me to make such {alterations} \omissions of repetition or changes of expression/ as I think proper and even necessary for the appearance in print

On these conditions only I agree to take charge of this Business, because, without this liberty, I could not produce a Work fit for appearing under the Name of dr Black. I must further observe, that it may perhaps

333

appear advisable, in future Editions, to change the form of the Work, and to make additions to those merely elementary lectures, which dr. Black had adapted to the use of persons who were only entering on the Study of Chemistry—For this there are plenty of Materials, which dr Black has not thought proper to insert into his Course of daily Lectures.

The only form of Compensation for this Employment of my time that I think becoming myself is my having a share in the whole Copy Right, and in the profits derived from the Editions, or from the entire sale of the Copy Right; and I am willing that my Quantum or Proportion, whether the half, or the third, or any other proportion, shall be left to the decision of two Gentlemen, one chosen by You, and the other by me (or by persons deriving legal Authority from us) with power to them to choose an Umpire or thirdsman in case of difference in opinion. I will make these Gentlemen Judges of my Trouble, and will abide by their decision.

Please to consider the above, of which I send you another Copy, and if it meets with your Consent, be pleased to signify the same by a few lines subjoined to one of the Copies. I shall consider that as your acceptance of the conditions mentioned in it, and as my Authority for proceeding with the Work. This I shall enter on immediately, and will carry it forward with all the despatch that my health will permit, and I doubt not but that it shall be ready in the proper time for publication next Winter

I am, with great Esteem and regard

Dear Sir
Your faithful
humble serv[an]t
John Robison

Letter 220

WATT TO ROBISON

* B.R.L. Boulton and Watt Letter Books.

Prof[esso]r Robison   *Soho Feb[ruar]y 19 1800*

Dear Sir

The other day I received the packet of my letters to Dr. Black safe, and Mrs. Matthews desired me to say that she had delivered the other packet according to your directions, that she would have answered your kind

letter but had nothing to say in the postage. She desires her Comp-
[liment]s and that when you have any thing to do in which she can serve
you, you need make no apologies as she will not consider it as trouble

I have not yet looked over all the letters, having been much molested
lately with headaches and Rheumatisms that with the cold weather have
made me very stupid The latter disease has affected my hands very much
which makes writing awkward and painful, they however seem to be
mending

I made an attempt to procure a situation for your son with Messrs.
Peel, but have not succeeded I have not heard from him since he was informed of the result, but if anything else should occur I shall write to him

We have at present commenced an attack on M[ess]rs Hornblowers,
as our most cordial Enemies, but the trial cannot come on this term and
perhaps may be otherwise settled

I still think of being in Scotland the ensuing summer but previous to
that must make a short Journey into Wales

Mrs. Watt joins me in best wishes to you Mrs. Robison Miss Robison
and all your family, hoping you have got over the winter tolerably well,
of which we shall be glad to hear

I remain
Dear Sir
Your's affectionately
James Watt

Letter 221

ROBISON TO WATT

Cover addressed: 'To James Watt Esq./Heathfield/Birming-
ham'. endorsed in Watt's hand, 'Proffessor Robison February
25 1800 His sending to me my letters to Dr. B[lack]   Opinion
of Mr. De Luc—distillation *in vacuo*—Schemes for publishing
the lectures   French Chymists, Birth of his youngest son' and
numbered '25'. Dol.

[25 Feb[ruary] 1800]

My very good Freind
    don't be afraid of the length to which this letter may run, nor imagine
that it either requires immediate perusal, or will oblige you to write a
long, or indeed any Answer. I only ask the bestowal of a few minutes,

335

when you might otherwise be perhaps yawning and have nothing to do; and a little patience to read what I have to say, to be answered as you may find yourself in the humour.

Mr. George Black, with whom alone I have any connexion, is the Son of your Acquaintance Mr. George Black of Belfast. He left Edin[bu]r[gh] this day, and before we parted he put into my hands the sealed pacquet of your Letters. He had indeed sent me them several days ago, but sent for them again in order to put up some more which he had found in another place. A Gentleman of my Acquaintance is probably going to London by the West Road in a few days, and engages to put the packet into the charge of a Freind in Coventry who will get it conveyed to you in perfect safety; and if he does not do this he will deliver it to Mrs. Matthews with his own hand. One Letter from you remains in my hands Mr. Black saw it written by another hand, and relating (as he thought) entirely to the subject of latent heat. It is dated [blank] and contains a Series of most valuable Experiments, and I am happy that it has been retained, altho' it contains half a page of private Correspondence of no moment added by yourself. Mr. Black also gave me a Scroll of a Letter from Dr. Black to you, which points out to me the very thing I wish to be informed about. It is dated [blank] and alludes to some pressing instances from you to publish his peculiar doctrines and some profers by Mr de Luc and yourself to be his Editors. The doctor then says that he has already done a part of what you have pressed on him, and that it was his fixed Resolution to finish it next Summer—He also undertakes to add *your extensions of his doctrines, if agreeable to you, and some particular discoveries which were wholly your own*; the words have a stroke below by way of Emphasis. I presume that this relates to your Notions as to the Composition of Water, which was published in the transactions for 1784 —I have a very imperfect remembrance of a *tracasserie* w[hi]c[h] took place in the R[oyal] Society about the reading or printing of your paper—some partiality to Mr. Cavendish. But I forget the Circumstances. Without committing You in the smallest degree, I must surely give these things, w[i]t[h] the most accurate arrangement of dates that I can procure. Pray give me the necessary Information on this point —This same scroll of the doctors brings another thing to my remembrance. The doctor there speaks very highly of Mr. de Lucs Genius, and expresses great Confidence in his Candour, should he be his Editor. I remember, long before this, when I had read his Recherches sur les Modif[ications] de l'Atm[osphere] I had a different opinion of both—Dr. Hutton, from whom I had the book, thought as I did, viz

336

that Mr. de Luc had gotten some imperfect accounts of Dr. Blacks doctrine from some Swiss pupils (we recollected Chaillot, Odier, Silvestre, Perronneau and others) and that he had thus derived some notions of latent heat—the division of the therm[omete]r Scale, seemed also an unwarranted assumption, as a thing first done by himself—When I hinted these things to our freind, he did not seem to mind them much—But about 1785 or 6 found Hutton quite acharné against de Luc, and Dr. Black by no means pleased with him, either as a philosopher or as a Man of honour. I had not seen his *Meteorologie*, and wished to know his Notions of Electricity as an Agent in those operations of Nature. I remember the doctor's saying to me that I would find a great deal of Balderdash in it—and plagiarism from him and from Watt—and that he seemed out of humour. When I read the first volume and saw the *cold* account w[hi]c[h] he gave of Dr. Blacks doctrine, and afterwards saw the second part of that Volume, and your Letter in it, I became of Dr. Huttons opinion, and thought that the Man who had prevailed on you to repeat in his presence the leading Experiments, and, after all, did not acknowledge Dr. Black as the first Man *who had conceived Heat or Fire as a constituent part of all Fluid and Gases*, and who still continued to consider himself as having any Share, was not a person of Candour or delicate honour. The vague and indefinite expression in his Recherches is no foundation for any such Claim—it had no importance *in his own Eye* at the time—otherwise it would have *instantly modelled all his thoughts on the Subject*—The very undefined nature of those early, fleeting, thoughts makes them susceptible of any twist which it may afterwards be found convenient to give it—The *Recherches* are like a standing Net, placed to catch something of every discovery which shall be made as long as the World endures—When I read the abovementioned Scroll of a Letter, I no longer wondered at Dr. Blacks ill humour, and I am less pleased with Mr. de Luc ever since—Yet I should be sorry to do him any Injury through ignorance—and therefore I trust to you for information to preserve me from such a *faux pas*—

I find repeated Accounts in the Lectures of "Mr Watts project of distill[atio]n *in Vac[u]o*, and three different drawings of the apparatus, and an acc[oun]t of your Exper[imen]t in Edin[bu]r[gh]—but notes of Mem[orand]a to omit this and *several other Circumstances* (not mentioned). This is a caution to me to say little of it, and perhaps to omit some thing said by the doctor—this must be regulated by Yourself. I remember that when I taught about three Weeks for John Anderson, I took that opportunity of trying the boiling heats of different fluids *in Vacuo*, and gave Dr.

337

Black the gross Result, which he communicated in his Class. The proj-[ec]t of distilling *in Vacuo* struck me as very promising, and I had tried it with the very Apparatus with which I immediately imitated your seperate Condenser. I found that the same project had occurred to the doctor long before, for I find in a Mem[orandu]m book written *before* 1757 (while he was paying quarterly to his Laundress in Edin[bu]r[gh] \therefore probably a Student/) the following Mem[orandu]m "May distill[atio]n be carried on in Vacuo (in order to save fewel) with ad-vantage?" Indeed it is very obvious, and Fontana proposes it—but I think you told me that the sum of sensible and latent heat was rather greater in low temperatures and small pressures—Tell me how much of this should be made public.—In short, give me as much of your Correspondence with Dr. B as will tend to his honour, and what he would have printed himself.

There is one point which I beg you to consider carefully—Will it redound much to the doctor's Honour, or suit the high Rank he posses-ses at present, to be the Author of the best and plainest system of elementary chemistry, open to the comprehension of any thinking black-smith?—Or would it not be better to confine the publication to the doctrines of Heat, and the theory of Q[uick] Lime and the Gases—This will include all his philosophical Notions, and all that is *peculiarly his* — The only thing that can be said for the publication of the Course is that it *will certainly* sell well, and if we do not print it, *another will* (perhaps imperfectly and erroneously) from Notes taken by his hearers. It will be more profitable for me—but I wish rather to consult Dr. Blacks repu-tation—This puts me in mind of a further liberty which I mean to take with you. Mr. Black and I have agreed that the compensation for my labour is to be a share of the Copy-Right of the Work—to be deter-mined by two freinds. I shall name you as mine, because no person can so well judge of my labour. By the time you come to Glasgow, the greatest part will be done, and you will be able to form a very accurate opinion. I plainly see now (Feb[ruar]y 4) that it will be a more laborious Jobb than I first expected. The MS is full of repetitions, of allusions to processes going on—of Hints, from which the speaker is to enlarge etc. —And I see, on the whole, that the vigour of mind which urges on to investigation, and delights in experiment, has never been a strong feature of the doctors Character, and that he has been satisfied with a just conception of the subject, and with applying to his own purpose the observation and experiments of others. His small, very small share of health and animal spirits has long damped his scientific Ardour, and

338

he has even been indolent, and without the Assistance of yourself and some other friends, I question whether he would ever have put his doctrine of latent heat on a footing that would have given satisfaction to the public. He saw clearly the broad principle, and took no pains to ascertain by measurable experiments the equality of the absorbed and Emerging heats. A single Exper[imen]t of his own, and one of yours, are all that seem to be thought suffic[ien]t. But, particularly, when the French Chymists made the great Revolution and Mr. Guyots Letter in 1787 (which the d[octo]r shewed me) announced their new Nomenclature, so full of barbarisms in Language, and deficient in justness of Conception, saying that their great Object was to give the *Coup de Grace a la pauvre phlogistique*, and to make us forget every thing, even that there had been known such things as Fixed Air, Vitriolic Acid etc. etc., and when I endeavoured to rouse him to a resistance of this despotism, and Dr. Hutton urged him to correct the Nomenclature, and to preserve the Supremacy of Combustion, as almost forming the characteristic feature of Chemistry—the poor doctor said some days after, that he had been thinking of it, but that the multitude of things which must be combined before a correct Nomenclature could be formed, jaded and fatigued his Spirits, and made him unhappy In short, he indolently adopted the whole, and even the most flattering deference paid him by Mr. Lavoisier in his Letter, could not rouze him to consider himself as a Man that was looked up to by philosophers—His Answer to Lavoisier was more like a pupil than a Brother philosopher By the bye, Lavoisiers public treatment of Dr. Black in the Memoire by him and de la Place, accords very ill with this Letter, and shews the letter to be only the flummery of an arrogant Frenchman.—Since that time, our dear Friend found that he was no longer the Standard of chemical Science—and tho' I believe that he had no share of real Vanity, yet the incitement arising from consciousness of philosophical Rank in the Estimation of others, was now greatly diminished.—and hence forward Dr. Black seems to have turned his whole attention to rendering his Lectures as popular and profitable as possible, by a neat exhibition of Experiments.—he multiplied these, without any new Views—and I find all his subsequent writing to be nothing but scraps of correction, and \occasional/ accommodation to the antiphlogistic doctrines Yet surely there is a fair field of Speculation laid open to a philosophic Mind like Dr. Blacks by the facts which these new doctrines have brought together The Connection between the {parts} \particles/ of tangible Matter and the Cause of Heat and Light is now seen in many more

339

Situations—in a sort of Gradation, from the Arithmetical expansion of a Solid to the formation of a permanent Gas. The important truth that the immediate cause of chemical Union is a moving force, like Gravity, or any other pressure, is made evident, by its being counteracted by pressure, and therefore being of the same kind—the seemingly general law, that the differences of temperature indicated by equal expansions of the thermometer produce equal *multiplications* of the bulk of Vapours and Gases, promises much instruction as to the manner in which the expanding Cause is connected with the tangible Matter—But, alas, like our departed freind, I am only fretted by finding myself no longer able to make those exertions of Mind and Body that those objects and hopes incite me to. I have been obliged to drop some very interesting Subjects in my own line, and must not thing [think] of trying any Cruizes on the Chemical Coasts. Indeed I fear that I have undertaken a task above my strength—But you can safely see that it was flattering, in many points of View—and I hope not to discredit either the doctor or myself, if I only get a moderate relaxation from suffering. Add to this that these pressing times call for every exertion to help the boiling of one pot.

Colonel Burnet left this place yesterday for London, by the West Road, and has engaged to have your Letters sent safely to your hands—Mr. Lawson called here yesterday, but I was at my Class. My freind Mr. Houstoun is delighted with his Engine, and now disgusted with every other. He says he can't bear to look at his other Engine and \that/ the Winding Machine, which stands close by the side of yours, must come down as soon as any body will give him the price of old Iron for it. In the mean time, he says that it will put money into your pocket, for it is like the bungling Zany on the Stage, to shew off yours to advantage. I hope soon to see one in the hands of Mr Geddes at the Glass Works, who will also do it all Justice

This Lettre has been often interrupted. This day (Feb[ruar]y 25] I rec[eive]d yours, acknowledging the Rec[eip]t of the Papers, at which I am very glad. I sympathise sincerely with your increase of indisposition. But the Summer always brings some mitigation to the sufferings of frail people like you and me   I stand much in need of it, both because my continual Sufferings are sensibly and steadyly increased, and because every paroxysm alarms me. I have no assistance now, and a very little addition to my pain would put an end to my earning my Family's bread. I thank you for your kind remembrance of us, and your freindly Endeavours in behalf of my Son. I trust that he will not discredit them. But I am growing very uneasy about him, because no door seems to be open, and I now see too late, that my solicitude to give him Education, and some little Cultivation, is rather an obstruction to his advancement—Similis simili gaudet—Sansculotism is not without its influence even in England. Mrs. R and my daughter return their thanks and kind wishes. I don't know whether I told you that I have gotten an addition to my family, a fine little Boy, born in July, healthy and chearful, and now beginning to amuse me and to be amused by me. I find this a great acquisition, notwithstanding a serious thought sometimes stealing into my mind. I am infinitely delighted with observing the growth of its little Soul, and particularly with the numberless Instincts which formerly passed unheeded. I thank the French Atheists for more forcibly directing my attention to the Finger of God, which I discover in every awkward movement, and every wayward whim, They are all guardians of his life and growth and powers. I regret that I have not time to make Infancy, and the developement of our powers, my sole Study. I see many important things which have not been noticed—But I must recollect that he must be fed and clothed, and I must think of more profitable Subjects, contenting myself with amusement with my pretty plaything.

I have now tired your patience and shall give over, having nothing to entertain you with. I trust to our being both in better health and spirits when we meet in summer. Adieu then, and keep in your kind remembrance

My dear Sir
Your Sincerely aff[ectiona]te Fr[ien]d
John Robison
Edin[bu]r[gh] Feb[ruar]y 25 1800

Letter 222

WATT TO ROBISON

J. P. Muirhead, Mechanical Inventions of James Watt, 1853, vol. II, pp. 269-70.

Heathfield, March 7th 1800

* * My paper on the constituent parts of water was first written in a letter to Dr. Priestley, dated April 26th, 1783, and sent to him in

London, with a request he would lay it before the Royal Society. The notions it contained were scouted by those members to whom it [was] shown; and I thought it proper to desire it might not be read then, but lie in the President's hands, which it did till April 1784, when it was read, but was never printed, being superseded by a letter to Mr. De Luc upon the same subject, dated November 26th, 1783, which was read before the Society in April of 1784, and printed in the Transactions for that year, with a note in part explaining the delay; which see. ★ ★

Letter 223

ROBISON TO WATT

Cover addressed: 'To James Watt Esq./Heathfield/by Birmingham', endorsed in Watt's hand, 'J. Robison July 23d 1800 on Dr. B[lack]s Lectures   Mr. R[obison]s election to be a member of the Imp[eria]l Academy at Petersburgh' and numbered '26'. Dol.

Edin[bu]r[gh] July 23 1800

My dear Sir

during the Winter I could only keep an Amanuensis at work on Dr. Blacks Lectures, directing him to leave a blank wherever he was at any loss. This was not completed till the beginning of June. Since that time I have compared the transcript, he reading it while I looked at the doctors papers. I find that he has gone thro' the patch work with great Attention, and even Skill, when entangled in Scraps of various readings of which the good doctor himself has not always made his Choice—there are innumerable blanks marked x x x, where Dr. Black spoke off hand Allmost the whole of these were of very easy matters, which I supplied on the blank leaf as we went along—others are narrations of exper[imen]ts or descriptions of processes, and sometimes accounts of opinions which have had their day, and the like—of such I took a note—and when alone, I employ myself filling them up—I have hardly met with any thing that was new to me so as to be at much loss. Lest I forget it however I will mention one, w[hi]c[h] I beg you to inform me about—After describing the facts on which the latent heat of Steam is founded, and particularly its extrication in the condensation of Steam he adds "but there are other ways, besides the contact of cold bodies, by which Steam may be condensed, without

342

robbing it of its latent heat \when we shall see it emerge/" *Gunbarrel Exper[imen]t.* In a loose paper he has a memorandum about the Apparatus for this Experiment—viz a Gunbarrel w[hi]c[h] must be strong) fitted with an airtight piston having a little water boiling in it thro a small hole in the piston This barrel is to be set (I think) in a Glass Cylinder filled with boiling Water, and the piston (its hole being shut) is to be strongly pressed down—I do not see what ostensible appearance there is to be of the Condensation, and particularly of the emission of the latent heat. I think that the steam is to be condensed, but this will not be seen, nor will the 900° of emerging heat penetrate the barrel so as to make the water on the outside boil in such a manner as to make a shewy Class Experiment. If you know what is the proper form and phenomena (for it is very likely that I misconceive it) I beg you to tell me

I have been sadly mistaken as to the condition in which the Lectures stand, being misled by those I chanced to look over, and which had either been {so} well arranged at first or afterwards mostly transcribed By far the greater part are loose scraps of paper, patched and pasted over and over sending the reader backward and forward thro' several pages. They are full of references to processes going forwards, or which have been gone thro' in the Class, and pointings to things on the table—and thro' the whole, there is such an exertion to be plain that the language is always artless, and very often disgreeably redundant both in words and in phrases, turning the same thought over and over again. In short you can conceive nothing so unlike the elegance of conception and expression which was so conspicuous in our worthy freind. There is not two pages together that can appear in print in its present form. I am really in great distress. I was attached to Dr. Black by the most affectionate Respect, and I promised myself much pleasure in discharging my last duties by publishing what would support the high opinion entertained of him as among the first Chemical Philosophers (to say the least) in Europe and I do not think that this publication will do it, even tho' the language should be made more like a composition for the public Eye. The World expects from Dr. Black the refinements of Science—and the writings of the present day all affect a subtelty of reasoning, and a stated dissimilarity to the broad plain common sense arguments of former times. This is more expected from Dr. Black than from any Man—the Lectures contain nothing of all this. He abstains from all nice disquisition. I see that his great Aim has been to make a pleasing Course, exhibiting a very great number of the neatest Experiments, in which he eminently excelled. He was contented with the Character he has acquired, and he aims at originality of thought and view in no other part of the Course—His lectures on Heat are more than enough—more than is necessary for establishing his own doctrine. His theory of Lime is tedious beyond bearing and the reader (of any information) cannot but see the keeping up of the great discovery till the very last. The whole might be brought into 1/3 of the room by taking Magnesia before the Calcareous Earth. This however I cannot do—But the whole may still be compressed into half of its present size, and must be, for I cannot consent to the appearance of such spiritless composition. Our freind was fatigued {with} by the very thoughts of any composition which required long plans and Arrangements—Yet was he sensible of the procrastination in this Article, and has marked on the Cover "*this must be greatly shortened from prop[osition] 2d*

What greives me most is that the new doctrines came upon him when his health was bad, and he was much alarmed about his situation and he was quite unable for the fatigue of such nice discussion as was necessary for adopting them in a way worthy of Dr. Black, presenting in full force the superiority of the explanation of Combustion and calcination, and at the same time pointing out the philosophical difficulties which must still adhere to them. He saw them however [*sic*], nor did Hutton allow them to escape his notice; and he set about marking their consequences—But, after eight or ten days thinking on the subject, he said that it fretted him and depressed his Spirits, and he gave it up, and went into the Lavoisierian doctrines *tête basse*, more (I think) like a pupil than like a great Master. You know he never had much vigour of exertion, and now, seeing that the Chemical Throne was, at least, to be divided, he had no longer the incitement to painful study—He therefore contented himself with a piece meal accommodation of his Lectures to the new Opinions—and I do not think that he has done this neatly. Indeed he was then declining fast in health. In the Article *Inflam[matio]n* he gives a general Enunciation of the new opinion derived solely from the superior Weight of the incombustible remains[?] Then, in the *Acids* and their action in inflammables (which I always thought premature, even in the old theory) he says something of the decomposition of the Nitric Acid Then, having in the Theory of Lime evinced the existence of Fixed Air, and his notion of its sameness with the Air vitiated by Combustion and breathing, he takes occasion to say that this discovery excited Chimists to examine the eruptive

344

matters which occurred in other chemical processes, naming particularly Priestly and his discovery of phlog[isticate]d and dephlog[istic-
ate]d and Nitrous Airs, and Cavendishs discoveries of the Compos[itio]n
of Nitr. Acid and of Water—also Scheeles discoveries and Theories,
and then Lavoisiers juster notions of those flu[i]ds—In the Acc[oun]t of
Inflammable Substances he now gives the New doctrine of Combustion
{better} more pointedly but without (I think) sufficiently availing himself
of what he had already mentioned of the composition of W[ate]r and
N[itri]c Acid—In treating this Acid with ℣ he does this more distinctly,
and explains by it many chemical facts—And lastly, in considering the
calcination and reduction of metals, *but chiefly* the action of Nitric
Acid on Iron and on Mercury, he gives the doctrine in its complete
force—but I think that his transition from the Action of the Nitric
Acid on Alcohol to its action on Sugar, he makes a very improper
Episode on the Vegetable Acids and their reducibility to Vinegar—All
this is very different from the synthetic form which is always given
now to treatises of Chemistry, all of which begin with the Gazious
Fluids, as the most extensive Agents. I see plainly it was to free himself
from the heavy task of contriving a new Arrangement—He indeed
begins his particular doctrines with his reasons for not making a
particular Article of the Gases—what are they as a Class? Simple
substances having a certain union with Caloric—I may as well make a
Class of Solids, and of Fluids, and of Vapours—I am not at liberty to
alter his Method—and I shall have no difficulty in justifying it, if I be
allowed to give, in his Name, a full developement of reasons for
preferring it to the Synthetic method affected by the modern Chemists
—Dr. Blacks method is strictly analytical. The properties of an Alkali
are not completely understood till we have seen its peculiarities of
relation to the last of the Metals. Therefore it can be no objection that
the important properties of the Nitric Acid are not completely un-
folded till we have seen its Action on Mercury and Silver—and I
would warn the Students, in Limine, of the advantages of patiently
taking this gradual establishment of the most important doctrine in
Chemistry. They acquire a *most confident* knowledge of it, without
Effort, while they are learning something else. Had I begun by the
Acc[oun]t of the Gases, I must have contented myself with *a very
scanty* demonstration of the leading points, and I should have accustomed your Mind to the precipitate adoption of spacious Systems, which
seduce us by their seeming comprehensiveness, and their Systematic
explanation of every thing—this dazzles and fascinates the judgment,

and makes us contented with slight proofs provided our proportions are brilliant, and rich in their applications to other phenomena

I am ill situated here in this difficulty. I am little abroad to converse with others. I cannot find a true candid and intelligent frend of our departed Master, to whom I can safely tell my difficulties It [is] wonderful to me (who am little conversant with the World) to see the numberless ways in which a Man's conduct may be warped from the pure unmixed regard for the reputation of Dr. Black. I am really in doubt whether I should proceed further. I know that a large Edition will sell well, and be profitable to myself. But even if no more sacred principle swayed my conduct. I would not do a thing that would lessen the fame of the Man that I have so often praised for his Genius and his justness of thought. Vanity would hold back my hand. Ferguson says "Let us have an exact Copy of the Lectures—send it to the Bookseller, and you have no further charge. Sed longé alia est mihi mens. P.S.†—I come therefore to you my dear Sir as to one influenced by the same motives which made me fondly and rashly undertake this Task. I long to see you, and hope that you will devote some time to the perusal of the MS. It will not require Study for it is not in the minutiae of detail that I am dissatisfied with it, but in the broad lines and general complexion of the whole. I feel it in my power to free it from these defects, if I am only allowed a little liberty, which shall not deviate in one sentiment or fact from Dr. Black, and if they will give me a reasonable time. I must write every word of it over again with my own hand, or dictate it to an Amanuensis. Notwithstanding the time and labour it has already cost me, and which I could have employed profitably, I should be better pleased (at least in my present mood) with publishing nothing more than Dr. Blacks peculiar doctrines, because this will correspond to the public opinion of Dr. Black. But his Friends strongly urge the publication of the whole Course

I beg therefore my good freind, that you will inform me of the exact time you will be at Glasgow. There are some domestic Concerns that make it absolutely necessary for me to know beforehand how to appropriate my time. I trust that you will readily forgive me this importunity and will favour me as much as you can.

We are both sufficiently tired. I therefore bid you farewell begging you to offer my best Compliments to Mrs Watt and to all freinds, and believe me to be

Dear Sir
Yours most truly
John Robison

† or P.C.

Pray could you procure me one or two of Mr. Davidsons (I think his name is) Medals struck in honour of L[or]d Nelson's Victory

It will be agreeable to you to learn that on announcing the death of Dr. Black to the Imperial Academy of Petersburgh the President Baron Nicholay[1] an old Acquaintance named me as a person to suceed him as a foreign Member—and that the Emperor ratified the Motion, and I was unanimously elected—without a single Solicit[at]ion. von Nicholay named me as a Man well known to several of the Members Æpinus seconded the Motion—as did Euler[2] the Secretary. Lowitz[3] proposed another who is not named to me—The Emperor asked Dr. Rogerson about me—he spoke favourably, but very artfully and kindly declined any more, remanding the Emperor to General Kutuzof[4] under whom I had acted in the Marine Cadet Corps four Years, and who Rogerson knew to love me like his own Son—this clinched the Matter at once. Mr. Kutuzoff[4] also reminded His Majesty of an agreeable Anecdote which happened at a Masquerade at Peterhof the day that I was presented to him when Grand Duke—he smiled and said he was glad to hear so well of an old Acquaintance. I have received my diploma with a fine gilt Silver box holding the Seal

[1] Ludwig Heinrich von Nicolay (1737–1820), private secretary to the Prince von Galitzin in 1761, tutor to the Russian Crown Prince Paul, 1798–1803, President of the Imperial Academy of Sciences at St Petersburg.
[2] Leonhard Euler (1707–83), mathematician.
[3] J. T. Lowitz (1757–1804), physical chemist.
[4] Ivan Longinovich (Golenischev) Kutuzov (1729–1802), Admiral. For forty years head of the only naval training institution in Russia.

Letter 224

ROBISON TO GEORGE BLACK JUNIOR

No cover. Endorsed in an unidentified hand: 'Professor Robison August 1800'. Edinburgh University Library.

Edin[bu]r[gh] Aug[us]t 1 1800

Dear Sir

I doubt not but that you wonder at not having heard long before this how I go on with my task. I have just finished and revised the Transcript, and will here give you an account of my procedure.

During my own Lecture season I had an Amanuensis six hours a day at it—he was directed to leave a blank wherever he was at a loss, and

go forward. Every day I looked over the blanks, and noted them in a book. This was ended in the last week of May. We then began again. I took dr Blacks papers into my hand, and my scribe read over his Copy—I found that he had picked his way very well among the innumerable scraps, and patches, and alterations, and duplicate pages where it would seem that your Uncle had not made a final Choice—Very few mistakes had been made by my Clerk having been a pupil of dr Blacks, and a good Chemist—But I now found a puzzle of another kind many sentences followed by an etc or xxxx   I found these sentences to be merely Memorandums to lecture from extempore—there was no difficulty in them, being generally plain exper[imen]ts, or easy pieces of doctrine—These blanks I filled up as we went along—but they became more and more frequent as we advanced among the particular {doctrines} \properties/ of chemical bodies—and in many places these blanks took more writing by far than the text. I began to take fright, and almost lost courage, because I saw that they must multiply as we advanced. But, having undertaken the Task, and its being according to my own heart, I was resolved not to give up; and about eight days ago I got thro' it, only leaving two or three considerable Gaps, the filling up of which will require study and some enquiry into the state of chemical sentiments at present on those particular points.

I am now able to form a pretty just notion of the Impression which dr Blacks Lectures will make on the public, and will tell you my mind with that fidelity which your Confidence in me deserves at my hand. It will certainly be the clearest, simplest, and most intelligible Collection of Chemical knowledge in our Language; such that any sensible dyer or Blacksmith or druggist will understand completely, and by far the fittest for the elementary instruction of a Gentleman or any person entering

I see that your excellent Uncle made it his great Aim to be completely understood by the most illiterate of his hearers—and for this reason he avoids on all occasions all refined or abstruse reasonings, all subtile philosophical disquisition Indeed his slender thread of life, which required the utmost care to prevent it from snapping, made all intense study fatiguing to him. Satisfied with the clearness and justness of his conception of any point, he could put it in the same simple form and make it clear to the apprehension of his hearers without any abstruse reasoning—he never attempted to please their fancies with a fine theory which promised the explanation of everything; and he knew that his own discoveries gave him sufficient authority in all matters of controversy—therefore he never almost enters upon any chemical dispute—Unfortunately however the great Revolution in Chemical science happened just at the time that your Uncle was in very poor health and spirits—He saw at once the great value of Lavoisiers discoveries—but he also saw the difficulties and the cloud which still hangs over them, and he was for some time unwilling to subscribe to the new opinions. His dear friend dr Hutton, who fought the battle for poor phlogiston as long as he lived, strongly urged the dr not to give it up. I saw a letter from Mr Guyot which provoked me, shewing plainly that the new language in Chemistry was not so much intended for instructing the world as for securing the sovereignty in science to the French Junto. When I made this remark to Hutton, it made him mad and he urged dr Black day after day to state the objections to the new doctrines in their full force—dr Black accordingly began it—but after ten days, he told Hutton that intense thinking hurt him and sunk his Spirits and even hurt his health—He was resolved to adopt the chief of Lavoisiers doctrines because he thought them right, and folly in him to throw away his Comfort and his health in maintaining these objections—others would do this soon enough—and thus your Uncles low state of health made him really step down from the throne and modestly adopt Lavoisiers opinions in their whole extent.

I am in some measure sorry that the doctor went over so entirely—so like a pupil—he was no longer able to new mold his Lectures to these doctrines—He therefore lets the new system come in, by bits, among his old lectures, and has scarcely written a new page on these subjects, and has just patched them in among his old pages—not gracefully, and in one or two instances I think not properly—But I am not at liberty to make any changes in Your Uncles arrangement—These two instances however, I cannot allow to remain in their present form, and I must certainly put in about a couple of pages in support of his principle of Arrangement—Even this however I shall not do without Authority, but will avail myself of *some hints and thoughts for another Order*, which I find in a seperate parcel—Thus the book will \not/ contain a single thought that is not Dr. Blacks, and shall inform the Reader of this Insertion and my authority for it.

And now my dear sir it will perhaps surprise you to hear me say that I have some doubts whether the publication of your Uncles Class Lectures will answer your views. It is surely my interest to publish them, because I am certain that it will be a profitable work. But I doubt whether it will be suitable to the high Rank that dr Black so

349

deservedly holds in the public Eye. To be the Author of the best plain system of Chemistry will by no means hurt his fame—but it will not raise it—It is not this that is expected from him who was considered as the first of Chemical philosophers. The public looks for the highest refinements in the Science, and will perhaps be disappointed with not meeting with them—Beginners will be highly obliged by the publication—But those who give the Ton at present will see nothing that they look for. Besides, chemistry has been making prodigious strides since 1795, the last of dr Blacks years of activity. This, to be sure, could be added, but it would not be dr Blacks—My own wish would be to publish nothing but dr Blacks peculiar doctrines, namely his Theory of quicklime and discovery of the Gases, his principle for the Scale of the Thermometer, and his discovery of latent Heat—and I would not publish this in the form of his Lectures, but as extracted from his papers, and supported by dates and Notes, which will secure his claim to originality and priority in all these points—dr Ferguson seems to be of the same opinion

I make no Apology for this freedom of opinion, because I know that you and I have the same wish on the subject. I have already passed over the worst of the labour, and what is to come is little more than copying —therefore I ought to wish for publishing the whole—But do not take this as my decided opinion—Mr Watt is a complete Judge and is as much attached to the doctors memory as myself—I am to meet him at Glasgow, where he will pass the Autumn. I shall take the Manuscript with me and he will look over it—and our opinion will be formed

Mr. Geddes gives me some hopes of seeing You in this Country soon I long exceedingly for this, and will take it as a great favour if you will let me know the time of your coming over—direct for me here—and, if it be not too much trouble I would beg you also to write a few lines directed to J. R. of Boghall to Care of Ja[me]s Arthur Stabler Glasgow. I may chance to be at my farm, and this would probably save much time

Adieu my good sir. Pray forgive this tiresome Epistle, which has tried your patience. Mrs. Robison and my daughter desire to be kindly remembered to you, and will be happy to see you once more.

I remain with much Esteem

D[ea]r Sir
Your most obed[ien]t
and faithful Serv[an]t
John Robison

Letter 225

ROBISON TO WATT

Cover addressed: 'To Jas Watt Esq./at Miss McGregors/Argyle
Street/Glasgow', endorsed in Watt's hand, 'J. Robison September 9th 1800—his sending me Copies of Dr. B[lack]s lectures,
wants my opinion on what he should have for his Editorship—
French theories of combustion etc.' and numbered '27'. Dol.

Edin[bu]r[gh] Sep[tember] 9 1800

My dear Sir
   You doubtless wonder at my not having long ere now acknowledged the receipt of your obliging notification of your arrival at
Glasgow. I have been in such poor health and such dejection of Spirits
since that time, arising from mere fatigue of mind occasioned by some
things which have much engaged my thoughts, that I was really
unable to correspond with any person. An unlucky combination of
tasks which I had brought upon myself, some domestic concerns, and
a torrent of literary Abuse which was poured upon me from Germany,
all worked together on a Man fretted by unceasing pain, and, for the
first time, I think, in my life have put me out of temper. I have now
got pretty well through the thorns, and, were it not for the illness of
my little fondling, who is now suffering most severely by teething, I
think I could smile once more
   If these things had not so terribly crossed me and put every other
matter out of my thoughts, I should have sent You a Box containing
my Scroll of Dr. Blacks lectures, for the Sake of a chance that you
might sometimes have a leisure hour to look at it; hopeing by this to
find you a little more prepared to give me your opinion as to the
propriety of the publication. As I cannot be in Glasgow before the
End of next Week, I will still send them, and beg that you will bestow
an idle hour on them now and then. Please to keep in view these two
points 1st Will it be proper to publish them. 2d If they should be
published, what share of the Copy right will be a reasonable compensation to me. That you may the better judge of this matter I have
accompanied the Scroll with some of the original M.S, so selected as,
in my sincere opinion, and that of Dr Hope, to be an average specimen
of the state of the whole. I think they are better than the Average,
being on those Subjects in which Dr. Black took the greatest Interest.
The lectures on Vapour, as they appear in the Scroll, are more different

351

from the doctors Notes than any other—owing to this that by some mistake the proper Notes had been misplaced, and I had scarcely any but scraps to proceed upon—After having gone over all that were neatly classed in paper Cases, I found among a quantity of Rubbish, titled *Old Notes and Extracts from Books*, the genuine Lectures on Vapour, extremely confused and patched, indeed, but still much preferable to what I had employed, filling up blanks as I could   I have not yet transcribed these, because, by that time, I was completely tired of the Job. I presume that you will see that all must be written anew. If the style of Lecture is to be retained, still the language must be made fit for a printed composition. It will require some care to correct its negligences and pleonasms and yet retain its perspicuous simplicity— All allusions to yesterday, to things on the table or pans on the fire, must be omitted, without loseing any thought—I said, from the first, that I would not engage on any other terms than a share of the whole Copy-right, nor for a smaller share than 1/3d—I apprehend that you will not think me mistaken when I say that I could more easily write a System of Chemical Lectures containing those doctrines than make a Copy of Dr. Blacks MS Lectures, fit for publication

These are wonderful Steps which are every day making in Chemical Analysis—the Analysis of the Alkalis and Alkaline Earths by Guyton by Henry and others, will presently lead, I think to [the doctrine of] a reciprocal convertibility of all things into all. It brings to mind a Minister lecturing on the first Chapter of one of the Gospels, where, after reading "Adam begat Abel, and Abel begat" etc., to save himself the trouble of so much cramp names, he said "and so they all begat one another to the 15th Verse" I expect to see Alchymy revive, and \be/ as universally studied as ever.

I am delighted with Herschels discovery of refracted heat, and do not despair of finding heat refracted etc. by some bodies impervious to Light—and I think it now high time for some person to stand up for Combustion, if they will not for phlogiston. It is illogical and foolish to banish from Chemistry the name and the notion of the most remarkable phenomenon in material Nature, and thus sink it in the general fact of Oxygenation or deoxygenation. Combustion, or Fire if you will is the phenomenon the most peculiarly chemical—But in the Revolutionary Committee assembled at Paris in 1787 the new Nomenclature was resolved on, not more to promote Science than to fix the Scientific dominion of the Gallic philosophers, by making us forget everything which was not derived from them. I think this plain from Mr Guyots Letter to Dr. Black of that date, which I shall publish along with Mr. Lavoisier's

My good freind Mr. Huston is sadly tormented just now by the fire damp in his Colliery; and I counselled him to apply to you for advice, imagining that you know what have been the most successful schemes for getting protection from it. I hope I shall be able to carry him some instruction from you when I come to Glasgow—Mean time, I remain

d[ea]r Sir

Your faithful h[um]ble Serv[an]t

John Robison

Letter 226

ROBISON TO WATT

Cover addressed: 'To James Watt Esq./at Miss McGregor's/ Argyle Street/Glasgow', endorsed in Watt's hand, 'October 2nd 1800 J. Robison—Sending one of the MS delayed by his own illness—wants me to judge what his share of Profits should be comes to Glasgow soon' and numbered '18'. Dol.

Edin[bu]r[gh] Oct[ober] 2. 1800

My dear Sir

It must appear odd to you that you have not heard from me before now—But I have been exceedingly out of order for almost three weeks, and almost out of life, by an obstinate dysentery, which has kept me continually sick and languid and spiritless, so that I was really unable to make up the parcel of papers which I proposed to send you before our meeting

I now hope to be in Glasgow on Monday, and I trust to that freind-ship which has so long united us, that you will help me to discharge, with satisfaction to myself, the task which I so rashly undertook—I urge you to it also by your regard for my chief Object, the reputation of our honoured freind   I do not mean that you shall critically examine the whole papers—but merely that you shall look into them, in those Articles that you think most important—particularly the doctrine of latent heat, the theory of quick lime, and the Articles most connected with the theory of Combustion—the Management of the theory of quicklime appears to me peculiarly needing amendment and compression—his Students of a Second Year always complained of it as a tedious spinning out of the subject—and that they had the whole thing in their \heads/ before they were half through his detail

The lectures on Vapour also need amendment—you will be so kind as to compare my Scrolls with the original, and you will see that I was often at a loss what text to adhere to—but part of the difference was owing to another Cause. I did not find out the *real* original till after I had made it out in the best way I could, from another parcel put into the slip by mistake, and I have not yet made out another Copy.

Also (and I request this as a particular favour) try to form an opinion of the trouble I have had in making out the Scroll and the still greater trouble I must have in writing out a new Copy, fit for the press. I still hope, notwithstanding your gentle declinature, that you will accept the office of being my Arbiter—the other, or Mr Black's, will probably be Mr Geddes of the Leith Glass Works, with whom I am intimate, and who is as affectionately attached to Dr. Blacks reputation as either you or I, and \is a person/ of the most honourable way of thinking and acting. I am certain that I should not have undertaken the task, had I not been assured that you would have guarded me against doing any thing unbecoming Dr. Black—and I know none who is so able to judge of the labour of the task—the Arbitration does not require You to say how much money should be given me for my trouble. I engaged in it only on condition of having a certain share in the whole property or Copy Right—not only in the first Edition, but also in any future Editions; besides my property in any additions which may be necessary in order to introduce what new discoveries have been made since Dr. Black gave over altering his MS Lectures in 1796 or 7. I find that I shoud not be contented with less than one third—When you look into the d[octo]rs MS, and my Scroll, and think on what I must yet do, to make a Copy fit for the press, I am convinced that you will agree that I should have much less trouble in simply writing a System of Chemistry, containing a clear exposition of all Dr. Blacks peculiar doctrines, than in fitting his Lectures for the press—But it was not for profit that I undertook it. I hoped for doing Credit to myself, while I discharged my last duties to my freind—All I wish for is that I may not throw away my time, which is all my fortune, and what belongs to my family

I write all this, lest I should forget anything when we meet—for alas my memory of detached things now fails me most alarmingly. I shall remain in Glasgow, or within call of you, till the 25th of this Month, when I must return to open Shop for the Winter. I wish I could find a Bedchamber and Parlour any where in your immediate Neighbourhood—Pray desire Miss McGregor's Servant to enquire after such a thing—it will be more agreeable than the noise and smell of an Inn

Mrs. Robison joins me in best Compliments to Mrs. Watt and begs your acceptance of her best wishes, and thanks for your kind congratulations on the addition to our family. My daughter would also join, were she here, for you are high in her esteem. She has given us the greatest Satisfaction by her choice, preferring a richly cultivated Mind and great moral worth to advantages which I believe the majority of young Lasses would have prized much more. A Lady of distinction said to her Fancy I don't know whether the Misses envy you; but all the Mothers do. Find me another Willy Erskine, and he shall have either of mine he pleases (two very elegant young Ladies)—I am sure that you are pleased with such a happy termination of one of the first concerns of

Your aff[ectiona]te Freind

J Robison

Letter 227

ROBISON TO WATT

Endorsed in Watt's hand, 'J. Robison Glasgow October 1800 upon his arrangement of Dr. B[lack]s lectures'. Unnumbered but appearing between numbered 27 and 28 in the bundle. The date, however, is clearly after 2 October 1800. Dol.

[October 1800]

D[ea]r Sir

I am not able, even if I were so disposed, to teaze you further about the Lectures—only let me inform you that where you observe in the d[octor]s Manuscript a red pencil mark drawn thro certain paragraphs, they refer to omissions which he made in two short Courses which he was urged to give, much against his will—Where you meet with x x x x x you will see plainly, after a few instances, that they refer to extemporary speaking, being generally accounts of well known processes, or facts, or opinions—I have filled up some of them, in a sort, on the blank pages of the Scroll—but this was always done in haste, and must not be considered as what shall appear in print—frequently you will observe in them prolix, and sometimes confused enlargement —this was merely catching what then occurred, lest it should be forgotten when I came to write in earnest.

What you find *within* the blue covers were so put up by doctor Black and what is not within them, but in the same Case or slip, were also found so by me—hence I inferred that they were only Memorandums, making no part of the spoken Lectures—these were (I think) within the blue Cover. Even in these you may perhaps find that I have sometimes gone on a wrong Scent, and followed an improper paragraph of the MS.—in such places, I beg You to put this Mark ✗ in the Scrowl. This will make me cast about and perhaps recover the right track of the doctor's discourse—I was most puzzled, and still am, how to manage those passages which refer to yesterdays lectures, or to specimens and things on the Table—or to processes going on for the Students Instruction, and, not seldom, for their Amusement. Our freind knew that this was no less necessary for whoever wishes to be a popular professor. I became sensible of this at last—altho' the disposition which most people feel to keep up their thriep[1] has hitherto prevented me from making any change in my own mode of lecturing

The Article on which the quondam pupils will have their Curiosity most agog is what relates to Inflammation and the new Theories of Chemistry—I think that you will see that Dr. Black has gone over to Lavoisier rather indolently, and not like himself—As a professor, and conscious of his own Rank in the opinion of the public, he should have done somewhat more than merely acknowledged the Value of LaVoisiers Observations and Exper[imen]ts. He should have stated the Objections which a Philosopher would still make, and the impropriety of adopting as a demonstrative *System*, the source of almost every chemical fact, the consequences which the French *Junto* have *forced* on the World. In short, he should not appear as the humble pupil— But alas, at the time of this revolution in science our worthy friend was no longer able for any vigourous exertion, or such steady obstinate thinking as was necessary for all this—he tryed it, and it not only jaded him before the end of a week, but it really made him ill, and Dr. Hutton gave over urging him. That he had some thoughts of going into this System, tete basse, appears from a sketch of a new plan of Lectures which you will find in the first parcel, stuck in under the

[1] N.E.D.: discussion, argument, strife.

strings—These are all the documents I can find of his plans. I have a complete series of all his arrangements of daily lectures and experiments with the preparations for a future lecture etc. But I see that he has not always adhered strictly to it. I am clear that considering the imperfect state of the science, Dr. Black did wisely, and philosophically, in not adopting the system which that plan indicates. To begin with the Gases, before any thing is known of the substances which are the subjects of those experiments on which the Existence and distinguishing properties of the Gases are founded, must have obliged him to content himself with very narrow and indistinct Evidence of the leading principle—the Student would be dazzled as he proceeds, with the happy and universal application to every phenomenon He would have been equally pleased, but the doctor begun thus "Suppose Gentlemen that our atmospheric Air consists of the three following substances having the following properties etc. etc." The student would have considered the happy application to the phenomena as complete evidence of the principle—This is the ruin of philosophy— Dr. Black, by adhering to his former Arrangements, brings out the very same general doctrines—but by degrees—by slow degrees are the various phen[omen]a of Nitrous Acid developed—and the existence and extensive agency of Oxygen is the result of an easy process, every step of which is convincing—this is Baconic, and in the order of Nature, but it wants the form of Synthetic Proposition and Corollary

When I touched on this in a former letter I hinted my intention of prefacing the *particular* doctrines with an *Apology* for the Author's abiding by his old Method—but now I shall preface it by a scientific *defence* of it, as the only proper method in an experimental science— You see however that Lavoisier (this is not surprising) and all his followers take the Systematic method—Nothing now pleases but a System—and Principle which will bend to nothing

I have put the MS on Mercury in the box—because it is there that the Evidence for the new doctrines may be considered as closed—a little occurs in the first lecture on Gold and Silver—but this is but little I will not trouble you further till you send me word that you wish to see me—My best Compliments to Mrs. Watt

I am

d[ea]r Sir

Yours truly

J. Robison

Letter 228

ROBISON TO WATT

Cover addressed: 'To Mr. Watt', endorsed in Watt's hand, 'J. Robison Glasgow October 1800 on Dr. B[lack]s lectures Dr. Crawford—Dr. Irvin' and numbered '29'. Dol.

[*October 1800*]

Dear Sir

Having extracted what appeared useful from the two Letters, I return them—I forgot to bid you attend to the manner in which Dr. Black has brought in the labours of Scheele,[1] Priestly, McBride,[2] Cavendish[3] and Yourself—Is it not awkward—head and shoulders—and could it not be rendered more smoothly flowing from the subject, without doing violence to the fidelity of the Edition. I think that this might be done merely by introducing each Gas just when it first appears as a chemical Agent, or where the Evidence for its Existence is most simple and uncontrovertible. Then the Authors are secured in their claim to originality or priority by carefully marking the dates. By the bye I should have brought You the MS of the Article Iron, where the knowledge of the composition of Water appears most necessary, and where the French Chemists have shewn the greatest Ingenuity—But as this part of the M.S. is (as far as I recollect) sufficiently distinct, and the Scrowl sufficiently clear, you have no difficulty. You would much oblige me if you would, in some idle hour, put down your notion of the *modus operandi* of the Galvanic Influence in the exper[imen]ts of Nicholson, Carlile, and Cruikshanks—I hear that davy, Dr. Beddoeses Man \has discovered/ that one End of Volta's Pile invariably detaches Hydrogen alone, and the other as invariably detaches Oxygen. I do not think that this will make the conception any easier—I wish exceedingly to meet with you in Edin[bu]r[gh]. My pile, consisting of 72 pieces of each Metal, is well fitted up I think, for a variety of experiments but I have not been able as yet to make much use of it. A very intelligent Chemist, a young Student, has promised me his attendance as soon as I return—I hope you will point out to me any thing that promises information—You will surely be so good as call on Mrs. Robison altho I should not be returned (which will not be till the 25th), and if you could forewarn her, so that she might bring Mr Geddes and You together it would give me great satisfaction

When you consider the hints for further Consideration by Dr.

358

Black which I left with you on Saturday, you will see that he has never troubled himself much with speculations on the immediate mode of action of particle on particle. his notion of rival attractions, and of one attraction weakening another etc. are not like those of a person accustomed to consider mechanical actions with that obstinate simplicity that is indispensably necessary for clear conceptions and accurate reasoning. Indeed I think all such speculations useless for the promotion of genuine *chemical* science, except as they may occasionally serve for exposing the futility of some attempts to the explanation of phenomena which are obtruded on the public

I find I was wrong in not looking at the letters which relate to the decomposing the Common Salt for the Alkali—in the history of that Article it would be unpardonable to omit Dr. Blacks claim to originality, and perhaps priority. If it be not too much trouble for you, it would greatly oblige me could you give me an account of it in a few lines, containing the dates and those of Mr Kiers Scheme, in as far as you judge yourself at liberty—If there be any thing in Dr. Blacks Scheme which you think proper to retain, I ask no more than what is necessary for establishing his Claim

I pray you also be so kind (if not in writing, yet in a *formal* intimation *vivâ voce*) as to tell me the story of Dr. Irvin and Craufurd—When I was with you my attention was distracted by too many things, and I forgot most of them—I think you say that *You* began to think the enquiry of the quantities of Heat necessary for equally raising the temp[eratu]re of bodies, of importance and made some exp[erimen]ts— on what?—when?—that Dr. Black made some what and when?— that Irwin [*sic*] made many—I have a great list, neatly written and calculated by the doctor, and dated—they all speak of the *Equilibrium* of Heat—you said that Crawfurd introduced *Capacity*, a mighty invention, but which set him on Tall Stilts, and has made him a great philosopher—Surely Cr[aufur]d did not attend Dr. Black—I think he attended my last Course—he certainly attended Dr. Irwin [*sic*], and there he *must* have heard the doctrine of changeable Equilibrium, and even Dr. Irwins application of it to liquefaction and Evaporation— and perhaps to the search of the absolute heat—I knew Crawfurd—he dined with us at Mrs. Lindsays two years ago When I left Gl[asg]o[w] he was incapable of conceiving the possibility of discovering the Zero of heat by means of the emerged heat and the proportions of the absolute heats—on the other hand Irvine had a clear conception, had a true mathematical taste, and delighted in reducing every thing to measure by means of Equations. He hunted for opportunities of doing this, and was very quick sighted in discovering the means of procedure Willy Traill and he were almost constantly occupied in this way. This problem therefore was most likely to occur to one or other of those youths but had few charms for one like Crawfurd—How he afterwards contracted a liking for such things I don't know, and am persuaded that some friend has helped him to the mathematical solutions—What was it that Pat Wilson awarded to him against Irvine—be prepared to tell me all this when I see you again—and pray tell me how long I may expect to have you in Glasgow—this will greatly affect my motions—

Pardon this long Bore from

Yours ever J Robison

Also tell me the names of the Swedes, Genevois or others who transfused Dr. Blacks thoughts clandestinely—was Chaillot able—I have heard him boast of his acquaintance with the *Sçavans* of Geneva

[1] Carl Wilhelm Scheele (1724–86), chemist. The discoverer of oxygene, chlorine, manganese, etc.

[2] David MacBride (1726–78), a Dublin surgeon, studied in Glasgow, author of *Experimental Essays*, London, 1767, which included an important section on 'fixed air'.

[3] Henry Cavendish (1731–1810), grandson of the 2nd Duke of Devonshire, and chemist.

Letter 229

ROBISON TO GEORGE BLACK JUNIOR

No cover or endorsement. Edinburgh University Library.

Boghall near Glasgow Oct[obe]r 18 1800

Dear Sir

I imagine that You was almost beginning to despair of hearing from this quarter, or any thing further about Your Uncles Lectures. Indeed it was not till within these very few days that I was in a condition to form a decided opinion about them, as I told you that I had such confidence in Mr Watts opinion. Many things, and particularly distress in my family, by the sickness of my little Infant, have put it out of my power to leave Edin[bu]r[gh] sooner. Mr Watt also was rambling among his relations in the highlands—At last we met, and Mr Watt took the papers into very serious examination. He was at first inclined to wish that the publication had not been thought or spoken of, but as the

360

public were made to expect it, he thinks that this should not be disappointed, and he imagines that the book will meet with a very favourable reception if conducted in a proper manner. About this we had much conversation, and we have come to a perfect agreement as to the Style of Composition that must be adhered to. This is, in short, to make the Work merely the Lectures as delivered in the Class, without making any attempt to give them a more correct and systematic form. Mr Watt has given me another Notion of the subject from what I had allowed myself gradually to form. He considers it as a *History of Chemistry*, for forty years, by one of its greatest Masters. dr Black never attempted to give a *System* of Chemistry. He was unfriendly to all systems of an experimental Science, and with respect to chemistry, he thought a system was an Absurdity, because, altho' we think ourselves very wise, and have made many discoveries in it, the science is still but beginning, in its Infancy, and therefore it is nonsense to pretend to teach a system of it. dr Black pretended no such thing—but to make his hearers good Chemists—not able to talk about theories, but able to examine the Chemical properties of bodies, and to apply their knowledge to the various purposes of Life which depend on Chemistry. His Lectures therefore *profess no system*, and, for this reason, may chance to be little thought of by the refined Theorists. But they will contain complete Instruction for those who are not acquainted with Chemistry, and wish to learn it. The philosophers, who want only Refinements and new discoveries, will perhaps be disappointed—the System mongers will throw the book aside—But the public will be instructed.

Such is the View that Mr Watt entertains of the Work, and I believe it to be a very just one. There is no man better informed, both with respect to all the new chemical discoveries, and the new doctrines, and with respect to what is most wished for by the generality of Readers. These considerations have overcome the Reluctance which I had to publish any thing that I thought unlike dr Blacks profound Views—The simplicity which runs thro' the whole, and which makes it look more like the work of an operative chemist than that of a great philosopher, is a high recommendation of the performance

As soon as I return to Edin[bu]r[gh] (in a fortnight) I shall begin, and shall not cease till I have written the whole over for the Press—But, as all this must be the Work of my own hand, it cannot be accomplished soon. I think that I may begin to print the first part about June or July, and it will be finished about Christmass, and while this is going on at the press, the second part will be getting ready, so that the press may go on—It will not perhaps be proper to begin dealing with the Book-sellers till this first part be ready—this will give them something to judge by. Mr Blacks [sic], who live in London, will take charge of this Matter, or will at least give their Assistance. I am not certain but that it will be necessary for me to employ some Artist to make drawings of the various Apparatus, furnaces etc which are minutely described in the Course of the Work. I presume that the Expence attending this will be considered as chargeable on my Employers, and perhaps also the Expence of writing out the first Scrowl from the doctors detached papers—as to the second or fair Copy corrected for the press, that is the Work in which I am employed, and for which I am to be compensated by a share in the Copy right—I have not yet been able to prevail on Mr Watt to be my Arbiter, but I still hope to succeed—No Man can judge so well, and no Man will do it more honourably.

I have trespassed most unmercifully on your patience, but really I could not but give you an account of the measures that were to be adopted —We have only now to wish success to the Work. I must wish for some health, to enable me to go through with it. I fear that it will be a tough Jobb, but a willing heart can do a great deal. It will be a great Encouragement to me to have the pleasure of a letter from you now and then. I should be sorry that an acquaintance, begun in a business, more of affection than of gain, should be confined to this single subject. True indeed I am aged and frail, while you are in the prime and vigour of Life, so that we are not just the most suitable Companions for a bottle. But a Gentleman esteemed by so good a Judge as dr Black will always be highly prized by me, and I would also flatter myself that a plain old fashioned Man, who was not (I hope) unacceptable to your Uncle, will not be thought unworthy of your friendly remembrance. If any of your friends are coming this Way, or young Men coming to their studies, and you think that my *sober family* can give them any entertainment, you will do me a favour by making me acquainted with them. Alas, my house is much soberer than when you was here. My daughter has grown weary of it, and \has/ chosen a Com-panion for herself, and Mrs R and I am left to play darby and Joan by ourselves. I thank heaven however that she has not gone far from us But still it makes a great blank at our fireside—I shall be much pleased to hear that you have also taken a Companion to yourself. I don't consider a Man as making a steady part of the Community till he fixes himself by taking a Wife. He does every thing with a double Relish when he sees a beloved Object the better for it, and sharing it with him

362

—Forgive all this prattle, and recollect that I am always the professor, giving advice and instruction to such as will take it. don't follow your Uncle in this particular, but secure some body at home to keep you Company in the long nights of Winter. This is much pleasanter than writing Lectures and leaving your friends to find an Editor—publish your own works in the shape of pretty little Boys and Girls—these far excel volumes in 4°—But enough of this nonsense—God bless you whether married or single—Let me have the pleasure of hearing from you at your leisure—and believe me in great sincerity

Dear Sir   Your's
J. Robison

Letter 230

ROBISON TO WATT

Cover addressed: 'To Mr. Watt care of/Miss McGregor/Argyle Street', readdressed 'care of Miss Cochran/Crawfordsdyke/ Greenock', endorsed in Watt's hand, 'J. Robison Boghall October 19 1800   Mr. Geddes's engine   Mr. Lowitz experiments on the crystalization of salts, by presenting a crystal of the kind', and numbered '30'. Dol.

19 October 1800

Dear Sir

I am quite ignorant how far it is in your power to further the suit of my freind Mr Geddes, but I earnestly join in the Request, and assure you that you cannot bestow a favour on a Man more worthy of it, not only by reason of his uncommon talents as a Man of business but also for the honour and liberality of his Sentiments and Conduct. I may add that I know none who will be more zealous or more successful in supporting your well earned Reputation. I therefore put him into your hands hoping that you may be able to give such orders as will both insure the excellency of the Engine and hasten its appearance at Leith—Altho' you may think the business of Scotland but a trifle, I am confident that it will not be unacceptable to you to have an Engine in Mr. Geddeses hands with a Rival or two in the Neighbourhood. It is such a thing as you should wish

I have a letter just now from Mrs. Robison, who begs to be kindly

363

remembered by You and Mrs. Watt. She bids me tell you that she had some time ago a letter from Miss Alston, anxiously enquiring whether Mrs. Watt and You were to be in Edin[bu]r[gh]. Miss Alston has been staying for some time at a Mr. Nobles at Lasswade near Edin[bu]r[gh], so that if Mrs. Watt writes by such addresse the Letter will reach Miss Alston   As I shall be here all this Week, and shall not go to Edin[bu]r[gh] till Sunday the 26th, you may order the papers to be nailed up, and I will send for them on Saturday—I hope still to meet with you in Edin[bu]r[gh]—Lest I should forget it, I wish you would mark such Notes as you think proper concerning the Mineral Alkali Affair   do you think that any thing can be made of it by the help of that pretty observation of Lowitzes, that if you touch a mixed saturated solution of Glauber Salt and Allum with a fragment of Glaubers Salt, that Salt only shoots into Crystals—or the Allum if you touch it with Alum—If therefore potash, saturated with fixed Air, be mixed with common Salt, and it be just ready to shoot, might not a crystal of very mild Soda have a similar effect

Pray are the Models or sections of Engines which you exhibited during the Law process of any further Use to you—if not, I should like to have them, and chearfully pay a reasonable price for them particularly that series which exhibited the Engine in its diff[eren]t Stages

Adieu and believe me
Yours always
J Robison

Boghall Oct[obe]r 19

Letter 231

ROBISON TO GEORGE BLACK JUNIOR

Addressed: 'Mr. Black' and endorsed in an unidentified hand: 'Doctor Robison January 1800'. Edinburgh University Library. 'January', however, is clearly too early for 1800. Perhaps January 1801.

[January 1801]

Dear Sir

I was surprised, the other day when Mr Geddes told me that dr Ferguson had expressed himself as hurt by not having had a Sight of the

364

Copy taken from dr Blacks Notes. There was nothing I so much wished for as his opinion, he being a Gentleman eminently qualifyed to judge of the propriety of the publication, and the way and form in which it should be brought forward.

As soon as the Copy was nearly completed, I put that Copy, and great part of the Original into a Box, with a Letter to dr Ferguson, directing his attention to those parts in which I thought the Notes most imperfect etc and I begged him to look them over, with the pen in his hand, to make his observations. I told him that Mr. Watt was to be in Scotland, and that I was to meet him at Glasgow where he was to reside some time, and had promisd to inspect them and give me his observations and instructions on many points. I therefore begged that he \dr F/ would look through the papers with all convenient speed, that I might get them with me

Colonel Burnett told me that he was going out to dr Fergusons next day, and would take the box in chaise with him, and desired me to send them to Mr Adam Fergusons in Chapel Street—I did so—I learned a few days after that Col Burnet had not gone as I expected I sent to him, and he said that he had been detained—he went out of town—About three Weeks after, I got Mr Watts Letter telling me that he would be in Glasgow on the 10th of August. I was exceedingly fretted at not hearing from dr Ferguson—that Night, my daughter chanced to see Col Burnet at a Ball and asked him about dr Ferguson—she learned that he had not yet been there, but that dr Ferguson was to be in town some days to meet another Gentleman. This fretted me immensely. I sent to young Mr Fergusons and found that the Box was still there—I immediately wrote another Letter to dr Ferguson, and sent it to his Son's, to wait his coming to town that day—I now told him that I was at Mr Watts Call, but still had a few days to spare, and begged him if he could spare as much time while in Town, as would serve for a hasty inspection of *certain parts* the most necessary.

I received for answer the enclosed Letter and the Box unopened—this was very distressing to me, you may be sure, as I had hoped for much useful observations from such an excellent judge of good writing—But I had no cause to take Offence I waited on dr Ferguson next day, and told him my thoughts of the Matter, and what I intended to do, with Mr Watts assistance—de Ferguson said that dr Blacks friends were obliged to me for my anxiety about his Reputation, which might perhaps save them from a blunder in publishing unadvisably—We had more conversation, and I believe were both perfectly of one opinion, except in this

365

single point that dr Ferguson thought that if a word was to be altered from what dr Black had written, the Lectures should not be published. I thought quite other wise, because Notes written merely for Memorandums must be extended and filled up etc etc

In about three Weeks after, I went to Glasgow and was a month there and Mr Watt looked over every page and made many notes with his pencil of which I have availed myself—he also brought me the whole of the Correspondence which related to Chemistry, and spoke very feelingly of the delicacy w[hi]c[h] you had shewed by sending him his own Letters

After my return from Glasgow, I could not spare the Copy to have dr Fergusons inspection, because I was every day employed upon it, filling up all blanks, altering the loose language of many parts, and pruning off many repetitions of lectures etc etc

At this moment I should be glad of dr Fergusons opinion—but I can no longer make great alterations because I have already done my best in every thing that regards the Science. If dr Ferguson would be so kind as to inspect it merely as a literary Composition, and give me his help to correct many faults of my own as a Writer, it would be indeed a very great favour—But I should fear that dr Ferguson, not taking time to view the whole Series, would not see the propriety of some changes that I have made in the order in which some things were placed, and would object that this was changing dr Blacks Lectures—I have no time to enter into a long defence, pro and con, of what I have done, from an anxiety to support dr Blacks Reputation—and I am neither in health nor spirits for such a task. My engagement was rash, considering my bad health and my other occupations—But I then thought, and I still think, that except Mr Watt there is scarcely another person who can do the same Justice to my excellent Master, by a thorough knowledge of the train of his researches, and many anecdotes in support of his claims to originality and discovery—It is this that has most contributed to keep up my Spirits thro' the whole, and I hope will carry me through

This is a very hurried Scrawl, but I thought the explication indispensable. If I am able I will call on you tomorrow about 12 or 1 and mention my notions about how we are to deal with the booksellers

I remain d[ea]r Sir
Yours very truly
J. Robison

Letter 232

FERGUSON TO WATT

Cover addressed: 'To James Watt Esq./Engineer at/Birmingham/Warwickshire', endorsed in Watt's hand, 'A[dam] Ferguson Esq. February 2d 1801 About to write a Memoir of Dr. Blacks life and requests information respecting his claims to the discovery of the doctrine of Latent heat' and numbered '6'. Dol.

Hallyards near Peebles
2d Feb[rua]ry 1801

Dear Sir,

As the other Friends and Relations of Dr. Black have put upon me the task \of preparing some account/ of his merit in Science and of his Character to be lodged with the Royal Society of Ed[i]n[burgh] for Publication or preservation as they may think proper, I am solicitous for every assistance I can procure having little of my own besides what I picked up in conversation with himself. I have never heard his title to the discoveries of fixed Air and latent Heat contested; but upon saying so to an acquaintance, he told me that Dr. Craufurd in his Treatise on Animal Heat etc ascribed the discovery of latent Heat to Mons[ieu]r De Luc; at the same time observing that Dr Black without out knowing of De Lucs discovery had stumbled on the same thing. This induced me to look into Dr. Craufurds Book, and find the matter nearly as I was told. Your Intimacy with Dr. Black at the time of his Experiments on this Subject may enable you to recollect the Date, and your attention to the progress of Science may enable you to set me right on the pretensions of Mons[ieu]r De Luc. The French Chymists too appear to me, by neglecting to bring to the test of Experiment that important question: How much of what may be called the Essential Heat of Fluids whether Liquid or Gas is *Latent* have left their Theory of Combustion deficient of any account why the intensity of sensible Heat and Flame should be so \nearly/ equal under all the extreams of manifest Heat \or Cold/ in the Atmosphere. I am well aware that when we little minds enter the lists of Fame in the pursuits of Science or Literature, we are too much disposed to level every eminence which we cannot reach and \in/ matters of invention or discovery, would Ascribe the merit to any one rather than the actual Author. But I have nothing to gain by detracting from Mr. De Luc and if Dr. Black could look down I am well perswaded he would not thank me for any

367

attempt to dress him in the spoils of any one else. Many are \better/ qualifyed to do Justice to his Chymical merits than I am: but hope for your assistance in the points I have mentioned or any others that may occur to you. I beg my affectionate Respects to Mr. Garbett and am Dear Sir with the most sincere Esteem Your most obed[ien]t and most humble Servant

Adam Ferguson

Letter 233

ROBISON TO GEORGE BLACK JUNIOR

No cover. Endorsed in an unidentified hand: 'Professor Robison/
October 1801'. Edinburgh University Library.

[*9 October 1801*]

Dear Sir,

I am very unwilling to give You any trouble, but my present situation obliges me to press for a settlement how we are to proceed in publishing your Uncles Lectures. I must{It is my} of necessity go to the Country, and must be back to open my Class on the 28th curr[en]t

It is my interest as well as yours to sell the Work to the best Advantage. We are both strangers to the manner of dealing with Booksellers—but it *must* be done by somebody—Now Sir, if you will commission me, and give me Authority, to transact this matter, in our joint Names, I will execute the commission in the best manner I can, and do nothing in the Bargain without the Advice of Mr James Russel and Mr Geddes, two Gentlemen very warmly attached to your Uncles Reputation.

Our Arbiters have not been named, nor my Compensation settled But I am willing to proceed on condition that I have one half of the property. It has occupied me for more than 12 Months, actually employed in nothing else, and on its Account I had no summer Class last Year, because I was then closely engaged with the Amanuensis, making out the first Copy. This was a Loss of £80 at least, besides £25 which I paid to him, as his Acc[oun]t of days and \his/ discharge will shew—You said that you did not know that there would be much writing—but (excepting about 20 lectures in all) the Doctors papers were not much more than Memorandums to speak from—before I got all inserted that is contained in the four bound Quartos, {of} which are in the Chest, my writing was *fully* equal to the doctors papers. These four Volumes would have been

368

a better text \than his Papers/ if it had not been [for] the complete Revolution in Chemical doctrines which took place since 1773, when these were written. I assure you, on my honour, that I have been more occupied, and much more fatigued, by the piecing and patching occasioned by this Revolution, than I should have been by writing a complete System of Chemistry. It is not difficult to see how this may be the Case—It was not till 1790 that dr. Black acquiesced in the new doctrines—and even then not completely. By that time his health, and strength, and spirits, had greatly declined. He was no longer able to sit down and study, and write new Lectures—He therefore stuck into his old lectures such patches as served his own purpose, and were well enough understood by himself, but must cost any other person much pains to mould into the new form. In many places dr Black has not been decided in what way he should proceed, and you will find several different ways (in different Years) of treating the same subject. I had all this to guess at, to write, and perhaps to write again, before I got it into the order in which I suppose dr Black finally meant to place it. This both tired and fretted me very often.

Much labour is yet before me, and I cannot continue it on more scanty terms, and will rather give it up Be assured that I do not say this in bad humour or peevishness. I have no cause to be in bad humour. But I am fatigued, and repent that, with such bad health, I undertook the task. I did not do it for profit, but had no intention of sustaining a loss by my anxiety to publish something not unbecoming dr Black or myself. I thought that my acquaintance with the train of his Studies, and the assistance of Mr. Watt, would do the doctor more Justice than most of those who would take it in hand—it would surely be imprudent in me to continue a task attended with certain loss to myself, by keeping me from occupations of more advantage

On the above mentioned Conditions I am willing to proceed. If this be agreeable to You, please to let me know by a few lines, and I will then get a form of mutual Agreement, which we can both sign.

I have tired your patience as well as my own fingers, but cannot help it, not being able to come out.

I remain
Dear Sir
Your most obed[ien]t
h[um]ble Serv[an]t
J. Robison

St. James's Street
Oct[obe]r 9 1801

369

13—PIS * *

Letter 234

GEORGE BLACK TO ROBISON

Appended to previous letter.

[*10 October 1801*]

D[ea]r Sir

In reply to your letter of yesterday Evening (which I must confess surprized me much) I beg leave to refer you to our agreement of 20th January 1800—written by yourself—{also} a duplicate \of which is/ now in my possession—I shall ever consider myself bound to adhere to the terms therein specified, but can never consent to any other method of ascertaining the value of your time or trouble—

I remain etc.

G.B.

Letter 235

J. ROBISON TO GEORGE BLACK JUNIOR

Endorsed in an unidentified hand: 'Professor Robison 1800'. No cover. Edinburgh University Library. The dating, however, is incorrect, since this letter is clearly a reply to the note appended by George Black to Robison's letter to him, dated 9 October 1801.

[?*10 October 1801*]

Dear Sir

Business that must be finished before I went to the Country so occupied me yesterday that I had not a moment to employ in reply to your Letter

I had not the least inclination to depart from the Award of our Arbiters nor imagine that I have done so when, for the sake of dispatch I made the proposal of taking the half of this Edition If the work is good for any thing, my share of the Copy Right will, I trust, be much better, and this I by no means intended to relinquish. But time presses me. I must leave Edin[bu]r[gh]—the Arbiters are not yet named—the bringing the book to market seems as far off as ever till some person undertake it. I offered to do this and conduct the publication, and, in this *purely commercial transaction*, I think my terms no more than will give me a mere commercial compensation.

But, Mr Black, suppose that I had wished to depart from the original agreement—then reflect on this Circumstance. { When } When that was entered into, I had only three days perusal of the papers, and on that I founded my judgment of the Task   It was not till I and my Amanuensis had gone thro' them page by page and copied them, that I could judge of the whole as a consecutive Scheme, and the labour that it would cost me to fit the M.S. for public appearance under dr Blacks Name. In this the four quartos gave me no Assistance because all the Chemical doctrines had been changed since they were written. This first labour occupied us 140 days as you may see by the Acc[oun]t of the Amanuensis. But the labour before me gave me no uneasyness, because I knew that the Arbiters would consider it seriously.

But here a new subject of Concern came before me. I thought the lectures unfit for public Appearance, because they would not correspond with the Authors Rank among the philosophers of Europe. Then was my chief Motive taken away. In this I may be wrong, but this was my opinion, and you see by dr Ferguson's Letter that I had expressed it to him in a manner that he thought judicious and friendly. Indeed this was my chief reason for requesting him to look over the Manuscript—Mr Watt was of the same opinion but thought that the expectation which had been given to the public should not be disappointed, and that the preface, w[hic]h I gave him the heads of, would do away the chief Objections.

After this time I never pressed the publication, but on the contrary, in all my conversation with those who were so eager to see dr Blacks Lectures in print, I said that I did not think that they would be published —It was only because Mr Geddes and some others assured me that it was resolved on by Dr Blacks Relations that I now fell seriously to work.

It is this that has given me so much trouble and *anxiety*—that dr Black should not appear like the humble pupil of Lavoisier. And I repeat it this has given me more, much more trouble than to write a new System. You do not know the difficulty of making a Course of *Popular Elementary Lectures* appear in a manner not becoming a Person of high literary Reputation—This, anxiety gave me a fatigue of mind which no money can compensate

I was going to the Country—hearing you was coming I was glad to think that now measures could be settled for publication, and I staid in

371

town, with considerable inconvenience, and now can stay no longer. In this Situation, and with these sentiments, I confess that I was much hurt to see myself considered by You merely as a hired Person, working for wages, while I could not help thinking myself one of your Uncles most zealous and *faithful* friends   I am not a Manufacturer of books, or a scribbler, but a Man of Letters, in the same Station with your departed Friend, and I felt myself doing an Act of Friendship—And now, unless my well meant Services are received on that footing, I cannot continue to labour, for at least six months to come, without that only reward for my labour that can give me any Satisfaction—rather than receive the wages of a hireling, I will give up all that is past—my labour as nothing, and more than 100 Guineas actually out of my pocket.

You should surely also reflect that You \and your friends/ can sustain no loss nor trouble, whatever Reception the Work meet with—on the other hand, whatever may be the Award of our Arbiters, a small sale may leave me a great loser, even in a pecuniary view   I might have died before it was completed, and then all my trouble was lost—while on the side of Dr Blacks friends there is nothing but gain

Thus my good Sir I have opened my mind to you, and trust that you will no longer be *surprised* at the proposal I made—At the same time, I have perfect confidence in the honourable and Gentlemanlike Sentiments of your mind, and am only surprised and sorry to see you consider me in any other light than as the attached friend of my respected Master.

I remain with great Esteem
Dear Sir
Your's
J Robison

Sunday

Letter 236

ROBISON TO WATT

Cover addressed: 'James Watt Esq./Heathfield/by Birmingham/
Via Ferry bridge' and in another hand 'Proffessor Robison
January 8th [*recte* 18th] 1802 about his finishing Dr. Blacks
lectures which will make 1500 pages has appointed Dr. Rutherford as arbiter for his share of profits—has been 18 months
composing the MS' and numbered '32'. Dol.

Edin[bu]r[gh] Jan[uar]y 18 1802

My dear Sir

I have at length got thro' my task with Dr. Blacks Lectures, in the best
way that I was able. It has almost finished me, and I often pressed for
leave to give it up—it was quite unfit for my condition

I am now in as great puzzle as ever. I am commissiond to sell the
Edition and I have not the least notion how to go about it, or whom to
address   I have the same opinion about the work that I expressed to you
at the beginning, and don't imagine that it will be a saleable book—but
must now endeavour to get some compensation for the trouble it has
cost me

The booksellers judge, in part, by the size of the book. I have counted
the letters in 20 pages, and, comparing it with the Phil[osophical] Transactions of the R[oyal] Society of London, each page of which contains
about 1800 Letters and Spaces, I find that this Work will run to 1500 such
pages.

As you declined being my Arbiter with respect to the Share which I
was to have in the property, I named Dr. Rutherford—and he has seen
some part of it, that he might judge of the manner in which I have executed my task (altho this is no part of his Office) and I have the satisfaction
to hear him speak of it in very flattering terms. Mr. James Russel, a
Relation of Dr. Black, and a very good Chemist, expresses himself still
more to my commendation. So that I would fain hope that it will not be
a discredit to me. If the friends would give me another summer, I should
not fear—but I have been so flogged and jaded to get it ready that it has
destroyed my appetite my Strength and my Spirits—being forced to
work at it while I was in the throng of my Class duty—so that it will go
out of my hand without the last correction that I wish to give it. I would
curtail the History of Quick lime to one half, and would greatly abridge
the doctrine of latent heat   I have taken some pains to be correct in the

373

History of the Composition of Water—by the bye, Lichtenberg[1] in his preface to Erxleben's Nat[ural] Phil[osoph]y[2] has been better informd of the investigations of the British in this Matter and also in every thing relating to Dr. Black, than any foreigner I know.—As Lavoisier publishd Dr. Blacks letter without leave, I have inserted his, that it may appear how well his wheedling corresponds with his public nondeclaration of deference for our freind—and I could not help noticing how little de Luc's *"tenta le premier"* agrees with his repeated importunity to be the Editor of the doctrine of latent heat. This is done without your appearing in it at all. A fortunate unfinished long letter dated Jan[uar]y 30 1783 beginning "dear Watt" gives me all the information I wanted—I have some pages of pencil notes about decompounding Sea Salt by means of little prisms of quick lime, which are curious—but I see that they relate to some private transaction in company with you, and that a patent is spoken of—I have therefore said nothing about it.

How shall I proceed to get the Book sold—for I am totally ignorant of this traffic—Several here would fain have it—but they all insist on my making a demand, and they will not make an offer—I beg that you will take the trouble of thinking a little about this, and write me what I should ask for a book of this size, coming from an Author of Such Reputation— You must be sensible that eighteen months complete occupation for every hour, which I swear it has given me, should not be thrown away It has cost me a summers vacation, which would have brought me 60 or 80 Guineas, and above 30 for Amanuenses etc—I have been much told of the honourable character of Nichol the Kings bookseller. He buys no Copy—but he Agents for an Author and sells his performance for him— he did very handsomely for Cap[tai]n Wilson's Acc[oun]t of the Pelew Islands[3] and for Mungo Parks Journeys in Africa. If he be really a man of honour, I should think this the best mode for *me*, who am totally ignorant both of the traffic, and of the public opinion Pray what think you of this Scheme—you mentiond one Wallis—but whether as an individual purchaser or an Agent or Broker, I dont know—For me to write to individual Booksellers, wait their answers, and perhaps give each the MS in his turn for inspection, would be an endless work—and indeed I am almost dead already with it. I am sorry to trouble you, but trust to your kindness for indulgence—a Compensation for my trouble, I fear, is not to be expected—but as little loss as possible would be an essential service to my family—These very hard times have already stripped me bare of every little floating Cash that I had, and even obliged me to encroach on my little Capital, and the best thing now that could happen to my family would be my decease—for I can no longer compensate for the expence that my infirmities create—I *feel* that I deserve something handsome for this Job. For had the Lectures been published by any person not affectionately attached to Dr. Black, just as they could be made out from his Notes, with the Assistance of such MS copies as I have been able to procure, I am certain that they would not have supported his reputation. I wish they may now— But his freinds, knowing nothing but the public deference for Dr. Black, never can suppose this, and they wondered when I said that I had much trouble with the publication

I would not trouble you with writing. There is no secret in this—you can tell any of your Clerks what to say to me.

Accept of our best wishes for yourself and the family about your fireside and believe me

D[ea]r Sir
Your affectionate
and faithful Serv[an]t
J Robison

[1] Georg Christoph Lichtenberg (1744–99), astronomer and physicist.
[2] Johann Cristian Polycarp, *Anfangsgrunde der Naturlehre*, Funfte Auflage, mit Zusatzen von G. C. Lichtenberg, Göttingen, 1791.
[3] Captain Henry Wilson, *An Account of the Pelew Islands*, London, 1803. The Sir Edward Pellew Group are situated off the coast of N.E. Australia.

Letter 237

ROBISON TO WATT

Cover addressed: 'To James Watt Esq./of Heathfield/near Birmingham/by Ferrybridge', endorsed in Watt's hand: 'Proffessor Robison April 19th 1803 on his publication of Dr. Blacks lectures' and numbered '33'. Dol.

Edin[bu]r[gh] April 19. 1803

My dear Sir

I have this day sent the last sheet of Dr. Blacks Lectures to be printed off. Thank heaven I am now done with a most oppressive and dispiriting Job. The labour is inconceivable that it has cost me to fit such imperfect Memorandums for appearing in the form of a Book. You inserted your Counsel to place all references to Authors and quotations of all passages

375

on which any reasoning proceeded, at the bottom of every page—I began this—but the labour of hunting for them would have been as much as all the rest—the few which were noted in the MS appear to be the most insignificant—of which scarcely any use had been made, and put down merely to save the trouble of working them into the text. I am far within bounds when I say that it would have been twice as easy for me to write a System of Chemistry than to manufacture the sentiments of another. I dissuaded from publishing, even after I had made out the first transcript, and would willingly let my labour go for nothing—but Mr. Black (chiefly at the instance of Mr. Geddes) continued to urge the publication, and I went on with the Revision, till it would have been folly for me to throw away the labours of at least eighteen Months It must now take its chance, and I must try to bear without wining the many scratches that I must look for from the Public, which certainly expects from Dr. Black much more than mere elementary Lessons, which is all that is to be found here. The worthy doctor seldom engaged in refined speculations, and had no great talent for them. When plain common sense could not take hold of a thing, Dr. Black always let it sleep in quiet. Smith was perfectly well founded when he said that no man had less Nonsense in his head than Dr. Black—but the public are not displeased with ingenious nonsense, and are never pleased without it

I have presumed to set your name at the head of this Edition, by a few lines of address to You. I did not ask you leave, because I believe you would not have given it—and I don't know whether I have designed you properly—transeat cum ceteris erroribus—and the Preface, containing some account of our freind was a most distressing Job—it is a kind of writing for which I am totally unfit, and I begged at every door to get it taken off my hands—but in vain—and the folks have insisted that there should be something of that kind. It is a sad specimen of biography—but may amuse such as do not know much about composition

On the whole, it is the best I can do in my present condition. I never possessed great talents, and have often been much distressed by seeing more imputed to me than I deserve—I have a tolerably just notion what they are, and am conscious that my abilities are overrated—But whatever they may have been formerly, I am as conscious of my powers having suffered greatly by my bodily infirmities—the unremitting sensation of acute pain is no good companion in study—and when I keep it down a little by Opium, I am most distinctly conscious of losing the command of my thoughts—I have often catched myself pondering most anxiously on one question, when I had positively set my mind to ponder on another toto caelo different. I see marks of this even in this work—It is astonishing how many things I found to correct in almost every page, when I saw the shape of it in print—Had it been printed from the papers I sent to London, it would have disgraced me. I fear it is bad enough as it is

It will give me much pleasure to hear good accounts from your fireside—that you are all well and hearty—Mrs. Robison joins in best wishes for you all, and in the request to be kindly remembered among you—Please offer our best Compliments to Mr Boulton's family—and remember me to your Son James I have this very day received the first accounts of my Son John's arrival at Colombo in health and spirits—The Letter is not from himself, but from General McDowall, to whose patronage I had recommended him—and it is in terms of the most affectionate kindness, with assurances of every service in his power, and a most encouraging account of the impression which my Sons Conversation and manners have made on all who have seen him. This has greatly cheered my drooping spirits. I stand much in need of all the comfort that my childrens good Conduct can give me—for bodily sufferings, and the continual fears of any small increase of them, which would immediately render me unable to support my family in our sober station, really leave me no great inducement to continue any longer here. My chief satisfaction is the consciousness that I have made a great struggle, and have not shrunk from my duty.

Now my good friend fare you well, and when you have a little leisure, be assured that you cannot bestow it on one who will be more grateful than

Your very aff[ectiona]te Freind
J. Robison

Letter 238

WATT TO ROBISON

J. P. Muirhead, *Mechanical Inventions of James Watt*, 1854, vol. II, pp. 284-85.

Heathfield, April 26, 1803

*   *   I am glad you have completed your task, which I am sorry has proved so grievous. You judged right in thinking I should not have con-

377

sented to your own friendly intention of dedicating it to me. I am not a proper patron for Dr. B.'s Lectures: not enough known in the world, nor a sufficient adept in chemical science for my name to recommend the book; and, as Dr. B.'s friend, there were many with whom he was more intimate and more connected. Besides all this, I have a great aversion to standing in the front rank on any occasion. I can only regard it as a proof of your friendship, which, though grateful to me as such, I wish you could still turn aside and inscribe the book to some more appropriate person. I shall feel equally obliged by the intention. * *

We were very kindly received by my old friends at Paris, M. Berthollet, M. Monge, and M. De la Place, now become Senators. M. Prony[1] and M. Hassenfratz[2] were also exceedingly attentive; the former especially, and seems an exceeding good sort of a man as well as a very able mathematician. He appeared to be sorry that he had not taken more notice of me in his book on the steam-engine, and has offered to publish, in a succeeding volume, anything I please to furnish him with on the subject. Many others were very kind. We passed five weeks there, and, had the weather been warmer, I should have wished to prolong my stay. * *

[1] Gaspard Clair François Marie Riche de Prony (1755–1839), civil engineer, Professor of Mechanics in the École Polytechnique, 1794. Author of several works on hydraulics and mechanics, including his *Nouvelle Architecture Hydraulique* 2 vols., Paris 1790.
[2] Jean Henri Hassenfratz (1755–1827), chemist, friend of Lavoisier, Professor of Mineralogy in the École des Mines, 1795.

Letter 239

ROBISON TO HAMILTON

Cover addressed: 'To Gilbert Hamilton Esq./Merchant/ Glasgow', and endorsed in Watt's hand, 'J. Robison to G. Hamilton August 14 1803 complaint of my not noticing his Edition of Dr. Blacks lectures' and numbered '31'. Dol.

Edin[bu]r[gh] Aug[ust] 14. 1803

Dear Sir

I have just learned that Mr. Watt was in Glasgow the day I left it (the 25 ult[im]o). I was very unfortunate indeed not to know it. Yet should I have met with Mr. Watt with no small Anxiety and uneasyness. An author is seldom free of this, till he know how his labours have been received. Mr. Watt knows that I prize his opinion in the present instance above all others—As most of the work had been previously submitted to his inspection, and his amendments adopted implicitly, I had hoped that his opinion would be favourable. He knows also my Condition—fatigued and jaded with sixteen years of *unceasing* pain, and not a little dejected in spirits. His approbation would have been a most soothing Cordial, and I really thought that I so far enjoyed his freindship, that he would not have omitted intimating his satisfaction, had the performance pleased him—Indeed Sir, you cannot imagine how this disappointment distresses me—I must add another circumstance—When I had corrected the last Sheet, and sent it to the Press, I immediately wrote to my old friend, and told him that my toil was now over, and, now for the first time, I let him know that I had addressed the work to him—I had his answer, conceived in what seemed to me terms of coolness—in particular, he expressed not only disapprobation of the dedication, but considerable dissatisfaction and, I think, displeasure—I asked your opinion as to the propriety of the thing, and it seemed to meet your approbation —and I think that the terms in which it is expressed are moderate, and just, and creditable, as far as Mr. Watt is concerned. I wished to say much more, but dared not take that liberty. A Gentleman told me that he said in a company of several Persons that he never was a Pupil of Dr. Black. I am therefore mistaken as to that fact—of which I never doubted, having found him, on my return to College in 1763, most intimately connected with Dr. Black, and continually speaking of his Lectures and doctrines— possibly I took it for granted without its having been told me—But, even granting the mistake, as to his having regularly attended the Lectures, I must still consider Mr. Watt as Dr. Black's most illustrious Pupil, and think that it was not kind to say publicly a thing that hurt my credibility on so slight grounds—I dont mention this as a thing that I take offence at—were it so, I would justify myself to Mr. Watt himself—I mention it, merely in corroboration of the very distressing impression which Mr. Watts coldness has made on my spirits—I am easily crushed now, having long felt the heavy hand of Providence, in misfortunes and Embarassments of various kinds, and nothing could have so cheered my heart as the Encouragement of an old and much respected friend

I assure you, good Sir, that I am now so little touched by what the *public* may think of my Edition of Dr. Blacks Lectures that I have never made the smallest enquiry how it is relished in London. About eight days ago, Mr. Patrick Wilson wrote me from Ramsgate, signifying his great Satisfaction—but professing total ignorance of its reception in Town, not having been there for some months—I was particularly anxious to learn the opinion of Dr. Ferguson, and even uneasy, as he was long silent, after having got the first Copy that went abroad—At last I had a Letter, telling me that he had deferred writing till he could do it with confidence, after having gone over the whole. He then says "It has exceeded my expectations, and fully comes up to my wishes. You are right, considering the present taste, to be moderate in your expectations —But it certainly contains a great body of Chemical Science, well supported by the proper Evidence, and made acceptable to any person who really wishes to learn—and, considering the total revolution in the received doctrines, there was wanted such a Work, under the Authority of such a Name, to keep in remembrance that Chemistry was a respectable Science in the hands of our predecessors—otherwise I think it would be forgotten, in a very few Years, that such philosophers as Stahl, Margraaf, or Geoffroi ever existed—This pleased me much—for these were precisely the two points of view in which I wished the public to consider the work—I feared a less favourable judgment—for Dr. Ferguson was not altogether pleased with its being put into my hands, at the first—at length however, when he saw that my opinion coincided with his own, that it would be fully more prudent to keep the M.S. [word torn out] than publish what did not altogether correspond with the very high opinion entertained of his Freind, and saw the other Relations bent on the publication, he was pleased to find it in such cautious hands, of one so warmly attached to his Freinds Reputation

I was in a peck of trouble about the Life—this was a kind of writing for which I found myself totally unfit—but I could not get it dispensed with, and I struggled through it in the best manner I could—as a piece of Biography, it is unquestionably far below par—but having a store of anecdotes, and a feature of Character which could never displease by being often recurred to, I judged that it would please the bulk of ordinary Readers; and I hear that it does so *in this place*. I own I should be glad to hear of its good reception in Glasgow—If Mr. Watt be still among You, pray assure him of my best respects—and accept for yourself, the best wishes of

D[ea]r Sir Your most obed[ien]t
h[um]ble Serv[an]t
J Robison

Letter 240

MRS ROBISON TO WATT

Cover addressed: 'Mr. Watt Senior', endorsed in Watt's hand,
'Mrs. Robison Edinburgh December 19th 1803. Mrs. Hutton'
and numbered '34'. Dol.

Monday 19th Decem[be]r 1803 Edin[bu]r[gh]

My dear Sir

I received your acceptable Letter by Mr. Hutton—I introduced him
immediately to Mr. Geddes and Mr. Playfair and from your hint I
thought of Mr. J. Russell as a particular acquaintance of Dr. Huttons and
desired him to ask an Introduction from Mr. R to Mr. Wardrope (his
brothers Master) who was very kind to him   I desired of Mr. P. and
Mr. R. to help him to any other of the doctors friends, which they did.

I have little to say from my own knowledge but from frequent conversations with the young Man. I think He has been most respectably
received—which may be of much value if he does well in the world, and
I conclude has been benefited by his visit here—He was long in the dark
—could learn nothing more than seing Miss H. affectionate and kind. A
conversation with himself will explain better than I can, all our cogita-
tions—one of the difficulties was, Miss Hutton's compleat misapprehen-
sion of his situation in business "he had the ball at his foot." and it all
depended on his brother, and himself to make their fortune etc—I
instructed him the best way I could, to set Miss H. right but He found it
difficult and delicate.—When your Sons Letter came, (happily constructed) I advised him to ask leave to read it to her, which has been of great
use to him and shews him she is much interrested in his success   he tells
me she desired he would advise with you as she would put the greatest
confidence in your opinion   here my dear Sir I think is the point—you
will have it in your power to influence Miss H in whatever you see most
for the young Mans good—

He seems to think himself secure in the greatest cordiallity of the
Balfour family who are distant Relations by the d[octo]rs Mother and
were the only people I dreaded would stand nearer

I have advised him with all the thought, and care I could what to do, or
what to avoid—and I hope, and think, so far as I could judge, he has
conducted himself well.—

I once thought it needless to give you this trouble as I could say nothing
but what Mr. H would be happy to repeat to you, but second thoughts

are best, and I thought you would wish to hear he had appeared so favourably

We had a Letter from \my/ Son in Petersburg tother day, well, and doing well—he gives us a flattering and pleasing piece of intelligence. He says he had a Message from Dr. Rogerson (our kind friend) to shew him a present to his Father, from the Emperor, of a fine Diamond Ring in return, on presenting a Copy of his Work—Hugo adds it is accompanyd with a Letter, and is coming with the Ambassadors Secretary Mr. Nicolai. This I should take to be authentick. so may indulge myself in communicating what I am sure you will take pleasure to hear—

I hope Mr. R will execute his *intention* of writing along, but he is poorly today, and Mr. H goes on Wednesday morning.

I beg to be kindly remembered to Mrs Watt and Miss Macgregor. Mr. James, and Mr. Gregory, with hopes to hear he is quite well again.— I hope you wont omit to present me to Mr. Bolton particularly—my best wishes to Miss Bolton and Mr. R. Bolton, and as Mr. Robison is speaking of perhaps going to London in Summer I hope he will go by Birmingham   it will be the chief temptation with me again to Visit that city to see en passant, so many friends.—

I find I am where I always go to the end of my paper before I say Adieu to a favourite friend   I hope you will excuse the liberty—and that I may cease to transgress farther I will only add

I ever am with due regard
Yours most Sincerely   R Robison

Letter 241

ROBISON TO WATT

Cover addressed: 'To James Watt Esq./Heathfield/Birmingham', endorsed in Watt's hand, 'Proffessor Robison December 20th 1802 By Mr. Hutton—Scheme of his Manual for Engineers and others' and numbered '35'. Dol.

Edin[bu]r[gh] Dec[embe]r 20 1803

My dear Sir
Be assured that it will always be a great satisfaction to Mrs. Robison and me to be able to make this place more useful or agreeable to any of your freinds. I only regret that it is so little in our power to be of any

382

material service to them. Mr. Galton[1] will always find me at home, and glad of the opportunity of a little sober chat with a sober young man. If I can assist him in the prosecution of his studies, it will be an additional pleasure

Allow me to remind you of your obliging promise of furnishing me with some corrections etc on my account of Dr. Blacks Lectures—A second Edition is now called for, with tolerable prospect of a demand. Therefor I beg that you will now and then occupy a vacant hour on the subject. I shall not be able to make any *additions* to my remarks, unless the publication be delayed till toward the end of Summer, as the exper-[imen]ts which are necessary for settling some notions about heat and light require both leisure and sunshine. I shall not have a moment even to think of it till I shut up shop again at College.

I have got some money from our Magistrates to encrease my Apparatus with some models of Machines, and I have a great inclination to have one of your pocket Steam Engine. I have looked into your specification in our Patent Office here, and find it uncommonly distinct and full, so that I think I should have no great difficulty in getting a Model made here, were I a little more able to go about and oversee the execution. But this will by no means by an easy task. It occurs to me that perhaps there are at Birmingham Artists who are accustomed to such Jobs, as I hardly imagine that the Models and Sections which you produced in the Course of your process were made by your own Workmen. If I am right, perhaps it would not cost much trouble to some of your people to order such a thing for me. If there be no impropriety in this, and the price be some moderate sum, say 20 Guineas, it would be doing me a very signal favour—But if you have any objection to a model being made at any rate, I will think no more of it—You may perhaps remember that I once hinted to you the giving such a thing to the University of Glasgow. I still think that it would be a very becoming thing—and am certain that it would be highly valued by the Society. I know that you are considered as an Alumnus and \that/ the Society thinks that it has some share in your Celebrity.

Your Son James once told me (no it was Gregory) that they were much acquainted, at Soho, with making Galvanic Apparatus. If I could be supplied with one from thence, I should be vastly glad—I am ignorant of what has been lately done in that way, and any apparatus that I should order here has a chance of being very deficient. Pray let me know whether this can be done without much trouble, and ab[ou]t what price

But the cheif request that I have to make is that you would be so

383

kind some day of leisure as to tell me a little more of what you hinted of your surmises about the constitution of Water, and its decomposition by electric or galvanic treatment. If I did not misunderstand you, you seemed to think that the two Gases detached from it in these Exper[imen]ts are Water united to the two electricities, and that the recomposition of Water by the electric Spark was only the detaching each electricity from the Water combined with it in the form of Gas, the two electricities uniting and escaping in Light and heat. I can see that such a doctrine promises support to de Luc's conjectures about thunderstorms etc.—but I am unwilling to admit two electricities, since the redundance and deficiency of one does as well, and, I think, agrees better with the phenomena of electric attraction and repulsion— And I cannot see, by any notion that I can form of Electricity, how the electric Spark is to cause the separation of the Electricities from the Water.—What is the difference between a common electric Spark, and the Spark taken in the Water, and composing the Gases with it, or taken in the mixture of Gases, and recomposing the Water—How does the electric Spark both compose and decompose the Gases? \Should not the two Electricities appear in Herschels separating the heat and light by refraction?/†

Two days of severe illness had interrupted my scribbling—and in the mean time, your young Man Hutton arrived here. Mrs. Robison read me a passage of your Letter to her, which spoke of the favourable Reception of Dr. Blacks Lectures. Such accounts chear me not a little and I need it all in my present trim, which is indeed very desponding. Your Observations and Corrections will be a great favour to me—not that I have sanguine Expectation from a 2d Edition, but I shall be glad to have it as free from mistakes as possible. I am not able to furnish my mind chemically at this day of life, and can add nothing to the Work myself.

The severe weather has again reached me at the fire side, and by giving me a Cold, and thus quickening my pulse, increases my pain beyond sufferance, for that life is burthensome to me, and I wish it over. I can do no more for my family. Indeed I have the comfort of seeing them in a fair way of supporting themselves in the same sober station with their parents—and it is folly to wish for more—When I had them to place in the world, and found myself unable to assist them, it sunk my spirits greatly—but I found friends in proportion as I needed them, and have been extremely fortunate. Indeed my Sons have been docile,

† This sentence inserted in Robison's own hand.

384

and so sober in their Conduct, that I have all the reason that human affairs can admit to hope favourably for them. And as for myself, considering the small pains I took to conciliate the favour of others, my treatment by the world has more than satisfied evry claim or expectation. I am only sorry that my talents and exertions have not deserved the opinion that is formd of them. The Credit I have gotten in my profession greatly exceeds what I deserve. I know this full well, and I am sometimes put in a little embarassment, when I find more expected of me than I am able to perform—I was much gratified a few days ago by the very favourable opinion expressed by Dr. Ferguson of my Edition of Dr. Black's Lectures—Even his moderate commendation at first, which I mentioned to you, had greatly pleased me, because I knew that he is a very cautious bestower of Commendation—and I have the highest respect for his judgment, both as a philosopher and as a Man of Taste and Learning—What he said the other day was indeed most flattering—I tell you all this, because I think you take some interest in what concerns me. The good opinion and good wishes of the good are now the only thing that can chear my Evning of Life— My Wife has told you how kindly my book was received by the Emperor of Russia. It will be immediately translated by a Mr Belaieff, one of my old pupils in the Marine Academy.

I fear that I shall not advance far on my project of a book more in my own Line, which I have long had at heart viz: a body of Mechanical Doctrine for the instruction of the Engineer, Civil or Military. Having given more attention to the Arts depending on my peculiar Science than most theorists, I think I can be useful in this way—but my state of health is such that I am able to do very little, even in writing—and as to making experiments, still greatly wanted for accommodating our mathematical theories to the practice of the Arts, I am altogether unable. I should have begun the project twenty years ago. Were I near the focus of Arts where You are, I should pick up many bits of instruction, and if my health next summer be somewhat better, and the Country have quiet, I may perhaps draw nearer the sun for a few weeks. I am not without hopes of getting an experimental Mill erected by a Nobleman who takes an interest in these things. This is intended cheifly for obtaining some information concerning the resistance opposed by the more general Works performed by Mills—*ex. gr.* Grist Mills—what is the actual reaction at the pinion of the Milstone—what change is made by an increase of Velocity, or by feeding faster with grain, or by grinding finer etc.—in like manner boreing Mills, Stump-

385

ing Mills—Another Object is to see what changes are produced by different ways of employing the water etc. When the Plan of Experiments is better digested I will communicate it to you, and will hope for some instructions—But, if not in the Air, perhaps my Castle will be in the Water, as unstable an Element, and may come to nothing

I hope young Hutton has done himself considerable service by coming here. I learn from Mr Playfair that he has made a very favourable impression. Miss Hutton is a most worthy Woman, and has shewn a very strong attachment to her Brother by so far getting the better of her delicacy and her respect for the famd institution of Marriage. I did not expect that she would have gone as far as she has done. I am now convinced that you have much in your power for Mr Hutton For she expresses the strongest Confidence in your Opinion of what is fitted for him, and will be much disposed to second your Views—by charging him so expressly to follow your Counsel in every thing, she gives you a right to intimate to her what you think suitable to his Situation and prospects, and I dare say will shew great deference for what you shall say

Now my dear sir farewell—keep me sometimes in your remembrance, and when at leisure, let me know so much by some answer to the philosophical queries in this Letter I mentiond to you some experiments on the quantity of steam from an ounce of Water—you will find them in Vol 41 of the Philosophical transactions, and I think them worth your perusal. The Author's Name is Payne, but I know nothing more about him—Remember me kindly to Mrs. Watt, and to your Sons. I wish to hear more favourable Acc[oun]ts of Gregory's Health I am truly sorry to learn that Mr. Boulton suffers so much. He has fought a tough battle with his disorder and all the infirmities of advanced life, and still has, I hope, spirits to snatch an Enjoyment in spite of trouble. my best wishes attend him—Adieu, believe me ever most cordially

Your affect[iona]te Freind
J Robison

[1] Samuel Tertius Galton of Birmingham attended the University of Edinburgh for one term and then returned to join the family's newly-formed bank of Galton, Galton and James.

ROBISON TO WATT

Endorsed, 'Proffessor Robison/July 30th 1804/by Dr. Thompson' and numbered '36'. Dol.

30 July 1804

My dear Sir

Dr. Thomson who presents this must be so well known to you by his Chemical Writings that I can do him no service by recommending him to those Civilities which you are always ready to shew to Persons of Merit. I know too well your own Need of repose to trouble you with solicitations of this kind, which I frequently receive, and decline as civilly as I can. But I make no doubt but that you will thank me for making personally known to you one, who, in very early life, has been able to give the public such an immense body of chemical knowledge. These Studies (indeed I should say all Studies) are now much stranger to me now than they have been, and I am but a poor judge of chemical Merit. But the speedy call for a second Edition shews that Dr. Thomson's performance is in great Esteem. I am pleased with this, because I know Dr. Thomson to be a most worthy Man, who will do Credit to the humble recommendation of D[ea]r sir

Your affect[iona]te Freind

etc

J Robison

July 30 1804

Letter 243

CHARLES ROBISON TO WATT

Endorsed in Watt's hand, 'C. R. Robison Edinburgh Proffessor Robison's death January 30th 1805' and numbered '33' in bundle headed 'Glasgow and Edinburgh 1805, No. 1 to 35'. Dol.

Sir

I am sorry to inform you that my Father Prof[esso]r John Robison died here this Morning

I am Sir
Your most Obed[ien]t
hum[bl]e serv[an]t
Edinburgh   Chas. R. Robison
30 Jan[uar]y 1805

Letter 244

WATT TO CHARLES ROBISON

J. P. Muirhead, *Mechanical Inventions of James Watt*, 1854, vol. II, pp. 289-90.

Heathfield, Feb. 5th, 1805.

DEAR SIR,——It was with great concern that I received yesterday your advice of the loss of my dear and much esteemed friend your father. It adds to my sorrow, that from the afflicting circumstances in my own family for this last twelve-month, I have not corresponded with him as I ought to have done had my mind been more at ease.

The loss you have sustained is a very great one, yet it must be some consolation that he is relieved from the state of suffering in which he has so long continued; that he will be sincerely regretted by all who had the happiness to know him; and that he has lived long enough to have by his writings raised monuments to himself that will long outlive the date of frail mortality. I shall, while I live, warmly remember his friendship to me, his virtues, the clearness of his head, and the uncommon extent of his knowledge and science, as well as the unwearied application with which he pursued it under the pressure of a painful disease. I shall not at present intrude further upon your sorrows, being

sensible that time alone can alleviate the feelings of his family, and
enable them to bear this affliction.   *   *

Letter 245

WATT TO R. MUIRHEAD

J. P. Muirhead, *Mechanical Inventions of James Watt*, 1854, vol. II,
p. 290

Heathfield, Feb. 7th, 1805.

*   *   It was with great concern that I learned the other day
of the death of my worthy friend Professor Robison. He was a man of
the clearest head and the most science of anybody I have known, and
his friendship to me ended only with his life, after having continued
nearly half a century.   *   *

Letter 246

MRS ROBISON TO WATT

Cover addressed: 'James Watt Esq./Heathfield', endorsed in
Watt's hand, 'Mrs. Proffessor Robison February 14 1805
Account of her husbands last illness' and numbered 32 in bundle
headed 'Glasgow and Edinburgh 1805 No. 1 to 35'. Dol.

Edin[bu]r[gh] 14th Feb[ruary] 1805

My d[ea]r Mr Watt
My Son Charles received your kind Letter—I feel very unable to
address so particular a friend. There are so many Ideas crowd[ed] on my
mind from so many years hearing you constantly spoken of, by Mr.
Robison, that I feel quite overwhelmed,—but, at the same time I cannot
be satisfy'd without writing immediately to a Friend He valued so
much.—
I am yet also much shock'd by the sudden and unexpected event. I
had formed an expectation that Mr. Robisons constitution seemd so
unimpaired, that He was in no other way affected by his Malady, than,

389

the much to be regreted Pain, and that He had the same chance to live long as other Men—I have only this Winter had an unhappy interruption sometimes to this opinion in his Legs swelling—this did alarm me but I have so long been witness of his uncommon suffering that I was not so much awake to his danger as I would have been of another person. however I believe if I could reconcile myself to the absence of so great and so good a Man—all has happen'd as the best for him, to have seen him linger, or lost his faculties, would [have] been still more severe.—

On Sunday before, He look'd as healthy and good looking as ever, and on Monday went to his Class and walked home as usual.—at Dinner he spoke slightly of a little cold, at Tea he said his cold had increased, but seemed not himself to have the slightest suspicion of any thing more, he went to bed early.—as He was worse in the morning I sent for Mr. Russell, who also thought merely of a Cold. He was siezed while Mr Russell staid, with a bilous vomiting, which did not still, alarm him. on that *continuing*, I became so, and sent for Dr. Gregory, who told me He was very bad indeed. —when I enquired soon after this, if he felt any better, He said no, nor did not expect to be, that it was just ending as He had ever expected it to do. he did \not/ pursue any discourse in consequence, but spoke occasionaly as easily and unconcernedly, and as much himself as ever, till his last breath, which was at seven in the Morning on the Wednesday 30th January. It will yeild you great satisfaction to hear he thus Died in the full vigour of his mind. Mr Playfair has been appointed to the Class, and it is to be taught out this season by Mr. Macnight who a short time he had taken as his assistant, in case he needed it, but he never was employd but a few days *last* winter while Mr. Robison had a bad cold.

I have been obliged to consider of various things just now, among others the propriety of immediately having by some Eminent hand— his Life written. I beg your advice and opinion on this, and any other subjects concerning as may occur to you I think, however you may advise me, my d[ea]r Sir, it will be very desirable you will without delay set down the many things you know which your long acquaintance and similar acquirements enable you, so ably, and particularly to to state—such materials, ignorant as I am to decide on such a matter, I see must be necessary. I hope then my d[ea]r Sir you will favour your friend in this, I can scarce urge indulge me.—

You would receive I suppose a Copy of Mr. Robisons last work. There is in manuscript nearly finished a second Vol[ume] which as it was intended for, I feel no impropriety in giving to the press.—all the other Manuscripts, Mr. R. leaves with his Books, to John my Son in India.

Mr. Robison often wished to have written to you of late, but diffidence only prevented him intruding on a mind he knew possessed all the consolation that was possible to apply his *never* failing kindness you would not doubt.

You will be pleased also to hear we just had a short while since, got his portrait compleated by Mr. Raeburn   It is reckoned a fine picture, and likeness

I think I have endeavoured to repeat what it appears to me you might wish to know I shall be happy to be permitted to apply for advice in any things, which Alas, I already feel in many things I stand in need of.

I beg leave to return my you the kind wishes of Mrs Watt and your Son and Mr. Bolton and family—and remain my d[ea]r Sir,

Yours Sincerely
R. Robison

P.S. excuse the confusion of this
Letter, I am unable to write another

Letter 247

WILSON TO WATT

Cover addressed: 'To/James Watt Senior Esq./Heathfield/near/ Birmingham', endorsed in Watt's hand, 'Dr. P. Wilson February 22d 1805' and numbered '15' in bundle headed 'Miscellaneous 1805 No. 1 to 59'. Dol.

Ramsgate No. 9 Effingham Place
22d Feb[ruar]y 1805

My Dear Sir

On this occasion my sister wishes me to return Mrs. Watt her kind thanks for her affectionate Letter in return to hers of the 23d October last which conveyed to You our most sincere sympathy on account of the affecting loss You had sustained; and which was to ourselves the source of deep regret.

We hope that the interval of time that has since elapsed has alleviated your distress, and that this will find You and Family in the enjoyment of the blessing of good Health; of which indeed we should be most happy to be informed, at some moment of your leisure.

You would be truly sorry at hearing of the Death† of our old and excellent Freind Professor Robison† of Edin[burgh]. This happened on Wednesday 30th Jan[uar]y after having lectured, as usual, to his Class, on the Monday preceding. I received the unexpected and melancholy accounts on the 4th Feb[ruar]y, when I was *just about* inviting him, to acknowledge his kindness in sending me a copy of his recent valuable publication on "Dynamici and Astronomy", which reached me only two days soonner. We have lost a most valuable Friend, who was distinguished by very eminent talents for Science, and by his constant endeavours to make Science and Philosophy subservient to the great cause of virtue and Piety—

It was with much satisfaction that I learnt, some time ago, of my little Tract in the Phil[osophical] Magazine for last Sept[ember], published 18th being much commended by several of the leading mathematicians about the London Royal Society.

I made it publick merely in the way of throwing *good seed* in the ground, and in order to inculcate the necessity of sifting† some of the most important principles of Opticks by actual experiment;† rather than *indolently* to rest under so much hypothesis—I have something further of the same kind on hand, which probably I may soon also publish.

My sister and I feel sincerely obliged by Your and Mrs. Watts kind invitation to see You at Heathfield. Were I at liberty to make visits so distant from London, we have no friends to whom we would soonner resort for a season. But the nature of my worthy Brother's and my own joint affairs require me always to be within a short reach of London; in so much that, of late, I have found myself too distant, even here, for occasional Emergencies of being quickly in Town; on which account, before the ensuing Autumn, we propose removing near to London.

Most likely however we shall be here through the Summer; in which case it would be a great enjoyment to us, were You and Mrs. Watt and Miss McGregor to think of visiting this shore, during any part of the Season—

By the end of March I intend being up on one of my trips to London —to stay 12 or 14 days—when I will not fail to enquire for You, in the possible chance of Your being there—I may be always heard of at Andrew Strahan's Esq M.A. Little New Street old Fleet Street—

† Doubly underlined.

392

My Sister joins me in most affectionate Regards to Yourself, and
Mrs. Watt, and Miss McGregor and to Your Son

I remain Dear Sir
ever most faithfully
Your's
Pat Wilson

James Watt Sen[io]r Esq.,
  Heathfield

Letter 248

PLAYFAIR TO WATT

Cover addressed: 'James Watt Esq./Heathfield/Birmingham',
endorsed in Watt's hand, 'J Playfair Edinburgh March 2d 1805
concerning Dr. Robison' and numbered '31' in bundle headed
'Glasgow and Edinburgh 1805 No 1 to 35'. Dol.

Edin[bu]r[gh] 2d March
1805

Dear Sir
     The answers I have to give to your inquiries about the last illness of
our late excellent Freind will not convey to you I fear such particular
information as you could wish. He had been uncommonly well during
the winter; his spirits were good; he lookt very well, and his complaints
tho not removed seemed in no respect to have increased. On the Monday before his death he gave his lecture as usual, or rather with more
than ordinary spirit, and the day being good he walked home, and that
even by a more circuitous road than he usually took. In the afternoon,
or I believe in an hour or two after he got home, he complained of
coldness and went to bed. He soon became very ill, was seized with
reachings and vomiting, and in the Even[in]g when Mr. Russel saw
him he thought his situation extremely critical. He had however
nothing of the retention of Urine of which he sometimes complained.
Dr. Gregory and Mr. Russel saw him on Tuesday Morn[in]g and they
both considered him as dying. The whole system as Dr. G said seemed
to be undermined at once. He continued quite sensible however and

393

as far as I can understand did not suffer much from this time to his Death, which was on Wednesday Morning.

Thus an event that had no doubt been preparing for many Years both by the internal and unknown Malady that distressed him, and by the hurtful regimen which that malady and a natural tendency to inaction of body induced him to follow, came at last very unexpectedly, and deprived the world of \a/ great combination of Talents and Genius. Mr. Robison was not opened which is much to be regreted, and nothing more is known of his Malady than when he was alive.

In what state he has left his Papers I am not yet able to say, tho I delayed writing you in order that I might have some satisfactory information to give you. I imagine that at least another Vol[ume] of the Work on Natural Philosophy, of which the 1st Vol[ume] appeared last summer, will be found ready for the press; but what more there may be I think is uncertain.—Mrs. Robison is pretty well; I told her I had heard from you and meant to write. She desired to be remembered. Mr. R left three sons, one is in India another at Petersburgh, and the third here following the law.

Which of Mr. Robisons Freinds will be pitched on to give an account of his life I do not know; No body would be so fit for it as yourself. At any rate it were much to be wished that you would at your leisure commit to writing such Anecdotes or remarks or details of any kind on that subject as seem to you of importance.

The distress you may be assured Sir that you have lately suffered in your own family meets with the sympathy of all your Freinds here, and many more who have not the happiness to be personally known to you. I am sorry to think that Mr. Boultons health is a subject also of Anxiety, but I hope it is better than when you wrote.—I have a life of Hutton that I would send you if I knew how. If in anything relative to our late Freind you wish for farther information, I shall be glad to supply it if I can.

Yours etc.
John Playfair

Letter 249

WATT TO P. WILSON

J. P. Muirhead, *Mechanical Inventions of James Watt*, 1854, vol. II,
pp. 290–91.

Heathfield, March 12th, 1805

*   *   I understand Mr. De Luc, who is lately returned to
England, is writing an answer to Dr. Robison's censures upon him,
which he feels most severely. I wish Dr. R. had not said so much; it is
hard at fourscore for a man to be obliged to write in self-defence. I do
not enter into the matter in dispute, but I know Mr. De Luc to be a
very worthy man, and I do not conceive that he had the intentions
Dr. R. attributes to him.   *   *

Letter 250

DE LUC TO WATT

Cover addressed: 'To James Watt Esq./Heath-field/Birming-
ham/free/T. Sarum', endorsed, 'Mr. De Luc March 15th 1805
Controversy with Edinburgh Review etc.' and numbered '2' in
bundle headed 'Miscellaneous 1805 No. 1 to 59'. Dol.

Windsor, March fifteenth 1805

My dear Sir
   It is very long since we have not written to one another, a circumstance which is but too easily accounted for. On my Side, I have been
so overwhelmed with thoughts and labour on a painfull Subject, that of
the present State of the minds on the Continent with respect to
Revelation [*sic*], which threatens Society at large and the happiness of
individuals here and hereafter, that I have even renounced for all that
time the blessing of living with my two dear friends at Windsor. And
on our Side, what pain have you not suffered, with a last Stroke which
has fixed it! I hope you know enough my tender friendship for you
and Mrs. Watt, for having attributed to discretion, that I have not

written to you in these painfull circumstances; I have prayed and I pray still, that God may give you both the Strenght [sic] of supporting such a mournful event.

I attribute to the Situation of mind in which you must have been for a long time, that you have not perceived two circumstances which have concerned me at Edinburgh, the publication of Dr. Black's lectures by Mr. Robison, in which he has accused me of the most infamous proceeding, and the repetition of that accusation in the No. V of the Edinburg Review. You know too well the truth in that respect, and you have shewn \me/too much friendship, for having remained Silent, if these accusations had been known to you. I judge by my own feelings; for nothing could have prevented me from coming forward, if the case had happened to you.

With this persuasion, my dear Sir, I apply to you for support in my defence, which honour commands me, else I have too much upon my hands, for having taken notice of a mere critick. I send you a letter —directed to the Conductors of the Edinburgh Review; be so good as to read it with attention, and if you find nothing in it but true, to send it yourself to the Reviewers at Edinburgh. I mention this in the letter, so that if it appears in the Review, it will be known from that single circumstance that the facts concerning you are true. If I had failed in some particular of any importance, be so good as to point it out to me, in order to correct it. I thought so little that I could be attacked in my honour and probity, that it is very fortunate for me, that in the natural course of my expositions, circumstances have been mentioned in my works, which alone defeat the accusations against me.

You will see that in writting the letter, I did not know Mr. Robisons death, another very disagreable circumstance for me, which the more requires your Support: however I would not change my letter, which will shew how I intended to behave with him notwithstanding his evident wrong, and I have only mentionned that circumstance in a Post Script. I hope the Reviewers will not refuse to publish my letter, especially coming through you; it is not on a controversy of *opinions*, which they might not accept, it relates to facts essential to fix the *character* of a man, which they have branded on the authority of others, without any inquiry. But if, contrary to my expectation and to their own credit, they refused to publish it, I would publish it myself, with their refusal, for I will not remain under such an accusation.

Miss De Luc has written to Mrs. Watt, in her anxiety for poor Mr. Boulton, which I heartily share with her; may we receive better news!

She unites with me in best wishes for you and Mrs. Watt and I remain with unalterable friendship and regard

My dear Sir
Your most affectionate
humble Servant
De Luc

Windsor March 15, 1805
I come from town and I here [sic] that Miss De Luc has received a letter from Mrs. Watt for which she is much obliged to her, I have not time to say any more You will receive these under two franks

Letter 251

MRS ROBISON TO WATT

Endorsed, 'Mrs. Proffessor Robison March 17th 1805—Her character of Proffessor Robison' and numbered '17' in bundle headed 'Glasgow and Edinburgh 1805 No. 1 to 35'. Dol.

Edin[bu]r[gh] March 1805

My dear Sir
    I fear I obtrude upon you, but I wish to return you my best thanks for your kind promise of contributing what you can recollect in supplying materials to assist in composing the Life

Mr Erskine my Son-in-law yesterday informed me Mr. Playfair had undertaken this work. I am glad it meets your approbation. I myself wished Mr. Stewart to do it, as he has had so much experience and celebrity in this kind of writing. but he had made a resolution to refuse, (for particular reasons) engaging himself again in that way, but promises me to give every assistance and as Mr. P. and he are on the happiest footing of intimacy, I hope they will conduct it well between them, but I much regret that the most amiable parts of Mr. Robisons character is least known to them and the world. His Talents were great and his knowledge most extensive, but as perfection is forbid to this state, there was a kind of mist I was sensible that often obscured his amiable bright character from those that did not often see him. It was much produced by his *wonderful sensibility* and *delicacy* which naturally caused him to be hurt, with many things not felt by common minds. and even by minds of refinement who mixed with the world they were

397

accustomed to allow for, and overlook what can neither be prevented nor approved. This irritability often made him appear unlike the benevolent gentle Man he was, in so *eminent a degree*, and kept the world at a distance. as to his Talents and acquirements I have less anxiety—They are in part known and will be much easier understood by the world—but his Religion and piety which made him patiently submit without ever a fretful or repining word in nineteen years of *unremitting* pain, his humility, in his modest opinion of himself, his kindness in labouring with such industry for his family during all this affliction, his moderation for himself, to indulge as *unbounded generosity* to all around him, joined to his Talents, from a character, so uncommon and so noble as won't be easily conceived by those who have not like me had the contemplation of it. I am afraid my dear Sir to appear, in treating so frankly of this subject, that from me it may be looked upon as my partiallity but I hope to you who had the opportunity, and so much discernment, you cannot think so—may I expect then my dear Sir your warm support in this view of the Character, any thing from you will have much weight. I wish I could convey his wonderous worth, but I am much mortifyd that that [sic] the chief knowledge of it rests in so inefficient an agent—

You anticipate what I meant to mention of the publication of Mr. Rs works. we have the indisputed right to print in seperate volumes the articles from the Encylopedia. if we had not that, we never could have got it Twenty five thousand p[oun]ds is lately given for an agreed Number of copies and tho we cant withdraw the articles from or sell them to another dictionary, we sink its value immensely by doing this. I have also mentioned this to John Rennie as a Man whose opinion of the best form of publication, will weigh much with the Booksellers. I wish to offer it to several, to get the best price I can for the copy-right— I will be happy in every thing to hear your sentiments—and whatever occurs to you my d[ea]r Sir to instruct or direct me I hope you will be kind enough to take the trouble of mentioning

The Trustees are thinking also of having a large print from the portrait, and a smaller one for the Works.

I think I have now gone thro the points I wished to mention, and will no longer detain your attention I have to add my best wishes to Mrs. Watt and Mr. James and to be kindly remembered to Mr. Bolton Miss B. and her brother—and I [am] my d[ea]r Sir with much regard

Yours much obligd

R Robison

Letter 252

DE LUC TO WATT

Cover addressed: 'James Watt Esq./Heath field/near/Birmingham', endorsed, 'Mr. De Luc March 23d 1805' and numbered '3' in bundle headed 'Miscellaneous No. 1 to 59'. Dol.

My dear Sir

I have received your very friendly letter of the 19th instance, and I answer it immediately, in order that its very disagreeable Subject does not intrude long in another which now occupies me, by remaining in my mind.

I am as ready to listen to your remarks on the form of my apology, as I was sure that you would take interest in the defence of my character. I therefore beg you to communicate to me your ideas upon that form, after having considered the following general objects.

It is not enough, it is even nothing to my feelings in this occurrence, to express that my conscience is free from reproach; it must be the case of every honest man. But the accusation contrasts farther with my character, which has always made me find Satisfaction in praising others, while I felt a bashfulness very great in speaking of me. I have given in my letter an instance of these dispositions concerning Dr. Black himself, and I could shew you many similar in my works.

Moreover, had I been only accused of having *copied* Dr. Black, availing myself of some *accidental* information, for giving as my own, discoveries that belonged to him; as would have been the case if the insinuation concerning Dr. Odier were true; I hate so much *claims*, that I would not have taken notice of it. But to accuse me of having *abused* of my acquaintance with you and your *confidence* in me, for *obtaining* communications from Dr. Black, and to have afterward *defrauded* you both; to bring that accusation on a man of my age and not unknown in the world: to circulate it so, that it becomes impossible for me to make my apology follow it every where; this is such an offense, that you may indeed have found much *temper* in my exposition. I had present to my mind Mr. Robison's connexion with you, and I devised every thing that could lessen his wrong, but I cannot let any appearance fall on me; on which I must present you some considerations suggested to me by your first ideas.

You tell me that you will examine your *correspondance* and *memorandums* of 1782 and 1783. I shall be glad of it, but that may only concern what I have said of the objects of our intercourse, and I cannot find any object that relates to Dr. Black and me. His theory of *latent heat* being generally known at that time, what could have I desired to *publish* with his *consent*? Is it a *determination of quantities*? But I had no interest in that object for my pursuit; and surely no possibility of a *wish to appropriate*, \as I am accused/, experiments which I had never attempted. The *absolute* quantities, I repeat, did but very indirectly interest my own views, and whatever may have been at that time your correspondance with Dr. Black; it cannot relate to any *consent* asked from me to him. Your modesty would lessen what I had said on the merit of your more exact determination of *latent fire* in Steam; I published your remarks in that respect, though not persuaded. But my view in giving the details of that object, had been to shew the strong attention with which you had studied it, from which you had been led to the beautifull and important application of a thorough knowledge of that great quantity of *latent fire*, \that/ of destroying the Steam *out* of the cylinder of the engine; an idea which was much admired at Paris, in the exhibition made by Mess. Perier. As for my own purposes, which were the general object of *evaporation*, its *laws*, and its connexion with *meteorology*, I wanted no information from Dr. Black, it was from you alone; I received them, and I have acknowledge [*sic*] it with pleasure and gratitude.

This is what I have stated in my letter, and I could not consent to submit it to the judgement of any other friend of Dr. Robison but yourself, and as you alone have been concerned in these transactions, and that truth must appear. In short the wrong must be fixed were it is, and the having reduced it to *inconsideration* in Dr. Robison, I feel as an act of Christian charity. For, nothing short of a derangement of mind could afford an excuse for such a violent and unprovoked offense. The more I think of it, the less I can bear the thought of such an event having happened to me, the first of that kind in my life, notwithstanding the many serious conflicts in which I have been engaged, and I had none with him.

Another consideration which I must not omit, is this. Every apology is dull for readers, where there is no other interest. I was then obliged to create some interest in the subject itself; that interest is certainly in the history of the subject connected with my pursuit, and it is only by the way that it appears how wrongly I have been accused; I could not change that form.

With respect to the Reviewers, I wish also that they be not applyed to before hand, for fear to provoke some indirect refusal; if they refuse, it must be on direct application: I have furnished them also an excuse, though I had much to reproach them. I think they must themselves for their own credit, \wish/ to publish my apology, for I find that they have generally the repute of a *cynical* turn of mind, which disgusts

These, my dear Sir, are the general remarks which I beg you to have in mind with respect to those that you will be so good as to communicate to me. I wish sincerely to please you, but I must not leave such *stain* upon my reputation when I shall be no more in this world; and a dry apology cannot answer either the purpose of its been *read*, or be worthy of me.

We are much affected by the painfull account you give us of M. Boulton's State; may God help him! We have had also the pain of seeing Mrs. De Luc very ill, and she has been obliged to go to Bath, but thank God, we hear that she is a little better. You have our very sincere wishes for you, Mrs. Watt and your Son, and I remain invariably—

My dear Sir
Your faithfull friend and Servant
Windsor March 23, 1805.   De Luc

Dans ce moment je recois une lettre de Geneve du 22 fev. contenant une declaration du Dr. Odier sur les objets suivans. Que son arrivée a Edinburgh a été seulement en Septembre 1767, qu'il ne m'a ecrit d'Angleterre que trois lettres, qui se sont trouvées parmi des papiers que j'avois laissés à Genève. La première, est d'Edinburgh de 27 Juillet 1771, elle est en reponse à une lettre que je lui avois écrite après la communication que m'avait faite son père d'un Mémoire qu'il avoit publié sur les Sons et les corps sonores, et il ne parlait que de cet objet. La seconde est du 24 Janvier 1772; il y reprend le même sujet d'après ma reponse à sa première, et e finnissant il me parle pour la première fois d'une Theorie du Dr. Black sur la chaleur latente, il l'a dit fort ingénieuse, mais il renvoie de m'en parler a son retour. Le troisième est de Londres, du 26 Octobre 1772. Point encore d'explication sur la theorie du Dr. Black, et mon Ouvrage sortait alors de dessous la presse. Je lui avais communiqué mes expériences sur les rapports de la chaleur avec le thermometre de mercure; il m'apprenait que Dr. Black en avait fait de semblables, donc les resultats étaient un peu differens des miens.

Tels sont donc les faits positifs, je les substituerai dans le P.S. a la lettre que vous avez en main, aux informations indirectes que j'avais eues; mais je

401

*laisserai subsister l'historique de la lettre meme, parcequ'il m'importe qu'on
voie que l'ouvrage même suffisait pour prevenir l'accusation contre moi.*

*Si ce que vous me destinez avait quelques failles, ayez la bonte de me les
envoyer sous couvert de l'Evêque de Salisbury à Windsor.*

Letter 253

DE LUC TO WATT

Cover addressed: 'James Watt Esq./Heath-field/Birmingham',
endorsed, 'Mr. De Luc March 25 1805' and numbered '4' in
bundle headed 'Miscellaneous 1805 No. 1 to 59'. Dol.

31 March 1805

My dear Sir

I have received your three packets, for which I am much obliged to
you. It is a great pain for me to hear that you are out of Spirits and
unwell, at a time especially when I am obliged to plague you, on
account of the painfull Situation your deceased friend has placed me in.
I will as much as can be consistant with my honour, Spare his memory.
You wish \it/ in consideration of his family and friends; but I must no
less consider mine, after the accusation he has laid on me, of having
defrauded the men who *trusted my promise*. In that respect however I
could rely on the resentment I see in all those who know me, and the
general impression of a long life; were it not for a consideration, which
makes my full defence a *duty* to me.

I have spent a great part of my life in endeavours to recall men laid
[*sic*] astray, to their only true mean of happiness, the belief of *Revelation*. In particular I have faught the last eight years its detractors, in
France and Germany, and thus excited their hatred against me; but
they have only shewn it by impotant means, because they could not
attack my moral character. What then might be, in those countries, the
consequence of Mr. Robison's accusation, if not publickly repulsed? It
would give to my adversaries an opportunity of traducing as a *defrauder*,
the man who has made himself a champion of *Religion*. Must I then be
reduced to print a paltry sheet, without any authenticity, and to hand it
about myself, or have it handled in the corners of the Streets? This, my
dear Sir, is what I beg you to consider

402

I have already told you, and I repeat it as the truth, that this foul accusation is my sole object, though I must go farther on its account. Had M. Robison said, that Dr. Black had been my *model*, and that I had *followed* him without acknowledging his *right*, I would not have said a word to *claim* mine; our works exist, and I would have left \it/ to the judgement of natural philosophers. But having been accused, on the ground of *private transactions*, of *defrauding* Dr. Black's *confidence*, with the view to convert to my *fame*, what was due to his I must absolutely make it evident, that my own works were sufficient to prevent such an accusation. A bare and flat demonstration that I am not a *rogue*, without any interest for the reader, would be intolerable to me, and that reference to my works is what requires some length

You communicates to me what you had written to Dr. Black in 1782 and 1783, and his answers; but from what I have already \remarked/ in my last letter, you will judge easily that it does not change what I had said from my recollection. The question is whether I had wished, for any *interest*, either *personnal*, or arrising from my *views*, to obtain some *permission* from Dr. Black; and it is evident that it cannot be. His discoveries on *latent fire* (which he called *latent heat*) were so well known that the wish of *appropriating* them to me would not have been of a *rogue*, but of a *mad man*; and how could M. Robison, without being himself out of his senses, associate these contradictory ideas; "that in order to *pass* for the *author* of the doctrine," I had wanted to publish, "what Dr. Black had taught to *very numerous classes of Students from various parts of Europe*, every year after 1760?"

As for the object of *determination* of *quantities of heat*, it is no less evident that I could not have any sordid view in it, since I could have no appearance even of share in the merit, having never attempted those *determinations*. If this was an object interesting to me, on account of my *System*, it was only as leading to a *comparison* of the quantity of *latent fire* in the product of *common evaporation* and in *Steam*; but these were your own experiments; I could therefore have no other interest in publishing them, but what related to that *comparison*, and as answering the same motive that Dr. Black gives for acquiescing to your demand; "that of ascertaining clearly and fully your *sole right* to the honour of the improvement of the Steam Engine." I do not doubt, since it appears so in your letter, that I joined in your request; but you may see from what precedes, that I could not have any other motive than the two mentioned.

When therefore I wrote my work, unconscious of any *engagement*

403

with Dr. Black, I never thought of *claim*, either for him or for me. I exposed simply a system which had been formed by degrees in my mind; and as in the course of that exposition I was to state fundamental facts concerning *congelation* and *vaporisation*, I naturally mentioned those which were already published in my former work, with those that I had learned from you. I could not explain these last, without speaking of *absolute quantities*, and thus came on the right of Dr. Black, as having *attempted the first* their *determination*. You made me aware, that by using that *expression*, it might be supposed that he had not begun by the discovery of the *fact itself*. I felt it, and so much so, that instead of correcting that expression in two places, by changing the leaves, as you advised me to do, I prefered to let it stand, in order to take that opportunity of introducing in the *appendix* of that volume, your account of Dr. Black's *discoveries* and their *dates*.

Nothing consequently can be more simple and fair than my proceedings; however, I can judge that the foundation of Dr. Robison's attack, is these very letters of which you have given me an extract. But what spirit can have prompted him, against a man who never offended him, to transfer to my *second volume*, what he could not know but by reading it in the *Appendix* to the *first* with the circumstances mentioned? to change thus my conduct as much as from *white* to black? the *wound* that he has given me, cannot be healed without *wounding* deeply his reputation, except by my apology bein[g] inserted in the Edinburgh Review. Relying still on that [word indecipherable] way of some *publicity*, I shall follow your proposed alterations to the utmost of forbearance. But I depend also, my dear Sir, on your sending my letter to the Reviewers. This is the slightest manner of *implicating* you in that affair, so painfull to me, after you have been publickly *named* in it, not by me, but by the friend whose reputation you wish to spare. I think also that you would do well to make understand to the Robisons, that you have prevailed on me not to shew any resentment, provided my apology be inserted in the Review; in order that they concur to it, was it only by its being known to the Reviewers, that the family has no objection against it: and the Reviewers themselves are not without interest in my request.

The whole of that plan is dist[r]acted by my wish of having that affair drop softly. For if I were deprived of that natural mean of making my apology known, as however I would endeavour to make it appear, and under the same form that would have been refused, I could not but preface it by the most severe reflexions on the *unfeeling injustice* both of the Author and the Reviewers, who ought to have thought of the old Adage, that *calumny* (and such could be their accusation) once *Spread*, whatever may be the endeavours to make the *apology* follow it, leaves always a *Stain* on the innocent.

I haste to express to you my sentiments in this letter, in order to have my mind at liberty to comply to your wishes in changing the letter to the Reviewers, which, as soon as written again (a labour that comes a cross many others) I shall send you.

God bless you, my dear Sir, I remain

Yours sincerely

De Luc

Windsor, March 31th [*sic*], 1805

Letter 254

JEFFREY[1] TO WATT

Cover addressed: 'James Watt Esq./Heathfield/Birmingham', endorsed, 'Fr[ances]Jeffray Edinburgh March 26th 1805 Mr. De Luc's answer to critiscism' and numbered '34' in bundle headed 'Glasgow and Edinburgh 1805 No. 1 to 35'. Dol.

Edin[bu]r[gh] 26 March

1805

Dear Sir

I have just had the honor of receiving your letter of the 21st upon the subject of M. De Luc and lose no time in assuring you that the Editor of the Edin[burgh] Rev[iew] will have the greatest satisfaction in inserting in the Appendix of their journal any explanation which that gentleman may think proper to offer of the circumstances alluded to by Mr. Robison and his reviewer—It is some time indeed since I was assurd from another quarter that Mr. Robisons information and conclusions upon the subject were altogether erroneous; and I am confident that it will afford pleasure both to the individual who thought it his duty to give publicity to the accusation and to every person connected with the review to have an opportunity of publishing to the world such an account of the transaction as may entirely exculpate Mr De Luc from any imputation of impropriety—

There is only one thing to be attended to—As M. De L's statement cannot form an article in the review it must necessarily be annexed as an appendix and it is possible that he may have extended the [paper to] such a length as to render it impossible for us to admit it without great inconvenience—You may rely however upon our disposition to stretch a point for his accommodation and if it can be comprised within six or seven pages of our smallest printing he may depend upon its insertion with my first No which appears after its arrival—I flatter myself that this will afford him scope enough—but if he should be inclined to publish \elsewhere/ a more ample statement of the case it might perhaps suit his convenience to prepare an abstract or abridgment of it for us—

While we are thus anxious to afford Mr De Luc every facility for vindicating himself from any erroneous accusation you will easily understand that we are so far jealous and tenacious of our reputation as not to submit quietly to any insinuation of malignity or gross inattention in the discharge of our duty; and as I have perfect access to know that the reviewer of Mr R's publication intended nothing more than a summary of his authors observation I flatter myself that Mr. De Luc will not think it necessary to impute to him either any improper motives or any culpable negligance—Indeed it is only upon the supposition that his vindication is to consist chiefly in a statement of facts that I have expressed my willingness to admit it—The review has all along abstained from controversial discussions in public and cannot be expected to print an accusation to which it has solemnly tendered the privilege of replying—

Have the goodness to remember me very kindly to your Son to whom I would have written before now had I not been excessively hurried. If he still wants the letters for which he formerly applied to me they shall be sent according to his direction—they have been packed up for him for these three months and would have been sent to London if it had not been for an accident—It will give me great pleasure at all times to hear from him

I am Dear Sir
Your very obliged and obed[ien]t Serv[an]t
F. Jeffrey

1 Francis Jeffrey (1773–1850), critic, and editor of the *Edinburgh Review*.

DE LUC TO WATT

Dol.

6 April 1805

My dear Sir

I answer immediately your kind and very interesting letters of the 1st and 2d of this month (which I have found here in returning from London) in order to relieve you from the anxiety of sending yourself my letter to the Reviewers: I now take it on myself, with the principal conditions they prescribe; no *complaint* against the Author or Reviewers; I only must secure my justification, which in that gentle way, requires more length than they expect. But this will be between them and me; I shall write to them a private letter, explaining my reasons, and offering to take upon me the expense of what shall excede their allowance, which I shall reduce as much as possible.

I beg you, my dear Sir, to explain to me this passage of your Second letter: "But I thing [*sic*]—you may expect a *reply* to your *answer*, though I should hope free from *unfounded assertion*; and as to *fair arguments*, I know you have no objection to it." However I will endeavour to *answer* without any possibility of *reply*, and to this I beg your assistance. I will state nothing but *facts*; if I am right in these, what do you think they could *reply*? Consider that *priority* never entered in my thoughts: if it would be proved even that Dr. Black had taught his doctrine of *latent heat* before I had made any of my experiments, this would be nothing against my Statement. Have I *imitated* him in the first *period*? Have I *defrauded* his *confidence* in the Second? Those are the only objects of my answer, or historical account of my pursuits.

This view of the object, as I understand it, will, my dear Sir, make you comprehend what puzzles me in the above passage, and I hope it will not give you too much trouble, to point out to me on what I am to expect a *reply*, that I may endeavour to avoid it.

We rejoice at the good news on Mr Boulton's state of health, and wish you could give us a better account of your own. Miss De Luc will soon write to Mrs. Watt, and I remain

My dear Sir
Yours most Sincerely
De Luc

Windsor April 6th 1805

DE LUC TO WATT

Cover addressed: 'James Watt Esq/Heath-field/Birmingham', endorsed, 'Mr. De Luc April 16th 1805—His having finished his answer' and numbered '6' in bundle headed 'Miscellaneous Letters 1781-1790'. Dol.

Windsor, April 16th 1805

Dear Sir,

Your kind letter of the 11th has accomplished all I could wish, with the view of shortning the disagreable episode in my occupations, which has occasioned our last correspondance; I wished to prevent any plausible *reply*, and you have directed me in that respect as far as human foresight can extend.

First of all, I have suppressed *every part* of my Apology that your *pencil* had sentenced, and I have omitted many other passages, or turn of phrase, with the same spirit of forbearance; so that, except from the *accusation* itself, which was to remain in the beginning of my letter, the reader will never think of Mr. Robison or the Reviewer himself in the rest, by any complaint against them. But in that plan, I have \been/ obliged to change the whole, giving it quite another turn, which, notwithstanding the Suppressions, has produced the same length

In that plan what could be the objects of a fair *reply*, either from Dr. Black's or Dr. Robison's friends? Would they again maintain the accusation of *plagiarism* or *fraud*, the only objects of my answer? *Impossible!* Would they raise a new attack against me, with the view of lessening my merit as *natural philosopher*? They would, I think, hurt themselves more than me; for it would be unprovoked, as I give them no clue by either praising myself or my works. I know the real deffects of the first \of these works/ better than \do/ themselves, and I have successively pointed them out in other works.

The friends of Dr. Black in particular will see moreover, how little I thought of *fame*, from the instance I give of having both in Germany and France, without any thought of *myself*, attributed to Dr. Black the *whole* of the object which they have so much at heart, *latent heat*. But those imputations have induced me, as a first consequence, to write to Paris, in order to correct the same expressions, which were near going to the press in another work.

In fact, that attack was the only circumstance that could have engaged me to those retrospects; but thus I have been led to shew, in the very *bud* of my thoughts, a *clearer*, and more *producive* idea of the phaenomenon, than that of *latent heat*. For *heat*, is an *effect*, which can not be *latent*, since it is the object of the *thermometer*, but *fire*, the cause of *heat* can be *latent* by chymical combination, † It is for not having understood that essential difference of ideas, that Dr. Robison pretends that my first work contained only some *crude ideas* of the *combinations of heat*: they were indeed in the *bud*, far from *ripe*; but with the idea of *combination of fire*, I have been led, from the beginning, in a quite different road than that of Dr. Black; it may be wrong, but not *stolen* from him, and it is all I contend for.

With respect to Dr. Robison's friends, as he \had/ no share to claim in these pursuits, would they, by any sort of *reply*, move his ashes which I leave quiet? They ought on the contrary to prevail on Dr. Black's friends to let this affair fall *into oblivion*. For a new attack would only bring again, with more disadvantage, the attention of the impartial public on a conduct in which, though I attribute it to *erroneous recollections*, you have judged yourself, "that he must have laboured under some other *prejudice*, though the cause is unknown to you". It is also unknown to me, but unconscious of any *wrong*, I am not affraid of an inquiry.

Having, in this affair, no view of defending my *ideas*, or their *expressions*, I confess to you, that I have not read, nor am I disposed to read Dr. Robison's *Note*, already pointed out by the Reviewer, and to which you refer me, for what may be opposed to me with respect to the merit of my first work. If the Reviewer has not imbittered that Note, it must have a character intolerable for a man of honour; and having no thought of vindicating my *philosophical merit*, I will not put myself to a new trial of forbearance. I therefore leave my letter as it is, with the alterations made according to your advice and new informations; it is finished, and only the copy I have to send, to to be revised; this week I hope will not pass, before it be in 'its way to Edinburgh, directed as you have advised me, in a frank of the Bishop of Salisbury; and then I shall drive all thought of it out of my mind, till the answer of the Reviewers, to whom I shall write a private letter.

We all join in good wishes for you and Mrs. Watt, in your future jaunt, hoping that it will do you both good; and with my sincere

† [in margin] producing no *heat*: the word *latent* I have borrowed since from Dr Black, but nothing else in the accused object.

409

thanks for the proofs of friendship you have given me in this disagreable occasion, I constantly remain,

Dear Sir

Your most affectionate friend

De Luc.

Letter 257

J. P. Muirhead, *Mechanical Inventions of James Watt*, 1854, vol. II, pp. 293-99.

J. Watt's Recollections of his Friend Dr. J. Robison.

April, 1805.

*   *   Our acquaintance began in 1756 or 57, when I was employed by the University of Glasgow to repair and put in order some astronomical instruments, bequeathed to the University by Dr. Macfarlane, of Jamaica. Mr. Robison was then a very handsome young man, and rather younger than I. He introduced himself to me, and I was happy to find in him a person who was so much better informed on mathematical and philosophical subjects than I was, and who, while he was extremely communicative, possessed a very clear method of explaining his ideas. Between two young men of ardent minds, and engaged in similar pursuits, a friendship was soon formed, which has continued until death has deprived me of my friend; and has suffered no other interruption than what has been caused by our absences from each other, and the necessary attentions to our respective duties in life. Soon after this, I settled as mathematical-instrument-maker in the College of Glasgow, and was frequently favoured by Mr. R.'s company, until he left the College about the end of 1758, and went to sea, I believe, in one of his Majesty's ships. During this period he turned my attention to the steam-engine, a machine of which I was then very ignorant, and suggested that it might be applied to giving motion to wheel-carriages, and that for that purpose it would be most convenient to place the cylinder with its open end downwards, to avoid the necessity of using a working-beam. The latter idea he had published some time before in the 'Universal Magazine.' In consequence, I began a model, with two cylinders of tin plate, to act alternately, by means of rack motions, upon two pinions attached to the axis of the wheels of the carriage; but the model, being slightly and inaccurately made, did not answer expectations. New difficulties presented themselves. Both Mr. R. and myself had other avocations which were necessary to be attended to; and, neither of us having then any idea of the true principles of the machine, the scheme was dropped.

I, however, went on with some detached experiments on steam until 1763, when I set about the matter more seriously, and discovered the principles upon which my improvements on the steam-engine are founded. Mr. R. returned to Glasgow in 1763 or 64. Among other places, he had been in the West Indies, and I remember his mentioning to me his feelings upon his landing in Jamaica, and his admiration of the vegetables there, especially the trees—so extremely unlike those of Europe—as well as some of the phenomena of the climate. He mentioned that, for the purpose of astronomical observation, he had gone up among the mountains there; and that though at 7 o'clock in the morning he had found the sun intolerably hot on the S.E. side of the mountain, he had found it so cold at 9 o'clock of the same morning on the N.W. side, that he found a large wood-fire exceedingly agreeable while he breakfasted. He mentioned many other circumstances that—though they interested me much then—are now obliterated from my memory.

After his return to Glasgow, I think it was, that he became tutor to Mr. Macdowal, of Garthland, and his brother; and during that time I recollect his mentioning that, during a very intense frost, the window of his room, being very badly fitted, admitted rather more cold air than was agreeable, which he remedied by applying water with a brush to the bad joints, and, in proportion as it froze, applying more until the joints were stopped. I do not recollect his being present or assisting me in any of my experiments on steam, or of the improvements upon the steam-engine; but on this head I send a copy of his evidence in B. and W.'s trial with Maberly, in the Court of Common Pleas, at Guildhall, in 1796. I remember also that in 1765, on seeing a perspective machine, with a double sliding motion at right angles to each other, which Dr. Lind had brought from India, and had made some improvements upon, Mr. R. suggested that the same thing might be better accomplished by a double parallelogram (as some parallel rulers were then made),—an idea which I pursued, and, by some improvements and additions of my own, made a useful instrument.

From the period of Mr. R.'s return to Glasgow, our interviews were rare: he had his duties to attend to and I, having become the father of a family, and loaded with cares of many kinds, had less time for mere philosophical conversations; our friendship, however, subsisted, and we were happy when we met upon any occasion. I cannot recollect the date when he went to Russia, nor do I know much of his transactions there, only in general that he was much esteemed, as was testified to me by Sir Charles Knowles, to whom he had recommended me. I remember also the receiving a letter from Mr. R., in or about 1773, proposing to me to come to Russia, where he had recommended me to fill some station I did not conceive myself equal to, and which I respectfully declined. In 1774 I left Scotland to settle in Birmingham, where I have resided ever since, and have had very few opportunities of meeting with Mr. R. But in 1796, when Boulton and Watt were assailed by a combination of pirates, who wished to rob them of the fruits of their industry, and disputed my claim to the invention of the improvements upon the steam-engine, Mr. Robinson, not withstanding the painful disease under which he laboured, and his necessary attention to the duties of his class, procured leave of absence, and made a journey to London to appear as witness in our cause, where his testimony had very great effect both upon the judge and jury; but be the latter circumstance as it may, the zeal with which he espoused my cause, and the disregard to his own personal inconveniences when they came in competition with it, can never be forgotten by me while I remember anything.

To give Dr. R.'s character is beyond my power, but somethings I may mention as hints to those who are more capable. He had the quickest and clearest comprehension of every question in science of any person I ever knew, and added to that a very pleasing manner of explaining it to others, though he was rather impatient if he found he was not attended to or comprehended. He used to complain of his own want of industry, but it was without cause, for nobody was more studious than himself; though, perhaps, he was sooner tired than duller men, with those studies which presented little upon which he could exercise those inventive powers he possessed in so eminent a degree. Yet, if this was so, his intense application in more mature life, and his productions even when labouring under an excessively severe malady, show that his complaints of himself were more imputable to the impatience of youth, and to the despondency and doubts of his own powers, to which he was unfortunately subject, than to any other defects in his character or disposition. He was kind and affectionate, constant in his friendships, and would take more trouble for his friends than he would for himself. Naturally diffident, he was reserved in his conversation with strangers,—at least with those whose characters he was not well informed of; but with his friends, nobody was ever more open and communicative, though he was always more ready to listen than to offer his opinion.

He had a high sense of honour and propriety, and nothing could offend him more than a breach of them in others. He entertained a high respect for the constitution of his country, and detested the novel doctrines of Jacobinism, which made him pass censures too severe upon several of the French philosophers (otherwise extremely estimable men, and to whom science is much indebted), without, perhaps, duly weighing the circumstances in which they were placed. His displeasure with some of them was probably augmented by his thinking them deficient in giving that praise and honour to Dr. Black which his discoveries merited: and, however any person might think himself unjustly censured by Dr. R., I can safely say that I am sure he was actuated by no selfish, envious, or malignant motive in anything he has written.

His errors must be attributed to the failings of human nature, and to the painful malady under which he laboured; which, however, he bore with the utmost patience.

Letter 258

Endorsed in Watt's hand, 'Mr. Robison's letters in my possession
at his death'. Dol.

Mr. Proff[esso]r Robisons letters—1805
No letters in my possession prior to Oct[obe]r 2d 1781; that letter mentions 2 others which I seem not to have received and recommends Mr. Peter Ewart to our service as a Mill wright or Engineer, the answer to it does not appear, but I believe I recommended him to learn the business as far as he could in Scotland first.
Oct[obe]r 22d 1783 says will pay attention to my recommendation of Mr. Pearson—that he was composing a System of Mechanicks, in which he considered machines in motion in place of a State of Equilibrium, finds by experiment that a horse drawing a boat performs the most work (estimated by the force with which he stretches the rope) when he moves

413

with 2/5 of the velocity with which he can move, performing no work, during the ordinary\working hours/ of the 24 and that he is then exerting $\frac{9}{23}$ of the force which he can continue to exert on a fixt obstacle for the same time—mentions a scheme of a Steam Engine, by a Mr. Ker, on Blakeys principle and another by the same in which the piston was fixed and Cylinder moveable, says that he himself published a Scheme of the Latter kind in the Universal Mag 26 years ago—Mention that 17 years since he had filled balls of varnish with inflamable air, which floated but burst before they could dry—

Aug[us]t 15 1786—recommends Dr. Rogerson—

Feb[ruar]y 3d 1788, requesting me to procure a silver Cup—Mentions his having been very ill

Mar[ch] 7th 1788 Orders the cup—Mentions some thing of Symingtons Engine—Dr. Bs. illness and recovery—

Mar[ch] 7th 1793, Reccommending Mr. Booker

May 12—about putting his son to business—

Oct[obe]r 25th 1796 Objections to his coming to England—his bad health had been ill 5 years, proposes to teach his class this winter will endeavour to get his assisstant to do it for him

Dec[embe]r 1796 \London/ previous to his examination in our cause, wishes our counsel to let him tell his tale in his own way—

Dec[embe]r 1796 \London/ correction of what he said respecting his conversation with Messrs. Model and Epinus—plan of a Mutual for Engineers and Mill wrights—

Feb[ruar]y 3d 1797 His embarrassments on his return to Edinburgh on account of the Article *Water works* he had promised to the Encyclopedia, plan of a book in practical Mechanics April 7th 1797 His sisters death, receipt of B and Ws draft £31..1..6. His own bad health—and Dr Bs Dr Huttons death—May 3d 1797, requesting one of Sir Isaac Newtons letters to Facio from Mr. Boulton—His search after Sir Isaac's extraction Jan[uar]y 14th 1798 Recommends Mr. Thomson as operator to the Pneumatic institution, his own troubles, copyright of proof of a conspiracy, threatnings ag[ains]t him on that account

May 4th 1798, His son John going to Manchester, Machine erected at Oulton in Cheshire—Zurich or Spiral Wheel for raising Water, Dr. Bs very bad health

Glasgow Sep[tembe]r 22d 1798 to Mr. Miller about placing his daughters with Mrs. Wright—

Dec[embe]r 15th 1798—His sons visit to me, His observations on Iceland Crystal—

Dec[embe]r 11th 1799 Dr. Blacks death—on the Friday preceding
—18th—   about his undertaking to edite the D[octo]rs
Lectures account of his first acquaintance with him with dates
Feb[ruar]y 25th 1800 his sending off \to me/ my letters to Dr. B by a
friend His opinion of Mr. De Luc—notes about my exp[erimen]ts on
distillation *in vacuo*—schemes for publishing Dr Bs lectures—
French chymists—Birth of his youngest son—
July 23, 1800, on Dr Bs lectures, his opinions on the notes put into his
hands and his doubts of the propriety of his publishing any more than the
D[octo]rs peculiar doctrines—his election as a member of the Royal
Accademy at Petersburgh
Sep[tembe]r 9th 1800, his sending me the copies of Dr. Bs lectures and
wanting my opinion of the share of the profits he sh[oul]d have for his
Editorship not less than ⅓—ab[ou]t french theories of consumption [*sic*]
etc
Oct[obe]r 2d 1800, His sending off the D[octo]rs MS had been delayed by
his own illness—begs me to consider what his share of the proffits of the
Book should be—Means to come to Glasgow immediately—
Oct[obe]r 1800, Glasgow. Wholy upon his plans for digesting Dr. Bs
lectures—
Oct[obe]r 19th Boghall—Dr. Bs lectures, Mr. Geddes's Engine
Mr. Lowitz experiment on causing salts to cristallize by presenting a
Crystal of the Salt
Jan[uar]y 8th 1802, Has finished his Copy of Dr. Bs lectures which will
make 1500 pages—has appointed Dr Rutherford for his arbiter as to his
share of the profits—De Luc—Lichtenberg—Has been 18 Months in
composing the MS has foregone a summers course which would have
brought 60 g[ui]n[ea]s and paid 30 for an amanuensis—Wants advice as
to a bookseller
Ap[ri]l 19th 1803 has sent the last sheet to the press, dedication to me—
His son arrived at Columbo well
Aug[us]t 14th 1803 to Mr. Hamilton is afraid that I am displeased with
his edition of Dr. Bs lectures and explains himself
Dec[embe]r 20 1803 By Mr Hutton his scheme for a Manual for
Engineers etc.

Copy of Mr. Watt's Remarks on Mr. Robison's Edition of Dr. Black's Lectures. communicated to Mr. Playfair 4 Jan[uar]y. 1809.—
Dedication p. III. I acknowledge to have received much information and instruction from Dr. Black and from Yourself on many subjects, but it was you that first turned my attention to the Steam Engine sometime about the Year 1759. (It was to make it move Wheel Carriages, that was the first scheme, but that was adandoned by me for want of knowledge at that time and of Perseverance.) It is impossible for me now to particularize the knowledge I acquired in conversation both from you and Dr. Black; but I shall afterwards show that though that knowledge was certainly conducive to my after inventions, yet it certainly did not directly point \out/ the improvements I have made upon the Steam Engine, as may be inferred from the page quoted. I may from what I now say be accused of vanity, but I owe something to truth, and as I would not wish to attribute to myself any thing I know to be my friends, neither ought I to decorate his brow with any of the few laurels I can lay claim to. It is however a painful task to diminish in any degree the fame which you have thought his due.—In what follows in p IV you pay me a compliment I never deserved. I shall however always be proud that you have thought me to have done so. *Laudari a laudato viro.*
Preface p.VIII. You must have been much misinformed concerning my attending Dr. Blacks Lectures. I never did so, and certainly would have possessed more solid knowledge of chemistry than I do, if I had been wise enough to have done so. Every thing I learnt from him was in conversation and by doing small mechanical jobs for him. These Conversations and those I had with you served to give me true notions in Science and to develope the powers of my Mind, such as they were; and I hope that after so long an acquaintance you will not suspect me of flattery when I say that I have never known a young Man of your then Years who possessed so much science or so quick a comprehension, joined to great inventive powers. To this I ought to add the great pleasure you seemed to take in instructing me.—
P. IX. You again are guilty of paying me too high a Compliment. I was no more fit to have edited Dr. Blacks lectures, than to govern a Nation. I had neither sufficient knowledge of chemistry, nor the necessary industry; nor did I so well recollect his train of thoughts as you have done,

who enjoyed his Society in later periods of his life, from which I had been separated for almost 30 Years before his death. Moreover I gave you very little help by my correspondence or observations in the task which you have perfomed with so much honour to yourself.

P.XLIV. I shall narrate what I remember of the Experiments of the latent heat of steam in giving an Account of my own operations

In 1780, when Magellan in a publication of his injuriously attributed the discovery of latent heat to Wilcke of Sweden, I wrote to Dr. Black for the date of his Discovery and received a very full answer, which I have now unfortunately mislaid. But from the quotation which Magellan thought fit to print from my letter to him, Dr. Black had made that discovery previous to 1758 or even to 1757. I suppose alluding to the latent heat absorbed by melting ice.—

My letter to Magellan contained *inter alia* as follows, "Dr. Black gave "the doctrine of Latent heat in his Lectures at Glasgow immediately on "his being made Professor there, which was in the year 1757–58, or in "the year 1758–9 at latest, and taught every winter at Glasgow until "1766–7 when he was made Professor at Edinburgh"

This I know I copied from the D[octo]rs letter to me. Some Account of the D[octo]rs Theory is given in Roziers Journal at the time it was published in Duodecimo about 1773 or 4. Magellan behaved like a rascal and did not publish half what I wrote to him, and that with deductions.—

Dr. Black has done me sufficient justice in the description *he* has given of my improvements upon the Steam Engine, but the history of my ideas on that subject may be misconceived from what he has said upon them. A short account of their progress may therefore not be improper.

My first attention was turned to that subject by a conversation with my friend Mr. Robison, then a student at Glasgow, some time about the year { 1761 or 1762 } \1759/. He threw out an idea of applying that power to the moving of wheel carriages and to various other purposes. A Model of its application was begun, but from various causes was never proceeded in. Afterwards, I tried some Experiments on the force of Steam in a Papin's digester, and formed a species of Steam Engine by fixing to it a narrow Syringe with a solid piston, accompanied with a cock which would admit the Steam from the digester into the Syringe, or shut it off at pleasure, and when the staple of the cock was turned in a certain direction would open a communication between the inside of the Syringe and the open Air, whereby the Steam contained in it would escape. When the communication was open between the Digester and

417

the inside of the Syringe, the Steam entered, and by its action in the Piston raised a considerable weight with which it was loaded. When the weight was raised as high as was thought proper the communication with the Atmosphere was opened, the Steam made its escape and the weight descended. These operations were performed with perfect regularity; but it was easy to see that an Engine so constructed would be liable to the most material objections which lay against Savery's construction, namely the danger of bursting the boiler, and the difficulty of making the joints tight, and that a great part of the power of the Steam would be lost, because no vacuum was formed to assist its action.—

Remarks on Mr. Robison's Edition of Dr. Blacks Lectures *continued*.—

As I had not at that time paid much attention to the subject and had other avocations, it was then pursued no farther; but in the Winter of 1763, having occasion to repair a Model of Newcomen's Engine which belonged to the Natural Philosophy class of the University of Glasgow; when I had got it in working order, I found that the Boiler, though large in proportion to the Cylinder could not supply it with Steam to work at a proper rate unless the fire was violently urged with bellows.

I observed also, that the Cylinder which was about 2 Inches diameter, could only give power enough to work a pump of the same diameter and about 2 feet high, which effect was much less in proportion to the Cylinder than was generally performed by larger \Steam/Engines.

On considering the causes of these defects it appeared, 1st that as Steam is condensed by the contact of bodies colder than itself and in proportion to the quantities of such cold bodies with which it comes into contact, and the internal surface of any cylinder being many times greater in proportion to its contents than that of the large Engines employed in Collieries, much more Steam must be condensed before the Cylinder could be filled so as to permit the piston to rise; 2dly that as water was supposed to boil *in vacuo* at much lower heats than it did under the pressure of the atmosphere, a vacuum could not be produced in the cylinder unless that vessel were cooled by the injection below the point at which water would boil in an exhausted Vessel.

Note.

For this I was indebted to the Experiments of Dr. Cullen on the boiling of Ether *in Vacuo* and some conversations I had on the subject of that experiment with Dr. B. and Mr. R[obiso]n†

† A line has been drawn enclosing this paragraph, as above.

Therefore the greater the degree of exhaustion which was demanded, the more the Cylinder must be cooled by the injection, and the greater quantities of Steam must be condensed before the Cylinder could be filled again, all which was confirmed by trying to work the Model under various loads, or higher and lower columns of Water in the Pump.

_____

Mem[orandu]m
This letter, to Dr. R. was begun sometimes after the publication of Dr B's lectures but was never compleated and by Mr. Robison's death was rendered useless as to him
J.W. 1808.

_____

The date of 1759 seems to be right, as Robison was absent about 4 Years, and returned in 1763, *vide* Preface to Dr. Black's lectures p.p. VII, VIII, XXXIV.

_____

Mem[orandu]m made at the request of JW. Jun[io]r in Jan[uar]y 1808.
The *common* Engines I erected, were a very small one to pump water to a turpentine still-tub at Carron Wharf 1765; a 24 Inch Cyl[inde]r for Mr. Bruce of Kennet in partnership with Mackell about 1766; a larger, I beleive 45 Inch at Newton of Air, with the same in 1767 or 8, and these were all in which he was concerned with me.—One or two short stroke Engines 18 or 20 Inch Cylinders for Mr Colville of Torryburn, date uncertain, but before 1769. One or two of the same sort for Dr.Roebuck prior to 1770; and and these are all I recollect at present.—

Letter 260

WATT TO BANKS

Addressed: 'The Right Hon[our]able/Sir Joseph Banks K B, Bart./Soho Square/London'. Royal Society Library: BLA. W. 17.

W 17
Heathfield Mar[ch] 1st 1815

My Dear Sir
I received your kind letter of 23rd with much pleasure as a testimony of your being tolerably free from your Tormentor, and of your very flattering remembrance of me

419

In reply to M Biot's query, at the instigation of my friends, and to my own great annoyance, I spent all my working hours of the winter of 1813 and spring of 1814 in writing a commentary on my Friend Dr. Robisons memoir upon the Steam Engine in the *Encylopedia Brittanica*, for the use of Dr. Brewster[1] who is editing all the Proffessors works and I put therein some account of all I have done on the subject of the{ *Calorique* }*Chaleur*/ *Specifique*, or in plain english of the heats at which water boils under various pressures, on its Latent heat etc. My Commentary has been finished by me ever since May last and is now in the hands of a friend for ultimate correction. The first volume of my Book is announced by Murray[2] (I think as in the press) and as my M.S. will soon be in Dr. Bs. hands I hope it will soon be before the Publick

Mean while nothing relating to the subject is in my possession and if it were, I should not do either Mr. Biot or myself justice by sending much less than the whole I have written, which would be to me, *in Grandum renovare dolorem*, and without it were accompanied with Dr. Robisons text would not be always intelligible—All that I can at present say upon the subject is that In the year 1765 I made some experiments upon the heats of water boiling under pressures greater than that of the atmosphere, say when it supported columns of mercury of 15 inches 60 inches 75 inches and sime higher ones in order to ascertain nearly the ratios of the heats to the pressures to assist me in my researches upon the improvement of the Steam Engine. These experiments being made in a rude way were not exact, though they were enough so for my purpose

In 1772 I made other experiments, in which I was assisted by Dr. Irvine Sen[io]r, both upon the boiling of water under pressures greater and lesser than that of the atmosphere, but the subject being difficult, these also did not satisfy me and in 1793 I requested my friend Mr. John Southern to repeat them at Soho and his results I have every reason to believe were as accurate as the subject permits, but of none of these have any copy by me. In the mean time I beg leave to refer Mr. Biot to some experiments upon the subject published by Mr. Dalton[3] which agree very nearly with those made by Mr. Southern, \from which/ As far as I recollect Mr. De Betancourts[4] exp[erimen]ts differ considerably.

I shall urge Dr. Brewster to complete his edition of Dr. Rs works, which will be a very valuable Book, but Dr. B has so much in hand that I fear he{ will }can not get on fast.

Mean while I beg you will make my acknowlegements to Mr. Biot for the honour he has done me by his reference to me on this subject and \say/ that I am sorry I cannot gratify him more fully at present.

I am still going on with my scheme and have made some progress and would have made more had not some unhappy Rheumatisms disabled me from ever doing much, without bringing on myself suffrings greater than the work deserved I am now considerably better, provided I am idle but that is not quite agreable

My only Grandson a youth of 21 is threatened with a fatal consumption. He is now at Plymouth under the care of Dr. Skey and we mean very soon to send him to sea to Madeira, Bermudas, or the Cape of Good Hope   Would you be so kind as to ask your experienced friends which of these they deem the most proper, especially what sort of winter there is at the Cape? We however trust more the effect of the sea than of the Land—I hope you will excuse the liberty of the request, I know nobody could serve me better in this case

I have delivered your messages to Messrs Galton[5] and Boulton who desire their best respects in return

My Son joins me in respectful comp[limen]ts and best wishes to your Lady Banks and Miss Banks and I remain always

My Dear Sir

Your grateful and obliged serv[an]t

James Watt

The Right Hon[oura]ble
Sir Joseph Banks KB, Bart.
Soho Square
London

[1] Sir David Brewster (1781–1868), Professor of Physics in the University of St Andrews, who had a particular interest in optics.
[2] John Murray (1778–1843), publisher.
[3] John Dalton (1766–1844), author of the atomic theory.
[4] Augustin de Bétancourt (1760–1826), military engineer, entered the Russian service. Author of a *Mémoire sur la force expansive de la vapeur d'eau*, Paris 1790.
[5] Samuel Galton, junior (1754–1832), F.R.S., member of the Lunar Society of Birmingham.

Part 2

The Notebook

The folios of the Notebook that are illustrated between pp. 432–3 are as follows:

folio		picture		text page	
10r		A		435	
11r		B		435	
14r		C		436	
17v		E		439	
21r		D		440	
23r		F		442	
24r		G		443	
31r		H		450	
38r		I		459	
40v		J		464	
42v		K		468	
43v		L		469	

Introduction to the Notebook

The Notebook is fragmentary and discontinuous except for the record, in their original and corrected states, of the experiments to determine the latent heat of condensation of steam. Some entries are dated, others undated; but the document contains some important historical details, especially those that are dated. It is mostly written on only one side of the paper of a small octavo notebook, of which only 83 pages are written on and many others are blank. It is foliated and the last sheet [53] is not numbered. This document, in view of its historical interest, is here reproduced in as exact a transcript as possible,* and the only two chemical symbols occurring in it, ▽ for water and ☿ for mercury, should prove no difficulty to the reader, who is asked to observe also that, where foliations are missing in the sequence below, the missing numbers indicate blank pages. The entries range irregularly over fifty years, from about 1765 to 1814.

The opening pages consist of notes on copal varnish, probably for use on Watt's instruments. Then follows a note on his improvement of the 'machine' for perspective drawing, an improvement that he wished to claim for himself. Both of these entries are undated.

The next entry, beginning on f. 7r is dated, with the year only, '1765'. It begins with a reference to Robison's idea of a leverless 'fire-engine', that is, a steam-engine, that would work without a lever or beam by the simple device of inverting the cylinder over the mouth of the pit. Watt was to make a model, which he began but never completed, because, he says, Robison went abroad and he was himself at that time 'ignorant' on this subject (he changed this to 'having . . . little knoledge', which may have seemed to him a better way of recording this). It seems, however, from what he wrote that he went on experimenting with the idea that such a machine might be used for other purposes, but that he made no 'conclusive experiments' until the winter of 1763–64. Robison, according to the notebook, was now again in Glasgow, as we know also from other sources, and thus

---

* Except that full points and colons after or below superior letters have been omitted. Thus 'Christ:' 'Dr.' 'Cyl:' appear in the transcript 'Christʳ' 'Dʳ' 'Cylʳ'. In addition the sketches which appear on some pages of the Notebook have not been reproduced in the transcript. Instead photographs of these pages have been inserted as plates and cross referenced. See p. 431.

he renewed his acquaintance with Watt, whom he had previously known since the latter had been appointed mathematical instrument-maker to the University of Glasgow in December 1757. Their previous association, although close, must have been short, since Robison left Glasgow in 1758.

Watt's duties at the University did not, however, enable him even to scrape a living, and he began to make instruments for sale. In 1759 he set up a partnership with John Craig and opened a shop in the Salt-market, removing late in 1763 to the Trongate. In the winter of 1763–64, as he recorded in his notebook, he was called on to put in order a small model of a Newcomen engine used for the class in natural philosophy in the University. This is largely well-known history, but in the notebook we have it in Watt's own words as written down at that time. He was, he wrote, surprised at the large amount of fuel consumed with a cylinder only two inches in diameter and he ascribed this to the heat 'lost thro the Metallic Cylinder', a very reasonable and common-sense conclusion. When he discussed this matter with Robison, the suggestion arose of making the cylinder of wood instead of metal. Abandoning Robison's earlier idea of a leverless or beamless engine, he experimented with wooden cylinders and also considered the condensation of the steam in the cylinder by using a jet of cold water. The notebook shows that these experiments with wooden cylinders were not successful, but records no use of a jet of water to effect condensation. Rates of evaporation of water were studied; Savery engines in series were considered; and the expansion of water when converted into steam was determined as 'above 1600 times its bulk', a very good result in what was no very refined experiment. This result is entered on *ff.* 14*r* and 15*r*, and it calls for some comment, as the values for 'some experiments formerly tho Less accurately made' are added in a note on *f.* 14*v*: further, the inner tube is unnecessary and was not described by Black, with whom Watt made this experiment, as has been shown elsewhere (see McKie, *Ann.Sci.*, March 1967, p. 27), where it is also shown that the revised value of 1600 (actually 1664), as compared with 1800, was determined in 1767.

On *f.* 17*r* there is an important entry. Watt is here quoting values for what were later called 'specific heats' for iron, copper and tin, first determined in experiments made by Black and Irvine; and that he obtained these values from the former is clear from his reference to tin ('tin is said by Dr Black . . .'). In the immediately following words the phrase should read, not 'heating *to* the boiling point', but 'heating

426

at the boiling point'; Black, from whom Watt here stated that he derived this information had already not only discovered this fact but also determined the value of the latent heat of vaporization of water, and would have told him that water heated *at* the boiling point 'did every minute receive Considerable additions of heat'. Watt's entry in his notebook was confusing and the next entry (*f.* 17*v*) shows how very confused he was; for he mixed 1 part of boiling water with 30 parts of cold water and found that the mixture was 'only heated to the arithmetical mean', which, as Watt reported it, is clearly impossible, since this would occur only with equal parts of cold and hot or boiling water. If he meant 'steam' rather than boiling water, such a result would be obtained. The next experiment with the kettle and a 'frigeratory' suggests that he may have intended to write 'steam' rather than 'boiling water', because he then condensed steam by passing it into cold water, which he found to become 'boiling hot'. He turned to Black to ask if it was possible that water under the form of steam could contain more heat than it did when, as water, it was heated to 212°, its boiling-point. Watt then recorded that Black told him that this had long been a tenet of his. Black, of course, had gone much further and had determined the latent heat of vaporization of water in his classic experiment of 4 October 1762. Watt added that Black tried the experiment with the still 'about a week later', that is, a week after this recorded discussion. From other sources we know that Black made this experiment with Irvine on 9 October 1764. Watt's account is dated generally, as we have noted, merely with the year, namely, 1765, and thus it appears that these pages were written in Watt's notebook somewhat after the event, at some date in the following year. On the other hand, Watt may here be referring to another experiment by Black, subsequently described by Black to his class in chemistry in the University of Edinburgh on 2 December 1766 (see McKie, *loc. cit.*, pp. 21-2) and this seems inherently more probable. In this experiment Black found that a half-gallon of steam condensed in cold water raised the temperature of the cold water by an amount that indicated that the steam contained 800° of heat (according to the system of measuring heat then in use and, of course, on Fahrenheit's scale). But Watt gives the value of 1012, which, however, is readily explained because 1012 = 800 + 212, and Watt, as will be seen below, always added 212 to give the total heat that he supposed to be involved.

After these details were given, Watt noted (*f.* 20*v*) that the experiments that follow in the notebook preceded many of those already described (those we have here dealt with), but in an order impossible now to tell, but they were all made prior to 1765, 21 to 24 December; and that they were copied from an older book by John Buchanan at Harpers Hill about 1782. So far in the notebook the writing is in Watt's hand, but at this point it changes, presumably to Buchanan's.

There follow (ff. 21r–40r) the descriptions of experiments re-copied by Buchanan with additions mostly on the verso of these pages in Watt's hand. The first of these experiments relates to the determination of the temperatures at which water boils under pressures above that of the atmosphere, but the summary of results (f. 23r) is not completed, the temperatures being omitted; Watt here inserted (f. 24r) in his own hand 'The preceeding exp^{ts} prior to 1765'. On f. 21v he later added a note to the effect that in 1803 Southern recalculated the pressures and he quoted these revised values. A further determination of 'the proportional expansion of steam' at different temperatures then follows and Watt inserted another note (f. 23v) with further details.

We now meet an account of later experiments, dated 17 August 1773, in Buchanan's handwriting on the boiling-point of water under pressures less than atmospheric. Under the date 1 March 1774 further experiments with a modified procedure are described (ff. 27r–30r) with water, saturated brine and spirit of wine; and there is a note to the effect that on 10 January 1781 it was found that the thermometer was inaccurate (4° too small between the fixed points), although it was not known whether this had been allowed for in the experiments, as there was no memorandum made on it. The table of results (f. 29r) is entirely in Watt's hand, except for the terminal insertion 'Stationary Barometer 29,4'; the continuation of the table of results (f. 30r) is entirely in Watt's hand.

Evidently the further experiments (f. 31r–f. 34r) belong to the same period, except for the statement dated 'May 1777' giving the specific gravity of Hassall brine (Cheshire); they related to the boiling-point of water at pressures above atmospheric. The tabulated results are recorded in Watt's hand on ff. 33r, 33v and 34r. On ff. 34v–35r, there is a table, partly in Buchanan's and partly in Watt's hand, taken from J. A. de Luc; on ff. 36r and v, and 37r there is a table, in Buchanan's hand, of comparisons of the Réaumur and Fahrenheit scales.

From f. 37v to 46r there is a long record of experiments on latent heat. The experiment recorded on f. 46r as made on 26 February 1783 is easily dealt with; it is a repetition of one of Black's classic experiments by the method of mixture on the latent heat of fusion of ice made in

428

Glasgow in the winter of 1761–62. Watt obtained a value of 138¾ and Black had given 139 or 140. As for the other experiments in this section of the notebook, they are concerned with the latent heat of condensation of steam. These pages appear to be in Buchanan's hand: they are certainly not in Watt's handwriting, except for the very extensive corrections, at least so far as the end of $f.$ 42r. These pages have demanded very close scrutiny. As will be seen, what was here recorded originally from February to March 1781 was 'corrected', wrote Watt, in 1814. There were two corrections necessary, as Watt recorded ($f.$ 45ar); first, he had assumed in his original calculations that the ounce avoirdupois was equivalent to 432 grains instead of 437½ grains, and, secondly, he had added the weight of the condensed steam to the weight of the cold water to give the weight of water subjected to the rise of temperature, whereas the weight of the condensed steam should have been omitted from this figure, and, after multiplying this sum by the rise in temperature, and dividing the product by the weight of the condensed steam, he had added the temperature of the cold rather than the hot water to give the total sensible and latent heat. These details will be dealt with in our notes on the notebook (pp. 480–90). The series opens with five experiments, so numbered; there follow three experiments, originally so numbered; after these come another three, also so numbered; but, these three series were, when the corrections were made in 1814, renumbered as one series with Experiments numbered 1 to 11. Full details are given below.

On $ff.$ 42v and 43r, there are abstracts from Smeaton's paper in the *Philosophical Transactions* (1776, **66**, 450–475) on the relation between power and velocity of heavy bodies moving from rest.

From $f.$ 43r to $f.$ 45v the results of determinations of the latent heat of condensation of steam 'in vacuo' are given for an experiment dated 4 January 1783. Watt was, as is well known, concerned to reduce the consumption of fuel in his engines. He had long thought that at temperatures below that at which water boiled under the pressure of the atmosphere the latent heat contained in the steam increased as the temperature, and likewise the pressure, decreased. Therefore, boiling under reduced pressure would increase the heat latent in the steam. He even went so far as to suppose that throughout the range of temperature the sum of the latent and the sensible heat was a constant. Southern, on the other hand, thought that latent heat did not vary with the temperature. Southern was here in error as the latent heat increases as the temperature of evaporation is decreased; and Watt also was incorrect, apart from being too optimistic about the rate of evaporation as the temperature decreased. The experiment of 4 January described in Watt's notebook scarcely needs any further comment.

On *f.* 45a*r* to *f.* 45b*r* we find some observations made in April 1814 on the experiments on latent heat described and detailed on *f.* 37*v* to *f.* 42*r*. Watt here recorded the nature of the errors that he had made in his original calculations and then gave a table of these results, with an average value of 945·3 for the latent heat of condensation of steam; but he felt that he must reject two of the results and therefore gave the value of 949·9. He was still not satisfied and arranged for Southern to repeat the experiments with larger quantities of water and also with steam at temperatures above the boiling-point of water, but he noted that he had no account of these experiments.

The remainder of the notebook, from *f.* 47*r* to *f.* 53*r* is taken up with some further studies on the elastic powers of steam at various temperatures, evidently made in March 1803. Watt stated here that the previous experiments on this problem (*f.* 21*r* to *f.* 23*r*) were merely *apperçus* and added his further considerations, giving the years in which he came back to this problem and giving revised tables of his results with the results of others who had worked in this field and very usefully gave comparative details in these tables. No comment seems to be needed on these pages. Bétancourt's *Mémoire sur la force expansive de la vapeur de l'eau* mentioned at the foot of *f.* 48*v*, was published in 1790, and Prony's *Architecture hydraulique*, referred to in the same place, appeared in two volumes in 1790 and 1796; with the reference to Southern's repetition of the experiments at Watt's request in September 1796, we have a date for these entries as late as that year, if not later.

The Notebook

Copal Varnish

[1r] Fill a Vial one third full of Copal broken into small pieces, add as much Oil of Spike Lavender as will fill the Vial sett it in a gentle heat for 3 or 4 days Q.D.E. Melius

Then take another Vial put into it as much of the Gelatinous mass formed by the Spike & Copal as will fill it a bout $\frac{1}{4}$ then add oil of Turpentine till the Vial is full sett it in a Gentle heat for 6 or 7 Days & pour of the Clear for use. J. Pringle Esqu[r]: This does not apear to be a perfect solution of Copal as there remain[s] a Quantity of a Mucilaginous stuff at the Bottom of the Vial that will not Dissolve either in oil of spike or turpentine however Long digested, it is also very slow in Drying unless in an oven & even when [2r] Dry it has a yelow Cast not being near so Coulourless as the Copal of Which it is made —

There appears to be two kinds of Copall one of them is Some What yellow some pieces of it being opake & is Considerably mixed with dirt the outside in General being opake & Crumbly however there are among pieces that are as transparent & Coulourless as any Copal Whatever but these are Commonly pickt out and mixed with the other sort which is harder in General more Coulourless & in Larger pieces & without any dirt or Dustiness on the skin. The first kind Dissolves in part by being boiled in alkohol what does not disolve being Converted into a Substance ressembling turpentine this residuum dissolves speedily in Ether tho not totaly the Residuum is [3r] very Light & has Little or no Substance. The Spirit of wine extracts the whole Colour so the solution in Ether is a very white varnish tho rather brittle — if to this solution in Ether oil of turpentine be added & the ether Distilled of[f] a part is suspended in the oill the rest being precipitated in form of turpentine Which again disolves in small Quantity of Ether making a very Good Varnish a small Quantity of the oil Turpentine being mixed with it which seems to improve it it is still better by adding a Small Quantity of fat oil tho that Imparts a slight yillow tinge to it

[4r] In order to do Justice it is necessary to show how far I can call this machine my own.

Sir Christ[r] Wren in the Philo: Trans is first I have heard of that men-

3   a measure of water was put in so as
always to have a surface 2 Inch dia
or thereabouts time of ev⁹ nearly
the same

4. a measure of water was put in
& eva⁹ in ~~given~~ certain time

5. another meas⁹ being ~~added put~~
in a ~~piece~~ Cylinder of wood (previously
soaked in boyling water and of such
diameter as to take up more than
half the area of the pan) was put in
& loaded with lead so as to make it
touch the pan bottom the evaporation
was compleated in same time as when
the water had double the surface

therefore the evap⁹ of water is neither
in proportion to the surface nor
quantity of it but as the quantity
of heat that enters it

I had often observed that the best way of
heating bodies was to bring them
in contact with the burning fuel
the great distance from the fire
to the boyler in fire engines seemed

A

in consequence to be wrong

after many fruitless thoughts on
the Subject I saw no boyler so perfect
in that respect as the Common
kitchen (an Invention for which we
are beholden to the Chinese) here the
fuel is always in Contact with the
sides of the boyler Containing the water
the outside may be assured with this
advantage that being little heat will
be able to penetrate it the Inside
of very thin Iron which will Considerably diminish the Expence and
being Continually Covered with water
it cannot burn this boyler I put in
practice & its effects answered my
expectation evaporating prodigious
Quantitys of water & consuming
little fuel

Exp. 1. a Florence Flask with about
an ounce of water it had a glass tube
inserted at its mouth & reaching
near the surface of the water
the tube was wrapt round with
thread so as to fit the mouth of the
Flask & then made tight with putty
it was placed in a white iron oven
before the fire till the water was intirely
evaporated and as the air was heavier
then the steam it must have been
driven out first as it lay nearest
the mouth of the tube so it may be
concluded that the flask was filled

C

"This Vessell made of Copper.
having a gage pipe & immersed in
a Cistern of Mercury at a. and
a thermometer with its bulb in the
Inside at b. being close shut. —
excepting a Snifting Valve also at b. to Inch
Diameter. the Boiling Water point of the Ther

D

10. I found that the Quantity of water used for injection in five engines was much Greater than I thought was necessary to cool the Quantity of water contained in the steam down to below the boiling point. I mixed 1 part of boiling water with 30 parts of Cold water & found it only heated to the arithmetical mean betwixt the two heats & that it was scarcely sensibly heated to the finger.

I took a Glass tube & inserted it into the nose of a tea kettle

the other end being immersed in Cold water I found on making the kettle boil that tho there was only a small increase of the water in the Refrigeratory that it was become boiling hot, this I was Surprised at & on telling it to Dr Black & asking him if it was possible that water under the power of steam could contain, more heat than it did when water

In order to determine the proportional expansion of Steam in different heats a Thermometer was made thus —

The bulb was filled with mercury except a small Vacuum at A into which was introduced a very small quantity of Water, the Capillary end at A which had been left open was then hermetically Sealed, a small quantity of air being necessarily included

It was then put into a pan with Lintsid Oyl so as totally to Cover the bulb, the oil being heated to 218°. the Mercury in our Thermom. begun to move along the Tube, which it Continued to do untill the oil was heated to 232°. when it became almost Stationary it had then filled 12 inches of the Tube

The oil being allowed to cool slowly The Mercury returned into the Ball slowly

F

August 17th. 1773
a Tube was bent as in the drawing, the Ball and the Tube as far as the Bend was filled with Water; the rest, or perpendicular part of the Tube was filled with Mercury. The Water was Cleared from air by plunging the open end of the Tube into a Cistern of Mercury, and thereby taking off the

G

the heats Corresponding to the heights, —
and the second the results of a Similar
Experiment tried in August last, —
The third Column shows the Results of
some Experiments tried with a tube
having a ball at bottom Containing ℥
& water, which was heated first in
Brine to 229° and afterwards in —

H

23d February 1781. — Latent heat
A pipe of Copper was provided about 5 feet long
3 Inches of one of its ends bent downwards, the Copper
was about 1/50 Inch thick, and the Diameter of the
Pipe was 5/8 of an Inch ═══════════════
The Straight end of the Pipe was fixed on the
Spout of a Tea Kettle from which the pipe inclined
upwards so that the Bent ends was about 2 feet
higher than the Spout of the Tea Kettle.
The Tea Kettle was filled with Water halfway up
the entry of the Spout, The Lid was fixed Steam tight
with some oat meal dough.
A Tin pan 4 Inches deep, and 6 Inches diar had
2½ pounds of Water put into it, which filled it
nearly to 2¼ Inches deep — This Pan was placed
upon a Stand, and the very point of the bent end
of the Pipe was Immersed in the Water, being first
Shut with a Cork, through which a Small passage
was kept open by a bit of Goose Quill —

I

Latent heat 5 March 1781

A short copper pipe was procured about
2 feet Long, and ¾ Inch Diar. 6 Inches of one
end of the pipe was bent downwards, and the
streaight end was fixed on the nose of the Tea
Kottle. The experiments were then prosecuted
as formerly. ~~Exp^t^~~

"6" Cold v. - - 47½° 175.00

m^r^ Smeatons Exp^ts^ on Rotative motion
Phil: Trans:^ns^ 1776 —

	inches
Dia^r^ of Cyl^rs^ of Lead or the heavy bodies	2.57
Lengths of Do	1.56
Dia^r^ of the hole therein	.72
weight of each 3^lb^ avoir^ds^	
Greater distance of the middle of each	
Body from the center of y^e^ axis —	8.25
the smaller distance of d^o^ —	3.92
10 turns of the ~~bigger done~~ smaller barrel = }	25.25
5 D^o^ of the smaller D^o^ —	

Experiment on Latent Heat
of water distilled in vacuo Jany 4ᵗʰ 1783

A Vessel was made in the following form

The Vessel was made of white Iron and well
soldered so as to be perfectly air tight
The opening at A was shut by a good Cork
The small opening, B & C which were only
¼ inch diameter were shut by brass plugs
ground very carefully into Brass sockets
The opening D which was very small was
also shut by a Brass plug
A pint of water was poured into the inside
vessel and as much into the outside vessel
The whole was then set upon a Chaffing dish
and made to boil. The steam was suffered
to issue at B & C untill it was supposed
all the air was extended, the aperture C
was then shut and just immersed in a

tion[ed] a machine of this kind[1] the Machine he has described has a ~~very~~ great number of Imperfections which no Doubt have been the Cause of its never Coming into Common use but which do not deprive him of the merit of being the first Contriver of the perspective machine. — Dr Hurst an english Clergyman now at Calcutta apears to have been the first that made the Machine to answer in practice tho still attended with some Inconveniences [4v] This Instrument was Composed of a Mahogany bourd 13 In Long 10 broad & about ½ an Inch thick at the bottom of this bourd (which was fixed on its edge) were 2 friction wheels that supported the cross head of a square resembling an Inverted

this ⅃

T in the stalk of ~~which~~ was a slit from top to bottom in which a straight Ruler ending at Top in atriangle slid up & down at the bottom of the

ye point of the

Ruler was a socket for a pencil then as⟋Ruler could be moved from Right to Left by the Motion of the ⅃ on the friction wheels and from up to down by the Motion of the Ruler in the slit it is evident that the point of the Ruler† and consequently the pencil could be moved in the ~~any~~ Direction of any Line

[5r] The Ingenious Mr Ja^s Lind[2] being accquain[ted] with Dr Hurst at

that

Calcutta saw his Machines and on his coming to London had one of them made by the help of which he has made a great number of accurate drawing[s] ~~as he generaly carried his Machine about~~ this Machine I saw at Glasgow & being employed to make one for Dr Black I wanted as much as I could to remedy some of its Incon[ven]- iences which were. That ~~being~~ from its Structure it was very difficult
+ to draw a Diagonal or Curve line ~~it being Con~~ it was also very trouble- some to carry about being put up in a box 15 In Square & about 2½ In deep & having besides a 3 Leg staff such as that of a Theodolite[3]

† The four words which follow are written vertically in the left-hand margin and marked with a caret for insertion here.

[1] Wren's 'Instrument invented divers years ago . . . for drawing the Out-lines of any Object in perspective' was described in Phil. Trans., 1669, 4, 898. It was much admired by Pepys, to whom Oldenburg showed it; and Pepys ordered one from Browne, an instru- ment-maker, recording that 'the sight of this do please me mightily' and it 'gives me great content' (Diary, 30 April and 8 May 1669).

[2] James Lind (1738–1812), M.D., who went out as surgeon in an East Indiaman in 1766 and visited China.

[3] Watt's apparatus for drawing in perspective is illustrated in H. W. Dickinson's James Watt, Craftsman & Engineer (Cambridge, 1935, Plate II), from a specimen preserved in the Science Museum, London.

433

About 6 or 8 years ago My Ingenious friend Mr John Robison having ~~Contrived~~ conceived that a fire engine[4] might be made without a Lever — by Inverting the Cylinder & placing it above the mouth of the pit proposed to me to make a model of it which was set about but having

never Compleated he going abroad[5] & I ~~being~~ at that time ~~Ignorant~~ little knoledge of the machine however I always thought the Machine other as

Might be applyed to ~~more~~ valuable purposes ~~than~~ as drawing Water. on making some Experiments with a Di∫gester on the force of Steam I thought that in that way a machine for some purposes might be made advantageously, but never made any Conclusive experiments till the winter 1763 [8r] when being employed to put in order a small model

4

of a fire engine belonging to the natural phil: Class & made by nathan

Jo: Sisson I mett with considerable difficultys in the execution owing to the very bad Construction of some of its parts but having at Last overcome all difficultys & made it to work regularly I was surprized at the Imense Quantity of fuel it consumed in proportion to its Cylinder which was only 2 In dia^r & which I imputed to the heat Lost thro the Metallic Cylinder   Mr Robison being now returned it was hinted in some of our Conversations together that if the Cylinder was made of wood it would not occasion the Loss of so much heat being less susceptible of heat or cold than Mettals (this I find has actualy been put in practice by the Duke of Bridgewaters engineer Mr Brindley tho I did not know that till long after) I being now resolved to endeavour to Improve the Machine read, what is said on it by Bielidor[6] & Desaguliers[7] & then saw the Impracticability of my freinds [8v] Scheme without

[4] A 'fire engine' is, of course, a steam-engine, an engine for raising (pumping) water 'by fire'.

[5] Robison, born in 1739, entered the University of Glasgow as a student of Humanity in November 1750 and graduated in Arts in April 1756. He left Glasgow for London in 1758 (this would be included in Watt's phrase 'going abroad') and, after service in Canada with the Royal Navy and other duties at sea until 1762, he did not return to Glasgow possibly until 1763 or even 1764. This would fit Watt's phrase '6 or 8 years ago' on this page of his notebook bearing the date 1765. Meanwhile, Black had made his classic discoveries in heat.

[6] Bernard de Forest Belidor (1693–1761), writer on architecture and engineering, compiled among other works La science des ingénieurs (1st edn., Paris, 1729) and Architecture hydraulique (4 vols., Paris, 1737–53).

[7] John Theophilus Desaguliers (1683–1744), F.R.S., author of numerous works on mechanics and physics and of many papers in the Philosophical Transactions.

some other method than what is now practised of making the piston air tight but was resolved to make a model of the Mach: in the common way only with a wooden Cylinder. & to begin by Making the boyler perform with as little heat as posible. it has been proposed but never that I could find put in execution to make a small boyler and to throw in a jets of water only at such times as the Steam was wanted tho the boy^r was kept Constant[ly] hot & thereby save fuel it being supposed that the water would in this Case be more Briskly Evaporated

1 a small Iron pan was sett on the fire a measure of water was put into it & evaporated in 20 minutes from the time of its being put in

2 the fire & in continuing the same another measure was put in drop after drop one drop being evaporated before another was added the whole was gone in 22 minutes or thereabouts

[10r]

3 a measure of water was put in so as always to have a surface 2 Inch dia[^{r}] or thereabouts time of ev^n nearly the same

4. a measure of water was put in & eva^d: in ~~given~~ Certain Time
Cylinder·

5. another mea^e being ~~added~~ put in. a ~~piece~~ of wood (previously soaked

† in boyling water and of such diameter as to take up more than half the area of the pan) was put in & Loaded with lead so as to make it touch

+ the pan bottom the evaporation was compleated in same time as when the water had double the Surface. Therefore the evap^n of water is

+ neither in proportion to the surface nor quantity of it but as the quantity of heat that enters it

I had often observed that the best way of heating bodies was to bring them in Contact with the burning fuel the great distance from the fire to the boyler in fire engines seemed [11r] in Consequence to be wrong

---

[9v] + rather in Less time

after many fruitless thoughts on the subject I saw no boyler so perfect in that Respect as the Common tea kitchen (an Invention for which we are beholden to the Chinese) here the fuel is always in Contact with the sides of the boyler Containing the water the outside may be of wood with this advantage that very little heat will be able to penetrate it the Inside of very thin Iron which will Considerably diminish the Expence and being Constantly Covered with water it cannot burn. This boyler I put in practice & its effects answered my expectation evaporating prodigious Quantitys of Water & consuming little fuel +   †

† Photograph: see p. 431.

435

[10*v*] + It burned 4^{lb} of coals p^r hour & in that time evap^d 20^{lb} of Water

[12*r*] I next made a Cylinder of Fir ½ In thick at bottom ¼ at top 6 In dia^r & 18 long hooped with 3 Iron hoops & having compleated My engine I gave it a tryal. The Cylinder answered very well at first but afterwards on being soaked with steam the pressure of the air contracted it in the midle so as to prevent the descent of the piston: it was

† therefore necessary to make a Stronger Cylinder & possibly it may be necessary to make it of oak ‡ which is less liable to Compression

In the working of this machine I perceived that the water issuing from the sinking pipe was always near boyling hot & that when the Steam was weak ~~that~~ it was a long time after opening the Steam-Cock before

[11*v*] † another Cylinder was made of hard fir ⅜ In thick at the two ends & ⅝ In at the middle yet it became pliable by steam as well as the other.

‡ I found the oak of my boiler in those parts of the Inside that were above ▽ became so soft that I thrust a sharp piece of white Iron ½ In into it w^t my fingers

[13*r*] any Steam came out of the snifting valve   on Consideration I found that the water in the Cylinder could not be forced out by the steam till it was near the heat of boyling water as it would till then undoubtedly Condense all the Steam Coming in Contact with it & I have since found that the Quantity of steam Condensed would be many fulls of the Cylinder

about this time I conceived the Idea of making a Machine Something like Capt Savarys but to raise water to any height by suction only by making a series of Receivers one above another so that each would raise the Water to the sucking pipe of the other the steam to be conveyed to them thro copper pipes surrounded with Chaff to prevent the escape of heat

[14*r*] But before anything could be known certainly about the best manner of Constructing Fire engines there were several facts necessary to be determined

Ex. 1. a Florence Flask with about an ounce of water it had a Glass tube Inserted at its mouth & reaching near the surface of the water   †

† Photograph: see p. 431.

436

The tube was wrapt round with thread so as to fitt the mouth of
the Flask & $\underset{\text{then}}{\int}$ made tight with putty it was placed in a White
✝ Iron oven before the fire till the water was Intirely evaporated and
as the air was heavier than the steam it must have been driven out
first as it Lay nearest the mouth of the tube   so it may be Concluded

---

[13v] ✝ it was above an hour in evaporating so could not be thought
much hotter than boyling water.

---

that the flask was filled [15r] with steam only, the whole was then let
× to cool & weighed $\underset{}{\overset{\&}{\int}}$the flask being made very dry within & weighed
+ again was found to be 4 grains lighter. the full of the flask of water
was found to be ~~4966~~ grains Consequently the water had been expanded
to above 1600 times its bulk which also nearly agrees with some experiments formerly tho Less accurately made
[There follows here a deleted line and a half, which seems to read:
'N.B. This Experiment was [tryed?] by Dr. Black.']

Ex. 2d. it was found the Boiler Consumed 5 lib of Coals in an Hour & half
3d. 1 lb evaporated in 27 minutes 210 Cubic Inches of Water so that
it produced rather less than 7 Cubic feet of steam in a minute
4. a pipe of Lead $\frac{1}{10}$ thick 9 foot Long 1 In diam^r: put into a box 4 In
Square & as long as itself filled with Sawdust to prevent the evaporation [16r] of heat was applyd to the mouth of the boiler & in 16

[14v] × It was rather more than 4 but not $4\frac{1}{2}$
+ The full of the flask was 17^{oz} 2^d averdu:
I reckoned only 24^{Grains} in a drop weight whereas there are $27\frac{1}{3}^{\text{Grains}}$
so that the expansion is 1849 a Cubic Inch becoming a Cubic foot &
a little more a drop weight is the 16th part of an avoir dupoise ounce,
& the true bulk of steam by this experiment is 1860,7. that is supposing the Steam to weigh only 4 g^r, but if supposed $4\frac{1}{3}$ then the bulk is
1730·7

---

seconds the steam came out transparent at the end of it.

437

4 a Small engine of Savarys kind ⊖ being Applyed to the end of the pipe was found to make a Stroke every 8 seconds two more pipes of equal dimensions being added & the Machi[ne?] applyd to the farthest no sensible odds Could be perceived in time of its Strokes tho its distance from the boiler was tripled

5. on using a brisker fire the Steam Came thro the pipe mentioned in N°.3. in 8 Seconds the Quantity of ~~water~~ Condensed being about ¾ Cubic Inch +ᴛ⊣

6 The pipe at first droped about a drop pᴿ second but on being an hour heated it did not drop 8 Drops in a minute & probably if the heat had been Continued Longer it would have been still diminished & only 7 foot of steam passed thro a pipe of [17r] an Inch bore in a minute

---

[15v] ⊖ the Cylᴿ was 6 inches diaᴿ & a foot stroke
⊣this is about 6 Inches pr minute

---

tho
~~the~~ with a pressure equall to 25 In of water which it would always have in an engine 100 feet might have passed in the same time as nearly 42ᵗⁱᵐᵉˢ the Quantity of Steam as of water can go thro a hole in the same time +

7 ~~The hole of the Steam pipe being Shut the Water rose in the gage pipe 1 foot in [6 or 8?] Seconds 2 feet in 12 Seconds~~

7 a piece of Iron being heated to 120° & then plunged into water at 60° was found to have heated the water as much as ~~so much W~~a an equall bulk of ▽ heated to 120°

8 Copper was found the to do the same

9 tin is said by Dᴿ Black only to hold the half of the heat of an equall bulk of water.

10. Doctor Black considering that ▽ during the time that it/was heating to the boiling point did every minute receive Considerable additions of heat. yett so soon as [17v] I found that that the Quantity of water used

---

[16v] + 1813 It is suspected that there has been some great inaccuracy in making the the experiments by the application of Savary's Cylinder otherwise the destruction of Steam must have been much greater

---

438

for Injection in fire engines was much greater than I thought was necessary to Cool the Quantity ~~of water~~ of water contained in the Steam down to below the boiling point. I mixed 1 part of boiling water with 30 parts of cold water I found it only heated to the arithmetical mean betwixt the two heats & that it was scarcely sensibly heated to the finger. I took a/Glass tube & inverted it into the nose
bent

of a tea kettle the other end being Imersed in Cold water I found †
~~a small encrease of the water in the the~~ on making the kettle boil that tho there was only a small increase of the water in the frigeratory that it was become boiling hot   this I was surprized at & on telling it to Dr Black & asking him if it was possible that water under the form of steam could contain, more heat than it did when water [18r] it was heated to 212°

---

or [18v] He told me that had long been a tenet of his & explained to me his thoughts on the subject & in about a week after he tryed the experiment with the Still

---

or boiling hot it would receive no more heat tho the fire &c continued the same   that the steams that go off do not appear sensibly hotter to the thermometer than 212 & that the Quantity of water that is evaporated in a minute is small in proportion to the ~~whole~~ heat that is certainly added to the water   he Thought that these steams certainly carried off or contained more heat than was sensible to the thermometer & that in Certain Circumstances they might part with that heat to other bodies— he Accordingly took a Common still & having put a ~~certain~~ Quantity of water into it he adapted a Refrigeratory as usual this he filled with a measured Quantity of Water of a k/own heat he then distilled till there
n
came into
~~was in~~ his reciver a certain ~~part~~ proportion of the Water contained in his Refrigeratory   he found the ▽ in the Refrig^y had acqu [19r] acquired from this water as much heat as ~~the~~ it would have got from an = quantity of ▽ heated to 1012
In Company with Mr Ja^s Lind I repeated this Experiment
We put into the Refrigeraty 18 measures of ▽ at [blank]° we Distilled over one Measure & found the ▽ in the Refrig^y heated to [blank]° the Experiment lasted ¾ of an hour the water in the Refrig^y standing in

† Photograph: see p. 431.

the room ½ hour after only Lost [1 ?]° [20r] Strengthened with these facts I could now judge of the merits of Savarys engine in Comparison with Newcomens

Savarys engine being more simple & having no pistons has in Consequence less friction than Newcomens

and the vacuum being perfect it can suck water to 28 or 29 feet

Newcomens engines as now Constructed do not raise more than a Column of water of 16 or 18 feet high & the diameter of their Cylinders

If a series of Savarys engines were placed above one another so as to act

the
in succession if there were 10 of them Each of them would have all/time to fill itself with water that the other 9 were filling with steam Consequently the sucking pipes might be very small

as the Cylinders could be made of wood the expence would be much smaller than Newcomens especialy as there would be no house needed

---

after
[20v] The experiments here/narrated preceded many of those which are contained in the foregoing pages, but in what order it is impossible now to tell, but they were made prior to 1765 — Dec 21 to 24th. They were copied from an older book by John Buchanan at Harpers hill about 1782 —

[21r] This vessell made of Copper having a Gage pipe Immersed in a Cistern of Mercury at A. and a Thermometer with its bulb in the inside at b. being close shut — excepting a Snifting Valve also at b. $\frac{1}{10}$ †

Inch Diameter, the Boiling Water point of the Thermometer was examined, and found exact. the Snift being shut, the Mercury rose in the pipe to 15 Inches, the thermometer rose to 236° the Mercury rose to 30 Inches. The Thermometer at 252° the steam was let out, the whole examined a Second time, and found to Correspond, the Mercury being wholly in the Cistern, the Top of the Gage pipe — which was 34 Inches long was Sealed — hermetically the 1st Mercury was raised to 12 inches, the Thermometer at 252°—

Mercury 2d at 16½ Inches, Thermometer at 264°

3d Mercury at 22 inches. Thermometer 292°

4 Mercury at 25 inches Thermometer 312°

† Photograph: see p. 431.

this being near the Melting of Tin, and Several parts of the Vessell being made tight with it, it durst be pushed no farther
On examining the Tube of the Gage pipe It was found to be a little Conical 12 Inches [22r] of the wide or lower end being filled with

---

[21v] In 1803 Mr Southern recalculated the pressures shewn by these experiments by considering the conical tube as represented by the spaces contained between a hyperbola & its asymptote which are more easily calculated than the supposititition [sic] of its being a true cone & come exceedingly near to the truth and gives the elasticities of the compressed air in inches of mercury, as in the 1st Colum

	air	☿	total	Heat
Case 1st =	47·47	12	59½	252
2^d =	59·25	16·25	75½	264
3 =	88·55	22·	110½	292
4 =	118·8	25	143¾	312

(See Mr S.^{s} paper on the subject put up with other papers on Steam (1803)

Mercury, and Moved to the upper end, it filled 13 Inches. —
Tube 34 Inches long, 12 inches of the bottom or lower end, equal to 13 of the upper end —
ıse 1st Condensed Air,........ 22 inches
    Mercury .... 12 inches
12 of bottom = 13 of Top
        atmos: inches

then $\dfrac{13}{34}$ .. leaves $\dfrac{21}{34}$ = 1,63 = 48,9

$252°..........☿ =.................... = \dfrac{12}{60·9}$

---

se 2^d Condensed Air — — — — = 17½
     ☿ — — — — = 16½
  Thermometer 264°
on Account of Narrow part of —   }   Inches
  Tube Say Air Compressed to ½ bulk } = 60
                 16½
☿ — — — — — — — — — — — — —   76½

Case 3^d Air — — — — — — — — 12 inches
  ☿ — — — — — — — — 22
  Thermometer 292°

        atmos: inches
  12 inches = 11 = 3,1   ——————— = 93
  ☿— — — — — — — — — — — — — 22
                                    ———
                                    115

Case 4: Air 9 inches ☿ 25 inches Therm^{er} 312°
Say Air 8 inches. Atmos: then Compressed to 4,25
= 127 Inches. ☿ 25 = 152$\frac{1}{2}$. ———

[23r] We may then thus place the scale of heats in proportion to pressure
Vacuum — — — — — — — — —
Open Air
An additional Atmosphere
2 Atmospheres
2 – – do
4$\frac{1}{2}$ – – do
  In order to determine the proportional expansion of Steam in different heats a Thermometer was Made thus —
†
  The bulb was filled with Mercury except a small Vacuum at A into which was introduced a very Small Quantity of Water, the Capillary end at A which had been left open was then hermetically Sealed, a Small quantity of Air being necessarily included
  It was then put into a pan with Lintseed Oyl so as totally to Cover the bulb, the oil being heated to 218°. the Mercury in our Thermom^r begun to move along the Tube, which it continued to do untill the oil was heated to 232° when it became almost Stationary   it had then filled 12 inches of the Tube   The oil being allowed to cool slowly The Mercury returned into the Ball slowly [24r] till it came to 12 inches. the heat of the oil being then 224° it proceeded quicker untill the Mercury

[23v] The oil was heated altogether to about 312° & by the last
80   the steam
~~100~~°, was expanded about 2 inches or $\frac{1}{4}$ of its former bulk —

† Photograph: see p. 431.

442

The experiment was repeated several times after & always when a little air was contained, the mercury proceeded slowly until the heat was about 20 degrees higher than when it began to expand, & this happened equaly when a saturated solution of common salt was employed instead of the oil, & though the heat was not then sufficient to expand the steam to its full bulk, the mercury remained stationary until the ball was heated by a fire when it expanded to its full dimension —

On employing water perfectly freed from air, when the thermometer in the bath stood at 214° The steam was formed with rapidity, & on being suffered to cool till the bath came to 210° was so suddenly condensed that it broke the ball

---

had got wholly into the bulb, the oil was then 208°
—— N B. It moved faster about the Middle of its expansion, than at either end   the preceeding exp^{ts} prior to 1765

August 17th 1773

a Tube was bent as in the drawing, the Ball and the Tube
† as far as the Bend was filled with Water; the rest, or perpendicular part of the Tube was filled with Mercury. —

The Water was Cleared from Air by plunging the open end of the Tube into a Cistern of Mercury, and thereby taking off the ~~atmosphere~~ of the atmosphere. The Air thus Generated being let out, the operation was repeated, and the Water made to boil in Vacuum, by which more Air was disentangled and let out again, The Ball was then immersed into a pan with Cold Water, the lower end of the Tube being immersed in a Cistern of Mercury   The Water in the Pan was gradually heated by a Lamp, and the descent of the Barometer, and ascent of Thermometer, placed close to the Ball of the Barometer were Carefully noted in three Experiments, the time of heating from 60° to 208° being about ¾ of an hour. In the [25r] two first Experiments the rise of the Mercury in the Cistern was not attended to; but in the last the Scale was raised from time to time so as just to touch the Surface of the Mercury

4th The Ball being Emptied was filled with fountain Water, and the Stem with Mercury   The Air was not Separated from the water but no disentangled air was left in the Ball   The Ball was plunged into Boyling Water which was allowed to cool exceedingly slowly a small flame

† Photograph: see p. 431.

being kept at it for that purpose. In this Experiment the ascent of the Mercury in Barometer, and descent in Thermometer were carefully noted.

In all the 3 first Experiments a little Air was freed from the Water, not with standing the same water was Constantly used, which had been boiled in the Air to one half its bulk before it was used, and the Mercury seldom rose higher than twenty Eight Inches

On the Ball's being suffered to cool again tho' it stood at 29, at the beginning of the Experiment.

In the fourth Experiment, the Quantity of Air generated ~~when Generated~~ when reduced† to the density of the atmosphere was ,833 of an inch of tube, which as the Ball contained 39 Inches of the Tube was equal to $\dfrac{1}{46,8}$ of the Water

† Followed by two deleted words

		1		2		3		4	
▽ added	B	T	☿ Supp^d	T	☿ Supp^d	T	☿ Supp^d	T	☿ Supp^d
29.07	29	60		60		60	0.25		
28.84	28¾	..		..		80	0.48		
28.91	28½	..		..		90	0.71		
28.38	28¼	..		..		99	0.94		
28.14	28	..		102		100	1.18		
27.22	27	..		114		118	2.10		
26.29	26	..		127		127	3.03		
25.37	25	134		135		134	3.95	56	
24.44	24	140		140		139	4.88	98	
23.52	23	146		146		144	5.80	119	
22.59	22	151		151		150	6.73	128	
21.66	21	156		156		156	7.66	136	
20.74	20	160		162		161	8.58	143	
19.81	19	164		165		165	9.51	148	
18.96	18	167		..		170	10.36	154	
18.	17	171		171		173	11.32	158	
17.03	16	..		174		174	12.29	162	
16.11	15	..		176		176	13.21	166	
15.18	14	181½		179		178	14.14	170	
14.26	13	184		182		180	15.06		
13.33	12	186		184		182	15.99	177	
12.41	11	187		188		..	16.91	180	
11.48	10	189		190		188	17.84	182	
10.55	9	191		192		190	18.77	184	
9.63	8	193		194		..	19.69	188	
8.7	7	195		196		194	20.62	190	
7.77	6	197		198		196	21.55	192	
6.85	5	199		199		198	22.47	194	
5.92	4	..		201		201	23.40	196	
5.	3	204		203		203	24.32	199	
4.07	2	205½		205		204	25.25	200	
3.14	1	208		207		206	26.18	204	
	0	..		208		208		208	

The former Experiments on boiling in Vacuo, were tried over again, but the Cold having frozen the Water, and burst the Ball used in the former Experiments, a Straight Barometer Tube with a Ball at Top was employed, and a hole made in the bottom of the pan near one side to let the Tube out   It was made Water tight by lapping Paper round the Tube, and forcing it into a Socket Soldered to the pan bottom. The Water was purged of Air as formerly, and by shaking it in Vacuo like the Water hammer which always detached Quantitys of Air; but as new Water had to be added to supply the place of the Air, I found I had no Chance of Clearing it entirely tho' I went so far as to be able to raise it upright when it supported a Column of 34 inches of Mercury, and did not form a Vacuum till it was shaken, when it fell down suddenly, but upon being inclined the Speck did not disappear, but when it supported 27 inches of perpendicular Mercury the Tube being inclined, the Speck was not larger than a pin head. In this state, when the Tube was perpendicular I found the Mercury to stand at 28,75 inches, the Column of Water above it was about $6\frac{1}{2}$ inches = $\frac{1}{2}$ inch of $\ascnode$. The whole height being thus 29,25 when the stationary Barometer stood at 29,4   The pan was then heated exceedingly slowly by the Lamp, and the water in it stirred perpetually, to make the heats as equal as possible [28r] the Results will appear from the following Table N° 2. — Those in Number 1st are a 5 Sett tryed with the former Tube, and not entered here both of them are Corrected for the Column of $\triangledown$ above the Mercury. In N° 2 the Mercury rose to 28,6 after the Experiment when the $\triangledown$ had cooled to 48° — N° 3 Contains Experiments of the same kind made upon Saturated brine — When the Brine was perfectly Saturated by boiling and was put into the Tube, it precipitated a Quantity of Salt, which disturbed the experiment, I was therefore obliged to take it out, and filter it, during which time it attracted Moisture from the Air, and appeared by its boiling point, not to be perfectly Saturated, though it was more free from Air than Common Water, yet it parted with what it had exceeding difficultly, and would part with none upon being Shaken by the Water hammer, though it opened in all parts of the liquor.

N° 4. is an Experiment upon Spirit of Wine, which also Contains Air, and was freed from it in the same manner with the rest, ~~but~~ though not perfectly   NB A mixture of Salt and Snow Cools this Thermom^r to 6° below. 0° —— 10 Jany 1781. On examining the Thermom^r with

446

which all these Experiments were tried I find the distance between the freezing & boiling ▽ points 4° too small. Whether this had been Attended to in the Experim^ts is uncertain as no Memorandum is made of it & the Thermo^r has 2 boiling points marked on it

| | | 1 | | | 2 | |
Therm^r	Bar^r	Column supported	Column supported	Ther^r	Barometer
70	29,75	0.25	0,15	55	29,25
80	29,5	0.5	0.65	74	28.75
88	29,25	0.75	0.80	81	28,60
94	29,04	0.96	1.30	95	28,1
110	28,12	1.88	1.75	104	27,65
123	27,19	2.81	2.68	118	26,72
133	26,26	3.74	3.60	128	25,80
140	25,34	4.66	4.53	135	24,87
146	24,41	5.59	5,46	142	23,94
152	23,49	6.51	6,40	148	23.
156	22,56	7.44	7.325	153	22,075
160	21,64	8.36	8.25	157	21,15
163	20,71	9.29	9.18	161	20,22
166½	19,78	10.22	×10.10	164	19,3
169	18,86	11.24	×11.07	167	18,33
172	17,92	12.08	×11.95	172	17,45
175	17,	13.	×12.88	175	16,52
178	16,07	13.93	13.81	177½	15,59
181	15,15	14.85	14.73	180	14,67
183½	14,22	15.88	15.66	182½	13,74
185½	13,3	16.7	16.58	185	12,82
188	12,37	17.63	17.51	187	11,89
190	11,45	18.55	18.45	189	10,95
192	10,52	19.48	19.38	191	10,02
194½	9,6	20.4	20.34	193½	9,06
196½	8,67	21.33	24.26	196½	8,14
198½	7,74	22.26			
200½	6,82	23.28			
202½	5,89	24.11			
204	4,96	25.04			
206	4,	26,			
208	3,12	26.88			
210	2,19	28.81			
213	0·	30.			

Stationary Barometer
29,4

Stationary barometer 30 inches.

448

	3			4	
Brine		Supported	Supported	Spirit of Wine ther[r]	
29,49	46	0.01	0.22	34	29·18
29,14	76	0.36	.929	40	28·471
28,92	85	0.58	1.897	67	27,503
28,69	92	0.81	2.806	84	26·594
	104		3.744	95	25,656
	109		4.728	103	24,672
27,78	113	1.72	5.63	110	23,77
26,87	129	2.63	6.58	114	22,82
25,96	139	3.54	7.12	120	21,88
25,05	147	4.45	8.46	$124\frac{1}{2}$	20,94
24,14	154	5.36	9.4	128	20,
23,23	160	6.27	10.34	132	19,06
22,3	165	7.2	11.32	135	18,08
21,38	169	8.12	12.21	139	17,19
20,47	173	9.03	13.15	$141\frac{1}{2}$	16,25
19,56	177	9.94	14.1	144	15,30
18,65	180	10.85	15.03	$146\frac{1}{2}$	14,37
17,74	183	11.76	15.974	$148\frac{1}{2}$	13,426
16,83	187	12.67	16.908	151	12,492
15,91		13.59	17.85	$152\frac{1}{2}$	11,55
15,	$193\frac{1}{2}$	14.5	18.8	155	10,6
14,16	$195\frac{1}{2}$	15.34	19.75	157	9,65
13,25	$198\frac{1}{2}$	16.25	20.71	160	8,69
12,34	$201\frac{1}{2}$	17.16	21.65	$162\frac{1}{2}$	7,75
11,4	$203\frac{1}{2}$	18.1	22.59	164	6,81
10,47	$205\frac{1}{2}$	19.03	23.53	166	5,87
9,56	207	19.94	24.47	167	4,93
8,64	208	20.86	25.4	168	4,
7,7	210	21.8	26.35	169	3,05
6,76	212	22.74	27.3	171	2,1
5,84	214	23.66			
4,90	216	24.6	Stationary Bar[r] 29.4		
3,98	218	25.52			
3,	220	26.5			
Station[y] 29.5					

[31r] To determine the heats at which Water boils, when pressed by a Column of ☿ above 30 inches. a Tube of 55 Inches long had one end of it put through a hole in the lid of a digester within which it was immersed in a Cistern of ☿. A Thermometer was put through another hole the bulb being in the inside, and kept ½ an Inch from the Brass-Work of the digester by means of a Wooden Collar   The whole being made tight and half filled with water, it was heated by means of a lamp, and the Thermom^r & Barometer noted. —

The Air in the upper part of the digester expanding by heat, the Column of Mercury was forced up before the Water boiled. A small hole was made to let out the Air, the Water was heated up to 212°, and the hole was Stopped —

Still some Air remained for the Column was 2½ Inches high at 213½.° Making that deduction, the first Column shows the heats Corresponding to the heights, And the second the results of a similar Experiment tried in August last, — The Third Column shows the Results of some

† Experiments tried with a tube having a ball at bottom Containing ☿ & water, which was heated first in Brine to 229° and afterwards in [32r] Lintseed oil. — The Oil has so low an Equilibrium, and transmits heat so unequally, that it was with the utmost difficulty, — and many alternate heatings and Coolings that any thing could be determined by it — I think now they are tolerably exact, but purpose to try them again in ☿ heated to the proper degree. —

N B. The Specific Gravity of Sp.v. to ▽ is 9 to 10, and of Brine to ▽ ?? 12 to 10

May 1777 Hassel Brine in Cheshire to Water as 64 to 53. —

† Photograph: see p. 431.

Bar	Ther:	Bar:	Ther:	Salt ▽	
0	213½			1	214
1	215			1½	215
2	217			2	216
3	218	3	220	3	218
4	220½	4	223	4	220
5	222	5	224	8	226
6	223½	6	225	$10\frac{6}{8}$	229
7	225	7	227		
8	226½	8	228		
9	228	9	229	Lintseed Oil	
10	229½	10		11½	230
11	231	11	231	17½	238
12	232½	12		13	232
13	234	13	233	15¼	236
14	235	14		$29\frac{7}{8}$	255
15	236½	15	236	$30\frac{7}{8}$	256
16	237½	16	237		
17	238½	17	238		
18	240	18			
20	242½	19	241		
22	244½	20			
24	247	21	243		
26	248½	22			
28	250½	23	245		
30	252½	24			
32	255½	25	247		
34	257	26			
36	259½	27	250		
38	261	28			
40	262½	29	252		
42	264½	31	253		
44	266½	33	255		
46	269	35	257		
48	269½	37	259		
50	271	39	260		
52	272½	41	261		
		43	263		
		45	265		
		47	266		
		49	268		

Atmos--pheres	Inches of Mercury	Most Correct Obsrva-tions	Corresponding Series 33. to 38	Differences
4096	122880		1325,39393	179,36574
2048	61440		1146,02819	155,76499
1024	30720		990,2632	135,2696
512	15360		854,9936	117,471
256	7680		737,5226	102,015
128	3840		635,5076	88,592
64	1920		546,9156	76,936
32	960		469,9796	66,8129
16	480		403,1667	58,0218
8	240	This series erroneous Mean 151°	345,1449	50,3874
4	120		294,7575	43,7575
2	60		251,	38,
1	30		213,	33,
0,5	15		180,	28,6578
0,25	7,5		151,3422	24,887
,125	3,75		126,4552	21,61239
,0625	1,875		104,84281	18,76865
,03125	0,9375		86,07416	16,29909
,015625	0,4687		69,77507	14,15447
,007812	0,2343		55,62060	12,29203
,003906	0,1171		43,32857	10,67465
,001953	,05859		32,65392	9,27
,000976	,02929		23,38392	8,05
,000488	,01464		15,33392	6,990789
,000244	,00732		8,343131	6,070948
,000122	,00366		2,272183	

Atmospheres	Inches of Mercury	Most Correct observations	Corresponding Series 32 to 38	Differences
4096	122880		1597,64338	
2048	61440		1352,28094	245,36244
1024	30720		1140,39678	211,88416
512	15360		961,96801	178,42877
256	7680		811,71273	150,25528
128	3840		685,18196	126,53077
64	1920		578,62973	106,55223
32	960		488,90153	89,7282
16	480		413,34093	75,5606
8	240		349,71093	63,63
4	120		296,125	53,58593
2	60		251,	45,125
1	30		213,	38,
0,5	15		181,	32,
0,25	7,5		154,05264	26,94736
,125	3,75		131,36013	22,69251
,0625	1,875		112,25065	19,10948
,03125	0,9375		96,158536	16,092114
,015265	0,4687		82,607283	13,551253
,007812	0,2343		71,195702	11,411581
,003906	0,1171		61,585950	9,609752
,001953	,05859		53,4935273	8,0924227
,000976	,02929		46,6788556	6,8146717
,000488	,01464		40,9401847	5,7386709
,000244	,00732		35,1076198	4,8325649
,000122	,00366		31,0380915	4,0695283

Table of Observations on the heat of Boiling

Dates		Places of Observations	Heat of the Air
July	13	Beaucaire	$14\frac{1}{4}$
	29	Ibid	$18\frac{1}{2}$
	28	Ibid	20
	31	Pierrelate.	19
Aug^t	1	Aurio [Auriol]	$19\frac{1}{2}$
	2	St Valier	$17\frac{1}{2}$
	4	Lyon	$15\frac{1}{2}$
	6	Ibid.	16
July	6	Monluel	$15\frac{1}{2}$
	7	Lyon	15
	5	Embournay	15
Aug^t	7	Sardon	19
Sept^r	29	Genève.	19
	6	Ibid.	$14\frac{3}{4}$
July	3	Ibid	$12\frac{1}{2}$
Oct^r	20	Ibid	5
Sept	16	Monetier sur Salève	14
Nov^r	20	Geneve	$2\frac{1}{2}$
Sept^r	16	Grange des arbres, Saleve.	$13\frac{3}{4}$
	16	Grange Tournier, Ibid.	$16\frac{3}{4}$
	21	Grange des Fonds, Sixt.	15
	22	Chemin de Grasse, Chevre. Ib.	$10\frac{1}{2}$
Aug^t	26	Grange des Communes Ib.	$8\frac{1}{2}$
	26	Abbaye de Sixt.	$16\frac{1}{4}$
Sept	22	Grasse Chèvre　　　　Ib.	10
	25	Plan-de-Léchaud.　　Ib.	$5\frac{1}{4}$
	d.	Ibid (le soir)	11
Aug^t	25	Grenairon.　　　　Ibid	$10\frac{1}{4}$
Nov^r	20	Geneve	2
Sept^r	25	Glacier de Buet　　Ibid	$6\frac{1}{2}$

[This table is taken from Jean André de Luc's *Recherches sur les modifications de l'atmosphère* (Geneva, 2 vols., 1772: vol. ii, p. 340) with some slight changes in order. The other half of the table is shown on the next page.]

Water by Mr De Luc in 1770

Height of the Barometer	Height in $\frac{1}{192}$ of an inch	Degrees of Reaumurs Ther- mometer	Difference from Calculation	Degrees by the Rule
28.5$\frac{2}{16}$	5458	81,09	+ 2	81,11
28.2.7	5415	80,93	+ 1	80.94
28.2.4	5412	80 93		80,93
28.1.2	5394	80,82	+ 3	80,85
27.11.0	5360	80,72		80,72
27.10.0	5344	80,68	− 2	80,66
27.9.7	5335	80,64	− 2	80,62
27.9.7	5335	80,62		80,62
27.6.13	5293	80,47	− 2	80,45
27.6.8	5288	80,47	− 4	80,43
27.5.11	5276	80,35	+ 3	80,38
27.5.3	5267	80,31	+ 4	80,35
27.1.14	5214	80,16	− 8	80,13
27.0.15	5199	80,10	− 3	80,07
27.0.9	5193	80,04		80,04
26.4.15	5071	79,60	− 7	79,53
26.3.15	5055	79,50	− 4	79,46
25.11.7	4983	79,19	− 3	79,16
24.10.9	4777	78,20	+ 5	78,25
24.5.15	4703	77,80	+11	77,91
24.1.1	4625	77,45	+10	77,55
23.8.2	4546	77,18		77,18
23.4.6	4486	76,89	+ 1	76,90
25.11.4	4980	79,13	+ 1	79,14
22.11.14	4414	76,54	+ 1	76,55
21.10.7	4199	75,47	+ 1	75,48
21.10.2	4194	75,47	− 2	75,45
20.4.15	3919	73,92	+ 7	73,99
25.11.2	4978	79,15	− 2	79,13
19.7.15	3775	73,21	− 2	73,19

Reaumur's Thermometer				Fahrenheits Thermo^r	
degrees of equal heats	degrees of Thermom^r	degrees of Fahrenheits Thermom^r	degrees of Fahrenheits of = heats	degrees of = heats	Corresponding degrees of Thermometer
0	00000	00000	000	0	0000
1	0,931	2,09475	2,25	2	1,862
2	1,863	4,19175	4,5	4	3,726
3	2,798	6,29550	6,75	6	5,596
4	3,734	8,4015	9,	9	8,4015
5	4,672	10,512	11,25	11	10,2784
6	5,611	12,62475	13,5	13	12,15716
7	6,553	14,74425	15,75	15	14,04214
8	7,496	16,866	18,	18	16,866
9	8,441	18,99225	20,25	20	18,7577
10	9,387	21,12075	22,5	22	20,6514
11	10,336	23,256	24,75	24	22,55127
12	11,286	25,3935	27.	27	25,3935
13	12,237	27,53325	29,75	29	26,83913
14	13,191	29,67975	31,5	31	29,20864
15	14,146	31,8285	33,75	33	31,1212
16	15,004	33,759	36,	36	33,759
17	16,062	36,1395	38,25	38	35,903
18	17,023	38,30175	40,5	40	37,828
19	17,985	40,46625	42,75	42	39,7563
20	18,949	42,63525	45,	45	42,63525
21	19,915	44,80875	47,25	47	44,5716
22	20,883	46,98675	49,5	49	46,5121
23	21,852	49,167	51,75	51	48,4544
24	22,823	51,35175	54,	54	51,35175
25	23,796	53,541	56,25	56	53,302
26	24,771	55,73475	58,5	58	55,2583
27	25,747	57,93075	60,75	60	57,2155
28	26,725	60,13125	63	63	60,13125

Reaumur's Thermometer				Fahrenheits Thermo^r	
Degrees of = heats	Degrees of Thermom^r	Degrees of Fahrenheits Thermometer	Degrees of Fahrenheit of = heats	Degrees of = heats	Corresponding Degrees of Thermometer
29	27,705	62,33625	65,25	65	62,0974
30	28,687	64,54575	67,5	67	64,06763
31	29,670	66,7575	69,75	69	66,3967
32	30,655	68,97375	72	72	68,97375
33	31,642	71,1945	74,25	74	70,9547
34	32,631	73,41975	76,5	76	72,9398
35	33,621	75,64725	78,75	78	74,9268
36	34,613	77,87925	81,	81	77,87925
37	35,607	80,11575	83,25	83	79,8751
38	36,603	82,35675	85,5	85	81,8751
39	37,600	84,6	87,75	87	83,8769
40	38,599	86.84775	90,	90	86,84775
41	39,6	89,1	92,95	92	88,8585
42	40,603	91,35675	94,5	94	90,87338
43	41,607	93,61575	96,75	96	92,89
44	42,613	95,87925	99,	99	95,87925
45	43,621	98,14725	101,25	101	97,9049
46	44,631	100,41975	103,5	103	100,1766
47	45,642	102,6945	105,75	105	101,9661
48	46,655	104,97935	108,	108	104,97935
49	47,67	107,2575	110,25	110	107,0142
50	48,687	109,54575	112,5	112	109,3588
51	49,705	111,83625	114,75	114	111,1052
52	50,725	114,13125	117,	117	114,13125
53	51,747	116,43075	119,25	119	116,18666
54	52,771	118,73475	121,5	121	118,24612
55	53,796	121,041	123,75	123	120,3074
56	54,823	123,35175	126,	126	123,35175

Reaumur's Thermometer				Fahren^{ts} Thermom^r	
Degrees of = heats	Degrees of Ther- mom^r	Degrees of Fahren- heits Thermom- eter	Degrees of Fahren^t of = heats	Degrees of = heats	Correspond- ing Degrees of Ther- mometer
57	55,852	125,667	128,25	128	125,422
58	56,883	127,98675	130,5	130	127,49637
59	57,915	130,3875	132,75	132	129,5725
60	58,949	132,63525	135,	135	132,63525
61	59,985	134,96625	137,25	137	134,7204
62	61,023	137,30175	139,5	139	136,8096
63	62,062	139,6395	141,75	141	138,9
64	63,103	141,98175	144,	144	141,98175
65	64,146	144,3285	146,25	146	144,08178
66	65,191	146,67975	148,5	148	146,18587
67	66,237	149,03325	150,75	150	148,291
68	67,286	151,3935	153,	153	151,3935
69	68,335	153,75375	155,25	155	153,5061
70	69,387	156,12075	157,5	157	155,6251
71	70,441	158,49225	159,75	159	157,7481
72	71,496	160,866	162,	162	160,866
73	72,553	163,24425	164,25	164	162,9957
74	73,611	165,62475	166,5	166	165,1273
75	74,672	168,012	168,75	168	167,2652
76	75,734	170,4015	171,	171	170,4015
77	76,798	172,7955	173,25	173	172,5461
78	77,863	175,19175	175,5	175	174,6926
79	78,931	177,59475	177,75	177	176,8454
80	80,000	180,	180,	180	180,

[38r] 23ᵈ February 1781.   Latent heat
A pipe of Copper was provided about 5 feet long 3 Inches of one of its
ends bent downwards. the Copper was about $\frac{1}{50}$ Inch thick, and the
Diameter of the Pipe was $\frac{3}{8}$ of an Inch —   †
The Straight end of the Pipe was fixed on the Spout of a Tea Kettle
from which the pipe inclined upwards so that the Bent end was about
2 feet higher than the Spout of the Tea Kettle. —
    The Tea Kettle was filled with Water halfway up the entry of the
Spout, The Lid was fixed Steam tight with some oat meal dough.
    A Tin pan 4 Inches deep, and 6 Inches dia^r had $2\frac{1}{2}$ pounds of Water
put into it, which filled it nearly to $2\frac{3}{4}$ Inches deep — This Pan was
placed upon a Stand, and the very point of the bent end of the Pipe was
Immersed in the Water, being first Shut with a Cork, through which a
Small passage was kept open by a bit of Goose Quill —
    The Water in the Kettle was made to boil some time before the
point of the Pipe was Immersed in the Pan, and it was observed that no
sensible quantity of Steam was Condensed into Water so as to fall in
drops from the small portion of the Pipe which was bent downwards —
the Steam which was condensed in the Inclined part of the pipe, returned into the Kettle —
    When the end of the pipe was immersed in the cold water, the
Steam issuing from it was condensed with a Crackling Noise, and
began to heat the Water in contact with it.
    Over —

[39r]   Latent Heat   Continued
The Water in the Pan being constantly stirred, with a Circular motion,
the heat was diffused thro' the whole, and the experiment was continued untill it was judged that the Water in the Pan had acquired a
proper degree of heat
                        Experiment 1st
The Heat of the Water in the Pan at beginning the Experiment was
$43\frac{1}{2}°$ When the Experiment was ended the heat of the Water was $89\frac{1}{2}$.
differe 46° — The Weight of water, at beginning of Expt. was $2\frac{1}{2}$
pounds = 17500 Grains —
After the experiment, by the addition of Condensed Steam, the Weight
of the water was 18260 Grains   Consequently the Steam Condensed
into Water was 760 Grs   Then 17500 Grains × by $46\frac{1}{2}°$ the Increase of
the heat arising from the Condensation of the Steam = 8·137500°

† Photograph: see p. 431.

459

which $\div$ by 760 Grains, the Weight of the Water, which, when in the form of Steam contained that heat is $= 1070$; but to this must be added the heat of the Water after — the Experiment $89\frac{1}{2}° = 1159\frac{1}{2}°$ which is the Sum of the Sensible and Latent heat of the Steam, reckoning from the O. point of Fahrenheits Scale, from which if we deduct $212°$ the Sensible heat of the Steam, remains $947\frac{1}{2}°$ its Latent heat —

The Water was weighed very accurately. The Tin Pan, and a piece of oiled paper fitted to its inside being first counterpoised, when they were quite dry: after the water had received [40r] its heat from the Steam it was thoroughly mixed so as to be all of one heat. Immediately after the Thermometer had shown what the heat was, which was in less than half a Minute, the Water was covered with the disc of Oiled paper to prevent evaporation which would otherwise have unavoidably lessened its Weight during the operation of Weighing. The Thermometer with which the heats were measured, became Stationary in less than 10 Seconds—The duration of the Experiments was generally from four to Six minutes. The first and Second experiments were tried without the Cork in the mouth of the Pipe, which was used in the *three* remaining ones —

The Second Experiment was supposed to have lost a little Weight as some few drops of Water were forced out by the Steam.

The Pan was set in a Cold place after the experiment, where the Air was at $40°$ and stood there for half an hour, when it was conjectured that it was come to the heat of the Place. 2 pounds of Water at $76°$ was then poured into it, and after the mixture, the heat was found to be $75\frac{1}{2}°$ — then for every $35\frac{1}{2}°$ with two pounds of Water there must be $\frac{1}{2}°$ allowed for the heat of the Pan, and $\frac{1}{2}°$ for each $44°$ with $2\frac{1}{2}$ pounds of Water —

[37v]

Latent[8]

Experiment 1st   [See Note 1, pp. 480–1.]
Cold $\triangledown$ ——— $43\frac{1}{2}°$
Hot $\triangledown$ ——— $89\frac{1}{2}°$

	Grains	
Weight of Cold $\triangledown$ $2\frac{1}{2}$lb $=$	17500	17500
D° of $\triangledown$ Condensed	760	760
D° of Mixture ———	17900	17900

[8] Watt's calculations of the latent heat of condensation of steam demand such detailed consideration that we have found it necessary to give this in a series of notes printed here on pp. 480–90 following the text of the notebook.

× by increase of heat 46° & heat of
Pan ½°

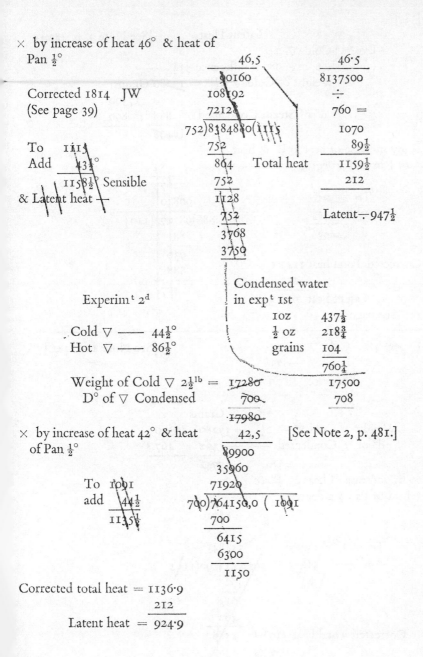

                                       46,5   46·5

                                   90160   8137500

Corrected 1814 JW   108192   ÷
(See page 39)   7212   760 =
                752)8184880(10885   1070

To   1115   752   89½
Add   43½°   864   Total heat   1159½
   1158½° Sensible   752   212
& Latent heat   1128
                  752   Latent 947½
                 3768
                 3750

                       Condensed water
      Experimᵗ 2ᵈ   in expᵗ 1st
                       1oz   437½
  Cold ▽ —— 44½°   ½ oz   218¾
  Hot ▽ —— 86½°   grains 104
                          760¼
Weight of Cold ▽ 2½ˡᵇ = 17280   17500
   D° of ▽ Condensed 700   708
                  17980

× by increase of heat 42° & heat   42,5   [See Note 2, p. 481.]
of Pan ½°
                      89900
                      35960
     To 1091   71920
     add 44½   700)764150,0 (1091
      1135½   700
                   6415
                   6300
                   1150

Corrected total heat = 1136·9
              212
   Latent heat = 924·9

Latent Heat　　　[See Note 3, p. 482.]

Exp^t 3^d Cold ▽ 44$\frac{1}{2}$°

　　hot　▽ 98 — difference 53$\frac{1}{2}$° ——

　　Weight of Cold ▽ 2$\frac{1}{2}$^{lb} = ~~17280~~ Grains

　　　　　　　　　　　　　　　　　17500

d° of Steam Condensed　　888　899

　　　　　　　　　　　　　~~18168~~

× by increase of heat 53$\frac{1}{2}$° & heat ⎱
of Pan half a degree ——— ⎰ = 　54

　　　　　　　　　　　　　72672

To　~~1104~~°　　　　　90840

Add　~~44$\frac{1}{2}$~~°　　888)981072(1104

　　~~1148$\frac{1}{2}$~~°　　888

　　　　　　　　　　　　930

Corrected Total heat 1149·1　888

　　　　　　　212　　　　4272

　　Latent heat 937·1

See page 39

Exper^t 4th　Cold ▽.　44$\frac{1}{2}$°　　　　[See Note 4, p. 482.]

　　　hot　▽ — 73$\frac{1}{2}$

　　difference　29°

　　　　　　　　　　　　Grains

Weight of Cold ▽ — 2$\frac{1}{2}$^{lb} = ~~17280~~ 17500

d° of ▽ Condensed ———　~~462~~　467,5

　　　　　　　　　　　　~~17742~~

× by Increase of heat 29°$\frac{1}{2}$° & ⎱
heat of Pan $\frac{1}{2}$ a degree　　⎰——29,5

　　　　　　　　　　88710

　　　　　　　　　159678

To —— 1132　　35484

Add —— 44$\frac{1}{2}$　462)5233890(1132

　　1176$\frac{1}{2}$　　462

　　　　　　　　　613

　　　　　　　　　462

Corrected Total heat 1102·1　1518

　　　　　　73·5　1386

　　　　　　1175·6　1329

　　　　　　212

Latent heat　936·6

462

[See Note 5, p. 482.]

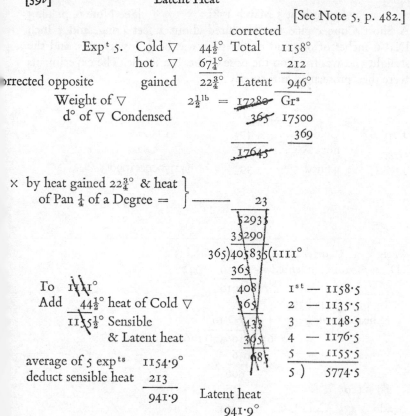

corrected

Exp^t 5.   Cold ▽   44½° Total   1158°
        hot ▽   67¼°   212
rrected opposite   gained   22¾° Latent   946°
    Weight of ▽   2½^{lb} = ~~17280~~ Gr^s
    d° of ▽ Condensed   ~~365~~ 17500
                                369
                           ~~17645~~

× by heat gained 22¾° & heat ⎫
  of Pan ¼ of a Degree = ⎭ ──── 23

                        ⎰293⎱
                      3⎰290⎱
            365)40⎰835⎱(1111°
                    36⎰
To   11⎱1°   40⎰   1st — 1158·5
Add   44½° heat of Cold ▽   ⎰6⎱   2 — 1135·5
   11⎰5½° Sensible   ⎰43⎱   3 — 1148·5
        & Latent heat   36⎰   4 — 1176·5
                          ⎰8⎱   5 — 1155·5
average of 5 exp^{ts} 1154·9°   5)   5774·5
deduct sensible heat   213
                ─────   Latent heat
                941·9   941·9°

NB. In the Five preceeding, and Three first succeeding Experiments, the Water &^{c} was weighed with Averdupoise Weight, and only 432 Grains were allowed to the Ounce, whereas in reality there are 437¼ Grains in the ounce But upon Calculating them by the last of these We^{ts} the results were found to be so nearly the same, that no alteration is necessary —

Latent heat 5 March 1781   [See Note 6, p. 482.]

A Short Copper pipe was procured about 2 feet Long, and $\frac{3}{4}$ Inch Dia^r 6 Inches of one end of the pipe was bent downwards, and the straight end was fixed on the nose of the Tea Kettle. The experiments were then prosecuted as formerly

†

$\overline{Exp^{t}\,1}^{st}$

Exp^t 6th Cold $\triangledown$ .. — 47$\frac{1}{2}$°   17500
           hot .. $\triangledown$ .. — 87°   40
           gained   — 39$\frac{1}{2}$°   642)70000(1090·3
                                              87
                                          ——————
                                          1177·3
                                           212
                                          ——————
                                           965·3

Weight of $\triangledown$ used 2$\frac{1}{2}$^{lb} = 17280 Grains
D° of Steam Condensed — 636   642
                        ——————
                        17916

$\times$ by heat gained 39$\frac{1}{2}$° ⎱
  & heat of pan $\frac{1}{2}$° — ⎰ — 40°
                        636)716640(1126
                            636
                            ——————
                            806
                            636
                            ——————
To 1126°   1704
add 47$\frac{1}{2}$° Cold $\triangledown$ 1272
   1173$\frac{1}{2}$°   ——————
                            4320
                            3816
                            ——————
                            Latent heat
                             965·3°

9 March 1781
Mr Boulton's long thermom^r gave the air in the Room 55$\frac{3}{4}$°
My Thermom^r gave it 55$\frac{1}{2}$°
Exp^t 6th so much exceeds the others as to make it a doubtful one

---

† Photograph: see p. 431.

Latent heat   5 March 1781
~~Expt 2d~~ Cold ▽ . . . .   49°
Expt 7 hot   ▽ . . . .   84½° gained 35½°

                                    Grains
                                                        ~~17500~~
Weight ▽ used 2½lb   =   17500
   d° of Steam condensed —   588·5   [See Note 7, pp. 483–4.]
× by heat gained 35½° ⎱   17500   water in pan
& by heat of Pan ½° — ⎰   36

              588·5)630000(1070°·5
                                    84·5
          Total heat   1155°
                                    212°
          Latent heat —   943°

~~Expt 3d~~   Cold ▽ 47°
Expt 8th   hot ▽ 87½ gained 40½°

                            Grs.
Weight ▽ used 2½lb   =   17500
   d° of Steam condensed =   675   [See Note 8, pp. 484–5.]
                                    17500 cold water
× by heat gained 40½° ⎱
  & heat of Pan — ½° ⎰—   41°

              675)717500(1063°
                                    87·5
          Total heat   1150·5
          Sensible D°   212°
          Latent heat —   938°·5

NB The cork & quill fitted into the tube as in the former
experiments —

Latent heat 16ᵗʰ March 1781

Present   Doctor Priestly

Experiments made with the long Pipe, the Cork in the bent end as formerly

Expᵗ 1ˢᵗ – 9ᵗʰ

Cold ▽ ———	45°
hot ▽ ———	86½
difference	41½

Grains   [See Note 9, pp. 485–7.]

Weight of Cold ▽ 2½ˡᵇ avoir =	17500
D° – – – of Steam Condensed – – –	680·5
× by heat gained 41½° ⎫	17500
& by heat of Pan ½° ⎭ – – – –	42
	35000
	70000

680,5(735000(1080°

To 1080	
Add 86½° heat of hot ▽	
1166½ ——	
212	
954·5 Latent heat	

corrected Mar 1814

Latent heat 16 March 1781

Expert ⚡ 10th

Cold ▽ 45°

hot ▽ 85½°   difference gained 40½°

	Grains
We^t of Cold ▽ 2½^{lb} =	17500
D° of Steam Condens'd	664,25
× by heat gained 40½° ⎫	17500
& heat of Pan ½°— ⎭	41
	17500

                    70000
       664·29)717500(1080·16   [See Note 10,
                    66425   p. 487].
To 1080·16   532500
Add   85·5 heat of hot ▽   531400
   1165·66   110000
   212   66425
   953·66 Latent heat   43575

Expert ⚡ 11th

Cold ▽ 45°

hot ▽ 102 heat gained 57° ——

	Grs		
We^t of Cold ▽ 2½^{lb} =	17500	6 1173½	[These
D° of Steam Cond^d —	975	7 1153	figures
	17500	8 1150	are partly
× by heat of Pan ½° ⎫	57·5	9 1167	erased.]
& heat gained 57° ⎭	87500	10 1166	

                    122500
                    87500   [See Note 11,
       975)10062500(1032   pp. 487–8.]
                    975
To   1032   3125
add   102 heat of hot ▽   2925
   1134   2000
   212   1950
   922 Latent heat   50

corrected Mar 1814

467

[42*v*]

Mr Smeatons Exp^{ts} on Rotative motions
Phil: Trans^{ns} 1776

†

	inches
Dia^{r} of Cyl^{r} of Lead or the heavy bodies	2·57
Length of D° — — — ————	1·56
Dia^{r} of the hole therein ————	·72
weight of each 3^{lbs} avoir^{se}	
Greater distance of the middle of each Body from the Centre of y^{e} axis —— }	8·25
The smaller distance of d° ————	3·92
18 turns of the ~~bigger scale~~ smaller barrel = 5 D° of the smaller D° ———— }	25·25

[43*r*] Table of Experiments

N°	oz. avoir in Scale	Barrel used M. bigger N. smaller	The Arm: W. whole H. half	Time of descent of weight	Number of turns wound on Barrel	Time of 20 Revolutions equable Motion
				″		″
1	8	M	W	—14¼	— 5—	29
2	8	N	W	—28¼	—10—	29¼
3	8	N	W	—14¼	— 2½—	58½
4	32	M	W	— 7 —	— 5—	14
5	32	N	W	—14 —	—10—	14¾
6	32	N	W	— 7 —	— 2½—	28¾
7	8	M	H	— 7—	— 5—	14¾
8	8	M	H	—14—	—10—	15
9	8	N	H	— 7—	— 2½—	30½
1	2	3	4	6	5	7

† Photograph: see p. 431.

Experiment on Latent Heat
of water distilled in vacuo Jany 4th 1783   †
a Vessel was made in the following form
The vessel was made of white Iron and well soldered so as to be
perfectly air tight
The opening at A was shut by a good Cork
The small openings B & C which were only ⅛ inch diameter were shut
by brass plugs ground very carefully into Brass Sockets
The opening D which was very small was also shut by a Brass plug
A pint of water was poured into the inside vessel and as much into the
outside vessel The whole was then sett upon a Chaffing dish and made
to boil. The steam was suffered to issue at B & C untill it was supposed
all the air was extruded, the aperture C was then shut and just immersed
in a

vessel of water to prevent the air from entering   the Steam was suffered
to issue some time longer at B & it was also shut and immediately
immersed a little way in ▽   Cold water was then poured into the
Balneum untill it reached to A. A kind of vacuum was instantly
produced in the internal vessel and the 2 double cones communicating
with it. Then the Double cone B was immersed in a tin pan 6 inches
deep and 8¼ inches diameter filled within an inch of its mouth. The
water was weighed into this pan as follows   Troy weight

	oz	dr	gr
Two fills of a small copper still			
with a narrow mouth, each	53	– 4 –	
	53	– 4 –	
	106	– 8 –	
40 Grains of ▽ stuck to to the inside			
of the Still each time ————	– 1	– 20	
	106	– 6	– 40
Water weighed in a Tin can ———	24	– —	– —
total ▽ in refrigeratory ————	130	– 6	– 40

Heat of ▽ in ye refrigeratory
  at Beginning———————————————————— 52° —
  D° at the end ——————————————— 61°
      Heat gained ———— 9+
Heat of ▽ which issued from y^e Cone 62
Heat of balneum at beginning 134°
D° at the end ———— 158

† Photograph: see p. 431.

469

Distillation in Vacuo

	oz	gr
weight of ▽ condensed in the Cone	1	. 54
▽ supposed to adhere to D°		.. 6

= 1 oz   1 dr

Duration of the experiment was 9 minutes
The heat of the Chaffing dish was prevented from coming at the refrigeratory by a sconce of Bricks, and the heat of the air of the room was about 58°
When the experiment was finished the air was lett in at D.
From several circumstances it appeared that the air originally contained in yᵉ still had not been perfectly expelled as the degree of heat it required to make it boil indicated only about $\frac{2}{3}$ vacuum
The double cone B weighed 1000 Grains and as it was about 134° of heat at the beginning and was cooled to 62° by the refrigeratory it lost 72° which × by its weight is = to 7200 but as its capacity for receiving heat is less than that of water I estimate it only at 5200   The ▽ in the refrigeratory weighed 62800 gr which × by 9° of heat = 565200 from wᶜʰ

deducting the 5200 given by the Cone there remains 560000 ÷ by 534 grains the ▽ condensed in the Cone = 1048° + 62 yᵉ heat which it retained = 1110 the apparent sum of the latent and sensible heat; but the Tin refrigeratory received 9° of heat for which no allowance has been made — The whole vessel weighed 24$\frac{1}{2}$ oz. but it had a wire round its mouth & a bevel which were not in contact with the water — The bevel weighd $\frac{3}{4}$ᵒᶻ and was some what more than = to one $\frac{1}{2}$ of the wire round the mouth of the pan, but for that wire, yᵉ bevel, & the sides of the pan not in contact with the water I allow 4$\frac{1}{2}$ ounces there remains 20 ounces which being tinned Iron I suppose to be [. . . seven lines obliterated . . .]

Distillation in vacuo

I suppose to be = to 2 ounces of ▽ (that is to $\frac{2}{3}$) of its bulk of water)
An error was committed on the other page in computing the quantity of heat given by the tin cone by its weight instead of its Bulk The calculations should stand as follows

130^{oz} 6^{dr} of water   = to [?] ────
28^{oz} tinned Iron   = the 2 oz water

$$132{\cdot}6$$

which is = to grains   63620
× by degrees gained   9°

$$\overline{572580}$$

subtract heat given by cone
143 × 72 = 10296 ÷ by ⅔ =7000
÷ by the weight of   565580
condensed ▽ in cone ────── 534

gives 1059 Latent heat + 62 heat retained = 1121 sum of sensible and latent heat

NB no allowance is made for water adhering to Cone because it was equally wet at the beginning of experiment and I even suspect that there was some water condensed in it before put into refrigeratory

[45a *r*]

Ap¹ 1814 Observations on the experiments on Latent heat p 38 to 42.

These experiments were made with great care, but two material errors were committed in the mode of calculating them. The first was the assuming the avoir dupois ounce at 432 grains; whereas it contains 437½

This was perceived in the course of the experiments & the 9th 10th & 11th were calculated properly in that respect, but the others remained uncorrected, till this time.

The second error consisted in adding the condensed Steam to the weight of the cold water and after multiplying that sum by the heat gained, ~~adding~~ & dividing by the weight of the condensed Steam, adding the degrees of heat of the *cold* water, in order to find the total sensible and Latent heats.

Whereas the weight of the cold water *alone* should be × by the heat gained and divided by the weight of the condensed steam, to which should be added the heat of the hot water, to give the total Sensible and Latent heat, from which if the sensible heat of boiling water = 212 be deducted the remainder is the latent heat, as is directed in p. 38. As it happened however these errors nearly ballanced one another so that the results did not differ materialy.

On looking over these experiments this year on the occasion of correcting Dr Robisons article on Steam & Steam

Engines

Engines in the Encylopedia Brit^a I perceived the second Error & have recalculated the whole experiments so that I believe they are now right in that respect, and they stand as follows

1st — 947·5° latent heat
2. — 924·1 — D°
3. — 937·1 — D°
4. — 963·6 — D°
5. — 946· — D°
6. — 965·3 — D°
7. — 943 — D°
8. — 938·5 — D°
9. — 954·5 — D°
10. — 953·66 — D°
11. — 922· — D°

÷ by 11)$\overline{10395·36}$(945·3 average Latent heat

But as two of the exp^{ts} the 2^d & 11th give that heat considerably less than the others if their sum 1846° be substracted & the remainder 8549·26 be divided by 9 the quotient gives 949·9 for the average latent heat which I believe is near the truth. Be that as it may I was not satisfied with the experiments on account of the discrepancy, & at a future period requested Mr Southern to repeat them on larger quantities of water, which he did in [blank] on Steam of the heat of 212° & in [blank] on Steam of higher temperatures at the temp^{re} of 224° 270° & 295° operating upon 28$\frac{1}{2}$^{lb} of water, he found the latent heat in the

3

[45br] 3 experiments 890° 920° & 933° but allowing for the heat which escaped during the time of the exp^{ts} he found those heats to be 942° 942° & 950°
Of the Exper^{ts} on the latent heat at the temp^{re} of 212° I am not furnished with an account

A Table of the particulars of the foregoing Experiments—

N° of Experiment	Quan^y of cold water in pan	Temperature of ye cold water	Weight of the Condensed Steam	Temperature of ye heated water	Encrease of Heat	Total, sensible & Latt. heat	Latent heat
	Grains		Grains				
I.	17500	43°.5	760	89°.5	46°.5	1159°.5	947°.5
2.	17500	44°.5	708.	86.5	42.5	1136.9	924.9
3.	17500	44.5	899.	98.	54.	1149.1	937.1
4.	17500	44.5	467.5	73.5	29.5	1175.6	963.6
5.	17500	44.5	369.	67.25	23.	1158.	946. . .
6.	17500	47.5	642.	87	40	1177.3	965.3
7.	17500	49.	588.5	84.5	36.	1155.	943. .
8.	17500	47.	675.	87.5	41.	1150.5	938.5
9.	17500	45.	680.5	86.5	42.	1166.5	954.5
10.	17500	45.	664.25	85.5	41.	1165.66	953.66
11.	17500	45.	975.	102.	57.5	1134.	922.
I	2	3	4	5	6	7	8

46r]
Latent heat of Snow Feby 26th 1783

32 oz Troy
Two pound of ▽/was heated to 127° and weighed accurately
Two parcels of Snow 8 oz each were weighed separately, and laid ready in the open Air while the water was heating
The heat of the air was 27°

Surface
of the Snow immediately under its   25°

473

The vessel containing the water was placed in a room about 40° of heat & before the Snow could be put into it was cooled by the spontaneous evaporation to 124° and I suspect rather lower
8 oz of the snow was disolved & the heat of the mixture was 76°
Then the warm $\triangledown$ had lost 48° of heat which $\times$ by 4 its quantity gives 192° from which substract 51° the sensible heat gained by the Snow, remains 141° the latent heat

The other 8 oz of Snow was added & the heat of the mixture was $44\frac{3}{4}$ —
Then the warm $\triangledown$ had lost $76 - 44\frac{3}{4} = 31\frac{1}{4} \times 5 = 156\frac{1}{4} - 19\frac{3}{4}$

gained by the snow $= 136\frac{1}{2}$ — and taking the whole together — 124 — $44\frac{3}{4} = 79\frac{1}{4} \times 2 = 158\frac{1}{2} - 19\frac{3}{4} = 138\frac{3}{4}$ So we may say the latent heat $= 140$

[47r]
Elastick powers of Steam at various
Temperatures Mar 1803

Page
My Experiments in 176 [5] — see 21
with the open tube gave

	pressure inches		heat
	45 =	—	236°
	60 =	—	252
with the sealed tube	$59\frac{1}{2}$ =	—	252
	$75\frac{1}{2}$ =	—	264
erroneous ——	$\{110\frac{1}{2}$ =	—	292
	$\{143\frac{1}{2}$ =	—	312

These experiments were considered merely as appercus, to give some idea of the progression & were intended to be repeated with greater accuracy, which however was long delayed. I believe they were the very first experiments ever made upon the subject, which at the time was so little understood that for some time I thought the boiling point in vacuo was about 100^d — I however soon became sensible that could not be so, it being plainly much lower, & indeterminate as to a *perfect* vacuum, which the Curve projected from these experiments showed.

In 1773 on reading M^r De Luc's book on the atmosphere I resumed the experiments

and

[47v]

Note. The thermometer by which the exp⁵ in — 74 were made being examined in —83 the Boiling ▽ water point was found to be placed 2° too high & the freezing point ⅙ too low where consequently the scale was 6°. too short for it the freezing point 32° of the scale corresponding to 36° of the thermometer, & the boiling point 212° of the scale standing at 214° of the thermometer

The above is a mistake of one therm^r for another

[48r]

and begun upon these below 212° as related in pp. 24 &^{ca} which still did not prove satisfactory   I continued them in 1774 & also made some upon heats above 212° which seemed to confirm these made with the open tube in 1763. I also made experiments upon the vapour of brine & on that of spirit of wine p. 30 and I laid down a curve from those made upon water, which drawing still subsists the points however fixed from
                                                    sealed
the experiments with the ~~open~~ tube in 1763 are from an erroneous calculation of the experiments. The set of experiments I thought most exact is that in Col. 2^d p. 29 — those made upon brine at same time keep paralel to it, & those on Spirit of wine do the same except the two or 3 at the lowest temperatures — I did not however ~~then~~ perceive this fact till pointed out by Mr Dalton in a late memoir.

    I could not at that time find out any series that corresponded with
                                        8 or
my observations but in 1779. I observed that if the pressures were taken in a Geometrical ratio the differences of the temperatures would be so also very nearly, & consequently the temperatures
                                                    themselves

Betancourt   Dalton Robson [These two names can be seen faintly]

Temp-erature	pressure	Geom. Series	Mᵣ Pronys calculⁿ	Mᵣ Schmidt	
				Temperat	elasticity
40.°	0.01			43°.25	0.11
50.	0.13			45.5	0.15
56.	0.23	50°.		54.5	0.28
60.	0.30			59.	0.38
67.5	0.46	66°.5		61.25	0.44
70.	0.53			65.77	0.55
80.	0.85			68.60	0.61
81.3	0.93	84.9		72.5	0.76
90.	1.28			77.	0.90
100.	1.78			81.5	1.01
102.	1.87	105.5		88.25	1.30
110.	2.40			92.75	1.42
120.	3.12			99.5	1.93
127.	3.75	127.9		106.25	2.23
130.	4.08			110.75	2.68
140.	5.41			115.25	3.20
150.	7.25			119.75	3.40
151.5	7.5	153.1		122.	3.64
160.	9.5			212.	28.
170.	12.				
179.5	15.	181.			
180.	15.2			The inches are French but	
212.	30.	212.		the degrees are Fahrenheit	
244.5	60.	246.4			

See Mᵣ Betancourts memoir & Mᵣ Prony's Hydraulic Circuit

themselves. On this footing the two sets of Series in p 34 were calcu-lated, the first of which is full of arithmetical errors in the lower being cast up by a clerk
temperatures A set of experiments — Col 1ˢᵗ p. 29 which I had not regarded as correct, agreed best with these series, I however still suspect its accuracy

In 1769 Ziegler had published his thesis on this subject, but I knew nothing of the book till long after & even now do not understand his experiments

In 1790 Mr Betancourt published his experiments on the same subject, which I found to differ from mine especialy in the heats above 212° they also seemed erroneous from his having made no allowance for a quantity of air which remained in his digester after having

inch

exhausted it by the air pump, about 4½ lines or ,375, his results stand on the opposite page reduced to English inches & Fahrenheits thermometer, from a curve in which I laid them down by Reaumurs scale & french inches, as far as 180°. the remainder are reduced from the observations by calculation. The red ink figures are the points of Duplication corresponding to the Geometrical Series — — — which Series was

[49v]

Mr Southerns Exp^{ts} in 1796

Temperature	1 Set	2^d Set	Mean
	Elasticity	Elasticity	Elasticity
	in inches	in inches	
52°	0.44	0.42	0.43
62.	0.53	0.52	0.525
72.	0.73	0.73	0.73
82.	1.03	1.02	1.025
92.	1.42	1.41	1.415
102.	1.98	1.92	1.95
112.	2.67	2.63	2.65
122.	3.58	3.54	3.56
132.	4.68	4.65	4.665
142.	6.05	6.00	6.025
152.	7.86	7.80	7.83
162.	9.98	9.96	9.97
172.	12.54	12.72	12.63
182.	16.01	15.84	15.925

477

~~Every~~ which series was formed by assuming the points of 212° & 181° as standards & supposing the zero of the thermometer to be depressed 100°, consequently calling these numbers 312° & 281°, & then continuing the series by Logarithms, afterwards substracting 100° from each Number so found. These experiments form an undulating curve between that of my Experiments in page 29 N° 2 & that of Mr Daltons —

Having reasons to doubt of the accuracy of my own experiments, as well as of that of Mr Betancourts, I requested Mr Southern to repeat them, which he did in Sepr 1796 — The apparatus he used was nearly the same as that I employed in 1774, namely a Straight Tube with a ball at the top, passing through the bottom of a oval tin pan filled with water so as completely to cover the ball — The dia^r of the Ball was
Inches   & its length 40 inches
about 2¼ & that of the tube about ¼ inch. — As much Mercury as the tube would contain was put into the ball, which had as much
distilled

distilled water added to it as the ball would contain so as to permit it to be boiled in it — The ball was heated & the water boiled in it for 10 minutes. The tube was then filled up with water well boiled, & inverted, that is to say the ball was placed upwards & the mouth of the tube placed in a cistern of Mercury, a vacuum being thus formed by the descent of the Mercury, the tube was reclined & showed a small bubble of air which was extricated by reinverting the tube & supplying the empty space with boiled water, which operations were repeated & the tube suffered to stand 3 or 4 days with the ball uppermost until it was found that the bubble of air generated was exceedingly small & there were no hopes of reducing it. The tube was then fixed in its place in the pan, & after properly mixing the water in the pan that it might be all of an equal heat, the Thermometer, which had a scale of about [blank] inch to the degree shewed the heat to be 52° & the height of the mercury in the tube as shewn by a floating scale was 28·33
Inches
inches surmounted by a column of water of 13·30 = ·98 of an
inch

= in all to 29·31 inches   Inches

inch of Mercury∕which being subtracted from 29·75 the height of the
                 Inches
common Bar^r gave 0·44 for the pressure of Steam at 52° — An Argand
lamp was now applied to the pan & it was heated to 62° & kept
stationary there until the heat & height of the mercury in the tube
were satisfactorily ascertained — & the same method was pursued for
every 10° to 182° —

These experiments were repeated & form the table in p. 50

A   A Mr Schmidt also made some experiments on this subject.
I have never seen his publication but have extracted from Mr Kirwans
treatise upon the variations of the atmosphere the numbers in the
Table page 49

N°	Heights of the Barometer Inches	Boiling Point by Observation °	Boiling Point by M^r De Luc's rules °	Error	Boiling point by interpolation from N° 1.2.6.7.14 and 15	Error
1	26,498	207,07	208,54	+0,47	207,18	+0,11
2	27,241	208,64	208,84	+0,20	208,52	−0,12
3	27,954	209,87	210,03	+0,16	209,80	−0,7
4	28,377	210,50	210,81	+0,31	210,56	+0,6
5	28,699	211,27	211,34	+0,7	211,11	−0,16
6	28,898	211,50	211,67	+0,17	211,47	−0,3
7	28,999	211,60	211,85	+0,25	211,64	+0,4
8	29,477	212,55	212,74	+0,19	212,42	−0,13
9	29 805	212,95	213,15	+0,20	213,03	+0,8
10	30,008	213,22	213,47	+0,25	213,49	+0,27
11	30,207	213,58	213,79	+0,21	213,71	+0,13
12	30,489	214,15	214,23	+0·8	214,19	+0,4
13	30,763	214,37	214,66	+0,29	214,65	+0,28
14	30,847	214,83	214,79	−0,4	214,79	−0,4
15	30,957	214,96	214,96	0	214,96	0

Notes on Watt's Determinations of the Latent Heat of Condensation of Steam

Watt's calculations of the value of the latent heat of condensation of steam need some detailed consideration and we set this out here in a series of notes on the various experiments recorded in his notebook. He began by taking the ounce avoirdupois as equal to 432 grains and later corrected this to $437\frac{1}{2}$ grains. He made another miscalculation, which will be explained as we proceed, but afterwards he concluded that these errors cancelled one another.

Note 1. In experiment 1 the cancelled calculation is arithmetically correct, but otherwise wrong; for Watt added the weight of water condensed from the steam to the weight of water in the refrigeratory, as if the whole of this water had been raised in temperature, and then multiplied this total by the rise in temperature of the cold water, whereas the weight of the condensed water is not subject to the rise in temperature; having obtained this product, he then divided it by the weight of the condensed water and to this quotient he added the 'heat' of the cold water (instead of hot water) to give the sum of the sensible and the latent heats, from which sum he subtracted 212°, the sensible heat of the steam, to give the latent heat of its condensation. His arithmetical analysis of the physical data that he was studying was, therefore, to say the least, confused, but he subsequently realized his errors in adding the 'heat' of the cold water and in adding the weight of the condensed water, and for Experiment 1 the whole calculation is corrected on the right of the page; the weight of cold water is multiplied by the rise in temperature, the product is divided by the weight of the condensed water, and to this quotient the 'heat' of the hot water is added and the 'heat' (212°) is subtracted, giving the latent heat of condensation of steam, and here his method is correct. Oddly enough, he set down a figure of 17900 in the corrected calculation on the right of the page, but his product 8137500 is correct, since he had multiplied 17500 by 46·5. As for the initialled 'J.W.' by Watt on the left of the page and marked 'Corrected 1814 (see page 39)', the date of 1814 seems surprisingly late.

To understand Watt's corrected method, it is helpful to show what would now be done with such experimental data. Let t_1 and t_2 be the temperatures (Watt would have said 'heats') of the cold and of the hot water respectively, m_1 and m_2 the weights respectively of the cold water and of the water condensed from the steam, and L the latent heat of condensation of steam per unit weight. We then have:

$$m_1 (t_2 - t_1) = m_2 (212 - t_2) + m_2 L.$$

Watt's method of calculation may be set out in the same symbols as:

$$\frac{m_1 (t_2 - t_1)}{m_2} + t_2 - 212 = L,$$

which is the same as the expression we have given, since it may be written:

$$m_1 (t_2 - t_1) + m_2 (t_2 - 212) = m_2 L, \text{ or}$$
$$m_1 (t_2 - t_1) = m_2 (212 - t_2) + m_2 L.$$

This, of course, applies to his corrected calculations, not to those made at the time of the original experiments. Watt accordingly corrected his calculations as late as 1814. In Experiment 1, he would have obtained $1158\frac{1}{2}$ — 212 or $946\frac{1}{2}$ as the latent heat, and his corrected result on the right of the page gave him $947\frac{1}{2}$, which, he persuaded himself, showed that the errors cancelled one another. It will be noticed that in the corrected calculation for Experiment 1 he entered a value of $760\frac{1}{4}$ grains for the weight of the condensed water, and here he evidently determined its weight as $1\frac{1}{2}$ oz. and 104 grains, but the 104 grains would not be capable of exact determination by difference on as large a mass as $2\frac{1}{2}$ lb. of water, and he probably estimated this last part as some fraction of an ounce and then converted it into grains. We would not place any great reliance on these weights, and Watt himself does not appear to have done so, but it remains interesting to realize how he obtained his numerical results.

Note 2. Here again we have the incorrect calculation by the addition of the 'heat' of the cold water, giving a result of 1091 + $44\frac{1}{2}$ or $1135\frac{1}{2}$ (deleted on the left), which would have given a final figure of $923\frac{1}{2}$ if Watt had completed it. On the right the incorrect calculation is deleted but the corrected form is not given. However, from his data he would have obtained $1050 \cdot 4 + 86 \cdot 5$, or $1136 \cdot 9$, which appears below as 'Corrected total heat', giving the latent heat as $924 \cdot 9$.

481

Note 3. Much the same occurs here as in Experiments 1 and 2. The deleted erroneous calculation would have given a value (not entered) of $1148\frac{1}{2}$ — 212, or $936\frac{1}{2}$, whereas the corrected figure is $1149\cdot1$ — 212, or $937\cdot1$, which is recorded, although the revised calculation is not entered.

Note 4. As before, the original and incorrect calculation, which is deleted, would have given a value (not entered) of $1176\frac{1}{2}$ — 212, or $964\frac{1}{2}$, and a corrected, but unrecorded, revision of this gave $963\cdot6$. But Watt here made a slip in his arithmetic and set down $1102\cdot1$ instead of $1104\cdot2$, which would have given a value of $965\cdot7$.

Note 5. Once more we have the deleted and the corrected calculations. The former would have given a value of $1155\frac{1}{2}$ — 212, or $943\frac{1}{2}$, if Watt had completed the subtraction, and the corrected one gave 1158 — 212, or 946, but the corrected calculation is not shown. On the right, half-way down the page, Watt determined the average result of Experiments 1 to 5, but, with the exception of Experiment 4, these results are the incorrectly calculated values, and so he deleted the attempted but incompleted average except that on the left he took it as $1154\cdot9$ instead of $1154\cdot5$, and then from this subtracted 213 instead of 212, obtaining $941\cdot9$ instead of $942\cdot9$, but evidently deletion was intended here also. The entry relating to this experiment concludes with a statement relating to his error in the number of grains in the ounce avoirdupois.

Note 6. This is numbered Experiment 6, although it is first numbered Experiment 1, as if a new series was being begun. But it is dated, while the earlier experiments are not dated; and it is dated 5 March 1781 and it shows that, even at this late date, Watt was still using the wrong value for the number of grains in the ounce avoirdupois and also adding the 'heat' of the cold instead of the hot water. The incorrect evaluation is deleted and the correct one set down on the right in part but not completely, giving a value of $965\cdot3$, whereas the uncompleted erroneous one would have given $961\frac{1}{2}$. In considering his revised result, however, Watt rejected it as doubtful because it 'so much exceeds the others'. For the same reason, he could have rejected the result of Experiment 4.

482

Note 7. On *f.* 41r, as printed above, the part marked by enclosed lines is an insertion pasted over other data and calculations, which read on the right as below, the upper edge of the pasted slip cutting through the figure 17500 as shown above:

$$
\begin{array}{r}
17500 \\
36 \\
\hline
\end{array}
$$

582 630000 (	1082,4
582	84,5
4800	1166,9
4656	212
1440	954,9
1164	
2760	
2328	
432	

Latent heat 954,9

It will be seen that Watt had not yet corrected his error about the number of grains equivalent to the ounce avoirdupois and that in the corrected calculation, pasted over this, he had made only an approximation by adding $6\frac{1}{2}$ grains instead of nearly $7\frac{1}{2}$, the weight of water condensed from the steam becoming 588·5 instead of 582. To the right of this he had, it seems, calculated the latent heat correctly by adding the 'heat' of the hot water instead of the cold, subtracting 212 and obtaining a value of 954·9, but we are doubtful about his having made this change at this date (5 March 1781), because in another calculation under the pasted slip on the extreme left (see below) he still adds the 'heat' of the cold water.

To the left of this, immediately under the heading 'Grains', there is another calculation beneath the figures as they appear on the corrected slip; but it will be seen below that this calculation makes use of some of the data shown on the slip covering them; and we distinguished the figures used in both by marking them * below:

Grains

17500*

588,5*

—————

17500*

36†

—————

107172

53589

582φ)643032‡

582

—————

610

582

—————

2832

To —1104°

Add— 49 Cold▽

1153

[†This figure appears between 17500* and 36*.

φThis appears under 588,5* as the divisor in the calculation.

‡This appears under 630000*.]

The quotient, which is omitted, would be 1104, which Watt has used in the deleted calculation on the left, adding, however, the 'heat' of the cold instead of the hot water. The deleted calculation would have given a value of 941 for the latent heat, but it is necessary to point out that at this date Watt was still making this major error of adding the 'heat' of the cold instead of the hot water, although this correction appears earlier in these obliterated data on this same page, as we have pointed out in the preceding paragraph. His arithmetic, so far as we have been able to decipher it correctly, is puzzling; When 643032 is divided by 582, the result is 1104, which Watt uses in the calculation on the left, but it is not clear why he has the figure 643032, and 36 times 17500 is 630000. One possibility is that he set down 362 in error for 582 as the weight of the steam condensed and this would have given, according to his method of calculation at that time, a product of 643032.

Note 8. There is a further insertion pasted over the lower half of ƒ. 41r and here shown in enclosed lines. Beneath this slip is another calculation as follows, the figures retained in the corrected version being again marked * by us:

Grs.

17500*
667
———
17500*
41*
———

667)717500*(1077†   [† The quotient is 10757, not 1077.]
667   87,5
——   ———
5050   1164,5
4669   212
——   ———
3810   942,5   Latent heat [Subtraction gives 952,5,
3335   not 942,5.]
——
4750
4669
——
81

On the left of the lower half of the page under the pasted slip, there
is another calculation:

To   1077°φ   [φ 1077° is corrected from 1062.]
add   87½ heat of hot▽
———
1164½‡ = 942,5†   [‡ 1164½ is corrected from 1149½.]
      Latᵗ heat   [† Subtraction of 212 gives 952·5,
                               not 942·5.]

Here again Watt had not yet corrected the error for the grains per
ounce avoirdupois. In the corrected calculation pasted over this, he had
added 8 grains instead of 8½, although he was calculating to the half-
grain. The quotient should be 10757, not 1077, and subtraction of 212
gives 952·5 not 942·5. It is not clear where he obtained the figures
1062 and 1149½, which were corrected to 1077 and 1164½, but these
may belong to an even earlier calculation; and possibly 1077 was
copied from a slip of paper on which he had made the calculation and
on which the figure was 10757. He had, however, added the 'heat' of
the hot water instead of the cold.

Note 9. There is a partially erased calculation on the lower half of this
page below the word 'Grains'. It reads as follows, but we have as
before marked * the corrected figures appearing in it and used in the
corrected version:

485

```
          Grains
          17500*
           680,5*
          ─────────
          18180,5
          17500*
            42*
          ─────────
          35000        [35000 and 70000 appear over erased figures
          70000         which we cannot read.]
  680,5)763581†(1122°φ    [† This figure appears under 735000*.]
          6805           [φ This figure appears under 1080°*.]
          ─────────
          8308
          6805
          ─────────
          15031
          13610
          ─────────
          14210
          13610
          ─────────
```

To the left of this calculation there are some obliterated figures that we cannot read but these, as in other similarly placed calculations, would have given a result as follows:

$$1122°$$
$$86\tfrac{1}{2}°$$
$$\overline{1208\tfrac{1}{2}°}$$
$$212$$
$$\overline{996\tfrac{1}{2}} \text{ Latent heat,}$$

a value that Watt probably rejected as too high in comparison with his other results.

The main calculation here is, however, illuminating and most significant for the question that we have raised earlier as to the date when Watt ceased to include the weight of the condensed steam in the total weight of the water that was raised in temperature by the condensation. His figure 763581 is, in fact, although the details that he has inserted of his calculation do not show it, the product of the total weight of water, 17500 grains + 680·5 grains, or 18180·5 grains, and the rise in temperature of 42°, which amounts to 763581, the figure that appears in his calculation. Therefore, on 16 March 1781, he was still making this fundamental error, and possibly the puzzling figures for

Experiment 8, where we found decipherment difficult, conceal the same fact. It will be further observed that the revised calculation is marked 'corrected Mar 1814', which we again observe is surprisingly late, unless, with his many preoccupations, he had not studied these results again since they were first obtained; on the contrary, however, this physical constant was fundamental in his other work.

Note 10. This calculation is written on a slip, marked here in enclosed lines, pasted over an earlier calculation beginning under the figure 70000, which reads as follows, figures that appear in both being marked * by us, as before:

$$
\begin{array}{r}
70000^* \\
664{,}25^*\overline{)74473425}(1121 \\
66425 \\
\hline
80484 \\
66425 \\
\hline
140592 \\
132850 \\
\hline
77425 \\
66425 \\
\end{array}
$$

On the left of this calculation under the corrected result we read:

To 1121°
Add 45°
―――――
1166°

[This would have given a result, on subtracting 212°, of 954 for the latent heat, but Watt does not seem to have completed the calculation.]

As for the calculation, 74473425 is the product of the total weight of water and the rise of temperature, and no further comment seems necessary on this point. It will be noticed that Watt still adds the weight of the cold, instead of the hot, water.

Note 11. Again a re-calculation is pasted on a slip, which we have marked by enclosed lines, and which reads as follows beginning under the figure 87500, figures that appear in both being marked by us * as before:

487

$$87500^*$$
$$129325$$
$$92375$$
$$975^*)\overline{10623125}(1089$$
$$\underline{975}$$
$$8731$$
$$\underline{7800}$$
$$9312$$
$$8775$$

Here again in the calculation, 10623125 is the product of the total weight of the water and the rise of temperature, and no further comment is necessary. The quotient of the division is correctly given as 1089, but again Watt must have added the heat of the cold water, 45°, to obtain the figure of 1134 that he used a few lines later.

To the right of this calculation under the list of results numbered 6 to 10 there appear the following figures, the first of which seems to be the result of Experiment 11:

$$1134$$
$$6934\dagger$$
$$\text{aving}\phi \quad 1157,1$$
$$\text{ded[uc]}^t \quad \underline{213\ddagger}$$
$$\text{Latent} \quad 944,1$$

[† This figure is the total of the results of Experiments 6 to 11: 1173, 1153, 1150, 1167, 1166 and 1134 respectively, giving 6943. ϕ = averaging: 6943/6 = 1157,1.
‡ This should, of course be 212, and the value for the latent heat should be 945,1, not 944,1.]

In concluding this study of Watt's notebook, it would not be out of place to refer to the statement so often made that Black's discovery of the latent heat of vaporization of water or the condensation of steam was an important factor in Watt's invention of the separate condenser. It will be noticed that Watt himself, in his notebook, would appear to have been more interested in the latent heat of condensation of steam. But it seems to us that far more important for his invention was Black's discovery of what were later called specific heats; and he was early aware of their significance in solving the problem of saving the heat lost by the older method of cooling the cylinder by means of cold water, and therefore great loss of heat, when at the next stroke it had to be heated again by the entry of fresh steam. What of the latent heat of the steam condensed in the separate condenser? Some part of it helped to maintain the temperature of the cylinder with which, on account of its metallic contact with the condenser, it was thus in efficient thermal communication. Where, however, did the latent heat given out by the condensation of the steam in the condenser go? It would seem that most of it was used in heating the condenser and the cold water surrounding it and that it was therefore lost. Watt's interest in the latent heats both of vaporization of water and of condensation of steam may be regarded as merely of importance to him in under-standing the physical details of the cycle water/steam/water. The separate condenser saved little of the latent heat involved in the cycle: that heat was largely lost down the sink-pipe. An example with arbi-trary figures might be given. Suppose an iron cylinder weighing 2 cwt with a capacity of 5 gallons. Converting all values to the metric system, we find that the cylinder weighs approximately 100,000 grammes and its capacity is approximately 22 litres. The loss of heat in cooling and then reheating the cylinder $= 2 \times 100,000 \times 0.12$ (specific heat of iron) $\times (100 - 10)$, assuming that the temperature falls from $100°$ to $10°C$. This gives the loss as 2,000,000 gramme-calories (approximately). 5 gallons are equivalent approximately to 22 litres, and that volume of steam weighs 18 grammes (nearly). The latent heat given out by 18 grammes of steam in condensing $= 18 \times 540 =$ 10,000 gramme-calories (nearly). Thus only 1 part in 200 is lost by the heat given out in the condenser, and this is a maximum.

The dates of Watt's measurements of the latent heat of condensation of steam are not always given, but for those that are dated it will be seen that they were made in 1781. However, on some of these it is indicated that they were not corrected until 1814, over thirty years later. At first sight, this seems curious. However, it seems probable that the persistence of Watt's more fundamental error in calculation, which was clearly derived from his lack of understanding of the physical details of the process that he was attempting to measure, was due to his stating his final results while keeping his arithmetical evaluations to himself. This would not be unusual with Watt, who was naturally secretive about his work; and, with regard to Experiment 9 ($f. 41v$), we may say that, if Priestley, who was present at the experi-ment, had seen Watt's detailed calculation, that alert analytical mind would very probably have observed the fundamental error that his friend was making and would have drawn attention to it, whereas it remained uncorrected until March 1814. The only explanation that seems to fit the facts is that Watt did not reveal the details of his calculations.

Index

Adair, Mr. Sergeant, 245
Aepinus, Franz Ulrich, 248, 252 n.2
Alkali
   Manufacture of, from salt, 16–17, 17 n.1,
      18–19, 20–21, 25–26, 90–91, 92–94, 95,
      111–112, 359, 364
   Keir's experiments on, 27
   Alexander Fordyce's petition to Parlia-
      ment, 90, 91–92, 93–94, 111–112
Alloa Company, 303, 304, 313–314
Anderson, James, 33, 34 n. 3
Anderson, John, 60, 60 n.1, 253, 337–338
Argand, Aimé, 150
Ayr Bank (See Douglas, Heron and Co.)
Ayr harbour, 30, 31 n.3

Baader, Joseph von, 173, 174 n.1
Bache, 97
Ballooning and Balloons, 128, 132
Banks, Sir Joseph, 419
Barr, Robert, 214, 214 n.3
Baskerville, John, 13, 14 n.3
Bath, 227, 279, 281, 282, 307
Beddoes, Dr. Thomas, 148 n.1, 196 n.3,
   207–208, 209–210, 210–211, 213, 217,
   222, 224, 226 n.2, 306, 307, 310,
   314–315
Belidor, Bernard de Forest, 446 and n.6
Bergman, Torbem Olaf, 78, 79 n.1, 128,
   140
Berrington, Dr. Thomas, 155, 154 n.1
Bernoulli, Daniel, 260, 291 and n.2
Berthollet, Claude Louis, 177 and n.1, 378
Biot, Jean Baptiste, 420
Birmingham, 14, 43, 43 n.1, 45, 49, 51, 55,
   56, 59, 65 and n.1, 67, 71, 76, 80, 82,
   83 n.1, 85, 86, 88, 90, 95, 97, 98, 102,
   103, 105, 106, 109, 111, 112, 114, 117,
   121, 123, 124, 129, 130, 132, 136, 139,
   144, 145, 149, 152, 155, 158, 161, 163,
   165, 166, 170, 174, 175, 181, 183, 184,
   185, 186, 189 190, 194, 195, 197, 200,
   203, 204, 206, 212, 219, 223, 225, 227,
   232, 235, 237, 241, 262, 271, 273, 275,
   276, 278, 281, 283, 285, 287, 289, 292,
   294, 298, 300, 302, 304, 307, 309, 311,

Birmingham—continued
   313, 314, 317, 319, 320, 335, 336, 341,
   342, 373, 375, 377, 382, 386 n.1, 388,
   389, 393, 395, 399, 402, 408, 419
   Duc de Chaulnes at, 128
   Dr. Sylvestre at, 147
   Newcome Cappe at, 171–172
   Cottrel from, 178
   Labrott at, 178
   Disorders in, 187
   Volatile alkali produced in, 297, 209
   Platina refined at, 215
   Penknife made at, 216
   Robison at, 260–261
   Ewart at, 261
   'Brimingham', 263
   James Hutton jr, at, 304, 382
   Death of Dr. Withering at, 306
   Dr. Thomson at, 387
Black, Alexander, 44, 54
   Character of, 53
Black, Dr. Joseph
   Copper still asked for from Watt, 8
   Organ made for, by Watt, 8, 145
   Comments on Watt's experiments in
      Delft and stoneware firing, 10–11
   Asks Watt for shoe-varnish, 16
   Alkali patent, 16–17
   Alkali experiments, 18–19, 20–21
   Asks Watt for a pattern, 22–23
   Mineral specimens requested from Watt,
      23, 41, 45, 65–66, 67–68
   Asks Watt for manganese, 23
   His second cousin, Adam Ferguson, 37
      n.1
   Account of Watt's debts, 40, 108,
      109–110
   Account of his brothers' financial difficul-
      ties, 44
   Seeks employment for his brothers at
      Boulton's, 44, 51–53
   Shows Watt's copying-machine to a
      Writer to the Signet, 68
   on Watt's copying-machine, 68, 71–72,
      75, 101–102
   Discovery of a new flux, 68, 75, 78
   Quartz used for polishing, 69–70

491

Black, Dr. Joseph—continued
Asks for secret of separating silver from copper, 70, 72
His theory of latent heat, 76–77, 80–81, 82, 83–84, 85–86, 87–88, 91–92, 117–118, 120, 124–125, 336–338, 342–386 passim, 395–410
Account of his theory of latent heat in Rozier's Journal, 86
Tests water in Meason's engine, 114–116
Refuses to describe his theories for Keir and de Luc, 120
Assigns to Watt sole honour of steam-engine, 123
Comments on Henry Cort's iron, 140–141, 142–143, 151
His visit to Birmingham, 142, 159
Requests from Watt a sketch of apparatus by Withering, 145
Enquiries about varnish, 154–155
Asks about steam-engine for Leith glass-works, 157, 194
Prescribes for Boulton, 163–164
Proposed trip, 164
Attends Rennie in London, 169, 170
Tells Watt of a new cement, 172
About Jessy Watt, 179–181, 197–198, 200–201
Commissions sedan chair, 183
Informs Watt about scagliola, 187
Advises on Boulton's health, 201
Courses of lectures, 208, 343–344
Observations on bleaching, 209
Orders rolling press through Watt, 215, 217
Memorial concerning Watt's improvements, 253–256
Friendship for Watt, 253, 318
Spitting blood, 267
Receives specimens of Boulton's coinage, 281–282
His death, 317–321
His will, 325
Theory of quick lime, 338
His deference to Lavoisier, 339–340, 344, 356–357
Simplicity of his manner of lecturing on chemistry, 348
Meets Watt and Robison at Glasgow, 321
Black, George, junior, 323–327, 331–332, 360, 364–366, 370–372
Returns Watt's letters to Black, 331–332
Black, James, 44, 151

Blair, Alexander, 95, 96 n.1
Blakey, William, 121, 122 n.1, 131
Booker, John, 189, 190
Boulton, Matthew
Robison meets him at Dr. Darwin's, 13–14
Urges Watt to perfect his steam-engine, 13–14
Black seeks employment for his brothers in his works, 44–49, 51–53, 55, 57–58, 61
Reduces number of employees at Soho, 50
Partner in copying-machine business, 73
In Cornwall, 96
Apprenticeship at his Soho works, 114
Calling on Dr. Black, 129, 140–141
Elected to Royal Society of Edinburgh, 135–136
His ferromania, 143
In London, 158
Black prescribes for him, 163–164
Owns Isaac Newton's letter to Nicholas Facio, 272
Contracts for copper coinage, 274, 280, 308
His thermometer, 474
Boulton, Matthew Robinson, 274, 286, 306, 308
Boulton, Mrs., 129
Brewster, Sir David, 420, 421 n.1
Brindley, James, 446
Bristol, 26, 209, 307, 309
Bristol wells, 196
Bruce, Mr., 419
Buccleugh, Duke of, 89, 96, 98
Supported Watt's application for extension of steam-engine patent, 71
Butler, Justice, 217
Burnett, Colonel, 317, 340, 365
Buxton, 170, 175, 281, 289

Canals
New canal at Birmingham requiring three engines, 14
Watt's plans for Tarbert and Crinan 34–35, 36
Laurie employed as surveyor on, 58, 58 n.1
Watt made an offer as canal-surveyor, 25
Cappe, Newcome, 171, 172 n.1, 172–173
Capper, 216

Carmichael, Dr. John, 213, 214 n.2, 224, 279, 287, 311
Carron, 15 n.6, 60, 141
Watt's acquaintance with processes at, 24
Newcomen engine at, 419
Catherine the Great, 153
Invites Watt to Russia, 24
Cavendish, Harry, 345, 358, 360 n.3
Chacewater, 71, 72, 74
Engine at, 41–42, 43
Cheltenham, 181
Chemical symbols, Table of, xvi
Chemistry
Hill's laboratory, 15
(See Alkali)
(See Minerals)
Manganese, 23, 111
Decomposition of vitriolated tartar and nitre, 27
Salt of Sylvius, 27
Acid contained in flus spat, 35–36, 36–37
(See Cullen)
(See Priestley)
(See Black)
Vitriolic acid, 37, 116, 209
Muriatic acid, 37
Acid of spar, 38
Experiments with terra ponderosa, 68–69, 100–101
Brass, 75
Soldering flux, 75
(See Watt, James)
(See Galvanism)
To extract the acid from Tartar, 101
Scheele's experiments, 111
Magnesium, 111
Experiments on water in engines, 114–116
(See Copal Varnish)
New cement, 172
(See Lavoisier, Berthollet, de Foureroy)
(See Keir, James)
Experiments on strontian, 198–199
Volatile alkali, 207, 209
Sal ammoniac, 209
Hydro carbonate made by Watt, 221–222
(See Pneumatic Medicine)
De Saussure's wax, 225
Nitrate of ammonia, 306
Cope and Biddle, chemists, 311, 315
Ammonia, 315
Composition of water, 341–342, 384

Chemistry—continued
Magnesia, 344
Quick lime, 353
Christ Church, 279
Clerk, Commissioner George, 31, 31 n.1, 32, 34, 35, 36, 38, 43, 123, 129
Cockermouth, 14
Coke, used in firing Delft and stoneware, 8–11
Colombo, John Robson jr. arrives at, 377
Colville, Mr., 419
Cookworthy, William, Quaker chemist in Plymouth, 11 and n.2
Copal Varnish, 156, 444
Cope and Biddle, chemists, 311, 313 n.1, 315
Copying-press
Watt's invention and improvement of, 71–72
Boulton, Keir and Watt partners in, 73
Form of, 73–74
Possibility of misuse of, 88
For Duke of Buccleugh, 89
Shown by Black to a Writer to the Signet, 92
Ink for, 96–97, 98–99, 103
Plan for a table for, 101–102
Engraving of a stand for, 102
Cort, Henry, 140–141, 141 n.3, 142–143, 151
Cosgarne, 113
Cotterel, 178
Coutts and Company, bankers, 210
Coventry, 336
Cowes, 279
Craig, Jonathan, Watt's partner, 28–29, 29 n.2
Crawford, Adair, 76, 78 n.3, 87, 117, 124, 177, 359–360, 367
Creech, William, 92, 92 n.1
Crell, Lorenz Frederich von, 84, 85 n.3
Crinan, 34–35
Cullen, Dr. William, 34 n.3, 36 n.2, 75
Cummings, Alexander, 72 and n.1

Dalton, John, 420, 421 n.3, 485
Dartmouth, Lord, 57 n.2
Darwin, Dr. Erasmus, Robison meets him, 13–14 and 14 n.1
Davidson, John, 71 n.2
Davy, Humphrey, 307, 311 n.1, 315, 358
de Bétancourt, Augustin, 420, 421 n.4, 481, 488

493

de Biencourt, Charles, 127, 127 n.1, 128
de Fourcroy, Antoine François, 177 and n.1
de la Métherie, J. C., 283 and n.1
de La Place, Pierre Simon, Marquis, 122, and n.2, 129, 139, 283, 378
  Passage translated by Keir, 284
de Luc, Jean André, 117, 119 n.1, 128, 142, 245, 336–337, 342, 367, 428, 484
  About to publish on heat, 121, 123
  Conducts heat experiments with Watt, 124–125
  His controversy with the Edinburgh Review, 395–410
de Chaulnes, Duc, 128, 129 n.2
de Lessert and Co., 188, 189 n.1
de Magalhaens, João Jacinto, 76–77, 77 n.1, 78–79, 80–81, 82, 83, 85, 86–88, 89, 90
de Montamy, Didier François, 28, 29 n.1
de Prony, Gaspard, 378 and n.1
de Saussure, Horace Bénedict, 225, 226 n.1
Delft
  Watt's share in Delftfield Pottery Company, 8
  Watt's interest in firing of, 9–10, 11–13
Derby, 170
Desaguliers, J. T., 446 and n.7
Desnitskii, Simeon, 84, 84 n.2, 85
Douglas, Heron & Co., 30, 31 n.2
Duguid, Patrick (See Leslie, Patrick Duguid)
Dumfries, 113

Edinburgh, 8, 15, 16, 17, 19, 20, 22, 29, 31, 31 n.3, 33, 38, 39, 43, 51, 54, 55, 57, 59, 61, 62, 63, 64, 65, 70, 71 and n.1, 72, 74, 75, 80, 82, 83, 85, 90, 91, 93, 94, 99, 100, 106, 111, 112, 117, 121, 123, 124, 127, 128, 130, 134, 138, 142, 147, 149, 150, 153, 159, 161, 165, 166, 168, 171, 173, 175, 180, 182, 186, 190, 195, 197, 198, 202, 203, n.1, 204, 205, 206, 208, 209, 210, 212, 214, 216, 219, 223, 225, 227, 229, 232, 233, 235, 236, 239, 241, 262, 263, 268, 269, 271, 275, 276, 278, 281, 285, 287, 289, 290, 292, 293, 294, 298, 300, 302, 304, 307, 309, 311, 313, 314, 317, 320, 326, 328, 331, 332, 333, 342, 347, 351, 353, 360, 361, 364, 368, 370, 373, 375, 378, 381, 382, 389, 393
  Marquis de Biencourt at, 127
  (See Royal Society of Edinburgh)
  Oyster Club, 176 n.1

Edinburgh—continued
  Artificial marble made in, 185
  Guyot in, 188
  Pneumatic medicine in, 211
  Robert Barr at, 214 n.3
  Black's death at, 317
  Robison's death at, 388, 392, 397
Edinburgh Review, 396, 399–410
Edinburgh University (See University of Edinburgh)
Edgeworth, Richard Lovell, 14, 15 n.4
Encyclopaedia Britannica, Articles by Robison in, 250, 260, 264–265
Euler, Leonhard, 260, 347 and n.1
Ewart, Peter, 113, 113 n.1, 114, 168, 327–328

Fabbroni, Giovanni Valentino Mattia, 95, 96 n.2
Fairy, 22 and 23 n.1
Farquhar, George, 84, 84 n.1
Ferguson, Dr. Adam, 36, 37 n.1, 71, 322, 323, 346, 365–366, 371, 380, 385
Financial Crises
  1772, 33–34
  1779, 50, 51 n.3
Fire-engine (See Steam-Engine)
Fitzmaurice, the Hon. Mr. 84, 85
Forbes, Sir William of Pitsligo, 71, 202, 203 n.1, 204, 205
Fordyce, Alexander, 90–91, 91 n.1
Forster, Johann Reinhold, An easy Method of Essaying and Classing Mineral Substances, 36, 36 n.1
Franklin, Benjamin, his Electrical Jack, 61, 61 n.1
Freer, Robert, 140, 141 n.2
Furnaces
  For Delft and stoneware fixing, 8–12
  Blown by steam-engines, 60

Gahn, Johan Gottlieb, 84, 85 n.4, 85
Galton, Samuel Tertius, 383, 386 n.1
Galton, Samuel, junior, 421 and n.5
Galvanism, 273–274, 383–384
Garbett, Samuel, 66, 67 n.5, 96, 100, 128, 129, 169, 368
  Carries letter from Watt to Black, 67
Garnan mine, 177
Geddes, Archibald, 157, 157 n. 1, 194, 293, 326, 340, 363, 364, 368, 371, 376
German, who has made self-moving wheel, 57

Glasgow, 8, 11, 12, 17, 18, 20, 21, 22, 23, 24, 28, 30 n.1, 32, 33, 77, 84, 85, 87, 135, 189, 191, 222, 225, 227, 257, 258, 378
Glass trade at, 25–27
Financial distress at, 33
Glasgow wharf, London, 46, 48
Watt purchases land near, 195
Philosophical Society at, 198, 199
McGregor in business near, 218 n.1
Masonic lodge at, 259
Robison's sister dies at, 268
Mr. and Mrs. Watt at, 295
Robison at, 295, 296, 297, 353, 355, 358, 366, 411
Watt at, 295–297, 351, 355, 358
Glasgow University (See University of Glasgow)
Glasgow University Philosophical Club
Black reads paper, 84
Hutton reads papers, 147
Hope reads paper, 198, 199
Glaze, for stoneware, invented by Watt, 12
Gleig, George, bishop of Brechin, 285, 287 n.2
Goodwyn, Dr. Edmund, 208 and n.1
Gordon Riots, 94, 94 n.1
Greenock, Watt at, 363
Greville, Charles, 56, 57 n.1
Guyot, A., 147, 147 n.1, 188, 198–199, 200, 202–203, 204, 206, 339

Hamilton, Gilbert, 27 and n.1, 143, 163, 195, 212, 283, 378
Handley, Thomas, 22 and n.1
Hassall, Cheshire, 428
Hassel (See Hassall)
Hassenfratz, Jean Henri, 378 and n.2
Hateley, Joseph, 14, 15 n.5, 239
Heath, Justice, 217
Henderson, Logan, 70, 71 n.1
Henry, Thomas, 213, 214 n.4
Herschel, William, 169, 169 n.3, 245, 352
Hill, Ninian, 15 n.1, 16, 19
Hogg, Thomas, 31 n.2, 33
Hope, Dr. Thomas Charles, 198 and n.1, 199, 220, 277, 299, 323, 351
Hopetoun, Countess of, 113
Hopetoun, Earl of, 34 n.4
Hornblowers, Cornish engineers, 188, 189 n.2, 235, 242, 245, 318, 335
Houlbrooke, 182

Houston, George of Johnstone, 252, 340, 353
Humboldt, F. H. A. von, 273–274, 275 n.1
Hutton, Dr. James, 33, 34 n.1, 173, 186–187, 197, 200, 205, 208, 210, 217, 218, 221
Reports on Watt's engine at Wanlock Head, 70
Visit to Birmingham, 142, 159
Reads papers to Glasgow University Philosophical Society, 147
Visits Isle of Man, 169
His natural son, James Hutton, 276–277
Death, 276
Critical of De Luc, 337
Hutton, James, junior, 276–277, 301, 304, 305, 386

Ingen-Housz, Jan, 215, 216 n.1
Inglis, Laurence, 98
Iron production
Henry Cort, 140–143, 151
McKenzie, engineer for iron furnaces 144
Irvine, Dr. William, 77, 84, 87, 124, 359–360, 426–427
Sets out for London, 23 and n.2
Isle of Man, Dr. Hutton visits, 169

Jackson, Cyril, 169, 169 n.1
Jary, M., 45, 47 n.1, 48
Jeffrey, Francis, 405–406, 406 n.1
Johnstone, Dr. Edward, 64, 65 n.1

Kaolin, 11
Keir, James, 116, 120 n.1, 176, 209
Tells Watt about his alkali experiments, 25–26, 26 n.1, 26–27
Enters caveat on alkali production, 25
Has thoughts of renting a coal and salt work in Scotland, 25
Asks Watt's advice on glass sales, 26–27
Secret of dissolving the silver from copper, 70, 72
Partner in copying-machine business, 73
Discovery of a form of brass, 73, 75
And ink for copying-press, 93
His method of alkali manufacture, 95
His partnership with Alexander Blair, 95
Building a very great works, 109
To take out a patent for alkali manufacture, 111–112
Supplies Black with an apparatus, 112

Keir, James—*continued*
  About to publish a new edition of his
    Dictionary, 118
  Refused information about latent heat
    from Black, 120
  Has reached *acid* in his *Dictionary*, 159
  Publishes first part of his *Dictionary*, 181
  Comments on Robison's book, 283–284
Kerr, Robert, 131, 132 n.1 148–149
Keswick 14
Kinneil, 18 n.1, 19, 21, 92
  Watt objects to alkali experiments at, 18
Kirwan, Richard, 164, 164 n.1, 489
Klaproth, Martin Heinich, 181, 182 n.2
Knowles, Sir Charles, 257
Kutuzov, Ivan Longinovich, 347 and n.1

Labrot, 178, 179 n.1
Landriani, Marsiglio, 181, 182 1
Lauderdale, Earl of, 92
Laurie, John, 58, 58 n.1
Lavosier, 129, 139, 177, 339, 352–353, 317
  Stated by De Luc to be at work on heat,
    122
le Blanc, Mr. Sergeant, 246
Lead Hills, 33, 34 n.4, 101
Lee, George, 113 n.1, 291 n.1
Legge, George, 57 n.2
Leith, 58, 157, 194, 218, 272, 293, 318,
    325, 354, 363
Leslie, Patrick Duguid, 76, 78 n.2, 87
Lichfield, 13
Lichtenberg, George Christoph, 374,
    375 n.1
Lind, Dr. James, 31 n.2, 92, 169, 451
Liverpool, 26
London, 23, 46, 47 n.2, 48, 52, 53, 76, 80,
    84, 85, 88, 91 n.1, 93, 109, 119 n.1,
    151 n.1, 177, 216, 241, 242, 264, 275,
    312, 419
  Waterworks in, 50–51, 55, 57
  German inventor in, 55, 57
  Albion Mill, 133 n.1
  Robison at, 168, 238, 242, 299
  Black at, 170
  Sedan chair from, 183
  Jonathan Wathen in, 211 n.1
  Vessels running between Leith and, 220
  Maberley at, 228, 230
  Boulton seeking copper coinage con-
    tract at, 274
  James Hutton junior at, 276
  Wrong-headed people of, 278

Lord Chief Justice, 216–217, 246
Lowitz, J. T., 347 n.3 and n.1, 364
Lunar Society, 185
Lymington, 279

Maberley, John, 228, 229 n.3, 230, 244
MacBride, David, 358, 360 n.2
Mackell, engineer, 419
Mackenzie, Alexander, 241
Macquer, Pierre-Joseph, 66, 67 n.2
Magellan (See de Magalhaens)
Manchester, 113, n.1, 192, 327
  Thomas Henry at, 213
  Peter Ewart at, 232
  George Lee at, 291
Marr, Capt., 88, 89 n.1, 90
Marshall, Claud, 29, 30 n.1
Martin, Benjamin, 299–300, 300 n.1
Matlock, 170
Matthews, William, 47 n.2, 78
McGowan, John, 166, 175, 176 n.1, 177
McGregor, James, 218 and n.1
McKenzie, Murdoch, 144, 145 n.1
Meason, Gilbert, 110, 114, 155
Menish, Dr. William, Watt staying with
  him, 14–15 n.7, 84, 85
Miller, Margaret, Mrs., 227, 229 n.2
  education of her children, 294–295,
    295–296
Minerals
  Lead veins in Derbyshire, 14
  Limestone in Derbyshire, 14
  Manganese asked for by Black, 23
  Greenock ore, 23
  Flus spat, 35
  Calcarious Earth, 36
  Black asks for specimens of Tin Ore, 41
  Yellow pyritous ores in Cornwall, 43,
    46, 48
  Black declines to send a list of Cornish
    minerals, 44
  Caple, 46
  Unusual copper ore from Cornwall, 64,
    65–66
  Terra Ponderosa, 68–69, 100–101
  Zeolite, 68
  Gypseous Spar, 68
  Fluor from Roskere mine, 78
  Crystallization of fluor in Cornwall, 79
  Alum, Priestley's experiment with, 106
  Gypsum, Priestley's experiment with,
    109

Minerals—*continued*
  Coarse rubies, sapphires, hyacinths and garnets in Cornwall, 116
  Iron, 140–141, 142–143, 144–145
  Hutton's paper on formation of fossils and origins of the earth, 147
  Quicklime, 172
  Large tin crystals from Cornwall, 176
  Gold in Cornwall, 176–177
  Calcarious stones in the Cotswolds, 181
  Grit in Wales, 182
  Bristol lime, 182
  Artificial marble, 185
  Quartz melted by lightning, 187
  Strontian discovered by Hope, 198–199
  Two geological letters from Watt to Hutton (1795–1796), 221
  Iceland Spar, 299–201
  Freestone at Castlesemple, 300
  Black on Quick Lime, 344, 373
  Lowitz's experiments with alum and Glauber's Salt, 364
Model, J. G., 248, 252 n.1
Monge, Gaspard, 177 and n.1, 378
Monro, Dr. Alexander, 292
Monro, Dr. Alexander, junior, 292 and n.1
Montgolfier, Joseph Michael, 128, 129 n.1
Morton, Earl and Countess Dowager of, 301
Muirhead, J. P., *The Origin and Progress of the Mechanical Inventions of James Watt*, 5, 8–13, 292–293, 319–320, 377–378, 389, 395, 410–413
Muirland, Mr. cotton-spinner, 290
Murray, John, 420, 421 n.1
Musical instruments
  Organ for Dr. Black, 8, 259–260
  made for James Watt, 31–32, 259–260

Naval mutiny, 274, 277
Newcastle-upon-Tyne, 27, 237, 240
  Glass trade at, 26–27
  Alkali manufacture at, 90
Newcomen, Thomas, 233, 245, 419, 452
Newton, Sir Isaac, 272
Nicolay, Ludwig Heinrich von, 347 and n.1
Nollet, Abbé Jean Antoine, *Leçons de Physique Experimentale*, 10, 11 n.1
North, Lord, 99

Odier, Dr. Louis, 278, 280 n.1, 281, 337, 399–402
Oulton, hydraulic machine at, 291

Owen, Dr, Pryce, 152, 153 n.2
Oxford, 169, 260

Parker, William, 150, 151 n.1
Patent law
  Alkali patent, 16–17, 22, 25, 90–95
  Thomas Handley consulted on, 22
  Small's patent for one-wheel clock, 27 and n.2
  Duke of Buccleugh's support for extension of Watt's steam-engine patent, 71
  Black, Watt and Keir share patent, 90–91, 93
  Argand's patent contested, 150–151
  Boulton and Watt's law-suits, 195, 209, 212–213, 223, 228, 229 n.3, 229–248, 248–252
  Robison's help requested in patent case, 229–232
  Boulton and Watt vs. Hornblower and Maberley, 244–248
Pearson, Mr. 129
  Advised by Robison to delay attending lectures, 130
Penelly lead mine, 68
Perier, Jacques Constantin, 49, 51 n.1, 400
Petunse, 11
Pirates of Watt's steam-engine, 184, 201, 217, 224–225, 230, 238, 244–248, 274, 335
Playfair, John, 116 and n.1, 306, 386, 393–394, 397
Plymouth, 11
Pneumatic Institution, 285, 309
Pneumatic machine, Dr. Beddoes; Watt contrives apparatus for, 217, 219–220, 223–225, 225–226, 232
Polgooth, 177
Polycarp, Johann Christian, 374, 375 n.1
Pott, Johann Heinrich; 'Pottian' experiments by Watt, 10 and n.3
Priestley, Dr. Joseph, 66, 67 n.3, 106, 109, 176, 224, 306, 341, 358, 442–443
  About to publish a new volume, 106
  Obtains dephlogisticated air from Gypsum, 109
  His experiments described by Watt, 118, 122, 125–127, 146–147, 152–153, 158–159, 167, 176–177
  Misrepresented by Robison, 283
Priestley Riots, 185, 186 n.1, 187

Queensbury, Duke of, 34 n.4

Ramsgate, Patrick Wilson at, 379, 391
Raspe, Rudolf Erich, 178, 179 n.1
Ravenhead Glass Works, 170, 171 n.1
Redruth, 40, 41
Rennie, John, 132–133, 133 n.1, 134–135,
　136–138, 161, 398
　Peter Ewart in his employ, 168
　Attended by Dr. Black in London, 169,
　170
Reynolds, William, 184, 185 n.1
Robison, Charles, 388–389
Robison, John
　A lesser man than Black or Watt, 3
　Thanks Watt for a route southwards, 14
　Invites Watt to go to Russia, 24
　Experiments on the gravitation of the
　　earth, 112, 114
　Advises Mr. Pearson to delay attending
　　lectures, 130
　Article by, in the Universal Magazine, 132
　Recommends Rennie to Boulton and
　　Watt, 132–133, 134–135
　Secretary of Royal Society of Edin-
　　burgh, 135
　Recommends Kerr to Boulton, 149
　Requests Watt to obtain a silver cup for
　　him, 159–161
　Recommends Ewart, his cousin, to
　　Boulton and Watt, 168
　Introduces Mr. Booker, 190–191
　Asks Watt's advice about his son, 191–
　　193, 290–291, 298–299, 320
　Helps Watt in patent case, 229–248, 262
　His discussion in St. Petersburgh of
　　Watt's engine, 248–249
　Composing a system of practical
　　mechanics, 249–252
　Articles in Encyclopaedia Britannica, 250,
　　260, 264–265
　Wishes to conduct mechanical experi-
　　ments, 251–252, 265–266, 385–386
　Requests drawings of steam-engines, 252
　Asks for a sketch of a trussed beam for
　　Houston, 252
　Memorial of Watt, 256–260
　His early interest in mathematics and
　　natural philosophy, 256
　First acquaintance with Watt, 256–257
　Enters Navy, 257
　Helps in trial of Harrison's chronometer,
　　257
　Secretary to Sir Charles Knowles, 257
　Visits Soho, 261, 265–266, 266–267

Robison, John—continued
　Asks for sketch of Watt's house, 267
　Observations on his own character, 268
　Enquires about Sir Isaac Newton's
　　letters, 272
　Suggests that Watt give model of his
　　engine to to Glasgow University,
　　272–275
　Proposes a new doctorate, 273
　Misrepresents Priestley and de la Place,
　　283–284
　Recommends Thomas Thomson,
　　285–287
　Writes on free-masonry, 286
　On the optical properties of Iceland
　　Crystal, 299–300
　Attends Martin's lectures, 299–300
　First acquaintance with Black, 321–322
　His editing of Black's lectures, 322–341,
　　342–386
　Asks Watt's advice about editing Black's
　　lectures, 322–326
　Tries the boiling heats of different fluids
　　in vacuo, 337–338
　Elected to membership of Imperial
　　Academy, 347
　Receives diamond ring from Emperor
　　Alexander, 382
　Wants model of Watt's pocket steam-
　　engine, 383
　His plan for a manual for engineers and
　　millwrights, 385–386
　His death, 388–394
　His criticism resented by De Luc,
　　395–410
　Memoir of, by Watt, 410–412
　Gives evidence in Boulton and Watt
　　case, 411–412
　His leverless steam-engine, 446
　Meets Watt and Black at Glasgow, 321
　Visits Soho, Birmingham, 260–261
　Article on 'Waterworks', 264
　Introduces Kier and his lamp to Boulton
　　and Watt, 148–149
　Enquires of Watt about an engine for
　　Leith glass-works, 363
　Employed to make observations for trial
　　of Harrison's chronometer, 257
Robison, Mrs., 243, 250–251, 294–296,
　322, 384, 389–391, 397–398
　Receives allowance from Watt,
　　269–270, 271, 272, 275
　Visited by Black, 275

498

Roebuck, Dr. John, 15 n.6, 33, 216, 230, 239, 242
Share in alkali business with Black and Watt, 16–18
Kinneil, 18 n.1
Partnership with Watt in steam-engine, 254
His failure to understand the nature of steam, 254
Roebuck, John, junior, 301, 302–303, 304, 313–314
Rogerson, Dr. John, 153, 154 n.1, 347, 382
Rooke, Mr. Justice, 217
Rotheram, Dr. 215
Royal Society of Edinburgh, 176 n.1
Watt and Boulton elected to, 135
Rumford, Count, 224
Russell, James, 31 n.3, 368
Russia
Watt invited to, 24
Cannon from Carron for, 24
Discussion of Watt's steam-engine in, 248, 262
Rutherford, Daniel, 373

Salt, Alkali manufactured from, 18–19. See Alkali.
Salt of Sylvius, 27
Savary, Thomas, 122, 131, 418, 426, 448, 450, 452
Scagliola, 187
Scheele, Carl Wilhelm, 107, 107 n.1, 109, 111, 358, 360 n.1
Scientific instruments
Thermometers, 23, 39
Tongs made for Black by Wilson, 23
Drawing machines, 31
Bill for, to Professor Russell, 32–33
Divided plate for graduating thermometers, 39
For measuring specific gravities of liquids, 167
Watt's invention and manufacture of, 39, 167, 445
Shrewsbury, 152, 155
Sinclair, Richard, 46, 48
Sisson, Jonathan, 446
Small, Dr. William, 242
Robison meets him, 13–14 and 14 n.2
Speaks to Keir about alkali, 21, 25–26
Has written to Watt on glass trade, 25
Has made a clock with one wheel, 27

Smeaton, John, 41, 41 n.1, 429
Publishes comparison of his own engine with Watt's, 66, 67 n.1
Smith, Adam, 75, 76 n.1
Soho manufacturing, 13, 162, 251, 260–261, 334
Book-keeper at, 46, 48
Galvanic apparatus made at, 383
Southampton, 279
Southern, John, 165, 196 and n.1, 428–430, 453, 482, 487, 488
St. Helens, 170, 171 n.1
St. Petersburg
Booker, agent at, 189
Robison at, 248, 262, 327, 347
Steam-engine
Edgeworth's engine, 14
At Chacewater, 42
At Nantes, 45, 48
At Paris, 49–50
At Shadwell, 57
Furnaces at Birmingham driven by, 60
Smeaton's observations on Watt's, 64, 67 n.1
At Wanlockhead, 70, 114–116
At Wheal Virgin, 72, 74, 84
Analysis of water in, 114–116
Tilt-hammer powered by, 119
Blakey's engine, 122
Savary's engine, 122, 131, 418, 426, 448, 450, 452
Kerr's plan for a, 131–132
Robison's scheme in the Universal Magazine, 132
Waggons powered by, 155
For use in Leith glass-works, 157, 194
Symington's at Wanlockhead, 162, 163 n.1
For Ravenhead glass works, 170, 171 n.1
At Ravenhead, 170
Pirates of Watt's, 184, 201, 217, 224–225, 230, 238, 244–248, 274, 335
Pirates of Boulton and Watt's, 195
Watt's account of his inventions for, 233–234, 242
Watt's trial of his condenser for, 233–234
Newcomen's engine, 245, 452
Houston's engine, 340
Models used in law-cases, 364
Model of Watt's pocket engine, 383
Robison's article on, 420, 481–482
Robison's idea of a leverless, 426

Steam-engine—*continued*
Wooden cylinder for, made by Brindley, 426, 446
Model steam-engine made by Sisson, 446–447
Watt's trial of the Newcomen model of, 446–447
Boiler for, 447
Injection in, 447
Trial between Watt's engine and a common engine, 64
Watt recalls early experiments concerning, 446 *et seq.*
Black analyses boiler-water in Meason's, 114–116
Stokes, Dr. Jonathan, 152, 153 n.1
Stonefield, Lord, 155 n.1
Stoneware, Watt's interest in firing of, 9–10
Stourbridge, 25, 152
Strontites, 198
Sylvestre, Dr. P., 147, 148 n.1, 337
Symington, William, 162, 163 n.1

Tarbert, 34–35
Tea kitchen (kettle), 103, 447
Thermometers, 39
Made by Watt for Black, 23
Boulton's, 474
Thomson, Dr. Thomas, 285–287, 287 n.1
Thomson, William, 169, 169 n.2, 387
Thornton, Robert John, 211 and n.2
Tretiakov, John, 84, 84 n.2, 85
Trustees for the Encouragement of Fisheries and Manufactures, promise aid to Robison, 131, 144
Tuffen, Mr., 312

University of Edinburgh, 31 n.3, 34 n.3, 37 n.1, 45, 85
Black's lectures at, 85, 123, 215, 323 et. seq.
Mr. Pearson at, 129
Robert Freer at, 141 n.2
Dr. Stokes at, 152
Dr. Baader at, 173
Dr. Webster at, 175
Dr. Carmichael at, 214 n.2
Daniel Rutherford at, 216 n.1
Dr. Withering at, 229 n.1
Robison's classes at, 235–236, 242, 244, 265, 290
Papers relating to Newton at, 272
New doctorate proposed at, 273

University of Edinburgh—*continued*
Playfair, Professor of Geometry at, 306
Dr. Crauford at, 359
University of Glasgow, 3, 23 n.2, 36 n.2, 84, 85, 87
Lectures at, 84–86
Dr. Cappe at, 171
Gregory Watt entered at, 188
Black lecturing at, 253
Watt, instrument-maker at, 253–254, 256
Robison, student at, 256, 359–360
Professors at, 256, 260, 322
Proposal to donate models of Watt's engine to, 273
Thomas Thomson at, 287 n.1
Robison and Black meet at, 321
Dr. Irvine at, 359–360
David MacBride at, 360 n.2

Voltaic pile, 358

Wallerius, Johan Gotschalk, 66, 67 n.4
Wanlockhead, 34 n.4
Symington's engine at, 162
Waterworks
At Richmond, Shadwell, and Chelsea, 51 n.2
Robison's article on, 264
Watford, 13–14
Wathen, Jonathan, 211 and n.1
Watt, Anne Mrs. *passim*
Watt, Gregory, 188, 189 n.3, 225, 238, 270, 274, 278, 288, 383
Watt, James
His range of interests, 3, 257–258
Mechanical Inventions, ed. J. P. Muirhead, 5, 8–13, 292–293, 319–320, 377–378, 389, 395, 410–413
His interest in firing Delft and stoneware, 8–10, 11–13
Share in the Delft work, 8–9, 10 n.1
Asked for organ and copper still by Black, 8
Asked to build organ for Free-Mason's Lodge, 8 n.1, 259–260
'Pottian' experiments by, 10
Invents glaze for stoneware, 12
Stays with Dr. Menish, 14
His interest in manufacturing alkali from salt, 16–17, 17 n.1, 18–19, 20–21, 25–26, 26–27, 90–91, 92–94, 95, 111–112, 359, 364

500

Watt, James—*continued*
Black asks him for shoe-varnish, 16
Alkali patent, 16–18
Objects to alkali experiments at Kinneil, 18
Trial of his model of steam-engine, 20
His improved steam-engine (fire-engine), 20, 233–234, 253–256
Tries his new condenser, 21
Makes pattern for Black, 22–23
Makes thermometers for Black, 23
Invited to be Master Founder of Ordnance in Russia, 24
Acquaintance with processes at Carron, 24
Advises Keir on outlets for glass, 26
Partnership with Craig, 28–29
makes musical instruments, 31–32, 259–260
His plans for canals and harbours, 34–35, 255, 258
Misuse of Latin words, 37
Debts to Black, 40
Cornish confidence in his steam-engines, 41–42
French privilege for steam-engines granted, 42, 45
Model of blowing-engine for Anderson's class, 60
Extension of his patent supported by Duke of Buccleugh, 71
Extension and improvement of his copying-press, 73–74, 79, 80–81, 89, 96–97, 98–99, 102–3, 111
Informs Magellan of Black's theories of heat, 76–77, 80–81, 82–83
Attitude towards inventor's secrets, 80–81
Petitions Parliament re. alkali manufacture, 90–91
Experiments on latent heat, 91, 103–107, 400, 420, 426–430
Income from steam-engines, 97, 98, 306
Uses tea-kettle in experiment, 103, 469
Asks Black to tell De Luc about latent heat, 117–118
Present at Priestley's experiments, 118, 122, 125–127, 166–167, 176–177
Describes steam tilt-hammer, 119
His invention of steam-engine, 122, 253–256, 259
Decomposition of water, 125–126

Watt, James—*continued*
Elected to Royal Society of Edinburgh, 135
Paper for R.S. on dephlogisticated air, 145
Describes Priestley's experiments, 146–147, 158–159
Supplies Hutton with a map of Cornwall, 173
Enquiries about artificial marble, 185–186
Law suits, 195, 209, 212–213, 228, 229–232, 232–252, 262–263, 274, 292–293, 300–301, 302, 308, 310–311, 335
His interest in pneumatic medicine, 196, 207–208, 209–210, 210–211, 212, 213–214, 215–216, 217, 219–220, 221–222, 232, 263, 278–280, 285–286, 287–288, 289, 307, 309–310, 311–312, 313, 314–316
Presents elastic buckles to Watt and Hutton, 197
Interest in bleaching, 207
Invents rotative couch, 222
Requests Robison's help in patent case, 229–241
Invents separate condenser, 233–234, 253–254
Molested by Glasgow corporations, 253
Mathematical instrument-maker to Glasgow university, 253
Repairs model of Newcomen engine, 253–254, 446–447
Friendship for Dr. Black, 253
Memorial of, by Black, 253–256
Partnership with Roebuck, 254
His character, 254–255, 258–259
Terms of his first patent, 255
Memorial of, by Robison, 256–260
His self-education, 258
The nature of oxygenous gases, 267, 269
Summer tour of S. England, 1797, 279
His paper on the composition of water, 336, 341–342
Asked to judge Robison's share of profits, 354, 368–369, 373–374
Never Black's pupil, 379
Appealed to by De Luc in dispute with *Edinburgh Review*, 395–410
First meeting with Robison, 410
Comments on Robison's edition of Black's lectures, 416–419
(See Scientific Instruments)

Watt, James—*continued*
Experiments with Papin's Digester, 417
His building of Newcomen engines, 419
Interest in specific heats, 426–427
Drawing-machine invented by, 445
Makes wooden cylinder for steam-engine, 448
Meets Black and Robison at Glasgow, 321
Invents instrument for measuring specific gravities of liquids, 167
His political opinions, 185, 195
Watt, James, junior, 158, 194, 195, 196 n.1, 236, 266, 270, 274, 280, 286, 298–299, 306, 308, 318, 383
Watt, Jessy, 179, 180 n.1, 181, 197–198, 200–201, 203–204
Webster, Dr. Charles, 174, 175 n.1
Wedgwood, Josiah, 139–140, 141 n.1
Weston, Mr., solicitor, 237
Wheal Virgin mine, 74, 96
Wilcke, Johan Carl, 79, 79 n.2, 80, 82, 85
Wilkinson, John, 60, 60 n.2, 148 n.1, 174 n.1, 184, 185 n.1, 213
Wilkinson, William, 213, 214 n.1
Williamson, Mr. 85
Wilson, Captain Henry, 374, 375 n.3

Wilson, Dr. Alexander, 8 n.2, 135
Wilson, Dr. Patrick, 84, 111, 135–136, 379–380, 391–393, 395
Wilson, Thomas (Boulton and Watt's agent in Cornwall), 70
Wilson, William, 92
Winander mere (See Windermere)
Winchester, 279
Windermere, 14
Windsor, 31 n.2, 119 n.1, 169, 395, 401, 405
Withering, Dr. William, 82, 83 n.1, 183–184, 204, 214, 215, 225, 274, 279, 288
Hammering iron red-hot, 82
Translation of Bergman, 128, 129, 140
Apparatus for aerated water, 145
His death, 306
Withering, Dr. William, junior, 227, 229 n.1, 232, 278, 281, 286, 292
Woodstock, 260
Wren, Sir Christopher, 444–445
Wright, Mrs., 296

York, 171
Young, Dr. Thomas, 124, 124 n.1